Integrating Sustainable Development into International Investment Agreements

A Guide for Developing Country Negotiators

J Anthony VanDuzer, Penelope Simons and Graham Mayeda

Commonwealth Secretariat

Commonwealth Secretariat
Marlborough House
Pall Mall
London SW1Y 5HX
United Kingdom

Published by the Commonwealth Secretariat
Edited by Wayzgoose and editors4change Ltd
Typesetting and index by Techset Composition
Cover design by Rory Seaford Design
Printed by Hobbs the Printers, Totton, Hampshire

Copies of this publication may be obtained from

Publications Section
Commonwealth Secretariat
Marlborough House
Pall Mall
London SW1Y 5HX
United Kingdom
Tel: +44 (0)20 7747 6534
Fax: +44 (0)20 7839 9081
Email: publications@commonwealth.int
Web: www.thecommonwealth.org/publications

A catalogue record for this publication is available from the British Library.

ISBN (paperback): 978-1-84929-086-9
ISBN (e-book): 978-1-84859-142-4

Foreword

The Commonwealth Secretariat has produced this practical handbook, entitled *Integrating Sustainable Development into International Investment Agreements: A Guide for Developing Countries*, to help enable developing countries to design international investment agreements (IIAs) that support their development needs. The Guide marks the culmination of an intense and successful consultative and expert-group process held in the Commonwealth Caribbean, Pacific, South Asian and African regions. It has also been subjected to a rigorous peer review process comprising renowned experts in the field to ensure that it meets international standards.

The Guide identifies an area of crucial need among its poorest, smallest and most vulnerable members; and is providing a cost-effective, instructive and already deeply appreciated tool across the Commonwealth's developing country membership. It is designed to be a useful reference for policy-makers, legal experts, legal researchers and civil society groups with a stake in the effects of IIAs on development. It explains how IIAs can be more effective tools to attract investment and to ensure that investment leads to sustainable development.

It is expected that the Guide will be of use to developing countries in negotiating bilateral investment treaties, while various provisions may also be suitable for inclusion in economic partnership agreements, investment provisions in preferential trading agreements and other international economic agreements relating to investment.

The Guide analyses the costs and benefits of existing approaches from a sustainable development point of view. It provides a menu of options for states negotiating IIAs, including new ideas for treaty provisions that can enhance the prospects for ensuring that investors' activities contribute to sustainable development.

The challenges of negotiating and living with IIAs

Most IIAs are bilateral investment treaties (BITs) between capital-exporting countries and capital-importing countries. These treaties offer protection for foreign investors operating in host countries. Countries hope that by offering protection, an IIA will increase inflows of foreign investment from existing and future investors. But the evidence of the link between IIAs and foreign investment inflows is weak, and not all foreign investment contributes to sustainable development. At the same time, the forms of IIA typically sought by countries can constrain the ability of host countries to regulate foreign investors operating within their borders. IIAs may make it difficult for countries to achieve essential public policy objectives, including their development goals and the maintenance of environmental, human rights and labour rights standards.

The constraints that IIAs impose on host states, combined with costly and often inconsistent decisions by investor–state arbitration tribunals regarding the meaning of broadly worded IIA obligations, have led many countries to rethink what obligations an IIA should include.

How can the Guide help address challenges related to IIAs?

The Guide is designed to explain how IIAs can do a better job of promoting sustainable development in host states. It explains how IIAs, if combined with a mix of other policies, can increase foreign investment inflows and support the efforts of host countries to regulate foreign investment inflows in order to ensure that they contribute to sustainable development.

The Guide achieves these goals by:

1. Identifying emerging best practices in existing agreements;
2. Suggesting new and innovative provisions; and
3. Discussing how states can achieve better coherence between their IIAs, their other international commitments and their domestic policy.

Essential features of the Guide

The Guide contains the following features, which are designed to explain how IIAs can do a better job of promoting sustainable development in a manner that serves the needs of its different intended users most effectively. It:

- Discusses the basic purposes of IIAs;
- Describes the links between IIAs and inward investment flows and those between investment inflows and sustainable development;
- Presents the various current approaches to IIA provisions;
- Identifies new ways to modify traditional IIA provisions;
- Describes new types of sustainable development provisions that can be included in future agreements relating to sustainability assessments, human rights, labour rights, environmental protection and corruption;
- Explains the policy implications of all provisions discussed and evaluates their costs and benefits; and
- Provides sample provisions.

Who is the Guide intended for?

The Guide is intended to serve the needs of a variety of users, including serving as:

- A resource to help policy-makers to make more informed policy choices;
- A negotiators' handbook;
- A technical reference for legal experts and researchers; and
- A source of information on IIAs for civil society groups and advocates.

Key policy issues discussed in the Guide

The Guide discusses many of the potential social, cultural and environmental effects of IIAs. It also explains the current debates regarding the legal interpretations of various IIA provisions. Issues discussed include:

- Do IIAs contribute to economic growth?
- How can IIAs contribute to sustainable development?
- How can IIAs encourage investment more effectively?
- What is the impact of IIAs on regulatory sovereignty?
- How can investors' home states be engaged to support sustainable development in host states?
- Can IIAs be used to implement international human rights obligations and promote corporate social responsibility?
- How do IIAs interact with WTO obligations, other investment agreements and domestic policy?
- Should IIAs include investor–state dispute settlement?
- What kinds of changes can be made to investor–state arbitration procedures to make them less onerous for states and more predictable?

The Guide is not intended to be prescriptive and is not without limitations. It does not compare IIAs with investment contract commitments or insurance, which may be used as substitutes for, or complements to, IIAs as ways to encourage investment. Nor does the Guide's focus on IIAs suggest that IIAs constitute the best or only approach to attracting and retaining foreign investment. Other policies may be preferable, or have greater impact.

Rather than surveying all possible approaches to attracting investment, the Guide aims to help developing countries with existing IIAs and the negotiations of new ones. Its main purpose is therefore to provide a source of useful information and analysis for countries that have negotiated, or are considering negotiating, IIAs.

The Commonwealth Secretariat is indebted to Professors Anthony VanDuzer, Graham Mayeda and Penelope Nelson at the University of Ottawa in Canada who have worked tirelessly over the past five years to write this Guide, along with the support of the technical manager overseeing this project. Special thanks as well to the Secretariat's Publications team for their editorial contributions.

I welcome this important publication, and hope that it will be widely read and actively utilised.

Dr Cyrus Rustomjee
Director, Economic Affairs Division
Commonwealth Secretariat

About the authors

Tony VanDuzer is a professor and former Vice Dean of Research with the Faculty of Law (Common Law Section) at the University of Ottawa, as well as an Adjunct Research Professor at the Norman Paterson School of International Affairs at Carleton University in Ottawa. He has written widely on investment and trade in services issues and completed several major studies for the government of Canada, including an analysis of the impact of the WTO General Agreement on Trade in Services to health, education and social services in Canada (2004) and a study of Canadian foreign investment policy (2005). He has participated in technical assistance projects related to trade and investment issues in more than 25 transition and developing economies over more than 20 years. He was a Member of the Academic Advisory Council to Canada's Deputy Minister for International Trade from 2002 to 2006.

Penelope Simons is an associate professor at the Faculty of Law (Common Law Section), University of Ottawa, Canada. She has been engaged in research on corporate human rights accountability since December 1999 when she participated in the Canadian Assessment Mission to Sudan (Harker Mission), appointed by Canada's Minister of Foreign Affairs and International Trade, to investigate allegations of slavery as well as links between oil development in Sudan and violations of human rights. Her research focuses on the human rights impacts of domestic and extraterritorial activity of extractive corporations, state responsibility for corporate complicity in human rights violations and the human rights implications of transnational corporate activity facilitated by international economic law. She is the co-author with Audrey Macklin of *The Governance Gap: Extractive Industries, Human Rights, and the Home State Advantage* (Routledge, forthcoming 2013) which examines the human rights implications of corporate activity in zones of weak governance and argues for home state regulation.

Graham Mayeda is an associate professor at the Faculty of Law (Common Law Section), University of Ottawa, Canada. His recent work has focused on the impact of international trade and investment law on developing countries. He is also interested in foundational issues in international law such as the role of global justice in structuring international legal regimes. In particular, he is interested in issues of justice raised by developing countries and methods for interpreting international law that can be more responsive to these claims. While on sabbatical at New York University Law School in 2011, he conducted research on the influence of Canadian, American and UK anti-terrorism policy on poverty alleviation and development work conducted by these countries. More recently, he has studied how international and domestic administrative law regimes can be used to promote and protect the interests of developing countries in international legal regimes. Outside of international law, his research has branched into legal theory, theories of judgment, social rights and public protest, and environmental law. He has a background in philosophy and specialises in East Asian and contemporary European ethics.

Acknowledgements

The Commonwealth Secretariat and the authors gratefully acknowledge the assistance provided by the following reviewers:

Dr Aradhna Aggarwal, Senior Fellow, National Council of Applied Economic Research, New Delhi, India

Mr Ahmed Aslam, Permanent Mission of Pakistan to the WTO, Geneva, Switzerland

Dr Debapriya Bhattacharya, Executive Director, Centre for Policy Dialogue, Dhaka, Bangladesh

Professor Yaw Benneh, Legon Centre for International Affairs, Faculty of Law, University of Ghana, Legon, Ghana

Ms Nathalie Bernasconi-Osterwalder, Senior International Lawyer and Leader of Investment Program, International Institute for Sustainable Development, Geneva, Switzerland

Professor David Collins, The City Law School, City University London, London, UK

Mr Jean-Paul Cumberbatch, First Secretary – Commercial Division, Barbados High Commission London, UK

Dr Daniel Franks, Senior Research Fellow, Centre for Social Responsibility in Mining, Sustainable Minerals Institute, University of Queensland, Brisbane, Australia

Mr Edwin Laurent, Head of Section and Adviser, Economic Affairs Division, Commonwealth Secretariat, London, UK

Ms Nicola Kirkup, Head of International Trade in Services and Investment, Department of Business, Enterprise and Regulatory Reform, London, UK

Ms Mahnaz Malik, Associate, International Institute for Sustainable Development, London, UK

Dr Howard Mann, Senior International Law Advisor, International Institute for Sustainable Development, Ottawa, Canada

Mr Fujita Masataka, Chief, Investment Trends, UNCTAD, Geneva, Switzerland

Ms Wase Musonge, Programme Officer, South Centre, Geneva, Switzerland

Professor Andrew Newcombe, Faculty of Law, University of Victoria, Victoria, Canada

Professor Ruth Okediji, William L Prosser Professor of Law, University of Minnesota Law School, Minneapolis, USA

Dr Chantal Ononaiwu, Trade Policy & Legal Specialist, Office of Trade Negotiations, CARICOM Secretariat, Bridgetown, Barbados

Dr Federico Ortino, Reader in International Economic Law, The Dickson Poon School of Law, King's College, London, UK

Mr Lincoln Price, Private Sector Liaison, Office of Trade Negotiations, CARICOM Secretariat, Bridgetown, Barbados

Ms Veniana Qalo, Economic Adviser, Economic Affairs Division, Commonwealth Secretariat, London, UK

Dr Mohammad Razzaque, Economic Advisor, International Trade & Regional Co-operation, Commonwealth Secretariat, London, UK

Mr Sergey Ripinsky, Investment Specialist, UNCTAD, Geneva, Switzerland

Mr Jeff Rodwell, Director, Investments & Ventures, Commonwealth Business Council, London, UK

Dr Nichodemus Rudaheranwa, Economic Advisor, International Trade & Regional Co-operation, Commonwealth Secretariat, London, UK

Dr Cyrus Rustomjee, Director, Economic Affairs Division, Commonwealth Secretariat, London, UK

Ms Shazinaz Bibi Sahadutkhan, Private Sector Investment Expert, ACP Secretariat, Brussels, Belgium

Ms Roseline Seleka, Programme Officer, Protocol on Finance and Investment, South African Development Community, Gaborone, Botswana

Mr Teddy Soobramanien, Economic Adviser, Economic Affairs Division, Commonwealth Secretariat, London, UK

Professor M Sornarajah, CJ Koh Professor of Law, Faculty of Law, National University of Singapore, Singapore

Dr Dirk Willem te Velde, Growth and Investment Programme Leader, Overseas Development Institute, London, UK

Professor Gus van Harten, Osgoode Hall Law School, York University, Toronto, Canada

The authors would also like to thank the University of Ottawa students who provided their research assistance in connection with the Guide: Michelle Bloodworth, Carolyn Burkholder-James, Will Boyer, Carolyn Cornford, Gregg Erauw, Jonathan Khan, Jessica Luscombe, Devanne O'Brien and Dee Pham.

Any errors or omissions remain the responsibility of the authors.

Please note: The Guide is not intended as legal advice and neither the Commonwealth Secretariat nor the authors are responsible for actions taken on the basis of information provided by the Guide.

Contents

List of cases

List of treaties

Multilateral agreements

Agreement on Trade-Related Investment Measures, signed 15 April 1994, in force 1 January 1995, Marrakesh Agreement Establishing the World Trade Organization, Final Act Embodying the Results of the Uruguay Round of Multilateral Trade Negotiations, GATT Doc. MTN/FA, Annex 1A, 1868 UNTS 18.

General Agreement on Tariffs and Trade 1994, signed 15 April 1994, in force 1 January 1995, Marrakesh Agreement Establishing the World Trade Organization, Final Act Embodying the Results of the Uruguay Round of Multilateral Trade Negotiations, GATT Doc. MTN/FA, Annex 1A, 1867 UNTS 187, 33 *International Legal Materials* 1153.

General Agreement on Trade in Services, signed 15 April 1994, in force 1 January 1995, Marrakesh Agreement Establishing the World Trade Organization, Final Act Embodying the Results of the Uruguay Round of Multilateral Trade Negotiations, GATT Doc. MTN/FA, Annex 1B, 1869 UNTS 183, 33 *International Legal Materials* 1167.

Bilateral investment treaties and other international investment agreements

Argentina–New Zealand, Agreement between the Government of the Argentine Republic and the Government of New Zealand for the Promotion and Reciprocal Protection of Investments, signed 27 August 1999, not yet in force.

Association of Southeast Asian Nations, Comprehensive Investment Agreement, signed 26 February 2009, in force 29 March 2012.

Association of Southeast Asian Nations, Framework Agreement on the ASEAN Investment Area, signed 7 October 1998 in force 25 May 1999.

Association of Southeast Asian Nations–Australia–New Zealand, Free Trade Agreement, signed 27 February 2009, in force 3 January 2010.

Australia–Argentina, Agreement between the Government of Australia and the Government of the Argentine Republic on the Promotion and Protection of Investments, signed 23 August 1995, in force 11 January 1997.

Australia–Chile, Free Trade Agreement, signed 30 July 2008, in force 5 March 2009.

Australia–Egypt, Agreement between the Government of Australia and the Government of the Arab Republic of Egypt on the Promotion and Protection of Investments, signed 3 May 2001, in force 5 September 2002.

Australia–India, Agreement between the Government of Australia and the Government of the Republic of India on the Promotion and Protection of Investments, signed 26 February 1999, in force 4 May 2000.

Australia–New Zealand, Investment Protocol, signed 16 February 2010, not yet in force.

Australia–Singapore, Free Trade Agreement, signed 17 February 2003, in force 28 July 2003.

Australia–Thailand, Free Trade Agreement, signed 5 July 2004, in force 1 January 2005.

Australia–United States, Free Trade Agreement, signed 18 May 2004, in force 1 January 2005.

Australia–Vietnam, Agreement between Australia and the Socialist Republic of Vietnam on the Reciprocal Promotion and Protection of Investments, signed 5 March 1991, in force 11 September 1991.

Austria–Tajikistan, Agreement for the Promotion and Protection of Investment between the Republic of Austria and the Republic of Tajikistan, signed 15 December 2010, not yet in force.

Azerbaijan–Estonia, Agreement between the Government of the Republic of Azerbaijan and the Government of the Republic of Estonia on the Promotion and Reciprocal Protection of Investments, signed 7 April 2010, not yet in force.

Barbados–Germany, Agreement between Barbados and the Federal Republic of Germany for the Promotion and Protection of Investments, signed 2 December 1994, in force 11 May 2002.

Belgium–Luxembourg–Colombia, Agreement between the Belgium–Luxembourg Economic Union, on the one hand, and the Republic of Colombia, on the other hand, on the Reciprocal Promotion and Protection of Investments, signed 4 February 2009, not yet in force.

Belgium–Luxembourg–Ethiopia, Agreement between the Belgium–Luxembourg Economic Union on the one hand, and the Federal Democratic Republic of Ethiopia, on the other hand, on the Reciprocal Promotion and Protection of Investments, signed 26 October 2006, not yet in force.

Botswana–China, Agreement between the Government of the Republic of Botswana and the Government of the People's Republic of China on Promotion and Protection of Investments, signed 12 June 2000, not yet in force.

Canada–Armenia, Agreement between the Government of Canada and the Government of the Republic of Armenia for the Promotion and Protection of Investments, signed 8 May 1997, in force 29 March 1999.

Canada–Barbados, Agreement between the Government of Canada and the Government of Barbados for the Reciprocal Promotion and Protection of Investments, signed 19 May 1996, in force 17 January 1997.

Canada–Chile, Agreement on Labour Cooperation, signed 6 February 1997, in force 5 July 1997.

Canada–Colombia, Agreement on Labour Cooperation, signed 21 November 2008, in force 15 August 2011.

Canada–Colombia, Free Trade Agreement, signed 21 November 2008, in force 15 August 2011.

Canada–Costa Rica, Agreement between the Government of Canada and the Government of the Republic of Costa Rica for the Promotion and Protection of Investments, signed 18 March 1998, in force 29 September 1999.

Canada–Ecuador, Agreement between the Government of Canada and the Government of the Republic of Ecuador for the Promotion and Reciprocal Protection of Investments, signed 29 April 1996, in force 6 June 1997.

Canada–Jordan, Free Trade Agreement, signed 28 June 2009, in force 1 October 2012.

Canada–Lebanon, Agreement between the Government of Canada and the Government of the Lebanese Republic for the Promotion and Protection of Investments, signed 11 April 1997, in force 19 June 1999.

Canada–Mexico–United States, North American Agreement on Environmental Cooperation, signed 14 September 1993, in force 1 January 1994.

Canada–Mexico–United States, North American Agreement on Labor Cooperation, signed 14 September 1993, in force 1 January 1994.

Canada–Mexico–United States, North America Free Trade Agreement, signed 17 December 1992, in force 1 January 1994.

Canada–Panama, Free Trade Agreement, signed 14 May 2010, not yet in force.

Canada–Peru, Agreement between the Government of Canada and the Government of the Republic of Peru for the Promotion and Protection of Investments, signed 14 November 2006, in force 20 June 2007.

Canada–Peru, Free Trade Agreement, signed 29 May 2008, in force 1 August 2009.

Canada–United States, Free Trade Agreement, signed 2 January 1988, in force 1 January 1989.

Caribbean Community, Revised Treaty of Chaguaramas Establishing the Caribbean Community Including the CARICOM Single Market and Economy, signed 5 July 2001, in force 5 February 2002.

Caribbean Community–Cuba, Trade and Economic Cooperation Agreement between the Caribbean Community and the Government of the Republic of Cuba, signed 5 July 2000, not yet in force.

Chile–Austria, Agreement between the Republic of Chile and the Republic of Austria for the Promotion and Reciprocal Protection of Investment, signed 8 September 1997, in force 22 October 2000.

Chile–South Africa, Agreement between the Republic of Chile and the Republic of South Africa for the Reciprocal Promotion and Protection of Investments, signed 12 November 1998, not yet in force.

China–Belize, Agreement between the Government of the Republic of China and the Government of Belize on the Promotion and Reciprocal Protection of Investment, signed 16 January 1999, in force 16 January 2001.

China–Côte d'Ivoire, Agreement between the Government of the People's Republic of China and the Government of the Republic of Côte d'Ivoire on the Promotion and Protection of Investments, signed 23 September 2002, not yet in force.

China–Germany, Agreement between the People's Republic of China and the Federal Republic of Germany on the Encouragement and Reciprocal Protection of Investments, signed 1 December 2003, in force 11 November 2005.

China–Guyana, Agreement between the Government of the People's Republic of China and the Government of the Republic of Guyana on the Promotion and Protection of Investments, signed 27 March 2003, in force 26 October 2004.

China–Jamaica, Agreement between the Government of the People's Republic of China and the Government of Jamaica on the Protection and Promotion of Investments, signed 26 October 1994, in force 15 November 1996.

China–New Zealand, Free Trade Agreement, signed 7 April 2008, not yet in force.

China–Peru, Free Trade Agreement, signed 28 April 2009, in force 1 March 2010.

Colombia–India, Agreement for the Promotion and Protection of Investments between the Republic of Colombia and the Republic of India, signed 10 November 2009, in force 2 July 2012.

Common Market for Eastern and Southern Africa (COMESA), Investment Agreement, adopted 23 May 2007.

Denmark–Poland, Agreement between the Government of the Kingdom of Denmark and the Government of the Republic of Poland for the Promotion and Reciprocal Protection of Investments, signed 1 May 1990, in force 13 October 1990.

Dominican Republic–Central America Free Trade Agreement, signed 2 August 2005, in force 1 January 2009.

Energy Charter Treaty, signed 17 December 1994, in force 16 July 1998.

Ethiopia–Malaysia, Agreement between the Government of the Federal Democratic Republic of Ethiopia and the Government of Malaysia for the Promotion and Protection of Investments, signed 22 October 1998, in force 25 June 2004.

European Community–CARIFORUM, Economic Partnership Agreement, signed 15 October 2008, in force 29 December 2008.

European Free Trade Association–Singapore, Free Trade Agreement, signed 26 June 2002, in force 1 January 2003.

European Free Trade Association–Ukraine, Free Trade Agreement, signed 24 June 2010, in force 1 June 2012.

European Free Trade Association–United Mexican States, Free Trade Agreement, signed 27 November 2000, in force 1 July 2001.

European Union–Morocco, Association Agreement, signed 26 February 1996, in force 1 March 2000.

European Union–Russia, Agreement on Partnership and Cooperation between the European Communities and the Russian Federation, signed 24 June 1994, in force 1 December 1997.

European Union–South Korea, Free Trade Agreement, signed 15 October 2009, in force 1 July 2011.

Finland–Kyrgyzstan, Agreement between the Government of Finland and the Government of the Kyrgyz Republic on the Promotion and Protection of Investments, signed 3 April 2003, in force 8 December 2004.

France–Mexico, Agreement between the Government of the Republic of France and the Government of the United Mexican States on the Reciprocal Promotion and Protection of Investments, signed 12 November 1998, in force 12 November 2000.

France–Uganda, Agreement between the Government of the Republic of France and the Government of the Republic of Uganda on the Reciprocal Promotion and Protection of Investments, signed 3 January 2003, in force 20 December 2004.

Germany–Antigua and Barbuda, Treaty between the Federal Republic of Germany and Antigua and Barbuda concerning the Encouragement and Reciprocal Protection of Investments, signed 11 May 1998, in force 18 February 2001.

Germany–Trinidad and Tobago, Treaty between the Federal Republic of Germany and the Republic of Trinidad and Tobago for the Encouragement and Reciprocal Protection of Investments, signed 8 September 2006, in force 17 April 2010.

Hong Kong–New Zealand, Agreement between the Government of Hong Kong and the Government of New Zealand for the Promotion and Protection of Investments, signed 6 July 1995, in force 5 August 1995.

Hong Kong–United Kingdom, Agreement between the Government of the Hong Kong Special Administrative Region of the People's Republic of China and the Government of the United Kingdom of Great Britain and Northern Ireland for the Promotion and Protection of Investments, signed 30 July 1998, in force 12 April 1999.

India–Bangladesh, Bilateral Investment Promotion and Protection Agreement, signed 9 February 2009, in force 7 July 2011.

India–Korea, Free Trade Agreement, signed 7 August 2009, in force 31 December 2009.

India–Malaysia, Comprehensive Economic Cooperation Agreement, signed 18 February 2011, in force 1 July 2011.

India–Singapore, Comprehensive Economic Cooperation Agreement between the Republic of India and the Republic of Singapore, signed 29 June 2005, in force 1 August 2005.

Indonesia–Jamaica, Agreement between the Government of the Republic of Indonesia and the Government of Jamaica concerning the Promotion and Protection of Investment, signed 10 February 1999, not yet in force.

Italy–Jamaica, Agreement between the Government of the Italian Republic and the Government of Jamaica for the Promotion and Protection of Investments, signed 29 September 1993, in force 9 November 1995.

Jamaica–Argentina, Agreement between the Government of the Jamaica and the Government of the Argentine Republic on the Promotion and Reciprocal Protection of Investment, signed 8 February 1994, in force 1 December 1995.

Japan–Bangladesh, Agreement between Japan and the People's Republic of Bangladesh Concerning the Promotion and Protection of Investment, signed 10 November 1998, in force 25 August 1999.

Japan–Peru, Agreement between Japan and the Republic of Peru for the Promotion, Protection and Liberalisation of Investment, signed 22 November 2008, in force 10 December 2009.

Japan–Singapore, Economic Partnership Agreement, signed 13 January 2002, in force 30 November 2002.

Japan–Vietnam, Agreement between Japan and the Socialist Republic of Vietnam for the Liberalization, Promotion and Protection of Investment, signed 14 November 2003, in force 19 December 2004.

Korea–Jamaica, Agreement between the Republic of Korea and the Government of Jamaica for the Promotion and Protection of Investments, signed 10 June 2003, not yet in force.

Korea–Japan, Agreement between the Government of the Republic of Korea and the Government of Japan for the Liberalisation, Promotion and Protection of Investment, signed 22 March 2002, in force 1 January 2003.

Korea–Trinidad and Tobago, Agreement between the Government of the Republic of Korea and the Government of the Republic of Trinidad and Tobago for the Promotion and Protection of Investments, signed 5 November 2002, in force 27 November 2003.

Kosovo–Austria, Agreement between the Government of the Republic of Kosovo and the Republic of Austria on Promotion and Protection of Investments, signed 22 January 2010, not yet in force.

Malaysia–New Zealand, Free Trade Agreement, signed 26 October 2009, in force 1 August 2010.

Mauritius–Singapore, Agreement between the Government of the Republic of Mauritius and the Government of the Republic of Singapore for the Promotion and Protection of Investments, signed 4 March 2000, in force 19 April 2000.

Mauritius–Swaziland, Agreement between the Government of the Republic of Mauritius and the Government of the Kingdom of Swaziland for the Promotion and Reciprocal Protection of Investments, signed 15 May 2000, not yet in force.

Mexico–Argentina, Agreement between the Government of the United Mexican States and the Government of the Republic of Argentina for the Promotion and Reciprocal Protection of Investments, signed 13 November 1996, in force 22 June 1998.

Mexico–Cuba, Agreement between the United Mexican States and the Republic of Cuba for the Promotion and Reciprocal Protection of Investments, signed 30 May 2001, in force 29 March 2002.

Mexico–Germany, Agreement between the United Mexican States and the Federal Republic of Germany on the Promotion and Reciprocal Protection of Investments, signed 25 August 1998, in force 23 February 2001.

Morocco–Italy, Agreement between the Government of Morocco and Government of the Italian Republic on the Promotion and Protection of Investments, signed 18 July 1990, in force 1 January 1992.

Netherlands–Jamaica, Agreement between the Kingdom of the Netherlands and the Government of Jamaica for the Encouragement and Reciprocal Protection of Investment, signed 18 April 1991, in force 1 August 1992.

Netherlands–Oman, Agreement between the Government of the Kingdom of the Netherlands and the Government of the Sultanate of Oman on Encouragement and Reciprocal Protection of Investments, signed 17 January 2009, not yet in force.

Panama–Taiwan, Free Trade Agreement, signed 21 August 2003, in force 1 January 2004.

Papua New Guinea–Australia, Agreement between Papua New Guinea and Australia for the Promotion and Protection of Investment, signed 30 September 1990, in force 20 October 1991.

Saudi Arabia–Malaysia, Agreement between the Government of the Kingdom of Saudi Arabia and the Government of Malaysia concerning the Promotion and Reciprocal Protection of Investments, signed 25 October 2000, in force 14 August 2001.

Sri Lanka–India, Agreement between the Government of the Democratic Socialist Republic of Sri Lanka and the Government of the Republic of India for the Promotion and Protection of Investment, signed 22 January 1997, in force 13 February 1998.

Sweden–Malaysia, Agreement between the Government of Sweden and the Government of Malaysia concerning the Mutual Protection of Investments, signed 3 March 1979, in force 6 July 1979.

Sweden–Mexico, Agreement between the Government of the Kingdom of Sweden and the Government of the United Mexican States concerning the Promotion and Reciprocal Protection of Investments, signed 3 October 2000, in force 1 July 2001.

Switzerland–Iran, Agreement between the Swiss Confederation and the Islamic Republic of Iran on the Promotion and Reciprocal Protection of Investments, signed 8 March 1998, in force 1 October 2001.

Switzerland–Mauritius, Agreement between the Swiss Confederation and the Republic of Mauritius on the Promotion and Reciprocal Protection of Investment, signed 26 November 1998, in force 21 April 2000.

Thailand–Jordan, Agreement between the Government of the Kingdom of Thailand and the Government of the Hashemite Kingdom of Jordan for the Promotion and Protection of Investments, signed 15 December 2005, not yet in force.

United Kingdom–Belize, Agreement between the Government of the United Kingdom of Great Britain and Northern Ireland and the Government of Belize on the Promotion and Protection of Investment, signed 30 April 1982, in force 30 April 1982.

United Kingdom–India, Agreement between the Government of the United Kingdom of Great Britain and Northern Ireland and the Government of the Republic of India for the Promotion and Protection of Investments, signed 14 March 1994, in force 6 January 1995.

United Kingdom–Jamaica, Agreement between the Government of the United Kingdom of Great Britain and Northern Ireland and the Government of Jamaica on the Promotion and Protection of Investments, signed 20 January 1987, in force 14 May 1987.

United Kingdom–Mexico, Agreement between the Government of the United Kingdom of Great Britain and Northern Ireland and the Government of the United Mexican States, signed 12 May 2006, in force 25 July 2007.

United States–Chile, Free Trade Agreement, signed 6 June 2003, in force 1 January 2004.

United States–Colombia, Trade Promotion Agreement, signed 22 November 2006, in force 15 May 2012.

United States–Dominican Republic–Central America, Free Trade Agreement, signed 5 August 2004, in force 1 January 2009.

United States–Jordan, Free Trade Agreement, signed 24 October 2000, in force 17 December 2001.

United States–Lithuania, Treaty between the Government of the United States of America and the Government of the Republic of Lithuania for the Encouragement and Reciprocal Protection of Investment, signed 14 January 1998, in force 22 November 2001.

United States–Morocco, Free Trade Agreement, signed 15 June 2004, in force 1 January 2006.

United States–Nicaragua, Treaty between the Government of the United States of America and the Government of the Republic of Nicaragua concerning the Encouragement and Reciprocal Protection of Investment, signed 1 July 2005, not yet in force.

United States–Peru, Trade Promotion Agreement, signed 12 April 2006, in force 1 February 2009.

United States–Rwanda, Treaty between the Government of the United States of America and the Government of the Republic of Rwanda concerning the Encouragement and Reciprocal Protection of Investment, signed 19 February 2008, in force 1 January 2012.

United States–Singapore, Free Trade Agreement, signed 6 May 2003, in force 1 January 2004.

United States–Uruguay, Treaty between the United States of America and the Oriental Republic of Uruguay concerning the Encouragement and Reciprocal Protection of Investment, signed 4 November 2005, in force 1 November 2006.

Vietnam–Finland, Agreement between the Government of the Socialist Republic of Vietnam and the Government of the Republic of Finland on the Promotion and Reciprocal Protection of Investments, signed 21 February 2008, in force 4 June 2009.

Environmental treaties

Cartagena Protocol on Biosafety to the Convention on Biological Diversity, adopted 29 January 2000, entered into force 11 September 2003, 2251 *United Nations Treaty Series* 205, 39 *International Legal Materials* 1027 (2000).

Convention on Access to Information, Public Participation in Decision-making and Access to Justice in Environmental Matters, adopted 25 June 1998, entered into force 30 October 2001, 2161 *United Nations Treaty Series* 447; 38 *International Legal Materials* 517 (1999).

Convention on Biological Diversity, adopted 5 June 1992, entered into force 29 December 1993, 1760 *United Nations Treaty Series* 79, 31 *International Legal Materials* 818 (1992).

Convention on Environmental Impact Assessment in a Transboundary Context (Espoo Convention), signed 25 February 1991, 1989 *United Nations Treaty Series* 309, 30 *International Legal Materials* 800 (1991).

Convention on International Trade in Endangered Species of Wild Fauna and Flora, adopted 3 March 1973, entered into force 1 July 1975, 993 *United Nations Treaty Series* 243.

Convention on Long-Range Transboundary Air Pollution, adopted 13 November 1979, entered into force 16 March 1983, 1302 *United Nations Treaty Series* 217; 18 *International Legal Materials* 1442 (1979).

Kyoto Protocol to the United Nations Framework Convention on Climate Change, adopted 11 December 1997, entered into force 16 February 2005, 2303 *United Nations Treaty Series* 148, 37 *International Legal Materials* 22 (1998).

Montreal Protocol on Substances that Deplete the Ozone Layer, adopted 16 September 1987, entered into force 1 January 1989, 1522 *United Nations Treaty Series* 3, 26 *International Legal Materials* 1541 (1987).

Stockholm Convention on Persistent Organic Pollutants, adopted 22 May 2001, entered into force 17 May 2004, 2256 *United Nations Treaty Series* 119, 40 *International Legal Materials* 532 (2001).

United Nations Convention on the Law of the Sea, adopted 10 December 1982, entered into force 16 November 1994, 1833 *United Nations Treaty Series* 3, 21 *International Legal Materials* 1261 (1982).

United Nations Convention to Combat Desertification in those Countries Experiencing Serious Drought and/or Desertification, Particularly in Africa, adopted 14 October 1994, entered into force 26 December 1996, 1954 *United Nations Treaty Series* 3, 33 *International Legal Materials* 1332 (1994).

United Nations Framework Convention on Climate Change, adopted 9 May 1992, entered into force 21 March 1994, 1771 *United Nations Treaty Series* 107, 31 *International Legal Materials* 849 (1992).

Vienna Convention for the Protection of the Ozone Layer, adopted 22 March 1985, entered into force 22 September 1988, 1513 *United Nations Treaty Series* 293, 26 *International Legal Materials* 1516 (1987).

Anti-corruption treaties

African Union Convention on Preventing and Combatting Corruption, adopted 11 July 2003, entered into force 5 August 2006, 43 *International Legal Materials* 5 (2004).

Inter-American Convention against Corruption, adopted 29 March 1996, entered into force 6 March 1997.

OECD Convention on Combating Bribery of Foreign Public Officials in International Business Transactions, adopted 21 November 1997, entered into force 15 February 1999, OECD Doc DAFFE/IME/BR(97)20.

UN Convention against Corruption, adopted 31 October 2003, entered into force 14 December 2005, GA Res 58/4, UN Doc A/58/422 (2003), 43 *International Legal Materials* 37 (2004).

International Labour Organization conventions

Convention (No. 29) concerning Forced or Compulsory Labour, adopted 28 June 1930, in force 1 May 1932.

Convention (No. 87) concerning Freedom of Association and Protection of the Right to Organise, adopted 9 July 1948, in force 4 July 1950.

Convention (No. 98) concerning the Application of the Principles of the Right to Organise and Collective Bargaining, adopted 1 July 1949, in force 18 July 1951.

Convention (No. 100) concerning Equal Remuneration for Men and Women Workers for Work of Equal Value, adopted 29 June 1951, in force 23 May 1953.

Convention (No. 105) concerning the Abolition of Forced Labour, adopted 25 June 1957, in force 17 January 1959.

Convention (No. 111) concerning Discrimination in Respect of Employment and Occupation, adopted 25 June 1958, in force 15 June 1960.

Convention (No. 138) concerning Minimum Age for Admission to Employment, adopted 26 June 1973, in force 19 June 1976.

Convention (No. 169) concerning Indigenous and Tribal Peoples in Independent Countries, adopted 27 June 1989, in force 5 September 1991.

Convention (No. 182) concerning the Prohibition and Immediate Action for the Elimination of the Worst Forms of Child Labour, adopted 17 June 1999, in force 19 November 2000.

Human rights and other treaties

Convention against Torture and Other Cruel, Inhuman or Degrading Treatment or Punishment, adopted 10 December 1984, in force 26 June 1987, 1465 *United Nations Treaty Series* 85.

Convention on the Elimination of All Forms of Discrimination against Women, adopted 18 December 1979, in force 3 September 1981, 1249 *United Nations Treaty Series* 13.

Convention on the Rights of the Child, adopted 20 November 1989, in force 2 September 1990, 1577 *United Nations Treaty Series* 3.

Inter-American Convention on International Commercial Arbitration, adopted 30 January 1975, in force 16 June 1976.

International Convention for the Protection of All Persons from Enforced Disappearance, adopted 20 December 2006, in force 23 December 2010, reprinted in (2007) 14 *International Human Rights Reports* 582.

International Convention on the Elimination of All Forms of Racial Discrimination, adopted 21 December 1966, in force 4 January 1969, 660 *United Nations Treaty Series* 195.

International Convention on the Protection of the Rights of Migrant Workers and Their Families, adopted 18 December 1990, in force 1 July 2003, 2220 *United Nations Treaty Series* 3.

International Convention on the Rights of Persons with Disabilities, adopted 20 December 2006, in force 3 May 2008, 2515 *United Nations Treaty Series* 3.

International Covenant on Civil and Political Rights, adopted 16 December 1966, in force 23 March 1976, 999 *United Nations Treaty Series* 171.

International Covenant on Economic Social and Cultural Rights, adopted 16 December 1966, in force 3 January 1976, 993 *United Nations Treaty Series* 3.

United Nations Convention on the Recognition and Enforcement of Foreign Arbitral Awards, adopted 6 July 1958, in force 7 June 1959.

Abbreviations and acronyms

AALCC	Asian–African Legal Consultative Committee
ADB	Asian Development Bank
ADR	Alternative dispute resolution
APPI	Agreement on the Promotion and Protection of Investments
ASEAN	Association of Southeast Asian Nations
BIPPA	Bilateral Investment Promotion and Protection Agreement
BIT	Bilateral investment treaty
CARICOM	Caribbean Community
CARIFORUM	The Forum of the Caribbean Group of African, Caribbean and Pacific (ACP) states
CAT	*Convention against Torture and Other Cruel, Inhuman or Degrading Treatment*
CECA	Comprehensive Economic Cooperation Agreement
CEDAW	*Convention on the Elimination of All Forms of Discrimination Against Women*
COMESA	Common Market for Eastern and Southern Africa
CPED	*International Convention for the Protection of All Persons from Enforced Disappearance*
CRC	*Convention on the Rights of the Child*
CRPD	*Convention on the Rights of Persons with Disabilities*
CSR	Corporate social responsibility
DSU	WTO *Dispute Settlement Understanding*
EBRD	European Bank for Reconstruction and Development
ECE	Evaluation committee of experts
EIA	Environmental impact assessment
EPA	Economic partnership agreement
EU	European Union
FDI	Foreign direct investment

FET	Fair and equitable treatment
FIPA	Foreign investment promotion and protection agreement
FTA	Free trade agreement
GATS	*WTO General Agreement on Trade in Services*
GATT	*General Agreement on Tariffs and Trade*
GMOs	Genetically modified organisms
Guiding Principles	Guiding Principles on Business and Human Rights developed by the United Nations Special Representative of the Secretary-General on the Issue of Human Rights and Transnational Corporations and Other Business Enterprises
HRIA	Human rights impact assessment
IBA	International Bar Association
ICCPR	*International Covenant on Civil and Political Rights*
ICERD	*International Convention on the Elimination of All Forms of Racial Discrimination*
ICESCR	*International Covenant on Economic, Social and Cultural Rights*
ICRMW	*International Convention on the Protection of the Rights of Migrant Workers and Their Families*
ICSID	International Centre for Settlement of Investment Disputes
IFC	International Finance Corporation
IIA	International investment agreement
IISD	International Institute for Sustainable Development
ILO	International Labour Organization
IMF	International Monetary Fund
IP	Intellectual property
ISO	International Organization for Standardization
MFN	Most favoured nation
MIGA	Multilateral Investment Guarantee Agency of the World Bank
MNE	Multi-national enterprise
NAAEC	*North American Agreement on Environmental Cooperation*
NAALC	*North American Agreement on Labor Cooperation*
NAFTA	*North American Free Trade Agreement*
NAO	National administrative office

New York Convention	*United Nations Convention on the Recognition and Enforcement of Foreign Arbitral Awards*
OECD	Organisation for Economic Co-operation and Development
PTIA	Preferential trade and investment agreement
SA	Sustainability assessment
SOE	State-owned enterprise
SRSG	Special Representative of the Secretary-General on the Issue of Human Rights and Transnational Corporations and Other Business Enterprises
TNC	Transnational corporation
TRIMs Agreement	*WTO Agreement on Trade-Related Investment Measures*
TRIPS Agreement	*WTO Agreement on Trade-Related Aspects of Intellectual Property Rights*
UNCITRAL	United Nations Commission on International Trade Law
UNCTAD	United Nations Conference on Trade and Development
UNDRIP	*United Nations Declaration on the Rights of Indigenous Peoples*
Vienna Convention	*Vienna Convention on the Law of Treaties*
WTO	World Trade Organisation

PART I. BACKGROUND

Chapter 1

Introduction

1.1 The rationale for a guide to international investment agreement provisions for developing countries based on sustainable development

1.1.1 Exploring how international investment agreements can do a better job of promoting foreign investment and accommodating appropriate host state regulation

Whether and how to negotiate international investment agreements (IIAs) are significant policy issues for virtually all countries. Most IIAs in place today are bilateral investment treaties (BITs) between capital-exporting developed countries and capital-importing developing countries. Developed countries are interested in the protection that these treaties offer to their investors operating in host developing countries. Developing countries hope that by committing to provide protection, IIAs will improve the prospects for future inflows of foreign investment. This has been called the 'grand bargain' of BITs.[1]

However, there is reason to doubt the value of the bargain represented by existing IIAs. Evidence of the link between entering into IIAs and increased foreign investment inflows, the main benefit sought by developing countries, is weak. In addition, investment inflows have not always contributed to sustainable development.[2] At the same time, critics assert that the forms of IIA typically sought by developed countries can constrain the ability of host developing countries to regulate foreign investors operating within their borders. IIAs may make it difficult for countries to achieve essential public policy objectives, including their development goals and the maintenance of environmental, human rights and labour rights standards.[3]

The constraints that IIAs impose on host states, combined with costly, inconsistent and sometimes surprising decisions by investor–state arbitration tribunals regarding the meaning of broadly worded IIA obligations, have led many countries to rethink what obligations an IIA should include. In some cases, countries have revised the models that they use as the basis for negotiations. A few countries, such as Ecuador, have sought to terminate their obligations altogether.

---

1 For example, J W Salacuse and N P Sullivan (2005), 'Do BITs Really Work? An Evaluation of Bilateral Investment Treaties and Their Grand Bargain', 46 *Harvard International Law Journal* 67.

2 K von Moltke and H Mann (2005), *A Southern Agenda on International Investment?: Promoting Development with Balanced Rights and Obligations for Investors, Host States and Home States*, International Institute for Sustainable Development, Winnipeg.

3 M Sornarajah (2010), *The International Law of Foreign Investment*, 3d ed., Cambridge University Press, Cambridge.

This guide (the 'Guide') is designed to assist developing countries to negotiate IIAs that do a better job of promoting their sustainable development. It explains how IIAs can increase foreign investment flows into developing countries and addresses how these agreements can support the efforts of host developing countries to regulate foreign investment inflows in order to ensure that they contribute to sustainable development.

The Guide achieves these goals by:

1. Identifying emerging best practices in existing agreements;
2. Suggesting new and innovative provisions;
3. Acting as a resource for developing country negotiators; and
4. Describing how states can achieve coherence among their IIAs.

1.1.2 Identifying emerging best practices

New model agreements contain innovative provisions of which developing countries should be aware. The international regime for investment, composed principally of more than 3,000 BITs and preferential trading agreements with investment provisions, has matured to the point at which there is broad consensus on many of the core categories of investor protection obligations. At the same time, the specific content of these obligations is evolving in important ways. Model agreements recently adopted by some countries in response to the growing number of investor–state arbitration cases incorporate innovations that strike a better balance between investor protection and the preservation of policy-making flexibility for party states. These models provide useful new approaches to incorporating sustainable development into IIAs.

Also, IIAs are being negotiated in increasingly diverse contexts. For instance, developing countries are negotiating more IIAs amongst themselves in bilateral and regional groupings. At the same time, a growing number of developing countries are becoming exporters of capital as well as importers. Some agreements between developing countries provide alternative approaches to the provisions that could be included in other investment agreements.

The Guide identifies emerging best practices from existing treaty models and discusses the costs and benefits of the different approaches they represent.

1.1.3 Identifying new kinds of provisions

As noted, evidence on the effects of IIAs on foreign investment flows is weak. The Guide includes examples of new, more effective ways to encourage investment flows. For instance, the traditional investor protection provisions that dominate existing IIAs could be supplemented with provisions that require technical assistance from investors' home states to support the development of transparent and effective regulatory schemes in host states that will be more predictable and less burdensome for investors. In addition, provisions could be included in an IIA to require home states to directly facilitate investment in host states by their investors.

The Guide also discusses new sorts of provisions that are designed to preserve the ability of states to regulate investment in a manner that ensures that foreign investment is harnessed to achieve development objectives without creating strong disincentives to investment. Such provisions may be useful to host states hoping to use IIAs more effectively to achieve sustainable development.

1.1.4 Supporting developing country negotiators

In addition to suggesting new provisions that may lead to a better bargain for developing countries than existing IIAs, the Guide is intended to be directly useful for countries negotiating new IIAs. There are often significant differences in economic and political power between developed and developing countries. Negotiators from developing countries frequently lack experience with IIAs, compared with their developed country counterparts. The information and analysis provided in the Guide helps to redress these chronic inequalities of bargaining power between developed and developing countries. The Guide aims to compensate in a modest way for the inadequate resources that developing countries can devote to evaluating the effects of entering into an IIA on investment flows and on their social and economic policies.

Inequalities between developed and developing countries are more easily exploited when negotiations are based on a pre-existing IIA model drafted by developed countries with only their interests in mind. When such a model is used, it can be difficult for developing countries to deviate from it. The Guide will make it easier for developing countries to negotiate IIAs consistent with their sustainable development objectives. The provisions that are discussed provide alternatives to existing IIA models that may be a new starting point for negotiations. In addition, the Guide will be a useful reference tool during negotiations to evaluate the costs and benefits of different approaches.

In addition to IIA negotiators, the Guide aims to support those implementing investment treaties and those involved in activities that may be subject to treaty obligations, including investment promotion agencies, domestic policy-makers and legislative drafters. Officials in government legal departments and others who may be called on in the event of a claim made under an IIA may also find the Guide helpful.

1.1.5 Enhancing policy coherence

Almost every country is a party to at least one IIA, and states continue to negotiate new agreements. The more IIAs that a country enters into, the more likely it is that conflicting obligations will arise. To avoid such conflicts, IIAs must be compatible. It is impossible to achieve perfect compatibility. Every agreement will reflect the unique result of negotiations between states. However, the Guide is intended to support consistency in investment treaties and will encourage greater policy coherence by improving understanding of the nature and effect of obligations, both in existing treaties and those being negotiated, and of how IIA obligations interact with each other. The Guide also discusses how to ensure coherence between IIAs and domestic policy on investment with a view to ensuring that IIA commitments support domestic policy goals.

1.2 What is in the Guide?

The first few sections of the Guide provide an overview of the context for IIA negotiations. They discuss:

- The basic purposes of international investment agreements;
- Links between IIAs and inward investment flows; and
- Links between investment inflows and sustainable development.

This overview will assist users of the Guide by identifying some of the objectives of both developed and developing countries in negotiating IIAs and explaining the need for new kinds of IIA provisions. In addition, the ways in which the Guide addresses this need are introduced.

The remainder of the Guide discusses options for IIA provisions, including samples of specific provisions, along with a discussion of their costs and benefits. These examples are not intended to be prescriptive. Each state must determine what bundle of commitments is appropriate given its unique circumstances, including its policies regarding openness to foreign investment and its capacity to regulate investment. The sample provisions are included primarily to illustrate how sustainable development policies, such as the protection of the environment or the promotion of human rights, could be better achieved through the innovative drafting of IIA provisions.

The provisions discussed in the Guide fall into three general categories:

- **Core investor protection obligations**: These are the obligations found in most existing IIAs. They include for example, national treatment, most favoured nation (MFN) treatment, fair and equitable treatment, compensation for expropriation and limits on restrictions on the transfer of funds by investors. Provisions in this category are the traditional host state obligations to investors. Like most international obligations, these provisions do impose some constraints on host state freedom to regulate. The Guide discusses more nuanced, sophisticated and balanced versions of these core obligations that increasingly have been adopted in national IIA models and that provide greater and more certain freedom for host state regulation to achieve domestic policy goals. The Guide also discusses the prospects for qualifying and limiting investor protection commitments through reservations and exceptions.
- **Investor protection obligations not found in most treaties**: These include provisions such as prohibitions on performance requirements that are found only in some IIAs. While these may have a positive impact on investment flows, they raise other policy issues for host countries, including concerns about their impact on a state's flexibility to adopt measures to obtain its development objectives.
- **New obligations to promote sustainable development**: The Guide provides examples of new kinds of obligations, such as obligations on home states and investors, that depart substantially from provisions in traditional IIAs, and are designed to better ensure that states can achieve their development goals, including attracting increased foreign investment. However, in some cases these

innovative provisions may discourage foreign investment in seeking to promote sustainable development.

1.3 What is not in the Guide?

The Guide does not compare IIAs with investment contract commitments or insurance that may be used as substitutes for, or complements to, IIA obligations as ways to encourage investment. The Guide's focus on IIAs does not suggest, however, that IIAs constitute the best or only approach to attracting and retaining foreign investment. Other forms of commitment may be preferable in some circumstances. For example, investment contracts have some advantages over IIAs. Unlike investment treaties, investment contracts can be used to bind the investor to specific commitments to the host state. In addition, it is easier for a state to assess the costs and benefits of specific transactions than to make this kind of assessment for the wide range of investments typically covered by an IIA. In an IIA, a state accepts broad commitments in relation to an unlimited number of future investments of various kinds by foreign investors for a long period of time, subject only to any limitations in the treaty. Even though they may be better in some cases, contract commitments and other strategies to attract investment are simply outside the scope of the Guide.

The goal of the Guide is modest. Rather than surveying all possible approaches to attracting investment, it aims to help developing countries with existing IIAs and the negotiation of new ones. In this regard, the Guide tries to address a significant practical challenge. Despite the potential utility of contracts and other alternatives to IIAs, developing countries will continue to be confronted with opportunities, and in some cases pressure, to negotiate IIAs. The Guide does not suggest that all countries will be better off negotiating IIAs. Some countries may determine that the costs of IIA commitments exceed the benefits and decide not to enter into these agreements. The discussion in the Guide should assist countries considering that option. The main purpose of the Guide, however, is to provide a source of useful information and analysis for countries that have negotiated, or are considering negotiating, IIAs.

Chapter 2

The Context for International Investment Agreement Negotiations

2.1 Existing IIA practice

2.1.1 Why states sign IIAs

This section explains the basic reasons states decide to enter into IIAs and how these reasons inform the negotiating positions of the parties. The basic purposes of existing IIAs can be simply stated as follows:

- To protect foreign investors from a treaty party state (the investor's *home state*) against discriminatory or unfair treatment by governments in the other party state (the *host state*);
- To ensure that the host state legal regime for foreign investors from the home state is stable, transparent, consistent and fair; and
- To promote foreign direct investment in host states by providing these protections to investors from the home state.[1]

The main way in which these purposes are achieved in existing IIAs is through provisions designed to protect foreign investors. The prospect of increased foreign investment inflows is only an incidental and, as discussed in Section 2.2 (Links between signing IIAs and attracting increased foreign investment), somewhat uncertain result of granting investors the protection that is provided for in IIAs.

In particular cases, developing countries will have a wide range of other motivations for entering into IIAs. Some may want to use investment treaties as a kind of external constraint to lock in domestic market-opening reforms, as well as to signal this intention to foreign investors from all states. Signing an international treaty makes it more difficult for the government to change its policies, laws and regulations regarding foreign investors.

Countries may negotiate an IIA as a way of keeping up with other developing countries that have signed agreements. Virtually all countries seek foreign investment, and the network of IIAs is already large and continually expanding. The competition

1 J W Salacuse and N P Sullivan (2005), 'Do BITs Really Work? An Evaluation of Bilateral Investment Treaties and Their Grand Bargain', 46 *Harvard International Law Journal* 67. Some BITs concluded with the United States and Canada, and more recently with Japan, contain commitments regarding access to host state markets (UNCTAD (2007), *Bilateral Investment Treaties 1995–2006: Trends in Investment Rulemaking*, UN publication, Sales No. E.06.II.D.16 at 23, United Nations, New York and Geneva).

for investment can be intense.[2] A country may seek to sign an IIA with a developed country that has already signed IIAs with neighbouring countries as a strategy to ensure that it is not discriminated against in the competition with its neighbours to attract investors from the developed country.

Countries may view signing a BIT with another country as a first step towards establishing a closer economic relationship with that country on a broader basis, possibly including entering into a comprehensive preferential trading agreement. The existence of a BIT between a developed and a developing country has been shown to increase the odds that they will enter into a preferential trading agreement. In addition, the combination of a BIT and a preferential trade agreement has been shown to attract more investment than a BIT alone.[3] Finally, a factor that often contributes to a developing country's desire to sign a BIT is pressure from the other party seeking protection for their investors.

While the desire to lock in openness to investment, keep up with the competition, build goodwill to pave the way for preferential trade agreements or respond to the pressure of other states may all play a role in some cases, the express purpose of all IIAs is the protection and promotion of foreign investment.

Box 2.1 Typical provisions in a bilateral investment treaty

1. Definitions and scope of agreement provisions
2. Basic investor protection obligations
   - National treatment
   - Most favoured nation (MFN) treatment
   - Fair and equitable treatment
   - Prohibition on expropriation without compensation
   - Prohibitions on restrictions on transfer of funds
3. Reservations and exceptions
   - General exceptions

(Continued)

2 Z Elkins, A Guzman and B Simmons (2006), 'Competing for Capital: The Diffusion of Bilateral Investment Treaties, 1960–2000', 60 *International Organization* 811.

3 J Tobin and M Busch (2010), 'A BIT is Better than a Lot: Bilateral Investment Treaties and Preferential Trading Agreements', *World Politics* 62, 1–42. In the past, BITs may have been signed on behalf of a government for political reasons, such as an opportunity for a government leader to demonstrate a general interest in an improved economic relationship with the other party state. Since most developed countries had a standard form of agreement, it was easy to put together a treaty to sign. Now that investor–state arbitration has made the costs of investment treaties much clearer, it seems unlikely that this practice will persist.

(Continued)

- Annexes setting out reservations for existing measures and areas of regulation

4. Transparency requirements
5. Investor–state dispute settlement

The relative importance of protection and promotion, however, are typically quite different for IIA parties. This may not be obvious from the form that these agreements take. In all existing investment treaties, the obligations are stated to be mutual and reciprocal in nature. That is, subject to some reservations,[4] the same protections that Canada agrees to give to investors from Trinidad and Tobago under the foreign investment protection agreement between the two countries must be provided by Trinidad and Tobago to investors from Canada. However, capital-exporting countries such as Canada are typically interested in securing protection for their investors, whereas the dominant motive for most capital-importing countries to sign an IIA is to increase foreign investment from capital-exporting treaty partners.

In the context of an IIA negotiated between a developed country and a developing country, there will usually be few investors from the developing country party with investments in the developed country party that will benefit from protection under the IIA. In such cases, the parties rarely expect that an IIA will induce investment from the developing country into the developed country. In this situation, there is very little cost to a developed country from entering into the treaty. It will never be called on to fulfil its investor protection obligations.

Developing countries, on the other hand, are interested in foreign investment from developed countries to stimulate economic development and contribute to host state revenues, providing them with the resources needed to alleviate poverty and, more generally, to achieve their political, social and economic goals. In order to try to attract investment, they subject themselves to the obligations to protect investors set out in the IIA, even though the investor protection obligations may impose real constraints on domestic policy-making flexibility.

Where developing countries are negotiating IIAs with each other, they may have interests both as capital exporters in investor protection and as capital importers in attracting investment. In 2010, 30 per cent of outward investment originated in developing countries. Some developing countries, such as China, have significant interests as exporters of capital to developed countries. In short, while, traditionally, developing countries have negotiated IIAs as capital importers, more and more developing countries have interests as exporters too, especially in their negotiations with neighbouring developing countries.

4 Where reservations are permitted in a treaty, different reservations taken by each state result in some formal asymmetry of obligations.

2.1.2 Why investors want IIA protection

It is important to appreciate the concerns that investors from developed countries have about protecting their investments because these concerns inform the demands and expectations of developed countries during IIA negotiations. Investors from capital-exporting developing countries are likely to have the same concerns.

Investor concerns regarding the risk of arbitrary and discriminatory treatment by host states

Fundamentally, foreign investors are concerned about the risk of arbitrary and discriminatory treatment by domestic governments in host states. IIAs create standards of behaviour for the host states in which investors operate that reduce the risk of such treatment and, more generally, promote a secure and predictable legal regime for investors.[5] Investors cite several reasons for their concerns and the need to have IIA provisions to address them.

Weak protection for investors under host state domestic law and under customary international law: Investors may be concerned that customary international law[6] does not provide sufficient protection for foreign investors to guarantee them a stable investment environment. For example, virtually all IIAs prohibit expropriation without certain procedural guarantees being met and require compensation to be paid. It is argued that such treaty provisions can guarantee a higher and more certain standard of compensation than weak and contested customary international law standards.[7] Foreign investors may also be concerned that domestic law standards of treatment in a host state provide inadequate protection of their interests. IIAs can create higher, more comprehensive and more effective standards for investor protection that operate independently of domestic law in host states.

Host state incentives to treat foreign investors will diminish after the investment is made: One of the most important motivations for seeking protection against host state actions through IIAs is to overcome what has been described as the problem of 'dynamic inconsistency' or the 'obsolescing bargain'.[8] Countries seeking to attract foreign investment have an incentive to liberalise their domestic regimes and take other steps to encourage investors to locate within their borders. However, once investments have been made, host countries may be tempted to make their regimes less

5 D L Swenson (2005), 'Why Do Developing Countries Sign BITs?', 12 *University of California Davis Journal of International Law and Policy* 131.

6 Customary international law is international law that exists independent of treaty law and is composed of 'rules of law derived from the consistent conduct of States acting out of the belief that the law required them to act that way' (Shabtai Rosenne (1984), *Practice and Methods of International Law*, Oceana, New York, at 55).

7 UNCTAD (1998), *Bilateral Treaties in the Mid-1990s*, United Nations, New York and Geneva.

8 M Hallward-Driemeier (2003), 'Do Bilateral Investment Treaties Attract FDI? Only a Bit … and They Could Bite', World Bank Policy Research Paper, WPS 3121, World Bank, Washington, DC, at 2; R Vernon (1971), *Sovereignty at Bay: The Multinational Spread of US Enterprises*, Basic Books, New York.

favourable to foreign investors or even to expropriate foreign investments. They may be pressured by domestic investors or civil society groups to give preferential treatment to local investors, or they may wish to acquire a profitable foreign investment and operate it as a state-owned enterprise or put it under the control of domestic investors.

One reason foreign investment is subject to the risk of this kind of government action is that foreign investment is often not very mobile. Once investors incur non-recoverable or 'sunk' costs that would be lost if the investor withdrew its investment before it generated significant returns, a state has some freedom to modify its rules to make the domestic environment less favourable to the foreign investor without causing the investor to leave. An investor that has partially constructed a mine in a country may not be able to recover its costs by selling the mine property if the local government changes the rules in ways that make the mine financially less feasible. In such situations, the host state has greater freedom to change its regime for foreign investors in order to extract greater benefits from them.[9] Concern about this dynamic inconsistency problem is one of the primary reasons that investors lobby their governments to negotiate IIAs. To some extent, commitments in IIAs restrain host countries from changing the rules in ways that are inconsistent with the basic expectations of foreign investors.

Some have questioned the significance of the dynamic inconsistency problem and the need to resort to IIAs to address it.[10] In almost every case, a country will be concerned about attracting investment, not just today, but also on a continuing basis in the future. Any country that wishes to be an attractive destination for foreign investment would be unwise to engage in the kinds of changes to its investment policy and practice that the problem of dynamic inconsistency would predict. On the other hand, states do make these kinds of changes from time to time.

Another reason to doubt the seriousness of the dynamic inconsistency problem is that there are a number of alternative ways for foreign investors to obtain protection against risks associated with state behaviour, including investment insurance and guarantees in investment contracts. Insurance for foreign investors against political risks associated with contracts with host states may be available from the World Bank's Multilateral Investment Guarantee Agency (MIGA) or national agencies in the investor's home state. In some cases, agencies in the host state may provide insurance. Political risk insurance may cover a variety of

---

9 E Neumayer and L Spess (2005), 'Do Bilateral Investment Treaties Increase Foreign Direct Investment in Developing Countries?', 33 *World Development* 1567 at 1570.

10 J W Yackee (2007), 'Do BITs Really Work? Revisiting the Empirical Link between Investment Treaties and Foreign Direct Investment', Legal Studies Research Paper No. 1054, University of Wisconsin Law School. See also UNCTAD (2009), *The Role of International Investment Agreements in Attracting Foreign Direct Investment to Developing Countries*, United Nations, New York and Geneva, discussing the methodological problems with the empirical studies, at 56–8); K P Sauvant and L E Sachs (2009), 'BITs, DTTs, and FDI Flows: An Overview', in K P Sauvant, and L E Sachs (eds), *The Effect of Treaties on Foreign Direct Investment: Bilateral Investment Treaties, Double Taxation Treaties and Investment Flows*, Oxford University Press, Oxford.

risks associated with state action, including expropriation of land, confiscation of assets and revocation of permits. Contractual protection can be tailored to address specific investor concerns about host state conduct. For example, an investor may be able to negotiate a promise by the host state not to change the rules that govern the investment.[11] This commitment may be backed up by an undertaking by the state to submit to arbitration if the investor claims that the state has not fulfilled its obligations.

An IIA may not be important for particular investors who can take advantage of these alternative forms of protection. However, these alternatives can result in additional costs for investors and states because they must be negotiated each time an investment transaction occurs. Once a treaty is negotiated, IIA protection operates to protect all investments by investors of a party state against actions of the other party state over a long period of time. Alternative arrangements are also less transparent than an IIA. Protections for investors negotiated in individual contracts may be known only to the parties, and their lack of transparency may increase the risk of corruption involving the government officials who negotiate them. In addition, if contracts are hidden from the public, democratic checks on government agreements with investors will be undermined.

It is hard to evaluate the extent to which IIAs are really necessary to attract foreign investment. As discussed, there are alternative mechanisms for protecting investors. In addition, reputational considerations may deter a government from changing policies in ways that are harmful to investors after they have made their investment. In practice, however, there is some evidence that investors view the investor protections in IIAs as important. The most obvious evidence is the large and continually expanding network of IIAs. MIGA and many national investment insurance providers, including those in France and Germany, require the existence of an IIA between the investor's state and the host state as a condition of their agreement to insure an investment, apparently because of their perception that IIAs play a role in mitigating the risk of state behaviour that will negatively affect investments. Some major transnational corporations, such as Dow Chemical, that have the sophistication and resources to negotiate protection directly with host states nevertheless view the presence of an IIA with a country as an important consideration when deciding whether to invest in the country.[12]

Investor concerns regarding the effectiveness, fairness and independence of host state courts and administrative tribunals and other remedies

Foreign investors are often sceptical about their ability to obtain relief from domestic courts and administrative tribunals when they complain about host state conduct. They may view domestic institutions in a host state as corrupt,

11 This kind of clause is referred to as a 'stabilisation clause'.

12 Tobin and Busch, op. cit. More discussion of the evidence regarding the links between signing an IIA and attracting investment is provided in Section 2.2 (Links between signing an IIA and attracting increased foreign investment) and Appendix 1 to the Guide.

incompetent or not sufficiently independent of the state. Local civil procedures may not provide relief in a timely way or, if relief is obtained, the procedures for collecting compensation or other remedies may not be effective against the state and state agencies.

Traditionally, the only alternative to pursuing relief through domestic procedures for a foreign investor was to lobby its government to pursue the claim on its behalf. This is called 'state espousal' because obtaining relief was dependent on the investor's home state 'espousing' the investor's claim and raising it with the host state government. Relying on 'state espousal' has several disadvantages from an investor's point of view. The home state's interest in pursuing a claim on behalf of one of its investors against another state will depend on a number of factors, such as the economic and political importance of the investor and its investment, as well as a complex matrix of political considerations related to the relationship between the investor's state and the host state. Regardless of the merits of an investor's claim, these kinds of considerations may discourage a state from pursuing the claim.

As a consequence of concerns about the effectiveness of domestic procedures in the host state and the alternative of state espousal, investors urged their governments to negotiate for the inclusion of investor–state arbitration in IIAs. This dispute settlement mechanism allows a foreign investor from one party state to submit to binding arbitration a claim that another party state has breached its obligations under the agreement. Unlike state espousal, it is solely up to the investor to decide whether to initiate a claim, how to argue its case and whether to settle its claim. If the arbitral tribunal finds that the state complained against has breached its IIA obligations, it can make an award of financial compensation in favour of the investor against the state to compensate the investor for any loss that it suffered as a result. In addition to providing a process for investors to seek compensation in particular cases, the host state's agreement to submit to investor–state arbitration demonstrates a strong and credible commitment to comply with the obligations set out in the IIA for the benefit of investors from the other party state.

Critics of these procedures argue that the threat of investor–state arbitration has a chilling effect on domestic legislators, discouraging them from acting or implementing policies which, though they may promote legitimate policy goals, are, or even might be, contrary to IIA obligations. For instance, legislators might hesitate to terminate a concession granted to a foreign investor to provide some service, such as waste collection, with the goal of returning to the public delivery of the service, out of concern that the investor might claim that the termination is a breach of the fair and equitable treatment obligation in an IIA. This chilling effect is exacerbated by uncertainty regarding the standards for investor protection found in IIAs that has resulted from inconsistent and surprising decisions by investor–state tribunals. Another concern for states is the cost of investor–state cases. Damage awards in investor–state suits can be very costly. The expense of defending an investor–state claim can be considerable, even if the state is successful. For all these reasons, a state may try to manage its risk of claims being made by refraining from some kinds of regulatory initiatives. Nevertheless, despite these and other concerns about investor–state arbitration, provisions for such a procedure are found in the vast majority of treaties currently in place and under negotiation.[13]

2.2 Links between signing IIAs and attracting increased foreign investment

Developing countries compete for foreign investment and many governments consider IIAs to be a necessary component of a strategy to attract it. But is this a good strategy? Do IIAs attract investment? It may seem surprising, but academics and others have only recently tried to determine whether signing a foreign investment treaty actually leads to increased foreign investment inflows. Proponents of IIAs have had to confront the brute fact that some developing countries, of which Brazil is the best example, have been extremely successful in attracting foreign investment from countries with which they do not have IIAs.[14] Other countries have signed IIAs and attracted little investment.

The success of some countries in attracting investment without having IIAs in place, and the failure of those that have signed them to attract investment, simply reflect the fact that there are a large number of variables that affect the decisions of foreign investors regarding whether to invest in a particular country. IIAs will never be more than one factor in investor decision-making.[15] There is no doubt that the domestic policy environment in a state, including its openness to investment and trade, efforts at investment promotion and involvement in preferential trading arrangements, as well as its transparency, are also significant factors. Market variables unique to each state are also important, such as:

- The size of and rate of growth of the domestic market;
- *Per capita* income;
- Geographical proximity to investors' home states; and
- The ease of investing in a market, including the availability, cost, reliability and quality of inputs into production, such as labour, electricity, telecommunications and the transportation infrastructure.

The relative importance of these factors will vary depending on the nature of the investor's investment. For example, an investor planning to set up a chain of retail stores to sell to the local market in a country will be more interested in the number of consumers and their *per capita* income than a mining company that intends to

13 A more detailed discussion of the costs and benefits of investor–state arbitration is set out in Section 7.1 (Investor–state dispute settlement) of the Guide. The consensus among developed countries on the desirability of investor–state arbitration was broken in 2011, when the Australian government announced it would no longer seek to have investor–state arbitration included in the IIAs it negotiates. Government of Australia (2011), 'Trading Our Way to More Jobs and Prosperity', Gillard Government Trade Policy Statement, Department of Foreign Affairs and Trade, at 14.

14 Hallward-Driemeier, op. cit.; Salacuse and Sullivan, op. cit.

15 A review of the studies of the effects of IIAs on investment flows is provided in Appendix 1 to the Guide.

export all of its production. The mining company will be more concerned about efficiency considerations, such as the cost and reliability of local power, and the quality and quantity of local mineral resources. Many global businesses try to allocate specific portions of their production process to countries in which that portion can be most efficiently carried out. This kind of business might allocate its research and development to one country, its component manufacturing to another country and final assembly to a third country. In each case, its investment decision will be based on distinct locational advantages in each country.

2.2.1 Empirical evidence

Researchers have recently tried to determine whether IIAs actually achieve one of their main goals: increased foreign investment flows into signatory countries. Studies have looked at two main expected effects on investment flows:

- **Commitment effect**: Signing an IIA creates an international commitment by a host country to comply with investor protection obligations in the treaty in relation to investors from the other party state. The expected effect is increased investment by investors from the other party state.
- **Signalling effect**: Signing an IIA sends a signal generally to foreign investors that a country is serious about protecting the rights and interests of foreign investors. The expected effect is increased investment from all countries.

To determine whether there is a commitment effect, studies have looked at investment flows between pairs of countries that have signed a BIT. Some of these studies show a significant positive correlation between a developing country signing a BIT with a developed country and increased foreign investment from that country. Other studies have found little or no evidence of such an effect. A similar inconsistency exists in studies seeking to determine if a signalling effect exists. Some studies have found a positive effect on total investment inflows into a country from all countries as a result of the country signing a BIT, while others have not. Most studies have found the other forms of treaties with investment provisions, such as preferential trade and investment agreements (PTIAs), have had a positive effect on investment inflows.

In some of the studies that found a positive relationship between signing an IIA and investment inflows, the results varied depending on particular circumstances. For example, several studies have found that the relationship between IIAs signed by a country and investment inflows to that country varied with the number of agreements entered into. At some point, signing an additional agreement was found to have little marginal effect.

Commentators have suggested that the inconsistency in the results of studies looking at the relationship between signing an IIA and investment inflows is due to problems with data and econometric modelling techniques.

2.2.2 Problems with empirical models

Most studies have looked simply at the correlation between IIAs and investment inflows and assumed that if the relationship was positive over time, meaning that signing an IIA was associated with increased investment either from the IIA partner or generally from all countries, then it was the IIA that caused the increased investment. It is possible, however, that the reverse is true: higher levels of bilateral investment could encourage countries to negotiate IIAs rather than the other way around. This might occur, for example, where investors in a host state sought the protection of an IIA between their home state and the host state after making their investment, and their government then negotiated an IIA with the host state.

Alternatively, investment flows may be affected by variables that models have not taken into account. Most significantly, few studies to date have tried to control for the effect of investment-liberalising changes made by a host state to its domestic regime. Often such changes are made contemporaneously with entering into a BIT.[16] Where a study shows a positive relationship between signing a BIT and investment inflows, but does not try to eliminate the effects of pro-investment domestic reform, it may overstate the investment-inducing effect. Some of the new investment might be attributable to the changes to the domestic regime. While the impact of the changes to the domestic regime is uncertain, the failure to control for such an impact in an empirical study makes conclusions regarding the investment inducing effects of BITs unreliable.

In one of the few studies that have rigorously examined these kinds of problems, Aisbett concluded that it is impossible to say that IIAs caused increased investment flows.[17] In her view, the results found by some earlier studies are unreliable because they do not deal adequately with the possibility of reverse causation or other potential causes for the results observed.[18]

2.2.3 Problems with data

There are a number of problems with using existing data to explain the relationship between investment flows and signing investment treaties. The data on investment flows for certain sectors, such as services, and for some countries, particularly least developed countries, are not always comparable or reliable.[19] This is particularly true for data on bilateral flows.[20] Investment flow data are also plagued by problems associated with the complex organisation of transnational businesses. Sometimes investments may be identified as coming from a particular foreign country in which the entity making the investment is organised, but the real source of capital is another country. For example, an investment by an investor of one state may be identified as

16 J W Yackee (2007), op. cit. Studies have tried to address trade openness in their models. One study that tried to control for this found a positive correlation between IIAs and investment inflows (P Busse *et al.* (February 2008), 'FDI Promotion through Bilateral Investment Treaties: More than a BIT?', Kiel Working Paper No. 1403, Kiel Institute for the World Economy, Kiel).

17 E Aisbett (2009), 'Bilateral Investment Treaties and Foreign Direct Investment: Correlation versus Causation', in Sauvant and Sachs, op. cit.

18 Ibid.

19 J W Yackee (2010–2011), 'Do Bilateral Investment Treaties Promote Foreign Direct Investment?: Some Hints from Alternative Evidence', 51 *Virginia Journal of International Law* 397 at 410.

20 Ibid. at 410–11.

originating in another state if it has been flowed by the investor through a subsidiary organised under the laws of that other state that the investor controls. Such a structure might be adopted for various reasons, including seeking to take advantage of a low tax rate in the state in which the subsidiary is incorporated. Similarly, a national of a state may make an investment in their own state but flow the investment funds through a wholly owned subsidiary corporation organised under the laws of another state. This kind of 'round-tripping' investment may be recorded as a foreign investment from the other state, even though it is really a domestic investment. In connection with these kinds of investments, investment flow statistics may not accurately reflect the true source of an investment.

Also, the use of aggregate investment data may mask possible variations in the investment flow effects of IIAs from sector to sector. Different kinds of investments are likely to be affected by IIA commitments in different ways, though it is not clear what the effect will be. For example, investments in sectors where the international movement of capital is relatively easy, such as financial services, might be greatly affected by IIAs, while investments in sectors such as natural resources might not be affected by IIAs signed by a country that does not possess resources available for exploitation.[21] An alternative and opposite analysis is also possible. Investments with more sunk costs benefit more from the protections in an IIA. Thus investments in sectors such as natural resources, where sunk costs are higher, might be more affected by IIAs. Other sectors, such as financial services that involve significantly lower sunk costs that cannot be recovered if the investment is terminated, might be little affected by IIA protection. Also, it may be that small and medium-sized businesses value IIA protection more highly since large transnational corporations are often in a position to negotiate for commitments directly from the state.[22] None of these kinds of considerations have been accounted for in the models used to date, even though it seems likely that the impact of an IIA will vary depending on the type of investment.

2.2.4 IIAs with different strengths

Studies that use long-term data lump together treaties with varying provisions that may provide quite different levels of protection for investors.[23] In particular, many early

21 This is suggested by Swenson, op. cit. Busse et al., op. cit., came to the opposite conclusion in their study (at 23).

22 UNCTAD (2009), *Role of International Investment Treaties*, op. cit., at 52–3.

23 Swenson, op. cit. Swenson developed a model that looked at the investment effects of signing a BIT, including effects occurring not only just after the BIT was signed, but also for a period prior to signing during which investment might be stimulated by the anticipated signing of the agreement. She also attached more weight to lag effects than do some other models. She found that new BIT signings in the early 1990s were not positively related to increased FDI, but that signings of BITs in the late 1990s were positively related. In contrast, T Siegmann (2007), 'The Impact of Bilateral Investment Treaties and Double Taxation Treaties on Foreign Direct Investment,' University of St Gallen Law and Economics Research Paper Series, Working Paper No. 2008–22, found that BITs from 1985 to 1995 had a significant effect on investment flows, which treaties signed after 1995 did not.

treaties did not provide for investor–state arbitration, which significantly reduces the value of the investor-protection provisions in these treaties.[24] Few empirical studies control for the relative strength of IIA obligations. It may be that a more significant positive effect on investment inflows is associated with IIAs incorporating stronger commitments. However, studies that have looked at the effects of strong US BITs have come to conflicting conclusions.[25]

2.2.5 Alternative evidence

In an attempt to address some of the methodological and data problems associated with the empirical studies discussed above, some researchers have surveyed investors to try to get a sense of the relative importance of the presence of an IIA for their decisions about where to invest. In a 2007 survey of transnational corporations for UNCTAD, more than 70 per cent of the respondents reported that the existence of an IIA with a country from which they would benefit did play a role in their decision about whether to invest in that country. Just fewer than 25 per cent of the respondents said that IIAs were relevant 'to a very great extent'. Only 23 per cent did not consider them 'at all.' Nine per cent of respondents answered 'don't know'.[26] Of 33 factors, the existence of an investment treaty ranked about in the middle in terms of its relative importance. It ranked higher in relation to investments in transition economies. Other surveys of the factors that corporate decision-makers take into account in deciding whether to invest in a country, however, have concluded that there is no evidence that IIAs are a significant factor in investors' decisions on where to invest.[27]

2.2.6 Conclusion

While a majority of studies to date have found a positive relationship between a country signing an IIA and increased investment into that country, other studies dispute those results on a variety of grounds related to problems with methodology and data. This does not necessarily mean that IIAs do not help to attract investment. Nevertheless, the conflicting evidence suggests that that if there is a role it is relatively small. Also, the impact of IIAs is likely to be complementary to other policies and circumstances that make a host country more attractive to foreign investors. The effect of signing an IIA may also vary depending on the nature of the investment.

In addition, whatever the evidence of benefits associated with concluding IIAs in the form of increased foreign direct investment (FDI) inflows, it is not clear that they are higher than the substantial costs developing countries incur in negotiating, signing,

---

24 Yackee (2007), op. cit., at 413.

25 See Salacuse and Sullivan, op. cit. Salacuse and Sullivan found a strong positive effect associated with signing strong US BITs. See also K P Gallagher and M B L Birch (2006), 'Do Investment Agreements Attract Investment? Evidence from Latin America', *Journal of World Investment Law and Trade 7* at 961. Gallagher and Birch find no evidence that signing a US BIT affected investment flows.

26 L Kekic and K P Sauvant (2007), *World Investment Prospects to 2011: Foreign Direct Investment and the Challenge of Political Risk*, Economist Intelligence Unit and the Columbia Program on International Investment, London and New York, at 96.

27 E.g. Yackee (2007), op. cit.

ratifying and complying with the obligations typically contained in such treaties. This caution is even expressed by some of those researchers who found that FDI inflows did result from IIAs.[28]

2.2.7 Guide features promoting investment

In response to the relatively weak evidence of the investment-inducing effects of existing IIA models, the Guide describes two features that are designed to stimulate more foreign investment than existing agreements in a more direct way. First, it discusses ways in which developed country parties can support the creation and implementation of a robust and transparent domestic regime for foreign investment in developing country parties. Such a regime should help to attract foreign investors by ensuring that their investments are subject to clear and predictable rules, as well as being more effective to obtain host country public policy goals. Second, the Guide discusses various obligations that can be placed on the investors' home states to promote investment in host states.

2.3 Links between foreign investment and sustainable development

In July 2008, the UN Secretary-General released a report that reviewed the implementation of the 2002 UN Monterrey Consensus on Financing for Development.[29] It concluded that action was needed to encourage larger and more consistent foreign investment flows to a broader group of developing countries and to ensure that investment activity led to development.[30] The need was described as particularly pressing for many small economies, which have seen growth rates decline compared with larger low- and middle-income states. How can the goal of increasing investment flows be linked to sustainable development? The Guide suggests various ways of achieving this.

To link foreign investment and sustainable development, the first task is to determine how investment and development are related, or how they ought to be related. Attracting foreign investment is an essential part of the development strategy of most developing countries. Important international instruments relating to sustainable development recognise that attracting foreign investment is crucial for developing countries to achieve economic growth that will translate into increased welfare for their citizens.[31] In addition, citizens naturally want to participate in the economic activities in their country, such as markets for goods, financial services and capital.

---

28 Neumayer and Spess, op. cit., at 1583; T Büthe and H V Milner, 'Bilateral Investment Treaties and Foreign Direct Investment: A Political Analysis', in Sauvant and Sachs, op. cit., at 214.

29 UN Secretary General (2008), *The Latest Developments Related to the Review Process on Financing for Development and the Implementation of the* Monterrey *Consensus*, UN Doc. A/63/179.

30 Ibid. at para. 18.

31 Principle 12 of the *Rio Declaration on Environment and Development*, UN Doc. A/CONF/151/26 (Vol. 1).

Such access is an important aspect of the freedom that citizens of developing countries seek to achieve through their development policies.[32]

However, investment inflows alone cannot produce sustainable development. How can these inflows be directed towards promoting sustainable development policies? The answer depends in part on each state's development goals. Traditionally, IIAs have focused exclusively on investor protection as a way of encouraging investment, but they did not otherwise address development. In this section, we discuss alternatives to the traditional IIA model that adopt a different approach to sustainable development, and we demonstrate how IIAs can be used to achieve sustainable development goals.

2.3.1 Defining sustainable development and the right to development

To make the link between foreign investment and development, we first have to be clear on the meaning of a highly contested term 'sustainable development'.

'Sustainable development' can mean different things in different contexts. In *international environmental law*, it relates to the protection of the natural environment in order that future generations can continue to enjoy it as present generations do.[33] In *development and human rights* circles, its meaning is broader, encompassing environmental sustainability, but also equitable development to reduce poverty, improve the health of people throughout the world, promote peace, protect human rights and pursue gender equality.[34] From an *economic* point of view, achieving sustainable development entails liberalising trade and investment policy in order to facilitate the access of goods to markets and to stimulate foreign investment flows.

The United Nations has articulated a *right to development*. It incorporates many aspects of the definitions of sustainable development current in the environmental, human rights and economics literature. The UN approach has many facets that suggest different ways in which IIAs and investment link to sustainable development.

Box 2.2 The right to development

The various elements of the right to development are articulated in many international declarations and documents.

(Continued)

32 Amartya Sen (1999), *Development as Freedom*, Anchor, New York, at 6, 38–39 and 111–145. The five dimensions of freedom identified by Sen are: (a) political freedoms; (b) economic facilities; (c) social opportunities; (d) transparency guarantees; and (e) protective security (at 10).

33 World Commission on Environment and Development (1987), *Our Common Future*, UN Doc. GA/42/427, at 43.

34 UN Millennium Project (2005), *Investing in Development: A Practical Plan to Achieve the Millennium Development Goals*, Routledge, London, at 3. Arjun Sengupta defines the right to development as follows: 'The Right to Development, which is an inalienable human right, is the right to a particular process of development in which all human rights and fundamental freedoms can be fully and progressively realized' (A Sengupta, 'The Human Right to Development', in B A Andreassen and S P Marks (eds) (2006), *Development as a Human Right*, Harvard University Press, Cambridge, MA, 9, at 11.

(Continued)

Declaration on the Right to Development, Art. 1

UN Doc. A/Res/41/128 Annex (1987)

The Right to Development is an inalienable human right by virtue of which every human person and all peoples are entitled to participate in, contribute to, and enjoy economic, social, cultural and political development, in which all human rights and fundamental freedoms can be fully realized.

Vienna Declaration and Programme of Action

UN Doc. A/CONF/157.23 (1993)

[T]he right to development, as established in the Declaration [on the Right to Development], [is] a universal and inalienable right and integral part of fundamental human rights.

Report of the Independent Expert on the Right to Development, Dr Arjun Sengupta

UN Doc. E/CN.4/2000/WG.18/CRP.1 (11 September 2000) at para. 64.

The right to development 'is the right to a particular process of development that allows the realization of economic, social, and cultural rights as well as civil and political rights and all fundamental freedoms by expanding the capabilities and choices of the individual'.

2.3.2 Current IIAs do not link development and foreign investment

Existing IIAs focus on guaranteeing investor protection in order to stimulate foreign investment; few contain provisions designed to ensure that investment leads to development. Indeed, many have criticised IIAs as imposing constraints on the ability of host country governments to adopt the policies needed to promote sustainable development.[35]

IIAs can constrain the ability of host country governments to regulate foreign investors in a number of ways. First, an IIA contains international legal rules that in many cases trump the application of the domestic law of the host state to a foreign investor. For instance, the constitutional law of the host state may allow a government to expropriate the property of an investor without paying compensation if this property will be used for a public purpose such as to build a road or create a national wildlife preserve. However, most IIAs require the state to compensate the investor fully for the economic value of any property that the government takes regardless of the importance of the public purpose of the expropriation.

Second, because they create a separate regime of international legal rules that apply to foreign investors but do not apply to domestic investors, and because they create a

35 E.g. M Sornarajah (2010), *The International Law of Foreign Investment*, 3d ed., Cambridge University Press, Cambridge.

mechanism for foreign investors to seek compensation for the adverse effects of laws and regulations of the host state that does not exist in domestic law, traditional IIAs can make it difficult for developing countries to implement sustainable development policies if they impose losses on foreign investors.

To illustrate this point, recall that most IIAs create a mechanism for foreign investors of one treaty party to complain about laws and regulations that the government of the other treaty party has passed if they cause a loss to the investor by breaching an obligation in the agreement. The complaint mechanisms in the IIA are separate from the recourse available to a foreign investor in domestic law. For instance, a country may place a cap on the price of water in order to ensure that poor people can have access to a clean and safe source of drinking water. It may be possible for an enterprise, whether foreign or domestic, that owns a water utility to challenge this cap by using the domestic law of the host state, such as administrative law, contract law, property law or even constitutional law. However, a *foreign* investor protected by the IIA will have an additional option to challenge the cap: it may bypass the domestic law remedies and invoke the IIA to complain that the investor protections provided in the investment treaty have been violated. Such a claim will be accompanied by a demand for compensation from the host state. In consequence, the bases for seeking relief that are open to a foreign investor under an IIA are far broader than those open to a domestic investor, and pursuing these remedies might undermine the government's sustainable development policy.

Designing an IIA that does a better job of promoting sustainable development than traditional agreements is challenging. In part, this is because the relationship between foreign investment and sustainable development is not straightforward.

2.3.3 The costs and benefits of foreign investment for sustainable development

Studies of the link between foreign investment and economic development have so far been inconclusive; increasing foreign investment does not necessarily result in economic growth. These studies have found that the nature of the relationship between foreign investment and economic growth depends on a variety of factors that vary from one host country to the next.[36]

In part, variability in the impact of foreign investment is due to the fact that foreign investment can have both costs and benefits (see Box 2.3).[37] Foreign investment can

---

36 Gallagher and Zarsky, for example, reviewed 11 studies and found that only two found a positive relationship between foreign investment and economic growth; one found a negative relationship; and the others concluded that the nature of the relationship depends on a variety of situation-specific factors (K P Gallagher and L Zarsky (2005), 'No Miracle Drug: Foreign Direct Investment and Sustainable Development' in L Zarsky (ed.) *International Investment for Sustainable Development: Balancing Rights and Rewards*, Earthscan, London; Sterling, VA, at 13). See also E S Prasad, R G Rajan and A Subramanian (November 2007), 'Foreign Capital and Economic Growth', NBER Working Paper, No. W13619, National Bureau of Economic Research, Cambridge, Massachusetts.

37 Some of the voluminous literature on the effects of foreign investment is referred to by Neumayer and Spess, op. cit.

supplement local sources of investment capital, contributing to increased employment and local tax revenues. It can also have a variety of positive spillovers, such as improving productivity and innovation in the domestic industry, transferring new technologies and production and management techniques to domestic producers, and creating better-paid jobs for local employees.

However, there may also be costs. Domestic investment may be crowded out, and domestic competition and entrepreneurship may be suppressed. Foreign investment could worsen income inequality as traditional industries atrophy, and workers from those industries may find it difficult to enter new ones. Investment may encourage the host state to rely on the exploitation of local natural resources of interest to foreign investors instead of developing other productive sectors of the economy.[38] In some cases, the activities of foreign investors have had a negative impact on the protection of the environment.[39]

The activities of foreign investors in host countries can have a significant impact on the promotion and protection of human rights. Tragic instances of the violation of human rights by foreign investors operating in developing countries are well known. International human rights law imposes obligations on states to protect and fulfil the human rights of individuals subject to their jurisdiction and to provide remedies for violations. States have a responsibility to regulate effectively the operations of foreign investors subject to their jurisdiction to ensure that they do not violate human rights. Few human rights treaties impose duties directly on non-state actors such as investors. For the most part, existing IIAs do not do so either.

The particular mix of costs and benefits of foreign investment for each country will depend on a host of local factors, including the nature and abilities of its human

---

38 The Secretary-General of the United Nations points out that 'foreign investment in natural resource exploitation [does] not automatically translate into durable development gains …' (UN Secretary General, *Latest Developments*, op. cit., at para. 16).

39 The former Sub-Commission on the Prevention of Discrimination and Protection of Minorities (now the Human Rights Council Advisory Committee) noted that foreign direct investment by transnational corporations can negatively interfere with a number of human rights, including 'the right of peoples to self-determination and to permanent sovereignty over their natural wealth and resources; the right to development; the right of everyone to a standard of living adequate for the health and well-being of himself and his family and the continuous improvement of living conditions; the right of everyone to the enjoyment of the highest attainable standard of physical and mental health; the right to full and productive employment; the right of everyone to the enjoyment of just and favourable conditions of work; the right to form and join trade unions, the right to strike and the right to bargain collectively; the right of everyone to social security; the right of everyone to enjoy the benefits of scientific progress and its applications …'. ECOSOC (1995), *The Realization of Economic, Social and Cultural Rights: The Relationship between the Enjoyment of Human Rights, in particular, International Labour and Trade Union Rights, and the Working Methods and Activities of Transnational Corporations*, UN Doc. E/CN.4/Sub.2/1995/11 para. 89. See S Joseph (1999), 'Taming the Leviathans: Multinational Enterprises and Human Rights', 46 *Netherlands International Law Review* 171, where she notes that 'in view of their vast economic power and ubiquitous presence, and consequent intrusion into many aspects of peoples' lives, it is not surprising that MNE activity can and does occasionally impact detrimentally on the enjoyment of internationally recognised human rights' (at 172).

capital, the effectiveness of its environmental, labour and human rights standards, its regulatory capacity and its ability to absorb technology. As well, while it is clear that foreign direct investment has the potential to aid development in developing states, positive development outcomes are not guaranteed because the activities of foreign investors are oriented towards the maximisation of profit and not the promotion of development.[40]

Because many elements of domestic policy affect how increased foreign investment flows translate into greater economic prosperity for citizens, the Guide does not prescribe provisions to strengthen the link between foreign investment and sustainable development. Instead, it highlights the potential policy implications of adopting different approaches to integrating sustainable development into IIAs in order to help decision-makers in developing countries adopt a suitable approach to IIA commitments. In addition, it points to resources such as international treaties, non-binding 'soft law' documents and the work of the UN Special Representative on Human Rights and Transnational Corporations that can be useful to governments in determining appropriate standards for foreign investors operating in their territories. Finally, the Guide addresses various steps that policy-makers can take in order to link their domestic sustainable development policy to the promotion of foreign investment. Box 2.3 summarises some of these steps.

Box 2.3 Integrating sustainable development into domestic policy on foreign investment

Over the last 60 years, developing countries have chosen to pursue different approaches to sustainable development. The purpose of the Guide is to help governments understand the link between their development policy and IIAs in order to enable them to promote their unique concept of development.

Examples of the link between sustainable development and investment

Positive links between development and investment: Foreign investment can spur economic growth, including through increased employment and positive spill-overs such as technology transfer. The economic benefits of these investments can be used to promote the development goals of the host state by providing government revenue for funding social programmes.

Negative links between development and investment: Foreign companies operating within the host state may:

- Pollute the environment;
- Fail to provide adequate working conditions or pay adequate wages;

(Continued)

40 ECOSOC (1995), ibid., para. 91.

(Continued)

- Require workers to work unacceptably long hours;
- Violate the human rights of citizens of the host state;
- Instigate conflict with local communities or social groups;
- Be involved in government corruption and bribery; and
- Fail to involve indigenous peoples in decision-making and ignore their rights and interests.

Making investment work for development

To strengthen the link between investment and development and ensure that foreign investors contribute to the well-being of citizens in a host state, governments can do several things.

1. Review their development policy and determine what aspects of sustainable development are priorities for them.
2. Try to anticipate how foreign investment may affect the achievement of these priorities. This involves considering how the kinds of foreign investments the government wishes to attract may affect:
    a. The environment;
    b. Human rights;
    c. Labour rights;
    d. The rights of indigenous peoples;
    e. The interests of local communities;
    f. Social policies (e.g. human health, employment);
    g. Domestic financial policies.
3. Consult with local communities in which investments exist or are planned and seek their participation throughout the life-cycle of the investment.
4. Consult with industry stakeholders, as they understand local conditions that can inform government policy.
5. Review their country's international obligations in the areas of human rights, labour rights, environmental protection and the rights of indigenous peoples. The international agreements ratified by the state contain standards that can be used for setting benchmarks and establishing best practices for investors.
6. Put in place effective domestic regulations for foreign investors in order to prevent future problems, mitigate existing risks, hold investors accountable

(Continued)

(Continued)

for past harms and enhance benefits of the investment for the community and for investors.

7. Include mechanisms in IIAs to ensure that the host state has the capacity to regulate and enforce compliance with the environmental, labour and human rights standards it has put in place and the capacity to protect the rights and interests of indigenous peoples.[41]

2.4 Making choices: sustainable development in the sample provisions in the Guide

2.4.1 A comprehensive and centrist approach to sustainable development

In drafting the Guide, the primary goal has been to illustrate various ways in which a traditional IIA can be modified to contribute to sustainable development. While the general approach of the Guide is to provide options and indicate their consequences for various areas of government policy such as finance, human rights and environmental protection, the Guide also includes sample provisions. These provisions are legal text that illustrates how investment and development policy translate into legal obligations in particular ways.

In order to draft these sample provisions and discuss the costs and benefits of different approaches, the Guide adopts a particular interpretation of sustainable development. It is important to be aware of this. As was explained above, countries may interpret 'sustainable development' in different ways; indeed, different interpretations will be required depending on whether a country is talking about trade policy, financial policy, environmental policy or social welfare policy. However, drafting sample text requires the definition of terms. In consequence, the Guide adopts a particular definition of 'sustainable development'. Instead of focusing purely on economic growth or environmental sustainability, it employs a holistic and comprehensive notion of development that encompasses a broad range of considerations such as environmental protection, human health and welfare, human rights and the rights of indigenous peoples.

The sample provisions reflect a comprehensive concept of sustainable development that is also centrist in its political approach and reflects the work of the United Nations Special Representative on the Right to Development. The approach to sustainable development in the Guide affirms that increasing foreign investment flows can be of benefit to developing countries, and it acknowledges that IIA investor protection provisions play a role in encouraging and promoting economic growth. However, it also acknowledges the potential negative effects of increased foreign investment

41 For a more comprehensive discussion of how to align investment policies with sustainable development see UNCTAD (2012), *Investment Policy Framework for Sustainable Development*, United Nations, New York and Geneva.

and the need to mitigate them. This approach is consistent with the international obligations that most countries have accepted by ratifying major international treaties in the area of human rights, labour rights, environmental sustainability and the rights of indigenous peoples. In taking on these obligations, countries accept part of the responsibility for regulating the negative effects of foreign investment.

2.4.2 Alternative approaches to sustainable development

The sample provisions do not adopt other interpretations of sustainable development that have been espoused by various developing countries and their advocates over the years. For instance, the Guide's use of 'sustainable development' does not reflect periodic calls for states to abandon the existing economic order despite the disadvantages that many developing countries suffer within this order.[42] Nor does it reflect any particular view about the historical origin of the inequality of the current international legal regime, which some development advocates trace to the history of colonialism and its continuing effects.[43]

At the other end of the spectrum from postcolonial approaches, the Guide does not adopt the view that every possible effort must be made to attract foreign investment to the exclusion of promoting environmental sustainability or important human rights. The sample provisions in the Guide reflect the view that foreign investment can be a means of promoting the economic growth that is necessary for citizens to pursue their goals. Economic growth can be properly managed so as to distribute its benefits and help alleviate poverty.

2.4.3 Supporting developing countries through co-operation and their integration into international decision-making

Although these alternative approaches to sustainable development are not reflected in their entirety in the sample provisions in the Guide, some of the concerns that animated the call for a 'new international economic order' and for overcoming the effects of decolonisation have been incorporated.

First, the sample provisions recognise the need to build partnerships and co-operation among IIA parties. A developing country's ability to participate effectively in IIA negotiations may be hampered by the country's lack of capacity, including inadequate information about the potential effects of the IIA, lack of expertise, lack of resources to implement the obligations set out in the IIA, and political and institutional weaknesses.[44] One way of overcoming these challenges is to promote co-operation

42 In 1974, two historic resolutions were passed by the United Nations declaring a New International Economic Order: The Declaration of a New International Economic Order (GA Res. 3201 and 3202 (S-IV), 1 May 1974 (adopted without a vote); and the Charter of Economic Rights and Duties of States (GA Res. 3281 (XXIX), 12 December 1974 (vote of 120–6, 10 abstentions).

43 See A Anghie (2005), *Imperialism, Sovereignty, and the Making of International Law*, Cambridge University Press, Cambridge, and A Escobar (1995), *Encountering Development: The Making and Unmaking of the Third World*, Princeton University Press, Princeton, NJ.

44 Ibid. at 93.

between developed and developing countries and among regional blocks of developing countries. The sample provisions in the Guide provide examples of how greater co-operation may be encouraged.

Second, the sample provisions promote full and effective participation of developing countries in global decision-making relating to investment. The cornerstone of co-operation is equality. The Brundtland Report, a classic statement of sustainable development dating from 1987, advocates that if the world is to move towards sustainable economic relations, international law should promote equality among states and eliminate inequalities in political power and influence between developing countries and large corporations.[45]

To reflect the emphasis in the Brundtland Report and other international legal documents on promoting international co-operation between developing and developed countries and between citizens and their governments, the Guide acknowledges the need for full and effective participation of developing countries in global decision-making in areas such as finance, technology transfer, debt management and trade policy. It also encourages consultation between communities and government by incorporating sample accountability mechanisms and by including examples of transparent processes for making decisions relating to investment.

2.4.4 Elements of sustainable development employed in the Guide's sample provisions

In adopting a comprehensive and centrist interpretation of sustainable development, the Guide relies on formulations of sustainable development that are broadly accepted by the international community.[46] In these formulations, economic growth is regarded as compatible with the preservation of the environment and positive social development[47] including the alleviation of poverty in developing countries.[48]

---

45 One of the aspects of ensuring a fair balance between the responsibilities of investors and developing countries is to recognise the responsibilities of investors though mechanisms such as corporate accountability. This is set out in the *Johannesburg Declaration on Sustainable Development: From Our Origins to the Future: Plan of Implementation of the World Summit on Sustainable Development* (2002), UN Doc. A/CONF.199/20 [the *Johannesburg Plan*], at 15, para. 18; 38, para. 49; and 66, para. 140.

46 In particular, we have relied on the following: *Our Common Future*, op. cit.; *Rio Declaration on Environment and Development* (1992), UN Doc. A/CONF.151/26 (Vol. I); *Johannesburg Plan*, ibid.; and UN Millennium Project (2005), *Investing in Development: A Practical Plan to Achieve the Millennium Development Goals*, op. cit.

47 For instance, the *UN Declaration on the Right to Development* (1987), adopted GA Res. 41/128 UN GAOR, 41st Sess. at 3, Annex, UN Doc.A/Res.41/128 Annex, recognises that sustainable development encompasses more than just the environment. Article 1 states: 'The right to development is an inalienable human right by virtue of which every human person and all peoples are entitled to participate in, contribute to, and enjoy economic, social, cultural and political development, in which all human rights and fundamental freedoms can be fully realized'.

48 In 1998, the Commission on Human Rights, in a decision endorsed by the Economic and Social Council, established an Independent Expert on the right to development and an open-ended Working Group to monitor and report on progress in the implementation of the right to development. In his

The following is a list of some of the ways in which this concept of sustainable development is reflected in principles for regulating foreign investment. These principles have informed the drafting of the Guide:

1. Increase investment inflows through investment protection and promotion;
2. Develop transparent and effective regulation of investment;
3. Put in place effective laws and regulations in policy areas that have a nexus with investment;
4. Build partnerships and co-operation among IIA parties;
5. Promote full and effective participation of developing countries in global decision-making relating to investment;
6. Involve domestic stakeholders in developing sustainable investment policy; and
7. Facilitate the protection of the environment, human rights, labour rights and the rights of indigenous peoples.

2.4.5 Summary: the principles of sustainable development reflected in the Guide

The discussion and sample provisions in the Guide reflect the view that if foreign investment is to promote sustainable development, investment must contribute to meeting the needs of people in the host country. The Guide recognises the need to promote and protect human rights, the environment and other development priorities in a way that is consistent with both the home and host states' international obligations.

In addition, the Guide acknowledges that developing countries should have adequate technical preparation and proper information when negotiating investment agreements. There must be due regard for the political and institutional weaknesses of developing countries, and IIA commitments should reflect an effort to overcome

---

third report, the Expert stated that the right to development is composed of many elements, including: 1. economic, social and cultural rights, including: (a) the right to food; (b) the right to health; (c) the right to education; (d) the right to housing. 2. civil and political rights. 3. poverty alleviation through sustained economic growth. 4. providing financial, technical and institutional resources that enable improvement in the well-being of the entire population and the realization of the rights to be sustained. The international community's commitment to the eradication of poverty is also clear in the endorsement of the *Millennium Development Goals* and the *UN Millennium Declaration* (*UN Millennium Declaration*, A/RES/55/2, adopted 18 September 2000). It is also recognised in documents relating to sustainable development (see *UN Framework Convention on Climate Change* (1992), 1771, *United Nations Treaty Series* 107, signed 9 May 1992, in force 21 March 1992, preamble; *The UN Convention on Biological Diversity* (1992), *United Nations Treaty Series* 79, preamble; and the *Copenhagen Declaration on Social Development* (1995), UN Doc.A/CONF.166/Res./1 paras. 6–7); International Law Association (2002), *New Delhi Declaration of Principles of International Law Relating to Sustainable Development*, Res. 3/2002, 209 UN Doc. A/57/329, reprinted in International Law Association, *Report of the Seventieth Conference*, *New Delhi 2002*, at 211–16, para. 2.4.

these. As noted, one of the Guide's primary purposes is to support developing countries in their IIA negotiations.

To ensure that international investment rules yield outcomes consistent with sustainable development, they should be developed through wide consultation with people in the host country,[49] and decisions about the negotiation, application and interpretation of agreements should be transparent and consistent.

2.4.6 Overview of mechanisms for promoting sustainable development discussed in the Guide

The Guide provides many options to those developing countries looking to integrate concepts of sustainable development into their international investment policy. Some of the provisions discussed are not found in existing IIAs.[50]

In addition to the broad-ranging discussion of the many approaches available to host states, the sample provisions illustrate some of these specific approaches such as:

a. **Encouraging investment:** IIAs can encourage investment by providing core investor protections[51] supported by investor–state arbitration,[52] and by imposing obligations on investors' home states to promote investment in host states and to provide technical assistance for them to develop robust, transparent and effective regulatory schemes.[53]

b. **Protecting the regulatory flexibility of host states to achieve their development goals:** IIA provisions can be designed that do not prevent host states from achieving their development goals. The Guide contains the following suggestions:

    - Identifying sustainable development as the main goal of the agreement and explicitly recognising the right to regulate to achieve sustainable development in the IIA's preamble and statement of objectives;[54]
    - Drafting the substantive obligations in IIAs to provide flexibility to regulate to achieve sustainable development;[55] and

49 See *New Delhi Declaration*, op. cit., Principle 5.1; see also A Boyle and D Freestone (1999), 'Introduction', in A Boyle and D Freestone (eds), *International Law and Sustainable Development: Past Achievements and Future Challenges*, Oxford University Press, Oxford, at 15–16.

50 UNCTAD notes that there is an emerging trend for investment agreements to include provisions designed to achieve non-economic objectives such as the protection of health, safety, the environment, and human and labour rights (UNCTAD (2007), *Bilateral Investment Treaties 1995–2006*, op. cit.). The Guide discusses provisions that are part of this trend, but also those that go beyond existing agreements.

51 See Chapter 5 (Substantive Obligations of Host States Regarding Investor Protection).

52 See Section 7.1 (Investor–state dispute settlement).

53 See Section 8.2 (Technical assistance).

54 See Section 4.2 (IIA preambles).

55 See Section 5.3 (National treatment), Section 5.4 (Most favoured nation), Section 5.5 (Fair and equitable treatment and the minimum standard of treatment), Section 5.6 (Limitations on expropriation and nationalisation), Section 5.7 (Compensation for losses), Section 5.8 (Free transfer of funds), Section 5.10 (Transparency).

- Including exceptions and reservations in the IIA to ensure that legitimate state measures intended to promote development are not contrary to it.[56]

c. **Partnerships with the investors' home states to support sustainable development:** IIAs can create obligations on investors' home states to support the efforts of host states to regulate in pursuit of sustainable development. The obligation to provide technical assistance for the development and implementation of host state regulatory schemes is just one example.[57]

d. **Sustainability assessments:** IIAs provisions can be designed to require that foreign investors conduct a sustainability assessment of their investment that takes into account the environmental, social and human rights impacts of proposed investments. This assessment can be used to create a management plan designed to ensure that the investments contribute to sustainable development on an ongoing basis.[58]

e. **A grievance procedure:** An IIA can include a grievance procedure for people negatively affected by an investment.[59]

f. **Standards for investors:** IIAs can contain standards that foreign investors must meet, including requirements to comply with the domestic law of the host state,[60] to meet human rights standards[61] and core international labour standards,[62] as well as to avoid complicity in grave violations of human rights[63] and refrain from bribery and other forms of corruption.[64]

g. **Developing domestic measures and enforcement mechanisms for promoting sustainable development in the host and home states:** In order to ensure that foreign investors (who are not parties to the treaty) are accountable for their actions in the host country, IIAs can be designed to require the host state and the investor's home state to:

  - Provide in their domestic laws for appropriate levels of environmental protection and the protection of human rights, labour rights and the rights of indigenous peoples in accordance with their international obligations;[65]

---

56 See Section 5.12 (Reservations and exceptions).
57 See Section 8.2 (Technical assistance).
58 See Section 6.6 (Sustainability assessments).
59 See Sections 6.6 (Sustainability assessments) and 6.13 (Enforcement of investor obligations).
60 See Section 6.7 (Investor obligation to comply with the laws of the host state).
61 See Section 6.8 (Investor obligation to respect internationally recognised human rights and undertake human rights due diligence).
62 See Section 6.10 (Investor obligation to comply with core labour standards).
63 See Section 6.9 (Investor obligation to refrain from the commission of, or complicity in, grave violations of human rights).
64 See Section 6.11 (Investor obligation to refrain from acts, or complicity in acts, of bribery and corruption).
65 See 6.12 (Other rights and obligations of party states).

- Impose criminal liability for investor complicity in grave violations of human rights and corrupt activities contrary to treaty obligations;[66] and
- Provide for investors to be held civilly liable in their domestic courts in these circumstances as well as in situations in which an investor breaches and IIA standard relating to core labour rights, fails to comply with domestic law, or fails to comply with the management plan developed in connection with a sustainability assessment.[67]

h. **Counterclaims by states in investor–state arbitration and limitations on investor access to investor–state arbitration:** IIAs can be designed to limit investor access to investor–state arbitration where the investor is not in compliance with standards set in the agreement. They can also be used to provide a counterclaim mechanism for a state against which an investor has made a claim. This would allow the state to obtain relief for injuries suffered as a result of non-compliance by the investor with obligations imposed on it under the treaty.[68]

These sample provisions reflect a comprehensive and centrist approach to sustainable development that includes the protection of the environment and the promotion and protection of human rights, labour rights and the rights of indigenous peoples. This is not the only approach to sustainable development. Each state must determine its own policy. Nevertheless, whatever approach a state elects to follow, the Guide provides options that should be of assistance.

---

66 See Section 6.13 (Enforcement of investor obligations).

67 See Section 6.13 (Enforcement of investor obligations).

68 See Section 6.17 (Counterclaims by states in investor–state arbitrations) and Section 7.1 (Investor–state dispute settlement).

Chapter 3

Using the Guide

3.1 Introduction

3.1.1 General purpose of the Guide

Section II of the Guide identifies categories of IIA obligations accompanied by a discussion of the purpose of each category, alternative approaches to formulating provisions in each category and a sample provision with a discussion of its specific features and rationale. This chapter provides a general introduction to using the Guide.

The main focus of the Guide is on provisions in bilateral investment treaties. The provisions discussed may also be used as the basis for the negotiation of other forms of international economic agreements that relate to investment. For example, many of the provisions could be used in regional investment agreements or in investment chapters in bilateral or regional free trade agreements. Investment provisions in these kinds of agreements often include the same kinds of obligations as those found in BITs, though the organisation of the investment provisions in these agreements may be different. For example, in some of these agreements, investment in services or in specific sectors, such as telecommunications and financial services, is dealt with separately from the general obligations applicable to investment.[1] Some of the provisions discussed in the Guide may be useful as a starting point for negotiations relating to investment provisions in economic partnership agreements, though the architecture of these agreements and their provisions on investment tend to be different from those in BITs.

3.1.2 Using the Guide in IIA negotiations

It is up to each state to decide what kinds of provisions it should seek when negotiating an IIA, in light of its own unique circumstances, including its domestic policy on foreign investment and its other international commitments affecting investment. There can be no guarantee that any particular sample provision in the Guide or any of the other options discussed will be optimal for a particular state. Indeed, a state may decide that certain provisions should be excluded altogether. Some states may even decide that it is better to refrain from concluding IIAs with any country on the basis that their costs outweigh their benefits, or they might conclude IIAs only with

1 C Fink and M Molinuevo (2008), 'East Asian Free Trade Agreements in Services: Key Architectural Elements,' 11 *Journal of International Economic Law* 263, at 279–286 (substantive obligations) and 300–303 (investor–state dispute settlement); A Mattoo and P Sauvé (2010), 'The Preferential Liberalization of Services Trade', NCCR Working Paper No. 2010/13, Bern, at 49–53.

selected states such as regional partners, states in a comparable economic position or states with which they have a special historical or economic relationship.

Once a state has decided to negotiate an IIA, it is unlikely that it will be successful in obtaining the agreement of its negotiating partner to include all the provisions that it desires in the final agreement. Each agreement will reflect the outcome of bargaining and the trade-offs that such bargaining entails. Consequently, each state must evaluate the cost and benefits of particular provisions, and make strategic decisions about which provisions it considers essential and which it is willing to change as a concession to the demands of the other party. To inform the choices that states must make when negotiating, the discussion that accompanies each category of provision explains the costs and benefits and the likely effects of alternative versions of the provision.

3.1.3 Using the Guide to better understand the relationship between IIA obligations and domestic law and other international obligations

Two overarching issues that states must consider in the context of IIA negotiations are: (i) the relationship between prospective IIA obligations and their other international obligations; and (ii) the relationship between prospective IIA obligations and their domestic law. These issues must be taken into account so that a state can ensure that its policies are coherent. Considering these issues will also help the state to avoid unintended consequences resulting from the interaction between various legal obligations. Some of the general challenges associated with the inter-relationships between IIA obligations and domestic law and between IIA obligations in different treaties are discussed in Sections 3.2 and 3.3, below.

3.1.4 Using the Guide to better understand existing IIA obligations

The Guide is intended not only to inform future IIA negotiations, but also to assist states in evaluating their existing commitments under IIAs already in force. States should carry out a comprehensive assessment of their existing IIAs because recent experience in investor–state arbitration has demonstrated that some kinds of provisions may carry significant and at times unforeseen risks. In the survey of IIA provisions, the Guide discusses these risks and how to address them. One aim of this discussion is to help states understand their existing obligations and how to avoid the risk of investor–state claims. In addition, a state may decide, based on its understanding of the impact of provisions in its existing agreements, to renegotiate or even withdraw from an IIA.

3.2 IIAs and domestic investment policy

3.2.1 General considerations

All treaty commitments constrain state sovereignty in some way. That is their purpose. The challenge for host states negotiating IIA commitments is to ensure that they understand the constraints and are satisfied that they contribute to the achievement of their domestic policy goals.

In the best case, the decision to enter into an IIA should be made only after the state has developed a broad policy on foreign investment, both inward and outward, having regard to its overall development strategy. In particular, states should ensure that their IIA commitments will be compatible with their current foreign investment policy. To avoid inappropriate commitments, states must review both their rules for foreign investment entry and their rules governing sectors in which foreign investment is permitted. Negotiating IIA commitments is especially challenging because IIA commitments tend to be of long duration. As a result, before accepting commitments, a state should also think through to what extent they may constrain future policy choices, perhaps in areas in which it has no developed policy at the moment. These preliminary steps should be taken prior to entering an IIA, because once a state has made IIA commitments, its freedom to make decisions on investment policies will be restricted by the obligations in the IIA.

Some states may welcome the way in which an IIA limits its sovereignty. For example, IIA commitments may be a way to secure a host state's market opening or market-based reforms, such as privatisation programmes.[2] Once IIA commitments have been entered into, it will be difficult for later governments to undo these reforms, because doing so may infringe the rights of investors under the IIA, thus giving rise to investor complaints.

The challenge of sorting out the implications of IIA commitments for domestic policy is particularly important in relation to investment treaties because they typically contain a distinctive form of enforcement mechanism: investor–state arbitration. This kind of dispute settlement mechanism permits private parties, through arbitration, to seek compensation from a state where its domestic measures breach its IIA obligations.[3]

3.2.2 Specific examples of the interaction between IIA commitments and domestic investment policy

Right of establishment

Each state negotiating an IIA must consider the commitments it proposes to undertake in the context of how open its domestic market is to foreign investment. Some countries have adopted a policy of opening most of their domestic economy to foreign investment. Others limit foreign investment in different ways. For many developing countries, controlling what foreign investments are permitted to enter is the most effective way for them to regulate foreign investment. Some capital-exporting states, however, seek an IIA commitment from another state (the host state) to allow its investors to enter the host state and carry on their businesses. An IIA provision that guarantees that foreign investors will be able to enter and operate in the host state is called a *right of establishment*. If a host state's policy is to allow foreign investors to

2 The interaction between IIAs and domestic policy is further discussed by JA VanDuzer (2008), 'Foreign Investment and Development: The Role of Domestic Policy and International Investment Agreements', in Commonwealth Secretariat (2008), *Commonwealth Finance Ministers Reference Report 2008*, Commonwealth Secretariat, London.

3 See Section 7.1 (Investor–state dispute settlement).

enter its market and carry on business, then granting a right of establishment would not require any change in government policy. However, such a provision would preclude a future return to a policy of excluding or limiting foreign investment. It is precisely this limitation on future policy change by the host state that is the mechanism by which IIA commitments encourage foreign investment. A right of establishment commitment provides certainty and predictability for foreign investors that they will be able to bring their capital into the domestic market. Granting a right of establishment may also represent a commitment by a state to remove existing restrictions on access to its market.

However, it may be inappropriate for a host state to agree to a right of establishment in several circumstances:[4]

- As a matter of domestic policy, the state does not permit foreign investment, either generally or in particular sectors. These kinds of policies would be inconsistent with a right of establishment commitment. An agreement to a right of establishment would be a commitment to liberalise the state's domestic regime.
- The state does not have a developed policy on the entry of foreign investment and lacks: (i) a robust system for making decisions about permitting particular foreign investments; or (ii) the capacity to regulate foreign investors who enter the country. If the state were to develop a policy limiting foreign investment into the country in the future, its implementation might be inconsistent with a right of establishment commitment.

No state grants unrestricted entry to foreign investors. At the very least, states will stop investments that pose national security concerns. Many states have sensitive sectors in which investment is prohibited for various policy reasons. If a state chooses to negotiate a right of establishment, the state must ensure that its commitments are consistent with its domestic regime, whatever it is, and that any commitment that it undertakes leaves it sufficient flexibility to control investment entry in accordance with its domestic policy. The various ways in which this may be done, such as through reservations and exceptions, are explored in the discussion of the sample provisions in the Guide.

The definition of 'investment'

Another issue related to the interaction of domestic policy and IIA obligations is the definition of investment in an IIA. This definition is critical to delimiting the scope of the host state's obligations under the agreement. It determines what kinds of interests held by investors of the other party state are entitled to claim the benefit of the investor protection obligations.

From a host state's point of view, another consideration is that the definition of investment should identify the kinds of investments that a state wants to attract as a matter of domestic policy. In addition, some forms of investment could be excluded

4 For a full discussion of this issue, see Section 5.2 (Right of establishment).

to ensure that host state policy-making flexibility in relation to these kinds of investments can be maintained. For instance, a state may not want to include bonds and other financial obligations that it issues within the definition of investment in order to preserve its flexibility to deal with these obligations in times of financial crisis. Sometimes policy concerns that arise in regard to the definition of investment can also be addressed in a more specific way through appropriate exceptions to the investor protection obligations in the agreement. For example, even if a state's financial obligations were included in the definition of investment, an exception might be included in the IIA to permit state actions to respond to a financial crisis.

Throughout the survey of categories of provisions in the Guide, an effort is made to identify domestic policy concerns. In particular, the Guide identifies certain provisions that may require the host state to maintain a level of openness to foreign investment or have a well-developed policy or regulatory capacity in relation to foreign investment. The Guide discusses alternative forms of provisions to address these concerns.

3.3 IIAs and other international obligations

As noted above, states may wish to use the Guide to conduct a risk assessment of their existing IIA commitments. This will allow them to determine how their commitments restrict their flexibility to make policies regarding foreign investment and other subjects that are related to investment such as financial policies, the regulation of economic sectors in which foreign investments exist and so on.

In addition, before negotiating a new IIA, states must consider how existing IIAs and their trade commitments interact with proposed new investment obligations. For example, if a state is a member of the World Trade Organization (WTO), it will have to consider the relationship between prospective IIA commitments and its obligations under the WTO's *General Agreement on Trade in Services* (*GATS*), which applies to some forms of investment. The possible interaction between IIAs and *GATS* is complex and will vary significantly from one country to the next.[5] While a full discussion of *GATS* is beyond the scope of the Guide, some of the main issues are identified in Box 3.1.[6] An overview of the *GATS* is set out in Appendix 2.

The challenge of identifying the impact of new IIA commitments on existing IIAs is significant because the inter-relationship between IIAs is complex and highly variable. In addition to the general challenge of trying to ensure that IIA commitments are consistent with domestic policy and each other, most favoured nation (MFN) clauses, which appear in some form in most IIAs and *GATS*, raise particular problems. Though they vary in scope, MFN clauses in IIAs generally oblige each party to treat investors

---

5 The scholarly literature on this subject is just beginning to develop. See R Adlung and M Molinuevo (2008), 'Bilateralism in Services Trade: Is There Fire Behind the (Bit-)Smoke', 10 *Journal of International Economic Law* 1.

6 Negotiations are ongoing in the WTO with respect to, among other things, new services commitments under *GATS*. In this context it is equally important for countries to consider the impact of new *GATS* commitments on their IIA obligations.

from the other party no less favourably than investors from any other country. MFN clauses in existing agreements can have the effect of committing a state to extend the benefit of commitments undertaken in new IIAs to investors from the states that are party to its existing agreements. As a result, a country negotiating an IIA should review all their existing international trade and investment obligations so it understands to what extent MFN commitments in those agreements means that accepting new commitments in an IIA will grant new rights to investors from other countries with which they have IIAs. In addition, states may wish to consider restricting the scope of MFN provisions in new or renegotiated IIAs. By doing so, it may be possible to limit the extent to which the new or renegotiated IIA would incorporate commitments from existing or future treaties.

The MFN provision in *GATS* is discussed in Box 3.1. The challenges that MFN clauses in IIAs create and strategies to deal with them are discussed in more detail in the survey of particular kinds of provisions in the Guide.[7]

Box 3.1 Interaction between GATS and IIA commitments

Two interactions between IIAs and GATS

1. IIAs can expand the scope of *GATS* commitments: While IIAs and *GATS* may contain similarly worded commitments, an IIA protects far more forms of investment than *GATS*. Unlike *GATS*, IIA obligations are not limited to investors supplying services through a commercial presence as defined in *GATS*. Also IIA obligations may be the subject of investor–state arbitration under an IIA. *GATS* does not provide for this kind of dispute settlement.
2. *GATS* may extend IIA protections to WTO members: A host state may be required to extend certain IIA protections to service providers from WTO member states with which the host state does not have an investment agreement by virtue of the MFN provision in the *GATS*. This provision requires the state to treat service providers that are nationals of parties to the *GATS* no less favourably than those of parties to its IIAs.

The nature of these interactions between *GATS* and IIAs is described below following a general introduction to the *GATS* as it applies to investment.

How does GATS apply to investment?

Under *GATS*, each WTO member has two kinds of obligations. Some apply to its measures that relate to services trade in all sectors. Others apply only to measures that relate to services trade in sectors that the WTO member has agreed to list in a national schedule of commitments. Unlike WTO obligations relating

(Continued)

7 See Section 5.4 (Most favoured nation).

(Continued)

to goods trade, *GATS* obligations apply to services delivered through a '*commercial presence*', which includes certain types of investments. In general, a service supplier from one WTO member is supplying a service through a commercial presence in the territory of another WTO member if:

- The supplier has a subsidiary (usually a corporation) or an unincorporated branch of its operation within the territory of that other member for the purpose of supplying the service; and
- The subsidiary or branch is owned or controlled by natural persons that are nationals of the first member or legal persons (usually corporations) organised under the laws of the first member.

A bank incorporated in the UK that is supplying banking services through a locally incorporated subsidiary in South Africa that it controls is an example of a UK service supplier supplying services in South Africa through a commercial presence.

Commercial presence under *GATS* does not include all of the forms of investor and investment that are eligible for protection under existing IIAs. Most obviously, commercial presence for the purposes of *GATS* does not include investments that do not involve the supply of a service, such as an investment to operate a local manufacturing business. Even in relation to services businesses, such as accounting or construction services, commercial presence does not include many forms of investment protected under an IIA. For instance, it does not include investments that do not give the foreign investor control over the local business such as a minority shareholding in a business. This kind of investment is often protected in IIAs.

These differences between the kinds of investments covered by an IIA and *GATS* are the key to how an IIA can affect the scope of *GATS* obligations.

Overview of GATS *obligations*

The most important *GATS* obligation applying to all services sectors is the most favoured nation obligation. MFN requires each WTO member to treat services suppliers from any WTO member state no less favourably than it treats service suppliers from any other state. Each WTO member was permitted to file a list of specific exemptions from the MFN obligation when it joined the WTO and many did so.

Each WTO member has its own national schedule of commitments that identifies particular sectors with respect to which it has assumed additional obligations under *GATS*. For services sectors that a WTO member has listed in its national schedule of commitments, the member has an obligation to provide national treatment to foreign services suppliers from other WTO member states. This

(Continued)

(Continued)

obligation means that the member may not treat such service suppliers any less favourably than its domestic suppliers. Also, for sectors they have listed, member states cannot impose certain kinds of barriers to market access, such as limitations on foreign ownership. These obligations apply to services suppliers operating through a commercial presence as well as through other modes of supply.

Both the national treatment and market access obligations for listed sectors can be circumscribed by limitations that the member has written into its schedule. In practice, the limitations in members' schedules typically carve out specific existing measures of the member that would otherwise be inconsistent with the national treatment or the market access obligation. Most states, other than those that have joined the WTO since it was formed in 1994, have made weak commitments in their services schedules that, at most, oblige them to maintain the degree of openness that they provided to their domestic markets when GATS came into force in 1995. Negotiations are ongoing, however, and it is possible that stronger liberalising commitments will be a feature of a successful conclusion of the current Doha round of negotiations.

GATS *obligations and IIAs*

A state's international commitments under GATS require careful consideration in the context of negotiating an IIA for a number of reasons. Two concerns are identified below.

Policy coherence

GATS raises a general policy coherence challenge when a WTO member is negotiating an IIA. To the extent that a state already has obligations under GATS, it must evaluate whether the obligations entered into under IIAs are consistent with them. If a state has already agreed to a certain obligation under GATS, a similar commitment in an IIA may not appear to represent a substantial additional commitment. For example, accepting an obligation to admit a foreign investor from another state in an IIA may seem to have only a marginal effect if the state has already committed through GATS to unlimited national treatment and market access in relation to that country's services suppliers operating through a commercial presence. Such a commitment would amount to an obligation to admit them to the domestic market.

Even if an IIA commitment seems identical to a state's prior GATS commitment, the IIA provision is broader in fact because it is not limited to investors supplying services through a commercial presence as defined in GATS. In addition, if the IIA contains investor–state dispute settlement procedures, the IIA commitment differs from the GATS obligation because, in most IIAs, an investor can claim compensation for its breach through investor–state arbitration.

(Continued)

(Continued)

MFN obligation

The *GATS* MFN obligation may require that IIA commitments be extended to services suppliers from other WTO member states. A state's MFN obligation may apply in this way unless the state has included in its exemption list a sufficiently broad MFN exemption to exclude preferences under IIAs at the time it became a member of the WTO. Few countries did so. *GATS* also provides a general exception from MFN treatment for obligations undertaken in a broad-based economic integration agreement requiring the substantial liberalisation of services trade as defined in Article V of the *GATS*. Few existing IIAs will meet the requirements of *GATS* Article V, though free trade agreements with investment commitments will qualify in some cases.

The *GATS* MFN obligation will be a serious concern only to the extent that the commitments undertaken in an IIA exceed those made to other states through *GATS*. After all, only if higher obligations are assumed in an IIA will the *GATS* MFN obligation extend them to other WTO members' services suppliers. However, the commitments in IIAs are likely to exceed *GATS* and other international commitments in several ways. For example, as noted, under most IIAs an investor has a right to seek compensation for expropriation by a host state through investor–state arbitration. It is possible that the MFN clause in *GATS* would apply to require a state to give a right to initiate investor–state dispute settlement against the host state to some investors in a host state who are services suppliers from WTO member states that had not signed an IIA with the host state. Similarly, the MFN obligation in a state's IIAs may require that the commitments that the state has made under *GATS* be extended to investors from states protected under those IIAs, even if those states are not WTO members.

PART II. SURVEY OF IIA PROVISIONS AND COMMENTARY

Chapter 4

Provisions Defining the Scope of IIA Application and Other Preliminary Matters

4.1 Introduction

In preparing the Guide, a wide variety of IIA models were studied, including the model agreements used by:

- United Kingdom – UK Model Investment Promotion and Protection Agreement (IPPA);[1]
- India – Indian Model Bilateral Investment Promotion and Protection Agreement (BIPPA);[2]
- Canada – Canadian Model Foreign Investment Promotion and Protection Agreement (FIPA);[3]
- USA – US Model Bilateral Investment Agreement (BIT);[4] and
- Norway – Norwegian Draft Model Agreement on the Protection and Promotion of Investment (APPI).[5]

In addition, the model investment treaty proposed by the International Institute for Sustainable Development (IISD model treaty),[6] which contains a variety of features not found in any existing treaty, and the models proposed by the Asian–African

1 Model Investment Promotion and Protection Agreement, copy on file with the authors. The model was used with some variations in the Agreement between the Government of the United Kingdom of Great Britain and Northern Ireland and the Government of the United Mexican States for the Promotion and Reciprocal Protection of Investments done at Vienna on 12 May 2006, in force 25 July 2007, UK Government, available at: www.official-documents.gov.uk/document/cm72/7218/7218.pdf (accessed 29 May 2012).

2 Indian Model Text of Bilateral Investment Promotion and Protection Agreement, online: Department of Economic Affairs, available at: http://finmin.nic.in/the_ministry/dept_eco_affairs/icsection/Indian%20Model%20Text%20BIPA. asp (accessed 29 May 2012).

3 Canada's New Model Foreign Investment Promotion and Protection Agreement, available at: www.international.gc.ca/trade-agreements-accords-commerciaux/assets/pdfs/2004-FIPA-model-en.pdf (accessed 29 May 2012).

4 2012 US model BIT, available at: www.ustr.gov/sites/default/files/BIT%20text%20for%20ACIEP%20Meeting.pdf (accessed 29 May 2012).

5 Norwegian draft model APPI (19 December 2007), copy on file with the authors. In June 2009, following extensive consultations, the Norwegian government announced that it would not proceed to finalise a new model agreement.

6 H Mann, K von Moltke, LE Peterson and A Cosbey (2005), IISD Model International Agreement on Investment for Sustainable Development, International Institute for Sustainable Development, Winnipeg, available at: www.iisd.org/pdf/2005/investment_model_int_agreement.pdf (accessed 29 May 2012).

Legal Consultative Committee (AALCC models) were studied.[7] A large number of existing IIAs were also reviewed, including some of the IIAs entered into recently between developing countries, such as the Investment Agreement for the COMESA Common Investment Area[8] (COMESA Investment Agreement), the ASEAN Comprehensive Investment Agreement[9] (ASEAN Agreement) and the investment chapter of the India–Singapore Comprehensive Economic Cooperation Agreement (India–Singapore CECA).[10]

Reference is made to these various models and existing IIAs in the discussion of specific provisions included in the Guide. One of the purposes of doing so is to identify the source of the provisions being discussed; another is to allow countries negotiating IIAs to use precedents that have been endorsed by other countries in support of their negotiating position. All of the existing treaties referred to in the Guide are listed in the List of Treaties set out at the beginning of the Guide.

4.2 IIA preambles

Cross reference

Section 4.4 Statement of objectives 92

4.2.1 The role of preambles in IIAs

A preamble to an IIA consists of statements at the beginning of the agreement expressing the parties' general intentions and goals in entering into the treaty. While it does not create or limit obligations in the treaty directly, the interpretation of obligations and their application in particular situations will be informed by the compatibility of the interpretation or application with the preamble. Those interpreting the treaty, including investor–state tribunals, should prefer the interpretation that best achieves the goals set out in the preamble and is otherwise consistent with it.

The relevance of the preamble for interpreting the obligations contained in an IIA is confirmed by the *Vienna Convention on the Law of Treaties* (*Vienna Convention*), which provides the basic framework for interpreting international treaty obligations.[11]

---

7 The treaty models were proposed by the Asian–African Legal Consultative Committee in the 1980s and are available at: www.aalco.int/PROMOTION%20AND%20PROTECTION%20OF%20INVESTMENTS.pdf (accessed 26 April 2012). UNCTAD (2007), *Bilateral Investment Treaties 1995–2006: Trends in Investment Rulemaking*, United Nations, New York and Geneva, provides a comprehensive review of IIA provisions from around the globe.

8 The Twelfth Summit of COMESA Authority of Heads of State and Government, held in Nairobi, Kenya, 22–23 May 2007, adopted the Investment Agreement for the COMESA Common Investment Area (CCIA). COMESA stands for the Common Market for Eastern and Southern Africa.

9 Association of Southeast Asian Nations, Comprehensive Investment Agreement, signed 26 February, 2009, in force 29 March 2012.

10 Investment Chapter of the Comprehensive Economic Cooperation Agreement Between the Republic of India and the Republic of Singapore, signed 29 June 2005, in force 1 August 2005.

11 *Vienna Convention on the Law of Treaties*, signed 23 May 1969, 1155 *United Nations Treaty Series* 331, reprinted in 8 *International Legal Materials* 679, signed 23 May 1969, in force 27 January 1980.

Article 31(1) of the *Vienna Convention* requires, in part, that treaty provisions be interpreted in light of their context. A treaty must be interpreted

> ... in good faith in accordance with the ordinary meaning to be given to the terms of the treaty in their *context* and in light of its object and purpose. (Emphasis added.)

The *Vienna Convention* goes on to define the context as consisting of the preamble as well as the treaty text and any annexes to the treaty.[12] Consistent with the *Vienna Convention*, all provisions in a treaty, including reservations and exceptions, must be interpreted in light of the expressly stated objectives of the treaty, which may appear in the preamble. Any other statements in the preamble form part of the interpretive context.

4.2.2 Use and interpretation of preambles in IIA practice

Where they have preambles at all, most IIAs refer only to protecting and attracting investment. For example, in the Indian model agreement, the preamble states:

> Desiring to create favourable conditions for greater investment by investors of one Contracting Party in the territory of the other Contracting Party;
>
> Recognising the reciprocal protection of investments under this agreement would foster individuals using initiative and will increase prosperity for both states;
>
> Have agreed as follows:[13]

Other preambles identify a more expansive set of goals. In the preamble of the India–Singapore CECA, for example, the parties recognise 'their right to pursue economic philosophies suited to their development goals and their right to regulate activities to realise their national policy objectives'. Other IIA preambles also affirm the party states' right to regulate.[14] Some mention specific policy objectives such as sustainable development and the party states' commitment to human and

---

12 Tribunals rendering decisions in investor–state arbitrations under Chapter 11 of the *North American Free Trade Agreement* (signed 17 December 1992, in force 1 January 1994, reprinted in (1993) 32 *International Legal Materials* 605) have sometimes accorded greater weight to the overall object and purpose of the agreement (e.g. *ADF Group Inc. v. the United States of America*, ICSID Case no. (AF)/00/1, Final Award, 9 January 2003, suggesting NAFTA should be interpreted 'in the context of the entire structure of NAFTA to understand the real shape and content of the bargain struck' (at para. 149)). Interpretation based on the true object and purpose of the treaty, which is sometimes referred to as a 'teleological approach', has been rejected in WTO cases by the Appellate Body in *Japan – Taxes on Alcoholic Beverages* (*Complaint by the European Communities, Canada and the United States*) (1996), WT/DS8, 10, 11/AB/R (Appellate Body Report). In *United States – Import Prohibition of Certain Shrimp and Shrimp Products (Complaint by India et al.)* (1998), WT/DS58/AB/R (Appellate Body Report), the Appellate Body expressly suggested that there is some scope for such an approach, though the approach actually applied in the case may be interpreted as consistent with the text based approach mandated by the *Vienna Convention*, op. cit.

13 Indian Model BIPPA, preamble. The UK model IPPA has almost identical language in its preamble.

14 E.g. Panama–Taiwan Free Trade Agreement, signed 21 August 2003, in force 1 January 2004.

labour rights, and environmental standards.[15] The preamble to the COMESA Investment Agreement, for example, reaffirms the importance to the parties of 'sustainable economic growth'.[16] The preamble of the ASEAN Agreement recognises the different levels of development of the member states and the need for 'special and differential treatment', as well as the link between investment flows and development.

How a preamble is drafted can have a significant effect on the way its various elements are used in interpreting the substantive provisions of the agreement. For instance, in the North American Free Trade Agreement (NAFTA),[17] a regional trade agreement among Canada, Mexico and the USA, the principal purpose of the agreement as stated in its preamble is to 'create an expanded and secure market for the goods and services produced in [the Party states'] territories'.[18] This statement has caused dispute settlement panels to narrowly interpret reservations and exceptions in NAFTA that limit the size or security of the market.[19] In NAFTA's preamble, the parties also resolve to 'preserve their flexibility to safeguard the public welfare'. This aspect of the preamble has not been relied on in cases decided under NAFTA's dispute settlement mechanisms because of the way it is expressed. Expanding and securing the market for goods and services is clearly identified as an objective of the agreement. In contrast, safeguarding the public welfare is not expressly referred to in the preamble as a positive objective of the agreement. Accordingly, it has been given less interpretive weight. This approach to interpretation of the different aspects of the NAFTA preamble is confirmed in a separate objectives provision, which states that the objectives of the agreement are to 'eliminate barriers to trade in, and facilitate the cross-border movement of, goods and services' and to 'increase substantially investment opportunities'. Nowhere in the objectives provision is public welfare mentioned.[20]

---

15 E.g. United States–Uruguay, Treaty between the United States of America and the Oriental Republic of Uruguay concerning the Encouragement and Reciprocal Protection of Investment, signed 4 November 2005, in force 1 November 2006; European Community–CARIFORUM Economic Partnership Agreement, signed 15 October 2008, in force 29 December 2008.

16 The COMESA Investment Agreement (2007) follows the IISD model treaty in this regard. See similarly the preamble to the Canada–Colombia Free Trade Agreement, signed 21 November 2008, in force 15 August 2011, and to the United States–Colombia Trade Promotion Agreement, signed 22 November 2006, in force 15 May 2012, as well as to the *Energy Charter Protocol on Energy Efficiency and Related Environmental Aspects*, 17 December 1994, 34 *International Legal Materials* 446.

17 NAFTA (1992).

18 In *In the Matter of Cross-Border Trucking Services* (USA-Mex-98-2008-01), Final Report of the Panel, 6 February 2001, the panel noted that international tribunals in other contexts frequently refer to the preamble of a treaty for the purpose of determining the principal object of the treaty, in accordance with Article 31 of the *Vienna Convention*, citing *The Lotus* (1927), P.C.I.J. Ser. A, No.10, 17; *Free Zones of Upper Savoy and the District of Gex* (Order) (1929), P.C.I.J., Ser. A, No. 22, 12; *Asylum (Colombia, Perú)* (1950), ICJ Rep. 266, 276, 282 (at para. 219, note 233).

19 *Cross–Border Trucking*, ibid. This is consistent with the approach generally adopted in international jurisprudence. See J K Koh (1982), 'Reservations to Multilateral Treaties', 23 *Harvard International Law Journal* 71.

20 NAFTA (1992), Art. 102(1)(a).

This brief discussion illustrates two points regarding the role played by preambles in IIAs:

- **Preambles are an important part of the interpretive context and, if they are to be included in an IIA, careful thought must be given to the manner in which they are worded.** The wording will indicate the relative importance to be attributed to different objectives of the parties. It is desirable for the parties to clearly identify their most important considerations as objectives of the agreement.
- **The significance of preambles for interpreting an agreement may be affected by other provisions in the agreement, including objectives provisions.** Accordingly, it is important to ensure that any objectives provision reflects the same priorities as the preamble in order to maximise the likelihood of consistent interpretation. Otherwise, the objectives provision may be given priority over more general wording in the preamble.

Box 4.1 Summary of options for an IIA preamble

1. *No preamble*
2. *Preamble that refers only to investment promotion and protection*
3. *Preamble that refers to objectives beyond investment promotion and protection*

4.2.3 Discussion of options

1. *No preamble*

This is the most common practice in existing IIAs. Because a preamble is an important part of the interpretive context, not including one means that interpreters of the IIA have less direction regarding how its obligations should be interpreted. This leaves more discretion to the interpreter. Interpretive direction can be given through an objectives provision in the absence of a preamble.

2. *Preamble that refers only to investment promotion and protection*

This is the most common form of preamble in IIAs that have one. Because this form of preamble identifies only two objectives, the promotion and protection of investment, it prioritises these objectives for any interpreter of the agreement, including an investor–state tribunal. An interpreter might feel compelled to disregard other policy considerations that might be relevant. So, for example, if a state sought to regulate to protect the environment, this legitimate public purpose might be disregarded as a factor relevant to the application of the treaty to the measure. Interpretive direction in an objectives provision can qualify or complement the direction in a preamble. To ensure consistent interpretation, the objectives provision and the preamble should be consistent.

3. *Preamble that refers to objectives beyond investment promotion and protection*

In this form of preamble, found in some IIAs, the parties have an opportunity to identify and prioritise their intentions in entering into an IIA to include a broad range of considerations, including contributing to sustainable development. This helps to ensure that various policy priorities are taken into account by the interpreters of the treaty. The interpretive direction in such a preamble can be complemented by an objectives provision.

4.2.4 Discussion of sample provision

The sample preamble is much longer than those found in most existing agreements, with a view to setting out a vision of an IIA that goes beyond simply the promotion and protection of investment. Recognising the important interpretive role of the preamble, the sample preamble emphasises several goals that would inform an IIA designed to help achieve sustainable development. First, the preamble begins by setting out the pre-eminent objective of achieving sustainable development through increased foreign investment. This is emphasised and confirmed by the statement in the sample objectives provision set out below.[21] Next, the preamble recognises the significant role of two elements in achieving this objective: co-operation among the host state, the home state and investors, and the existence of favourable conditions for investment.

Other values inherent in a commitment to sustainable development and which are to inform interpretation of the parties' obligations are specifically identified: the protection of health, safety and the environment; the promotion and protection of internationally and domestically recognised human rights; labour rights; the rights of indigenous peoples; the commitment of the parties to democracy; the rule of law; and the parties' determination to prevent and combat corruption and to promote corporate social responsibility. The sample preamble also specifically refers to the right of party states to regulate to achieve their development objectives.

Drafting the preamble with such a fully elaborated description of what the parties are seeking to achieve should help to ensure that the reservations and exceptions in an IIA that are intended to preserve host states' ability to regulate in the public interest for the achievement of sustainable development are not interpreted in a restrictive manner, as has been done under NAFTA and in some other investor–state arbitration cases dealing with other IIAs.[22]

States should consider whether they want to include additional or different objectives from those set out in the sample preamble to reflect their own priorities and the specific context in which a treaty is being negotiated. In a regional treaty, for example, the

---

21 See Section 4.4 (Statement of objectives).

22 E.g. the conclusion reached in *SGS v. Philippines*, ICSID Case no. ARB/02/06, Decision of the Tribunal on Objections to Jurisdiction, 29 January 2004, that it is appropriate for a tribunal to resolve questions of interpretive doubt under a BIT in favour of the investor.

parties may want to include a reference to achieving regional integration.[23] In some negotiating contexts, countries may want a shorter, more focused set of objectives than is set out in the sample preamble.

4.2.5 Sample provision: preamble

AGREEMENT BETWEEN ——— AND ————

FOR THE PROMOTION AND PROTECTION OF INVESTMENTS

———————— and ————————, hereinafter referred to as the 'Parties'

Recognising that investment is critical for sustainable development, and understanding that the promotion of investment requires co-operative efforts by investors and both Parties, those that are host to investors and those that are their home states;

Seeking to encourage, create and maintain equitable and favourable conditions for investors of one Party and their investments in the territory of the other Party on the basis of equality and mutual benefit with a view to encouraging investment that contributes to sustainable development;

Seeking to ensure that investment is consistent with and facilitative of the protection of health, safety and the environment, the promotion and protection of internationally and domestically recognised human rights, labour rights and the rights of indigenous peoples;

Recognising that each Party has, in accordance with general principles of international law, the right to pursue its own development objectives and priorities and the right to take regulatory or other measures to ensure that development in its territory is consistent with the goals and principles of sustainable development and with other social and economic policy objectives, including the promotion and protection of human rights, labour rights, the rights of indigenous peoples, and the protection of the environment;

Reaffirming their commitment to democracy, the rule of law, human rights and fundamental freedoms in accordance with their obligations under international law, including the principles set out in the United Nations Charter, the Universal Declaration of Human Rights, customary international law and provisions of international agreements relating to the environment, human rights, labour rights and the rights of indigenous peoples binding on the Parties and desiring to have this Agreement interpreted in a manner consistent with these commitments;

Determined to prevent and combat corruption, including bribery, in international trade and investment and to promote corporate social accountability;

---

23 E.g. the preamble to the COMESA Investment Agreement (2007) and the preamble to the Protocol on Finance and Investment of the Southern African Development Community, signed 18 August 2006, in force 16 April 2010.

Recognising that the provisions of this agreement shall be interpreted in a mutually supportive manner;

Have agreed as follows: …

4.3 Definitions

Cross references

Section 4.5	Scope of application	94
Section 5.6	Limitations on expropriation and nationalisation	152
Section 5.12	Reservations and exceptions	224
Section 7.1	Investor–state dispute settlement	408
Section 8.2	Technical assistance	499

The definition provisions of an IIA are important for several reasons. First, definitions provide clear and predictable meanings for terms used in the agreement. Second and more importantly, definitions determine the scope of the agreement. As discussed above,[24] the key definitions in this regard are 'investor' and 'investment'.

From the perspective of investors, the definitions of these terms should be as broad as possible to ensure that their investments in the other state, however they are structured and regardless of the form or nature of their investment, receive the protection of the treaty. In contrast, a capital-importing state[25] will want to ensure that these definitions are targeted at the kinds of investments and investors that the state wants to attract by assuming IIA obligations and that it does not include categories of investors or investments of a particular kind that it does not want to protect. For example, if a state does not want to provide protection to foreigners from the other party state who are buying recreational property rather than investing in a business, it will need to reflect this in the definition of investment in the treaty or in some other way.

In addition, defining investment and investor establishes the scope of a host state's obligations and, as a result, the state's exposure to investor–state claims. As a consequence, a capital-importing state will want to make certain that it is comfortable assuming the substantive obligations in the IIA in relation to all the kinds of investments and investors that fit within the definition. This requires assessing the compatibility of the obligations undertaken regarding the defined categories of investment and investor with the host state's current domestic policies and policies

24 See Section 3.2.2 (Specific examples of the interaction between IIA commitments and domestic investment policy).

25 In this section and throughout the Guide, the expressions 'capital-importing state' and 'capital-exporting state' will often be used. It is recognized that many states are both importers and exporters of capital. Such states have interests as capital exporters and capital importers and their approach to IIAs should reflect an assessment of their overall interests, balancing their interests as exporters and importers in each negotiation. For such states, references to 'capital-importing state' and 'capital-exporting state' should be understood to refer the interests that a state has as a capital importer and those that it has as a capital exporter.

that it can foresee pursuing in relation to those kinds of investments and investors in the future. Possible conflicts between domestic policy and protecting certain kinds of investors and investments are discussed in detail below.

Countries also use definitions to specify the territorial scope of their obligations and the extent to which obligations apply to sub-national governments. Examples of how these kinds of limitations may be addressed are provided in the sample provision below.

Definitions, other than 'investment' and 'investor', that are included in the Guide sample definitions are discussed in the sections of the Guide on the substantive treaty provisions in which the defined term appears. In actual IIA negotiations, the sample definitions in the Guide may need to be supplemented by definitions specific to the IIA being negotiated.

4.3.1 Definition of investment

Investment is a broad concept that can include a wide range of interests. One approach to defining investment for the purposes of an IIA is to limit investments to interests in enterprises that are carrying on some productive activity in the host state. In some trade agreements, such as *GATS*, a narrow enterprise-based approach is used. In relation to investments, the agreement applies only to a service supplied through a commercial presence, which is defined as a corporation or a branch of a corporation that is owned or controlled by suppliers from WTO member states.[26] It is possible to have a more expansive list of interests in enterprises that qualify as investments. In NAFTA, for example, equity and debt securities issued by an enterprise are included (NAFTA, Art. 1139).[27] The investment does not have to give the investor ownership or control of the enterprise. Most IIAs, however, define investments to include an even wider range of property rights, assets and interests that are not limited to interests in an enterprise.

Issue 1: General approach – should the definition be open or closed?

In a large proportion of IIAs, investment is defined in an open-ended manner to include virtually every possible kind of investment. For example, many agreements define investment as 'every kind of asset' owned or controlled directly or indirectly by an investor of another party state, followed by an illustrative, non-exhaustive list of assets.[28] More recently, some countries, such as Canada, have opted for a closed or exhaustive list of assets that qualify as investment, and have provided specific

26 *GATS* also applies to services supplied through non-investment modes: services supplied (i) across the border by a foreign supplier to a consumer in another country, (ii) to a consumer who travels to the supplier's jurisdiction and (iii) though a services supplier who enters the consumer's jurisdiction. See the discussion of *GATS* in Appendix 2.

27 NAFTA (1992), Art. 1139.

28 E.g. Indian model BIPPA, Art. 1(b); US model BIT, Art. 1; UK model IPPA, Art. 1(a); Norwegian draft model APPI, Art. 2; ASEAN Agreement (2009), Art. 4; Sri Lanka–India, Agreement between the Government of the Democratic Socialist Republic of Sri Lanka and the Government of the Republic of India for the Promotion and Protection of Investment, signed 22 January 1997, in force 13 February 1998; India–Bangladesh, Bilateral Investment Promotion and Protection Agreement, signed 9 February 2009, in force 7 July 2011. The COMESA Investment Agreement (2007) simply refers to 'assets' followed by an indicative list and some exclusions (Art. 1.9).

exclusions from the definition.[29] Typically, the exclusions are intended to clarify the meaning of investment rather than to adopt a narrow or restrictive meaning. The IISD model treaty also contains a closed list definition, but it is much narrower in scope. For example, it excludes all portfolio investment.[30] The use of a closed definition and of exclusions allows states to ensure that IIA commitments are more precisely targeted at particular kinds of investments – those they want to attract.

As indicated above, capital-exporting states have usually favoured open definitions, because such a definition covers the widest range of investments by its investors. Investor arbitration tribunals have interpreted such definitions broadly, as appears to be intended, to include any kind of asset, including assets that are not normally considered an investment, such as money in a bank account and claims related to ordinary commercial transactions.[31] Because of this broad interpretation, open definitions provide the greatest reassurance to investors that their interests will be eligible for protection regardless of the form or nature of their investment. In addition, investments vary tremendously in their form and effect, and any limiting criteria that are imposed will inevitably be somewhat arbitrary.

However, from a host state's point of view, an open definition has several disadvantages:

- **Some of kinds of assets that will be eligible for protection will not produce the benefits commonly associated with investment, such as increased local employment and technology transfer, and will make little or no contribution to development;**
- **The scope of an open definition is inherently unpredictable, so states will find it difficult to determine what foreign interests qualify for protection and to ensure that they act consistently with their obligations; and**
- **With an open definition, protection will be extended to some kinds of investments that may not be attracted by the protection of an IIA.**

Regarding the last point, investments in sectors such as the extractive industries involve high sunk costs and are more likely to be the subject of regulatory action. Investors in these sectors may be more concerned about the risk of adverse action by a state because, typically, they have substantial effects on the local community in which they operate that may be the subject of state standards. Also, these kinds of investments must be in place for a long time before they become profitable, increasing the likelihood that state policy may change and new, possibly more onerous rules for the investment will be put in place. By comparison, IIA protection is less likely to attract investments that have no sunk costs or in relation to which the risk of government interference is low because they have little local effect and are of short duration, such as bonds and other financial investments. Investors with these kinds of investments are likely to be less interested in IIA protections from government interference.

---

29 Canadian model FIPA, Art. 1.

30 IISD model treaty, Art. 3(C).

31 *SGS v. Philippines*, op. cit.

Some kinds of investments may be sufficiently mobile for investors to be able to move their capital out of the host state to avoid state actions that they do not like. It may be easier to withdraw a financial investment from a host country following some local government action, as compared with a direct investment. For example, in most cases it will be easier to dispose of a corporate bond issued by a business in a host state than an unfinished factory. In addition, for some financial investments, country-specific risks may be reduced for an investor where the investor has a large number of diversified investments in different countries. If an IIA does not contribute significantly to reducing the risks associated with host state actions for an investor with particular kinds of investments, it will not encourage investors to make such investments. At the same time, the inclusion of these categories of investment in an IIA definition of investment expands the host state's obligations and its risk of investor–state claims.

For all these reasons, host states may opt for a closed definition. UNCTAD has identified the use of closed definitions as an 'emerging trend'.[32] The issue then becomes what assets should be included. This issue is also relevant, however, if an open definition is used, since even an open definition may have criteria that must be satisfied for an investment to be eligible for IIA protection and it may exclude certain investments from its scope. Ultimately each state must resolve this issue on the basis of its domestic policy, but there are a number of common issues that will need to be taken into account in limiting the scope of an IIA definition of investment. These are discussed in the next sections.

Issue 2: What specific identified assets should be included (or excluded) in a definition of investment?

Whether the definitions are expressed to be open or closed, most contain a list of assets that are considered investments. The list in the German model BIT is typical:

I. Movable and immovable property as well as any other rights in rem, such as mortgages, liens and pledges;

II. Shares of companies and other kinds of interest in companies;

III. Claims to money that has been used to create an economic value or claims to any performance having an economic value;

IV. Intellectual property rights, in particular, copyrights, patents, utility-model patents, industrial designs, trademarks, trade names, trade and business secrets, technical processes, know-how, and good will; and

V. Business concessions under public law, including concessions to search for, extract and exploit natural resources.[33]

While this kind of listing is common, it raises a number of issues that countries must consider, including whether the definition should be limited to particular classes of

32 UNCTAD (2011), *Scope and Definition: A Sequel*, United Nations, New York and Geneva, at 114.

33 See the similar definition in the India–Singapore CECA (2005), Art. 6.1.

assets, how this should be done and whether there should be general limitations on what constitutes an investment.

Issue 2(a): Should the definition of investment be limited to foreign direct investment?

Foreign direct investment typically refers to transactions in which a foreign party obtains a lasting interest in some entity in the host country economy. It generally involves a long-term relationship and a significant degree of influence over the management of the entity.[34] Given the substantial investor protection obligations typically undertaken in an IIA and the prospect that they may be enforced through investor–state dispute arbitration, a state may prefer to limit the definition to interests that involve the characteristics of a direct investment. Many definitions, however, capture investments that do not have the attributes of foreign direct investment. For example, a definition may extend the protections in the agreement to short-term or highly mobile forms of investment that the host state is not interested in attracting.

Should an investment be required to have the 'characteristics of an investment'? One limiting approach adopted in some treaties is to require that an investment have the characteristics of an investment. For example, the US model BIT defines investment as follows.

> 'Investment' means every asset that an investor owns or controls, directly or indirectly, that has the *characteristics of an investment*, including such characteristics as the *commitment of capital or other resources*, *the expectation of gain or profit*, *or the assumption of risk* ...[35] (Emphasis added.)

The ASEAN Agreement takes a similar approach.[36] This approach has several advantages. It goes some way towards ensuring that the economic contribution of the investment is substantial because it requires interpreters of the treaty to look at the economic characteristics of the investment, not just its formal characteristics, and provides some objective criteria to distinguish investments from ordinary commercial transactions. Nevertheless, how this sort of definition will apply in practice is hard to predict for several reasons:

- **The characteristics of an 'investment' in this kind of definition are not exhaustive.** It remains to be seen if other criteria may be developed in investor–state cases.

34 OECD (1996), *OECD Detailed Benchmark Definition of Foreign Direct Investment*, 3rd ed (BD3), OECD, Paris. Investors have used creative legal mechanisms to disguise portfolio investment as FDI in order to avoid capital controls and so states will need to incorporate language to address this if they wish to limit their IIAs to FDI.

35 US model BIT, Art. 1. A similar definition can be found in many agreements, e.g. India–Malaysia Comprehensive Economic Cooperation Agreement, signed 18 February 2011, in force 1 July 2011.

36 In a footnote to the definition of investment, the ASEAN Agreement provides as follows: 'Where an asset lacks the characteristics of an investment, that asset is not an investment regardless of the form it may take. The characteristics of an investment include the commitment of capital, the expectation of gain or profit, or the assumption of risk'.

- **It is not clear what the identified criteria mean.** The following questions about the definition remain unanswered: (i) does a commitment of any amount of capital qualify as an investment or is there a minimum threshold? (ii) if so, what is the threshold? and (iii) if an investment involves an assumption of risk, how should this risk be assessed? In some investor–state arbitrations under the Convention on the Settlement of Investment Disputes (the ICSID Convention),[37] tribunals have applied similar criteria to those in the US model to define investment for the purposes of the treaty and the results have been inconsistent.[38] The interpretation and significance of the ICSID definition of investment is discussed in Box 4.2.
- **In the definition used in the US model BIT, it is sufficient if any one of the criteria is satisfied.** An investment meets the requirements of the definition if it 'has the characteristics of an investment, including such characteristics as the commitment of capital or other resources, the expectation of gain or profit, *or* the assumption of risk'. While, in most practical circumstances, it seems likely that an investment with one of the characteristics would also have the other two, the fact that the criteria are not cumulative makes their application less certain. Some treaties use a cumulative formulation to address this uncertainty.[39]

Should an investment be required to contribute to development in the host state? An issue related to the definition of investment is whether only investments that make some contribution to development should be protected. From a developing country point of view such a requirement might seem to be a useful way to target the commitments being undertaken in the treaty so that they encourage only those investments that will provide development benefits. Including a 'contribution to development' requirement in the definition of investment also indicates clearly that the treaty's goal of protecting investment must be balanced with the goal of ensuring that the treaty meets the expectations of capital-importing states that investment benefiting from the treaty will contribute to their development. Such a provision would complement and reinforce the statements in the preamble, and the objectives provisions to the same effect.[40] In the event of an investor–state claim, the presence of such a requirement would permit a respondent state to challenge the jurisdiction

37 *Convention on the Settlement of Investment Disputes between States and Nationals of Other States*, signed 18 March 1965, 575 *United Nations Treaty Series* 159, reprinted in 4 *International Legal Materials* 532. ICSID dispute resolution is commonly provided for in IIAs. See Section 7.1 (Investor–state dispute settlement). ICSID also refers to the institution that administers arbitrations and other procedures under the ICSID Convention, the International Centre for the Settlement of Investment Disputes.

38 See the survey of the case law in UNCTAD (2011), *Scope and Definition*, op. cit., at 48–65.

39 E.g. Belgium–Luxembourg–Colombia, Agreement between the Belgium–Luxembourg Economic Union, on the one hand, and the Republic of Colombia, on the other hand, on the Reciprocal Promotion and Protection of Investments, signed 4 February 2009, not yet in force, Art. I(2.3); Bilateral Agreement for the Promotion and Protection of Investments Between the Republic of Colombia and ___________, Colombian model agreement (2007), Art. 2.3.

40 See Section 4.2.1(The role of preambles in IIAs) and Section 4.4 (Statement of objectives).

of an arbitral tribunal to hear an investor's claim on the basis that the investment did not contribute to development.

Undoubtedly, however, a 'contribution to development' criterion would be difficult for both states and investors to interpret. In addition to the general uncertainty regarding what a contribution to development is, there will be situations in which both the investor and the host state expect an investment to contribute to development, but it fails to do so in practice. In the context of investor–state arbitration, a tribunal would have to deal with conflicting views regarding whether a contribution to development existed. The tribunal's job would be complicated by the fact that development, as discussed in Section 2.3, is not just a legal concept, but also has economic and social dimensions.

Some commentators have expressed the view that there is no need to include 'contribution to development' in the definition of investment because if the investment meets the other criteria mentioned above (commitment of capital or other resources, the expectation of gain or profit and the assumption of risk), it will necessarily contribute to development. However, not all tribunals have followed this approach.[41]

As discussed in Box 4.2, the 'contribution to development' criterion has sometimes been applied in cases under the ICSID Convention,[42] even where it does not appear in the IIA under consideration. This has occurred because an ICSID tribunal has jurisdiction only if the dispute arises out of an 'investment', and some tribunals have considered a contribution to development to be an essential characteristic of an investment. In the ICSID cases to date, tribunals have found it challenging to determine whether an investment does make a contribution to development.

As a consequence of the uncertainty relating to the concept of development, the availability of the protections of the treaty would become less certain for investors and host states if it were part of the definition of investment. It is probably impossible to draft a definition of investment that sets out clear and specific criteria capable of limiting the scope of the treaty to investments that promote sustainable development.

An alternative to including a requirement that the investment must contribute to sustainable development in the definition of investment is to limit the protection of the treaty to investments that have been approved by the host state and to have the host state evaluate the investment's contribution to development as a condition of approving it. If a state has the capacity to make such an assessment, there is less need to include such a requirement, with its attendant uncertainty.

41 R Dolzer and C Schreuer (2008), *Principles of International Investment Law*, Oxford University Press, Oxford, at 69.

42 *ICSID Convention*, op. cit.

Box 4.2 The requirement for an 'investment' under Article 25 of the Convention on the Settlement of Disputes between States and Nationals of other States

About two-thirds of all investor–state arbitrations take place under the rules of the International Centre for the Settlement of Investment Disputes (ICSID). For a dispute between an investor and a state under an IIA to be dealt with under the procedures of the ICSID Convention, the investor must have made an 'investment' within the meaning of Article 25 of the Convention. Different tribunals have adopted different approaches to determining whether this requirement is met.

There is some uncertainty about whether Article 25 requires a tribunal to apply a definition of investment that is independent of the definition of investment in the IIA that is alleged to have been violated. While some ICSID tribunals have found that the language used by the parties in their agreement determines whether there is an investment for the purposes of Article 25,[43] others have decided that the existence of an investment for the purposes of Article 25 depends on the fulfilment of criteria that are independent of the parties' agreement, as well as whatever definition they have agreed to in the treaty. One recent tribunal identified the following criteria as relevant.

> To summarize all the requirements for an investment to benefit from the international protection of ICSID, the Tribunal considers that the following six elements have to be taken into account:
>
> 1. a contribution in money or other assets;
> 2. a certain duration;
> 3. an element of risk;
> 4. an operation made in order to develop an economic activity in the host State;
> 5. assets invested in accordance with the laws of the host State;
> 6. assets invested *bona fide*.[44]

Some ICSID cases have also required that the alleged investment make a contribution to the host state's development in order for it to be considered an

(Continued)

43 E.g. MCI *Power Group LC and New Turbine Incorporated v. Ecuador*, (2007) ICSID Case No. ARB/03/6, IIC 296, Award. 26 July 2007.

44 *Phoenix Action Limited v. Czech Republic*, ICSID Case No. ARB/06/5, IIC 367, Award, 15 April 2009.

(Continued)

investment for the purposes of Article 25,[45] though in other cases this approach has been specifically rejected.[46]

Since the decisions of ICSID tribunals are not binding on subsequent tribunals, it is impossible to predict with certainty whether: (i) a tribunal in an ICSID arbitration will require that these kinds of objective criteria for the existence of an investment must be satisfied regardless of what the parties have agreed to in their treaty; and (ii) if such objective criteria are applied, a contribution to development will be required.[47]

The implications for drafting IIAs are:

- States should not rely on definitions of 'investment' adopted in arbitration awards. If they wish to ensure that a specific criterion will be used to define whether an investment is eligible for protection, regardless of whether the treaty provides for ICSID arbitration or not, that criterion should be put into the treaty definition of investment.
- Even specific criteria may be interpreted in surprising ways, so it is best to be as clear as possible in defining investment in an IIA.
- If an IIA provides for ICISD arbitration, regardless of what the IIA says, an arbitral tribunal may adopt additional criteria for the purpose of determining whether or not the requirements for an investment under Article 25 have been met.

Making such an assessment, however, will often be a challenge for host countries. To respond to this problem, the Guide includes a discussion of best practices in the area of assessing investments. For instance, it describes provisions that require investors to engage in assessments of the environmental, social and human rights impacts of their investments prior to implementing them and to provide the assessment to the host country government for review with the goal of developing a management plan for the implementation of the investment that is designed to ensure its compatibility with sustainable development.[48] The Guide also discusses the use of technical assistance provisions to support the development of the capacity of developing countries to assess the costs and benefits of foreign investment.[49]

---

45 *Salini Costruttori S.p.A. and Italstrade S.p.A. v. Jordan*, ICSID Case No. ARB/02/13, IIC 208, Award, 31 January 2006.

46 *Biwater Gauff v. Tanzania*, ICSID Case No. ARB/05/22, Award, 24 July 2008, at para. 312; *Malaysian Historical Salvors v. Malaysia*, (2009) ICSID Case No. ARB/05/10, Annulment Decision, 16 April 2009.

47 Some non-ICSID tribunals have applied objective criteria for the existence of an investment in determining their own jurisdiction, for example *Romak S.A. v. Uzbekistan*, PCA Case No AA280, Award, 26 November 2009, at para. 207; and *Mytilineos Holdings S.A. v. The State Union of Serbia and Montenegro and Republic of Serbia*, UNCITRAL, Partial Award on Jurisdiction, 8 September 2006 at paras 117–125.

48 See Section 6.6 (Sustainability assessments).

49 See Section 8.2 (Technical assistance).

Issue 2(b): Should portfolio investment be excluded?

Another way to narrow the definition of investment so that it includes only significant investments that contribute to development is to create specific exclusions for investments that do not satisfy these requirements. Some suggest that portfolio investment should be excluded on this basis.

Considerations related to whether portfolio investment should be included in an IIA definition of investment As noted above, most treaties use a broad definition of investment that includes what is referred to as portfolio investment, meaning investment in debt and equity securities that is intended only for financial gain and that does not create a lasting interest in or control over an enterprise. Portfolio investors are passive and do not have the ability to manage the business in which they have invested. Examples of portfolio investments are purchases of bonds and stocks that do not give the investor control over the issuer of the securities. Several arguments can be made in favour of excluding portfolio investment from investments protected under an IIA. These arguments parallel those made above in support of a definition of investment that is limited to investments that have the characteristics of an investment.

- **The exclusion of portfolio investment helps to ensure that only substantial investments that make a significant contribution to the host country economy would benefit from IIA protection, including access to investor–state dispute settlement.**[50] Portfolio investment does not generally produce the kinds of benefits attributed to direct investment, such as technology transfer.[51]
- **Portfolio investment is highly volatile and rapid swings in investment flows can be damaging to a host state.** For this reason, a definition of investment should not be targeted at portfolio investment. It is not a category of investment that states should seek to attract.
- **Protecting portfolio investment under an IIA increases the risk of investor–state cases by expanding the class of persons eligible to make claims.**
- **Portfolio investment does not need the protection of IIA investor protection commitments and will not be encouraged by such commitments:**
    - Portfolio investors are often able to reduce their country-specific risk by diversifying their investment holdings to include investments in many countries; and

---

50 The exclusion of portfolio investment in the IISD model was intended to ensure the achievement of this objective. As discussed below, under the IISD model investors also have obligations and for this reason as well the drafters decided that it would be impractical to include portfolio investment in the definition of investment (H Mann, K von Moltke, LE Peterson and A Cosbey (2005), IISD Model International Agreement on Investment for Sustainable Development, International Institute for Sustainable Development, Winnipeg, at 6).

51 UNCTAD (2011), *Most Favoured Nation: A Sequel*, United Nations, New York and Geneva, at 29.

- Portfolio investors are more likely to be able to recover the value of their investments and withdraw them from a host country if the host country acts contrary to their interests, compared with investors who have acquired ownership or control of real property, plants and equipment in the host country. Portfolio investors are less likely to have sunk costs that would require them to continue to hold their investments in the face of adverse host state action.

On the other hand, portfolio investment may be attractive to host countries and their businesses because it can make a contribution to sustainable development, at least in some cases. Even though the inclusion of portfolio investment extends treaty protection to many relatively small investments, the aggregate benefit of such investments to investors of the home state may be substantial and complementary to other sources of capital.[52] Successful direct investments may require other types of capital flows, including portfolio investment.[53] In addition, portfolio investment in locally owned businesses may be attractive because it permits the control of the business to remain in the hands of host state nationals.

The risk of multiple claims by portfolio investors with investments in the same business may be mitigated in practice because the costs for an individual investor to bring an investor–state claim, even if the investor's claim is ultimately successful, are so large that many possible claims by small investors may never be brought. This impediment will not operate, however, where many small investors with identical claims can pool their resources to bring a claim.[54] This might occur where there are multiple minority foreign holders of shares of a corporation carrying on business in a host state or multiple holders of bonds issued by such a corporation and all these investors are affected in the same way by host state actions.[55]

Defining portfolio investment in an IIA One of the challenges of excluding portfolio investment is how to define it, causing some to question the practicality of excluding it.[56] It is difficult to create a definition of portfolio that can be applied in a consistent and predictable way. One approach that has been used in some agreements has been

---

52 WTO Working Group on the Relationship between Trade and Investment, Note by the Secretariat, WT/WGTI/W/108, paras 50–54 (21 March 2002).

53 Ibid.

54 See, for example, 107 identical claims by individual members of the Canadian Cattlemen for Fair Trade as one claim, available at: www.state.gov/s/l/c14683.htm (accessed 29 May 2012).

55 E.g. *Abaclat and others v. Argentine Republic*, (2011) ICSID Case No. ARB/07/05, Decision on Jurisdiction and Admissability, 4 August 2011. One way to address the process costs of multiple identical investor–state claims is to provide a process for their consolidation. This is discussed below. See Section 7.1 (Investor–state dispute settlement). While consolidation of multiple similar or identical claims reduces the cost for states of defending them, the possibility of consolidation may deter investors from making claims.

56 Association of Southeast Asian States, Framework Agreement on the ASEAN Investment Area, signed 7 October 1998, excludes portfolio investment, but does not define it (Art. 2). The current ASEAN Agreement (2009) contains no such exclusion. The SADC Investment Protocol (2006) contains a proviso permitting each party state to exclude 'short-term portfolio investments of a speculative nature' but provides no further definition (Art. 1).

to limit the coverage of the IIA to foreign direct investment, which would have the effect of excluding portfolio investment.[57]

The OECD Benchmark Definition of Foreign Direct Investment[58] was produced by the Working Group on International Investment Statistics, representing the international community of FDI statisticians. Its purpose is to provide a definition of FDI that can be applied consistently by national statistical agencies. It is more than 200 pages long, but the basic definition is as follows:

> Foreign direct investment (*FDI*) is a category of investment that reflects the objective of establishing a lasting interest by a resident enterprise in one economy (*direct investor*) in an enterprise (*direct investment enterprise*) that is resident in an economy other than that of the direct investor. The lasting interest implies the existence of a long-term relationship between the direct investor and the direct investment enterprise. The direct or indirect ownership of 10% or more of the voting power of an enterprise resident in one economy by an investor resident in another economy is evidence of such a relationship.[59]

The definition in the IMF's *Balance of Payments and International Investment Position Manual* takes an identical approach. The IMF *Manual* defines portfolio investment, essentially, as anything that is not FDI.[60]

Even though the 10 per cent threshold in the OECD definition is arbitrary, in that some investments of less than 10 per cent will represent a significant degree of influence and some investments of greater than 10 per cent will not, it is used without exception for statistics gathering in the interest of consistent reporting. The same consideration does not apply in the context of a definition in an IIA. Nevertheless, in the absence of any other specific criterion, 10 per cent of voting shares in a corporation or other forms of ownership may be a useful way to define when an investment is no longer a portfolio investment, because compared with the other main criteria – a lasting interest – the 10 per cent threshold is more certain and predictable.

---

57 E.g. the Canada–United States Free Trade Agreement, signed 2 January 1988, in force 1 January 1989, Art. 1611; European Free Trade Association–United Mexican States Free Trade Agreement, signed 27 November 2000, in force 1 July 2001, Art. 45; and Denmark–Poland, Agreement between the Government of the Kingdom of Denmark and the Government of the Republic of Poland for the Promotion and Reciprocal Protection of Investments, signed 1 May 1990, in force 13 October 1990, Art. 1(1)(b). A similar approach is taken in the IISD model treaty, though the definition goes on to specify certain additional characteristics of an investment for the purposes of the agreement (Art. 2).

58 OECD (2008) *OECD Benchmark Definition of Foreign Direct Investment*, 4th ed, OECD, Paris.

59 Ibid., at 234.

60 IMF (2007), *IMF's Balance of Payments and International Investment Position Manual*, 6th ed, IMF, Washington, paras 6.8 to 6.24. The definition of portfolio investment in the *IMF Manual* essentially says that portfolio investment is anything that is not direct investment or reserve assets (para. 6.54). UNCTAD uses a similar definition. See UNCTAD (1996), *World Investment Report 1996*, United Nations, New York and Geneva, at 219.

As defined in the IMF *Manual*, the threshold includes interests that are held directly by an investor, as well as indirectly through an interest in an intermediary entity such as a corporation wholly owned by the investor. Determining the effective size of an interest held through several intermediary entities can be complex. Debt and other claims that do not involve the power to vote are not generally considered a direct investment relationship, unless a direct investment relationship otherwise exists between the parties through other forms of investment.[61]

Based on this discussion, 'portfolio investment' could be defined as follows for the purpose of excluding it from the definition of investment in an IIA.

> Portfolio investment has the meaning given to that term from time to time in the IMF's *Balance of Payments and International Investment Position Manual.*

This definition has the benefit of relying on a well-recognised and widely used international standard. However, the definition is subject to change over time as the IMF Manual is revised, and the manual definition is nuanced and complex to apply in practice.

Another approach would be the following:

> Portfolio investment is any investment that is an equity security or a debt security in an enterprise that does not give the investor a lasting interest in the enterprise or direct or indirect ownership of 10 per cent or more of the voting power of an enterprise.

This definition adopts the essence of the IMF and OECD definitions. The concept of 'lasting interest' is inherently flexible and requires a degree of judgment that could lead to a degree of unpredictability with respect to what it means. For example, it is not clear whether certain debt securities that impose requirements on management to maintain specific financial standards, and become voting securities if management fails to do so, would give a significant degree of influence to the investors such that they should not be considered portfolio investment. The additional requirement of less than 10 per cent of the voting power is somewhat arbitrary, but is more certain and predictable.

Issue 2(c): Should debt and other claims to money be excluded?

As in the German model agreement, most IIAs include 'claims to money which has been used to create an economic value or claims to any performance having an economic value' in their definition of investment.[62] This expression would include most debts and even some claims under commercial contracts. Because both of these kinds of transactions are outside what would conventionally be considered an investment, some IIAs contain limitations that narrow the scope of the definition of an investment to exclude them to some extent. There are two main approaches:

61 *IMF Manual* at para. 6.37. Some exceptions are provided.

62 M Malik (2009), *Report on Bilateral Investment Treaties*, Commonwealth Secretariat, London, at 7.

- **Claims to money are included only if they are linked to some more conventional kind of investment that fits within the definition of investment in the agreement.** Some IIAs entered into by Caribbean countries, for example, limit loans to those that 'are directly related to a specific investment'.[63]
- **Certain claims to money are specifically excluded.** For example, the COMESA Investment Agreement excludes 'claims to money deriving solely from commercial contracts for the sale of goods and services to or from the territory of a member State' and 'a bank letter of credit; or the extensions of credit in connection with a commercial transaction, such as trade financing.'[64] The Canadian model agreement similarly excludes claims to money arising out of commercial contracts for the sale of goods or services between national enterprises in different party states. The Canadian model also excludes financial transactions that do not involve the acquisition of property, as well as loans with a maturity of less than three years.[65]

The approach adopted in the COMESA Investment Agreement and the Canadian model has the advantage of being more specific and predictable for the benefit of both host states and investors. The exclusion of loans with a maturity of less than three years is an attempt to ensure that only loans that make a significant and stable financial contribution in a host country are protected as investments. Short-term investments are inherently more volatile. Nevertheless, a term of three years is somewhat arbitrary and may not be the optimal way to distinguish loans that support other kinds of investment activity.

A third approach is found in the US model agreement, which has a broad definition that includes claims to money, but adds the following footnote:

> Some forms of debt, such as bonds, debentures, and long-term notes, are more likely to have the characteristics of an investment, while other forms of debt, such as claims to payment that are immediately due and result from the sale of goods or services, are less likely to have such characteristics.

An investor–state arbitration tribunal would have to take this interpretative direction into account in determining whether an alleged investment has the characteristics of an investment as required by the US definition of investment. This approach might do a better job of targeting the definition at debt that supports investment, but it creates a greater degree of uncertainty than the other two approaches regarding how it would operate in practice.

---

63 For example, Germany–Trinidad and Tobago, Treaty between the Federal Republic of Germany and the Republic of Trinidad and Tobago for the Encouragement and Reciprocal Protection of Investments, signed 8 September 2006, in force 17 April 2010, and Korea–Trinidad and Tobago, Agreement between the Government of the Republic of Korea and the Government of the Republic of Trinidad and Tobago for the Promotion and Protection of Investments, signed 5 November 2002, in force 27 November 2003, and others described in Malik, ibid., at 7–8.

64 COMESA Investment Agreement (2007), Art. 1.9.

65 Canadian model FIPA, Art. 1.

Issue 2(d): Should intellectual property be excluded?

Existing practice Most IIAs include intellectual property in their definition of investment, though how they do so varies.[66] One common approach is exemplified by the German model set out above, which defines investment to include:

> Intellectual property rights, in particular copyrights, patents, utility model patents, industrial designs, trademarks, trade names, trade and business secrets, technical processes, know-how and good will.

Some other IIAs simply refer to intellectual property without specifying what is meant, or identify categories of intellectual property rights without using the words 'intellectual property'.[67] The Canadian model, for example, refers simply to 'intangible property.'[68]

Issues related to the inclusion of intellectual property rights in an IIA Protecting the intellectual property rights of foreign investors can raise a number of difficult challenges for host developing countries and the additional protection of such rights through IIAs has been the subject of some criticism.[69] All countries that are members of the WTO must comply with the obligations of the Agreement on Trade-related Aspects of Intellectual Property (the TRIPs Agreement), which identifies categories of intellectual property and sets minimum standards for the rights associated with each category, as well as the enforcement of those rights. Many countries have entered into preferential trade agreements that impose further obligations. As a consequence, one challenge is to ensure that that any IIA provisions that a country agrees to are

66 For example, the following models define investment to include intellectual property, either explicitly or through open-ended definitions: Indian model BIPPA, Art. 1(b); US model BIT, Art. 1; Canadian model FIPA, Art. 1; UK model IPPA, Art. 1(a); Norwegian draft model APPI, Art. 2; COMESA Investment Agreement (2007), Art. 1.9; SADC Investment Protocol (2006), Art. 1; ASEAN Agreement, Art. 4(c); India–Singapore CECA (2005), Art. 6.1(1); India–Malaysia CECA (2011), Art. 1. The same is true for most Caribbean and all Pacific BITS (Malik, op. cit., at 8, 43). The IISD model treaty does not expressly refer to intellectual property rights, but the commentary indicates that the drafters intended the intellectual property rights could be protected where the right is associated with an investment otherwise defined. Stand-alone rights, including rights under a licence, are intended to be excluded (H Mann, et al. (2005), *IISD Model International Agreement on Investment for Sustainable Development – Negotiators Handbook*, International Institute for Sustainable Development, Winnipeg, at 6.). The IISD's distinction has not been adopted in the Guide sample provision because it is difficult to express such a distinction clearly and effectively. It is not obvious that the IISD model is successful in excluding stand-alone rights. Also, it may be desirable for local businesses to be able to access technology through such licences.

67 E.g. Germany–Antigua and Barbuda, Treaty between the Federal Republic of Germany and Antigua and Barbuda concerning the Encouragement and Reciprocal Protection of Investments, signed 11 May 1998, in force 18 February 2001.

68 Canadian model FIPA, Art 1.

69 C M Correa (2004), 'Bilateral Investment Agreements: Agents of New Global Standards for the Protection of Intellectual Property Rights?', available at: www.grain.org/briefings_files/correa-bits-august-2004.pdf (accessed 29 May 2012).

consistent with its obligations. Developing countries often find their international obligations related to intellectual property onerous and struggle to comply with them. Nevertheless, in general, IIA provisions do not conflict with intellectual property obligations, since IIAs do not prescribe specific levels of intellectual property rights protection. Instead, the broad investor protection obligations largely protect entitlements in intellectual property that are granted under domestic law.[70] Nevertheless, protecting intellectual property rights as investments under IIAs can create problems. The following are two examples:

- **Protecting the patents of foreign investors in pharmaceuticals as investments under an IIA may impede the host country's ability to grant access to medicines for the poor.** Granting a compulsory licence of a patented drug to a local company to produce a needed medicine at a lower price could be considered an expropriation of an investment requiring compensation under an IIA if the patent is held by a foreign investor eligible for protection under the IIA. This is a risk even though the TRIPs Agreement expressly permits compulsory licensing so long as certain criteria are met.[71]
- **Protecting intellectual property of foreign investors under an IIA may result in protecting entitlements beyond what is protected under domestic law.** Despite TRIPs and other international intellectual property agreements that set standards for what must be protected, what is actually protected as intellectual property varies somewhat from one country to another. Some IIAs include goodwill, technical processes, trade names and other forms of intellectual property within their definition of investment. These are not categories of intellectual property rights that are required to be protected under intellectual property treaties and may not be protected under domestic law. Nevertheless, if they are defined to be an investment under an IIA, a host state will be required to treat these kinds of rights and interests in a manner consistent with the protections in the agreement.

From an investor's point of view, intellectual property rights are often critically important because the value of their investments is determined by technology and other assets protected by such rights.[72] For this reason, and because it would be inconsistent with existing practice, total exclusion of intellectual property rights will be difficult to negotiate. Even if it were possible, a complete exclusion might have a negative impact on the success of the IIA in attracting investment. In addition, developing country businesses are increasingly exporters of intellectual property. Consequently, often the issue in IIA negotiations will be how to ensure that the scope for IIA protection is appropriate.

70 E.g. *Eli Lilly v. Canada*, (2012), Notice of Intent, 7 November 2012, challenging aspects of Canada's patent law as not consistent with Canada's international obligations.

71 TRIPs Agreement, Art. 31. There may be defences that a state could raise to such a claim.

72 B Mercurio (2010), 'Reconceptualizing the Debate on Intellectual Property Rights and Economic Development', 3 *Law and Development Review* 64.

Options for narrowing the scope of intellectual property rights included in an IIA If intellectual property rights are to be protected as investments, a second set of issues relates to how broadly they will be protected. The following sets out several approaches to limiting the protection afforded.

- **Limiting protected intellectual property to rights that are connected to some other form of investment:** One issue for host states is whether intellectual property rights should be protected only when they are connected to some other form of investment in the host state or also on a stand-alone basis, such as in a licensing transaction unconnected to any other economic activity. Most agreements simply say that intellectual property rights are protected, which would apparently cover both situations. The COMESA Investment Agreement, however, provides that an intellectual property right has to be connected with an investment in the host state to be eligible for protection.[73] A host state might be concerned that protecting bare licences would extend protection to investors who have registered their rights but not contributed anything to the local economy. A patent on an industrial process that is not being worked by the foreign patent holder in the host country is one example. The patent holder could prevent others from using the patented technology even if they are not using it themselves. On the other hand, protection would encourage licensing of needed technologies to businesses operating in the host country.
- **Defining what is meant by intellectual property rights specifically:** A second issue is how broadly to define intellectual property rights. While some agreements include goodwill, technical processes, trade names, know-how and business secrets, as well as patents, copyrights, trademarks, industrial designs and utility models,[74] others do not define intellectual property rights at all[75] or exclude certain forms, such as goodwill.[76] In general, some definition of what is meant is helpful since what is intellectual property varies somewhat from state to state. Also, a state should consider to what extent it wants to agree in an IIA to protect categories of intellectual property that are not protected under its domestic law. The definition of investment in the India–Malaysia Comprehensive Economic Cooperation Agreement includes only intellectual property rights 'recognized pursuant to laws and regulations of each Party.'[77] Such an approach has the advantage of precluding an investor from making a claim under an IIA that is based on a conception of intellectual property not recognised in the host state.

---

73 COMESA Investment Agreement (2007), Art. 1.9. The definition in the Canadian model FIPA states that intangible property is protected as an investment only to the extent that it is acquired in the expectation or used for the purposes of economic benefit or other business purpose (Art. 1). This would appear to be broad enough to capture stand-alone licences.

74 Korea–Jamaica, Agreement between the Republic of Korea and the Government of Jamaica for the Promotion and Protection of Investments, signed 10 June 2003, not yet in force.

75 ASEAN Agreement (2009), Canadian model FIPA.

76 E.g. COMESA Investment Agreement (2007), Art. 1.9.

77 India–Malaysia CECA (2005), Art. 10.2(d).

Protecting goodwill or reputation as investments under IIAs creates particular concerns, since including these interests in the definition of investment means that an investor may be able to claim damages in investor–state arbitration on the basis that an action of the host state has a negative impact on the value or reputation of its business.

- **Include intellectual property in the definition of investment, but use exclusions and reservations to protect particular areas of policy making:** A final approach, which is complementary to the others, is to include intellectual property in the definition of investment, but to use exceptions and reservations to ensure that host states are permitted to regulate intellectual property rights in accordance with domestic policy. The following are examples:
    - o Even if intellectual property was a protected investment under an IIA, a state could preserve its right to issue compulsory licences of patented pharmaceuticals, a right specifically granted in the TRIPs Agreement, if the agreement provided that compulsory licences are not to be considered expropriations for the purposes of the IIA;
    - o Derogations from national treatment and MFN are permitted by TRIPs, and these could also be permitted by express exceptions in an IIA; and
    - o Another kind of exception that may relate to intellectual property interests, such as copyrights in music, literature and other art forms, is an exception from the obligations in the agreement for measures related to the promotion of culture.[78]

Issue 2(e): Should government securities and loans be excluded?

While most agreements are silent on this point,[79] the Canadian model FIPA specifically excludes government securities and loans of the host state.[80] By contrast, the Jamaica–Korea BIT specifically includes government-issued securities.[81] The likely rationale for excluding government securities and loans is a concern that if these investments were protected under IIA obligations, a government would be limited in its ability to restructure, reschedule or otherwise deal with its debt in times of financial crisis.[82] In addition such investments do not contribute directly to private sector economic activity.

On the other hand, excluding these obligations would presumably make it harder and more expensive for governments and state-owned enterprises to raise capital

78 A cultural exception is discussed below. See Section 5.12 (Reservations and exceptions).

79 The COMESA Investment Agreement (2007) excludes loans to a member state or state enterprise (Art. 1.9).

80 Canadian model FIPA, Art. 1. See also Colombia model agreement, Art. 2.1.

81 Korea–Jamaica BIT (2003), Art. 1.

82 It is also possible that the contract governing the debt provides for arbitration or enforcement in foreign courts which could be resorted to by investors, regardless of whether the debt was covered by an IIA or not.

from foreign investors. In some countries where state-owned enterprises do not operate with the benefit of a state guarantee of their obligations and must compete for capital against private enterprises, the blanket exclusion of debt issued by state-owned enterprises may put them at a disadvantage. Also, since the state is not responsible for their obligations, the inclusion of their obligations within the definition of investment would not impair a state's ability to manage its finances. One approach to addressing this problem would be to exclude the debt of state-owned enterprises that the state has guaranteed or for which the state has assumed direct or contingent liabilities.

As with intellectual property, it is possible that the specific concern regarding a host state's need to have flexibility to take action to respond to a financial crisis can be addressed using an exception. The use of a prudential exception for this purpose is discussed below.[83] Another alternative would be to include government securities and loans in the definition of investment but provide that no claim can be made in relation to these investments in investor–state dispute settlement.[84] This would not avoid the application of the obligations of the agreement but would prevent use of the investor–state process to claim compensation if a state breached an obligation in relation to this form of investment.

Issue 2(f): Should other exclusions be added?

Each state should consider what other exclusions might be incorporated in the definition of investment based on its domestic policy on investment, including categories of investment in which foreign participation is limited or prohibited. Examples of other exclusions include the following:

- **Property not being used for a business purpose:** Some IIAs exclude property that is being used for recreational, personal or other non-business purposes on the basis that the purpose of an IIA is to attract foreign capital that is to be used for productive business purposes.[85]
- **Agricultural land:** In many developing countries, foreign ownership of agricultural land is a sensitive issue. Often agriculture is a major area of economic activity and a successful agricultural sector is critical to national food security. Foreign investment can support increased agricultural production and enhanced food security. Nevertheless, concerns have been expressed that the protection of foreign investors' investments in agricultural land in IIAs can have negative consequences for food security because of the restrictions that are imposed on the ability of host states to regulate foreign investors who buy agricultural land, especially in weak states, and to comply with their international human rights

83 See Section 5.12 (Reservations and exceptions).

84 This was done in the United States–Peru Trade Promotion Agreement, signed 12 April 2006, in force 1 February 2009.

85 Japan–Singapore Economic Partnership Agreement, signed 13 January 2002, in force 30 November 2002, Art. 72(a); Canadian model FIPA, Art. 1 (regarding property that qualifies as an investment).

obligations.[86] States need to consider to what extent investment in agricultural land should be protected under their IIAs.

- **Assets of less than a certain value:**[87] Assets below a specified value threshold might be excluded from the definition of investment in an IIA in order to reduce the risk of investor–state claims by large numbers of small investors whose investments are not significant from an economic point of view. As discussed above, the small value of each such claim will discourage investors who hold them from bringing expensive investor–state claims, though this can be offset if the investors act collectively. In addition, some countries may want to protect small and medium-sized local businesses from competition. One way to do this is not to give foreigners carrying on small and medium-sized businesses incentives to invest in the form of the protection under an IIA. As discussed below, another approach is to limit the scope of the agreement by excluding investments in certain sectors characterised by small and medium-sized local businesses from the categories of investments under the IIA. For example, an IIA could exclude investments in hotels with fewer than 50 rooms.[88]
- **Changes in the form of the investment:** Most IIAs do not address what happens if an investment changes form. For these agreements, when an investment changes its form, the protection of the agreement continues to apply only to the extent that the new form meets the requirements of an investment under the IIA. A few IIAs expressly address whether a change in an investment should fall within the definition of investment. These agreements typically provide that a change in the form of the investment does not affect whether it is covered by the definition of investment.[89] Such an approach will be most attractive to investors because it ensures that their interests will be protected regardless of what happens to their investment. So, for example, if a shareholder in a corporation exchanged its shares for a debt claim against the corporation, the debt claim would be considered an investment, even if, on its own, the debt claim would not meet the requirements of the definition of investment in the IIA. For capital-importing states, however, it may be desirable to require that a changed investment must still fall within the definition of investment agreed to in the IIA to be protected, since that definition describes what they agreed to protect and an obligation to protect new forms of investment outside the definition is inherently unpredictable. In addition, protecting new forms of existing investments will not encourage new investment.

---

86 F Smith (2012), 'Food Security, Foreign Direct Investment and Multilevel Governance in Weak States', presented at Third Biennial Global Conference of the Society of International Economic Law, National University of Singapore; C Häberli (2012), 'Foreign Direct Investment in Agriculture: Land Grab or Food Security Improvement', presented at Third Biennial Global Conference of the Society of International Economic Law, National University of Singapore; and UNCTAD (2012), *World Investment Report 2012*, United Nations, New York and Geneva, at 79.

87 UNCTAD (2011), *Scope and Definition*, op. cit., at 117.

88 See Section 4.5 (Scope of application).

89 E.g. UK IPPA, Art. 1.

Issue 2(g): Should the definition of investment limit eligible investments to investments made in accordance with host state law?

Many IIAs include in the definition of investment a requirement that the investment be made in accordance with the laws and regulations of the host state.[90] Such a requirement can also be included in a provision expressly setting out the scope of the IIA.[91] Locating this requirement in a scope provision highlights its importance. Though the precise meaning of such a requirement depends on the wording used, in general, such a provision, sometimes called an 'admission clause', is designed to limit the protection of the agreement to investments that have been admitted or approved by the host state in accordance with whatever domestic requirements exist.[92] Such a provision provides an incentive for foreign investors to comply with host state requirements in order to ensure that they benefit from the protections of the treaty. This type of provision is particularly important for countries that use their investment admission process as one way, perhaps the only way, of ensuring that investments contribute to sustainable development.

If an IIA contained a requirement that an investment be made in accordance with the laws and regulations of the host state in order to receive the protection of the treaty, the failure of an investor to obtain the necessary approval for a particular investment would mean that its investment would not be protected and an investor–state arbitration tribunal would not have jurisdiction to hear a claim by the investor. The same result would follow if the approval had been obtained but through misrepresentations or fraud or other corrupt actions on the part of the investor. There are some important limits on the ability of the state to rely on the absence of an investment approval or an investor's non-compliance with domestic law that have been imposed in investor–state arbitration awards:

- **A state's subsequent withdrawal of an approval properly given to an investment cannot be used to deny the protection of the IIA to the investment.** While an IIA provision could be drafted to permit a state to deny protection in this way, most do not give the host state such a broad discretion. If a host state did have discretion of this kind, it would be able to decide when the protections of the treaty would be available and the value of the protections of the treaty to the investor would be seriously diminished.[93]

---

90 E.g. UK IPPA, Art. 1; Indian BIPPA, Art. 1(b); COMESA Investment Agreement (2007), Art. 1(9); ASEAN Agreement (2009), Art. 4(a). Other model agreements do not (e.g. Canadian model FIPA; US model BIT).

91 See Section 4.5 (Scope of application).

92 Some tribunals have found that a requirement for investments to comply with local laws exists even in the absence of an express provision in an IIA. See the cases discussed in UNCTAD (2011), *Scope and Definition*, op. cit. at 38.

93 C McLachlan, L Shore and M Weiniger (2007), *International Investment Arbitration, Substantive Principles*, Oxford University Press, Oxford, at 196.

- **A country that accepts an investment in practice cannot later challenge the jurisdiction of an investor–state tribunal when the investor makes a claim on the basis that some formalities were not satisfied in connection with the approval of the investment.**[94] In this regard, the host state must act in good faith.
- **The requirement that an investment be made in accordance with national laws and regulations does not mean that the protection of the treaty extends only to investments *as defined in national law*.** While it would be possible to draft a provision that limited treaty protection in this way, IIAs with their own definitions of investment that include an additional requirement that an investment be made in accordance with national laws and regulations are not likely to be. 'Investment' will be as defined in the treaty. Otherwise, there would be no reason to have a specific definition of investment.[95] National definitions may be idiosyncratic and subject to change, so that reliance on them would undermine the predictability of an IIA for investors.
- **The requirement that an investment be made in accordance with national laws and regulations is unlikely to be interpreted to mean that the protection of the treaty only extends to investments that comply with all host state legal requirements on an ongoing basis throughout the life of the investment, though that will depend on the language used in the provision.** A requirement for continuous legality would make it very easy for a host state to avoid complying with the substantive investor protection obligations of the treaty by changing the laws to make an investor's investment non-compliant.[96]

Box 4.3 Summary of options for a definition of investment

This section lists the basic options that must be considered in drafting a definition of investment. Options 1 to 3 are presented in descending order beginning with the broadest definition that is most favourable to investors, followed by options for limiting the scope of the definition in various ways.

1. *Open definition of investment – 'Every kind of asset, including ...'*
2. *Closed definition of investment – limited to the specific forms of assets identified*
3. *Possible limiting elements in a definition (whether open or closed)*
    a. An investment must have some or all of these attributes to be protected by the IIA:

(Continued)

94 *Desert Line Projects LLC v. Yemen*, ICSID Case no. ARB/05/17, Award, 6 February 2008.

95 A Joubin-Bret (2008), 'Admission and Establishment in the Context of Investment Protection', in A Reinisch (ed.), *Standards of Investment Protection*, Oxford University Press, Oxford, at 27.

96 In one case, a series of minor defects in filings by the investor were not found to render an investment one which was not made in accordance with the laws and regulations of the host state: *Tokios Tokelés v. Ukraine*, ICSID Case No. ARB/02/18, Decision on Jurisdiction, 19 April 2004, at 37–9.

(Continued)

i. have the characteristics of an investment, including such characteristics as the commitment of capital or other resources, the expectation of gain or profit, and the assumption of risk;

ii. contribute to the development of the host state; and

iii. be made in accordance with host state law.

b. An investment covered by the IIA does not include some or all of these categories of investment:

i. portfolio investment;

ii. debt and other claims to money;

iii. intellectual property;

iv. government securities and debt;

v. property not used for a business purpose;

vi. agricultural land;

vii. assets below a specified value threshold; and

viii. other categories of investment in accordance with the domestic policy of the host state.

Discussion of options

1. *Open definition of investment: 'Every kind of asset, including…'*

This is the broadest form of definition and is found in most older BITs. It provides the most comprehensive protection for investors. Regardless of the form of their interest, it is likely to be covered by this definition. Correspondingly, there is some uncertainty regarding its scope that will make it difficult for a state to predict whether some kinds of interests qualify as investments.

Even with such a definition, however, in an ICSID arbitration a tribunal may require that specific requirements for an investment be present for the tribunal to have jurisdiction. These may include the following though ICSID tribunals have not been consistent in how they interpret 'investment':

i. A contribution in money or other assets;

ii. A certain duration;

iii. An element of risk;

iv. An operation made in order to develop an economic activity in the host state;

v. Assets invested in accordance with the laws of the host state;

vi. Assets invested *bona fide*; and

vii. A contribution to development.

2. *Closed definition of investment: limited to the specific forms of assets identified*

This form of definition may still be very broad and so protect most kinds of interests. Nevertheless, because it is limited to defined categories of assets, it is more predictable for host states, permitting them to target the application of the agreement at the categories of investment that they want to attract, facilitating compliance with their obligations and management of their risk of investor–state claims.

3. *Possible limiting elements in a definition (whether open or closed)*

A definition of investment may require some or all of these attributes for the investment to be covered by the IIA:

i. Have the characteristics of an investment, including such characteristics as the commitment of capital or other resources, the expectation of gain or profit, and the assumption of risk;

ii. Contribute to the development of the host state; and

iii. Be made in accordance with host state law.

As noted with respect to a closed definition of investment, imposing limits on what is an investment for the purposes of an IIA permits states to: (i) target the obligations of the agreement at categories of investment that it seeks to attract; (ii) facilitate compliance with their obligations; and (iii) limit the categories of investments that can be the subject of an investor–state claim.

Requirements that an investment have the characteristics of an investment appear in many IIAs, including the US model treaty, and will be required in any ICSID investor–state arbitration. Such a requirement helps to ensure that protected investments make an economic contribution to the host state. At the same time, these requirements introduce some uncertainty regarding when an investment qualifies for protection under the treaty.

A specific requirement that an investment contribute to development is not commonly found in IIAs, although it is sometimes imposed by ICSID tribunals in arbitrations under the ICSID Convention regardless of what definition of investment is included in the applicable IIA. Such a requirement goes some way to ensuring that protected investments are limited to those that benefit the host state. At the same time, this requirement introduces significant uncertainty into the definition of investment. A definition that excludes portfolio investment is another way to target an IIA definition of investment at significant investments making a contribution to the economy of the host state.

Uncertainty regarding the scope of the definition makes the application of the agreement harder to predict. Such uncertainty may deter some investors and make it more difficult for states to comply with their obligations. Notwithstanding their uncertainty, these kinds of requirements for an investment to be eligible for protection can work to the advantage of host states. In some cases, there will be scope for a host state to argue that an investor–state arbitration tribunal does not have jurisdiction to hear an investor's claim because the investor has not made an eligible investment. Such jurisdictional challenges may be used to stop an investor bringing a claim that is an abuse of the investor–state process.[97] For example, if an investor set up a controlled subsidiary in a state that is a party to an IIA and then transferred an existing investment that it had made in the other party state to the IIA (the *host state*) to the subsidiary for the sole purpose of bringing an investor–state claim, the host state may be able to challenge the jurisdiction of the investor–state tribunal on the basis that the investment did not make a contribution to its development after the transfer to the subsidiary in the other party state.

The requirement that investments be made in accordance with host state law is included in many IIAs. Such a requirement allows the host state to control through its domestic policies what foreign investments obtain the benefit of the treaty. Such a power will be especially important for a state that has limited capacity to regulate an investor once it has entered the country. It also provides an incentive for foreign investors to comply with host state rules in order to ensure that they benefit from the protections of the treaty.

An investment covered by the IIA may exclude some or all of these categories of investment:

i. Portfolio investment;

ii. Debt and other claims to money;

iii. Intellectual property;

iv. Government securities and debt;

v. Property not used for a business purpose;

vi. Agricultural land;

vii. Assets below a specified value threshold; and

viii. Others in accordance with the domestic policy of the host state.

In general, the desirability of particular exclusions will depend on the policies of the host state. In some cases, policy sensitivities related to specific kinds of investments, such as intellectual property, can be addressed in other ways in an IIA, such as through exceptions and reservations, rather than by excluding those kinds of investment from the definition of investment.

It is also possible to limit the practical impact of obligations in relation to particular categories of investment by excluding them from the scope of the dispute settlement procedures in the treaty.

97 *Phoenix Action v. Czech Republic*, op. cit.

Discussion of sample provision

The sample provision provides an example of what a definition of investment could include. No single definition will be optimal for all states, in all circumstances. Host states must make individual choices regarding how broadly to define an investment considering their domestic policy and their own priorities for attracting investment in particular forms by including such forms within the definition of investment, recognising that as the definition of investment expands so does the scope of host state obligations and the corresponding risk of investor–state claims.

Closed definition

In the interests of clarity, predictability and precision, the sample definition of investment in the Guide provides a closed definition with several exclusions. This approach follows an emerging trend in IIA drafting and provides the best approach for host countries to manage the scope of their liability.

The sample provision in the Guide provides an example of a relatively narrow definition of investment compared with many existing IIAs. Most investments within the definition are interests in enterprises. It also imposes a general requirement that to be an investment, the asset must have the typical characteristics of an investment, including making a contribution to development. Even though this last characteristic is somewhat uncertain in scope, it has been required by a number of ICSID tribunals and so may be imposed in an arbitration under the ICSID Convention even if it is not in the treaty. In addition, ICISD cases considering the requirement provide some guidance regarding its scope of application.

Exclusions

Consistent with the Canadian and US model agreements and in the interests of clarity, certain specific exclusions have been incorporated in the definition:

- **Volatile short-term debt, defined in the Guide as debt with a maturity of less than three years**: The intention of this provision is to exclude loan transactions from the definition of investment that are volatile and less likely to make a direct contribution to new economic activity. While three years is admittedly an arbitrary benchmark, it is predictable and has been used in some agreements.

- **Debt securities issued by a state or a state enterprise**: These securities were excluded to ensure that states have flexibility to deal with their debt obligations in the event of a financial crisis. Excluding these securities may make it marginally more difficult or expensive for states and state enterprises to raise capital in international markets.

- **Claims to money arising out of commercial contracts for the sale of goods or services between national enterprises in different party states and property not used for a commercial purpose**: These kinds of interests are not investments as commonly understood and are unlikely to make a direct contribution to new economic activity. They are excluded in some IIAs.

Consistent with widespread IIA practice, the sample provision does not contain an exclusion for portfolio investment. Examples of such an exclusion are provided above and the sample indicates where such an exclusion could be included. As discussed, there is no easy way to define such an exclusion that is not either very vague or arbitrary. Nevertheless, some countries may want to incorporate such an exclusion in an IIA. There is no exclusion for investments below a specific value threshold because such a provision is uncommon and inevitably somewhat arbitrary.

Intellectual property included but exceptions added to protect host state policy space

Like the IIA models used by most countries, the Guide's definition of investment includes intellectual property used for business purposes, which is broad enough to include intellectual property rights in recognition of the general importance of intellectual property rights protection to investors. However, intellectual property rights protection is limited to categories of rights consistent with TRIPs that are recognised in the host state's law. As noted, reservations and exceptions may be included to protect a host country's ability to avoid specific adverse effects associated with the exercise of such rights. In particular, the Guide provides an example of a provision that excludes the granting of compulsory licences in accordance with a state's intellectual property obligations from what constitutes an expropriation requiring compensation.[98] In addition, the Guide describes how reservations may be used to protect host states' policy-making flexibility in relation to intellectual property[99] and how broad exceptions can protect interests that may be affected by intellectual property rights.[100]

Investment in accordance with law

Finally, to ensure that host states can require that investors make their investments in accordance with local requirements related to development and other policies expressed in domestic legislation, it is important to require that investments be made in accordance with the host state's law in order to be eligible for protection under the treaty. Because of the fundamental importance of this requirement, it is included in the Guide sample provision defining the scope of the treaty's application, rather than in the definition of investment.[101] It could, however, be incorporated in the definition of investment.

4.3.2 Definition of investor

However investment is defined, IIAs apply only to investments by *investors* of one party state in the territory of the other party state. For this purpose, investors may be either natural or legal persons. The only issue regarding who is an investor eligible

98 See Section 5.6 (Limitations on expropriation and nationalisation).

99 See Section 5.12 (Reservations and exceptions).

100 See Section 5.12 (Reservations and exceptions).

101 See Section 4.5 (Scope of application).

for protection is what link an investor must have with a party state in order to be considered an investor of that state.

In most cases, investors are likely to want the broadest possible definition of investor so that, however their business is structured and no matter how weak their connection to a state, they will benefit from the protection of the IIAs that the state has signed. Some capital-exporting states may also want a broad definition that is easy to satisfy. For example, a state that is pursuing a strategy of becoming an international business centre by encouraging foreign investors to set up in its jurisdiction as a platform to make investments in other countries will want to have a very open definition of investor that creates minimal hurdles for foreign businesses to obtain the protections in the IIAs that that the state has signed. This is the policy of Mauritius, for example. Other capital-exporting states may want to ensure that only investors that have made a substantial contribution to their economy can benefit from the protections in the treaties they negotiate with other states.

Capital-importing host states may have different preferences in this regard. A state that is targeting a limited class of investor in a particular sector may want to ensure that investors protected under the treaty are strongly connected to the treaty partner they are negotiating with in order to manage their exposure to investor–state claims. Such states will be concerned about the risk that investors will organise their corporate structure for the sole purpose of taking advantage of the treaty, sometimes known as *treaty shopping*. A very open and easily satisfied definition of investor in a treaty means that investors from many states will be able to take advantage of the treaty protections, multiplying the risk of investor–state claims. For some states, treaty shopping may not be an issue. If their goal is simply to maximise the investment they attract, they may not mind if an investor from a non-party state is able to organise itself to take advantage of the treaty so long as they receive the investment.

Natural persons

Most IIAs require natural persons to be nationals of a state in order to qualify as investors of that state.[102] Typically, nationality is determined conclusively by the domestic law of the state whose nationality is in issue. The Canadian model and some others provide that permanent residents of a state also qualify as investors of that state.[103] This may be because, as a high immigration country, many investors from Canada are permanent residents who are not yet citizens, with the result that limiting protection to people who are citizens would narrow the scope of protection unduly.[104]

---

102 US model BIT, Art. 1; UK model IPPA, Art. 1(c); COMESA Investment Agreement (2007), Art. 1.4.

103 Canadian model FIPA, Art. 1, Norwegian Draft model APPI, Art. 1. The ASEAN Agreement (2009) also permits investors to be permanent residents or citizens, as does Australia–Argentina, Agreement between the Government of Australia and the Government of the Argentine Republic on the Promotion and Protection of Investments, signed 23 August 1995, in force 11 January 1997 (only for Australians).

104 UNCTAD (2011), *Scope and Definition*, op. cit., at 74.

Actual residency in a state is seldom required, although parties to an IIA may consider it desirable to require some other link to a party state in addition to nationality as a condition of acquiring treaty protection, such as carrying on some economic activity in the state.[105]

Natural persons connected to more than one state

Where both permanent residents and citizens of a state are defined as investors of a state, it is possible that a single person could be a citizen of one party state to an IIA and a permanent resident of another. In this situation, a person who is a permanent resident (or a citizen) of a party state could try to seek the benefit of treaty protection for actions of that country that are contrary to the treaty, relying on their status as a citizen (or permanent resident) in the other party state. This occurred in one case under NAFTA.[106] The problem can be avoided by defining investors as including only nationals.

This solution does not work if a person has the nationality of both parties to an IIA. Few treaties address this problem, which in some cases can have practical implications. For example, developing country nationals often emigrate to developed countries and obtain the nationality of that country. If they return to their home country as investors they may seek to qualify for preferential programmes set up for the exclusive benefit of nationals. They may also seek protections under an IIA between their country of birth and the developed country whose nationality they have acquired as an investor of the developed country.

The doctrine of dominant or effective nationality, which has been developed in public international law to determine which nationality of a person should be given effect in dual nationality cases, has been rejected in a number of investor–state arbitration cases as a way to resolve this problem.[107] Consequently, if a state wants to address this problem it must do it expressly in the definition in the IIA. One kind of provision that assigns nationality in cases of dual nationality appears in the US–Argentina BIT, which provides 'that a person who is a dual citizen shall be deemed to be exclusively a citizen of the State of his or her dominant and effective citizenship'.[108] Another approach is adopted in the Canada–Lebanon Foreign Investment Protection Agreement, which provides simply that a person who is a Canadian and a Lebanese national has the nationality of the state in which they are present.[109] In the absence of these kinds of provisions, a dual national might be able to claim either nationality and use their

105 Ibid. at 123.

106 *Marvin Roy Feldman Karpa v. United Mexican States*, ICSID Case No. ARB(AF)/99/1, Award 16 December 2002, affirmed *United Mexican States* v. *Karpa* (2005), 74 *Ontario Reports* (3d) 180 (Court of Appeal).

107 *Micula v. Romania*, ICSID Case No. ARB/05/20, Decision on Jurisdiction and Admissibility, 24 September 2008.

108 US–Uruguay BIT (2005), Art. 1.

109 Canada–Lebanon, Agreement between the Government of Canada and the Government of the Lebanese Republic for the Promotion and Protection of Investments, signed 11 April 1997, in force 19 June 1999, Art. 1.

nationality of one state as the basis for their claim against another state of which they are a national. With respect to IIAs that provide for investor–state arbitration under the ICSID Convention, a few additional complications arise, as discussed in Box 4.4.

The sample provision in the Guide defines investors to include only nationals and has a test for effective nationality with a view to avoiding the problems discussed above.

Box 4.4 Nationality and the ICSID Convention

Under Article 25 of the ICSID Convention, disputes may be arbitrated under the rules of the Convention only if the dispute is between a contracting state and a national of another contracting state. 'National of another contracting state' means

a. Any **natural person** who had the nationality of a contracting state other than the party state to the dispute on the date on which the parties consented to submit such dispute to conciliation or arbitration as well as on the date on which the request was registered ... *but does not include any person who on either date also had the nationality of the contracting state party to the dispute*; and

b. Any **juridical person** which had the nationality of a contracting state other than the party state to the dispute on the date on which the parties consented to submit such dispute to conciliation or arbitration and any *juridical person* which had the *nationality of the contracting state party to the dispute* on that date and which, *because of foreign control, the parties have agreed should be treated as a national of another contracting state* for the purposes of this Convention. (Emphasis added.)

Natural persons: The effect of this provision is that, under the ICSID Convention, a natural person can initiate an arbitration only if the person:

- Has the nationality of a contacting state in accordance with the laws of that state; and
- Does not have the nationality of the state complained against (the *host state*).

Consequently, dual nationals who have the nationality of the host state cannot use the ICSID arbitration process. This is true regardless of whether the nationality of the host state would be the person's effective nationality under international law.[110] An IIA provision that assigns nationality to one state on some basis in cases of dual nationality may not be effective to overcome this limitation. Even if an IIA would permit a claim because an investor's effective

(Continued)

110 *Champion Trading v. Egypt*, ICSID Case No. ARB/02/9, Decision on Jurisdiction, 21 October 2003.

(Continued)

nationality is not that of the host state, ICSID arbitration may not be available. An investor in this situation would have to choose some other arbitral process if permitted under the IIA.

The ICSID treaty also identifies the dates when these nationality requirements apply: the date on which the parties consented to submit their dispute to conciliation or arbitration, and, in the case of claim by a natural person, the date on which the request was registered.

Legal persons: For corporations and other legal persons, typically the dual nationality problem does not arise. Nationality is defined in the IIA. As discussed below, usually the nationality of a legal person is attributed to the state in which the legal person is organised. However, Article 25 permits the parties to agree that a legal person that had the nationality of the host state on the relevant date but is under 'foreign control' can be treated as having the nationality of another party state to the ICSID Convention to permit the legal person to bring the claim. This provision addresses the common situation in which a foreign investor is carrying on business in the host state through a corporation incorporated in the host state that it controls (a *subsidiary*). In the absence of this rule, if the test for nationality under the IIA is the jurisdiction under which the corporation is organised, the subsidiary would have the same nationality as the host state and be precluded from ever making a claim in ICSID arbitration. The foreign investor that controls the subsidiary could, however, make a claim on its own behalf for injuries that it has suffered.

Only some IIAs permit claims against host states by host state-incorporated subsidiaries. In those that do, often the consent of the state to permit claims by foreign-controlled local subsidiaries is set out in the dispute settlement provisions of the IIA.[111] The requirement for 'foreign control' has been held by ICSID arbitration tribunals to be an objective standard that must be satisfied irrespective of any agreement between the parties regarding how nationality should be determined.[112] To ensure that the requirements for ICSID dispute resolution are met, IIAs should permit claims by subsidiaries only when they are foreign controlled.

Note: The requirements of the ICSID Convention apply only to arbitrations under the Convention. Arbitrations under other rules are not affected. Eligibility of an investor to make a claim under other arbitral rules will be determined exclusively by the applicable IIA and those rules.

111 E.g. Canadian model FIPA, Art. 23. Consent may also be given in a contract with the host state in relation to a particular investment.

112 *Vacuum Salt v. Ghana*, ICSID Case No. ARB/92/01, Award, 16 February 1994. See P Muchlinski (2007), *Multinational Enterprises and the Law*, Oxford University Press, Oxford, at 728–9.

Legal persons

Nationality based on a legal person being incorporated or organised in a state

With respect to legal persons (also called 'juridical persons'), most IIAs define investor of a state as meaning corporations and other forms of business organisation incorporated or organised under the laws of that state.[113] Often both for-profit and not-for-profit entities, as well as state-owned enterprises, are expressly included. The Canadian model FIPA and the US model BIT follow this approach.[114] The rationale for including not-for-profit entities is that they may make investments in commercial operations to produce revenues that they can apply to their charitable purposes. In addition, not-for-profit entities may make valuable investments, such as in schools or medical clinics that will be of interest to a host state.[115] Including not-for-profit entities in the definition of investor may encourage them to invest.

Another category of investor often expressly included in the definition of investor is party states and their entities, such as sovereign wealth funds, an increasingly important source of global capital. Concerns that sovereign wealth funds and other state-owned enterprises (SOEs) operate in a manner that is not transparent and may be responsive to their home state's policies, rather than host state interests or the commercial considerations that would determine the behaviour of private investors, have caused some states to question the desirability of investments by such investors.[116] Some states have adopted special investment screening requirements to address these concerns. In some cases, SOE investment will be permitted only if certain standards for transparency and independence from their home state are satisfied.[117]

In addition, some IIAs provide that an unincorporated branch of a business enterprise located in a state and carrying out business activities there is considered an investor of that state. This approach is followed in the Canadian and US model agreements.[118]

The US and Canadian model agreements employ a broad definition that includes all these types of investors. In the US and Canadian model agreements an 'investor of a party' means 'a Party or state enterprise thereof, or a national or an enterprise of a Party.' In turn, 'enterprise' is defined as follows:

---

113 UK model IPPA, Art. 1(d). The same is true for most BITS entered into by Caribbean and Pacific countries (Malik, op. cit., at 11, 44–5).

114 Some others follow this approach too, e.g. SADC Investment Protocol (2006), definition of company, Art. 1.

116 UNCTAD (2011), *Scope and Definition*, op. cit., at 80–1.

116 L Skovgaard Poulsen (forthcoming), 'Investment Treaties and the Globalisation of State Capitalism: Opportunities and Constraints for Host States', in R Echandi and P Sauvé (eds), *Prospects in International Investment Law and Policy*, Cambridge University Press, Cambridge.

117 See the discussion of Canadian policy in this regard in J VanDuzer (2010), 'Mixed Signals: What Recent Developments Tell Us about Foreign Investment Policy in Canada,' 10 *Asper Review of International Business and Trade Law*, 247 at 251–4.

118 Canadian model FIPA, Art. 1; US model BIT, Art. 1. The approach in the India–Singapore CECA (2005) is similar.

> Any entity constituted or organized under applicable law, whether or not for profit, and whether privately or governmentally owned or controlled, including a corporation, trust, partnership, sole proprietorship, joint venture, association, or similar organization, and a branch of an enterprise.

Most other definitions are not as comprehensive in that they do not expressly extend their coverage to not-for-profit entities or party states and SOEs specifically, though they still rely on incorporation or organisation as the test for nationality. For example the Indian model agreement simply defines Indian investors as 'corporations, firms, associations incorporated, constituted or established in any part of India'.[119] Not-for-profit enterprises may fall within this kind of definition. Indian SOEs incorporated in India will fall within this definition.

The simple incorporation or organisation test for the nationality of a legal person has two main advantages:

- It is simple for investors to qualify; and
- It is easy for both investors and host states to determine if an investor is eligible for protection under the IIA.

Potentially, however, the protection is very broad. Even though the investor must have made an investment, in a variety of situations described in Box 4.5, being able to claim the benefits of the treaty for an investment in one party state by simply incorporating a controlled subsidiary corporation in the other party state for the purpose of making the investment means that some protected investors may not be providing new capital to the host state. Furthermore, the state in which the subsidiary was incorporated may be concerned that an investor is benefiting from a treaty that it has negotiated without having any real economic activity in the state.[120]

Box 4.5 Treaty-shopping opportunities created by a simple incorporation or organisation test for the nationality of a legal person in an IIA

If an IIA provides that the nationality of a legal person is determined exclusively by the state in which it is incorporated or organised, investors have opportunities to structure their affairs to take advantage of the treaty. This means that a state may end up extending the promised protections in an IIA to a broad range of investors that have little economic connection with the other party state. It also means that, in some cases, investors will be able to secure protection when the

(Continued)

119 Indian model BIPPA, Art. 1. The ASEAN Agreement (2009) is similar.

120 In *Alps Finance and Trade AG v. Slovak Republic*, Award (redacted version), Investment Ad Hoc Arbitration, 5 March 2011, the tribunal described the concerns of states with respect to the connection that an investor should have to benefit from the protection of a BIT in the following terms: 'the object and purpose of the BIT, as reflected in its preamble, is to intensify the economic cooperation between states for the mutual benefit of both states and, to attract foreign investments with the aim to foster their economic prosperity' (at para. 236).

(Continued)

investment does not result in new capital being brought into the host state. The following are examples.

- *Example 1: Investor of third party state incorporates a subsidiary in a party state to an IIA to obtain treaty protection in another party state to the IIA*

  A natural person, who is a citizen of State A, or a corporation incorporated in State A (INVESTOR A) seeks to invest in State B but there is no IIA between State A and State B. There is an IIA between State B and State C that provides that an investor has the nationality of State C and, as a result, is entitled to the protection of the IIA if it is incorporated or organised in State C.

  INVESTOR A incorporates a subsidiary corporation in State C that it controls and provides it with capital to make the desired investment in State B.

  State B is obliged to give the protection of the IIA to the investment.

  In this situation, new capital did result from the investment, but it may have been capital that would have been invested in State A anyway. To this extent, the treaty protections are being extended to an investor, but may not have been necessary to induce the investment.[121]

- *Example 2: Investor in a party state to an IIA state incorporates a subsidiary in the other party state to the IIA to obtain treaty protection in their own state*

  A natural person, who is a citizen of State B, or a corporation incorporated in State B (INVESTOR B) seeks to invest in State B. There is an IIA between State B and State C that provides that an investor has the nationality of State C and, as a result, is entitled to the protection of the IIA if it is incorporated or organised in State C.

  INVESTOR B incorporates a subsidiary corporation in State C that it controls and provides it with capital to make the desired investment in State B.

(Continued)

121 Investors with the nationality of a party state to an IIA have standing only if they make an investment in another party state to the IIA. Most definitions of investor permit the investment to be made 'directly or indirectly'. This means that in Example I, where there is an IIA between State B and State C, an investor with the nationality of State C (INVESTOR C) is entitled to the protection of the IIA in relation to an investment in State B, even if the investment is directly owned by a corporation incorporated in State A, which, in turn, is controlled by INVESTOR C. See *Waste Management, Inc. v. United Mexican States*, ICSID Case No. ARB (AF)/00/3, Award, 30 April 2004; and *SOABI v. Senegal*, ICSID Case ARB/82/1, Decision on Jurisdiction, 1 August 1984.

(Continued)

State B is probably obliged to give the protection of the IIA to the investment.[122]

Since the source of the capital is INVESTOR B in State B and the investment is in State B, the net effect of this transaction is that no new capital has been invested in State B (though existing capital has been put to a different use) and INVESTOR B has the protections of the IIA. This may be a concern to State B only to the extent that the protections available to the INVESTOR B under the IIA and/or the mechanisms for their enforcement are better than the protections available to INVESTOR B under the domestic law of State B.

Additional links to a party state to an IIA as a condition of obtaining nationality

As a consequence of the risk of treaty shopping illustrated by the examples in Box 4.5, definitions in IIAs sometimes impose additional requirements for corporations and other legal persons to be considered to be sufficiently connected to a party state in order to be an investor of the Party under the treaty. Either some actual business activity being carried on in the state or the ultimate owners of the investment possessing the nationality of the state, or both, may be required. In some treaties, for example, legal persons are required to have their head office or headquarters in a state or to have substantial business operations in the state to be considered a national of that state, though different formulations of these requirements are used.

- In the UK model agreement, an investor must be 'engaged in business operations' in the territory of the treaty party in which it is organised to have the nationality of that party.[123]
- The COMESA Investment Agreement requires 'substantial business activity in the Member State in which it is constituted or organised' to be an investor of the state.[124]
- In the India–Singapore CECA, a corporation with 'negligible or nil business operations or with no real and continuous business activities carried out in

122 *Tokios Tokelés v. Ukraine*, op. cit. In this case, the investor did not structure the investment with the intention of taking advantage of the treaty protection. Nevertheless, the majority award suggests that this would be possible. This approach has been followed in subsequent cases such as *ADC v. Hungary*, ICSID Case No. ARB/03/16, Award, 2 October 2006, para. 360, but not others, e.g. *TSA Spectrum de Argentina S. A. v. Argentine Republic*, ICSID Case No. ARB/05/5, Award, 19 December 2008 at paras. 114–62. In that case the tribunal determined that a Dutch company was owned by Argentine nationals. The claim against Argentina was not allowed to proceed but on the basis that the investor was not under 'foreign control' as required by Article 25(2)(b) of the ICSID Convention.

123 UK model IPPA, Art. 1. The Canada–Jordan Free Trade Agreement, signed 28 June 2009, in force 1 October 2012, follows the same approach except that it refers to 'business activities' (Art. 1(k)).

124 COMESA Investment Agreement (2007), Art. 1(4).

the territory of the party' is excluded from the definition of investor of that party.[125]

- In the China–Jamaica BIT, a corporation has Chinese nationality only if it is 'domiciled' in China as well as incorporated there.[126] Domicile in this context probably means that the principal place of business of the corporation is in China.
- In the South Korea–Jamaica BIT, a corporation has the nationality of a state in which it is incorporated only if it has its 'seat' in the state.[127] A corporation's seat is located where it is effectively managed.[128]

One difficulty with all of these expressions is applying them in practice. Perhaps the most difficult to apply is the requirement to have business activities or operations, even if modified by the adjective 'substantial'. Substantial business activity has been found to exist where an investor has premises from which it conducts the investment business and a small but permanent staff.[129] Nevertheless, significant uncertainty remains regarding just what is required to meet this test.[130] 'Seat' has a well-established meaning: the principal place of business and location of effective management. The presence of a corporation's seat, however, may still represent a relatively slight connection to a jurisdiction. In one arbitration award, a corporation was found to have its seat in a country where its only connections were that it had one resident director and had an audit of its financial statements done in the country.[131] A few treaties require that an investor should both have its seat in a jurisdiction and carry out activities there in order to have the nationality of the jurisdiction.[132]

The German–Antigua and Barbuda BIT requires both business presence and control. A juridical person is considered to have the nationality of Antigua and Barbuda only

125 India–Singapore CECA (2005), Art. 6.1(6). The same agreement provides in a somewhat duplicative way that a party may deny benefits of the treaty to an investor that 'has no substantial business operations in the territory of the other Party' (Art. 6.9).

126 China–Jamaica, Agreement between the Government of the People's Republic of China and the Government of Jamaica, signed 26 October 1994, in force 15 November 1996.

127 Korea–Jamaica BIT (2003), Art. 1; Colombian model agreement, Art. 1.1.b. This provision also requires that the investor have substantial business activities in the same state.

128 UNCTAD (2011), *Scope and Definition*, op. cit., at 83.

129 *AMTO v. Ukraine*, Arbitration Institute of the Stockholm Chamber of Commerce, Arbitration No. 080/2005, Award, 26 March 2008, cited in UNCTAD (2011) *Scope and Definition*, ibid., at 96–7.

130 The COMESA Investment Agreement (2007) provides that determining whether substantial business activity exists requires an 'overall examination, on a case-by-case basis, of all the circumstances including, among other things: (a) the amount of investment brought into the country; (b) the number of jobs created; (c) the effect on the local community; and (d) the length of time the business has been in operation' (Art. 1(4)).

131 *Yaung Chi Oo Trading PTE LTD. v. Government of the Union of Myanmar*, ASEAN I.D. Case ARB/01/1, 42 *International Legal Materials* 540 (31 March 2003).

132 E.g. Switzerland–Iran, Agreement Between the Swiss Confederation and the Islamic Republic of Iran on the Promotion and Reciprocal Protection of Investments, signed 8 March 1998, in force 1 October 2001, Art. 1(1)(b), (c); Colombian model agreement Art. 1.1(b) (includes also entities controlled by nationals of a state).

if it has 'its main operation in Antigua & Barbuda and ... [the] operation is controlled directly or indirectly by citizens of Antigua & Barbuda'.[133] Few IIAs contain such a control requirement.[134] Given the complex corporate structures used by multinational enterprises and non-equity control mechanisms, determining who has ultimate control of operations will be a daunting challenge in some cases.

Another approach – denial of benefits

Another approach to ensure that the incorporation or organisation test for nationality is not abused by 'treaty shopping' is to add a provision that permits a party state to deny the benefits of the treaty to investors unless certain criteria are met in addition to incorporation or organisation in a state. Usually denial of benefits by a state is permitted where an investor does not have substantial business operations in the state and the investor is ultimately controlled by other investors who are not nationals or legal persons of that state.[135]

In principle, a denial of benefits provision may operate automatically, in which case it is effectively part of the definition of investor, or it may require some positive action by the denying state. With an automatic denial of benefits, the protections of the treaty are not available if some specific requirement, such as carrying out substantial activities in the jurisdiction, is not met. Under the Canadian model, however, a positive action is required. A state must give prior notification of its intention to deny benefits.

The practical effectiveness of such a discretionary denial of benefits clause may be limited. In one case involving a similar treaty provision, a state sought to deny benefits after an investor had initiated a claim in investor–state arbitration. The tribunal, however, ruled that it was too late.[136] To take advantage of the denial of benefits provision, the tribunal held that the state had to act prior to a claim being made. This would seem to mean that to take advantage of a denial of benefits provision like this, a state would have to monitor foreign investments constantly to determine if the criteria for denying benefits are met and then decide whether it wants to deny benefits in a particular case prior to being aware of any claim. If this were what was required, however, the provision would be practically useless. Even under the approach adopted in this case, however, it might be possible to rely on such a provision where an investor

---

133 Germany–Antigua and Barbuda BIT (1998).

134 Malik, op. cit., at 14, 45, regarding Caribbean and Pacific BITS.

135 Canadian model FIPA, Art. 18; US model BIT, Art. 17(2). This approach is also followed in the European Energy Charter Treaty, signed 17 December 1994, in force 16 July 1998 (Art. 17(1)) and the Indian model BIPPA (Art. 12). In the US and Canadian models, the protection of the treaty may also be denied where the ultimate owners of the investment are from a country with respect to which the denying state has some kind of measure that would be violated if the benefits of the agreement were accorded to the investment or the investors. A trade embargo would be an example of such a measure. No notice is required by the denying party in these circumstances.

136 *Plama Consortium Ltd. v. Republic of Bulgaria*, ICSID No. ARB/03/24, Decision on Jurisdiction, 8 February 2005.

has indicated that it may make a claim but before it has formally initiated arbitration proceedings.[137] This would be much more useful for states.

A more recent case interpreting a different denial of benefits clause gave the host state much more flexibility to deny benefits. It found that there was no time limit specified in the treaty for the exercise of the respondent state's right to deny benefits and permitted the denial after the investor's claim had been filed, noting that the denial was made within the time limit for filing a jurisdictional challenge under the applicable arbitral rules.[138]

It would be highly advantageous for a host state to be able to deny benefits after a claim had been filed because it could investigate whether the criteria for denial of benefits were met in relation to that particular investor and take a decision based on the specific facts of the case. At the same time, a denial of benefits clause that could be exercised after a claim had been filed would undermine the benefits of the treaty for some investors. In light of the conflicting views expressed by arbitral tribunals, in order to ensure that a state can deny benefits after a claim is made, the treaty should expressly permit the state to do so.

Box 4.6 Summary of options for a definition of investor in an IIA

1. *Natural persons:* A natural person is an investor of a party state if that person is
   a. A national of a party state as determined by that state; or
   b. A national *or* permanent resident of a party state as determined by that state.
2. *Legal persons:* A legal person is an investor of a party state if that person is incorporated or organised under the law of the party state. Any or all of the following criteria may be added. The investor
   a. Has (substantial) business activities in that state;
   b. Has its seat (or effective management) in that state; and/or
   c. Is owned or controlled by nationals (legal or natural persons) of that state.
3. *A state can deny benefits of the treaty to a legal person where it does not meet one of criteria a, b or c in option 2*

137 UNCTAD (2011), *Scope and Definition*, op. cit., at 98–9.

138 *Pac Rim Cayman LLC v. Republic of El Salvador*, ICSID Case No. ARB/09/12, Decision on the Respondent's Jurisdictional Objections, 1 June 2012, regarding Art. 10.12.2 of the US–Central American–Dominican Republic Free Trade Agreement, signed 4 August 2004, in force (for all countries) 1 January 2009 (at paras 483–5). The arbitration was under the ICSID Rules.

Discussion of options for a definition of investor

Investors may be either natural or legal persons.

1. *Natural persons*

Under most IIAs, a natural person is an investor of a party state if that person is either

a. A national of the party state as determined by that state; or

b. A national *or* a permanent resident of the party state as determined by that state.

The definition may go on to provide that where a natural person has dual nationality, their nationality belongs to the state with which they have the most effective connection or, alternatively, the state that they are in. Dual nationals that have the nationality of the host state, however, may be precluded from making a claim in ICSID arbitration. This may be true even if the IIA includes a provision that defines a person as having a single nationality for the purpose of the treaty, and, on the basis of the application of the provision, the person would not have the nationality of the host state. This problem arises only in arbitrations under the ICSID rules.

While high immigration states, such as Canada, may want to include permanent residents as well as nationals, this is likely to be a small and less important category of investor for other states that they may not want to include. It creates the possibility that a person may be a national of one party state to a treaty and a permanent resident of another party state. A state may avoid this problem by limiting the definition of investor to nationals. This is the most common approach in IIAs.

2. *Legal persons*

Many IIAs provide that a legal person is an investor of a party state if that person is incorporated or organised under the law of the party state. Some IIAs impose one or all of the following additional criteria. The investor:

a. Has (substantial) business activities in that state;

b. Has its seat (or effective management) in that state; and/or

c. Is owned or controlled by nationals (legal or natural persons) of that state.

In choosing how to define the nationality of legal persons for the purposes of their eligibility for protection under an IIA, each state will have to determine to what extent it is worried about treaty shopping and what additional criteria it wants to adopt. While some requirement for the seat of the investor and/or some business activity are common, a requirement for ultimate ownership or control to exist in a state is less common. An ultimate ownership or control requirement may be more difficult to apply in practice, because of the challenge of locating ownership within complex corporate structures.

3. *A state can deny benefits of the treaty to a legal person where it does not meet any one of criteria a, b or c in option 2*

As an alternative to including the limitations discussed in option 2 in the definition of investor, an IIA may include a provision that allows a state to deny the benefits of the treaty where an investor does not satisfy any or all of criteria a, b or c in relation to the other party state to the treaty. In principle, this would permit a state to deny the benefit of the protections of the treaty when it determined that an investor was merely incorporated in a party state and should not be given the protection of the treaty for some reason. However, if the treaty requires a state to take a positive step to deny benefits under the IIA, this step might have to be taken *before* the investor commences an investor–state arbitration. If the treaty is interpreted to require action before the claim is filed, the denial of benefits provision loses much of its practical utility. Specific wording in the treaty could be used to ensure that a state may deny benefits after an investor makes a claim and the state has an opportunity to consider whether benefits should be denied to that investor.

Discussion of sample provision

Natural persons

In the interests of clarity and administrative simplicity, the sample provision requires that for a natural person to be an investor of a party state they must be a national of that state, and that if they are a national of more than one state, they have the nationality of the state with which they have the closest connection. As an alternative, states may want to simply exclude their own nationals from the protection of an IIA, even if they also have the nationality of the other party state. Such an approach would avoid any conflict with the ICSID Convention, which would be useful if the IIA allowed for the possibility of ICSID dispute settlement.

Legal persons

The sample provision requires that, to be an investor of a party state, the investor must:

- Be an enterprise incorporated or organised under the law of the state;
- Have its seat in the state; and
- Carry on substantial business activities in that state.

Incorporation or organisation in a state is almost universally used as one of the criteria for a legal person to be a national of that state. The sample provision does not include an unincorporated branch located in the territory of a party. Without local incorporation or organisation, the party state may find it more difficult to regulate an investor. Enterprise is the expression used to define legal persons. Enterprise is defined broadly to mean 'any entity constituted or organised under applicable law, whether or not for profit, whether privately-owned or governmentally-owned, including any corporation, trust, partnership, sole proprietorship, joint venture or other association' so as to avoid formalistic limitations on what category of business organisation qualifies for protection. Not-for-profit and government-owned investors are included. States should consider whether SOEs should be included based, in part, on their capacity to regulate such investors effectively.

The requirement for the investor's seat is intended to provide a relatively certain test that would help to avoid treaty shopping. The seat requirement is, however, more restrictive and less flexible than the simple incorporation or organisation test, which is the only test in most IIAs. The substantial business presence in the state requirement was added to provide additional assurance that an investor has a real economic link to a state before it is eligible for protection under the treaty. Both seat and substantial business activity, however, remain somewhat uncertain. Both could be further defined by more detailed specific requirements, such as those listed in the COMESA Investment Agreement.

An ownership or control test has not been included because of the complexity of defining control in a way that will be effective and not unduly restrictive for investors in their choices of business structure. It is rarely used in IIA practice. Such a requirement could be used to ensure that investors are closely connected with a treaty party in order to benefit from the protections of the treaty. An ownership or control requirement is provided for in the sample denial of benefits provision.

Denial of benefits provision

A sample denial of benefits provision is included in the sample provisions. A party state can deny the benefits of the agreement to an investor that is incorporated or organised under the laws of the other party state, but is not owned or controlled by investors of the other party state. This is the most common form of denial of benefits provision and is found in the Canadian model among others. The sample provisions have been drafted to make clear that the state's right to deny benefits can be exercised after the investor's claim has been filed. Where the investor has initiated an investor–state claim, the denial can be made at any time prior to the expiry of the time within which jurisdictional challenges may be filed by the host state under the arbitral rules applicable to the claim. In order to deny benefits, a party state must give notice to the other party state.

4.3.3 Sample provision: definitions

Definitions[139]

For the purpose of this Agreement:

Commission means the commission of ministerial-level representatives of the Parties established under this agreement [see Guide Section 9.2 (Commission)].

Cultural industries means persons engaged in any of the following activities:

i. The publication, distribution or sale of books, magazines, periodicals or newspapers in print or machine readable form but not including the sole activity of printing or typesetting any of the foregoing;

ii. The production, distribution, sale or exhibition of film or video recordings;

iii. The production, distribution, sale or exhibition of audio or video music recordings;

139 Defined terms used in other sample provisions are also set out here.

iv. The publication, distribution, sale or exhibition of music in print or machine readable form; or

v. Radio communications in which the transmissions are intended for direct reception by the general public, and all radio, television or cable broadcasting undertakings and all satellite programming and broadcast network services [see Guide Section 5.12 (Reservations and exceptions)].

Days means calendar days, including weekends and holidays.

Enterprise means any entity constituted or organised under applicable law, whether or not for profit, whether privately owned or government owned, including any corporation, trust, partnership, sole proprietorship, joint venture or other association.

ICSID means the International Centre for Settlement of Investment Disputes.

ICSID Convention means the *Convention on the Settlement of Investment Disputes between States and Nationals of other States*, done at Washington, 18 March 1965 [see Guide Section 7.1 (Investor–state dispute settlement)].

Intellectual property rights, in relation to the obligations of a Party means copyright and related rights, trademark rights, rights in geographical indications, rights in industrial designs, patent rights, rights in layout designs of integrated circuits, rights in relation to protection of undisclosed information, and plant breeders' rights to the extent protected under the laws of the Party.

Investment means:

i. An enterprise;

ii. An equity security of an enterprise;

iii. A debt security of an enterprise:

   a. where the enterprise is an affiliate of the investor, or

   b. where the original maturity of the debt security is at least three years, but does not include a debt security, regardless of original maturity, of a state enterprise;

iv. A loan to an enterprise

   a. where the enterprise is an affiliate of the investor, or

   b. where the original maturity of the loan is at least three years,

   but does not include a loan, regardless of original maturity, to a state enterprise; and

   for greater certainty, a loan to, or debt security issued by, a Party or a state enterprise thereof is not an investment;

v. An interest in an enterprise that entitles the owner to share in income or profits of the enterprise;

vi. An interest in an enterprise that entitles the owner to share in the assets of that enterprise on dissolution, other than a debt security or a loan excluded from subparagraphs (iii) or (iv);

vii. Real estate, intellectual property or other property, tangible or intangible, acquired in the expectation or used for the purpose of economic benefit or other business purposes; and

viii. Interests arising from the commitment of capital or other resources in the territory of a Party to economic activity in such territory, such as under:

a. contracts involving the presence of an investor's property in the territory of the Party, including turnkey and construction contracts, and concessions, or

b. contracts where remuneration depends substantially on the production, revenues or profits of an enterprise;

provided that an investment must have the characteristics of an investment, including such characteristics as the commitment of capital or other resources, the expectation of gain or profit, and the assumption of risk and must make a contribution to development;

but investment does not mean:

ix. Claims to money that arise solely from:

a. commercial contracts for the sale of goods or services by a national or enterprise in the territory of a Party to an enterprise in the territory of the other Party, or

b. the extension of credit in connection with a commercial transaction, such as trade financing, other than a loan covered by subparagraph (iv); and

c. any other claims to money, that do not involve the kinds of interests set out in subparagraphs (i) through (viii);

x. [Other exclusions could be added here, including an exception for portfolio investment as defined in the IIA.]

Investor of a Party means

i. An enterprise constituted or organised under the law of a Party that has its seat and carries on substantial business activities in that Party; and

ii. A natural person who is a citizen of a Party, provided that that a natural person who is a dual citizen of both Parties shall be deemed to be exclusively a citizen of the Party of his or her dominant and effective citizenship;

that has made an investment.

Measure includes any law, regulation, procedure, requirement or practice.

New York Convention means the *United Nations Convention on the Recognition and Enforcement of Foreign Arbitral Awards*, done at New York, 10 June 1958 [see Guide Section 7.1 (Investor–state dispute settlement)].

Person means a natural person or an enterprise.

State enterprise of a Party means an enterprise that is owned or controlled through ownership interests by a Party.

Sub-national government means:

in respect of [Party] …; and

in respect of [Party] … [see Section 5.3 (National treatment)].

Territory means

in respect of [Party] …; and

in respect of [Party] …[140]

Tribunal means an arbitration tribunal established under this agreement [see Guide Section 7.1 (Investor–state dispute settlement)].

UNCITRAL Arbitration Rules means the arbitration rules of the United Nations Commission on International Trade Law, approved by the United Nations General Assembly on 15 December 1976, as amended [see Guide Section 7.1 (Investor–state dispute settlement)].

WTO Agreement means the Agreement Establishing the World Trade Organization done at Marrakesh, 15 April 1994.

4.3.4 Sample provision: denial of benefits

Denial of Benefits

1. A Party may deny the benefits of this Agreement to an investor of the other Party that is an enterprise of such Party and to investments of such investors if investors of such non-Party do not own or control the enterprise.
2. A Party shall give notice to the other Party of its intention to deny benefits to an investor of the other Party under Section 1.
3. Where an investor has made a claim against a Party under this agreement, the Party may deny benefits to the investor in accordance with this article at any time prior to the expiry of the time within which jurisdictional challenges may be filed by the Party under the arbitral rules applicable to such claim.

---

140 Countries should consider how to define the scope of their territory by reference to: (a) their land territory, air space, internal waters and territorial sea; (b) those areas, including the exclusive economic zone and the seabed and subsoil, over which the country may exercise, in accordance with international law, sovereign rights or jurisdiction for the purpose of exploration and exploitation of the natural resources; and (c) artificial islands, installations and structures in the exclusive economic zone or on the continental shelf over which the country has jurisdiction as a coastal state.

4.4 Statement of objectives

Cross reference

In addition to the preamble, an explicit statement of objectives is an important part of the interpretive context for a treaty as noted above.[141] A separate section setting out objectives is a useful way to give priority to particular objectives referred to in the preamble, though most agreements currently in place make limited use of such a provision.

4.4.1 IIA practice

Most national models, such as those used by Canada, the USA, the UK and India, and the Norwegian draft model, do not include a statement of objectives. In those that do, investment promotion is typically identified as an objective of the agreement. The COMESA Investment Agreement, for example, identifies investment liberalisation and promotion in its general objectives provision.[142]

Some IIAs express a wider range of objectives than investment promotion. In the part of the agreement setting out the main protections for investors, for example, the COMESA Investment Agreement goes on to state that the objective of the agreement is also to 'provide COMESA investors with certain rights in the conduct of their business within an overall balance of rights and obligations between investors and Member States.'[143] This language suggests that investor protection is not the sole overriding purpose of the agreement. Investment liberalisation and promotion is also the main objective identified in the ASEAN Agreement, but in a separate section on guiding principles, 'flexibilities to Member States depending on their level of development and sectoral responsibilities' is listed.[144]

Box 4.7 Summary of options for an objectives provision

1. *No objectives provision*
2. *Objectives provision that refers only to investment promotion and protection*
3. *Objectives provision that refers to objectives in addition to investment promotion and protection*

141 See Section 4.2.1 (The role of preambles in IIAs).

142 COMESA Investment Agreement (2007), Art. 2. Because it is a regional agreement, the objectives provision also refers to strengthening and increasing the competitiveness of COMESA's economic activities and jointly promoting COMESA as an attractive investment area.

143 COMESA Investment Agreement (2007), Art. 11.

144 ASEAN Agreement (2009), Arts. 1 & 2. The India–Singapore CECA (2005) has a more extensive statement of general objectives for the entire agreement in Art. 1.2, which includes 'to establish a transparent, predictable and facilitative investment regime'.

4.4.2 Discussion of options

1. *No objectives provision*

This is the most common practice in existing IIAs. Because an objectives provision is an important part of the interpretive context, not including one means that interpreters of the IIA have limited direction regarding how its obligations should be interpreted. The objectives of the treaty will be inferred from the provisions that it contains. Without an objectives provision an interpreter of the treaty has more discretion to determine its objectives and to interpret the agreement accordingly. An IIA that primarily contains investment protection provisions is likely to be found to be intended to protect investors to the exclusion of other goals. Some interpretive direction can be given through a preamble in the absence of an objectives provision.

2. *Objectives provision that refers only to investment promotion and protection*

By identifying only two objectives, the promotion and protection of investment, this kind of objectives provision prioritises these objectives for any interpreter of the agreement, including an investor–state tribunal. An interpreter is likely to feel compelled to disregard other policy considerations. Interpretive direction in a preamble can complement or qualify the direction in an objectives provision. An interpreter is likely to give more weight to an objectives provision. To encourage consistent and predictable interpretation, the objectives provision and the preamble should be consistent.

3. *Objectives provision that refers to objectives in addition to investment promotion and protection*

In this form of objectives provision, the parties have an opportunity to identify and prioritise their intentions in entering into an IIA to include a broad range of considerations, including contributing to sustainable development. The interpretive direction in an objectives provision can be complemented or qualified by a preamble. As noted, the objectives provision and the preamble should be consistent.

4.4.3 Discussion of sample provision

In the Guide's sample provision, the objective of attracting investment for the purposes of sustainable development is the sole objective identified. Certainly, another objective of the agreement, and one that may be of paramount importance to capital-exporting states, is the protection of investments; many of the IIA provisions discussed in the Guide provide such protection. Capital-exporting states may insist that this purpose be recognised expressly in the objectives provision. It might be argued in response that protection of investments is implicit in their promotion. The benefit of indicating the single objective of promoting foreign investment to support sustainable development is that it makes clear the paramount importance of investment promotion and the achievement of sustainable development through legitimate regulatory activities of the host state. The investment protection provisions in an IIA with this kind of objective provision should be understood as a means of achieving this objective.

Such an approach should discourage interpreters of the treaty from engaging in a weighing of the relative importance or balancing of investment protection against the promotion of investment and sustainable investment,[145] though some tribunals may view protection as a necessary and incidental aspect of an IIA that promotes investment.

4.4.4 Sample provision: objective

Objective

The objective of this Agreement is to promote foreign investment that supports and facilitates sustainable development in accordance with legitimate regulation by the host state, including the protection of internationally and domestically recognised human rights, labour rights and the rights of indigenous peoples and the environment.

4.5 Scope of application

Cross references

Section 4.2.1	The role of preambles in IIAs	42
Section 4.3	Definitions	48
Section 5.12	Reservations and exceptions	224
Section 7.1	Investor–state dispute settlement	408
Section 7.2	State-to-state dispute settlement	483
Section 8.2	Technical assistance	499
Section 9.3	Termination of IIAs	510

Provisions defining the scope of an IIA represent an opportunity for the parties to expressly indicate what is and what is not covered by the agreement. Few IIAs contain separate provisions expressly defining their scope of application.[146] Many IIAs simply define their scope through the definitions of investors and investments that are entitled to protection under the treaty. Nevertheless, there are several additional issues that can be dealt with in scope provisions.

4.5.1 IIA practice

Relatively few IIAs contain scope provisions that are identified as such, though many agreements contain provisions that expressly address their scope of application in some way. The scope issues typically addressed include the following:

- Defining when obligations begin to apply;
- Limits on the application of the agreement

145 The IISD model treaty identifies sustainable development as its sole objective (Art. 1).

146 India's model agreement limits its application to 'investments … accepted as such in accordance with its laws and regulations' (Indian model BIPPA, Art. 2).

  - to investments made in accordance with host state law;
  - in relation to certain policy areas, sectors or measures;
  - in relation to measures of sub-national actors; and
- Limits on what may be the subject of dispute settlement.

When do obligations begin to apply?

Some treaties expressly apply only to investments made *after* the treaty comes into force, though most apply to protect investments regardless of whether they had been made at the time the IIA became effective or after.[147] A few treaties that protect investments in place when the treaty came into effect provide that the agreement do not apply to disputes related to measures of the host state that were in place prior to that date, even if they continue to be in place afterwards.[148]

One of the main objectives of capital-exporting states in negotiating IIAs is often to protect existing investments in host states. In principle, however, extending protection to investments already in place will not induce new capital inflows. Consequently, for host countries, the benefit of protecting pre-existing investments is likely to be small.[149] There may, nevertheless, be a marginal benefit for host states to the extent that such protection encourages foreign investors to stay who, in the absence of such protection, might have left. Similarly, such an approach may create an incentive for investors with investments that pre-date the treaty to retain investment returns in the host country and to invest further.[150]

In Sections 6.6–6.11 (obligations of investors), the Guide describes provisions that impose obligations on investors that are intended to ensure that investment contributes to sustainable development. If such obligations on investors are included in an IIA, it is necessary to indicate when they begin to apply. From a host state point of view, such obligations would be most effective if they commenced at the time that the treaty came into force and applied to investments in place at that time as well as new investments.

Scope limited to investments made in accordance with host state law

As discussed in relation to the definition of investment above,[151] it is useful to limit the application of an IIA to investments made in accordance with the laws and

---

147 E.g. Indian model BIPPA, Art. 2; IISD model treaty, Art. 4; Canadian model FIPA, Art.1; US model BIT, Art. 1; India–Singapore CECA (2005), Art. 6.2(1); COMESA Investment Agreement (2007), Art. 12.2 (though only investments registered under the agreement are protected). The same is true for all Caribbean and Pacific BITS (Malik, op. cit., at 14, 46).

148 E.g. Colombian model agreement Art. II. Many treaties also provide that parties may deny the benefits of the treaty to certain investors in certain circumstances (e.g. Canadian model FIPA, Art. 18). See Section 4.3 (Definitions) 'investor'.

149 The Asian-African Legal Consultative Committee, op. cit., described the imposition of IIA obligations in relation to pre-existing investments as 'controversial'.

150 The duration of treaties is discussed below. See Section 9.3 (Termination of IIAs).

151 See Section 4.3 (Definitions).

regulations of the host state. While this can be done in the definition of investment, it can also be done in the scope of the agreement clause. The latter approach gives more profile to the limitation.

Some policy areas, sectors or measures excluded

Some IIAs contain scope provisions that exclude certain policy areas, sectors or measures from the application of the agreement, where both parties agree that these areas should not be covered, perhaps because of their sensitivity or their connection to state policy or security. Some agreements exclude policy areas such as government procurement, subsidies to local businesses and social services, such as health and education.[152] The Colombian model agreement excludes a policy area, taxes, and certain specific measures relating to the financial sector.[153] Alternatively, these kinds of exclusions may be set out as exceptions or reservations to the agreement.[154] In some cases, exceptions in an IIA have been interpreted narrowly as being contrary to the main goals of the agreement. One possible advantage of excluding a sector or activity in a scope provision, as compared with an exception or reservation, is that a scope limitation might not be interpreted narrowly in this way. Where states wish to exclude different policy areas, sectors and measures from the agreement, each may list them in a national schedule of reservations. Both reservations and exceptions are discussed below.[155] It is also possible to limit the scope of an IIA's application by agreeing to its application only to sectors that each state lists.[156]

Application to measures of sub-national actors

As a matter of general international law, a state is responsible for actions of all entities that can be attributed to the state. These include actions of courts, administrative tribunals and regulators, as well as sub-national levels of government. If any actor whose actions are attributable to the state performs actions that are contrary to an international treaty obligation, the state is internationally responsible in the absence of an applicable exception or reservation in the treaty.[157]

---

152 For example, the ASEAN–Australia–New Zealand Free Trade Agreement, signed 27 February 2009, in force 3 January 2010, excludes government procurement, subsidies and services supplied in the exercise of governmental authority (Art. 1).

153 Colombian model agreement, Art. II.4 and II.5. As discussed below under Section 5.2 (Right of establishment), it is also possible to provide that the IIA applies only to listed sectors. This approach is adopted in the ASEAN Agreement (2009), Art. 3.3.

154 See Section 5.12 (Reservations and exceptions), Section 5.3 (National treatment) and Section 5.4 (Most favoured nation).

155 See Section 5.12 (Reservations and exceptions).

156 This is called positive listing and is described in Section 5.2 (Right of establishment).

157 *Vienna Convention on the Law of Treaties*, Art. 27; UN (2001), Report of the International Law Commission, Fifty-third session (23 April–1 June and 2 July–10 August 2001), UN Doc A/56/10, United Nations.

If an IIA provides for investor–state arbitration, actions of all state actors can be the subject of claims. Some agreements create express exclusions for actions by municipalities and other sub-national actors.[158] These kinds of limitations are discussed below.[159]

Limitations on dispute settlement and umbrella clauses

A final possible limitation relates not to the scope of application of the agreement, but rather to the scope of access to dispute settlement procedures that are available under it. It may be desirable to provide that some of the obligations in the treaty cannot be the subject of an investor–state claim by an investor. While investors will want to ensure that they can claim if the host state has breached a specific investor protection obligation, there may be obligations in the agreement for which an individual investor is not a direct beneficiary and which should not be the subject of investor–state claims. An obligation for states to consult regarding technical assistance, for example, is an obligation that implicates only the party states and a failure of either state to perform would not be an appropriate basis for an investor–state claim.[160] These kinds of limitations are discussed below.[161]

In addition, some obligations may be sufficiently sensitive that states will not want them to be the subject of state-to-state dispute settlement. Where state obligations regarding areas such as environmental protection, human rights, labour rights and the rights of indigenous peoples, of the kind that are discussed in the sample provisions below, are being undertaken, states may decide to exclude them. These kinds of limitations are discussed below.[162]

Some treaties contain an *umbrella clause*, which provides that obligations that a state owes to investors but that are not specifically set out in the treaty are considered to be treaty obligations and can be the subject of the dispute settlement procedures under the treaty. As discussed below,[163] there are few benefits to host states associated with such clauses and they expand the scope of host state obligations in unpredictable ways.

---

158 The Canadian model FIPA excludes the application of some provisions to all existing measures of sub-national governments (Art. 9). The US model BIT excludes the application of some provisions from all existing measures of listed central and regional government entities as well as of local governments.

159 See Section 5.12 (Reservations and exceptions) and Section 5.3 (National treatment) and Section 5.4 (Most favoured nation).

160 See Section 8.2 (Technical assistance).

161 See Section 7.1 (Investor–state dispute settlement).

162 See Section 7.2 (State-to-state dispute settlement).

163 See Section 7.1 (Investor–state dispute settlement).

Box 4.8 Summary of options for a scope provision

1. *No scope provision*
2. *Include a scope provision*

   A scope provision can be used to do any of the following:

   a. Define when the agreement begins to apply and whether pre-existing investments are protected;
   b. Limit the application of the agreement to investments made in accordance with the laws and regulations of the host state;
   c. Limit the application of the agreement by listing policy areas, specific sectors and measures to which the agreement does not apply;
   d. Exclude the application of the agreement to sub-national governments; and
   e. Limit access to dispute settlement.

4.5.2 Discussion of options

1. *No scope provision*

This is the most common practice in existing IIAs. The scope of the agreement will be determined by the definitions of investor and investment and the language used in individual provisions. In the interests of clarity, it is helpful to have a scope provision, especially if the parties wish to have particular limitations on the agreement's application.

2. *Include scope provision*

If a scope provision is included, the parties need to decide how it will address the following issues.

a. Define when the agreement begins to apply and whether pre-existing investments are protected

This kind of limitation provides clarity to investors and states regarding the date the IIA begins to apply and the extent to which pre-existing investments are protected. The protection of investments in place at the time that the treaty comes into force is a common objective of capital-exporting states, but it will have a limited effect on inducing new investment. If the scope of the IIA is limited to investments made after the date the treaty comes into force, there will be differential treatment of investments that pre-date the treaty. It is also possible that there will be some uncertainty regarding the status of reinvestment by investors whose initial investment pre-dated the IIA.

A separate issue is how to deal with host state measures that pre-date an IIA coming into force. In the interests of assisting host states to manage their risk of investor–state claims, all claims relating to measures of the state prior to the agreement coming into force could be excluded. Such a provision should address whether measures that were put in place prior to the treaty coming into force but which continue to affect investors after that date can be the subject of an investor complaint.

Distinct considerations arise in relation to the commencement of obligations on investors. As discussed below in the Guide, one way to help ensure that IIAs contribute to sustainable development is to impose obligations on investors to comply with host state laws and to meet specific standards in relation to human rights, labour rights, indigenous peoples' rights, not engaging in bribery and corruption, and undertaking sustainability assessments of their investments. If obligations on investors are included in an IIA, it is useful to indicate when they begin to apply. From a host state point of view, investor obligations would be most effective in contributing to sustainable development if they commenced at the time that the treaty came into force and applied to investments in place at that time as well as new investments.

b. Limit the application of the agreement to investments made in accordance with the laws and regulations of the host state

This kind of limitation ensures that only investments that were properly approved under the state's domestic rules when they came into the host state territory qualify for protection. It is a very common and useful limitation that ensures that only investments that a state has determined are desirable under its domestic policy benefit from the obligations of the IIA. Such a limitation can also be included in the definition of investment.[164]

As discussed below, most IIAs do not give protection to investors prior to the admission of the investment.[165] For a treaty that provides for pre-establishment rights for investors, it may be necessary to specify a different earlier commencement date for the investor obligations. To be effective, obligations that are to apply prior to establishment must extend to investors seeking to make or who are in the process of making investments.

c. Limit the application of the agreement by listing specific policy areas, sectors and measures to which the agreement does not apply

This kind of limitation may be of interest to states that have policy areas, sectors or measures that are sensitive and in which foreign investment is not permitted or with respect to which a state does not want to undertake the commitments in the IIA. Scope limitations of this kind can be used to preserve flexibility to develop and implement national policies. Policy areas, sectors and measures can also be excluded in reservations and exceptions. Scope limitations and exceptions apply to both parties. Reservations are unique to each party. Alternatively, states can agree that the IIA will apply only to sectors that they list.

---

164 In IIAs that provide for pre-establishment rights a host state will be subject to limits on its ability to prevent investments from investors of the other party state. See Section 5.2 (Right of establishment).

165 See Section 5.2 (Right of establishment).

d. Exclude the application of the agreement to sub-national governments

Most capital-exporting states and their investors will want IIA obligations to extend to all government actors that could take actions that would affect them. Some states may not want to assume obligations at the sub-federal level, perhaps because local governments will either not be aware of IIA obligations or be unwilling to comply with them.

e. Limit access to dispute settlement

This kind of limitation does not restrict the obligations of party states, but only the extent to which they may be the subject of investor–state or state-to-state dispute settlement. States may decide that IIA obligations that are not intended to provide direct protection to investors should be excluded from the obligations that may be the subject of an investor–state claim. Some obligations may be so sensitive that a state may not want to be obliged to defend its compliance with them in state-to-state dispute settlement.

4.5.3 Discussion of sample provision

Applies to all investments by investors of another party, whenever made: In the interests of clarity and predictability, the sample provision in the Guide provides that the obligations of the treaty apply only to measures taken by the host state after the treaty becomes effective in relation to all investments by investors of party states, regardless of when the investment was made. In light of the fundamental importance of existing investor protection to capital exporting countries and the possible marginal benefits to host countries, the Guide provision extends protection to existing investments, as do most IIAs.

Claims arising out of events before the treaty comes into force excluded: In order to assist states to manage the risk of investor–state claims, it would be desirable to exclude the application of the agreement to disputes arising prior to the agreement coming into force. This could be done in the sample provisions on dispute settlement. It is done in the sample scope provision.[166] By referring to measures adopted after the treaty comes into force, the sample provision excludes all measures in place at the time that the IIA comes into force, including those that continue in force after that date. Investor–state claims can be made only in relation to measures adopted after the agreement comes into force. With the adoption of such an approach, it becomes unnecessary to use a reservation to list pre-existing measures that a state wants to exclude from the application of the treaty.

Investor obligations: The sample provision makes clear that any investor obligations included in an agreement also apply upon the agreement coming into force in relation to investments made before or after that date. This would be necessary only in an IIA that included obligations on investors. When particular IIA obligations on investors commence in relation to a particular investment is discussed below in the section on rights of establishment.[167]

166 See Section 7.1 (Investor–state dispute settlement).
167 See Section 5.2 (Right of establishment).

Sub-national governments not excluded: The sample provision does not address its application to sub-national government entities. Instead, the sample provision on reservations contemplates the possibility of excluding measures of sub-national governments.[168] If the party states wanted to exclude all measures of sub-national governments, it could be done in the scope provision.

Listed policy areas and sectors excluded: The sample provision includes a subsection that permits parties to list policy areas and sectors to which the agreement does not apply. The Guide also discusses how states may limit the scope of the agreement by listing sectors and specific measures that are excluded from the application of all or certain portions of the agreement using reservations and exceptions.[169] Subsidies and grants, government purchases of goods and services, and taxation measures, for example, are excluded in the sample provisions.

Scope limited to investments made in accordance with the laws and regulations of the host state: The sample provision limits the application of the treaty to investments made in accordance with the laws and regulations of the host state. Such a provision is sometimes called an 'admission clause'. The importance of this limitation was discussed above in relation to the definition of investment.[170]

Limits on investor–state and state-to-state dispute settlement: Possible limits are discussed below in relation to each form of dispute settlement.[171]

4.5.4 Sample provision: scope of application

Scope of Application

1. This agreement applies to measures of a Party adopted after this agreement comes into force relating to investors of the other Party and their investments, whether the investment is made before or after this agreement comes into force, provided that the investment has been made in accordance with the laws and regulations of the Party.
2. With respect to obligations on investors in [Guide sample provision Sections 6.6–6.11 (obligations of investors)], this Agreement applies to investors of a Party and their investments whether the investment is made before or after this agreement comes into force.
3. This agreement shall not apply to ... [list policy areas or sectors]

168 See Section 5.12 (Reservations and exceptions).

169 See Section 5.12 (Reservations and exceptions). Other limitations on the scope of particular provisions are discussed in the section discussing the provision.

170 See Section 4.3 (Definitions).

171 See Section 7.1 (Investor–state dispute settlement) and Section 7.2 (State-to-state dispute settlement).

Chapter 5

Substantive Obligations of Host States Regarding Investor Protection

5.1 Introduction

The dominant feature of existing IIAs is that they create substantive obligations that host states must observe in relation to investors from the other party state. In this chapter, the Guide discusses the main categories of the core obligations found in existing IIAs.

Recent investor–state arbitration decisions have raised some serious concerns regarding the potential scope of some of the generally worded substantive obligations found in many IIAs.[1] If domestic laws, regulations or policies violate these substantive standards and cause losses to an investor, the settlement of the dispute through investor–state arbitration can result in an award requiring the host state to compensate investors. A number of cases recently decided by investor–state tribunals have required developing countries to compensate the investor when domestic laws and regulations have had a negative effect on investments based on surprisingly broad interpretations of IIA obligations.[2] Compensation may be required even where a measure was intended to achieve important domestic policy goals, including policies related to development, financial stability and public health. Some critics argue that IIAs can negatively affect the capacity of host states to comply with their international human rights obligations,[3] especially in relation to economic, social

1 B Hoekman and R Newfarmer (2005), 'Preferential Trade Agreements, Investment Disciplines and Investment Flows', 39 *Journal of World Trade* 949 at 966.

2 See, for instance, *CMS Gas Transmission Company v. Argentine Republic*, ICSID Case No. ARB/01/8, Award, 21 May 2005; *Compañía de aguas del aconquija s.a. and Vivendi Universal S.A. v. Argentine Republic*, ICSID Case No. ARB/97/3, Award, 21 November 2000; *Sempra Energy International v. Argentine Republic*, ICSID Case No. ARB/02/16, Award, 28 September 2007; *Enron Corporation & Ponderosa Assets, L.P. v. Argentine Republic*, ICSID Case No. ARB/01/3, Award 22 May 2007.

3 As of 20 November 2008, the following Commonwealth members had ratified or acceded to the *International Covenant on Civil and Political Rights* (adopted 16 December 1966 in force 23 March 1976), 999 *United Nations Treaty Series* 171: Australia, Bangladesh, Barbados, Belize, Botswana, Cameroon, Canada, Cyprus, Dominica, The Gambia, Ghana, Grenada, Guyana, India, Jamaica, Kenya, Lesotho, Malawi, Maldives, Malta, Mauritius, Mozambique, Namibia, New Zealand, Nigeria, Papua New Guinea, St Vincent and the Grenadines, Samoa, Seychelles, Sierra Leone, South Africa, Sri Lanka, Swaziland, Trinidad and Tobago, Uganda, United Kingdom, United Republic of Tanzania, and Zambia. As of 20 November 2008, the above member countries (excluding Belize, Botswana, Mozambique, Samoa and South Africa), but with the addition of the Solomon Islands, had ratified or acceded to the *International Covenant on Economic, Social and Cultural Rights* (adopted 16 December 1966, in force 3 January 1976) 993 *United Nations Treaty Series* 3.

and cultural rights.[4] It is also argued that IIA obligations may restrict the ability of host states to make regulations to protect the environment.[5]

Limitations that IIAs impose on the ability of governments to enact new laws and regulations that apply to foreign investors are of particular concern from the point of view of sustainable development where the host state is considering creating new legal mechanisms to protect the environment, or protect or promote human rights, labour rights or the rights of indigenous peoples. Box 5.1 sets out an example of this.

Box 5.1 *Vivendi v. Argentina*

An example of the difficulties IIAs can pose for the power of states to enact future laws and regulations is the case of *Vivendi v. Argentina.*[6] The case dealt with a decision of the government of the Argentine province of Tucumán to change its policy regarding a water utility. The utility had been privatised under the government of President Carlos Menem, but local politicians became dissatisfied with the service provided by the French investor who had been granted the concession, because of both a perceived decline in water quality and an increase in the price of water for the community. The provincial government took various steps to replace the foreign owner, Vivendi, which then complained that Argentina (via its province, Tucumán) had violated its obligations under the BIT between France and Argentina. The tribunal found in favour of the foreign investor. The case illustrates a scenario in which a government was required to pay costly compensation under an IIA to a foreign investor when it sought to change a policy with significant human rights implications (in this case, the right to water), based on legitimate governmental concerns.

4 States have both immediate and continuing obligations under international human rights treaties to respect, protect and fulfil the rights in relation to each individual subject to their jurisdiction – see for example, Article 2 of both the ICCPR and the ICESCR. The obligation to *protect* human rights requires states to take legislative, administrative and other measures in order to control and regulate the activities of non-state actors that may violate human rights, and in cases where a violation occurs, to investigate and prosecute such actors. See, for example, *Velásquez Rodriguez v. Honduras*, (1989) 28 *International Legal Materials* 294; *Herra Rubio v. Colombia* (161/1983), (1988) *HRC Report*, GAOR, 43rd Sess., Supp. 40, 190 [11]; *Ergi v. Turkey* (App. 23818/94) (1998) 32 EHRR 388; *Timurtas v. Turkey* (App. no. 23531/94) (2000) ECHR 13 June 2000; and A *v. UK* (App. no. 25599/94) (1999) 27 EHRR 611.

5 See, for example, K Miles (2011), 'Sustainable Development, National Treatment and Like Circumstances in Investment Law', in M-C Cordonier Segger, A Newcombe and M Gehring (eds), *Sustainable Development in World Investment Law*, Kluwer Law International, The Hague, at 266.

6 *Vivendi v. Argentina*, op. cit.

When awards are made, the required compensation can be quite costly.[7] Even where a state successfully defends an investor's claim, the costs involved can be substantial.[8] As a result, in order to comply with their obligations and manage the risk of claims being made, states must carefully determine the amount of freedom they wish to maintain to make changes to laws, regulations and policies that might affect investment, and ensure that such freedom is protected in the IIAs they sign.

Some countries have adopted different forms of clarifying language in their IIA models that limit the scope of application of core IIA obligations. Some of these approaches are incorporated in the Guide's sample provisions to help preserve host state flexibility.[9] The increasingly common use of exceptions and regulations to exclude the application of investor protection obligations from sectors, measures or policy areas is also discussed.[10] Given their technical nature, and the fact that they have been adopted by major developed countries in the IIA models that they use, these kinds of further specification of the party state's obligations may be acceptable to prospective treaty partners and are unlikely to have an impact on investment flows.

This section of the Guide discusses these core provisions, beginning with a fundamentally important issue that arises in some forms of IIA currently in use: whether the IIA grants foreign investors from party states a *right* to invest in other party states.

5.2 Right of establishment

Cross references

7 In the case of CMS *Gas*, op. cit., the award was US$133 million plus interest; in the case of *Vivendi*, op. cit., US$105 million plus interest; in the case of *Sempra*, op. cit., approximately US$128 million plus interest; and in the case of *Enron*, op. cit., US$106.2 million plus interest.

8 The costs of investor–state arbitration are discussed in more detail in Section 7.1 (Investor–state dispute settlement).

9 See Section 5.3 (National treatment), Section 5.4 (Most favoured nation), Section 5.5 (Fair and equitable treatment and the minimum standard of treatment), Section 5.6 (Limitations on expropriation and nationalisation), Section 5.7 (Compensation for losses), Section 5.8 (Free transfer of funds), and Section 5.10 (Transparency).

10 See Section 5.12 (Reservations and exceptions).

According to UNCTAD, '[t]he right to control admission and establishment remains the single most important instrument for the regulation of FDI'.[11] Control over the admission of foreign investors is likely to be especially important for countries that have a limited capacity to regulate foreigners operating within their borders. For example, foreign investors may engage in anti-competitive conduct that would be hard to address in the absence of effectively enforced competition laws, which few developing countries have.

Some IIAs contain provisions that have the effect of granting a right for foreign investors from one treaty party to enter the domestic market of the other party and carry on business. Such a right is sometimes called a 'right of establishment'. These rights could have implications for the protection of human rights and the environment, and the attainment of other development and regulatory objectives to the extent that they operate to preclude host states from screening prospective foreign investors and investments and thereby limit their ability to ensure that a particular foreign investment contributes to the protection of human rights or the environment and/or facilitates the progressive realisation of such objectives.[12] Granting a right of establishment could deprive the host state of an important tool that cannot easily be replaced through domestic regulation. At the same time, a right of establishment enhances the certainty and predictability of access to the host state market and may encourage foreign investment inflows.

5.2.1 IIA practice

As noted, most IIAs, such as the Indian model BIPPA, limit their application to investments that have been lawfully admitted according to the host state's domestic investment regime. Admission of new investments is permitted, but only subject to compliance with whatever requirements are imposed under the national law of the host state.[13] There is no right for foreign investors to enter the host state.

An increasing number of treaties, however, include limited rights that operate for the benefit of foreign investors before they have made an investment. The purpose of these rights is to commit party states to allow investors to enter the host country market and operate there.

---

11 UNCTAD (2003), *World Investment Report 2003: FDI Policies for Development: National and International Perspectives*, United Nations, New York and Geneva, at 102.

12 India has argued in the WTO that developing states need to retain this capacity to screen investments. See WTO, *Communication from India*, Working Group on the Relationship between Trade and Investment (2 October 2002), Doc. No. WT/WGTI/150 at para. 12.

13 E.g. Indian model BIPPA, Art. 2. See also India–Bangladesh BIT, Art. 2 and ASEAN–Australia–New Zealand FTA, Art. 2(a). In the UK model IPPA, states are obliged to admit investors from the other party, but only 'in accordance with its laws and regulations' (Art. 2.10). It is not obvious that this is different in effect from the Indian model BIPPA. None of the Pacific BITs, and only a few Caribbean BITs, include a right of establishment (M Malik (2009), *Report on Bilateral Investment Treaties*, Commonwealth Secretariat, London, at 14, 47). The India–Singapore CECA provides for a right of establishment in listed sectors only (Art. 6.3(1)). While the national treatment obligation in the ASEAN Agreement includes 'establishment, acquisition, expansion', the definition of covered investment includes only those that have been admitted in accordance with national rules (Art. 4). In the IISD model treaty (Art. 4(E)), it is provided that nothing in the treaty creates a right of establishment.

In a few treaties, an express commitment to grant entry is provided.[14] The Canadian and US models adopt a different approach. The national treatment and MFN obligations in these treaties extend to the pre-establishment phase, creating a right of establishment for foreign investors from the other party to the treaty by requiring treatment of them by the host state that is no less favourable than that accorded to domestic investors and other foreign investors with respect to establishing their businesses in the host state market.[15] The right of access is not an absolute right, but one that allows access to sectors that are open to domestic investment. Such rights do not create a requirement, for example, to privatise activities that are reserved to the state or that are state-sanctioned monopolies.

Another approach that is more limited and specific is to adopt a provision that prohibits the maintenance or adoption of particular restrictions on market access, such as a maximum permissible percentage of foreign ownership of a business, and limitations on the number of firms allowed to participate in identified activities, a kind of limitation that favours incumbent firms that may be mostly local. This is the approach taken in the *GATS*.[16]

All IIAs that provide for rights of establishment limit their scope of application by expressly excluding particular sectors or permitting the maintenance of certain restrictions, such as investment-screening regimes. There are two main ways in which exclusions of this kind may be provided for in an IIA:

- **A *positive list* of the policy areas, sectors and measures to which the right of establishment obligation applies; and**
- **A *negative list* of policy areas, sectors and measures to which the right of establishment obligation does *not* apply.**[17]

In principle, negative listing is not inherently more restrictive than the positive list approach. A party could achieve the same level of committed sectors and measures using either approach. However, negative listing forces states to make an inventory of their restrictions and make them transparent by listing them. If a state fails to include a sector or measure on its list, the right of establishment obligation will apply. By

14 E.g. 1998 Framework Agreement on the ASEAN Investment Area, Art. 7(1).

15 Canadian model FIPA, Arts. 3 and 4; US model BIT, Arts. 3 and 4. Also investors eligible for protection are defined to include persons seeking to make an investment (Canadian model FIPA, Art. 1; US model BIT, Art. 1). These obligations apply to state treatment of investors related to the establishment and acquisition of investments. See UNCTAD (2003), *World Investment Report 2003*, at 102; Oxfam International (2003), *The Emperor's New Clothes: Why Rich Countries Want a WTO Investment Agreement*, Oxfam International Briefing Paper 46, at 25. See also WTO, *Communication from India*, Working Group on the Relationship between Trade and Investment (2 October 2002), Doc. No. WT/WGTI/150, at para. 4, where India noted in 2002 that apart from a BIT between Japan and Korea, only US and Canadian IIAs require pre-establishment national treatment. The Norwegian Draft model APPI also contains a right of establishment in Art. 4. Right of establishment provisions are becoming increasingly common.

16 *GATS* Art. XVI. See discussion of *GATS* in Appendix 2.

17 Positive and negative listing is common in relation to a wide variety of IIA obligations, as discussed below.

contrast, under a positive list approach, a state need only identify those sectors with respect to which it is prepared to undertake a commitment. Consequently, a positive approach is less administratively burdensome and more likely in practice to leave the state with greater residual policy-making flexibility.[18]

A negative list or 'opt-out' approach is the more common model where rights of establishment are provided for. The Canadian model FIPA and the US model BIT follow a negative list approach. For example, the Canadian model treaty contemplates that each party may exclude certain sectors and measures from the application of the national treatment, MFN and some other obligations through the use of reservations.[19] Canada routinely uses reservations to protect its foreign investment screening regime as well as other discriminatory measures from challenge under its IIAs.[20] The US model BIT contains a similar provision excluding the application of national treatment and MFN obligations to certain sectors, sub-sectors and activities listed in a schedule to the agreement.[21]

Under a positive list approach, a state commits to providing a right of establishment, but only for sectors that the state agrees to list, and only subject to reservations for any conditions that must be satisfied in order for access to be permitted.[22]

Other possible limitations on a right of establishment include the following:[23]

- **Agreeing to negotiate right of establishment commitments at a later date:** This approach may be desirable for countries whose foreign investment policy generally or for particular sectors is evolving. An alternative that would create greater certainty for investors would be to commit to a right of establishment on particular terms at a fixed date in the future.
- **Agree to a right or establishment but exclude this commitment from investor–state dispute settlement:** This has been done in some Canadian IIAs.[24]
- **Agree to a 'best endeavours' right of establishment:** This is not a binding obligation but is an expression of host state intention that may provide some comfort to investors.

---

18 A third alternative would be to have a state commit to provide national treatment on a non-binding 'best endeavours' basis. This has been done in relation to pre-establishment commitments in some treaties such as the European Union–Morocco Association Agreement, signed 26 February 1996, in force 1 March 2000, Art. 31.

19 Canadian model FIPA, Art. 9.

20 E.g. Canada–Peru Free Trade Agreement, signed 29 May 2008, in force 1 August 2009. Additionally, in some agreements, disputes regarding the right of establishment are not subject to investor–state dispute settlement. E.g. Canada–Barbados, Agreement between the Government of Canada and Government of Barbados for the Reciprocal Promotion and Protection of Investments, signed 19 May 1996, in force 17 January 1997.

21 US model BIT, Art. 14.

22 The India–Singapore CECA (2005) provides for a right of establishment in listed sectors only (Art. 6.3(1)). This positive listing approach is followed in the IISD model treaty, Arts. 4 and 5.

23 This list is based on UNCTAD (2012), *Investment Policy Framework for Sustainable Development*, United Nations, New York and Geneva, at 61.

24 E.g. Canada–Barbados BIT (1997), Art. II.

5.2.2 Investor obligations and the right of establishment

As discussed below in the Guide, one way to help ensure that IIAs contribute to sustainable development is to impose obligations on investors (i) to comply with host state laws, (ii) to meet specific standards in relation to human rights, labour rights, indigenous peoples' rights, (iii) not to engage in bribery and corruption and (iv) to undertake sustainability assessments prior to making their investments.[25] If parties negotiating an IIA decide to include some or all of these provisions, some consideration will have to be given to when they should begin to apply. To be most effective, some obligations would have to start before an investment is admitted by the host state. For example, an obligation to undertake a sustainability assessment prior to making an investment would have to commence prior to host state admission of the investment if it were to have any effect. States may agree that treaty prohibitions on bribery and corruption should apply to a prospective investor during the host state's investment admission process to ensure that any bribery or corruption during that process is caught.

As noted above, most IIAs do not protect the investments of investors prior to the admission of the investment. For a treaty that follows this approach but contains investor obligations, it may be necessary to specify a different earlier commencement date for the investor obligations in the investor obligation provisions. For treaties that create investor protection obligations that operate at the pre-establishment phase, and impose investor obligations, the investor obligation provisions will still need to be drafted to make clear when each kind of obligation begins to apply.

Box 5.2 Summary of options for a right of establishment provision

1. *No right of establishment*
2. *Right of establishment subject to limitations*
    a. Limiting scope of right of establishment by specifying that only specific barriers to market access are prohibited;
    b. Positive list of sectors to which right of establishment obligation applies;
    c. Negative list of sectors to which right of establishment obligation does not apply;

(Continued)

25 See Sections 6.7 (Investor obligation to comply with the laws of the host state); 6.8 (Investor obligation to respect internationally recognised human rights and undertake human rights due diligence); 6.9 (Investor obligation to refrain from the commission of, or complicity in, grave violations of human rights); 6.10 (Investor obligation to comply with core labour standards); 6.11 (Investor obligation to refrain from acts, or complicity in acts, of bribery and corruption); 6.6 (Sustainability assessments).

(Continued)

d. Postponing right of establishment commitments to a fixed date or to be negotiated in the future; and

e. Limiting right of establishment commitments to 'best endeavours'.

3. *Unlimited right of establishment*

5.2.3 Discussion of options

Whether an IIA contains a right of establishment and, if it does, the scope of any permitted limitations are key issues that define the degree of openness secured by the treaty because the protection of pre-establishment rights limits the ability of the host state to use domestic law and regulations to keep out foreign investment. If the state does not have sufficient regulatory capacity to deal with the conduct of investors after their admission, it would be ill advised to grant a right of establishment, and no state gives foreign investors an unlimited right of establishment. To grant a limited right of establishment in an IIA, the host state must have a developed policy framework in place for the admission of foreign investments and be confident that its regime can be carved out of IIA in sufficiently broad terms to ensure not only that its existing policy and programmes are insulated from challenge, but also that foreseeable future changes to the policy may be made as necessary.

Whether a state should commit to granting a right of establishment in any of the forms identified above, even a best endeavours undertaking, is a matter that can be determined only by reference to the existing policy of the state on the admission of foreign investment. If a country has already adopted a policy of opening the domestic economy to foreign participation, the effect of an IIA provision guaranteeing that access would not require any change in government policy. Such a provision would, however, constrain a future return to a policy excluding or limiting foreign investment. As noted, it is precisely this limitation on future policy change by the host state that foreign investors hope to obtain from an IIA. Any retreat from the level of openness guaranteed by a right of establishment in an IIA could result in a claim for compensation by prospective investors under the treaty's investor–state arbitration procedure. If a state permits foreign investment on a limited basis, a commitment to a right of establishment in an IIA would represent a substantial liberalising policy shift for that state. The magnitude of the shift would depend on the precise terms of the commitment.

The Guide does not include a sample provision creating a right of establishment. As discussed above, only a few developed countries seek a right of establishment, and even for those that do, the right is always a qualified one. Also, the challenge of drafting adequate reservations (a negative list approach) or listing commitments (a positive list approach) to provide sufficient policy flexibility regarding the host state's right to refuse entry of foreign investors consistent with its existing and anticipated future foreign investment policy is significant and will be hard for many host states to meet, especially if their policy on permitting entry of foreign investors is not well developed. As between a positive and a negative list approach, it is administratively simpler to use a positive list.

A right of establishment represents a strong commitment to foreign investors that may encourage investment from investors of the other party state and even from other states. If a right of establishment is desired, it could be set out in a specific section. It is often found in the national treatment and MFN provisions as described below.[26] Some of the options for dealing with a right of establishment are discussed below in relation to these provisions.

5.3 National treatment

Cross references

Section 4.3	Definitions	48
Section 5.4	Most favoured nation	124
Section 5.5	Fair and equitable treatment and the minimum standard of treatment	138
Section 5.12	Reservations and exceptions	224

A national treatment obligation in an IIA prohibits party states from treating foreign investors from other party states and their investments less favourably than domestic businesses and their investments. The purpose of a national treatment obligation is to protect foreign investors against arbitrary or unfair discrimination by host states in favour of domestic businesses. National treatment typically prohibits both differences in treatment that are expressed in a host state measure (called *de jure* discrimination) and those that result in practice from the operation of a state measure that is not in its express terms discriminatory (called *de facto* discrimination).[27] Regarding *de facto* discrimination, in order to show a breach of the national treatment obligation, it is not necessary to show discriminatory intent on the part of the state. The fact of less favourable treatment is generally sufficient.[28]

National treatment is one of the most significant obligations found in IIAs, in part because host state measures that discriminate in favour of domestic firms are common, often tied closely to national development goals and politically very sensitive. Most host states have some programmes that grant advantages exclusively to domestic businesses in order to encourage their growth and their ability to compete with foreign investors. While these kinds of programmes are most common in developing countries with less developed industries, virtually all states have some kinds of preferences for domestic businesses. No state grants national treatment to foreigners in every situation without qualifications.

---

26 See Section 5.3 (National treatment) and Section 5.4 (Most favoured nation).

27 *ADF Group Inc. v. United States of America*, ICSID Case no. (AF)/00/1, Final Award, 9 January 2003, at para. 157.

28 *International Thunderbird Gaming Corporation v. Mexico*, UNCITRAL, Award, 26 January 2006; *Siemens v. Argentina*, ICSID Case No. ARB/02/8, Award, 6 February 2007. But see *Methanex v. US*, UNCITRAL, Final Award, 3 August 2005 at Part IV, Chapter B, para. 12.

This deceptively simple obligation can be quite difficult to apply in practice, especially in relation to host state measures that treat foreign investors differently for some legitimate policy reason. Its application often depends very much on the specific facts and some issues regarding the application of national treatment have not been fully resolved by existing arbitral cases.[29] Some options for ensuring that the national treatment obligation does not inappropriately constrain host states seeking to regulate to achieve legitimate policy objectives are discussed below.

5.3.1 National treatment is a relative standard

What national treatment requires is determined not by any objective norm, but by reference to the host state's treatment of its domestic businesses. This has three main implications.

- **If national treatment is agreed to, discrimination in favour of domestic investors or their investments by a host state must be either eliminated by the host state or excepted from the IIA obligation in some way, such as through a reservation or exception.** To the extent that the national treatment obligation requires states to remove discriminatory measures, it has a liberalising effect. Most other IIA obligations do not require liberalisation. Often, however, existing discriminatory measures are excluded from the agreement in some way.
- **Any new, more favourable treatment of domestic investors increases the minimum level of treatment that the host state must provide to foreign investors.** The level of protection for foreign investment may be ratcheted up in this way over time as the treatment of domestic investors improves. It is also the case that if a host state's treatment of its domestic investors worsens, the national treatment will only commit the host state to that lower standard. However, other IIA provisions, such as the fair and equitable treatment obligation, may limit states' ability to reduce the level of treatment of foreign investors in some circumstances, even where the treatment of domestic investors is worsened in some way.[30]

  It is important for countries considering negotiating an IIA to be aware that their obligations towards foreign investors under national treatment clauses will change over time with changes in their domestic regime. States need to bear the relative nature of the national treatment obligation in mind on an ongoing basis to ensure that they are in compliance with IIA national treatment commitments. In this regard, it is important to note that any difference in treatment is not always less favourable. In each case, the impact and purpose of the treatment by the host state must be considered.

29 R Dolzer and C Schreuer (2008), *Principles of International Investment Law*, Oxford University Press, Oxford, at 179.

30 See Section 5.5 (Fair and equitable treatment and the minimum standard of treatment).

- **It is consistent with the national treatment obligation to treat foreign investors and their investments** *more favourably* **than domestic businesses.** The most common formulation of national treatment is to require treatment 'no less favourable than' that accorded to domestic businesses,[31] which makes clear the possibility of better treatment for foreign investors.

5.3.2 IIA practice

Most IIAs require party states to provide national treatment,[32] but not all do. The trend in recent IIAs, however, has been to include a national treatment obligation. The formulation of the national treatment standard varies. The Indian and UK model treaties simply require a party state to treat the investments of investors of other party states in a manner that is no less favourable than the treatment accorded to investments of that party's nationals.[33]

Others, such as the Canadian and the US model treaties, limit the obligation to investors and investments that are 'in like circumstances' and to certain identified activities. For example, Canada's basic national treatment obligation regarding foreign investments provides as follows:

> Every Party shall accord to covered investments of another Party treatment no less favourable than that it accords, *in like circumstances*, to investments of its own investors with respect to the *establishment*, *acquisition*, *expansion*, *management*, *conduct*, *operation*, *and sale or other disposition* of investments.[34] (Emphasis added.)

The reference to 'in like circumstances' is intended to direct any interpreter of the provision, such as an investor–state tribunal, to ensure that the domestic investment whose treatment is chosen to compare with the foreign investor's investment is an appropriate comparator.[35] The reference in this provision to specific activities clarifies and defines the scope of the obligation. Both are discussed below.

Finally, the national treatment obligation set out above applies only to 'investments'. In the Canadian model, the national treatment obligation is expressed separately in

31 UNCTAD (1999), *National Treatment*, United Nations, New York and Geneva, at 37. See, for example, the AALCC draft model BITs, Art. 5, models A and B.

32 E.g. Indian model BIPPA, Art. 4; UK model IPPA, Art. 3; ASEAN Agreement (2009), Art. 5. Some other countries have not always required national treatment in their IIAs (e.g. Australia).

33 In practice there has been some variation in the scope of the national treatment obligation in agreements entered into by the UK. In the United Kingdom–Belize, Government of the United Kingdom of Great Britain and Northern Ireland and the Government of Belize on the Promotion and Protection of Investment, signed 30 April 1982, in force 30 April 1982, the obligation only applies to new measures introduced after the date of the treaty. The United Kingdom Jamaica, Agreement between the Government of the United Kingdom of Great Britain and Northern Ireland and the Government of Jamaica on the Promotion and Protection of Investments, signed 20 January 1987, in force 14 May 1987, permits 'special incentives' to nationals that do not significantly affect the investment and activities of the foreign investor in connection with the investment.

34 Canadian model FIPA, Art. 3(2).

35 For a more extensive discussion of the issues related to national treatment, see UNCTAD (1999), *National Treatment*, op. cit.

relation to 'investors' of the other party state.[36] Most national treatment obligations apply to both investors and their investments. Some obligations are expressed to apply only to investments. As discussed above, both investment and investor are extensively and carefully defined in IIAs.[37] Consequently, the failure to refer to investors might significantly limit the scope of the treaty and would reduce its benefit to foreign investors correspondingly. For example, a treaty that applied only to investments would not cover directly the treatment of foreign natural and legal persons of the other party but only of the investments they make. The distinction between the protection of investments and investors has not, however, been a significant issue in investor–state arbitration cases to date.[38]

5.3.3 The basis of comparison and 'in like circumstances'

The purpose of the national treatment obligation is to prohibit discrimination based on nationality. Consequently, measures that expressly state that foreign investors in identified categories are to be treated differently from identified categories of domestic businesses will generally be found to be a breach of the national treatment obligation if the treatment of foreign investors is less favourable. An investor–state tribunal would also have to be satisfied that the domestic investor alleged to be favoured by the measure was truly comparable to the foreign investor claiming a breach of national treatment. Where a government measure does not expressly prescribe discriminatory treatment and an investor argues that it is being treated differently and less favourably in fact (*de facto* discrimination), it is necessary to identify the appropriate domestic business to compare with the foreign investor to evaluate their relative treatment. Choosing an appropriate comparator has proven difficult in practice.

In most cases, for example, it would not be appropriate to compare the treatment of a foreign investor with a domestic investor in a different economic sector or of a very different size. While finding the right comparator is an inherent requirement of applying a national treatment obligation, many treaties, like the Canadian model mentioned above, direct an interpreter of the provision to investigate whether the foreign investor and a domestic investor alleged to have received more favourable treatment are truly comparable by specifying that they be 'in like circumstances'.[39]

A requirement that the foreign investor be 'in like circumstances' with the domestic investor in order for national treatment to apply helps to make clear that governments have scope to treat foreign investors differently from domestic businesses where doing so is necessary to achieve some legitimate public policy objective. In *Pope & Talbot*, an arbitral decision under NAFTA's investment chapter,[40] the tribunal had to determine

36 Canadian model FIPA, Art. 3(1).

37 See Section 4.3 (Definitions).

38 UNCTAD (2010), *Most Favoured Nation Treatment: A Sequel*, United Nations, New York and Geneva, at 104.

39 The UK model IPPA uses the same language. The UK–Belize BIT (1982), however, refers to 'in the *same* circumstances' (emphasis added), a stricter standard, meaning that fewer domestic businesses would be appropriate comparators.

40 NAFTA (1992), op. cit.

whether foreign and Canadian investors that were treated differently were in like circumstances with respect to the allocation of an export quota. The tribunal asked whether the difference in treatment was justified by a rational policy objective that was not based on a preference favouring domestic investors over foreign investors and did not unduly undermine the investment-liberalising objectives of NAFTA. The tribunal held that if the difference in treatment could be justified on this basis, then the foreign and domestic investors were not 'in like circumstances' for the purposes of the measure.[41] As a result, there could be no breach of the national treatment obligation.[42] The overall purpose of the enquiry is to ensure that the national treatment obligation is applied only to prevent discrimination on the basis of the foreign nationality of the investor or investment. In the Norwegian draft model agreement, as well as including a reference to 'in like circumstances,' a footnote was added reciting the parties' agreement to a standard for differential treatment that is similar to the test set out in *Pope & Talbot*.

The IISD model treaty also contains an 'in like circumstances' qualification, but goes on to expressly require the following factors to be taken into account when determining whether investors are 'in like circumstances':

- The effect of the investment on third persons and the local community;
- The effect of the investment on the local, regional or national environment or the global commons, including effects relating to the cumulative impact of all investments within a jurisdiction;
- The sector in which the investor operates;
- The goal of the alleged discriminatory measure;
- The regulatory scheme applied to the investor; and
- Other factors directly related to the investment of the investor in relation to the measure concerned.[43]

The IISD model directs interpreters of the treaty to give equal consideration to all factors, rather than favouring some over others. This approach, which has been adopted in the COMESA Investment Agreement,[44] is intended to ensure that the application of the national treatment obligation takes into account development and other

41 *Pope & Talbot v. Canada*, UNCITRAL, Award on Merits of Phase 2, 10 April 2001, at para. 79, applying the approach in OECD (1993), *Declaration on National Treatment for Foreign-controlled Enterprises*, OECD, Paris, at 22. See similarly *S D Myers Inc. v. Canada*, UNCITRAL, Partial Award, 13 November 2000, at para. 246, and *In the Matter of Cross-Border Trucking Services*, (USA-Mex-98-2008-01), Final Report of the Panel, 6 February 2001 at para. 258.

42 Some commentators suggest that this is an inherent limitation on the national treatment obligation, such that different treatment is never a breach of national treatment if rational grounds are shown for the difference. Dolzer and Schreuer describe this as 'widely accepted' but acknowledge that 'a precise definition of these grounds remains elusive' (Dolzer and Schreuer (2008), op. cit., at 181).

43 IISD model treaty, Art. 5(E).

44 COMESA Investment Agreement (2007), Art. 17. Under the COMESA Investment Agreement (2007) national treatment does not apply to certain sectors listed by each member state (Art. 18).

policy priorities as well as investment policy considerations in determining whether domestic and foreign investors are in like circumstances. Moreover, this approach avoids the approach adopted by tribunals in some investor–state cases, under which domestic and foreign investors are assumed to be in like circumstances simply because they are in the same sector or industry and consequently the host state is required to explain how the domestic and foreign investors are not in like circumstances. Such an approach places the burden on the host state to justify treating investors differently. Box 5.3 provides an example of how 'in like circumstances' can be applied to protect the policy-making flexibility of host states.

Box 5.3 Example of 'in like circumstances'

A host state enacts a measure to protect the environment by limiting use of a particular highly polluting industrial technology. In practice, foreign investors in the state are the only users of that technology. Domestic businesses in the same sector do not use the polluting technology. They use another technology that has much less serious environmental effects.

The foreign investors are not 'in like circumstances' with the domestic businesses for the purposes of the achievement of environmental protection objective of the measure and the measure is not a breach of national treatment.

Determining what is an appropriate domestic business to compare to a foreign investor is a complex and fact-specific enquiry. As a result, it is difficult to make reliable generalisations regarding what will be considered an appropriate comparison for the purposes of applying the national treatment standard. Nevertheless, one can say that there is nothing in the expression of the standard or the arbitral cases that requires a tribunal to compare the treatment of a foreign investor to the treatment of all domestic businesses in a particular sector as opposed to a particular domestic business or group of businesses. There is no hard and fast rule that all foreign investors must be given the best treatment given to any domestic investor in the host state or treatment that is no less favourable than the average treatment of domestic investors.

5.3.4 Limiting national treatment to specific matters, including pre- and post-establishment activities

National treatment applies only to matters governed by the treaty, specifically the treatment of investors and their investments. It does not extend to other matters, such as maritime shipping rules, except to the extent that they affect investors and their investments. Similarly, national treatment does not apply to tax matters if tax matters are excluded from the treaty.[45]

45 This is an example of the *ejusdem generis* principle of interpretation. Regarding the application of this principle in the MFN context, see ILC, Draft Articles on MFN, Report of the Commission on the Work of the Thirtieth Session, UN Doc.A/33/10, Yearbook of the International Law Commission, 1978 (Arts. 9 and 10).

Some states have agreed to limit the application of the national treatment obligation to specific matters. The national treatment obligation in the Netherlands–Jamaica BIT applies only to measures related to 'taxes, fees, charges and exemptions'.[46] The Canadian and US model agreements also limit the scope of the national treatment obligation to treatment relating to particular activities: 'the establishment, acquisition, management, conduct, operation, expansion and sale or other disposition of investments in its territory'.[47] This language makes clear that national treatment only applies to measures affecting these aspects of investments and helps to make the scope of the provision's application more predictable.

By referring to terms such as 'establishment', 'acquisition' and 'expansion', however, the national treatment obligation creates a right of establishment for foreign investors.[48] They must be treated no less favourably than domestic investors with respect to being allowed to operate in the host state. A national treatment obligation that does not include those kinds of words does not create a right of establishment, so long as the IIA makes clear that it applies only to investments admitted by the host state in accordance with its domestic regime. In general, pre-establishment rights are sought in order to achieve some actual liberalisation of conditions of entry to the host state, though a commitment to pre-establishment national treatment also obliges host states not to change the existing rules in ways that restrict entry. Pre-establishment rights are always accompanied by exclusions, usually in the form of reservations, to protect the host state's right to discriminate in specific sectors or through particular measures, typically reflecting existing state policy.[49]

If the parties to an IIA do not intend to create a right of establishment, in addition to omitting words such as 'establishment', 'acquisition' and 'expansion' from the national treatment provision, it is important to include a provision stating that the agreement applies only to investments admitted by a state in accordance with its laws and regulations. An example of such a provision is provided in the Guide sample scope provision.[50]

5.3.5 Excluding particular sectors or measures from national treatment

It is possible to limit the scope of a national treatment obligation to exclude particular sectors or measures with respect to which a host state does not want to be bound. As

46 Netherlands–Jamaica BIT (1991), Art. 4, though Art. 3 contains a broader non-discrimination provision.

47 Similar language is used in the Draft Norwegian APPI, Art. 3. Prior to 2004, the Canadian model treaty did not allow investors to initiate investor–state dispute settlement on the basis of a claim that national treatment had not been provided in relation to establishment or acquisition of a business.

48 Expansion includes an investment of new foreign capital to expand an existing business carried on by an investor. Similarly, acquisition includes acquisitions financed by new foreign capital. However, an expansion or acquisition would also include transactions or activities financed entirely in the host state. If an IIA contains a clear admission clause that ensures that any new investment must meet domestic requirements for admission, then expansion and acquisition could be included in the list of activities to which the obligation applies without creating a right of establishment; e.g. ASEAN Agreement.

49 See Section 5.2 (Right of establishment).

50 See Section 4.5 (Scope of application).

noted, most states have some preferential arrangements for local businesses. The Canadian model adopts a negative list approach to protect domestic preferences from the agreement. It permits each party state to exclude sectors and measures from the application of the national treatment and some other obligations by including them in a list of reservations.[51] The US model BIT contains a similar provision excluding the application of national treatment and some other obligations to certain sectors, sub-sectors and activities listed by each party in a schedule.[52] By contrast, the India–Singapore CECA takes a positive list approach to national treatment. The national treatment obligation is limited to sectors listed by each country.[53] All other sectors are excluded.

Another way to exclude sectors or measures from the scope of an IIA is to include general exceptions. Unlike reservations, exceptions operate for the benefit of both parties. It is increasingly common to have general exceptions to the national treatment obligation that protect measures in certain policy areas, such as health and the environment.[54] It may also be desirable to include an exception tailored to development. An example is found in the Italy–Morocco BIT.

> Investors of the two Contracting Parties shall not be entitled to national treatment in terms of benefiting from aid, grants, loans, insurance and guarantees accorded by the Government of one of the Contracting Parties exclusively to its own nationals or enterprises within the framework of activities carried out under national development programs.[55]

Such a broad exception creates significant uncertainty for foreign investors regarding whether they may rely on the national treatment obligation in relation to particular state actions. Such uncertainty might discourage investment. Also, it might be argued that such a development exception is not necessary to the extent that, for the purposes of a policy supporting local development, foreign and domestic investors will not be found to be in like circumstances. In the absence of some clear indication that discriminatory development policies are permitted, however, it is difficult to be confident that an investor–state arbitration tribunal would accept such an argument. As a consequence, some form of express exception may be needed to make sure that a host country has the flexibility to pursue its domestic policy. Exceptions that provide discrete lists of sectors and activities that are excluded from the scope of the national treatment obligation provide greater certainty to investors than a general development exception, but a general exception provides more flexibility for host states.[56] Examples of specific exceptions from the national treatment obligation for

51 Canadian model FIPA, Art. 9.
52 US model BIT, Art. 14.
53 India–Singapore CECA (2005), Art. 6.3(1).
54 See Section 5.12 (Reservations and exceptions).
55 Morocco–Italy, Agreement between the Government of Morocco and Government of the Italian Republic on the Promotion and Protection of Investments, signed 18 July 1990, in force 1 January 1992, Art. 3(3). See also the Netherlands–Jamaica BIT (1991), Art. 3(6). The ASEAN–Australia–New Zealand Free Trade Agreement has a different approach focusing on special and differential treatment (Art. 15).
56 UNCTAD (1999), *National Treatment*, op. cit., at 65.

government subsidies and government purchases of goods and services (often referred to as 'government procurement'), two common types of discriminatory policies maintained by host states, are provided below.[57]

5.3.6 The scope of the national treatment obligation as it applies to sub-national governments

As noted, a state is responsible for compliance by sub-national governments with its IIA obligations in the absence of a reservation or exception.[58] With respect to the application of national treatment to sub-national government measures, one of the issues is whether sub-national governments must grant foreign investors the same treatment they give to local investors within their sub-national region or whether it is sufficient if they grant the same level of protection that they accord to other domestic investors from outside the region.

In the Canadian model FIPA and the US model BIT, sub-national governments are obliged only to provide treatment that is no less favourable than the treatment that they grant to domestic investors from other parts of the country. Such a special national treatment obligation for sub-national governments permits them to discriminate in favour of local businesses and against foreign investors so long as the treatment given is at least as good as that given to investors from other parts of the country. In the absence of such a provision, an argument could be made that the category of national investors that constitutes the appropriate group for comparison with foreign investors for the purpose of national treatment is local investors within the region. If such an argument were successful, a sub-national government would have to give foreign investors no less favourable treatment than it gives to local businesses, even if such treatment were better than that given to other national investors of the host state from other parts of the country.

Investors will want to receive treatment by a sub-national government that is no less favourable than local investors from within the jurisdiction of the government. Host states, however, may not want to impose such a strict national treatment obligation on sub-national governments for political or other reasons. Sub-national governments may have limited awareness of IIA obligations or be unwilling to comply with them. Whether national governments can compel compliance by sub-national governments with IIA obligations will depend on each country's constitutional system and its politics. The importance of the issue will depend on the extent to which sub-national governments in the host state have the power to act in ways that will affect investors.

5.3.7 Interaction between national treatment and MFN

The national treatment obligation interacts with MFN obligations in an IIA in two important ways:[59]

57 See Section 5.12 (Reservations and exceptions).

58 See Section 4.5 (Scope of application).

59 Possible interactions are discussed in UNCTAD (1999), *National Treatment*, op. cit., at 55–60.

- **Where both standards are present in an IIA, one issue is which prevails in the event of a conflict**: Some agreements, such as NAFTA, expressly provide that the higher standard prevails.[60] In the absence of such a provision, it is likely that this is the most appropriate interpretation. Both provisions would be given effect.
- **Could an IIA that does not explicitly include a promise of national treatment, but that does provide for MFN, be interpreted to impose a national treatment obligation on a party if the party has agreed to a national treatment commitment in another agreement?** As discussed below, this kind of incorporation in a treaty of provisions from other treaties is possible in some circumstances.[61]

Box 5.4 Summary of options for a national treatment provision

1. *No national treatment obligation.*
2. *A post-establishment national treatment obligation that may be limited in one or all of these ways:*
   a. To specific activities (and *not* including activities such as establishment, acquisition or expansion);
   b. To foreign investors 'in like circumstances';
   c. To listed policy areas, sectors and measures (positive list) or excluding listed policy areas, sectors and measures (negative list);
   d. With respect to sub-national governments, to treatment no less favourable than such governments extend to other investors of the host state from outside the jurisdiction of sub-national governments;
   e. Subject to general exceptions; and
   f. To *de jure* national treatment, excluding *de facto* national treatment.
3. *A pre-establishment national treatment obligation that may be limited in the same ways as discussed in option 2.*

5.3.8 Discussion of options

1. *No national treatment obligation*

Most IIAs contain a national treatment obligation. It provides significant protection to foreign investors against discrimination in favour of domestic businesses which may be valued by them. Without such an obligation, host states have discretion to

60 NAFTA (1992), Art. 1104.

61 See Section 5.4 (Most favoured nation).

treat foreign investors differently. Some other obligations typically found in IIAs, including a prohibition on expropriation without compensation and the fair and equitable treatment obligation, may operate to prohibit discriminatory actions by host states.[62]

It is possible that an IIA could contain an obligation to grant national treatment but only subject to domestic law of the host state. In effect, this would not commit the host state to grant national treatment but only to ensure that any discrimination was authorised by law.

If an IIA does not contain a national treatment obligation, but (i) the IIA contains an MFN obligation and (ii) the state had entered into another IIA that provided a national treatment obligation, it is possible that an obligation on the state to provide national treatment would be incorporated into the IIA through the MFN obligation.

2. A *post-establishment national treatment obligation limited in one or all of these ways*

   a. Limited to specific activities (and *not* including establishment, acquisition or expansion)

This approach to drafting an IIA provision clarifies the scope of the obligation by limiting it to identified activities for the benefit of both investors and host states. Many IIAs refer to activities to which the obligation applies, such as the conduct, operation, and sale or other disposition of the investment.

   b. Limited to foreign investors 'in like circumstances'

A reference to 'in like circumstances' directs a tribunal to make sure that it considers a variety of factors to determine what domestic businesses should be compared to the foreign investor for the purposes of applying the national treatment obligation. Some view the national treatment obligation as inherently requiring such a determination, whether it refers to 'in like circumstances' or not. An express reference to 'in like circumstances' provides more certain direction to interpreters. An analysis of 'in like circumstances' that takes into account the purpose of the measure provides more scope for a state to engage in policies for non-discriminatory purposes that may have a negative effect on foreign businesses. This is because, for the purposes of a particular policy, a foreign investor and a domestic business may be found not to be in like circumstances. A national treatment obligation can provide even more direction to an interpreter of the obligation by identifying possibly relevant circumstances that should be taken into account to determine if a foreign investor and a domestic business are in like circumstances.

62 See Section 5.5 (Fair and equitable treatment and the minimum standard of treatment) and Section 5.6 (Limitations on expropriation and nationalisation).

c. Limited to listed policy areas, sectors and measures (positive list) or excluding listed policy areas, sectors and measures (negative list)

Most IIAs exclude the application of the national treatment obligation to some policy areas, sectors or measures to reflect preferences for local businesses in existing national rules and in sectors or areas of policy where a state wants to be able to discriminate against foreign investors in the future. A negative list approach requires a state to list a policy area, sector or measure if the obligation is to be avoided. A positive list approach requires a state to list a sector or measure for the obligation to apply. Positive listing is a less burdensome approach because it is not necessary to list sectors or measures to avoid the application of the national treatment obligation and it may result in a narrower scope of application for the obligation. It also means, however, that restrictions are not transparent to investors.

d. With respect to sub-national governments, limited to treatment no less favourable than such governments extend to other investors of the host state from outside the jurisdiction of sub-national governments

In the absence of an exception or reservation, the national treatment obligation applies to measures of sub-national governments. The Canadian and US model agreements create a relaxed national treatment obligation for sub-national governments that permits them to discriminate in favour of local businesses and against foreign investors so long as the treatment given is at least as good as that given to investors from other parts of the country. This may be desirable for some states. Depending on the importance of sub-national governments in the regulation of economic activity, such a limitation might be a concern for investors.

e. Subject to general exceptions

Exceptions can be used to carve out areas of state policy-making from the application of the national treatment obligation and are being increasingly used in IIA practice. Common exceptions from the national treatment obligation are government preferences for local businesses in extending subsidies or buying goods and services. Exceptions limit the benefits of the obligation for investors.

f. Limited to *de jure* national treatment

A final option to limit the scope of a national treatment obligation is to limit the national treatment obligation to state measures that are *de jure* discrimination. In other words, only measures that expressly discriminate based on the foreign nationality of investors would be prohibited. This approach would create a clear and predictable obligation, though one that is very limited in its scope. It is not an approach that is followed in any IIA currently. One of the concerns that investors would have is that it is often difficult to distinguish between measures that are *de jure* and those that are only *de facto* discriminatory. A specific concern in this regard would be that governments could draft measures that avoided language that was discriminatory, but then apply the measure in a discriminatory way. If an IIA prohibited *de jure* discrimination only, there would be no breach of the treaty in these circumstances.

3. *A pre-establishment national treatment obligation limited in the same ways as discussed in option 2*

A pre-establishment national treatment obligation means that foreign investors must be treated no less favourably than domestic businesses with respect to entry into the host state market to carry on business. If specific activities to which the obligation applies are listed, they will include activities such as establishment, acquisition and expansion of the investment that relate to entry into the host state's market. Reservations can be used to carve out any specific entry restrictions for foreign investment that a state wants to maintain, or sectors of activity to which the obligation does not apply. Alternatively, positive listing of sectors subject to the pre-establishment national treatment obligation could be used.

With respect to options 2 and 3, if (i) a state has imposed limitations on the scope of the national treatment obligation in an IIA, (ii) the IIA contains an MFN obligation and (iii) the state has entered into another IIA that contains a national treatment provision without these limitations, it is possible that the more favourable national treatment obligation will be incorporated into the treaty through the MFN obligation.

5.3.9 Discussion of sample provision

A national treatment obligation provides assurance to foreign investors that they will encounter a level playing field when they do business in the host state. It prohibits nationality-based discrimination. Some form of national treatment obligation is found in most, but not all, IIAs. Any limitation on the scope of national treatment will impair the benefit of the provision for investors.

In the sample provision, the national treatment obligation is qualified by reference to 'in like circumstances' to ensure that in applying the provision an appropriate comparator is sought. In general, this may help to ensure that host states have the right to pursue legitimate policy objectives even if the way that they do so incidentally results in a foreign investor being treated less favourably than a national. This approach is followed in many recent agreements other than those negotiated by some European countries. As in the IISD model agreement, a non-exhaustive list of factors to be taken into account in determining if investors are 'in like circumstances' is set out. While this is not an approach followed in existing agreements (other than in the COMESA Investment Agreement), it incorporates the general approach applied in a number of arbitration cases where tribunals have determined that in order to compare what is comparable it is necessary to take into account all relevant factors.[63] For further certainty, a version of the test developed in *Pope & Talbot* is included. A state measure that treats investors of the other party or their investments less favourably than its own investors or their investments is not inconsistent with the national treatment obligation if it is applied by the state in pursuit of a legitimate non-discriminatory public purpose and has a reasonable connection to the purpose.

The clarifying language from the Canadian and US models regarding the aspects of investments that are subject to the national treatment commitment has been

63 UNCTAD (2010), *Most Favoured Nation Treatment*, op. cit., at 26–7.

incorporated in the sample provision, except that words such as 'establishment', 'acquisition' and 'expansion' have not been included. If party states desire to create a right of establishment, words such as these should be included in the agreement. While an increasing number of treaties provide a right of establishment, most do not.

The Guide sample definition provision provides that sub-national governments are to be defined by each party in the definition section.[64] The sample national treatment provision clarifies and limits the obligations of sub-national governments in the same way as in the US model. Sub-national governments are obliged only to provide treatment that is no less favourable than the treatment that they grant to domestic investors from other parts of the country. Such a special national treatment obligation for sub-national governments permits them to discriminate in favour of local businesses and against foreign investors as long as the treatment given is at least as good as that given to investors from other parts of the country. With respect to legal persons, the sample provision permits discrimination in favour of locally incorporated or organised enterprises. Any other basis of discrimination in favour of locally organised businesses (such as discrimination based on the location of the operations of the business within the territory administered by the sub-national government) would not be protected.

Other sample provisions in the Guide provide examples of general exceptions and country-specific reservations applicable to the national treatment obligation, including specific exceptions for subsidies and government procurement.[65] Both may be necessary, especially if a negative list approach is followed. As noted, an alternative would be for the national treatment obligation to apply only to sectors and measures that a state had positively agreed to list. This option is provided for in brackets in the sample provision.

5.3.10 Sample provision: national treatment

National Treatment

1. Every Party shall accord to investors of the other Party and their investments treatment no less favourable than that it accords, in like circumstances, to its own investors and their investments with respect to the management, conduct, operation, and sale or other disposition of investments in its territory.

2. The treatment accorded by a Party under section 1 means, with respect to a sub-national government, treatment no less favourable than the treatment that the sub-national government accords, in like circumstances, to investors and to investments of investors of the Party of which it forms a part who are: (i) natural persons who are not residents in the territory administered by the sub-national government; or (ii) enterprises that are not incorporated or organised under the law of the sub-national government.

3. For greater certainty

---

64 See Section 4.3 (Definitions).
65 See Section 5.12 (Reservations and exceptions).

a. A determination of whether an investment or an investor are in like circumstances for the purposes of this article shall be made based on an assessment of all of the circumstances related to the investor or the investment, including:

   i. The effect of the investment on

      A. the community;

      B. the human rights of individuals and rights of indigenous peoples;

      C. the environment, including effects that relate to the cumulative impact of all investments within a jurisdiction;

   ii. The business sector in which the investor operates;

   iii. The goal of the alleged discriminatory measure; and

   iv. The regulations that apply to investments or investors;

b. A measure of a Party that treats investors of the other Party or their investments less favourably than its own investors or their investments is not inconsistent with this article if it is adopted and applied by the Party in pursuit of a legitimate public purpose that is not based on the foreign nationality of investors, including the protection of health, safety, the environment and internationally and domestically recognised human rights, labour rights or rights of indigenous peoples, or the elimination of bribery and corruption, and it bears a reasonable connection to the purpose.

[4. This article shall apply only to measures that a Party adopts or maintains with respect to sectors, sub-sectors or activities, as set out in its schedule to Annex 1 of this agreement.]

5.4 Most favoured nation (MFN)

Cross references

Section 4.5	Scope of application	94
Section 5.3	National treatment	110
Section 5.12	Reservations and exceptions	224
Section 7.1	Investor–state dispute settlement	408

A commitment to MFN in an IIA means that each party state commits to treating investors of the other party state and their investments no less favourably than it treats investors and investments of any other country. The investors that are the beneficiaries of an MFN commitment are assured that if other foreign investors are given treatment of a particular kind by the host state, their treatment should be no worse. The main goal of an MFN provision is to ensure equality of competitive opportunity among investors of different nationalities. The MFN obligation can be a key IIA provision for smaller developing countries, if it permits their investors to benefit from stronger commitments negotiated by other countries with more bargaining power.[66]

Like national treatment, MFN typically prohibits both differences in treatment that are expressed in a host state measure (*de jure* discrimination) and those that result in practice from a state measure that is not discriminatory on its face (*de facto* discrimination).[67] With respect to *de facto* discrimination, in order to show a breach of the MFN obligation, generally it is not necessary to show discriminatory intent on the part of the state. Less favourable treatment by the state is sufficient.

Many of the issues related to MFN provisions are the same as those related to national treatment:

- Does the obligation create pre-establishment rights, meaning that it protects investors before they have entered the host country with their investments?
- How should an appropriate comparator with a foreign investor be identified in order to assess whether there has been a breach of the obligation?
- Should the obligation be limited to specific activities?
- Should particular policy areas, sectors or measures be excluded from the obligation and should this be done on a positive list or a negative list basis?

Since these issues have been previously discussed in the section on national treatment, they will be only briefly discussed in this section.[68]

Controversy has arisen around the extent to which an MFN provision in one IIA can be used to incorporate treaty standards from *other* IIAs. In fact, this has been the issue in most investor–state arbitration cases dealing with MFN, rather than the level of treatment given by the host state to investors from different states under its domestic law. Investors now frequently claim that the presence of an MFN clause in an IIA between their state and a host state means they should be able to take advantage of the highest level of investor protection that a host state has agreed to in any treaty, rather than the specific level of protection negotiated between the investor's state and the host state. The failure by investor–state tribunals to take a consistent approach regarding this issue has contributed significantly to the challenge countries face in trying to predict the scope of their obligations and act accordingly. Much of the discussion in this section will focus on this issue.

5.4.1 MFN is a relative standard

Like national treatment, MFN is a relative standard. In the case of MFN, what the obligation requires is determined by reference to the host state's treatment of other

66 See Government of Canada (2002), 'Canada's Foreign Investment Protection and Promotion Agreements (FIPAs) Negotiating Programme 2002', available at: www.bilaterals.org/spip.php?page=print&id_article=497 (accessed 25 May 2012).

67 *ADF v. US*, op. cit., at para. 157.

68 See Section 5.3 (National treatment).

foreign investors. As a result, any new, more favourable treatment of foreign investors increases the level of treatment that the host state must provide to foreign investors who are protected by an MFN obligation, subject to any applicable exception or reservation. The level of protection for foreign investors who benefit from an MFN provision may increase over time as the treatment of foreign investors from other countries improves. The effective impact of MFN tends to be much less significant in practice than national treatment, however, because most countries do not have policies that protect foreign investors from one country and not others that are as important or politically sensitive as the policies that protect domestic businesses. As discussed below, an important exception to this generalisation is the preferential treatment given by many countries under bilateral and regional trade and investment agreements.

Finally, it is important to note that different treatment of foreign investors will not always be less favourable. In each case, the impact of the treatment by the host state on a particular investor must be assessed to determine if it is less favourable.[69]

5.4.2 IIA practice

Almost all IIAs require that MFN treatment be provided, though a few do not.[70] The India–Singapore CECA, for example, does not include an MFN provision.[71] As noted, despite their common presence in IIAs, MFN provisions are less significant than national treatment obligations because of the relatively limited incidence of host state discrimination between foreign investors based on nationality.[72] As a result, states may decide that the simplest way to avoid some of the problems with MFN provisions discussed below is simply not to include an MFN obligation in their IIAs.

As with the national treatment standard, the MFN obligation in some treaties simply requires treatment no less favourable than that provided to investments and investors of other states.[73] The MFN obligation in other treaties is qualified in that it only applies to specified aspects of an investment, and requires MFN treatment only if foreign investors from different states or their investments are 'in like circumstances'.[74] The Canadian and US model treaties follow this approach. For example, the US MFN obligation related to investments provides as follows:

---

69 In addition, UNCTAD has pointed out that the MFN obligation does not prevent preferences being granted to a foreign investor by contract that are not given to others. One explanation offered for this result is that a foreign investor who was not awarded a contract is not in like circumstances with the one that was (UNCTAD (2010), *Most Favoured Nation Treatment*, op. cit.).

70 In a recent study, UNCTAD found that approximately 80 per cent of the IIAs reviewed contained MFN provisions (UNCTAD (2010), *Most Favoured Nation Treatment*, op. cit.).

71 See, similarly, the India–Korea Free Trade Agreement, signed 7 August 2009, in force 31 December 2009, and the ASEAN–Australia–New Zealand FTA (2009) Investment Chapter, though there is a commitment to seek to negotiate an MFN commitment in the work programme established by the latter agreement (Art. 16).

72 Discrimination in the form of preferential agreements is common but this particular form of discrimination is usually permitted through a specific reservation or exception.

73 E.g. Indian model BIPPA, Art. 4; UK model IPPA, Art. 3.

74 E.g. Canadian model FIPA, Art. 4; US model BIT, Art. 4.

> Each Party shall accord to covered investments treatment no less favourable than that it accords, in like circumstances, to investments in its territory of investors of any non-Party with respect to the establishment, acquisition, expansion, management, conduct, operation, and sale or other disposition of investments.[75]

The purpose of the MFN obligation is to prohibit discrimination based on nationality. Consequently, measures that expressly state that foreign investors from one state are to be treated differently from foreign investors in another state will generally be found to be a breach of the MFN obligation if the treatment of foreign investors that benefit from that obligation is less favourable. Where such *de jure* discrimination is claimed by an investor, the issue for an investor–state tribunal will be whether the foreign investor that is discriminated against under the measure is being treated less favourably. A government measure does not need to prescribe discriminatory treatment on its face, however. An investor that is being treated differently and less favourably in fact (*de facto* discrimination) may also claim a breach of MFN. With claims of *de facto* discrimination, it is necessary to identify a foreign investor to compare with the foreign investor who is claiming less favourable treatment. Conceptually, the same challenges arise in finding an appropriate comparator as were discussed above in relation to national treatment.

In practice, finding the right comparator has not proved so difficult in relation to MFN. Nevertheless, in terms of drafting, the same considerations apply. Many IIAs include a direction to interpreters to ensure that they identify foreign investors that are truly comparable to a foreign investor who claims to have been less favourably treated by limiting the application of the MFN provisions to investors that are 'in like circumstances'. As with national treatment obligations, MFN obligations that contain 'in like circumstances' qualifications may provide more regulatory freedom for host states than obligations that are not restricted to investments and investors that are in like circumstances by ensuring that investor–state tribunals consider more carefully what is an appropriate foreign investment to compare with the foreign investment whose treatment is at issue. The need to find an appropriate comparator and the role of a reference to 'in like circumstances' were discussed above in Section 5.3 (National treatment). Since, essentially, the same issues arise for MFN as for national treatment, these issues will not be further discussed here.

5.4.3 Limiting MFN to specific matters, including pre- and post-establishment activities

As with national treatment, a key question is whether an MFN obligation applies in the pre-establishment stage of an investment or only after the investment has been admitted and established in accordance with the laws and regulations of the host state. As discussed above, most IIAs apply only post-establishment. States remain free to determine the conditions for entry of foreign investments and may change those conditions over time. Typically, this right is expressly preserved by an admission clause.[76] Once an investment has been admitted, the MFN obligation applies to

75 US model BIT, Art. 4(2). The same obligation is extended to investors as well (Art. 4(1)).

76 See Section 4.5 (Scope of application).

its treatment for the duration of its life. Some treaties, such as those negotiated by Canada and the USA, apply MFN to the pre-establishment phase of an investment, creating, along with the national treatment obligation, a right of establishment.[77] In the case of the MFN obligation, the right is only to permit establishment on terms no less favourable than those accorded to investors of other states. This would not create a right to enter the host state market for a foreign investor from a party state to an IIA unless other foreign investors were permitted to enter. Even then, the obligation would only be to treat foreign investors from the IIA party state no less favourably than investors from non-party states. No absolute right of entry is created. Often pre-establishment rights are sought in order to achieve some actual liberalisation of conditions of entry to the host state, as well as to obtain a commitment not to change existing rules in ways that restrict entry.

As with national treatment, the application of the MFN obligation to the pre-establishment stage is achieved by identifying the specific activities to which MFN applies and including those that are related to entry into the host state market. For example, the content of the MFN provision in the US model BIT set out above is limited to 'investments in its territory of investors of any non-Party with respect to the *establishment, acquisition, expansion,* ... of investments' (emphasis added). When this is combined with a national treatment obligation that also applies to these activities related to market entry, a right of establishment is created.[78]

As noted in Section 5.3 (National treatment), it is common to exclude particular sectors or measures from national treatment using either limited commitments through a positive list approach or reservations from a general commitment using a negative list approach.[79] General exceptions may also apply. The same issues arise under MFN and the same options for dealing with them are used in IIAs. For a discussion of these issues refer to Section 5.3 (National treatment).

5.4.4 Importation of standards from other treaties

One of the most controversial issues regarding MFN clauses is the extent to which they import standards of behaviour and even rules of investor–state dispute settlement from other treaties into a treaty that includes an MFN provision. To the extent that they do so, investors protected under an IIA with a state that contains an MFN clause are entitled to the most favourable protection provided under *any* treaty the state has signed. In the arbitral decision in *Maffezini v. the Kingdom of Spain*,[80] for example, it was held that, subject to certain limitations, an MFN obligation may apply to treaty-based dispute settlement procedures, with the result that an investor protected by an

77 E.g. Canadian model FIPA, Art. 4; US model BIT, Art. 4.

78 The US model BIT provides only one example of how to create pre-establishment rights. Creation of pre-establishment rights can be achieved using different words.

79 In a few IIAs, states do not agree to grant MFN treatment in some sectors unless the other party grants MFN treatment on a reciprocal basis. See UNCTAD (2010), *Most Favoured Nation Treatment*, op. cit., at 49.

80 *Maffezini v. the Kingdom of Spain*, Decision on Jurisdiction of 25 January 2000 and Award of the Tribunal of 13 November 2000.

MFN clause in an IIA could use a more favourable procedure found in another IIA to which the host state was a party, rather than the specific dispute settlement procedure provided for in the treaty to which the investor's home state was a party. In *Maffezini*, an Argentine investor with a claim against Spain argued successfully that the investor–state arbitration procedures in the Spain–Chile BIT were more favourable than those in the Spain–Argentina BIT, because the Spain–Argentina BIT required an Argentine investor to wait 18 months before bringing a claim under the BIT, while the Spain–Chile BIT had no such requirement. The Argentine investor was allowed to proceed against Spain without meeting the 18-month requirement because it was entitled to MFN treatment under the Spain–Argentina BIT. Subsequent cases have come to differing conclusions in specific situations about the extent to which MFN provisions should be interpreted in this way.

There are a wide variety of ways in which an MFN might import treaty provisions. These are set out in Box 5.5. Some recent model treaties now have provisions that specifically address this problem.

Box 5.5 Possible application of an MFN provision to incorporate provisions from third party treaties into the basic treaty between two states – five cases

Five situations in which an MFN obligation in an IIA could conceivably incorporate provisions from another treaty are described below. In this discussion, 'basic treaty' is used to refer to the treaty between a host state and the state of an investor making a claim against the host state that has an MFN provision, while 'third party treaty' is used to refer to a treaty between the host state and another state.

1. The same categories of investor protection exist in both the basic treaty and a third party treaty, but a more favourable version of the standard for investor protection exists in the third party treaty than in the basic treaty.
2. A standard of investor protection in a third party treaty does not exist in the basic treaty (e.g. national treatment).
3. A provision related to the scope of the treaty in a third party treaty is broader than the comparable provision in the basic treaty (such as the definition of investor or the time period during which the treaty operates).
4. A provision restricting investor protection in the basic treaty does not exist in a third party treaty (such as an exception).
5. A procedural provision in the third party treaty establishes (i) requirements for the admissibility of investor–state claims (e.g. the expiry of an 18-month waiting period for claims to be brought) or (ii) requirements for an investor–state tribunal to have jurisdiction that are more favourable than the

(Continued)

(Continued)

comparable provision in the basic treaty (e.g. defining what may be the subject of dispute settlement under the IIA).[81]

The many investor–state arbitration cases that have dealt with these issues have been recently surveyed by UNCTAD.[82] While the case law is not consistent, and particular decisions are tied to the specific facts of the case, UNCTAD offered some rough generalisations regarding the cases to date:

- Tribunals have not reached consistent conclusions on whether a more favourable version of an investor protection provision in a third party treaty can be incorporated into the basic treaty to replace a less favourable provision (Case 1), though the weight of authority would suggest that this is the right approach.[83] If it could be established that the treatment under the third party treaty was better, the MFN obligation could probably be relied on to incorporate that version of the provision into the basic treaty.
- Tribunals have been willing to consider incorporating from third party treaties a substantive standard that is not present in the basic treaty (Case 2), but not provisions relating to the scope of the treaty (Case 3) that would have the effect of expanding the scope of application of the basic treaty.
- Tribunals have not been willing to eliminate restrictions on investor protection in the basic treaty on the basis that they do not exist in a third party treaty (Case 4).
- With respect to dispute settlement procedures (Case 5), a majority of cases have permitted the incorporation into the basic treaty of more generous requirements for admissibility, though there is substantial disagreement in the cases regarding the propriety of doing so. In contrast, most tribunals have rejected the incorporation of more generous jurisdictional requirements from a third party treaty to expand the scope of tribunal jurisdiction in the basic treaty.

Several important implications for states arise from the arbitral jurisprudence relating to the incorporation of rules in third party treaties into the basic treaties between party states under an MFN provision.

- Existing IIAs should be reviewed to determine to what extent MFN clauses in those treaties could
  - Incorporate more investor-friendly provisions in a state's other existing treaties, or
  - Incorporate new more investor-friendly commitments in treaties a state negotiates in the future.

81 These categories are borrowed from UNCTAD (2010), *Most Favoured Nation Treatment*, op. cit., at 58–84.

82 Ibid.

83 Dolzer and Schreuer, op. cit., at 190.

- As a result of such a review, it may be prudent to seek to renegotiate MFN provisions in existing treaties or to adopt bilaterally or unilaterally an interpretation of such provisions with a view to limiting the scope of these provisions to incorporate more investor-friendly provisions from third party treaties.[84] Alternatively, a state could seek to renegotiate provisions in existing treaties that it considered too investor-friendly with a view to limiting their application.
- In IIA negotiations, particular attention should be paid to
  - Identifying the extent to which proposed MFN obligations may incorporate more investor-friendly provisions from existing treaties and treaties negotiated in the future, and
  - Drafting MFN provisions in ways that will specifically avoid the unwanted (or unanticipated) incorporation of more investor-friendly obligations from other treaties.
- If, in a new IIA, an MFN provision is agreed to that does not contain an exception or other form of limitation on the incorporation of more investor-friendly provisions in other treaties, a party state should review its existing IIAs to determine to what extent provisions from other treaties could be incorporated into the new IIA.

IIA practice – limits on MFN

Several approaches to drafting MFN provisions have been adopted in IIAs that address the incorporation of treaty standards from third party treaties into basic treaties between two states. As noted, the model treaties of Canada and the USA limit the MFN obligation to specific kinds of activities in relation to an investment: 'the establishment, acquisition, expansion, management, conduct, operation, and sale or other disposition of investments'. Since this language does not include dispute settlement, the limitation of MFN to these activities should have the effect of preventing the incorporation into a basic treaty of any rule regarding dispute settlement in a third party treaty.[85] Some treaties have gone farther and made an exclusion of such rules an explicit part of their understanding regarding what these limited activities include.[86]

In addition, there are certain kinds of exclusions from the MFN obligation that are commonly found in IIAs, such as exclusions for preferences granted in treaties to reduce the incidence of double taxation as well as free trade agreements, customs

84 Some treaties provide for binding interpretations by the parties (e.g. NAFTA (1992), Art. 1131). In any case, the *Vienna Convention on the Law of Treaties* establishes as a general rule of interpretation that any agreement between the parties regarding interpretation be taken into account (Arts. 31.3 and 31.4). See Section 7.1 (Investor–state dispute settlement) for a discussion of a mechanism for the adoption of interpretations by the party states.

85 This was the position taken by the negotiating parties to the Free Trade Agreement for the Americas in a footnote to the proposed MFN provision (cited in UNCTAD (2010), *Most Favoured Nation Treatment*, op. cit., at 85–6).

86 E.g. Canada–Peru FTA (2008), Annex 804.1; Colombian model agreement, Art. IV.2.

unions and other kind of bilateral or regional economic integration agreements.[87] Annex III to the Canadian model FIPA specifically excludes the application of MFN to other international agreements as well as to foreign aid programmes.[88]

Box 5.6 Summary of options for MFN treatment provision

1. *No MFN obligation;*
2. *A post-establishment MFN obligation that may be limited in one or all of these ways:*
   a. To specific activities (and *not* including activities such as establishment, acquisition and expansion);
   b. To foreign investors 'in like circumstances';
   c. To listed policy areas, sectors and measures (positive list) or excluding listed policy areas, sectors and measures (negative list);
   d. Subject to general exceptions; and
   e. To *de jure* discrimination
3. *A pre-establishment MFN obligation that may be limited in the same ways as discussed in option 2.*

5.4.5 Discussion of options

1. *No MFN obligation*

Most IIAs contain an MFN obligation. An MFN obligation provides protection against host state actions that treat investors from an IIA party state less favourably than investors from other states. With the exception of preferences resulting from investor protection and investor–state dispute settlement provisions in IIAs and preferences in some other international economic agreements, such discrimination tends to be less significant than discrimination against all foreigners, with the result that, practically, the MFN obligation may be considered both less important for investors and less burdensome for states. Nevertheless, in light of the uncertainty associated with the incorporation of other treaty provisions through an MFN provision, some states may decide not to include such an obligation.

It is possible that an IIA could contain an obligation to grant MFN treatment but only subject to the domestic law of the host state. In effect, this would not commit the host state to grant MFN treatment but only to ensure that any discrimination was authorised by law.

87 UNCTAD describes these as 'fairly standard' exclusions (UNCTAD (2010), *Most Favoured Nation Treatment*, op. cit., at 46). See for example, Indian model BIPPA, Art. 4(3); UK model IPPA, Art. 7; Colombian Model Agreement, Art. IV.3.

88 See Annex III to the Canadian model FIPA.

2. *A post-establishment MFN obligation that may be limited in one or all of these ways*

a. Limited to specific activities (and *not* including activities such as establishment, acquisition and expansion)

This approach to drafting an IIA provision clarifies the scope of the obligation by limiting it to identified activities for the benefit of both investors and host states. The specification of activities to which the obligation applies may be interpreted as excluding the application of the MFN obligation to dispute settlement procedures in other IIAs. In the interests of clarity, recent IIAs often include a specific exception from the application of the MFN obligation to dispute settlement procedures in other IIAs. By excluding activities such as establishment, acquisition and expansion, this provision does not extend to pre-establishment activities.

b. Limited to foreign investors 'in like circumstances'

A reference to 'in like circumstances' directs a tribunal to make sure that it considers a variety of factors to determine what foreign investors should be included in comparisons for the purposes of applying the MFN obligation. Some view the MFN obligation as inherently requiring such a determination, whether it refers to 'in like circumstances' or not. An express requirement to find that foreign investors are 'in like circumstances' provides clear direction to an interpreter of the provision. An analysis of 'in like circumstances' that takes into account the purpose of the measure may provide more scope for a state to engage in policies for non-discriminatory purposes that may have a discriminatory effect on foreign businesses from the other IIA party state. For the purposes of a particular policy, foreign investors from that state may not be in like circumstances with foreign investors from other states. An MFN obligation can provide more direction to an interpreter of the obligation by identifying possibly relevant circumstances that should be taken into account.

c. Limited to listed policy areas, sectors and measures (positive list) or excluding listed sectors and measures (negative list)

Most IIAs exclude the application of the MFN obligation to some sectors or measures to reflect existing domestic policy that grants discriminatory preferences to foreigners and/or areas of policy where a state wants to be able to discriminate in the future between foreign investors. A negative list approach requires a state to list a sector or measure if the obligation is to be avoided. A positive list approach requires a state to list a sector or measure for the obligation to apply. Positive listing is a less burdensome approach because it is not necessary to list sectors or measures to avoid the application of the MFN obligation. With a positive list, however, remaining discriminatory restrictions are not disclosed to the other party state or its investors.

d. Subject to general exceptions

Exceptions can be used to carve out areas of state policy-making from the application of the MFN obligation and are being increasingly used in IIA practice. Exceptions limit the benefits of the obligation for investors. In the case of MFN, IIAs often contain exceptions that apply only to MFN obligations, in the interests of rendering the effect of the MFN provision more predictable. Two important and common categories of exceptions from MFN obligations are for commitments in preferential trading agreements and dispute resolution procedures in other IIAs.

e. Limiting MFN to *de jure* discrimination

The scope of an MFN obligation can be restricted to state measures that are *de jure* discriminatory. In other words, only measures that expressly discriminate against a foreign investor from one country compared with foreign investors from other countries based on the investor's nationality are prohibited. This approach creates a clear and predictable obligation, but one that is very limited in its scope. This approach is not currently followed in any IIA. Investors may be concerned that it is often difficult to distinguish between measures that are *de jure* and those that are only *de facto* discriminatory. Also, governments could draft measures that do not use language that is discriminatory, but then apply the measure in a discriminatory way. If an IIA prohibits only *de jure* discrimination, there would be no breach of the treaty in these circumstances.

3. *A pre-establishment MFN obligation that may be limited in the same ways as discussed in option 2*

A pre-establishment MFN obligation means that foreign investors must be treated no less favourably than other foreign businesses with respect to entry into the host state market. If specific activities to which the obligation applies are listed, they will include activities such as establishment, acquisition and expansion. Positive listing or negative listing can be used to ensure that the obligation does not apply to discriminatory entry restrictions for foreign investment that a state wants to maintain.

5.4.6 Discussion of sample provision

The Guide sample provision follows the approach in many IIAs and limits the application of the MFN obligation to situations in which foreign and domestic investors are 'in like circumstances'. This approach helps to ensure that investor–state tribunals engage in a serious investigation with a view to determining that the comparator used to define what MFN requires in relation to a foreign investor is a truly comparable foreign investor from another state. Such an approach may enhance regulatory flexibility compared with the unqualified formulations of the MFN obligation in some other national models. As with the national treatment provision, a list of factors to be taken into account in determining whether investors or their investments are 'in like circumstances' is set out in the sample provision with a view to helping to define more clearly when different treatment is permitted. For further certainty, the sample provision expressly states that a state measure that treats investors of the other party or their investments less favourably than investors of another state or their investments is not inconsistent with the MFN obligation if it is applied by the state in pursuit of a legitimate public purpose not based on the nationality of the investor and bears a reasonable connection to the purpose.

In addition, like most IIA provisions, the sample provision is limited to certain identified situations with a view to clarifying the scope of the obligation.[89] Consistent with widespread practice, a right of establishment is not provided for in the sample provision. The references to 'establishment', 'acquisition' and 'expansion' in the list of activities to which the obligation applies, found in the Canadian and US models, have not been included.[90] Limiting the scope of application of the MFN clause to certain situations should also eliminate the risk that dispute settlement provisions in other agreements could be accessed through the MFN clause by investors from states not party to those agreements, as in *Maffezini*.[91] It seems likely that the importation of investor–state dispute settlement procedures, and even other substantive treaty standards, was not foreseen, at least in treaties negotiated prior to *Maffezini* and the other cases that address this issue. In the interests of greater certainty, the sample provision in the Guide creates a number of specific exceptions to the MFN obligation as discussed below:

- **All international agreements existing at the time the IIA comes into force**: As an alternative, it would be possible to exclude only existing bilateral and regional agreements that require party states to accord preferences to investors from other parties based on their nationality, which would include not only investment agreements and free trade agreements, but also double taxation agreements and other forms of economic co-operation and economic partnership treaties. This is the approach adopted in the COMESA Investment Agreement.[92] It would also be possible to create a more limited exclusion that applied only to agreements creating such preferences that a party state listed as exceptions to the MFN obligation. This would be a more transparent approach to reconciling these kinds of preferences with the MFN obligation in an IIA. However, such an approach would be more burdensome. A straightforward exception for all existing agreements was adopted as an example of a provision that provides administrative simplicity and a high level of certainty for host states regarding the scope of the obligation.
- **Defined categories of future international agreements that create preferences based on nationality**: The categories exempted are those found in most IIAs: agreements (i) establishing, strengthening or expanding a free trade area, customs union, common market, labour market integration commitment or similar international agreement; (ii) promoting investment; or (iii) relating wholly or mainly to taxation.

89 E.g. the Canadian and US model agreements (Canadian model FIPA, Art. 4; US model BIT, Art. 4). See, similarly, the draft Norwegian APPI (Art. 4) and others.

90 Expansion includes an investment of new foreign capital to expand an existing business carried on by an investor. Similarly acquisition includes acquisitions financed by new foreign capital. However, an expansion or acquisition would also include transactions or activities financed in the host state. If an IIA contains a clear admission clause that ensures that any new investment must meet domestic requirements for admission, then expansion and acquisition could be included in the list of activities to which the obligation applies without creating a right of establishment.

91 *Maffezini v Spain*, op. cit.

92 COMESA Investment Agreement (2007), Arts. 19.1 and 19.3.

- **Any dispute settlement procedures in any other international agreement.**
- **Other agreements:** The sample provision contemplates that states may identify their own categories of future agreements in addition to those that are listed in the Guide provision that would be excepted from the MFN obligation.

Limiting the scope of the MFN obligation in all these ways prevents the importation of standards into a treaty relationship where those standards go beyond what the parties intended. Inevitably, this approach is imperfect. When negotiating new agreements, states will have to bear in mind the requirements of these limited exceptions for future agreements. If any commitments undertaken in future agreements do not fall within the exceptions, they may have to be extended to investors from a party state to those earlier IIAs through the operation of the MFN clause. Alternatives would include: (i) exempting *all* future preferential agreements that a party state might enter into; or (ii) not including an MFN obligation at all. Of course carving more future agreements out of the MFN obligation will reduce its value to investors. Not including an MFN obligation in an IIA means that foreign investors get no protection against domestic measures preferring foreign investors from other states and further reduces the value of the agreement to investors. The approach taken in the Guide provision represents a compromise, providing limited benefits for investors in terms of the future international commitments of a host state but full protection in relation to domestic measures. Limiting MFN in the ways described is unlikely to be perceived as affecting significantly the interests of investors, since they do not affect the basic non-discrimination obligation with respect to state domestic measures.

Finally, as with the national treatment obligation, the Guide includes sample provisions that provide for exceptions and country-specific reservations applicable to the MFN obligations.[93] Examples include public procurement and subsidies. As discussed, an alternative would be to have the MFN obligation apply only to sectors and measures that a state positively agrees to list. This option is provided for in brackets in the sample provision.

5.4.7 Sample provision: most favoured nation treatment

Most Favoured Nation Treatment

1. Every Party shall accord to investors of the other Party and their investments treatment no less favourable than that it accords, in like circumstances, to investors of any other state or to their investments with respect to the management, conduct, operation and sale or other disposition of investments in its territory.
2. For greater certainty:
    a. A determination of whether an investment or an investor are in like circumstances for the purposes of this article shall be made based on an assessment of all of the circumstances related to the investor or the investment, including:
        i. The effect of the investment on

93 See Section 5.12 (Reservations and exceptions).

A. the community;

B. the human rights of individuals and the rights of indigenous peoples;

C. the environment, including effects relating to the cumulative impact of all investments within a jurisdiction;

ii. The business sector in which the investor operates;

iii. The goal of the alleged discriminatory measure; and

iv. The regulation that applies to the investment or investor;

b. A measure of a Party that treats investors of the other Party or their investments less favourably than investors of another state or their investments is not inconsistent with this article if it is applied by the Party in pursuit of a legitimate public purpose that is not based on the nationality of investors, including the protection of health, safety and the environment, internationally and domestically recognised human rights, labour rights or the rights of indigenous peoples, or the elimination of bribery and corruption, and it bears a reasonable relationship to the purpose.

3. This article shall not apply to:

a. Treatment by a Party under any bilateral or multilateral international agreement in force or signed by the Party prior to the date of entry into force of this Agreement;

b. Treatment by a Party pursuant to any future bilateral or multilateral agreement:

i. Establishing, strengthening or expanding a free trade area, customs union, common market, labour market integration commitment or similar international agreement;

ii. Promoting investment; or

iii. Relating wholly or mainly to taxation or …;[94] or

iv. Any dispute settlement procedures.

[4. This article shall apply only to measures that a Party adopts or maintains with respect to sectors, subsectors or activities, as set out in its schedule to Annex 1 of this agreement.]

94 Each country should consider what specific categories of agreements should be listed based on its existing and anticipated future international commitments. Agreements may relate, for example, to aviation, fisheries or maritime transport, including salvage. These are areas where access is frequently granted to investors from particular states on the basis of reciprocal access from the other party state. (See Canadian model FIPA, Annex III).

5.5 Fair and equitable treatment and the minimum standard of treatment

Cross references

5.5.1 Introduction

Most IIAs require party states to provide a minimum standard of treatment to the investments of investors of the other party state, which is described using the words 'fair and equitable treatment' (FET).[95] The general purpose of requiring fair and equitable treatment of investments is to protect investors against serious abuse and arbitrary or discriminatory actions by host states by requiring a standard of fair treatment. Unlike the national treatment and MFN standards, the FET standard is not a relative one. This means that regardless of how a state treats its own nationals and their investments, treatment of foreign investors and their investments cannot fall below the minimum standard defined in the treaty.

FET provisions have been the IIA provisions most frequently relied on by investors in investor–state arbitration claims and have resulted in the most successful claims. This is not surprising. The standard is inherently broad and open-ended. There are, potentially, an unlimited number of situations in which investors may claim that their investments have been treated by a host state in a manner that is not fair and equitable. In addition, investors have been encouraged to make claims based on FET because investor–state arbitration tribunals have interpreted the FET standard in a wide variety of ways, sometimes leading to surprising results. A number of commentators have expressed concerns that the FET standard as it has been applied creates a significant risk that it will be used to constrain a state's sovereignty and its ability to regulate in the public interest.[96]

As discussed below, there is now a well-developed debate about the content of the FET standard, but little certainty regarding what this obligation requires of states in particular circumstances.[97] The uncertainty of the standard makes it challenging for states to implement the FET obligation with confidence and encourages 'regulatory chill' – states concerned about complying with their obligations and managing the risk of investor–state claims may try to avoid any action that even might be a breach of the standard.

---

95 For example, the Indian model BIPPA, Art. 3(2) simply refers to fair and equitable treatment.

96 R Kläger (2011), 'Fair and Equitable Treatment and Sustainable Development', in Cordonier Segger et al., op. cit., at 241; G Mayeda (2007), 'Playing Fair: The Meaning of Fair and Equitable Treatment in Bilateral Investment Treaties (BITs)', 41 *Journal of World Trade* 273.

97 Ibid.

The essential problem is that the FET standard has no definable specific meaning.[98] This has made it useful as a gap-filling device because not all kinds of state misbehaviour can be caught by the more specific investor protection standards in IIAs, but has also rendered its application unpredictable. IIAs provide little guidance to tribunals regarding the interpretation of the standard, though statements regarding the purpose and priorities of the party states in IIA preambles and objectives provisions may be helpful in particular cases. The lack of predictability is aggravated by the fact that prior decisions in investor–state cases do not constitute binding precedents for subsequent decisions.

The discussion below surveys existing state practice regarding FET provisions in IIAs and identifies the main considerations regarding their application.

5.5.2 IIA practice

While almost all IIAs have some kind of FET provision, the expression of the standard varies considerably.[99] For states that have signed multiple IIAs with different versions of the FET obligation this diversity makes it difficult for them to keep track of their obligations.[100] Some treaties simply require party states to provide fair and equitable treatment.[101] Others combine an FET standard with additional treaty requirements for 'full protection and security', and obligations not to discriminate against or act unreasonably in relation to foreign investments.[102]

As will be discussed below, one of the difficult issues with respect to FET is to what extent it represents an expression of the minimum standard of treatment required of host states under customary international law as opposed to an autonomous treaty standard. How FET is characterised in this regard can have an impact on the content of the obligations. There are variations in treaty provisions in terms of how they describe the relationship between FET and international law. Some treaties require that fair and equitable treatment be provided 'in accordance with international law', suggesting that the standard is to be defined by reference to international law, including customary law, general principles of international law and other sources of international law. For example, NAFTA requires 'treatment in accordance with

98 UNCTAD (2012), *A Review of Fair and Equitable Treatment: A Sequel*, United Nations, New York and Geneva, at 2–3.

99 Not all agreements, however, contain such an obligation (e.g. India–Singapore CECA (2005); Australia–Singapore Free Trade Agreement, signed 17 February 2003, in force 28 July 2003; and the AALCC model agreements, though the inclusion of an FET obligation was suggested by Kuwait). Whether the minimum standard required by customary international law can be enforced through investor–state arbitration under an IIA with no FET obligation depends on the scope of the dispute settlement procedures. If the procedures are available only for breaches to the treaty then they cannot be used in this way, unless FET can be incorporated into the agreement through an MFN provision.

100 This kind of problem can be complicated by the presence of MFN provisions that may be argued to import the higher FET standard agreed to by a state into another treaty, as discussed in the previous section. See Article Section 5.4 (Most favoured nation).

101 Indian model BIPPA, Art. 3(2) simply refers to 'fair and equitable treatment'.

102 UK model IPPA, Art. 2, contains all of these obligations.

international law, including fair and equitable treatment and full protection and security'.[103] Other treaties tie FET only to the minimum standard imposed on host states by customary international law. The Canadian model treaty, for example, seeks to limit the scope of application of FET by defining the standard as 'treatment in accordance with the customary international law minimum standard of treatment of aliens, including fair and equitable treatment and full protection and security'.[104] The Canadian provision goes on to specify that fair and equitable treatment and full protection and security do not require treatment 'in addition to or beyond that which is required by the customary international law minimum standard of treatment of aliens'.[105] In 2001, the NAFTA Free Trade Commission issued a binding interpretation saying that the FET standard in that treaty means the customary international law standard for the treatment of aliens.[106]

More recent treaties have started to include additional language clarifying the meaning of the obligation in specific ways. The US model BIT specifies that the FET obligation includes a commitment:

> ... not to deny justice in criminal, civil, or administrative adjudicatory proceedings in accordance with the principle of due process embodied in the principal legal systems of the world.[107]

Additional specific treaty stipulations regarding the content of the standard include prohibitions on arbitrary, unreasonable or discriminatory measures.

Some treaties provide that breaches of other treaty rights do not result in a breach of the minimum standard of treatment. This clarifies the scope of the provision and avoids the application of some investor–state dispute settlement cases that have ruled the opposite.[108]

The COMESA Investment Agreement adopts a different approach. It expresses member states' understanding that the international minimum standard is not a single standard, that different states have different forms of administrative, legislative and

103 NAFTA (1992), Art. 1105.

104 Canadian model FIPA, Art. 5. The Norwegian Draft model APPI uses the same wording (Art. 5). See also the ASEAN–Australia–New Zealand FTA (2009), Chapter 11, Art. 6.

105 Ibid. COMESA Investment Agreement (2007) (Art. 14) and the US model BIT (Art. 5(2)) contain similar language.

106 NAFTA Free Trade Commission Notes of Interpretation, 31 July 2001.

107 US model BIT, Art. 5; and see COMESA Investment Agreement (2007), Art. 14. The ASEAN Agreement (Art. 11) specifies that FET 'requires' parties not to deny justice. The IISD model treaty is very similar (Art. 8). In some treaty models, these additional standards are referred to separately without being tied to FET.

108 This second type of specification appeared in provisions negotiated after the NAFTA (1992) decision in *S D Myers v. Canada*, op. cit., para. 261, which held that a breach of national treatment was a breach of NAFTA's FET standard. This conclusion was effectively reversed by the FTC Notes on Interpretation, 2001. As a general rule, the amount of compensation will not be different regardless of whether the conduct concerned is held in breach of one or two IIA obligations.

judicial systems, and that member states at different levels of development may not all achieve the same standards at the same time.[109]

As noted, the requirement that the host state provide 'full protection and security' to investments of foreign investors is often included in provisions relating to fair and equitable treatment, though it sometimes appears as a stand-alone obligation in an IIA.[110] The duty to provide full protection and security is generally understood to require the host state to take active steps, such as through police protection, to protect a foreign investor's investment from injury – traditionally understood as physical injury – resulting from civil unrest or local violence. It does not constitute an absolute commitment to protect in all circumstances. The state's obligation has been characterised as an obligation to take such steps as may be reasonable in the circumstances.[111] Some tribunals have extended its application to the protection of the security of legal rights and economic interests. In effect, this approach treats full protection and security as a part of FET.

5.5.3 Minimum standard of treatment required by customary international law versus an autonomous treaty standard[112]

Where treaties have referred simply to 'fair and equitable treatment,' the obligation on states has often been given a broader interpretation than treaty standards that are tied to the international minimum standard required by customary international law, though the content of both obligations is contested.[113] The purpose of tying FET to customary international law in IIAs is to try to ensure that FET is not interpreted as an autonomous treaty standard and to avoid overly broad interpretations of the provision. Part of the rationale for this approach is that customary international law standards must be demonstrated through state behaviour arising out of a sense of legal obligation, which must be objectively determined. If 'fair and equitable treatment' is not restricted to the customary international law standard, however, this standard could be understood as an open-ended and unpredictable requirement for a state to act fairly, leaving it to an investor–state arbitration tribunal to determine what is fair in particular circumstances. Some tribunals have followed such an approach, though a few have suggested that a state's misconduct must meet a minimum threshold of seriousness before a breach will be found.[114] Under this approach, not every case of unfairness will justify a finding of state liability.

Unfortunately, the content of the minimum standard itself is not well developed and the approach of arbitral tribunals has not been consistent, leaving significant residual uncertainty. The development of the customary international law standard and its recent application are described in the next section.

---

109 COMESA Investment Agreement (2007), Art. 14.3.

110 This language is typical of Caribbean BITs and found in all Pacific BITs (Malik, op. cit., at 17, 50).

111 Dolzer and Schreuer, op. cit., at 149–150, describing the obligation as one to provide due diligence.

112 Customary international law results from a general and consistent practice of states that they follow from a sense of legal obligation.

113 Most Caribbean BITs and all Pacific BITs use this language (Malik, op. cit., at 16, 49). This language is also used in the ASEAN Agreement (2009), Art. 11.

114 Malik, ibid., at 88.

5.5.4 Evolution of the customary international law minimum standard

Historically, the source of the FET standard is the customary international law minimum standard of treatment.[115] Some developing countries have traditionally denied the existence of an international minimum standard. They have argued that state sovereignty permits national governments to set the standard of fairness applicable to foreign nationals and their investments.[116] Numerous investor–state tribunals, however, have found that a minimum standard is required by customary law.

International arbitration tribunals have differed, however, in their interpretation of what the minimum standard requires. In contemporary investor–state arbitration, particularly in NAFTA cases, the starting point for defining the requirements of FET is often a famous case called *The Neer Claim* decided in 1926.[117] The case deals with whether Mexico failed to take adequate steps to investigate and prosecute the murderer of an American, resulting in a denial of justice.[118] The tribunal found that customary international law prohibits egregious or outrageous behaviour by a state towards a foreign citizen.

> [T]he treatment of an alien, in order to constitute an international delinquency, should amount to an outrage, to bad faith, to wilful neglect of duty, or to an insufficiency of governmental action so far short of international standards that every reasonable and impartial man would readily recognize its insufficiency.[119]

While this standard clearly sets a high threshold for challenging state action, its content is indeterminate. Since *Neer* addressed only the denial of justice in relation to individual aliens, it has not been clear what it requires in relation to foreign investors and their investments. Another significant question is to what extent the standard has evolved since the *Neer* decision.

---

115 Ibid., at 5.

116 Historically, developing countries, particularly in Latin America, have supported the *Calvo Doctrine*, which asserts the sovereignty of developing countries and their freedom from interference by other states, as well as the principle that foreign nationals ought not to be given treatment to which nationals are not entitled (D Shea, *The Calvo Clause: A Problem of Inter-American and International Law and Diplomacy* (1955), University of Minnesota Press, Minneapolis, at 19–20). Proponents of the doctrine oppose the development of minimum standards of treatment for foreign nationals in customary international law, since these standards do not respect the exclusive jurisdiction of the host country. See also D Manning-Cabrol (1995), 'The Imminent Death of the Calvo Clause and the Rebirth of the Calvo Principle: Equality of Foreign and National Investors', 26 *Law and Policy in International Business*, 1169; B Tamanaha (1995), 'The Lessons of Law and Development Studies', 89 *American Journal of International Law*, 470 at 478; T Guha Roy (1961), 'Is the Law of Responsibility of States for Injuries to Aliens a Part of Universal International Law?', 55 *American Journal of International Law* 863.

117 Some researchers argue that *Neer* does not represent an accurate statement of customary law: e.g. J Thornton (2012), 'Divining the Content of the Customary International Law Minimum Standard Treatment from the Jurisprudence of the US–Mexico General Claims Commission', *World Arbitration and Mediation Review* (forthcoming).

118 *Neer v. Mexico, Opinion*, United States–Mexico General Claims Commission, 15 October 1926, (1927), 21 *American Journal of International Law* 555.

119 Ibid.

In a 2009 NAFTA case, the tribunal held that the investor had not succeeded in proving that the standard had evolved beyond what it had been found to require in *Neer*. The tribunal described the standard in the following terms:

> The Tribunal therefore holds that a violation of the customary international law minimum standard of treatment, as codified in Article 1105 of the NAFTA, requires an act that is sufficiently egregious and shocking – a gross denial of justice, manifest arbitrariness, blatant unfairness, a complete lack of due process, evident discrimination, or a manifest lack of reasons – so as to fall below accepted international standards and constitute a breach of Article 1105. Such a breach may be exhibited by a 'gross denial of justice or manifest arbitrariness falling below acceptable international standards'; or the creation by the State of objective expectations *in order to induce* investment and the subsequent repudiation of those expectations. (References omitted.)[120]

A number of investor–state cases under NAFTA have agreed that a state action must be shocking or serious to breach the standard, as this quote suggests.[121] NAFTA tribunals have acknowledged that what is considered shocking or serious is likely to have evolved over time,[122] but the exact nature of the evolution is not clear. In addition, arbitral tribunals have confirmed that it is possible that the customary standard in *Neer* has changed through consistent state practice engaged in out of a sense of legal obligation. However, it has proved difficult for investors to successfully show that the standard has changed over time or that it imposes specific requirements.[123] In this regard, tribunals have not been consistent regarding what is needed to prove an evolution in customary law. Some tribunals have decided that arbitral tribunal decisions do not create or prove customary international law, though they may be looked at as illustrations of customary law if they are interpreting the customary international law minimum standard and not an autonomous FET standard.[124] Others have looked to the practice of states in signing IIAs with FET provisions as evidence of an evolving standard, but have not identified specifically what it requires.[125]

In 2010, a NAFTA tribunal determined that the autonomous standard has become part of customary law based on what it described as widespread and consistent practice.[126] Unfortunately, this award failed to explain the basis for its conclusions that the minimum standard has evolved in this way.[127] Recently, UNCTAD has

---

120 *Glamis Gold, Ltd. v. United States of America*, UNCITRAL, Award, 8 June 2009, at para. 627.

121 Some tribunals have adopted an apparently lower threshold. In *Waste Management*, for example, the tribunal synthesised the standard as prohibiting state behaviour that is 'arbitrary, grossly unfair, unjust or idiosyncratic' or that is 'discriminatory and exposes the claimant to sectional or racial prejudice' (*Waste Management v. Mexico*, op. cit., at para. 98).

122 *Mondev International Ltd v. United States*, ICSID Case No. ARB (AF)/99/2, Award, 11 October 2002.

123 *Glamis Gold*, op. cit., at para. 614, referring to other NAFTA awards.

124 *Glamis Gold*, ibid., at para. 605.

125 *Mondev*, op. cit., at paras. 114–19.

126 *Merrill and Ring v. Canada*, UNCITRAL, Award 31 March 2010. See also *Waste Management v. Mexico*, op. cit., at para. 98.

127 UNCTAD (2012), *Fair and Equitable Treatment*, op. cit., at 57.

suggested that there is evidence of a long-term trend in the cases towards *de facto* convergence in terms of the categories of state behaviour that may raise concerns under FET.[128] A remaining difference seems to be that a higher threshold for the seriousness of state conduct must be established if an FET standard is limited to the minimum standard of treatment under customary international law. Investors making claims under NAFTA, where the FET obligation is limited to the minimum standard in customary international law, have been less successful than investors seeking relief under other treaty standards on the basis of a breach of FET.[129] There is no guarantee, however, that a higher threshold for finding a breach of state action will be adopted in interpreting an FET obligation tied to customary law.

5.5.5 What the FET standard requires

General requirements

In terms of its specific content, the following synthesis of the categories of requirements imposed by FET was recently provided by UNCTAD:

a. Prohibition of manifest arbitrariness in decision-making, that is measures taken purely on the basis of prejudice or bias without a legitimate purpose or rational explanation;

b. Prohibition of the denial of justice and disregard of the fundamental principles of due process;

c. Prohibition of targeted discrimination on manifestly wrongful grounds, such as gender, race or religious belief;

d. Prohibition of abusive treatment of investors, including coercion, duress and harassment;

e. Protection of the legitimate expectations of investors arising from a government's specific representations or investment-inducing measures, although balanced with the host State's right to regulate in the public interest.[130]

---

128 UNCTAD (2012), *Fair and Equitable Treatment*, ibid., at 59–60.

129 Ibid., at 60–1.

130 Ibid., at 62–3. The OECD takes the view that the fair and equitable treatment standard goes beyond customary international law to impose the following additional requirements:

1. An obligation of vigilance and protection (i.e. an obligation to exercise due diligence in protecting foreign investments);
2. An obligation of transparency in the treatment of foreign investors;
3. An obligation of good faith, which includes an obligation to protect the basic expectations of investors created by the treaty;
4. An obligation to respect 'autonomous fairness elements', which seems to include fairness obligations beyond those required by international law and that are generally recognised in the legal systems of states with well-developed legal systems.

(OECD (September 2004), 'Fair and Equitable Treatment Standard in International Investment Law', Working Papers on International Investment No. 2004/3 at 26–39).

Protection of legitimate expectations

It is the obligation to protect the legitimate expectations of investors that has the greatest potential to cause difficulty for host developing countries. The concept of legitimate expectations is complex and has not been treated in a uniform way by investor–state tribunals. The key elements of the approaches taken to determining what are an investor's legitimate expectations are identified below:

- **Legitimate expectations of investors require host states to provide a stable and predictable investment environment:** Some investment tribunals have interpreted this aspect of the FET obligation broadly as requiring the host state to ensure that the conditions that induced the investor to invest are not to be disturbed.[131] Such a wide interpretation of the principle of fair and equitable treatment provides tribunals with substantial scope to grant relief whenever the legal and regulatory frameworks of a host state are changed. Some tribunals have expressly determined that a breach of legitimate expectations may occur in these circumstances, even if the state is acting in the good faith pursuit of a legitimate regulatory goal.[132] Such a broad approach to protection has been criticised as unreasonable on the basis that it prevents any regulatory reform.[133]
- **Legitimate expectations must include an expectation of the risk of regulatory change over time:** In response to the concerns noted in the previous point, some tribunals have recognised that while investors may generally expect a stable and predictable regulatory regime, especially the maintenance of the conditions upon which they based their initial decisions to invest, regulatory change is to be expected over time and this consideration should inform what is a legitimate expectation of investors.[134] More generally, in some cases tribunals have said that in identifying an investor's legitimate expectations, it is necessary to take into account the facts relating to the investment as well as 'the political, socioeconomic, cultural and historical conditions prevailing in the host state'. In *Vivendi II*, for example, it was recognised that a newly elected government that advocated different policies from its predecessors should be permitted to adopt a different approach to regulation.[135] In order to achieve its regulatory objective, however, a state must act in a manner otherwise consistent with all IIA obligations, including the other requirements of FET. In *Vivendi II*, the new government's change in policy affected a contract that the investor had entered into. The tribunal suggested that the state should

131 CMS Gas, op. cit.; *Tecnicas Medioambientales Tecmed S.A. v. Estados Unidos Mexicanos*, ICSID Case No. ARB (AF)/00/2, Award, 29 May 2003, at para. 154; *CME Czech Republic B.V. v. The Czech Republic*, UNCITRAL, Award, 14 March 2003, at para. 601; *Occidental Exploration and Production Company v. Republic of Ecuador*, Case No. UN 3467, Final Award, 1 July 2004, at para. 190.

132 *Enron v. Argentina*, op. cit., at paras. 164–168. This part of the decision was upheld by an annulment panel: *Enron v. Argentina*, Decision on the Application for Annulment, 30 July 2010, at paras. 298–316.

133 This approach was suggested in UNCTAD (2012), *Fair and Equitable Treatment*, op. cit.

134 E.g. *Saluka v. Czech Republic* UNCITRAL, Partial Award, 17 March 2006, at paras. 304–8; *Glamis Gold*, op. cit.

135 *Suez, Sociedad General de Aguas de Barcelona SA and Vivendi Universal SA v. Argentine Republic*, (2003) ICSID Case No. ARB/03/19, Decision on Liability, 30 July 2010 (called Vivendi II), at para. 7.4.31.

be able to seek to renegotiate the contract, but that the renegotiations should be transparent and non-coercive. They should not be accompanied by 'threats of rescission' based on unfounded allegations.

- **Legitimate expectations must take into account the level of development of the host state:** What an investor may legitimately expect from a developing country and its institutions cannot be the same as it would expect from a developed country.[136] This is really only a specific example of the approach mentioned in the previous point.
- **Legitimate expectations may be produced by specific acts of the host state in relation to the investor:** Specific representations by host country officials and contractual commitments are generally accepted as providing a basis for legitimate expectations.[137] With respect to contractual commitments, contractual performance may be a reasonable expectation, but not all breaches of contract should be treated as breaches of FET.[138]
- **An investor's behaviour may be relevant to determining the investor's legitimate expectations:** With regard to defining an investor's legitimate expectations, the investor's own behaviour will be relevant in some circumstances. For example, if the investor has engaged in fraud or misrepresentation, or otherwise acted so as to cause the state to act, it will be more difficult for the investor to establish that the state's action was inconsistent with its expectations.[139] In addition, the investor must have relied on what are alleged to be its legitimate expectations in making the investment in order to succeed in claiming a breach of FET on this basis.[140] Some tribunals have taken a different approach to this issue. Where a breach of FET is found, they have taken into account the behaviour of the investor and the interests of the state in assessing the damages to be paid to the investor. Tribunals have required investors to have carried out due diligence investigations to inform their expectations and where an investor has not acted reasonably in this regard, the tribunal has reduced the damages awarded to the investor.[141]

---

136 *Genin v. Estonia*, ICSID Case No. ARB/99/2, Award, 25 June 2001, at para. 367; *Parkerings-Compagniet v. Lithuania*, ICSID Case No. ARB/05/8, Award, 11 September 2007, at para. 344. It is not clear to what extent this is conceptually consistent where the standard is equated to the customary international law minimum standard which is intended to create a floor below which no state may go (UNCTAD (2012), *Fair and Equitable Treatment*, op. cit., at 34–5).

137 Ibid.

138 C Schreuer (2007), 'Fair and Equitable Treatment: Interactions with Other Standards', 4 *Transnational Dispute Management* 17.

139 For example, in *EDF v. Romania*, ICSID Case No. ARB/05/13, Award, 8 October 2009, the tribunal determined that Romania's prohibition of duty-free businesses at domestic airports was held to be a reasonable response to contraband activities being carried out by those businesses.

140 *Duke Energy v. Ecuador*, ICSID Case No. ARB/04/19, Award, 18 August 2008, at para. 340.

141 *MTD v. Chile*, ICSID Case No. ARB/01/07, Award, 25 May 2004: damages reduced by 50 per cent where an independent assessment would have revealed that the authorisation received was not permitted by local law.

- **An investor's legitimate expectations must be weighed against host states' legitimate interest in regulating for the public good:** A number of tribunals have recognised that in determining whether there has been a breach of FET, it is necessary to weigh whatever legitimate expectations an investor is found to have with the interest of the state in regulating. This does not mean that states may act however they choose to achieve their regulatory objectives. A state must act in a good faith and in a manner otherwise consistent with all IIA obligations, including the other requirements of FET.[142]

Box 5.7 Options for a fair and equitable treatment provision

1. *No FET obligation;*
2. *FET obligation linked to the minimum standard of treatment of aliens under customary international law;*
3. *FET obligation linked to international law;*
4. *Unqualified FET obligation to accord fair and equitable treatment (the autonomous standard);*
5. *FET obligation (whether or not linked to international law or the minimum standard of treatment of aliens under customary international law) with additional substantive content, such as a prohibition on denial of justice or treatment of investor and its investments that is manifestly arbitrary, discriminatory or abusive, to clarify its meaning;* and
6. *No FET obligation but specification of prohibited state actions as in option 5.*

5.5.6 Discussion of options

1. *No FET obligation*

The minimum standard of treatment under customary international law would still apply even if no FET obligation were included in a treaty. Probably this standard could not be enforced through investor–state arbitration under an IIA, though this would depend on the scope of the dispute settlement provisions in the IIA. Not including an FET obligation would be inconsistent with the dominant IIA practice and would undoubtedly be a concern for capital-exporting states. Nevertheless, in light of its unpredictability, some capital-importing states may seek to exclude it.

If an IIA contains no FET obligation, but (i) the IIA contains an MFN obligation; and (ii) the state party had entered into another IIA that contained an FET provision,

142 *Saluka v. Czech Republic*, op. cit., at paras. 304–8.

it is possible that the FET obligation would be incorporated into the treaty through the MFN obligation.

2. *FET obligation linked to the minimum standard of treatment of aliens under customary international law*

This is an approach intended to limit the scope of the FET obligation. In principle, an investor would have to prove what the standard required based on general and consistent state practice of states motivated by a sense of legal obligation, though tribunals have not always strictly adhered to these requirements. There is also uncertainty regarding what the standard requires. Some tribunals have determined that the categories of state action that can be addressed under the minimum standard of treatment are converging with those that can be addressed under an autonomous FET standard (option 4). The liability threshold may be higher under the customary international law standard, though this is not clear. Nevertheless, many IIAs, including the US and Canadian model agreements, adopt this approach with a view to limiting the scope of the obligation.

3. *FET obligation linked to international law*

The standard must be determined by reference to all sources of international law. Some IIAs adopt this approach. It is not clear how this standard is different in practice from option 2. A link to customary international law is more specific.

4. *Unqualified FET obligation to accord fair and equitable treatment (the autonomous standard)*

This obligation provides maximum assurance to investors, but allows for far-reaching review of host state actions by investor–state arbitration tribunals based on an uncertain standard of fairness.

5. *FET obligation (whether or not linked to international law or the minimum standard of treatment of aliens under customary international law) with additional substantive content, such as a prohibition on denial of justice or treatment of investor and its investments that is manifestly arbitrary, discriminatory or abusive, to clarify its meaning*

It is not clear how this standard is different in practice from options 2, 3 and 4. Most of the additional language used in treaties has described elements that tribunals have found to be part of the FET standard in any case. FET could be defined as including only those standards identified. This would clarify the scope of the obligation.

6. *No FET obligation, but specification of specific prohibited state actions as in option 5*

The scope of this obligation depends on the language used. It avoids the risk of an open-ended FET standard, but the terms used instead may introduce new uncertainty. Most of the language used to specify what is prohibited refers to aspects of what tribunals have found to be part of the FET standard such as a prohibition on denial of justice or treatment of investor and its investments that is manifestly arbitrary, discriminatory or abusive.

With respect to options 2, 3, 5 and 6, if (i) a state has imposed limitations on the scope of the FET obligation in an IIA, (ii) the IIA contains an MFN obligation and (iii) the state has entered into another IIA that contains an FET provision without these limitations, it is possible that the more favourable FET obligation will be incorporated into the treaty.[143]

5.5.7 Discussion of sample provision

The FET standard has been the subject of a large number of arbitral decisions that have not produced a consistent approach to interpretation – or consistent results. Some decisions have been criticised as imposing inappropriate constraints on state regulatory power. In this context, states may decide that the best course of action is not to agree to an FET provision at all. On the other hand, capital-exporting states and their investors may prefer a simple statement of FET as an autonomous standard to provide the broadest protection.

The Guide sample provision sets out an example of how an FET provision can be made somewhat more certain than existing provisions. In general this has been done by making explicit some of the limitations on the standard developed in the arbitral cases. It must be acknowledged, however, that significant residual uncertainty remains about how the provision will be applied in particular circumstances. As an alternative, a state may seek to include specific commitments without referring to the minimum standard of treatment or FET. While this approach avoids the uncertainty associated with the FET standard, referring to new treaty standards such as a prohibition on denial of justice or manifestly arbitrary treatment raises new issues of interpretation and uncertainty. The approach adopted in the sample provision may be summarised as follows:

- **FET tied to minimum standard established by customary international law:** As is common in many IIAs, the sample provision specifies that foreign investors can expect to be treated in accordance with the international minimum standard established by customary international law for the treatment of foreign nationals. This language follows the Canadian and US models among others. This has been achieved by referring to the standards of fair and equitable treatment and full protection and security, but qualifying these standards as equivalent to and subsumed within the minimum customary international law standard.

  By specifying that the content of these standards does not go beyond the minimum standard of treatment required by customary international law, the Guide provision seeks to restrict the ability of international tribunals to conduct a wide-ranging review of the legislative, regulatory and policy decisions of the host state based on what they think is fair. In the formulation adopted in the Guide, the standard that tribunals apply must be determined by reference to what customary international law requires. In principle, proof of customary international law requires consistent generalised state practice that is engaged in out of a sense of

143 This was done in *Bayindir v. Pakistan*, ICSID Case No. ARB/03/29, Award, 27 August 2009.

legal obligation. It must be admitted that tribunals have not been consistently rigorous in demanding proof of customary law in practice and have differed in what customary law requires. Also, the very existence of a customary standard is disputed by some countries. Consequently, tying the FET standard to customary international law leaves significant residual uncertainty.

- **FET limited to specific kinds of state actions:** The sample provision identifies state measures that are manifestly arbitrary, unreasonable or discriminatory, or that are a gross denial of justice and due process, as the exclusive content of the prohibition in the FET obligation. In effect, the enumeration of these standards incorporates the high threshold for finding that a state has breached the FET obligation that has been established in arbitration cases under NAFTA. It also reflects the categories of state action that have been identified in other treaties as examples of what FET requires.[144] No treaty to date has limited the categories of FET in this way.
- **Breach of another provision of the IIA does not mean that there is a breach of FET:** Section 3 of the Guide sample provision provides that breaches of other treaty rights do not result in a breach of the minimum standard of treatment, following the Canadian and US models among others. This clarifies the scope of the provision and avoids the application of some investor–state dispute settlement cases that have ruled that a breach of another IIA obligation is a breach of FET.
- **Level of development of host state to be taken into account:** Following the COMESA Investment Agreement, the sample provision specifically records the parties' acknowledgement that they may have different forms of administrative, legislative and judicial systems, and that parties at different levels of development may not achieve the same standards at the same time. The provision goes on to direct that the FET standard set out in the article must be interpreted taking this context into account.
- **Freedom to regulate is specifically recognised:** The sample makes clear that the FET obligation does not preclude the party states from adopting regulatory or other measures to pursue legitimate policy objectives, including measures to meet other international obligations. This provision is not found in other agreements,

144 E.g. ASEAN–Australia–New Zealand FTA (2009) Chapter 11, Art. 6.2(b) ('For greater certainty, fair and equitable treatment requires parties not to deny justice'); US model BIT, Art. 5(2)('"fair and equitable treatment" includes the obligation not to deny justice in criminal, civil, or administrative adjudicatory proceedings in accordance with the principle of due process embodied in the principal legal systems of the world'); ASEAN Investment Agreement, Art. 11.2 ('fair and equitable treatment requires each member State not to deny justice in any legal or administrative proceeding in accordance with the principle of due process'); Netherlands–Oman, Agreement between the Government of the Kingdom of the Netherlands and the Government of the Sultanate of Oman on Encouragement and Reciprocal Protection of Investments, signed 17 January 2009, not yet in force ('Each Contracting Party shall ensure fair and equitable treatment to the investments or nationals or persons of the other Contracting Party and shall not impair, by unjustified or discriminatory measures, the operation, management, maintenance, use, enjoyment or disposal thereof by those nationals or persons').

but reflects the approach taken in some investment arbitration awards and is intended to make clear that a balance is to be struck in applying the requirements of FET, including the protection of investors' reasonable expectations, that takes into account the host state's right and responsibility to regulate.

- **Tribunals are permitted to take into account case-specific factors in assessing compensation:** Consistent with some investor–state tribunal decisions, the sample provision directs tribunals to take into account the circumstances surrounding any breach of FET in assessing the appropriate compensation. These would include the investor's behaviour, such as whether it had been duly diligent in informing itself regarding the risks associated with the investment.[145] This provision is not found in other agreements. The inclusion of such a provision may be unnecessary if a requirement to take into account case-specific factors is included in the general rules governing damages in investor–state arbitration cases. Such an approach is discussed below.[146]

Finally, it is important to note that, even more than other IIA provisions, the scope of an open-ended obligation such as FET may be defined in part by other provisions in an IIA. Statements regarding the goals of the party states in negotiating a treaty in the preamble, an objectives provision or provisions elsewhere in the treaty should inform what protection is afforded by the FET standard in the treaty. The Guide sample provisions have been drafted to provide an appropriate interpretive context by emphasising the relationship between the investment and sustainable development and the right of host states to regulate.[147]

5.5.8 Sample provision: minimum standard of treatment

Minimum Standard of Treatment

1. Each Party shall accord to investments of investors of the other Party treatment in accordance with the customary international law minimum standard of treatment of foreign nationals, including fair and equitable treatment and full protection and security.
2. Fair and equitable treatment means treatment that is not manifestly arbitrary, unreasonable or discriminatory or a gross denial of justice or due process.
3. The concepts of 'fair and equitable treatment' and 'full protection and security' in section 1 do not require treatment in addition to or beyond that which is required by the customary international law minimum standard of treatment of aliens.

---

145 This approach was suggested in UNCTAD (2012), *Fair and Equitable Treatment*, op. cit., at 111. UNCTAD also suggested that damages could be limited to the investor's direct losses, and in no case should be allowed to exceed the amount of capital invested and interest at a commercially reasonable rate. The goal is to ensure that lost profits were not included and that awards would not be too onerous for cash-strapped governments in developing countries.

146 See Section 7.1 (Investor–state dispute settlement).

147 See Section 4.2.1 (The role of preambles in IIAs) and Section 4.4 (Statement of objectives).

4. A determination that there has been a breach of another provision of this Agreement, or of a separate international agreement, does not establish that there has been a breach of this article.
5. For greater certainty, the Parties recognise that they may have different forms of administrative, legislative and judicial systems, that parties at different levels of development may not achieve the same standards at the same time and that the standard set in this article must be interpreted taking this context into account.
6. This article shall not be interpreted to preclude the Parties from adopting regulatory or other measures that pursue legitimate policy objectives, including measures adopted to comply with other international obligations, so long as the manner in which such measures are implemented is consistent with this article.
7. The amount of any compensation under the Agreement [see Guide Section 7.1 (Investor–state dispute settlement)] to be paid to an investor as a result of a breach of paragraph 1 of this article shall be equitable, taking into account the relevant circumstances of the case.

5.6 Limitations on expropriation and nationalisation

Cross references

Section 5.5	Fair and equitable treatment and the minimum standard of treatment	138
Section 5.12	Reservations and exceptions	224
Section 7.1	Investor–state dispute settlement	408

One of the greatest concerns of foreign investors is that their investments will be expropriated by host-country governments. Existing IIAs permit expropriation so long as certain requirements are met, including the payment of compensation to the investor. While there is a fairly high degree of consensus regarding some of the requirements in IIA expropriation provisions, the types of government actions that constitute an expropriation and the standard for determining the compensation to be paid vary somewhat from one IIA to the next.

It is generally recognised that states have the right to regulate without having to compensate foreign investors for any adverse effects that they experience as a result. The main challenge in drafting expropriation provisions in an IIA is to define the scope of expropriation and the remedies available to investors in a manner that safeguards a state's right to regulate without having to compensate investors for any resulting costs while, at the same time, protecting investors against true expropriations without compensation. It is relatively easy to identify a direct expropriation requiring compensation where a state takes an investor's property for itself. However, states may act in various ways that have an adverse effect on investors without taking their property. In some cases, state actions may deprive the investor of its ability to use or take advantage of its property to such an extent that it is just as if the property had been taken from the investor. Some actions of this kind are characterised as indirect expropriations requiring compensation. An expropriation provision must address how much a state's action can interfere with an investor's rights of ownership before an expropriation of those rights requiring compensation takes place. In doing so, it is also necessary to take into account the nature and characteristics of the government measure. In most cases, non-discriminatory state regulation to achieve a legitimate public purpose is not considered an expropriation requiring compensation regardless of its effect on an investor.

5.6.1 IIA practice

Apart from any treaty obligations, states have a right to expropriate the investments of both foreign and domestic investors, subject to any requirements in their domestic law and, in the case of foreign investors, customary international law. Though an expropriation is generally a lawful act under domestic laws and customary international law, usually certain requirements must be satisfied. Typically expropriation is permitted only if the following conditions are met:

1. The expropriation is for a public purpose;
2. The expropriation occurs in a non-discriminatory manner;
3. The expropriation occurs in accordance with due process of law; and
4. Compensation is paid.

These requirements are reflected in IIA expropriation provisions as discussed in the next section.

Defining expropriation

The first issue in assessing whether an expropriation requiring compensation has occurred is to determine whether the government action is an expropriation. In defining when an expropriation has occurred, IIAs use different formulations. IIA provisions on expropriation often refer to expropriation that is 'direct' or 'indirect', or to measures 'equivalent to' or 'tantamount to' expropriation, though the use of these terms is not consistent.[148] For example, the UK model treaty applies to nationalisation, expropriation and 'measures having effect equivalent to nationalisation or expropriation'.[149] The US and Canadian models apply to state measures that expropriate or nationalise an investment 'either directly or indirectly'. In the Canadian model, indirect expropriation can occur only through 'measures having an effect that is equivalent to expropriation or nationalization'. Case law decided under NAFTA suggests that measures 'equivalent to' or 'tantamount to'

148 The COMESA Investment Agreement (2007) refers to nationalization and expropriation as well as measures tantamount to expropriation (Art. 20). Most Caribbean BITs and Pacific BITs are similar though some refer to 'equivalent' rather than 'tantamount' to expropriation (Malik, op. cit., at 26, 56).

149 UK model IPPA, Art. 5. The Indian model BIPPA (Art. 3) is substantially similar. The India–Singapore CECA (2005) (Art. 6.5) and ASEAN Agreement (2009) (Art. 14) simply refer to expropriation and nationalization.

expropriation are simply forms of indirect expropriation.[150] In general, there is no evidence to suggest that the different words used in the various models result in different interpretations.[151]

In order to avoid uncertainty regarding whether an indirect expropriation has occurred, some treaties, including the US and Canadian model agreements, provide further guidance on the scope of an indirect expropriation. In the US model, whether or not an indirect expropriation has occurred is to be determined using several criteria:

- An indirect expropriation must have an effect equivalent to a direct expropriation, even though there is no formal transfer of title or an outright seizure;
- The determination of whether an indirect expropriation has occurred requires a case-by-case analysis, including a consideration of the character and economic impact of the government action and the extent to which the action 'interferes with distinct, reasonable investment-backed expectations';[152]
- The fact that a measure or series of measures of a party state has an adverse effect on the economic value of an investment does not by itself establish that an indirect expropriation has occurred; and
- 'Except in rare circumstances,[153] non-discriminatory regulatory measures that are designed and applied to protect legitimate public welfare objectives, such as public health, safety, and the environment, do not constitute indirect expropriations'.[154]

The US model states that this standard for expropriation is intended to reflect customary international law.[155] The US model also requires that to be an

150 *Pope & Talbot Inc. v. Canada*, op. cit., at 96, 99; and *S D Myers v. Canada*, op. cit., at para. 181.

151 UNCTAD (2011), *Expropriation: A Sequel*, United Nations, New York and Geneva, at 22.

152 See Annex B of the US model BIT, and Annex B.13(1) of the Canadian model FIPA.

153 The IISD model goes farther, providing that *bona fide* measures of this kind *do not* constitute indirect expropriation. This approach is followed in the ASEAN–Australia–New Zealand FTA (2009) Investment Chapter, Annex on Expropriation and Compensation.

154 See Annex B of the US model BIT. The language used in the Canadian model FIPA and the Colombian model agreement is somewhat different (Annex B.13(1) of the Canadian model FIPA; Art. VI.2 of the Colombian model agreement). Similar provisions are found in the Agreement for the Promotion and Protection of Investments between the Republic of Colombia and the Republic of India, signed 10 November 2009, in force 2 July 2012, Art. VI.2(c), China–Peru Free Trade Agreement, signed 28 April 2009, in force 1 March 2010 (Annex 9), COMESA Investment Agreement (2007), Art. 20.6, and Dominican Republic–Central America Free Trade Agreement, signed 2 August 2005, in force 1 January 2009 (Annex 10). See also Australia–Chile Free Trade Agreement, signed 30 July 2008, in force 5 March 2009, Annex. The ASEAN Agreement (2009) has a similar set of factors in Annex 2 to the agreement (2009). See also other agreements listed in UNCTAD (2011), *Expropriation*, op. cit., at 28. See also the IISD model treaty, Art. 8(I). Certain other exclusions are also provided for in that model (Art. 8(H)).

155 This approach is followed in the ASEAN–Australia–New Zealand FTA (2009) Investment Chapter (Art. 9.1) and the Australia–New Zealand Investment Protocol, signed 16 February 2010, not yet in force (Art. 14).

expropriation a state action must interfere with a tangible or intangible property right or interest in an investment, which is narrower than an investment as defined in the US model.[156]

The China–New Zealand FTA includes the same qualifications, but goes beyond the Canadian and US models to provide that:

3. In order to constitute indirect expropriation, the state's deprivation of the investor's property must be:
    a. either severe or for an indefinite period; and
    b. disproportionate to the public purpose.
4. A deprivation of property shall be particularly likely to constitute indirect expropriation where it is either:
    a. discriminatory in its effect, either as against the particular investor or against a class of which the investor forms part; or
    b. in breach of the state's prior binding written commitment to the investor, whether by contract, licence, or other legal document.[157]

Another approach to limiting the scope of expropriation provisions is to include exception clauses in the IIA that carve out measures in particular policy areas from the scope of the treaty. The US and Canadian model treaties, as well as the India–Singapore CECA and the COMESA Investment Agreement, exclude from the application of expropriation provisions state actions to grant compulsory licences of intellectual property rights and to revoke, limit or create such rights, so long as the actions are compatible with the WTO TRIPs Agreement.[158] In addition, under the US model, tax measures may be challenged as an expropriation only if the competent tax authorities of each party fail to agree that the taxation measure is not an expropriation. Some countries also use general exceptions for measures related to areas such as public order and morals, health and the environment that apply to the expropriation obligation.[159]

156 It has also been replicated in some recent IIAs concluded by other countries: e.g. Australia–Chile FTA (2008) (Annex 10-B); Malaysia–New Zealand FTA (2009) (Annex 7); ASEAN Investment Agreement (2009) (Annex 2); ASEAN–Australia–New Zealand FTA, Annex on Expropriation and Compensation. However, in most IIAs, anything that qualifies as an investment of an investment of another party may be expropriated.

157 Similar language is found in ASEAN–Australia–New Zealand FTA (2009) Investment Chapter, Annex on Expropriation and Compensation.

158 US model BIT, Art. 7(G); Canadian model FIPA, Art. 13.5; India–Singapore CECA (2005), Art. 6.5(6); COMESA Investment Agreement (2007), Art. 20.6; Colombia model agreement, Art. VI.7. The IISD model treaty (Art. 9(G)) is substantially similar.

159 E.g. Canadian model FIPA, Art. 10; COMESA Investment Agreement (2007), Art. 22. General exceptions are discussed below under Section 5.12 (Reservations and exceptions).

Other requirements regarding expropriations

Public purpose

In all IIAs and under customary international law, expropriation, whether direct or indirect, may only be for a 'public purpose'.[160] Some treaties provide that public purpose is to be interpreted in accordance with international law.[161] In practice, a host country has considerable scope to assess for itself what constitutes a 'public purpose'. Indeed, apart from excluding an expropriation that is clearly and solely a reprisal against an investor or that transfers an investor's property to another private party for their own use, there appear to be few limits on the notion of 'public purpose'. While the taking of property must be to further some legitimate public interest, the cases to date does not provide much guidance regarding what constitutes a public purpose.

On a non-discriminatory basis

The requirement in all IIAs that expropriation must occur in a non-discriminatory manner also reflects customary international law. The most obvious example of a discriminatory expropriation is one based on the nationality of the investors.[162] Customary international law's prohibition of discriminatory expropriation does not, however, preclude expropriation where the entire sector is owned by foreign investors or by a particular foreign investor, so long as the state action is motivated by legitimate public policy, is not otherwise discriminatory and is in accordance with due process.

In accordance with due process

The requirement that an expropriation be in accordance with due process has not traditionally been mentioned as a feature of the customary international law of expropriation. However, it is common to the legal systems of most countries that investors must be treated fairly and in accordance with the principles of natural justice. IIAs have increasingly required that host states provide the guarantees of fair treatment contained in the notion of 'due process' to foreign investors.[163] In

---

160 UNCTAD (2011), *Expropriation*, op. cit., at 48.

161 E.g. Canada–Peru FTA (2008), Art. 811 (footnote 7).

162 *Oppenheimer v. Inland Revenue Commissioner* [1975] 1 *All England Reports* 538; FV Garcia Amador (1959), *Special Rapporteur's Report*, International Law Commission, at para. 62; for other situations of discrimination, see *Sociedad Miner el Tenient S.A. v. Aktiengesellschaft Norddeutsche Attinerie (Chilean Copper Case)*, 12 *International Legal Materials* 251 (Hamburg Superior Court 1973). M Sornarajah (2010), *The International Law of Foreign Investment*, 3d ed., Cambridge University Press, Cambridge, at 398, suggests that expropriations by former colonies of investments of nationals of colonial rulers in the context of achieving independence could be interpreted as discriminatory, since the expropriations solely involved the property of nationals of the colonial power but have nevertheless been permitted in some cases.

163 E.g. India–Singapore CECA (2005), Art. 6.5(1); COMESA Investment Agreement (2007), Art. 20.1; ASEAN Agreement (2009), Art. 14.1; NAFTA (1992), Art. 1110.

practice, due process requires that the expropriation be conducted in accordance with domestic rules, as well as international principles. In particular, there must an opportunity for the investor to have the expropriation decision reviewed by an impartial body that is independent of the state. Typically, recourse to domestic courts or independent administrative tribunals meets this requirement. In the interests of clarity, some IIAs set out specifically that such a right of review is required.[164] Other due process requirements may include prior notice of government acts that are likely to have a significant effect on the investor, such as an expropriation, though the existence of such a requirement is likely to depend on the circumstances. There may be no such requirement where the state is responding to an emergency situation and subsequently provides an opportunity to the investor to seek review of the action.

Compensation requirements

Once a government action is found to be an expropriation, typically the main controversy is over the amount of compensation that is required by international law to be paid to the investor. The standard of 'prompt, adequate and effective compensation' is found most frequently in IIAs.[165] Other standards include 'just compensation', 'equitable compensation' and 'appropriate compensation'.[166] These standards are generally understood as requiring less than full compensation where that is fair in the circumstances, though their precise content is unclear.

Prompt, adequate and effective compensation

In IIAs, the 'prompt, adequate and effective' standard has tended to be proposed by developed countries, while the alternative standards have historically been supported by developing countries, though many developing country agreements also refer to 'prompt, adequate and effective' compensation.[167] Each of the component terms has been given meaning by international tribunals. 'Prompt' means, at a minimum, 'assessed without delay . . . [with] . . . payment to follow soon after.' 'Adequate' means 'the full equivalent in monetary terms of the property taken.' 'Effective' refers to the form of the compensation; compensation should be received in a 'freely transferable currency' to ensure that the recipient can make use of it.[168]

164 Canadian model FIPA, Art. 13(4), COMESA Investment Agreement (2007), Art. 20.9, UK model BIPPA, Art. 7.3.

165 UNCTAD (2011), *Expropriation*, op. cit., at 62. The various standards in use are summarised at 64–5.

166 The United Kingdom–India, Agreement between the Government of the United Kingdom of Great Britain and Northern Ireland and the Government of the Republic of India for the Promotion and Protection of Investments, signed 14 March 1994, in force 6 January 1995, refers to 'fair and equitable' compensation.

167 E.g. India–Singapore CECA (2005), Art. 6.5(2); ASEAN Agreement (2009), Art. 14.1. The typical compensation provision in Caribbean and Pacific BITs is the same (Malik, op. cit., at 28, 57). The COMESA Investment Agreement (2007) requires prompt and adequate compensation (Art. 20.1).

168 E Lauterpacht (1962), 'The Drafting of Treaties for the Protection of Investment,' *International and Comparative Law Quarterly* (Supp. Publ. No. 3) 18 at 27; Sornarajah, op. cit.

Additional standards for the amount *of compensation*

With respect to the standard for the amount of compensation, most agreements now state that compensation has to reflect the actual value of the investment.[169] In some cases, more specific valuation standards such as fair market value are set out. The UK model treaty provides that '[v]aluation criteria shall include the going concern value, asset value including declared tax value of tangible property and other criteria, as appropriate to determine the fair market value'.[170] Some agreements also refer to equitable principles as being relevant to valuation.[171] For example, the COMESA Investment Agreement permits compensation to be adjusted to reflect 'aggravating conduct by the investor' and to be reduced if the investor has not taken reasonable steps to mitigate its loss.[172] Many agreements require states to provide an opportunity for investors to have state valuations reviewed by a domestic judicial or other body.[173]

Most IIAs include an obligation to pay interest[174] from the date of expropriation to the date compensation is actually paid, but there are a variety of approaches regarding the nature of these requirements.[175] One issue is that the date on which an expropriation takes place may be difficult to determine, especially if the government measure at issue is not a straightforward dispossession of the investor's investment. For example, is the date of the expropriation the date of the measure, the date that the measure becomes effective or the date on which the investor is finally dispossessed? A few IIAs deal with this issue by referring to the date on which the investor was dispossessed.[176] Most, however, are silent on this point. In cases of indirect expropriation where it is not clear that there is an expropriation requiring compensation, it is possible to argue that interest should start to run only when there is a finding that an expropriation has occurred.

---

169 E.g. IISD model treaty, Art. 8(B); Canadian model FIPA, Art. 13.2; US model BIT, Art. 6; Indian model BIPPA, Art. 5. The draft Norwegian model APPI (Art. 6.1) does not set a valuation standard, but simply refers to satisfaction of 'conditions provided for by law or by the general principles of international law'. The India–Singapore CECA (Art. 6.5(2)), ASEAN Agreement (Art. 14.2(b)), and COMESA Investment Agreement (Art. 20.2) all refer to 'fair market value'.

170 UK Model IPPA, Art. 7.2. See the similar provision in NAFTA (1992), Art. 1110(2), and the Canada–Peru FTA (2008), Art. 812(2).

171 E.g. Chile–South Africa, Agreement between the Republic of Chile and the Republic of South Africa for the Reciprocal Promotion and Protection of Investments, signed 12 November 1998, not yet in force; Australia–Thailand Free Trade Agreement, signed 5 July 2004, in force 1 January 2005.

172 COMESA Investment Agreement (2007), Art. 20.2.

173 E.g. IISD Model Treaty, Art. 8; Canada Model FIPA, Art. 13.4; Indian Model BIPPA, Art. 5(2); India–Singapore CECA (2005), Art. 6.5(4).

174 The India–Singapore CECA (2005) (Art. 6.5(2)) requires interest at an appropriate rate. The ASEAN Agreement (2009) simply refers to 'any accrued interest' (Art. 14.3). The COMESA Investment Agreement (2007) (Art. 20.2) requires interest at a 'commercially reasonable rate'.

175 The IISD Model Treaty (Art. 8(F)) contemplates that where awards are 'significantly burdensome' they may be paid over a period of three years or such other period as the parties agree. The UK–Jamaica BIT (1987) allows some deferral in cases of balance of payment emergencies.

176 The Colombian model agreement fixes the 'date of value' as 'immediately before the expropriatory measures were adopted or immediately before the imminent measures were of public knowledge, whichever is earlier' (Art. VI.3).

There may also be uncertainty regarding the rate at which interest accrues on delayed compensation payments. Interest rates may be specified in IIAs though most are silent on this point too. Some model IIAs refer to interest at a normal commercial rate for the currency of payment.[177] The Indian model treaty requires interest at a 'fair and equitable rate'.[178] Others refer to a specific domestic rate in the host country, such as the government rate on fixed deposits of a certain maturity.[179]

Finally, a few model IIAs deal with the risk to the investor associated with a devaluation of the currency in which payment is made taking place after the expropriation has occurred but prior to payment. The US model BIT provides such protection in cases where payment is not made in a freely usable currency.[180] Some other IIAs provide complete protection against losses resulting from currency devaluation in all circumstances.[181]

Additional standards for the form *of compensation*

Almost all IIAs set some specific requirements for the form of compensation. Some IIAs permit compensation to be in any freely convertible currency[182] or simply require that compensation be effectively realisable and freely transferable.[183] The latter is probably the most flexible standard. Other forms of IIA require compensation in the currency in which the investment was originally made or, with the agreement of the parties, some other convertible currency. Still other models require compensation in a freely usable currency. It will often be preferable for countries to pay compensation in their own currencies. While most currencies qualify as convertible, a 'freely usable currency' is likely to be a much narrower category. Some agreements provide that this expression has the meaning used by the IMF in its Articles of Agreement: currencies widely used to settle international transactions.[184] Only four currencies are recognised by the IMF as meeting this standard: the euro, pound sterling, Japanese yen and US dollar.

177 E.g. UK model IPPA, Art. 5(1).

178 E.g. Indian model BIPPA, Art. 5(1).

179 Vietnam–Finland, Agreement between the Government of the Socialist Republic of Vietnam and the Government of the Republic of Finland on the Promotion and Reciprocal Protection of Investments, signed 21 February 2008, in force 4 June 2009.

180 E.g. US model BIT, Art. 6(4).

181 E.g. Japan–Bangladesh, Agreement between Japan and the People's Republic of Bangladesh Concerning the Promotion and Protection of Investment, signed 10 November 1998, in force 25 August 1999. See also the COMESA Investment Agreement (2007), Art. 20.4.

182 E.g. Canada model FIPA, Art. 13(3).

183 E.g. Indian model BIPPA, Art. 5(1); UK model IPPA, Art. 5(1).

184 Art. XXX(f) defines a freely usable currency as 'a member's currency that the Fund determines (i) is, in fact, widely used to make payments for international transactions, and (ii) is widely traded in the principal exchange markets'. The US model BIT requires that compensation be fully realisable and freely transferable and, if not in a freely usable currency, will have a value equivalent to the value in a freely usable currency (Art. 6(4)).

Additional standards for the timing of payment of compensation

Most IIAs provide that payment must be '*prompt*', '*without delay*' or '*without undue delay*'.[185] These timing standards must take into account the normal period of time for payments of the kind in question. In some circumstances, such as where the expropriation is part of a government response to a national emergency, a longer delay may be reasonable. It is not clear to what extent these common formulations would accommodate delays in particular circumstances. The COMESA Investment Agreement provides specifically that payment may be in yearly amounts over a period to be agreed by the investor and the state if payment of an award would be 'significantly burdensome' for the host state. Interest is to be paid at an agreed rate until the full amount is paid.[186]

5.6.2 Understanding what constitutes an expropriation

IIA standards for what constitutes an expropriation triggering a compensation obligation may differ from domestic standards. In addition, the rules regarding expropriation under customary international law differ from the standards established in some IIAs as applied in cases interpreting IIAs. For this reason, it is important to specify in the agreement which body of law is to be applied. The standards of customary international law are often considered to be less onerous for states, though the precise standard is uncertain, difficult to articulate and contested. Whether the customary standard is higher or lower than a particular treaty standard also depends on what the treaty standard requires.

Some investment tribunals interpreting expropriation provisions in IIAs have given a broad meaning to expropriation with the effect of restricting the ability of states to regulate in the public interest. For instance, a few international investment tribunals have found that some forms of state regulation of the environment constituted expropriation.[187] In the remainder of this section the requirements for a finding of expropriation are considered.

Direct expropriation

In general, direct expropriation refers to a situation in which a state takes title to the property of a foreign investor or otherwise transfers the benefit of the foreign

185 E.g. Canadian model FIPA, Art. 13(3)(without delay); US model BIT, Art. 6(2)(b)(without delay); UK model IPPA., Art. 7(2)(without delay); Indian model BIPPA, Art. 5(1)(without unreasonable delay); Colombian model agreement, Art. VI.4 (without unjustified delay).

186 COMESA Investment Agreement (2007), Art. 20(5).

187 E.g. *Santa Elena v. Costa Rica* (2002), 15 *ICSID Review-Foreign Investment Law Journal* 72. This decision was followed in *Tecnicas v. Estados*, op. cit. See also H Mann and K. von Moltke (1999), *NAFTA's Chapter 11 and the Environment*, International Institute for Sustainable Development, Winnipeg; International Institute for Sustainable Development (2001), *Private Rights, Public Problems: A Guide to NAFTA's Controversial Investment Chapter*, International Institute for Sustainable Development, Winnipeg and World Wildlife Fund). The Canadian Government raised this concern in a 1998 issues paper that has not been made public but was reproduced in 17 *Inside US Trade* (12 February 1999) at 20–1. It is discussed briefly in J A VanDuzer (1999), 'What Have We Done? NAFTA States Have Concerns Regarding Investor–state Dispute Settlement Under NAFTA Chapter 11', 25 *Canadian Council of International Law Bulletin* 13.

investor's investment to itself, typically through an outright seizure or other transfer of title.

Indirect expropriation

What constitutes indirect expropriation is much more difficult to define. Indirect expropriation refers to the situation in which the state deprives the foreign investor of the ability to make use of its property in some substantial way, even when title remains with the investor. An indirect expropriation can occur even if the host state does not benefit from the limitation on the foreign investor's ability to use its property. It can also occur through a series of acts, sometimes referred to as 'creeping expropriation'. Defining an indirect expropriation requires specifying the degree of diminished control necessary to qualify as an expropriation. It is impossible to cite a single rule that precisely identifies the degree of control that must be lost for an expropriation to exist that can be applied in all circumstances. Host state actions listed in Box 5.8 are examples of state action that could be found to be an indirect expropriation.[188]

Box 5.8 Host state actions that could be found to be an indirect expropriation

- The host state forces the foreign investor to sell its property.
- The host state forces the sale by a foreign investor of its shares in an investment that is a corporation.
- Indigenisation measures, whereby the host state requires a gradual transfer of ownership from foreign investors to nationals of the host state.
- The host state assumes complete control over the management of an investment of a foreign investor.
- The host state induces others to assume physical possession of the property of a foreign investor.
- The host state fails to provide protection against a taking of the property of a foreign investor.
- Administrative decision-makers cancel licences and permits necessary for the functioning of a foreign investment.
- The host state imposes exorbitant taxes on the foreign investor's investment.
- The host state harasses a foreign investor by, for example, freezing bank accounts or promoting strikes, lockouts and labour shortages, such that it is impossible for the investor to operate.
- The host state expels the foreign investor from its territory in contravention of international law.[189]

188 UNCTAD (2011), *Expropriation*, op. cit., at 30.

189 For a full discussion of these various forms of indirect expropriation, see Sornarajah, op. cit., at 359–95. For examples, see R D Bishop, J Crawford and W M Reisman (2005), *Foreign Investment Disputes: Cases, Materials and Commentary*, Kluwer Law International, The Hague, at 854–83.

The measure must have the same effect as if the investment was directly expropriated

To be an expropriation, a measure must deprive the investor of all or almost all of the value of the investment. The measure must render the economic rights of ownership useless. Some tribunals have referred to the effect on the 'reasonably to-be-expected economic benefit' of the investment to help define what it is that the measure must interfere with.[190] An expropriation may be found where the owner is deprived of control over the investment, such as by the installation of government appointed managers of the investment, even though the owner retains title or physical possession.[191] Other examples are provided in Box 5.9. Where the impact of the measure is not permanent, the duration of the measures is relevant. Some tribunals have concluded that an expropriation could be found even if the measure is only temporary,[192] but when a temporary effect becomes sufficiently serious to constitute an expropriation is not clear.

Box 5.9 Indicators of a loss of control relevant to determining if an investment in an enterprise has been expropriated

- Interference with the direction of the day-to-day operations of the enterprise
- Detention of employees or officers of the enterprise
- Supervision of the work of employees or officers of the enterprise
- Taking the proceeds of enterprise's sales (apart from taxation)
- Interference with management or shareholders' activities
- Preventing an enterprise from paying dividends to its shareholders
- Interference with the appointment of directors or management of an enterprise [193]

None of these factors would necessarily be sufficient on their own, but they would be relevant to a determination as to whether there had been a loss of control of the investment.

Some tribunals have held that to assess the impact of an alleged indirect expropriation it is necessary to consider the effect on all elements of the investment together.[194] This typically involves an examination of the effect of the government action on the

190 *Waste Management v. Mexico*, op. cit., at para. 159.

191 UNCTAD (2011), *Expropriation*, op. cit., at 26, 86.

192 E.g. in *Wena Hotels, v. Egypt*, ICSID Case No. ARB(AF)/00/3, Award, 8 December 2000, at para. 4 (one year). See also *S D Myers v. Canada*, op. cit.

193 These factors were first listed in *Pope & Talbot v. Canada*, op. cit., at para. 100, but have been extensively cited in other investor–state cases.

194 *Telenor Mobile v. Hungary*, ICSID Case No. ARB/04/15, Award, 13 September 2006, at para. 70.

overall business of the investor.[195] Other tribunals have considered the impact of the host state action on any investment that falls within the IIA's definition of investment, such as particular rights under a concession contract or a long-term loan. Under the latter approach, each separate investment is capable of being expropriated.[196] A finding of expropriation will be harder to make if the impact on the entire business held by an investor is considered.

An issue that has arisen in this context is the extent to which contractual rights on their own are capable of being expropriated. In principle, if they are investments within the definition of investment found in the IIA they can be expropriated, but tribunals have determined that not every failure to perform a contract by a state is an expropriation. In general, a state must have gone beyond an ordinary breach of contract. The failure to perform the contract must be associated with an exercise of its sovereign powers. In *Waste Management*, an investor–state tribunal considered a claim by an investor that a municipality's persistent refusal or inability to pay sums that were owed to the investor under a concession agreement to collect waste constituted an expropriation. The tribunal determined that even though the anticipated benefits under the contract were not received by the investor as a result, in part, of actions by the municipality, there was no expropriation of the investor's contractual rights. In order for the rights to be expropriated, the tribunal stated that there would have to be an act of the state in its sovereign capacity, such as legislation or a decree to enact public policy. In addition, the usual civil remedies for breach of contract must have been foreclosed by the state's action.[197] A failure to honour what is, in effect, a commercial obligation of the state is not an expropriation.

Investor expectations concerning the investment may be relevant to assessing the magnitude of the loss to the investor

As noted, the specification of what constitutes an indirect expropriation adopted by some countries in their IIAs refers to an investor's expectations as relevant to determining the magnitude of what the investor has lost. In this regard, the requirement to establish an investor's expectations is likely to be higher in relation to expropriation than as discussed in relation to FET.[198] Tribunals have considered only expectations based on statements of host state officials or expressed in contracts to an investor that have been relied on by the investor.[199] General expectations regarding the stability and predictability of the host state regime have not been found to be sufficient to provide the basis for an expropriation claim.

Regulatory measures that have effects equivalent to expropriation are nevertheless not expropriations

One of the issues addressed by arbitration tribunals is whether a deprivation meeting the standards discussed above is, on its own, sufficient for a finding of expropriation.

195 See, for example, the approach of the tribunal in *Chemtura Corporation v. Canada*, UNCITRAL, Award, 2 August 2010.

196 Dolzer and Shreuer, op. cit.; UNCTAD (2011), *Expropriation*, op. cit., at 42.

197 *Waste Management v. Mexico*, op. cit., at par. 163. See also *Siemens v. Argentina*, op. cit.

198 See Section 5.5 (Fair and equitable treatment and the minimum standard of treatment).

199 UNCTAD (2011), *Expropriation*, op. cit., at 104.

Some tribunals have considered that deprivation alone is sufficient applying what is called the 'sole effects doctrine'. For these tribunals, the host state's motivation for the measure is irrelevant.[200] Other tribunals have rejected this approach.[201] The inconsistency in tribunal practice has caused some countries to include a specific provision saying that deprivation alone is insufficient.[202] Instead, deprivation is treated as a necessary but not sufficient condition for a finding of expropriation. The character of the measure, including, in particular, whether it is a regulatory act for a public purpose needs to be considered. Thus, while most regulatory measures will not result in a deprivation substantial enough to be considered an expropriation, even if a measure did reach this threshold, it may not be an expropriation.

In general, it is recognised that a state has power to regulate without paying compensation for any resulting negative effects on investors. Traditionally, this has been referred to as the 'police power' of states. The scope of this power to regulate is one of the more complex issues in international investment law. In general, non-discriminatory regulation for a public purpose undertaken in good faith is considered to be valid and not an expropriation,[203] though the existence of such a broad carve-out from expropriation is not universally acknowledged.[204] For this reason, some states have adopted specific language to describe what should be considered regulatory measures that do not constitute an expropriation in their treaty models, as noted above. Some of the elements of regulatory measures are listed below:

- **The measure is taken in good faith for a public purpose:** Under international law, states are presumed to act in good faith. The burden is on the investor to demonstrate a lack of good faith. A measure is not taken for a public purpose simply because a state says that is what it is doing, though significant leeway is accorded to states in this regard.[205] Consideration will be given to whether the measure is within the normal scope of regulatory activity.
- **The measure is non-discriminatory:** This requirement means that the measure does not target a foreign investor based on nationality or other bases of discrimination prohibited under international law.
- **The measure has been implemented in accordance with due process:** In this context, due process means that the process through which the measure was adopted and implemented complies with basic procedural requirements of domestic law and general requirements of procedural fairness.

---

200 E.g. *Fireman's Fund v. Mexico*, ICSID Case No. ARB(AF)/01/1, Award, 17 July 2006, at para. 176(f).

201 E.g. *LG&E v. Argentina*, ICSID Case No. ARB/02/1, Decision on Liability, 3 October 2006, at paras. 189 and 194.

202 See, for example, Canadian model FIPA, US model BIT and other agreements referred to above. UNCTAD identifies this as a 'clear trend'. UNCTAD (2011), *Expropriation*, op. cit., at 86.

203 UNCTAD (2011), *Expropriation*, ibid., at 110, describing this as the consensus view of commentators, states and investor–state arbitration tribunals.

204 A K Hoffman (2008), 'Indirect Expropriation', in Reinisch (ed.), *Standards of Investor Protection*, op. cit., at 165.

205 *Tecmed v. Mexico*, op. cit., at para. 122.

These requirements overlap substantially with the requirements for a lawful expropriation. Some commentators suggest that, for this reason, there is no general exception for regulatory actions that have effects equivalent to expropriation,[206] though some arbitral awards reflect a different view.[207]

A number of tribunals have required that the measure must bear some plausible relation or be proportional to the achievement of the public purpose.[208] There is no clear consensus on this requirement, however, which is why it is expressly provided for in some IIAs, as discussed above.

When a claim of indirect expropriation arises in an investor–state arbitration case, the state must initially show that the measure was taken for a public purpose, is non-discriminatory and is in accordance with due process to argue that it is within the police powers exception. Then the burden shifts to the investor to show that the state's action did not meet these standards. Overall, the assessment will be tied very closely to the facts surrounding the measure and its adoption and implementation.

5.6.3 Understanding what compensation is required to be paid

Some argue that customary international law requires that compensation for a *lawful* expropriation be 'appropriate' or 'just', and that this means that less than full compensation can be paid in some circumstances.[209] In cases of *unlawful* expropriation, where the customary international law requirements of public purpose or non-discrimination are not met, there is strong authority supporting a requirement to pay full compensation, including any consequential losses.[210] Investment treaties that require compensation at fair market value even for lawful expropriations in effect move the standard for all expropriations, lawful and unlawful, close to the same level. Some argue that this is inappropriate, at least for indirect expropriations in which typically no financial benefit is transferred to the state.[211]

In a recent report, UNCTAD suggests a number of valuation adjustments that states may wish to consider incorporating in their IIAs.[212] A state may want to limit compensation to direct losses not including loss of future profits and prohibit the calculation of compensation based on the discounted value of future profits at the

206 E.g. Hoffman, op. cit., at 165.

207 *Chemtura v. Canada*, op. cit.

208 UNCTAD describes this requirement as 'not universally recognised' in UNCTAD (2011), *Expropriation*, op. cit. at 97.

209 Ibid., at 41.

210 Ibid., at 142–4, citing *The Factory at Chorzów* (Claim for Indemnity) (The Merits), Germany v. Poland, Permanent Court of International Justice, Judgment, 13 September 1929, 1928 P.C.I.J. (ser. A) No. 17. See also A Reinisch (2008), 'Legality of Expropriations,' in Reinisch, op. cit., at 197–8 to the same effect.

211 UNCTAD (2011), *Expropriation*, op. cit., at 148.

212 Ibid., at 148–55.

date of the expropriation.[213] Limiting compensation in this way would reduce the size of awards in some cases, avoid awards of speculative damages and enhance the predictability of damage awards. While the value to an investor of a business at the time of its expropriation may be determined, in part, by the value at that date of the profits that the business might earn in the future, the amount of those future profits and the assessment of their value at the date of expropriation are inherently uncertain. Other bases for valuation, such as the liquidation value (the amount the assets could be sold for net of liabilities on a sale of the investment business) and the book value (the value that the assets are recorded at on the investment's accounting records), are less speculative. Investor–state tribunals have sometimes rejected discounted cash flow valuations as too speculative,[214] though they have been used to assess damages in some cases where the evidence of future cash flows was found to be reliable.[215] No treaty to date has specifically excluded discounted cash flow valuation.

A state may wish to allow investor–state arbitration tribunals to award less than the full fair market value of an investment based on the failure of the investor to mitigate its damages and other equitable considerations, such as when an investor's own actions caused the state to intervene. As noted, such a provision is included in the COMESA Investment Agreement.[216]

UNCTAD also suggests that states consider including an express prohibition on the award of punitive or moral damages. Punitive damages are intended not to compensate the investor for loss but rather to punish the state and send a message to the host state that its actions are not to be repeated. The award of punitive damages is precluded in the US model BIT.[217] In a number of cases, investor–state tribunals, as well as other international bodies, have decided that international law does not

213 The value of future profits is typically calculated using 'discounted cash flows'. Discounted cash flow valuation estimates the cash receipts expected from the investment in each future year of its anticipated economic life less each year's expected cash expenditures. The present value of these net cash flows is calculated by discounting the net cash flow for each year by a discount rate that reflects the expected rate of return on invested funds for the investor's business, taking into account expected inflation and the risk associated with the cash flows. One way to identify the appropriate discount rate is to look at the rate of return available in the same market on alternative investments of comparable risk. See World Bank (1992), *World Bank Guidelines on the Treatment of Foreign Direct Investment*, Washington, D.C.,World Bank.

214 E.g. *SPP v. Egypt*, Award on the Merits, 20 May 1992, at para. 36; *Metalclad v. Mexico*, ICSID Case No. ARB(AF)/97/1, Award, 30 August 2000, at para. 120; and *Tecmed v. Mexico*, op. cit.

215 E.g. *CME v. Czech Republic*, op. cit.

216 COMESA Investment Agreement (2007), Art. 20(2). See the same provision in IISD model treaty, Art. 8(B).

217 This limitation appears in the US model BIT as a general limitation on damages (Art. 34.3). Punitive damages are also excluded in the Canadian model BIT (Art. 44(3)), as well as some existing agreements: NAFTA (1992), Art. 1135(3); Canada–Peru BIT (2008), Art. 44(3); United States–Uruguay BIT (2005), Art. 34(3).

permit the use of damage awards to punish the state for its actions.[218] The goal is compensation for loss.

Moral damages are damages that are intended to compensate the investor, but not for its economic loss. Though the concept of moral damages is not well developed in investment arbitration cases it has a long history in international law and includes damages to compensate for 'mental suffering, injury to ... feelings, humiliation, shame, degradation, loss of social position or injury to ... credit or to ... reputation'.[219] Moral damages have been claimed by investors in a few investor–state arbitrations, but one recent survey found only one case in which such damages have been awarded. In that case, damages of US$1 million were awarded to the claimant to compensate for the malicious infliction of physical duress on the executives of the corporate claimant by the host state and for the loss of reputation by the claimant.[220]

As a practical matter, the circumstances giving rise to a claim for moral damages are likely to be rare in investor–state disputes, which typically centre on economic losses. In expropriation cases, compensation is being sought for the effective taking of a business. Moral injuries are more common in disputes involving other kinds of legal norms, such as human rights. Full reparation may involve compensation for moral damages, but some argue that full reparation is not what is required in all cases of lawful expropriation. Perhaps most important from a host state point of view, an obligation to provide compensation for moral damages is inherently unpredictable, in terms of both the threshold for awarding them and the assessment of the appropriate amount.[221] In addition, some advocates for moral damages in investor–state cases acknowledge that often awards of moral damages are often used both to compensate and to punish state behaviour.[222] Consequently, a state may wish to consider excluding moral damages.

Other limitations identified by UNCTAD as possibilities include (i) giving the state and the investor a period of time to negotiate compensation prior to an award of damages by the tribunal and (ii) providing for situations in which payment of compensation by the state may be delayed, including, for example, a financial crisis. Only the second of these appears in existing treaties.[223]

---

218 Commentaries to the Draft Articles on Responsibility of States for Internationally Wrongful Acts Adopted by the International Law Commission at its Fifty-Third Session, November 2001, Report of the ILC on the work of its Fifty-third Session, Official Records of the General Assembly, Fifty-sixth Session, Supplement No. 10 ((A/56/10), Ch. IV.E.2), at 279; and cases cited by P Dumberry (2010), 'Compensation for Moral Damages in Investor–state Arbitration Disputes,' 27 *Journal of International Arbitration* 247 at 276, and B Sabahi (2011), *Compensation and Restitution in Investor–state Arbitration: Principles and Practice*, Oxford, Oxford University Press, at 146–8.

219 Opinion in the Lusitania Cases, United States–Germany Mixed Claims Commission, 1923, VII U.N.R.I.A.A. 32, at 40, cited in P Dumberry, op. cit., at 249.

220 *Desert Line Projects L.L.C. v. Yemen*, ICSID Case No. ARB/05/17, Award, Feb. 6, 2008, cited by P Dumberry, op. cit.

221 Sabahi, op. cit., at 141.

222 Dumberry, op. cit., at 274–5.

223 COMESA Investment Agreement (2007), Art. 20(5). See the same provision in IISD model treaty Art. 8(F).

Box 5.10 Summary of options for expropriation provisions

1. *No obligation to provide compensation for expropriation*
2. *Qualified obligation to compensate for expropriation*

   This obligation would include a prohibition on direct or indirect expropriation of an investment of a foreign investor as defined in the IIA unless the expropriation is for a public purpose, non-discriminatory, in accordance with due process and accompanied by prompt, effective and adequate compensation, but could include a number of limitations on the unqualified obligation described in option 3 below, including any or all of the following:

   a. Clarifications regarding what is to be considered an indirect expropriation:

      i. An indirect expropriation of an investment can occur only when a measure of a state has an effect equivalent to a direct expropriation;

      ii. Whether an indirect expropriation has occurred requires a determination of the economic impact of the state measure, but the sole fact that a measure has an adverse effect on the economic value of an investment is not sufficient for it to be considered an expropriation (rejecting the 'sole effect' doctrine);

      iii. Non-discriminatory state measures that are designed and applied to protect legitimate public welfare objectives do not constitute indirect expropriations.

      These clarifications may themselves be qualified by further providing that:

      1. Limitation (iii) applies 'except in rare circumstances'; or
      2. Imposing an additional requirement that the measure must be in good faith, not arbitrary or disproportionate in light of its purpose;

   b. Limiting the interests protected against expropriation to tangible or intangible property rights, which is narrower than investment as defined in the IIA;

   c. Subjecting the expropriation obligation to exceptions:

      i. Exceptions specific to the expropriation obligation such as a provision that excludes a compulsory licence of intellectual property rights from what is an expropriation;

      ii. General exceptions for measures to protect health, the environment and other policy priorities;

(Continued)

(Continued)

d. Limitations on compensation:

   i. Limiting the basic standard to compensation that is 'appropriate', 'just' or 'equitable' rather than 'prompt, effective and adequate';
   ii. Limiting compensation to direct losses, not including loss of future profits, and prohibiting the calculation of compensation based on the discounted value of future cash flows;
   iii. Allowing investor–state arbitration tribunals to award less than the full fair market value of an investment based on the failure of the investor to mitigate its damages and other equitable considerations;
   iv. Prohibiting the award of punitive or moral damages;
   v. Giving the state and the investor a period of time to negotiate compensation prior to an award of damages by an arbitration tribunal; and
   vi. Providing for situations in which payment of compensation by the state may be delayed, including, for example, a financial crisis.

3. *Unqualified obligation to compensate for expropriation*

   a. A prohibition on direct or indirect expropriation of an investment of a foreign investor as defined in the IIA, unless the expropriation is for a public purpose, non-discriminatory, in accordance with due process and accompanied by prompt, effective and adequate compensation;
   b. Compensation shall be based on market value of the investment immediately before the time of expropriation;
   c. Compensation shall be paid in a freely convertible currency with interest from the date of expropriation;
   d. Interest is payable from the date of expropriation until actual payment in full at a specified rate; and
   e. Protection is provided against devaluation of the currency of payment from the date of expropriation until actual payment in full.

5.6.4 Discussion of options

1. *No obligation to provide compensation for expropriation*

Since an obligation to provide some compensation for at least some kinds of expropriation is fairly firmly established as part of customary international law, capital-exporting states are very unlikely to accept an IIA with no expropriation provision. Even without a provision, customary international law would still apply, though a customary international law claim for compensation could probably not be enforced through investor–state arbitration procedures in an IIA. This would depend, however, on the scope of the dispute settlement procedures in the agreement. It is also possible that a treaty-based obligation on a host state to pay compensation for expropriation would be incorporated into an IIA if the IIA contained an MFN clause, and the host state had entered into another IIA that included such an obligation.

2. *Qualified obligation to compensate for expropriation*

   a. Clarifications regarding what is considered to be an indirect expropriation

   The qualifications identified in the summary are present in a significant number of more recent treaties, including the Canadian and US model agreements. They are designed to clarify the standards that exist under customary international law, though some argue that the remaining protection for investors is less than that required by customary international law. Nevertheless, these qualifications represent, at most, an incremental shift from the customary international law standards and are accepted by some major capital-exporting states.

   b. Limiting the interests protected against to tangible or intangible property rights, which is narrower than investment as defined in the IIA

   This qualification is designed to further narrow the circumstances in which an expropriation may be found and excludes expropriation claims that are based exclusively on contractual rights. It is the approach adopted in treaty models used by the USA and some other countries. It also reflects the approach of some investor–state tribunal awards.

   A further limitation adopted by some investor–state tribunals would be to require that all aspects of an investor's investment be assessed in determining whether there has been an expropriation, rather than looking separately at any distinct interest that could qualify as an investment under the IIA definition of that term. Such an approach would limit the circumstances in which an expropriation could be found.

   c. Subjecting the expropriation obligation to exceptions

   Exceptions specific to the expropriation obligation, such as a provision that excludes a compulsory licence of intellectual property rights from what is an expropriation, appear in the treaty model used by Canada and some other countries. Some IIAs entered into by major capital-exporting states and some developing countries, however, do not include them. It is much less common for general exceptions to apply to the expropriation obligation. Some states may view general exceptions for measures to protect health, the environment and other policy priorities as inappropriate for an obligation that already exists in some form in customary international law. They may also view the limitations discussed above on the forms of state regulation that may be found to be an indirect expropriation requiring compensation as sufficient to address the need for policy flexibility, and therefore consider that further exceptions are duplicative and unnecessary. As a practical matter, there may be few regulatory measures that would fit within these kinds of general exceptions and that would have the same effect as if the investment had been taken from the investor. The vast majority of regulatory measures will have a less significant impact. Nevertheless, some states may still want exceptions because they clearly exclude the application of the expropriation provision and other investor protection obligations from the policy areas identified in the exception and so preserve their policy flexibility in these areas with greater certainty.

d. Limitations on compensation

i. Limiting the basic standard to compensation that is 'appropriate', 'just' or 'equitable', rather than 'prompt, effective and adequate'

Compared with the 'prompt, effective and adequate' standard, all of these other formulations of the basic standard for compensation are used in some IIAs and provide more scope for assessing damages in a way that provides for less than full fair market value compensation in appropriate circumstances, so long as any further specification of the standard in the agreement does not define the compensation required by reference to fair market value. At the same time, however these standards are both less certain and less commonly found than the 'prompt, effective and adequate' standard.

ii. Allowing investor–state arbitration tribunals to award less than the full fair market value of an investment based on the failure of the investor to mitigate its damages and other equitable considerations

These limitations have some basis in investor–state arbitration cases, but they do not reflect a consensus position. The COMESA Investment Agreement permits compensation to be adjusted to reflect any aggravating behaviour of the investor, such as behaviour that might have caused the state to act or otherwise contributed to the loss suffered by the investor, and permits damages to be reduced where the investor has failed to take reasonable steps to mitigate its losses. While few other existing treaties contain such limitations, they are consistent with widely accepted principles for the award of damages under international law.

iii. Prohibiting the award of punitive or moral damages

It is not obvious that investor–state awards where an expropriation has taken place should go beyond what is required to compensate investors for the losses that they have suffered as a consequence of a host state's breach of an IIA obligation. Punitive damages are not intended to provide compensation but to deter future conduct. In addition, punitive damages are prohibited under the US model agreement, and under some other agreements. They are generally not awarded for state actions contrary to international law. This category of damages is also inherently highly discretionary. A prohibition would prevent such damages from being awarded and ensure that host states would not be at risk of claims for such damages.

Unlike punitive damages, moral damages have been awarded in at least one investor–state case to date. They are intended to compensate for non-economic losses that may be very real, though they are likely to be rare in investor–state disputes, given the essentially economic nature of such disputes. Investor–state tribunals have significant discretion to determine in what circumstances moral damages may be awarded and their amount. They may also be used to sanction state behaviour. In the interests of managing their exposure to liability, states may seek a prohibition on moral damage awards in their IIAs.

iv. Giving the state and the investor a period of time to negotiate compensation prior to an award of damages by the tribunal

A requirement to provide an opportunity for states to negotiate compensation prior to an award would simply ensure that states have a period of time to settle a case, something that the parties could agree to at any time in any case. A treaty requirement would ensure that the tribunal permitted such an opportunity by not awarding damages until the expiry of some period of time after it found the host state to be liable.

v. Providing for situations in which payment of compensation by the state may be delayed, including, for example, a financial crisis

Deferral of payment in some cases may be implicitly permitted in treaties that require payment without 'unjustified delay' or use similar formulations regarding the time within which payment must be made. Under such treaties, some delays must be justifiable. An express provision that identifies the circumstances in which payment may be delayed, however, is rare. Providing for delays in payment would probably be a concern for capital-exporting states and their investors.

vi. Limiting compensation to direct losses, not including loss of future profits, and prohibiting the calculation of compensation based on the discounted value of future cash flows

Excluding compensation for loss of profits and precluding the calculation of compensation on the basis of discounted cash flows, even where they are reliable, could significantly reduce awards in some circumstances. Such a blanket limitation has no basis in existing practice. Consequently, while this kind of limit would reduce the exposure of host states, it may be viewed as inappropriately curtailing the compensation obligation by capital-exporting states and their investors.

All of these kinds of limitations on the damages recoverable could be applied to all investor–state claims and are discussed in more detail in Section 7.1 (Investor–state dispute settlement).

3. *Unqualified obligation to compensate for expropriation*

This is the most demanding version of an expropriation provision. It provides an obligation to pay compensation in relation to any direct or indirect expropriation of a foreign investor from the other treaty party. This model will be most attractive to investors and capital-exporting states because it imposes the highest level of obligation on host states. Most of its elements as set out in Box 5.9 are found in the Indian and German model agreements. Protection against currency devaluation appears in the US model and the COMESA Investment Agreement, but in few others.

5.6.5 Discussion of sample provision

The sample expropriation provision in the Guide takes into account features of the US model BIT, the Canadian model FIPA, the Norwegian draft model APPI, the Indian model BIPPA, the UK IPPA and other treaties. The Guide provision also contains some unique features that differentiate it from many models commonly in use. The goal of the provision is to balance the protection of investors against the expropriation of their investments without compensation with preserving appropriate regulatory flexibility of host states to regulate in order to promote their sustainable development.

Standard set in the treaty is intended to reflect customary international law: The Guide uses the language from the US model BIT to indicate that the standard set in the treaty is intended to reflect and not exceed the standard imposed by customary international law. This has the effect of tying down the discretion of an investor–state tribunal with respect to finding that there has been an expropriation by requiring it to be justified as an expropriation under customary international law. The impact of this limitation is likely to be small, however. Arbitral awards have adopted a variety of approaches to the customary international law standard. Some even argue that particular treaty standards are lower than what is required under customary international law. The limitation in the sample provision may, nevertheless, be useful to make clear that the standard in the IIA is not higher than that under customary international law.

Indirect expropriation does not necessarily occur just because of a loss in value of the investment: The Guide provision adopts the language used in the US and Canadian model treaties and incorporated in an increasing number of IIAs that clarifies, for further certainty, that a government measure that causes a loss in the value of an investment or the failure of an investment to meet the expectations of investors does not of itself qualify as an indirect expropriation.

Indirect expropriation and permitted regulation are distinguished: The Guide sample provision adopts the language used in the US and Canadian model treaties and found in an increasing number of IIAs worldwide that clarifies the meaning of indirect expropriation and distinguishes it from permitted regulation. The sample provision requires that in assessing whether an indirect expropriation has occurred, a case-by-case, fact-based enquiry should be undertaken that considers factors such as the character and purpose of the government action. The sample provision goes on to provide specifically that governments are able to legislate to achieve a wide range of legitimate public welfare objectives without their actions triggering liability to investors for compensation. In addition to the three examples of legitimate objectives commonly mentioned (public health, safety and the environment), 'economic security' has been added. Also, regulatory actions need only to be designed and applied to achieve such objectives. It is not necessary for states to be able to demonstrate that these objectives will be achieved in fact. The intention is to ensure that measures taken to stabilise the often-fragile economies of developing countries, so as to avoid a severe negative impact on the residents of those countries, will not be considered to be expropriations.

The sample provision also provides that for an expropriation to be found there must be interference with a tangible or intangible property right. This limitation is included in the US model treaty and reflects the decisions of some investor–state arbitration tribunals. It means that state actions in other types of investments that may be within the treaty definition of investment can nevertheless not be challenged as expropriations.

Exceptions are provided: In addition, the Guide sample provision expressly provides that compulsory licensing in a manner consistent with international obligations under applicable international agreements on intellectual property rights, such as the WTO TRIPs Agreement, is not an expropriation. Such an exclusion is provided for in the US and Canadian models and other agreements. The requirement for compliance with international rules binding on the host state is to assure investors that any compulsory licence will meet these standards. This raises the issue that in any case where a state seeks to take advantage of this exception to defeat an investor's claim, the state's compliance with the requirements of TRIPs or other international commitments will be adjudicated by an investor–state tribunal. To avoid this possibility, it could be provided that the compulsory licensing of intellectual property in accordance with the law of the host state does not constitute an expropriation. This approach provides less certainty to investors regarding the circumstances in which compulsory licencing can be used without breaching the expropriation provision.

The Guide includes other sample provisions that provide exceptions and country-specific reservations that could be made applicable to the expropriation obligation. These are discussed below.[224]

Standard of compensation: The basic standard for compensation in the sample provision is that it be 'prompt, adequate and effective'. This is the standard on which IIA practice is converging. While another standard could have been provided, the approach adopted in the sample provision is to adopt the most common standard, but also to include specific limitations on the amount of compensation in the interests of certainty and predictability, as well as to mitigate the concerns that capital-exporting countries will have with other less predictable standards.

224 See Section 5.12 (Reservations and exceptions).

In general, compensation is to be based on the market value of the investment at the time it was expropriated – again, a standard on which IIA practice is converging. Several specific limitations on damages have been included:

- Following the COMESA Agreement, the sample provision allows compensation to be adjusted to reflect any aggravating conduct by the investor or a failure by the investor to take reasonable steps to mitigate its damages. Few other agreements contain these kinds of qualifications. As discussed more fully below, both these qualifications are accepted principles of compensation in international law.[225]
- The sample provision also limits compensation to direct losses, not including loss of future profits, and prohibits the calculation of compensation based on the discounted value of future cash flows. Existing agreements do not contain these kinds of qualifications, but some investment tribunals have declined to award damages for these indirect losses where there was uncertainty regarding future cash flows.
- The sample prohibits the award of punitive damages, following the US model. Punitive damages have not been awarded in investor–state cases to date, but the provision has been included to prevent the introduction of such damages. Moral damages have also been excluded. Moral damages are, in principle, intended to compensate for non-economic losses and have been awarded in at least one case. Nevertheless, they have been excluded in the sample provision on the basis that they are rarely appropriate in an investor–state case and both the threshold for awarding moral damages and the assessment of their amount is inherently unpredictable.
- A provision requiring investor–state tribunals to provide an opportunity for a host state to negotiate compensation after a finding of liability has been included in the sample provisions dealing with investor–state dispute settlement.[226]

Form of payment: The only restriction on the currency in which payment is made is that it is freely convertible. So long as a state's currency meets this standard, it may use its own currency for payment. This approach reflects the practice in most IIAs. No provision has been included to shift the risk of currency devaluation between the date of expropriation and the date of payment to the state. Few IIAs contain such provisions.

Time of payment: The sample provision provides that there may be situations in which payment of compensation by the state is so burdensome that it must be delayed. One situation in which this might occur would be a financial crisis. This provision is based on the COMESA Investment Agreement. Few other IIAs have such a provision. Most simply require payment without delay. Accordingly, this provision may be a concern to capital-exporting states and investors. To address this concern, where payment is delayed, compensation must be accompanied by the payment of interest at a reasonable commercial rate for the currency in which the payment is made, consistent with the approach in the COMESA Investment Agreement.

---

225 See Section 7.1 (Investor–state dispute settlement).

226 See Section 7.1 (Investor–state dispute settlement).

Right to review of expropriation and compensation decisions: Consistent with widespread IIA practice, the sample provision gives an investor a right to seek review in the host state of host state decisions regarding expropriation and the value of any compensation paid. The sample dispute resolution provision in Section 7.1 (Investor–state dispute settlement) provides that these kinds of domestic procedures will have to be exhausted before an investor may commence investor–state dispute settlement proceedings to seek relief for expropriation or any other breach of an IIA.

5.6.6 Sample provision: expropriation and compensation

Expropriation and Compensation

1. Neither Party may expropriate or nationalise an investment of an investor of the other Party, either directly or indirectly through measures equivalent to expropriation or nationalisation (all of which are referred to in this Article as an 'expropriation'), except:

    a. For a public purpose;

    b. In a non-discriminatory manner;

    c. On payment of prompt, adequate and effective compensation in accordance with sections 2 and 3 of this article; and

    d. In accordance with due process of law.

2. The compensation referred to in subsection 1c. shall be paid without unjustified delay and be effectively realisable and freely transferable. Such compensation shall be in a freely convertible currency and include interest from the date of the expropriation, defined as the date upon which the measure constituting the expropriation becomes effective in relation to the investor, until the date of payment at a reasonable commercial rate for the currency in which payment is made.

3. The compensation referred to in subsection 1c. shall be equivalent to the fair market value of the expropriated investment immediately before the expropriation took place and not reflect any change in value occurring because the intended expropriation had become known earlier. Valuation criteria may include asset value, including declared tax value of tangible property and other criteria, as appropriate, to determine fair market value provided that compensation (i) shall be limited to direct losses of the investor, (ii) shall not include loss of future profits or be calculated on the basis of the discounted value of future cash flows, (iii) shall be adjusted to reflect any aggravating conduct by the investor, including conduct that caused the state to take the action that constitutes an expropriation, or a failure by the investor to take reasonable steps to mitigate its damages, and (iv) shall not include punitive or moral damages.

4. An investor of a Party affected by an expropriation shall have a right, under the law of the Party making the expropriation, to prompt review, by a judicial or other independent authority of that Party, of the decision to expropriate and of

the valuation of its investment in accordance with the principles set out in this article.

5. This article does not apply to the issuance of compulsory licences granted in relation to intellectual property rights, or to the revocation, limitation or creation of intellectual property rights, to the extent that such issuance, revocation, limitation or creation is consistent with applicable international agreements on intellectual property rights binding on both Parties.
6. For greater certainty, this article is intended to reflect customary international law concerning the obligation of states with respect to expropriation.
7. An action or a series of actions by a Party cannot constitute an expropriation unless it interferes with a tangible or intangible property right or property interest in an investment.
8. Proof that an action or series of actions by a Party has an adverse effect on the economic value of an investment of an investor of the other Party or interferes with the investment-backed expectations of the investor, standing alone, does not establish that an expropriation has occurred. The determination of whether an action or series of actions constitutes an expropriation requires a case-by-case, fact-based enquiry considering factors such as the character and purpose of the government action. A non-discriminatory measure by a Party that is designed and applied to achieve legitimate public objectives, such as the economic security of residents, public health, safety, the protection or promotion of internationally and domestically recognised human rights, labour rights, the rights of indigenous peoples, social justice and the protection of the environment, does not constitute an expropriation.

5.7 Compensation for losses

Cross references

Section 5.3	National treatment	110
Section 5.4	Most favoured nation	124
Section 5.5	Fair and equitable treatment and the minimum standard of treatment	138
Section 5.12	Reservations and exceptions	224
Section 6.13	Enforcement of investor obligations	372
Section 7.1	Investor–state dispute settlement	408

Many IIAs deal with losses experienced by foreign investors in connection with war, civil disturbance and other extraordinary events separately from expropriation. Because of the exceptional nature of these kinds of events, often they are not covered by private insurance. Customary international law is generally understood as not requiring compensation in these circumstances, unless the state has failed to act in a duly diligent way. Consequently, protection in the form of an IIA commitment is often sought.

5.7.1 IIA practice

Traditionally, almost all IIAs contain some kind of provision dealing with the protection of investors in extraordinary circumstances,[227] but there are some variations in their scope. Some are limited to damage caused by people,[228] while others extend to losses resulting from natural disasters[229] and, in a few cases, a broad and undefined category of national emergency.[230]

In situations that are covered, the compensation obligations vary. In most treaties, investors of party states are required to be accorded treatment no less favourable than that accorded to investors of other states with respect to any compensation, restitution or other settlement, a version of MFN treatment.[231] Many others guarantee treatment no less favourable than that accorded to domestic investors, a form of national treatment.[232] A third category of IIAs provides MFN and national treatment where losses are caused by human activity, but only MFN treatment in the case of losses due to natural disaster.[233] However structured, provisions of this kind do not specify standards for the compensation required because, unlike IIA provisions dealing with expropriation discussed above, the standard is a relative one determined by reference to the treatment of others.

A few IIAs provide an absolute obligation to compensate for a limited category of losses occasioned by actions of the host state's armed forces.[234] For this category of

---

227 Mexico–Argentina, Agreement between the Government of the United Mexican States and the Government of the Republic of Argentina for the Promotion and Reciprocal Protection of Investments, signed 13 November 1996, in force 22 June 1998, is an exception.

228 E.g. US model BIT, Art. 5.4 (losses limited to losses due to armed conflict or civil strife).

229 E.g. Canadian model FIPA, Art. 12 (losses to due armed conflict, civil strife or natural disaster).

230 E.g. Indian model BIPPA, Art. 6 (losses limited to war or other armed conflict, a state of national emergency or civil disturbance). See also India–Singapore CECA (2005), Art. 12; ASEAN Agreement (2009), Art. 12. The COMESA Investment Agreement (2007) (Art. 21.3) has a similar provision except that natural disasters are specifically excluded.

231 E.g. Ethiopia–Malaysia, Agreement between the Government of the Federal Democratic Republic of Ethiopia and the Government of Malaysia for the Promotion and Protection of Investments, signed 22 October 1998, in force 25 June 2004.

232 E.g. COMESA Investment Agreement (2007), Art. 21.1; Indian model BIPPA, Art. 6; India–Singapore CECA (2005), Art. 12; Canadian model FIPA, Art. 12 (simply referring to non-discriminatory treatment); US model BIT, Art. 5.4 (simply referring to non-discriminatory treatment).

233 E.g. Mexico–Cuba, Agreement between the United Mexican States and the Republic of Cuba for the Promotion and Reciprocal Protection of Investments, signed 30 May 2001, in force 29 March 2002.

234 E.g. US model BIT, Art. 5.5 (limited to losses due to requisitioning of the investment by host state armed forces and unnecessary destruction by armed forces); COMESA Investment Agreement (2007), Art. 21.2.

loss, some IIAs impose compensation requirements that are the same as those for expropriation,[235] while others set a different standard.[236]

Box 5.11 Summary of options for compensation for losses provision

1. *No obligation to provide compensation for losses*
2. *Compensation for losses provision limited to MFN treatment and/or national treatment or both and limited to particular kinds of causes*

   Causes triggering the obligation may include any or all of the following:

   a. War, armed conflict and civil disturbance
   b. Natural disasters
   c. National emergencies
3. *Compensation for losses provision that requires compensation in limited circumstances in addition to when compensation is required by MFN and national treatment*

5.7.2 Discussion of options

1. *No obligation to provide compensation for losses*

Even if no compensation for losses provision were included in an IIA, a state would still be bound to provide MFN treatment and national treatment with respect to its treatment of foreign investors to the extent that it had agreed to those obligations in the IIA. Consequently, if an IIA contains MFN and national treatment obligations, they may apply in relation to the compensation paid by a state for losses, even if there is no separate compensation for losses provision. In addition, a reasonable level of protection of foreign investors would be required under any full protection and security provision agreed to.

It is also possible that an obligation on a host state to pay compensation for losses would be incorporated into an IIA, if (i) the IIA contained an MFN clause, and (ii) the host state had entered into another IIA that provided such an obligation.

235 E.g. US model BIT, Art. 5.5 (requiring 'prompt, adequate and effective' compensation in accordance with the expropriation provision in the model).

236 E.g. Hong Kong–United Kingdom, Agreement between the Government of the Hong Kong Special Administrative Region of the People's Republic of China and the Government of the United Kingdom of Great Britain and Northern Ireland for the Promotion and Protection of Investments, signed 30 July 1998, in force 12 April 1999 (restitution or reasonable compensation); Mauritius–Singapore, Agreement between the Government of the Republic of Mauritius and the Government of the Republic of Singapore for the Promotion and Protection of Investments, signed 4 March 2000, in force 19 April 2000 (domestic standard). The IISD model treaty prohibits investors from assisting in or being complicit in violations of human rights committed by third parties or by the host state or its agents at any time, including during civil strife (Art. 14).

2. *Compensation for losses provision limited to MFN treatment and/or national treatment or both and limited to particular kinds of causes including any or all of the following: (i) war, armed conflict and civil disturbance; (ii) natural disasters; and (iii) national emergencies.*

If the host state's obligation is limited to providing treatment no less favourable than the treatment it provides to other foreign investors (the MFN obligation), it remains able to prefer national investors. This gives more flexibility to host states than a national treatment obligation, but less protection to foreign investors. Capital-exporting states and their investors would prefer national treatment. It is not clear in most treaty models how these protections differ from the basic MFN and national treatment obligation found in most IIAs. Their main purpose is to clarify that these obligations apply even in the extreme circumstances contemplated.

In terms of the causes of losses triggering a compensation obligation, natural disasters are out of the state's control and may create enormous and unpredictable stresses on host states. In these situations, the compensation of nationals might be the first priority and paying the same compensation to foreigners might be an onerous burden. National emergencies, which could include natural disasters, are an open-ended and unpredictable category of situations where host states may, at least in some circumstances, want to favour nationals. As with natural disasters, a national treatment obligation could prove to be a heavy burden. An MFN obligation would trigger obligations in practice only if the state compensated some foreigners. As a result, the MFN obligation would impose a more limited burden and one that the state is in control of by its actions related to the payment of compensation to foreigners.

War and civil disturbance are the most specific and narrowest category of events triggering an obligation to compensate for losses and are the subject of some protection in almost every agreement. Nevertheless, a national treatment commitment may prove onerous, depending on the magnitude of the events. An MFN commitment would be more manageable for host states.

If national treatment is to be avoided, however, the IIA should make sure that the general national treatment obligation is drafted in such a way as to exclude any payments to nationals to compensate for losses due to any of the identified causes.

No matter what limitations are imposed on compensation for losses, it also possible that a higher obligation on a host state to pay compensation for losses would be incorporated into an IIA if the IIA contained an MFN clause and the state had entered into another IIA that provided a more demanding compensation obligation, including, for example, a mandatory compensation obligation as described in option 3.

3. *Compensation for losses provision that requires compensation in limited circumstances in addition to when compensation is required by MFN and national treatment*

This is the most onerous provision for host states, but provides the best protection for investors. Treaties generally limit this kind of mandatory compensation obligation to losses caused by the host state requisitioning or destroying an investor's property, other than during combat or where required by the necessity of the situation. In some circumstances, these kinds of acts may trigger compensation under an IIA's expropriation provision even where no specific compensation obligation is included in the IIA. The obligation to compensate in these circumstances could be excluded in some cases on national security grounds if an appropriate exception is included in the IIA.[237]

In a very narrow range of circumstances, a state may be able to avoid its IIA obligations by relying on general customary international law rules dealing with *force majeure* and necessity.[238] *Force majeure* refers to situations that are beyond the control of the state that make it impossible for the state to comply with its obligations. A state may rely on necessity to justify its actions where those actions are the only means to protect its essential interests against a serious and imminent peril.

5.7.3 Discussion of sample provision

The Guide sample provision adopts the standard used in the US model BIT, which simply prohibits discrimination by the host state government with respect to whatever measures it undertakes to respond to armed conflict or civil strife contrary to the MFN obligation. This is the narrowest specification of the causes triggering a compensation obligation in existing IIAs. In this context, discrimination by a party state against investors from other party states would include more favourable treatment of foreign investors from non-party states. The standard for discrimination is defined by reference to the MFN provision in the IIA.[239] By setting a relative standard that is measured against compensation meted out to others, this provision leaves considerable discretion to the host state to decide what compensation is appropriate, taking its means into account.

The less predictable categories of situations referred to in some other treaties, such as natural disasters and national emergencies, do not give rise to obligations under the sample provision. The sample provision provides that the general MFN and national treatment obligations do not apply to state actions in response to these situations. No mandatory compensation obligation has been included for any particular kind of action. Such an obligation may be onerous for states that may be unable to compensate their own nationals and is included in only a few treaties. It is possible that a general expropriation obligation in an IIA may apply in any case where the action of the state constitutes an expropriation subject to any applicable general exception.[240]

---

237 See Section 5.12 (Reservations and exceptions).

238 These customary international law rules are codified in the ILC Draft Articles on State Responsibility, op. cit., Arts. 23 and 25.

239 See Section 5.3 (National treatment) and Section 5.4 (Most favoured nation). This approach follows the Norwegian Draft model APPI, Art. 7.

240 See Section 5.6 (Limitations on expropriation and nationalisation).

In the sample provision, an additional specific exclusion has been inserted that provides that investors are not entitled to the benefit of the article if they have been complicit in serious violations of human rights in connection with the armed conflict or civil unrest. This limitation does not exist in any IIA and may be a concern for capital-exporting states and their investors. Nevertheless, it has been included in the sample provision to create an incentive for investors to avoid such violations.

Sections 6.7–6.11 (obligations of investors) discuss sample provisions that complement this limitation. Sample provisions provide examples of standards for investors in relation to their observance of domestic law in the host state, including laws relating to human and labour rights, and the rights of indigenous peoples, as well as prohibitions on complicity in serious violations of human rights, and bribery and corruption. These sample provisions contemplate that in circumstances in which investors engage in conduct which breaches these standards, they may be held civilly liable to the host state or persons of the host state who suffer losses as a result in the domestic courts of the investor's home state, as well as in courts in the host state. They also provide that investors may be held criminally liable for violating prohibitions on complicity in corruption or serious violations of human rights.[241]

5.7.4 Sample provision: compensation for losses owing to armed conflict or civil strife

Compensation for Losses Owing to Armed Conflict or Civil Strife

1. Each Party shall accord to investors of the other Party and to their investments treatment in accordance with [Guide sample provision in Section 5.4 (Most favoured nation)] with respect to measures it adopts or maintains relating to losses suffered by investments in its territory owing to armed conflict or civil strife. [Guide sample provision in Section 5.3 (National treatment)] shall not apply to measures referred to in this section.
2. [Guide sample provision in Section 5.4 (Most favoured nation)] and [Guide sample provision in Section 5.3 (National treatment)] shall not apply to measures adopted or maintained by a state in response to a natural disaster or national emergency.
3. Section 1 shall not apply to investors of the other Party or to their investments where such investors or investments are complicit in the perpetration of egregious violations of human rights, including war crimes, crimes against humanity, genocide, torture, extra judicial killing, forced disappearance and forcible displacement, in the Party in connection with armed conflict or civil strife referred to in section 1.

241 See Section 6.13 (Enforcement of investor obligations).

5.8 Free transfer of funds

Cross references

Most IIAs provide some form of guarantee regarding an investor's freedom to transfer funds related to its investment out of the host state.[242] Investors consider flexibility to repatriate profits made from their investment, proceeds from the sale of the investment and other funds associated with their investment to be fundamentally important. On the other hand, states need a certain amount of flexibility in order to deal with problems such as capital flight and, more generally, to manage their monetary and financial policies, and to engage in law enforcement that may require limiting international transfers in some circumstances. Developing countries are especially vulnerable to sudden and significant financial flows that may require regulation.

Agreements that contemplate a right of establishment typically also provide for a right to transfer funds *into* host states.[243] Such rights complement and reinforce the investor's right to enter and operate in a host state.

Traditionally, many IIAs contained unqualified prohibitions on host state restrictions related to the transfer of funds by investors. In many more recent IIAs, transfer of funds provisions seek to accommodate the interests of host states and investors in a more balanced way by creating a basic prohibition on transfer restrictions, but listing extensive exceptions to provide host states with the flexibility that they need to engage in necessary financial and monetary management and law enforcement.

5.8.1 IIA practice

Transfers covered

Most IIAs commit host states to ensuring that investors can transfer funds related to their investments out of the host state without delay and in a specific currency.[244] As noted, agreements that provide a right of establishment typically also provide for a right to transfer funds into host states.[245] Usually the same obligations regarding freedom for transfers and any exceptions apply equally to transfers into and out of the host state.

---

242 E.g. IISD model treaty, Art. 11; Canadian model FIPA, Art. 14; US model BIT, Art. 7; Indian model BIPPA, Art. 7; UK model IPPA, Art. 6; Norwegian Draft model APPI, Art. 9; India–Singapore CECA (2005), Art. 6.6; ASEAN Agreement (2009), Art. 13; and the COMESA Investment Agreement (2007), Art. 15.

243 E.g. Canadian model FIPA, Art. 14; US model BIT, Art. 7.

244 Ibid. Most Caribbean and Pacific BITs contain such a provision (Malik, op. cit., at 29, 58).

245 E.g. Canadian model FIPA, Art. 14; US model BIT, Art. 7; ASEAN–Australia–New Zealand FTA (2009) Investment Chapter, Art. 5.1.

There are, however, differences in approach regarding whether the right to transfer applies to all funds or only to specific types of funds listed exhaustively in the agreement. The Canadian, US, UK, Indian, Norwegian and IISD models all extend the transfer requirement to all funds related to an investment and provide an extensive illustrative list of types of funds.[246] This is the most common approach.[247] The COMESA Investment Agreement sets out an exhaustive list of transfers that a member state is obliged to permit.[248] Often the wording of exhaustive list provisions is broad enough to cover most transfers that investors would want to make in practice.

Some IIAs limit the free transfer obligation by making it 'subject to its laws and regulations'. The COMESA Investment Agreement adopts this approach, which means that a host state is prohibited from applying only restrictions on transfer that are different from those that exist from time to time under its law.[249] Such an approach gives maximum flexibility to host states, but limited assurance to investors regarding their ability to transfer funds. Host states can define the rules regarding transfers of funds as they choose so long as the rules are in accordance with national law.

One final variation found in a few IIAs is to permit transfers out of the host country, but only after capital has been invested for a minimum period of time, usually a year, as in the Chile–Austria BIT.[250]

Currency in which transfers are to take place, applicable exchange rate and time frame

Another issue related to the design of funds transfer provisions is the currency in which transfers must be permitted. The UK, Indian and Canadian model agreements all provide that transfers are to be permitted in the currency originally used for the investment or any other freely convertible currency agreed on by the parties.[251] The US, Norwegian and IISD models simply require that transfers be permitted in a freely usable currency.[252] As noted above, 'freely usable currency' may be given the precise and limited meaning attributed to the expression under the IMF Articles of

246 E.g. ASEAN–Australia–New Zealand FTA (2009) Investment Chapter, Art. 5.1. The same approach is followed in the India–Singapore CECA (2005) (Art. 6.6 (1)); the ASEAN Agreement (2009) (Art. 13.1); and the Mauritius–Singapore BIT (2000) (Art. 8). The UK model IPPA (Art. 6) refers to the 'unrestricted transfer of [investors'] investments and returns'.

247 UNCTAD (2007), *Bilateral Investment Treaties*, 1995–2007, op. cit., at 61.

248 COMESA Investment Agreement (2007), Art. 15. Some other existing BITs contain similar language: e.g. China–Jamaica BIT (1994); Colombian model agreement, Art. V.

249 COMESA Investment Agreement (2007), Art. 15. Some other existing BITS contain similar language: e.g. China–Jamaica BIT (1994).

250 Chile–Austria, Agreement between the Republic of Chile and the Republic of Austria for the Promotion and Reciprocal Protection of Investment, signed 8 September 1997, in force 22 October 2000, *Ad* Art. 4(1).

251 UK model IPPA, Art. 8. Indian model BIPPA, Art. 7(3) (no agreement of the parties required); Canadian model FIPA, Art. 14.2.

252 US model BIT, Art. 7.2; IISD model treaty, Art. 11(B). See, similarly, ASEAN–Australia–New Zealand FTA (2009) Investment Chapter, Art. 5.2.

Agreement.[253] Only the euro, Japanese yen, US dollar and UK pound sterling are recognised as freely usable currencies.

Most agreements provide that the exchange rate applied to funds transferred should be the rate in effect at the date of the transfer.[254] The Indian model treaty and the Canadian model treaty refer to the 'market rate'.[255] The UK model, however, refers to the 'rate of exchange applicable on the date of transfer pursuant to the exchange regulations in force'.[256] In either case, if the host state has a floating currency exchange rate, the market will determine the applicable rate. For the first group of IIAs that refer to a 'market rate', it is not clear what happens if there is no market rate. In the case of the UK model, if a state has an officially administered exchange rate, that rate will be applied. Resort to the official rate may be advantageous or disadvantageous to the investor depending on the circumstances.[257] If the host country has an overvalued official exchange rate, investors will be disadvantaged because they will receive less foreign currency than under a market rate. Equally, if the official rate is artificially low, investors will receive a benefit.[258]

In terms of timing, most IIAs that address the issue require that transfers be permitted without delay. The India–Singapore CECA requires only that the transfer be permitted without 'undue delay'.[259] It is also possible to stipulate a maximum time period.[260]

Exceptions to funds transfer obligations

Neither the Indian nor the UK model treaty provides any exception to the funds transfer obligations. In contrast, many agreements set out an extensive list of circumstances in which transfers may be restricted for the application and enforcement of laws in particular areas. The Canadian, US and IISD models all contemplate that transfers may be restricted in connection with the good faith, non-discriminatory application of a state's laws relating to:

- Bankruptcy, insolvency or the protection of the rights of creditors;
- Issuing, trading or dealing in securities;
- Criminal or penal offences;

253 See Section 5.6 (Limitations on expropriation and nationalisation).

254 The IISD model treaty, Art. 11(B); US model BIT, Art. 7.2.

255 Indian model BIPPA, Art. 7(3); Canadian model FIPA, Art. 14.2. See, similarly, ASEAN–Australia–New Zealand FTA (2009) Investment Chapter, Art. 5.2.

256 UK model IPPA, Art. 8.1; US model BIT, Art. 7.1; Canadian model FIPA, Art. 14.1; ASEAN–Australia–New Zealand FTA (2009) Investment Chapter, Art. 5.1. Timing is not addressed in the COMESA Investment Agreement (2007).

257 This issue is not addressed in the Norwegian Draft model APPI.

258 Some treaties provide that, where there is no market rate, the rate shall be the cross rate obtained from those rates which would be applied by the International Monetary Fund on the date of payment for conversions of the currencies concerned into Special Drawing Rights; e.g. German model treaty, Art. 7(2).

259 India–Singapore CECA (2005) Art. 6.6 (1). The Indian model BIPPA refers to 'without unreasonable delay' (Art. 7(3)).

260 UNCTAD (2007), *Treaties 1995–2007*, at 61.

- Reporting regarding currency or other financial transfers; and
- Ensuring compliance with orders or judgments in judicial or administrative proceedings.

These kinds of restrictions are commonly imposed in practice by many countries. For example, a bankrupt foreign investor operating in host state will not be permitted to transfer is assets out the country to defeat the claims of local creditors. A similar list of exceptions is included in the India–Singapore CECA and the ASEAN Agreement.[261] The ASEAN Agreement adds taxation, social security, public retirement and compulsory savings programmes, as well as requirements for severance payments to employees as laws in relation to which restrictions on transfer of funds are permitted.

A number of agreements contain provisions that permit countries to restrict transfers in connection with the regulation of financial institutions, though the majority of IIAs do not contain such provisions.[262] For example, Canada's model permits restrictions on transfers by financial institutions in some circumstances in the interests of maintaining the soundness and integrity of financial institutions. These kinds of measures are sometimes referred to as based on 'prudential' considerations.[263]

Other treaties permit states to restrict transfers in balance of payments emergencies.[264] Such an emergency occurs when a host state's foreign currency reserves are exceptionally low. During such a period it will be extremely difficult for the state to convert its own currency into foreign currencies for the purpose of providing foreign currency for transfers of funds related to investments. In IIAs that contain such a limitation, it is common to require that restrictions on transfers be temporary, in accordance with IMF requirements,[265] and applied in good faith and on a non-discriminatory basis. These requirements are intended to assure foreign investors that host state restrictions for balance of payments purposes will not be imposed lightly or in ways that would disadvantage them in comparison with local investors. The IMF requirements do not relate to restrictions on capital transfers. Under the IMF rules, a member is prohibited from restricting payments related to current transactions, without the approval of the IMF. These include regular payments in connection with business activities, such as payments for goods and services, short-term bank loans

---

261 India–Singapore CECA (2005), Art. 6.6(2); ASEAN Agreement (2009), Art. 13.3.

262 Malik, op. cit., at 29.

263 Canadian model FIPA, Arts. 14.6 and 14.7. Some other agreements subject the transfer guarantee to domestic law generally. Some treaties have a general exception for a broader class of prudential measures as discussed below, e.g. US model BIT, Art. 20. See Section 5.12 (Reservations and exceptions).

264 IISD model treaty, Art. 11(G). Some broader formulations are also found. The India–Singapore CECA (2005) allows restriction on payments in the event of 'serious balance of payments or external financial difficulties' (Art. 6.7). In the Papua New Guinea–Australia BIT, a party may restrict payments in 'exceptional financial or economic circumstances'. The ASEAN–Australia–New Zealand FTA (2009) Investment Chapter has a similar list (Art. 5.3).

265 *Amended Articles of Agreement of the International Monetary Fund* (1992) 31 *International Legal Materials* 1309. Article VIII, section 2(a) prohibits restrictions on 'the making of payments and transfers for current international transactions' without the approval of the IMF.

and transfers of income from a business. Payment of proceeds from the sale of an investment is an example of a capital payment.

GATT and *GATS* require compliance with IMF requirements if restrictions are to be imposed on international transfers related to current transactions in goods and services.[266] These obligations apply to all WTO members. *GATS* obligations apply only in relation to sectors that a member has listed in its national schedule of commitments. *GATS* goes on to provide that in sectors where a member has undertaken market access commitments, it cannot impose restrictions on related capital transfers.[267]

Referring to compliance with the IMF requirements as a condition of eligibility for an IIA exception means that where a state seeks to take advantage of this exception to defeat an investor's claim that a state has breached a free transfer of funds obligation, the state's compliance with the IMF's requirements will be adjudicated by an investor–state tribunal. This may be considered anomalous since the IMF rules are not directly enforceable at the instance of private parties in other contexts. An alternative approach that avoids this problem would be simply to say that a state might restrict payments to address a balance of payments emergency and leave it up to an investor–state tribunal to apply that provision to the situation in which a state has acted. Such an approach, however, provides less certainty to investors.

It is also possible that a state might be able to justify a restriction on transfers of funds based on exceptions in an IIA that permit it to take action to protect its essential security interests, notwithstanding any obligation in the IIA.[268] Security exceptions are discussed below.[269]

Box 5.12 Summary of options for transfer of funds provision

1. *No obligation to permit transfer of funds*
2. *Obligation to permit the transfer of funds with exceptions and qualifications*
    a. Open or closed list of transfers that must be permitted
    b. Subject to exceptions

    As noted above, many IIAs contain detailed lists of situations in which restrictions are permitted, including the application of laws in some or all of these areas.

    i. Bankruptcy, insolvency or the protection of the rights of creditors

(Continued)

266 *GATT*, Art. XV, I Arts. XI and XII. Both *GATT* and *GATS* impose some additional requirements. *GATS* limits a member's ability to impose restrictions to situations involving a 'serious balance-of-payments and external financial difficulties or threat thereof'.

267 *GATS*, Arts. XI and XVI, footnote 8.

268 The OECD's Code of Liberalization of Capital Markets and Code of Liberalization of Invisible Operations both contemplate the possibility of restrictions in these circumstances.

269 See Section 5.12 (Reservations and exceptions).

(Continued)

ii. Issuing, trading or dealing in securities

iii. Criminal or penal offences

iv. Reporting regarding currency or other financial transfers

v. Ensuring compliance with orders or judgments in judicial or administrative proceedings

vi. Taxation

vii. Social security, public retirement and compulsory savings programmes

viii. Payments of remuneration and severance to employees.

Other exceptions in IIAs allow the restriction of payments by financial institutions in connection with prudential management to ensure the maintenance of the safety, soundness, integrity and financial responsibility of financial institutions and to address balance of payments emergencies.

3. *Unqualified obligation to permit transfer of funds*

5.8.2 Discussion of options

1. *No obligation to permit transfer of funds*

Based on existing IIA practice, not including a funds transfer obligation in an IIA would be very unusual. A transfer of funds provision grants protection to investors regarding what may be the most important business objective of their investment, to repatriate capital and profits to their operation in their home state. Not having a transfer of funds provision would be a significant gap in investor protection. At the same time, a transfer of funds provision can be useful to host countries because it clearly sets out what restrictions on transfers are permitted and insulates states that impose such restrictions from challenge by investors through investor–state arbitration. In addition, the general commitment not to restrict transfers may encourage investment on the basis that it ensures that investors can repatriate returns and other financial flows from their investments.

Even if no transfer of funds obligation is included in an IIA, it is possible that such an obligation on a host state would be incorporated into an IIA if (i) the IIA contained an MFN clause and (ii) the state had entered into another IIA that provided such an obligation. In addition, certain kinds of restrictions on transfers may be characterised as inconsistent with an IIA obligation to provide fair and equitable treatment or, in extreme cases, an IIA obligation not to expropriate without compensation, depending on their nature and their manner of implementation.[270] To avoid the application of these provisions, an express exception would be required.

270 A Kolo and T Wälde (2008), 'Capital Transfers under Modern Investment Treaties', in Reinisch, op. cit., at 227–242.

2. *Obligation to permit the transfer of funds with exceptions and qualifications*

a. Open or closed list of transfers that must be permitted

Based on current practice, the items identified in provisions that set out a closed list of transfers permitted include most categories of transfers that are likely to be of interest to an investor. Nevertheless, a capital-exporting state is likely to prefer an open list to ensure that any new forms of financial flows are covered. An open list, however, reduces the certainty of its scope of application for states compared with a closed list.

The practice of making the commitment to permit funds transfer subject to domestic laws and regulations found in the COMESA Investment Agreement would seem to significantly reduce the benefit of the provision for investors. Defining the restriction by reference to domestic law in the host state renders it uncertain, non-transparent and subject to change. It does, however, give maximum flexibility to the host state.

b. Exceptions

As noted above, many IIAs contain detailed lists of situations in which restrictions are permitted, including the application of its laws in some or all of the specific areas identified in the summary.

These exceptions relate to areas of domestic policy that are not discriminatory and are addressed in most countries' laws, and they are increasingly found in IIAs. Most states impose these same restrictions on transfer. Their inclusion provides certainty regarding the situations in which host states may act to restrict transfers for the benefit of both parties.

Other exceptions in IIAs allow the restriction of payments by financial institutions in connection with prudential management to ensure the maintenance of the safety, soundness, integrity and financial responsibility of financial institutions and to address balance of payments emergencies. The last exception may be tied to compliance with the IMF Articles of Agreement to provide more certainty to investors. With respect to payments related to current transactions in goods and services, WTO members have committed to compliance with the IMF requirements under the *GATT* and the *GATS*. Alternatively, an exception may be drafted to be self-judging, meaning that it is up to the host state to decide in its discretion whether there is a balance of payments emergency or not. With such a provision, compliance with the requirements of the Articles of Agreement of the IMF would not be necessary.

If a transfer of funds obligation is included in an IIA, but is made subject to exceptions, it is possible that an unqualified obligation on a host state would be incorporated into an IIA if (i) the IIA contained an MFN clause and (ii) the state had entered into another IIA that included such an unqualified obligation. In these circumstances, the exceptions would not apply.

3. *Unqualified obligation to permit transfer of funds*

While this form of obligation appears in many treaties and provides the maximum protection to investors, it does not expressly permit various kinds of restrictions for legitimate policy purposes as described in relation to option 2. The only real issue to be addressed with such an obligation is whether there should be an open or closed list of permitted transfers.[271] This was discussed in relation to option 1.

5.8.3 Discussion of sample provision

While funds transfer provisions have not raised the same kinds of problems in investor–state arbitration as IIA provisions on expropriation and fair and equitable treatment, the drafting of funds transfer provisions could usefully incorporate some of the innovations from the IIA models reviewed. The sample provision has been drafted to ensure that it strikes a balance between investors' interest in being able to transfer funds out of the host state without restriction and the host state's interest in regulating transfers for the legitimate purposes of law enforcement, the regulation of financial institutions and the financial management of its economy.

Payments subject to funds transfer obligation: The sample definition of what payments are subject to the obligation to permit transfers is broad, but, in the interests of certainty, is fixed. While this is not the most common approach in IIAs, fixing the categories of payments is not likely to raise concerns for capital-exporting states and their investors because the provision covers most types of transfers likely to be of interest to investors. Since most agreements do not contemplate a right of establishment, the sample funds transfer provision does not extend to transfers *into* the host state. It applies only to transfers *out of* the host state. Where a funds transfer provision is used in an IIA that also creates a right of establishment, consideration should be given to whether the funds transfer obligation should be extended to inward transfers, subject to any limitations provided in the agreement.[272] The sample provision also provides that investors' home states may not require their investors to transfer funds, or penalise its investors that fail to transfer funds following the Canadian model. The sample provision goes on to clarify that this prohibition does not prevent a host state from restricting transfers where permitted by the exceptions discussed below.

Required currency for transfer: The sample provision adopts the approach of the Canadian model and many other agreements,[273] which provides that transfers are to be permitted in the currency originally used for the investment or any other currency agreed to by the parties. The use of 'freely usable currency', which may include only a small number of major developed country currencies, has not been adopted. Unless

271 To the extent that an IIA has an exception permitting the enforcement of measures to ensure compliance with laws and regulations that are not inconsistent with the provisions of the IIA, some of the exceptions listed in option 2 may be covered. Such an exception is discussed below. See Section 5.12 (Reservations and exceptions).

272 See above Section 5.2 (Right of establishment).

273 UK model IPPA, Art. 8; Indian model BIPPA, Art. 7(3) (no agreement of the parties required); Canadian model FIPA, Art. 14.2.

otherwise agreed by the investor and the state party concerned, payments are to be made at the market rate of exchange applicable on the date of transfer. If there was no market rate of exchange and the parties could not agree on another rate of exchange, the default is the rate of exchange applicable on the date of transfer pursuant to the exchange regulations in force in the host state. This approach follows the UK model.[274]

Exceptions for law enforcement: The sample provision incorporates the practical exceptions for measures to give effect to the application of laws in various areas that restrict transfers for different public policy reasons, reflecting those in the COMESA Investment Agreement, the ASEAN Agreement and the India–Singapore CECA, as well as the Canadian and US model treaties.[275] An exception for taxation measures could be added to the list or a general exception for taxation may be included in an IIA. Such a general exception for taxation is discussed below.[276]

Exceptions for prudential measures: The sample provision permits states to restrict the transfer of funds involving financial institutions in order to maintain the 'safety, soundness, integrity or financial responsibility of financial institutions' following the Canadian and other models. A broader general exception for prudential policies to protect depositors and others with a stake in financial institutions as well as the stability of the host state's financial system as a whole is provided for below.[277] This exception is included in the general exceptions section because host state actions driven by these considerations may not be limited to restrictions on the transfer of funds out of the country.

Exclusion for measures taken to address balance of payments emergency: The sample provision contains an exclusion for measures taken in a balance of payments emergency.[278] In IIAs that contain such a limitation, it is common practice to require that restrictions on transfers be temporary, in accordance with IMF standards, and made in good faith and on a non-discriminatory basis. These qualifications are intended to assure investors that restrictions for balance of payments purposes will be rarely used and will be fairly implemented. This means that in any case where a state seeks to take advantage of this exception to defeat an investor's claim the state's compliance with the requirements of IMF rules will be adjudicated by an investor–state tribunal. As noted, an alternative to avoid this possibility, it could simply be provided that it is

274 An alternative default provision could be added, such as in the agreement between Brunei Darussalam and China (2000): '…in the event that the market rate of exchange does not exist, the rate of exchange shall correspond to the cross rate obtained from those rates which would be applied by the International Monetary Fund on the date of payment for conversions of the currencies concerned into Special Drawing Rights'.

275 US model BIT, Art. 7.1; Canadian model FIPA, Art. 14.1; India–Singapore CECA (2005), Art. 6.6(2); ASEAN Agreement (2009), Art. 13.3.

276 See Section 5.12 (Reservations and exceptions).

277 See Section 5.12 (Reservations and exceptions).

278 At a minimum, it might be useful to include an exception that permits restrictions in circumstances in which transfers may be restricted under other international agreements, such as in the exception in GATT Art. XII, which deals with balance of payments emergencies.

up to the state to determine if there is a balance of payments emergency and not refer to the IMF requirements.

5.8.4 Sample provision: free transfer of funds

Free Transfer of Funds

1. Each Party shall permit the following transfers relating to an investment of an investor of the other Party to be made freely and without delay out of its territory:
    a. Contributions to capital;
    b. Profits, dividends, interest, capital gains, royalty payments, management fees, technical assistance and other fees, returns in kind and other amounts derived from the investment;
    c. Proceeds from the sale of all or any part of the investment or from the partial or complete liquidation of the investment;
    d. Payments made under a contract entered into by the investor, or the investment, including payments made pursuant to a loan agreement;
    e. Remuneration to employees of the investor;
    f. Payments made pursuant to [Guide sample provision in Section 5.6 (Limitations on expropriation and nationalisation)] and [Guide sample provision in Section 5.7 (Compensation for losses)]; and
    g. Payments arising under [Guide sample provision in Section 7.1 (Investor–state dispute settlement)].
2. Each Party shall permit transfers relating to an investment of an investor of the other Party to be made in the currency in which the capital was originally invested, or in any other convertible currency agreed to by the investor and the Party concerned. Unless otherwise agreed to by the investor and the Party concerned, transfers shall be made at the market rate of exchange applicable on the date of transfer. If there is no such market rate or agreement, the rate shall be the rate of exchange applicable on the date of transfer pursuant to the exchange regulations in force in the Party.
3. Notwithstanding sections 1 and 2, a Party may prevent a transfer through the equitable, non-discriminatory and good faith application of its laws relating to:
    a. Bankruptcy, insolvency or the protection of the rights of creditors;
    b. Issuing, trading or dealing in securities;
    c. Criminal or penal offences and the payment of fines or penalties;
    d. Reports of transfers of currency or other monetary instruments;
    e. Ensuring the satisfaction of judgments in judicial or administrative proceedings;

f. Social security, public retirement and compulsory savings programmes; or

g. Payments of remuneration and severance to employees.

4. Neither Party may require its investors to transfer, or penalise its investors that fail to transfer, the income, earnings, profits or other amounts derived from or attributable to investments in the territory of the other Party.

5. Section 4 shall not be construed to prevent a Party from imposing any measure through the equitable, non-discriminatory and good faith application of its laws relating to the matters set out in subsections a. through g. of section 3.

6. Notwithstanding the provisions of sections 1, 2 and 4, and without limiting the applicability of sections 3 and 5, a Party may prevent or limit transfers by a financial institution to, or for the benefit of, an affiliate of or person related to such institution, through the equitable, non-discriminatory and good faith application of measures relating to maintenance of the safety, soundness, integrity or financial responsibility of financial institutions.

7. Notwithstanding section 1, in case of serious balance of payments difficulties or the threat of such difficulties, each Party may temporarily restrict transfers, provided that the Party's measures shall be consistent with the Article VIII of the Amended Articles of Agreement of the International Monetary Fund, in good faith and on a non-discriminatory basis.

5.9 Performance requirements

Cross references

Section 5.2	Right of establishment	104
Section 5.3	National treatment	110
Section 5.4	Most favoured nation	124
Section 5.12	Reservations and exceptions	224

Performance requirements are obligations that a state imposes on an investor to take some specific action with a view to achieving a domestic policy objective. In general, performance requirements seek to ensure that the potential benefits of foreign investment are realised. For example, an investor may be required to hire local workers or meet fixed targets for the volume of its exports. Performance requirements may be imposed by a state as a condition of permitting a foreign investor to bring its capital into the host state. They may also be imposed on an investor in relation to its ongoing operations, perhaps in exchange for some benefit such as a subsidy or tax break. Performance requirements are commonly used by many governments to ensure that their development goals are achieved.

Some commentators have criticised performance requirements as inherently redundant or inefficient. They argue that if it made business sense to do what was required by a performance requirement, the investor would do it without the performance requirement being imposed. Alternatively, if the investor would not have done what the performance requirement obliges the investor to do, it is inefficient and costly to the investor. On this basis, it is argued that the costs associated with performance requirements could deter investors from investing.[279]

Performance requirements are addressed under rules binding on WTO members. These rules intersect with IIA commitments in sometimes complex ways. The WTO rules and IIA practice are discussed below.

5.9.1 Some performance requirements are prohibited by the WTO Agreement on Trade-related Investment Measures (*TRIMs*)

Some performance requirements for investors that affect trade in goods are inconsistent with obligations under the *GATT* that require WTO members to provide national treatment to foreign goods and not to impose quotas on foreign goods entering the country. In 1984, a *GATT* panel decision, in a case brought by the USA against Canada, found certain requirements imposed by Canada's Foreign Investment Review Agency as a condition of its approval of foreign investments to be contrary to *GATT*. For example, a requirement that foreign investors source their inputs in Canada in order to be allowed to invest in Canada was found to be contrary to Canada's obligations to give national treatment under the *GATT* because it imposed a preference for Canadian goods over foreign goods.[280]

The application of these *GATT* rules to performance requirements imposed in connection with investments was confirmed by the *TRIMs* Agreement, which provides an illustrative list of trade-distorting investment measures. It includes, for example, a prohibition on restricting the ability of an investor to import inputs for its local production in the host state. The full list of *TRIMs* is set out in Box 5.13.

Box 5.13 Illustrative list of Trade-related Investment Measures contrary to the *GATT* set out in the WTO *TRIMs* Agreement

1. *TRIMs* that are inconsistent with the obligation of national treatment provided for in paragraph 4 of Article III of *GATT* 1994 [national treatment] include those which are mandatory or enforceable under domestic law or under administrative rulings, or compliance with which is necessary to obtain an advantage, and which require:

   a. The purchase or use by an enterprise of products of domestic origin or from any domestic source, whether specified in terms of particular products, in terms of volume or value of products, or in terms of a proportion of volume or value of its local production; or

(Continued)

279 UNCTAD (1998), *Bilateral Treaties in the Mid-1990s*, United Nations, Geneva.

280 World Trade Organization (WTO) (1984), *Canada – Administration of the Foreign Investment Review Act*, Report of the Panel adopted on 7 February 1984 (L/5504 – 30S/140), available at: www.wto.org/english/tratop_e/dispu_e/82fira.pdf (accessed 29 May 2012).

(Continued)

b. That an enterprise's purchases or use of imported products be limited to an amount related to the volume or value of local products that it exports.

2. *TRIMs* that are inconsistent with the obligation of general elimination of quantitative restrictions provided for in paragraph 1 of Article XI of *GATT* 1994 [prohibition on quotas] include those which are mandatory or enforceable under domestic law or under administrative rulings, or compliance with which is necessary to obtain an advantage, and which restrict:

a. The importation by an enterprise of products used in or related to its local production generally, or to an amount related to the volume or value of local production that it exports;

b. The importation by an enterprise of products used in or related to its local production by restricting its access to foreign exchange to an amount related to the foreign exchange inflows attributable to the enterprise; or

c. The exportation or sale for export by an enterprise of products, whether specified in terms of particular products, in terms of volume or value of products, or in terms of a proportion of volume or value of its local production.

As of 1 January 1995, WTO members have been subject to limitations on their ability to impose performance requirements that are inconsistent with the *TRIMs* Agreement.[281] For most WTO members, the imposition of performance requirements contrary to the *TRIMs* Agreement is prohibited. By virtue of a decision of the WTO Ministerial Conference in Hong Kong in 2005, however, least developed country members are excused from *TRIMs* obligations until 2020 in recognition of the possible development benefits associated with being able to impose such requirements.

5.9.2 Some performance requirements are prohibited by the WTO General Agreement on Trade in Services (*GATS*)

The obligations under the *TRIMs* Agreement apply only to trade in goods. It is possible, however, that some forms of performance requirements applied to investors in services sectors would be inconsistent with a country's commitments relating to

281 *TRIMs*' restrictions on the use of performance requirements apply only to measures that relate to trade in goods. The extent to which there are restrictions on measures relating to trade in services depends on a country's international obligations regarding trade in services. TRIMs' obligations were applied in *Indonesia – Certain Measures Affecting the Automobile Industry*, 2 July 1998, WT/DS54, 55, 59, 64/R.

services trade under the *GATS*. As noted above, some *GATS* obligations apply only to sectors that a country has listed in its national schedule of commitments.[282] For listed sectors, a WTO member cannot adopt specific kinds of limitations on market access and must provide national treatment to foreign services suppliers.[283] Some kinds of performance requirements may be prohibited by these obligations. For example, the imposition by a host state of requirements for an investor to use only domestic suppliers of construction services as a condition of granting approval for its investment to build a factory would probably be contrary to the *GATS* national treatment obligation if construction services were listed in the host state's national schedule of commitments. Some regional trade agreements also contain national treatment and other relevant obligations relating to performance requirements that could apply to services.

5.9.3 IIA practice

Although IIAs have not traditionally dealt with performance requirements, UNCTAD notes that restrictions on the use of performance requirements are increasingly found in more recent agreements.[284] Performance requirements may be imposed by states at two stages: (i) as a condition of admission of an investment; and (ii) in relation to the operation of an investment post admission. Performance requirement restrictions in IIAs address performance requirements at both stages.

Performance requirements as a condition of admission of an investment

A state may require investors to undertake certain actions as a condition of permitting them to invest in the country. Whether an IIA limits the ability of states to impose performance requirements as a condition of admission typically depends on whether the IIA creates a right for foreign investors of one party state to enter the market of the other party state and establish an investment. Rights of establishment were discussed above.[285] Where countries have undertaken no IIA obligation to permit the establishment of investments, they remain free to impose on investors whatever requirements they choose as a condition of permitting the entry of their investments into the local market, including performance requirements. The UK and Indian model agreements do not create a right of establishment and, consistently, do not impose restrictions on the ability of states to impose performance requirements as a condition of admission.[286] By contrast, where a state commits in an IIA to giving

---

282 See Section 3.3 (IIAs and other international obligations) and the overview of *GATS* obligations in Appendix 2.

283 The specific kinds of market access limitations that are prohibited, subject to any limitations on the market access obligation set out in a country's national schedule, are specifically listed in *GATS* Art. XIV. See the overview of *GATS* obligations in Appendix 2.

284 UNCTAD (2003), *World Investment Report 2003: FDI Policies for Development: National and International Perspectives*, United Nations, New York and Geneva, at 119–20.

285 See Section 5.2 (Right of establishment).

286 Indian model BIPPA; UK model IPPA. It may be that, in some cases, performance requirements imposed by states could be inconsistent with other IIA obligations, such as prohibitions on expropriation without compensation, the minimum standard of treatment and, if they are imposed in a discriminatory manner, national treatment and most favoured nation treatment.

foreign investors a right to establish themselves in the domestic market, the state implicitly gives up its right to impose performance requirements as a condition of access. In the Canadian and US model treaties, both of which provide a qualified right of establishment, express restrictions limit the ability of host states to impose performance requirements as a condition of permitting an investment to enter the market.[287]

Performance requirements related to the operation of an investment

Regardless of whether a right of establishment is provided for in an IIA, a state may impose performance requirements on foreign investors in relation to their activities in the host state after they bring their capital into the state, subject to any restrictions on the state's right to resort to performance requirements in the treaty. Both the US and Canadian model agreements restrict the ability of host states to impose performance requirements on investors after they are established in the market.[288] Most other IIAs do not impose specific restrictions on the use of performance requirements in this context.[289] Even without a specific provision dealing with performance requirements, however, any measure imposing performance requirements would have to be consistent with any other substantive standard in an IIA, including national treatment, MFN treatment and fair and equitable treatment.

Approaches to performance requirements provisions

A few treaties prohibit performance requirements in very general terms, but most recent treaties that address performance requirements contain detailed and specific provisions. Two main approaches are followed: (i) prohibiting performance requirements that are inconsistent with *TRIMs* and *GATS*; and (ii) prohibiting specific performance requirements, including performance requirements that are not inconsistent with *TRIMs* or *GATS*.

Incorporating TRIMs and GATS in an IIA

Some IIAs simply incorporate the obligations of the *TRIMs* Agreement, making them an obligation of the parties under the treaty. For example, the Canada–Costa Rica Foreign Investment Promotion and Protection Agreement contains the following clause relating to the *TRIMs* Agreement.

> Neither Contracting Party may impose, in connection with permitting the establishment or acquisition of an investment, or enforce in connection with the subsequent regulation of that investment, any of the requirements set forth in the World Trade Organization Agreement on Trade-related Investment Measures

---

287 Canadian model FIPA, Art. 7; US model BIT, Art. 8.

288 Canadian model FIPA, Art. 7; US model BIT, Art. 8.

289 For example, the India–Singapore CECA (2005) and the COMESA Investment Agreement (2007) do not prohibit performance requirements. In the India–Singapore CECA (2005), the parties reaffirm their commitments in this regard under the *TRIMS* Agreement (Art. 6.23).

> contained in the Final Act Embodying the Results of the Uruguay Round of Multilateral Trade Negotiations, done at Marrakech on April 15, 1994.[290]

This provision does not address *GATS* obligations. Following the approach in the provision set out above, an IIA could, however, specifically recognise the binding nature of all WTO commitments and contemplate that the party states will commit not to impose performance requirements to the extent that their other international obligations prohibit doing so. Other commitments in regional agreements could be addressed as well.

Some IIAs contain an 'application of other rules' provision that binds the party states to comply with any other international obligation to which they are both parties relating to investments and to provide the benefit of any such obligation to investors protected under the IIA.[291] Under such a provision the obligations of the *TRIMs* Agreement and the *GATS* would apply as part of the IIA so long as the IIA parties were WTO members.

Every WTO member is bound by its obligations under *GATS* and the *TRIMs* Agreement. Reiterating these obligations in an IIA, however, changes the impact of these obligations in at least one important way: they become enforceable through the dispute settlement procedures in the IIA. This could be avoided by specifically excluding any performance requirement commitments from the scope of the dispute settlement procedures.

Detailed specification of prohibited performance requirements going beyond TRIMs *(*TRIMs *plus)*

In both the Canadian and US model agreements, the prohibition on the imposition of performance requirements applies to specific kinds of requirements set out in the agreement. This list includes some performance requirements that would be permitted under the *TRIMs* Agreement and *GATS*, such as commitments to transfer technology. For example, the Canadian model treaty provides that neither state party can:

> ... impose or enforce any of the following commitments which relate to the *establishment, acquisition, expansion, management, conduct or operation* of an investment of an investor of a Party *or a non-Party*:

a. to export a given level or percentage of goods or services;

b. to achieve a given level or percentage of domestic content;

290 Canada–Costa Rica, Agreement between the Government of Canada and the Government of the Republic of Costa Rica for the Promotion and Protection of Investments, signed 18 March 1998, in force 29 September 1999, Art. VI. A similar provision is found in the ASEAN–Australia–New Zealand FTA (2009) Investment Chapter, Art. 5. The IISD model treaty 'recognizes' the limits imposed by the *TRIMs* Agreement (Art. 26), but it is not clear if this amounts to an obligation not to put in place performance requirements inconsistent with *TRIMs*.

291 UNCTAD (2007), *Bilateral Investment Treaties 1995–2006*, op. cit., at 65–6 describing the Germany–Thailand BIT, Art. 7. The same provision is Art. 8 of the German model BIT.

c. to purchase, use or accord a preference to goods produced or services provided in its territory, or to purchase goods or services from a person in its territory;

d. to relate in any way the volume or value of imports to the volume or value of exports or to the amount of foreign exchange inflows associated with such investments;

e. to restrict sales of goods or services in its territory that such investment produces or provides by relating such sales in any way to the volume or value of its exports or foreign exchange earnings; and

f. to transfer technology, a production process or other proprietary knowledge to a person in its territory, except where the requirement is imposed or the commitment or undertaking is enforced by a court, administrative tribunal or competition authority, to remedy an alleged violation of competition laws or to act in a manner not inconsistent with other provisions of this Agreement; ...[292] (Emphasis added.)

A subset of these requirements may not be imposed by a host state as a condition of granting an advantage, such as a subsidy, to an investor. Because the obligation not to impose performance requirements relates to the 'establishment, acquisition, [and] expansion' of an investment, it applies to the pre-establishment stage. In other words, under this provision, a host state would not be able to impose any of these performance requirements on a foreign investor as a condition of allowing the investor into its market. The reference to 'management, conduct or operation' means that the host country is also prohibited from imposing any of these performance requirements on a foreign investor at the post-establishment stage in relation to these activities.[293] The performance requirement prohibition in this model extends to measures related to services as well as those related to goods.

In the performance requirement provision in the Canadian model agreement, all of these obligations also apply in relation to how party states deal with investors from *non-party states*. For example, under the Canadian model provision, a party state could not approve an investment by an investor from a third party state in return for its agreement to a performance requirement, such as a commitment to transfer technology. The provisions apply in this way in order to ensure that investors from the other state party to the IIA are not treated unfavourably compared with investors from third party states.[294] In the example above, if the prohibition did not extend to performance requirements imposed on investors from third party states, there would be a risk that Canada's foreign investment review agency would approve an investment from a third party state where the investor gave an undertaking to transfer technology, instead of approving an investment of an investor of a

292 Canadian model FIPA, Art. 7.

293 A similar approach is followed in treaties negotiated by Japan (UNCTAD (2007), *Treaties 1995–2006*, op. cit., at 67).

294 See the similar provision in the US model BIT. The Canadian model FIPA provides for limited specific exceptions to these obligations (Art. 9).

party state who could not be asked to make such a commitment because of the performance requirement prohibition in the treaty. This sort of provision seeks to ensure a level playing field for all investors. It is also found in the US model BIT, but not in other IIAs.[295]

Norway's draft model treaty contemplates a provision similar to the Canadian model, but contains some additional general requirements. It provides that any additional restrictions on a host state's resort to performance requirements should be negotiated taking into account both the specific needs of Norway's investors as well as any particular concerns of the host state. All performance requirements that are imposed must be transparent, non-discriminatory and applied in the public interest. The draft Norwegian model also contains a provision clarifying that the imposition of requirements to use a technology to meet general standards related to health, safety or the environment should not be subject to the prohibition on performance requirements.[296]

IIAs that have detailed performance requirements provisions such as those described above typically also include reservations taken by each party to preserve their right to impose performance requirements in some circumstances. General exceptions may also be relied on in some cases to permit measures that are performance requirements that would otherwise be prohibited under the treaty.[297] For example, an exception for measures to protect and promote the interests of indigenous peoples could permit a performance requirement that investors buy their inputs from indigenous peoples in the host state, subject to availability, even if requiring preferences in favour of inputs supplied by host state nationals is generally prohibited in an IIA.[298]

Affirming host state rights to impose performance requirements

The IISD model takes an entirely different approach from the IIAs described above. It expressly *permits* the use of performance requirements to ensure that development benefits flow from foreign investment. The IISD model gives host states the right to impose performance requirements on investors in order 'to promote domestic development benefits.'[299] The IISD model treaty 'recognises' the limits imposed by the *TRIMs* Agreement, but it is not clear to what extent this amounts to an obligation not to put in place performance requirements inconsistent with *TRIMs*.

---

295 This example is hypothetical because Canada always excludes its foreign investment review regime from the application of the performance requirement prohibition in IIAs that it negotiates.

296 Draft Norwegian APPI, Art. 8. In the India–Singapore CECA (2005), the parties do reaffirm their commitments in this regard under the *TRIMS* Agreement (Art. 6.23).

297 E.g. Canadian model FIPA, Art. 9. Canada routinely excludes performance requirements that are imposed in connection with approving foreign investments under its investment review law.

298 Such a requirement may be contrary to *TRIMs*.

299 IISD model treaty, Art. 26.

Box 5.14 Summary of options for performance requirements provisions

1. *Affirming a host state's right to impose performance requirements*
2. *No obligation regarding performance requirements*
3. *Prohibition on performance requirements inconsistent with TRIMs*
4. *Prohibition on specific TRIMs plus performance requirements*

5.9.4 Discussion of options

1. *Affirming a host state's right to impose performance requirements*

This kind of provision makes clear the party states' intention to allow the imposition of performance requirements. No treaty has adopted such a provision, but since it simply expressly recognises a right that states would have in the absence of any provision prohibiting the use of performance requirements, its inclusion may not be a significant concern for investors or capital-exporting states. The effect of such a provision, however, is not clear, and it has never been the subject of interpretation by an arbitral tribunal.

Even with such a provision, a host state would have to comply with its obligations under *TRIMs* as well as those under *GATS* if it is a WTO member but those obligations are not incorporated in the IIA and would probably not be enforceable under IIA dispute settlement procedures. Whether *GATS* and *TRIMs* obligations could be raised in IIA dispute settlement, however, would depend on the scope of those procedures as set out in the IIA. Some IIAs contain a clause that incorporates host state obligations that are not expressly provided for in the treaty.

Affirming a right to impose performance requirements does not seem to create an exception from other obligations in the IIA, so it would still be necessary for the host state to comply with other IIA obligations, including national treatment and MFN, in imposing performance requirements. The scope of application of these other IIA obligations will depend on the applicability of reservations and exceptions in the treaty.[300] Also, if the treaty does not apply to investments prior to admission then there is no limitation on the performance requirements that may be imposed by the host state as a condition of admission. The protection of the treaty simply does not apply to investments that have not been admitted.

A prohibition on the imposition of performance requirements could be incorporated into an IIA that does not contain a performance requirements provision if (i) the IIA contained an MFN clause and (ii) the state had entered into another IIA that included such a prohibition. An affirmation like the one in the IISD model may make it less likely that a prohibition on the imposition of performance requirements would

300 See Section 5.12 (Reservations and exceptions).

be incorporated into an IIA on this basis. Incorporating a prohibition through an MFN provision would contradict the parties' intention expressed in the affirmation.[301] Nevertheless in light of the inconsistent approaches of arbitral decisions in this area, there is a residual risk that a performance requirement prohibition could be incorporated through an MFN provision.

2. *No obligation regarding performance requirements*

This is the most common approach to dealing with performance requirements. A host state would still have to comply with its obligations under *TRIMs* and *GATS* if it is a WTO member. Without an express provision, these WTO obligations are not incorporated in the IIA and would be not enforceable under the agreement's dispute settlement procedures, though whether this is the right conclusion would depend on the scope of those procedures as discussed in relation to option 1. As noted, some treaties include a provision that all obligations undertaken by a party state may be the subject of the dispute resolution procedures in the treaty.[302] A host state would still have to comply with other IIA obligations, including national treatment and MFN, in imposing performance requirements, subject to any applicable reservations or exceptions. Treaty obligations would not limit the imposition of pre-establishment performance requirements if the treaty applies only to investments that have been admitted.

It is also possible that a prohibition on the imposition of performance requirements by a state would be incorporated into an IIA if (i) the IIA contained an MFN clause and (ii) the state had entered into another IIA that provided such an obligation.[303]

3. *Prohibition on performance requirements inconsistent with TRIMs*

A prohibition of this kind obliges IIA parties to comply with *TRIMs* obligations, which would apply in any case for WTO member states. It has the benefit of making this commitment transparent. Such a provision may be preferable to a host state that is a WTO member compared with the forms of provision in the Canadian and US model agreements because it does not contain rigid specific *TRIMs* plus prohibitions on the host state's ability to resort to performance requirements. Instead it incorporates in the IIA a host state obligation to comply with its existing international commitments. A host state would also have to comply with other IIA obligations, including national treatment and MFN, in imposing performance requirements, subject to any applicable reservations or exceptions. IIA obligations would not limit the imposition of pre-establishment performance requirements if the treaty applies only to investments that have been admitted.

Including such a provision in an IIA would probably render *TRIMs* obligations enforceable under the dispute settlement procedures of the IIA, though the procedures could be drafted to exclude these obligations. While it may be attractive

301 See Section 5.4 (Most favoured nation).
302 See the discussion of umbrella clauses in Section 7.1 (Investor–state arbitration).
303 See Section 5.4 (Most favoured nation).

to capital-exporting states and their investors to be able to enforce prohibitions on performance requirements through investor–state arbitration, there is no strong case for bolstering these WTO obligations in this way. Doing so might deprive host states in practice of the flexibility necessary to use performance requirements to meet their development objectives. The foregoing analysis would apply equally to a provision that prohibited performance requirements that were inconsistent with *GATS*.

It is also possible that a broader prohibition on the imposition of performance requirements by a host state would be incorporated into an IIA if (i) the IIA contained an MFN clause and (ii) the state had entered into another IIA that contained such an obligation.[304]

4. *Prohibition on specific TRIMs plus performance requirements*

This is the strongest form of obligation and imposes significant constraints on host states. It is found in treaties negotiated by Canada, the USA and Japan. Such a provision may be attractive to capital-exporting states because it provides investors with protection against the imposition by host states of specific kinds of performance requirements that go beyond what WTO members have committed to under *TRIMs* and *GATS*. A host state would also have to comply with other IIA obligations including national treatment and MFN in relation to all performance requirements subject to any applicable reservations or exceptions in the treaty. Treaty obligations regarding performance requirements would not limit the imposition of pre-establishment performance requirements if the treaty applies only to investments that have been admitted.

Including such a provision in an IIA would render the prohibition on performance requirements enforceable under the dispute settlement procedures of the IIA, though the scope of those procedures could be limited to preclude this result.

5.9.5 Summary

The Guide does not include a sample provision prohibiting performance requirements, even though resort to performance requirements by host states may deter investment in some cases. While some agreements, notably Canadian, US and Japanese agreements, prohibit performance requirements, most do not. In addition, prohibitions on performance requirements prevent host states from linking foreign investment to the needs of the local economy. For example, for many states, the transfer of technology constitutes one of the key benefits of foreign investment.[305] A prohibition on mandatory technology transfer requirements may jeopardise the prospects for realising this benefit. The prospect for performance requirements to play a role in promoting development has been recognised by the WTO.[306] The empirical evidence on the

304 See Section 5.4 (Most favoured nation).

305 UNCTAD (2003), op. cit., at 129. This is the right 'to enjoy the benefits of scientific progress and its applications' (ICESCR, Art. 15(1)(b)).

306 Ministerial Declaration on Doha Work Program, adopted at Hong Kong, 18 December 2005, Annex F (WT/MIN(05)/DEC).

effectiveness of performance requirements in enhancing development, however, is mixed.[307] Requirements to transfer technology, for example, may deter investors from using their technology in the host state. It has been noted that such research has focused primarily on the economic effectiveness of these measures. There has been little focus on the use and effectiveness of performance requirements to advance other social policy objectives.[308] It may be that a performance requirement for foreign investors to source their labour inputs from indigenous peoples in the host state, for example, is an effective way to promote their interests.

5.10 Transparency

Cross references

To encourage investment by both foreign investors and domestic parties, an investment regime should be transparent and meet basic standards for fairness and due process in its administrative decision making and in the implementation of administrative policies. Transparency regarding the rules applicable to investments, as well as proposed legal and regulatory changes in the host country that might affect investments and high standards of fairness and due process for host state administration, produce a predictable environment in which foreign investors can make informed decisions with confidence regarding the legal requirements they must comply with and how they will be treated by the state. Investment may be encouraged as a result. Transparency regarding any incentives and other programmes that host states use to support investment, will directly contribute to effective investment promotion. Transparency regarding applicable rules also helps investors to ascertain whether they are being treated in accordance with those rules.[309] For all these reasons, IIA provisions requiring transparency and setting standards for government administration should facilitate and encourage inward foreign investment.

307 UNCTAD (2003), *World Investment Report*, op. cit., at 120.

308 L E Peterson (2004), *Bilateral Investment Treaties and Development Policy Making*, Winnipeg, International Institute for Sustainable Development, at 34.

309 Transparency in dispute settlement proceedings is an important issue for investors and host states and is discussed in Section 7.1 (Investor–state dispute settlement) and Section 7.2 (State-to-state dispute settlement). Transparency and the exchange of information regarding home state policies and by investors are discussed below Section 8.1 (Investment promotion).

At the same time, increased transparency and improved administrative procedures are likely to have other benefits in terms of facilitating stakeholder participation in government, improving government accountability and reducing opportunities for corruption, all of which will contribute to a better, more efficient environment for both domestic and foreign businesses, as well as improved governance and sustainable development.

For some countries, however, greater transparency and improved administration may require a substantial and costly shift from traditional ways of operating. As these obligations become more specific and onerous, the costs will increase. For developing countries, these kinds of obligations are most likely to be effective when accompanied by IIA commitments from developed country parties to provide technical assistance to support the development of more transparent, fair and effective host state regimes.

In this section, the IIA practice regarding transparency and administrative procedure obligations is discussed. The transparency requirements emerging from some investor–state arbitration cases interpreting the fair and equitable treatment standard are also briefly surveyed.

5.10.1 IIA practice

Most recent IIAs deal with transparency issues in some fashion,[310] though some do not.[311] There is, however, some variation in the nature and scope of obligations regarding: (i) disclosure of the requirements of the existing legal regime; (ii) disclosure of proposed changes to the existing regime; and (iii) requirements that go beyond basic disclosure requirements to impose procedural and substantive standards for domestic administrative procedures.

Basic requirements regarding disclosure of the existing legal regime

Many agreements impose requirements on party states to disclose publicly the requirements of their existing legal regimes. For example, the US model BIT contains the following provision:

1. Each Party shall ensure that its

    a. *laws, regulations, procedures, administrative rulings of general application*; and

    b. *adjudicatory decisions*

    on matters covered by the Treaty are promptly published or otherwise made publicly available.[312] (Emphasis added.)

Similar obligations are imposed in the Canadian model agreement, as well as in the India–Singapore CECA, the ASEAN Agreement and the COMESA Investment

310 UNCTAD (2011), *Transparency in IIAs*, United Nations, New York and Geneva, at 114.

311 E.g. UK model IPPA; Indian model BIPPA; Colombian model agreement.

312 US model BIT, Art. 10.

Agreement.[313] The precise scope of the commitments varies. While strong commitments are optimal from the perspective of capital-exporting states and their investors, the burden on the host state will increase as provisions impose more onerous obligations. The variations in what is required are discussed below.

What categories of information have to be disclosed? In general, the obligation to publish laws and regulations will not be onerous for many countries. Such disclosure is typically required under domestic law. The publication of 'procedures, administrative rulings of general application; and ... adjudicatory decisions', as in the US model, is a much more comprehensive obligation that imposes a heavier burden on host states. Adjudicatory decisions would include court, arbitration and administrative tribunal decisions. Some agreements impose more limited obligations. The ASEAN Agreement, for example, includes only 'laws, regulations and administrative guidelines of general application', excluding procedures and adjudicatory decisions. The India–Singapore CECA is similarly limited.[314] The ASEAN–Australia–New Zealand FTA Investment Chapter and some other IIAs create an obligation to disclose international agreements.[315]

What is the connection between the matters that are the subject of the disclosure obligation and the IIA that defines what has to be disclosed? In the US model, the disclosure obligation extends to 'all matters covered by the Treaty'.[316] In the COMESA Investment Agreement, disclosure is mandatory only in relation to 'measures' that pertain to or affect the agreement. Measures are defined as 'any legal administrative, judicial or policy decision that is taken by a member state, directly relating to and affecting an investment'.[317] Some other treaties adopt narrower approaches requiring a closer connection with the treaty obligations before disclosure is required. The Australia–US FTA applies only to measures that a party considers 'might materially affect the operation of the agreement or the other party's interests under this Agreement'.[318] Disclosing only measures that 'might materially affect' the operation of the agreement is a more limited commitment than that in the US model and would be easier to administer for host states.

---

313 India–Singapore CECA (2005), Art. 6.15; ASEAN Agreement (2009), Art. 21; and COMESA Investment Agreement (2007), Art. 4. Similar provisions are also found in the Canadian model FIPA (Art. 19) and the draft Norwegian APPI (Art. 31).

314 The Canadian model FIPA does not refer to adjudicatory decisions. The ASEAN Agreement (2009) requires notification of such agreements to the council appointed under the agreement (Art. 21.1(a)).

315 ASEAN–Australia–New Zealand FTA (2009) Investment Chapter, Art. 13.1. See also ASEAN Agreement (2009), Art. 21.1(a).

316 The Canadian model FIPA uses the same language (Art. 19.1) and the India–Singapore CECA (2005) is similar (Art. 6.15(1)). In the ASEAN Agreement (2009), the comparable language is 'relevant laws that pertain to, or affect investments' (Art. 21(1)(c)). Perhaps the broadest obligation of all is the approach used in Azerbaijan–Estonia, Agreement between the Government of the Republic of Azerbaijan and the Government of the Republic of Estonia on the Promotion and Reciprocal Protection of Investments, signed 7 April 2010, not yet in force, which applies to all measures that 'may affect' investments (Art. 2.4).

317 COMESA Investment Agreement (2007), Art. 1.10.

318 Australia–United States Free Trade Agreement, signed 18 May 2004, in force 1 January 2005, Art. 20.3.

Are disclosure obligations mandatory? In the US model set out above, the obligation is mandatory. While a mandatory obligation is typical[319] in the Canadian model, a state need only disclose 'to the extent possible'.[320] The ASEAN–Australia–New Zealand FTA investment chapter creates a mandatory obligation, but creates an exception for emergency situations.[321]

Is disclosure combined with an obligation to respond to specific questions regarding matters covered by the IIA? In some models, the disclosure obligation is made more onerous because it is combined with an obligation to respond to specific questions from the other party state regarding matters covered by the IIA. For these IIAs, the administrative burden of compliance could be extensive.[322] The US model requires each state to provide information upon the request of the other party state regarding any actual or proposed measure that the requesting party state considers might materially affect the operation of this treaty.[323] Some IIAs require the establishment of contact points to be responsible for facilitating communication between the party states.[324] Contact points staffed by designated government officials facilitate not only disclosure of laws and policies, but also communication between the party states regarding investment issues. While contact points may encourage investment, establishing and maintaining a contact point involves the expenditure of resources to develop and maintain the necessary administrative and technical capacity to operate it.

Some of these kinds of basic disclosure obligations are imposed on WTO members under *GATS*. The obligations in *GATS* are set out in Box 5.15.

Box 5.15 Transparency obligations in *GATS*

Some of the transparency requirements in IIA models can be found in the *GATS* and other WTO Agreements.

Article III of *GATS* requires WTO members to publish promptly all relevant measures of general application that pertain to, or would affect the operation of,

(Continued)

319 India–Singapore CECA (2005), Art. 6.15; and COMESA Investment Agreement (2007), Art. 4.

320 Canadian model FIPA, Art. 19.1. The Azerbaijan–Estonia BIT (2010) uses the same language (Art. 2.4).

321 ASEAN–Australia–New Zealand FTA (2009) Investment Chapter, Art. 13.1. This agreement also contemplates that publication be prompt and on the internet but, if that is not practicable, then some other way of making the information public shall be found (Arts. 13.2, 13.3).

322 India–Singapore CECA (2005), Art. 6.15(2); Japan–Peru, Agreement between Japan and the Republic of Peru for the Promotion, Protection and Liberalisation of Investment, signed 22 November 2008, in force 10 December 2009, Art. 9.

323 Canadian model FIPA, Art. 19; US model BIT, Art. 11.5.

324 United States–Rwanda, Treaty between the Government of the United States of America and the Government of the Republic of Rwanda concerning the Encouragement and Reciprocal Protection of Investment, signed 19 February 2008, in force 1 January 2012, Art. 11.1; ASEAN–Australia–New Zealand FTA (2009) Investment Chapter, Art. 13.1; ASEAN Agreement (2009), Art. 21.

(Continued)

GATS. 'Measures' is defined as 'any measure by a member, whether in the form of a law, regulation, rule, procedure, decision, administrative action or any other form'. Bilateral or plurilateral agreements on services must also be published (Article XXVII). Since *GATS* applies to 'commercial presence', its obligations extend to some investments in services.[325]

WTO members are also obliged to respond to requests for information regarding their measures and agreements. There are enhanced transparency obligations for sectors in relation to which a member has undertaken specific commitments, which means that the member has listed the sector in the member's national schedule of commitments. In addition to the general publication obligation, each member must establish one or more enquiry points to provide specific information to other members regarding its services regime. *GATS* does not oblige members to disclose confidential information the publication of which would impede law enforcement or otherwise conflict with the public interest, or which would prejudice legitimate commercial interests.[326]

In relation to services, all WTO members have to comply with these obligations regardless of what is provided for in any IIA to which they are a party.

Disclosure of proposed measures

In addition to disclosure regarding the existing regime, many treaties require some disclosure in relation to proposed measures.[327] The disclosure of draft or proposed measures by the host state is often considered important to investors in order to help them avoid unexpected changes in the host state's regulatory framework. Commitments to disclose proposed measures and provide affected investors with an opportunity to comment provides a level of assurance for foreign investors that their interests are being taken into account. Provisions that permit interested persons to comment on proposed measures also promote participation by domestic stakeholders in the process of developing host state rules.

The Canadian and US models require that any measure that a party proposes to adopt that applies to matters covered by the treaty should be published in advance and 'interested persons' as well as the other party state itself must be permitted to

325 See Section 3.3 (IIAs and other international obligations) Box 3.1.

326 A similar proviso regarding confidential information is contained in the India–Singapore CECA (Art. 6.14(2)), the ASEAN Agreement (Art. 21.2) and the COMESA Investment Agreement (Art. 4.4).

327 E.g. India–Singapore CECA (2005), Art. 6.15.

comment on the proposed measure.[328] The US and Canadian models define the range of proposed measures to be disclosed in the same way as for the basic disclosure obligation discussed above. Treaties that require disclosure of proposed measures reduce the burden of this obligation on host states in different ways.

- **Some IIAs limit the scope of what must be disclosed.** For example, the Canada–Panama FTA limits the obligation to measures that 'might materially affect the operation of the agreement or substantially affect the other party's interests' under the agreement.[329]
- **Some IIAs limit the disclosure obligation to what is required by the host state's domestic law.** The ASEAN–Australia–New Zealand FTA investment chapter provides that each party 'shall endeavour to provide a reasonable opportunity for comments by interested parties prior to measures that are subject of the basic disclosure obligation' but only '[t]o the extent provided for under its domestic legal framework'.
- **Disclosure is required only to the extent possible.** In both the US and Canadian models, in recognition of the more burdensome nature of the obligation to disclose proposed measures, the obligation obliges states to disclose only 'to the extent possible.[330]
- **Some IIAs require only that new measures be disclosed after they have been implemented.** The COMESA Investment Agreement does not require notice of a proposed change at all. Instead it requires member states to inform the public of any new measure or change to an existing measure that affects investments or the party's commitments under the agreement within 30 days of its enactment.[331] The ASEAN Agreement requires simply that new or changed laws that 'significantly affect investments or commitments of a member' be notified to the council created under the agreement.[332]

Consultation, exchange of information and co-operation

In addition to disclosure obligations, some treaties impose additional obligations regarding transparency. Some impose an obligation on each party state to consult with the other on request regarding any question related to the interpretation or

328 Canadian model FIPA, Art. 19.1; US model BIT, Art. 11.2. The US model goes on to impose a much more specific set of requirements regarding how central government regulations are to be published.

329 Canada–Panama Free Trade Agreement, signed 14 May 2010, not yet in force, Art. 20.03.

330 Canadian model FIPA, Art. 19.1; US model BIT, Art. 11.2. The same language is used in NAFTA (1992), Art. 1802 and China–New Zealand Free Trade Agreement, signed 7 April 2008, not yet in force, Chapter 13.

331 COMESA Investment Agreement (2007), Art. 4.3.

332 ASEAN Agreement (2009), Art. 21(b).

application of the IIA.[333] In addition, some treaties provide that upon the request by either party, 'information shall be exchanged on the foreign investment policies, laws and regulations of the other Contracting Party that may have an impact on new investments or returns covered by this Agreement'.[334] This kind of exchange is one way to facilitate the dissemination of information regarding the host state's regime and the opportunities and incentives it provides to foreign investors. Finally, some IIAs create a general obligation on the parties to co-operate on promoting transparency in relation to international trade and investment.[335]

Exceptions

Many IIAs contain exceptions that allow state parties not to disclose confidential information concerning particular investors or investments where disclosure would impede law enforcement, or otherwise be contrary to the public interest, or which would prejudice legitimate commercial interests of particular legal persons, public or private. Sometimes these exceptions are set out in transparency provisions.[336] In other IIAs, they are included in the general exceptions provisions. The Canadian model agreement, for example, creates a general exception for all obligations under the agreement for measures to protect confidential information.[337]

Who bears the transparency obligation?

Typical transparency obligations are expressed to apply to both states equally.[338] In practice, in most cases, it is capital-importing states that will need to bear the obligation in mind. Capital-exporting states and their investors will insist on compliance with transparency obligations. Capital-importing states may also be encouraged to comply in the hope of attracting investors. Some treaties expressly recognise the greater practical relevance of the transparency obligations to host states by describing the obligation as relating to measures of a party that may affect the investment of investors of the other party in its territory.[339]

Where a treaty contains obligations that go beyond investor protection by host states, however, transparency obligations in relation to investors' home states may be relevant. For example, if home states are obliged to co-operate with host states to address investor violations of IIA provisions or host state domestic rules relating to corruption or breaches of human rights, labour rights or indigenous rights obligations, then disclosure of relevant measures of the home state could become

---

333 E.g. Thailand–Jordan, Agreement between the Government of the Kingdom of Thailand and the Government of the Hashemite Kingdom of Jordan for the Promotion and Protection of Investments, signed 15 December 2005, not yet in force, Art. 9. The US model BIT provides that the parties are to consult periodically on ways to improve the transparency practices.

334 E.g. Thailand–Jordan BIT (2005), Art. 9.

335 E.g. Canada–Peru FTA (2008), Art. 1905.

336 COMESA Investment Agreement (2007), Art. 4.4.

337 Canadian model FIPA, Art. 11.5. See Section 5.12 (Reservations and exceptions) for an example.

338 E.g. Canadian model FIPA, Art. 19.1; US model BIT, Art. 11.2.

339 E.g. Azerbaijan–Estonia BIT (2010), Art. 2.

important.[340] Obligations of this kind are discussed below.[341] Similarly, if home states have investment promotion or technical assistance obligations, transparency commitments regarding the steps they have taken to fulfil these obligations may be relevant.[342] Consideration may also be given to the desirability of transparency obligations on investors and provisions enabling host states to require disclosure from investors.

Requirements for administrative procedures

A few IIAs seek to provide procedural protections for the benefit of individual investors in their dealings with party states. For example, the US model BIT goes beyond basic transparency commitments to require parties to provide certain protections for investors in administrative proceedings, including a right for an investor to receive reasonable notice of any proceeding that directly affects its interests and a reasonable opportunity to present facts and arguments at such a proceeding. Compliance with any requirements of domestic law is also required. Such rights are to be accorded 'wherever possible'. Party states are also required to have judicial and administrative tribunals for the purpose of providing prompt review of decisions relating to matters arising under the treaty.[343]

In addition to these procedural protections, the US model agreement sets out some general substantive standards that host state procedures should achieve. Tribunals reviewing administrative decisions must be impartial and independent of the agency responsible for enforcement and must not have any interest in the outcome of the matter. Persons participating in these reviews must have a reasonable opportunity to defend their positions, and decisions must be based on evidence and submissions.[344]

The IISD model treaty contains a provision on 'procedural fairness' that similarly combines procedural requirements for host state administrative actions with substantive standards. In some respects, the standards in the IISD model go beyond those in the US model. Under the IISD model, the parties must deal with investors in a manner that is not arbitrary or unfair and does not constitute a denial of justice. The IISD commitments also extend to judicial and legislative processes, as well as administrative procedures. To balance these far-reaching requirements, however, the IISD model recognises that there is no single international standard for achieving these objectives and acknowledges that there may be differences from one country to another depending on the level of development. In terms of specific process requirements, the IISD model follows the US model in requiring timely notice to investors of proceedings directly relating to them, and investor access to review or appeal procedures. The IISD model also requires that judicial and administrative proceedings be open to the public.

---

340 Some agreements also permit states to seek information from investors. Such a right will be more important where investors have obligations.

341 See Section 6.13 (Enforcement of investor obligations).

342 See Chapter 8 (Investment Promotion and Technical Assistance).

343 US model BIT, Arts. 11.6 and 11.7.

344 US model BIT, Arts. 11.4 and 11.5. A similar approach is taken in the ASEAN–Australia–New Zealand FTA (2009) Investment Chapter, Art. 14.

5.10.2 Transparency obligations deriving from FET

A number of investor–state arbitration awards have described transparency as an element of the fair and equitable treatment obligation. In *Tecmed v. Mexico*, for example, the tribunal described the FET obligation as requiring the following:

> The foreign investor expects the host State to act in a consistent manner, free from ambiguity and totally transparently in its relations with the foreign investor, so that it may know beforehand any and all rules and regulations that will govern its investments, as well as the goals of the relevant policies and administrative practices or directives, to be able to plan its investment and comply with such regulations.[345]

This approach has been applied in other cases.[346] It has also been criticised as setting an unreasonably high standard[347] that few states could meet and one that would be especially burdensome for developing countries.[348] Many cases have imposed standards for administrative procedures on host states under the FET standard.[349]

Box 5.16 Summary of options for transparency provisions

1. *No transparency obligation*
2. *Transparency obligation with a basic commitment to disclose existing and proposed laws*

   The main issue with this kind of obligation is the scope of the disclosure obligation. Existing IIAs require disclosure of some combination of the following kinds of measures:

   a. Existing laws and regulations, administrative procedures and rulings, judicial decisions, and international agreements;
   b. Draft or proposed laws and regulations (which may be combined with an obligation to provide an opportunity to comment on proposed laws and regulations).

   There is also some variation in IIA provisions regarding the connection that is required between the measure and investment in order to trigger the disclosure obligation. Obligations may attach to measures that:

(Continued)

345 *Tecmed v. Mexico*, op. cit.

346 *Azurix Corp. v. Republic of Argentina*, ICSID Case No. ARB/01/12, Award, 14 July 2006, at paras. 371–3; and *Lemire v. Ukraine*, ICSID Case No. ARB/06/18, IIC 424 (2010), Decision on Jurisdiction and Liability, 14 January 2010.

347 UNCTAD (2011), *Transparency*, op. cit., at 61. See also R Dolzer (2006), 'The Impact of International Investment Treaties on Domestic Administrative Law', 37 *NYU Journal of International Law and Politics* 953.

348 See Section 5.5 (Fair and equitable treatment and the minimum standard of treatment).

349 Ibid.

(Continued)

a. May affect investments;

b. Affect investments;

c. Substantially affect, materially affect or significantly affect investments.

In addition, treaty practice sets different standards with respect to whether the obligation is mandatory or only 'to the extent possible'.

Some treaties create an obligation to respond to specific questions on matters related to the treaty and establish a contact point to provide information regarding the host state's domestic regime.

3. *Obligations regarding consultation and co-operation*

Some agreements provide obligations for states to:

a. Consult on any question related to the interpretation or application of the IIA;

b. Exchange information on the foreign investment policies, laws and regulations of the other party that may have an impact on new investments or returns covered by the agreement; and

c. Co-operate in promoting transparency in respect of international trade and investment.

4. *Transparency obligation with additional specific commitments regarding domestic administrative procedures*

5.10.3 Discussion of options

1. *No transparency obligation*

Not all IIAs include a commitment regarding transparency. Some capital-exporting states, however, such as Canada and the USA, routinely seek commitments regarding transparency. In addition, there are benefits associated with transparency for host states in terms of improved governance and investment promotion. A commitment to transparency would provide assurances to investors of predictability in the host state's regime that might attract them. At the same time, a state considering a specific transparency commitment would have to consider the costs involved.

Even without a specific transparency obligation, a state would still have to comply with any other obligation in the IIA that imposes requirements related to transparency. Depending on the formulation of an FET obligation in an IIA and its interpretation by an investor–state tribunal, an FET obligation may impose transparency requirements.[350] It is also possible that a transparency obligation would

350 See Section 5.5 (Fair and equitable treatment and the minimum standard of treatment).

be incorporated into an IIA that contained an MFN clause if the state had entered into another IIA that provided such an obligation.[351]

2. *Transparency obligation with a basic commitment to disclose existing and proposed laws*

As noted, the main issue with this kind of obligation is its scope. From the perspective of an investor and its home state, more comprehensive and binding transparency obligations will be preferable. Host states will benefit from transparency commitments to the extent that they encourage investment, but must also consider the burden of transparency requirements. The obligation to disclose only laws and regulations is the least intrusive and may already be required under domestic law. A commitment to disclose administrative procedures and rulings, judicial decisions, international agreements and, especially, proposed laws and regulations may require significant changes to government operations and new resources. An obligation to establish an enquiry point is likely to be the most resource-intensive commitment.

The effective scope of the obligation is also affected by the degree of connection required between the measures that must be disclosed and investments. Disclosure of laws and so on that 'may affect' is a very high standard. Sometimes it may be hard to tell if a measure 'may affect' matters related to the treaty. By contrast, it is easier to tell if a measure actually affects or substantially, materially or significantly affects such matters. There may be some slight difference in the degree of obligation created by these last three expressions, but all require more than a trivial effect. The obligation is also mitigated if it is qualified by language such as 'to the extent possible'.

It is possible to establish differing degrees of obligation for existing and proposed measures. Some states commit to providing disclosure of existing measures and only after the fact disclosure for changes to measures and new measures. Exceptions to transparency commitments to permit states not to disclose confidential information are common. The impact of transparency commitments could also be limited by exempting them from the application of dispute settlement procedures. Basic transparency obligations are not intended to directly benefit individual investors, and so it may be appropriate to exclude them from obligations that could be the basis for an investor–state claim.

Regardless of what is specifically provided for in an IIA, it is possible that minimum requirements in this regard will be established by an FET obligation in an IIA.

3. *Obligations regarding consultation and co-operation*

In principle, these kinds of obligations may be included in an IIA whether or not there is a basic obligation to disclose the existing law in an area. Consultation and co-operation obligations may not be viewed as onerous. Consultation and co-operation are soft obligations that do not involve specific commitments to do a great deal. In addition, it is likely to be in each state's interest to be able to talk to the other about investment policy issues and find out about each other's policies regarding inward

351 See Section 5.4 (Most favoured nation).

and outward investment. Exchanging information regarding a host state's investment regime, including any incentives or opportunities provided, may help to promote investment.

4. *Transparency obligation with additional specific commitments regarding domestic administrative procedures*

States that already have robust domestic administrative procedures in place may be willing to undertake this more onerous set of obligations to send a strong signal to investors regarding their commitment to fairness and due process, as in the US model agreement. More robust domestic regimes that meet such standards for administrative procedures are more likely to produce sustainable development, and commitments to such standards will be attractive to investors. Consequently, states whose domestic regimes meet these standards may decide to commit to maintaining them. Other host states may not be in a position to undertake such commitments. It is possible to qualify the burden of these obligations by adding a provision such as appears in the IISD model, requiring these obligations to be interpreted in light of the level of development of the host country.

The impact of such commitments could be limited in practice by exempting them from the application of IIA dispute settlement procedures. Obligations regarding administrative procedures have a general benefit for investors, but may be relevant to the treatment of an individual investor too. Consequently, the argument for excluding such obligations from those that may be the basis of an investor–state claim is not as strong as for excluding basic transparency obligations, as discussed in option 2.

Depending on the formulation of any FET obligation and its interpretation by an investor–state tribunal, a state may have obligations related to the conduct of its administrative procedures arising out of the FET obligation.[352]

With respect to any of options 2, 3 or 4, it is possible that any more favourable obligation with respect to transparency or administrative procedures that a state has entered into in another IIA would be incorporated into an IIA that contained an MFN clause.[353]

5.10.4 Discussion of sample provision

The Guide provides a sample of a basic provision committing host states to transparency, with a view to encouraging investment and improving the quality and effectiveness of domestic regulation. It has the following elements.

Obligation on each party state to publish existing laws, regulations, procedures, administrative rulings of general application and any international agreement to which it is a party relating to any matter covered by the investment agreement: Such an obligation is found in many current IIAs. In addition, the Guide provision mirrors the commitments undertaken by all WTO members in GATS Article III. In

352 See Section 5.5 (Fair and equitable treatment and the minimum standard of treatment).

353 See Section 5.4 (Most favoured nation).

order to limit the burden of this obligation, the Guide provision obliges states to meet these requirements only 'to the extent possible' as in the Canadian model agreement, which provides some flexibility for host states.

Publication of proposed laws with a right to comment: The sample also creates an obligation to publish and provide an opportunity to comment on any new laws and regulations that the host state proposes to adopt relating to any matter covered by the investment agreement. Such a commitment is important to investors, contributes to good governance and appears in some IIAs. Nevertheless, such a commitment may not be feasible for states where it would require significant changes to government operations and new resources. In order to limit the burden of these obligations, the Guide provision obliges states to meet these requirements only 'to the extent possible'.

Exchange of information: The Guide includes a sample provision that creates obligations regarding the exchange of information between parties related to measures that may have a material impact on investment. In light of the possible concerns regarding the resource implications of such a commitment for host states, the Guide does not create a specific requirement for host states to establish a contact point for party states or investors seeking information on the domestic regime. However, putting in place a contact point may be valuable and appropriate for some states and, as noted, is required under *GATS* in some cases. The role of information exchange and enquiry points in promoting investment is discussed further below.[354] A consultation obligation is also included in relation to any actual or proposed measure or any other matter that a party state considers might materially affect the operation of the agreement.

No obligation to disclose confidential information: Many IIAs contain exceptions that allow party states not to disclose confidential information concerning particular investors or investments where disclosure would impede law enforcement or otherwise be contrary to the public interest, or which would prejudice legitimate commercial interests of particular legal persons, public or private. Sometimes these exceptions are set out in transparency provisions.[355] The sample provision provides an example of this. In other IIAs, they are included in general exceptions provisions.[356]

The obligations in the sample provision apply to all party states. In part, this approach, which is followed in most IIAs, recognises that there may be disclosure that should be required of the investor's home state to the extent that obligations of home states are included in an IIA. The Guide describes some possible home state obligations below.[357]

No obligation regarding administrative procedures: The willingness of developing countries to accept these kinds of commitments will depend not only on the level of development of their administrative systems, but also on the prospects for receiving

354 See Section 8.1 (Investment promotion).

355 COMESA Investment Agreement (2007), Art. 4.4.

356 E.g. Canadian model FIPA, Art. 11.5. The Canadian model agreement extends the exception to confidential information generally. See Section 5.12 (Reservations and exceptions) for an example.

357 See Section 6.13 (Enforcement of investor obligations) and Section 8.2 (Technical assistance).

technical assistance from developed country parties to support the development of such systems. Technical assistance provisions are provided for elsewhere in the Guide.[358]

5.10.5 Sample provision: transparency

Transparency

1. Each Party shall, to the extent possible, ensure that its laws, regulations, procedures, administrative rulings of general application and any international agreement to which it is a party respecting any matter covered by this agreement are published or otherwise made available in such a manner as to enable interested persons and the other Party to become acquainted with them.
2. To the extent possible, each Party shall:
   a. Publish in advance any law or regulation respecting any matter covered by this agreement that it proposes to adopt; and
   b. Provide interested persons and the other Party with a reasonable opportunity to comment on such proposed measures.
3. Upon request by a Party, information shall be exchanged on the measures of the other Party that may have a material impact on investments subject to this agreement.
4. A Party may request in writing consultations with the other Party regarding any actual or proposed measure or any other matter that it considers might materially affect the operation of this agreement. The other Party shall engage in consultations within 30 days of such request.
5. Nothing in this agreement shall require a Party to furnish or allow access to any confidential information, including information concerning particular investors or investments, the disclosure of which would impede law enforcement, or otherwise be contrary to the public interest, or which would prejudice legitimate commercial interests of particular legal persons, public or private.

5.11 Entry and sojourn of foreign nationals and restrictions on nationality requirements for senior management

Cross reference

Section 5.4 Most favoured nation 124

The effective operation of a foreign investment may require employees of the investor with high-level management authority or special skills to be able to work on a temporary basis in the host country. Nevertheless, few IIAs create any meaningful

358 See Section 8.2 (Technical assistance).

commitments with respect to the entry of foreign personnel into host states because of labour market, immigration and security concerns.[359]

Another issue related to foreign personnel is nationality requirements for senior managers. Host states often have an interest in ensuring that their nationals fill senior positions or particular technical specialist positions in foreign investment operations. Host states may view access to this type of position as a way to ensure that nationals get both technical training and management expertise. The benefits to individual nationals can spill over as they transfer their experience to others in the host state. Some states have rules that require that certain positions be held by nationals in the hope of capturing these benefits of foreign investment. Investors typically do not like this kind of rule because they want to be able to hire whoever they believe is best for the job regardless of nationality, including, often, their own nationals. Some IIA provisions limit the ability of host states to impose nationality requirements.

5.11.1 IIA practice

Entry and sojourn of foreign nationals

While most IIAs contain no commitments regarding the entry of foreign nationals, a few provide very limited commitments. For example, some agreements oblige a host state to give assistance to nationals from another party that are seeking permission to engage in activities associated with an investment in the host state.[360] Other IIAs commit host states to give sympathetic consideration to requests for permission to enter in these circumstances.[361] Another variant is agreements that do not create a right of entry, but commit the host state not to apply labour market tests based on the economic need for workers or numerical quotas for workers in relation to employees of investors from the other party state.[362]

The Indian model treaty does contain a commitment on the part of each state to permit non-citizens to enter the host state for the purpose of engaging in activities connected with investment, but only subject to the state's own laws applicable to entry requirements from time to time.[363] This caveat would seem to remove any

359 Neither the US model BIT nor the UK model IPPA addresses entry of personnel.

360 Botswana–China, Agreement between the Government of the Republic of Botswana and the Government of the People's Republic of China on Promotion and Protection of Investments, signed 12 June 2000, not yet in force, Art. 2.

361 France–Mexico, Agreement between the Government of the Republic of France and the Government of the United Mexican States on the Reciprocal Promotion and Protection of Investments, signed 12 November 1998, in force 12 November 2000, Art. 4.

362 United States–Nicaragua, Treaty between the Government of the United States of America and the Government of the Republic of Nicaragua concerning the Encouragement and Reciprocal Protection of Investment, signed 1 July 2005, not yet in force, Art. VII. See also Japan–Korea BIT (2003), Art. 8. This agreement allows for such tests to be applied after prior notification and consultation with the other party.

363 Indian model BIPPA, Art.11; Australia–India BIT. There are similar commitments in the US–Nicaragua BIT (Art. VII) and the Japan–Korea BIT (Art. 8), but they are limited to nationals of the other party who enter for the purpose of establishing, developing, administering or advising on the operation of an investment to which they, or a company of the other party that employs them, have committed or are in the process of committing a substantial amount of capital or other resources.

real binding effect from this provision. Similarly, the Canadian model obliges each party state to permit temporary entry of nationals of another party state that is the investor's home state to render services to the investor's investment in a capacity that is managerial or executive or that requires special knowledge, but only subject to the 'laws, regulations and policies of the host state'.[364] The Canadian provision is set out in Box 5.17. The COMESA Investment Agreement requires member states to permit investors to hire technically qualified persons from any country, but obliges investors to give priority to workers with the same qualifications in the host state.[365]

Box 5.17 Canadian model FIPA provision on entry of foreign nationals and restrictions on nationality requirements for senior management

Article 6

Senior Management, Boards of Directors and Entry of Personnel

1. A Party may not require that an enterprise of that Party, that is a covered investment, appoint to senior management positions individuals of any particular nationality.
2. A Party may require that a majority of the board of directors, or any committee thereof, of an enterprise that is a covered investment be of a particular nationality, or resident in the territory of the Party, provided that the requirement does not materially impair the ability of the investor to exercise control over its investment.
3. Subject to its laws, regulations and policies relating to the entry of aliens, each Party shall grant temporary entry to nationals of the other Party, employed by an investor of the other Party, who seeks to render services to an investment of that investor in the territory of the Party, in a capacity that is managerial or executive or requires specialised knowledge.

Restrictions on nationality requirements for senior management

Some IIAs limit the ability of host states to require that their own nationals occupy identified positions with businesses operated by foreign investors, though most do not address this issue. For example, a few IIAs provide that party states cannot require that senior management positions in the local operation of foreign investors of the other party state be held by persons of any particular nationality, including the nationality of the host state. Such provisions ensure that a foreign investor has freedom to choose who runs its investment. However, because this obligation imposes no requirement on party

364 Canadian model FIPA, Art. 6.3. The IISD model treaty is similar (Art. 9C) as is the Norwegian draft model IPPA (Art. 4.2.8) and the ASEAN Agreement (2009) (Art. 22).

365 COMESA Investment Agreement (2007), Art. 16. This would appear to mean that a host state can require that such priority be given. The COMESA Investment Agreement (2007) is part of a regional integration project and its provisions probably reflect that distinct goal.

states to admit foreign nationals into their territory, in practice investors will be limited in terms of whom they can choose as senior managers working in the host state. Only nationals and foreigners admitted in accordance with host state law will be eligible.

IIAs take several approaches to prohibitions on host state nationality requirements for senior managers. The Australia–Egypt BIT provides that each party shall permit investors of the other party to employ within its territory key technical and managerial personnel of their choice regardless of citizenship. In this agreement, the commitment is made subject to host state law, which would appear to eliminate the effective benefit of the commitments, since provisions in host state law could impose limitations or even an outright ban.[366] The US–Lithuania BIT contains the same obligation, but without this limitation.[367] The Canadian and US model treaties contain another version of such a provision. The general prohibition on nationality requirements is narrowed by an exception permitting host state requirements that a majority of the board of directors of an investment have a particular nationality or residence, so long as the requirement 'does not materially impair the ability of the investor to exercise control over its investment'.[368] Canada's provision is set out in Box 5.17.

The *GATS* and some other trade agreements contain provisions on the temporary entry of individuals, including NAFTA[369] and the EC–CARIFORUM economic partnership agreement (EPA). These obligations would have to be complied with by party states regardless of any other commitments in an IIA. *GATS* commitments are described in Box 5.18.

Box 5.18 *GATS* and the entry of foreign nationals and restrictions on nationality requirements for senior management

The obligations of the General Agreement on Trade in Services[370] apply to the supply of services by individuals, though the obligations are very limited. *GATS* obligations do not apply to natural persons seeking access to the employment market in a member state or measures regarding citizenship, residence or employment

(Continued)

366 Australia–Egypt, Agreement between the Government of Australia and the Government of the Arab Republic of Egypt on the Promotion and Protection of Investments, signed 3 May 2001, in force 5 September 2002, Art. 5.

367 United States–Lithuania, Treaty between the Government of the United States of America and the Government of the Republic of Lithuania for the Encouragement and Reciprocal Protection of Investment, signed 14 January 1998, in force 22 November 2001, Art. II.

368 Canadian model FIPA, Art. 6; US model BIT, Art. 9. See also the India–Singapore CECA (2005) (Art. 6.19(2)) and IISD model treaty (Art. 9). This qualification reflects requirements of domestic corporate law in Canada and some other jurisdictions.

369 NAFTA (1992) Chapter 16 commits each NAFTA party to grant temporary entry on specified terms for a number of categories of individuals including investors and intra-corporate transferees who are managers or have some specialized knowledge and who are employees of an investor of another party seeking to provide services to an investment of that investor in the first party. The EC–CARIFORUM EPA (2008) deals with temporary entry in Arts. 80–4.

370 See Appendix 2 of the Guide for an overview of *GATS*.

(Continued)

on a permanent basis. Members are also permitted to apply measures to regulate entry, such as visas. However, each member can make commitments in its national schedule of commitments relating to the movement of natural persons. Many developed countries but few developing countries did so.[371] A WTO member who has made commitments in its national schedule is obliged under *GATS* to provide the access agreed to in relation to services suppliers of other WTO members.

Members who made commitments typically grant rights of temporary entry into their territory for specific categories of persons who have technical or managerial expertise subject to requirements set out in their national schedules. In its national schedule, for example, Canada committed to granting temporary entry into Canada to a number of categories of individuals, including 'Intra-corporate transferees', who are individuals of one member who go to work at an investment in another member. Intra-corporate transferees are granted entry for up to three years. They are defined as follows in Canada's national schedule of commitments.

> **Intra-corporate transferees**
>
> Natural persons of another member who have been employed by juridical persons of another member for a period of not less than one year and who seek temporary entry in order to render services to (i) the same juridical person which is engaged in substantive business operations in Canada or (ii) a juridical person constituted in Canada and engaged in substantive business operations in Canada which is owned by or controlled by or affiliated with the aforementioned juridical person.
>
> Intra-corporate transferees must be in one of three categories.
>
> **Executives** — Natural persons employed by a juridical person who primarily direct the management of the juridical person or establish goals and policies for the juridical person or a major component or function of the juridical person, exercise wide latitude in decision-making, and receive only general supervision or direction from higher-level executives, the board of directors, or stockholders of the juridical person.
>
> **Managers** — Natural persons employed by a juridical person who direct the juridical person, or a department or subdivision of the juridical person, supervise and control the work of other supervisory, professional or managerial employees, have the authority to hire and fire or recommend hiring, firing, or other personnel actions and exercise discretionary authority over day-to-day operations at a senior level.
>
> **Specialists** — Natural persons who possess knowledge at an advanced level of expertise and who possess proprietary knowledge of the juridical person's product, service, research equipment, techniques or management.

371 *GATS Annex on Movement of Natural Persons Supplying Services under the Agreement.*

Box 5.19 Summary of options for an IIA provision on the entry of foreign nationals and restrictions on nationality requirements for senior management

1. No provision addressing the entry of foreign nationals or nationality requirements for senior management
2. Commitment regarding the entry of foreign nationals
3. Commitment prohibiting restrictions on nationality requirements for senior management

5.11.2 Discussion of options

1. *No provision on the entry of foreign nationals or nationality requirements for senior management*

This is the most common approach in current IIAs and gives host states the maximum flexibility with respect to who is permitted to enter the country in accordance with domestic labour market, immigration and security policies. It provides no commitment for the benefit of foreign investors to allow them to bring into the host state foreign individuals to work at their investments or protection against any host state rule that requires that locals be hired to fill particular positions.

Even without an IIA commitment of this kind, however, a host state would be subject to any similar commitment that it had made under *GATS* or in any other trade or investment agreement. Such an obligation could not be subject to the dispute settlement procedures of an IIA unless the treaty contains a clause that expressly permits investors to make claims based on other state obligations that are not expressly set out in the treaty. It is also possible that an obligation regarding entry or prohibiting nationality restrictions would be incorporated into an IIA that contained an MFN clause, if the state had entered into another IIA that provided such obligations.[372]

2. *Commitment regarding the entry of foreign nationals*

For some investors, a commitment to permit the entry of foreign nationals may be valuable, though the value will depend on the extent to which bringing in foreign nationals is part of the investor's business plan and to what extent the domestic rules in the host state otherwise impose restrictions on doing so. If host state rules would have to be changed as a result of such a commitment, then access for foreign nationals

372 See Section 5.4 (Most favoured nation).

will be improved. If host state rules are already liberal, then the IIA obligation serves only to prevent the introduction of new restrictions.

Regardless of their possible value, however, only a few treaties include such a requirement. In those that do, the commitment is subject to applicable national rules and so seems not to create any real obligation. Undoubtedly, the small number of IIAs with this kind of provision reflects significant host state concerns about managing entry into the country.

3. *Commitment prohibiting restrictions on nationality requirements for senior management*

Such a provision may be an absolute commitment or, as in some treaties, be subject to national law. In the latter form, it would seem to have limited effect. Neither type of commitment is included in many IIAs. This is probably because some host states want to be able to put in place requirements that their nationals hold senior management or specialist positions with a view to facilitating the transfer of technological expertise and skills and ensuring that senior managers are responsive to local conditions. There is no guarantee, however, that these benefits will be realised in practice.

A commitment not to impose nationality restrictions may have some value to foreign investors who have an interest in ensuring that they have freedom to choose whomever they consider to be the best person for a senior management position. Host state rules that restrict this freedom may have efficiency implications for the operation of the investment. Consequently, rules restricting senior management personnel to host country nationals may deter investment. The significance of a commitment not to impose such restrictions for investors will depend on the host state's domestic policy. If the host state does not impose nationality restrictions, then the only effect of the commitment is to prevent the introduction of future measures of this kind. The value of a host state commitment not to impose restrictions on nationality will be higher if it is accompanied by a commitment to grant entry for foreign individuals to work at the foreign investor's investment in the host state.

With respect to options 2 and 3, it is possible that any more favourable obligation regarding entry or prohibiting nationality restrictions that a state has entered into in another IIA would be incorporated into an IIA, if the IIA contained an MFN clause.

5.11.3 Summary

The Guide does not include a sample provision on the entry of personnel. Only a few model treaties include such a requirement. In those that do, the commitment is subject to applicable national rules and so seems not to create an effective obligation in any case. As a result, it is not clear what benefit would attach to such a provision. At the same time, for states that are concerned about managing their domestic employment markets and protecting the integrity and security of their borders, such a provision will be unattractive despite its possible appeal to some investors. The significance of host state policy concerns related to the entry of foreigners suggests that they will not want to risk any unexpected consequences associated with such a provision.

No sample provision restricting the ability of host states to stipulate that their nationals shall occupy senior management positions has been included in the Guide. Again, this is because such a provision is not included in the agreements of many countries. In addition, as noted above, host states may want to put in place such stipulations as a way of facilitating the transfer of expertise and skills. At the same time, restricting investors' freedom to choose whomever they consider to be the best person for a senior management position may have efficiency implications for the operation of the investment and may deter investment. Consequently, a prohibition on restricting senior management personnel to host country nationals may encourage investment to some extent by some investors. Nevertheless, the absence of such a commitment from many developed country IIA models suggests that the value of the commitment is small.

5.12 Reservations and exceptions

Cross references

As frequently noted in the Guide, concerns have been expressed that the investor protection obligations in IIAs prevent states from acting to achieve public policy objectives, even where state action is necessary to implement other international obligations.[373] Reservations and exceptions are provisions in IIAs that seek to ensure that states are not unduly constrained by IIA obligations. They are designed to ensure that state measures intended to achieve important public policy objectives are not at risk of being successfully challenged on the basis of their inconsistency with the investor protection obligations in the treaty. General exceptions often address

373 A Newcombe (2011), 'General Exceptions in International Investment Agreements', in Cordonier Segger et al., op. cit., at 365–6.

measures enacted for purposes such as the protection of public health, the environment and national security. Reservations may be used in a similar way to safeguard a state's freedom to act in a particular area but, unlike exceptions, reservations are separately listed for each party and typically are not symmetrical. They are customised to reflect the national policies and priorities of each party. Reservations can be used to permit the maintenance of specific legislation or programmes that would otherwise be contrary to the obligations in the treaty or to exclude whole sectors from the scope of the treaty or particular obligations.

The trend in IIAs is towards an expansion of the use of exceptions and reservations, though currently extensive general exceptions and reservations are included in relatively few treaties.[374] Some model treaties, such as the UK model IPPA and the Indian model BIPPA, contain few exceptions and do not contemplate reservations.[375] Others, such as the Canadian and US model treaties, create a detailed pattern of exceptions and reservations that refines the scope of the treaty's obligations in specific and complex ways.[376]

Another possible approach, analogous to an exception and discussed above, is to exclude matters from the scope of the treaty.[377] A final possibility discussed below in this section, but not found in many existing treaties, is to provide that a host state has a general right to regulate in the public interest.[378] Asserting a right to regulate is intended to ensure that a host state has a broad power to take action to achieve its public policy objectives in all areas.[379]

Each of these approaches has advantages and disadvantages as discussed below. Reservations, exceptions and scope restrictions are limited to the discrete areas of state activity to which they refer. In addition, some investor–state tribunals have interpreted exceptions and reservations narrowly on the basis that they undermine the main investment protection and promotion goals of IIAs. By contrast, a general right to regulate is intended to recognise that states have a broad general power and responsibility to regulate in the public interest that is not confined to any specific policy area. While the existence of this right is undeniable as a general proposition, it is difficult to give it specific legal content and it is not clear how it should be applied in relation to the investor protection provisions that dominate the content of

374 UNCTAD (2007), *Treaties 1996–2006*, op. cit., at 80–1.

375 UK model IPPA, Art. 7 discussed above; Indian model BIPPA, Art. 12 (excepting only measures to protect essential security interests or enacted in circumstances of a national emergency applied on a non-discriminatory basis). The IISD model treaty provides a few general exceptions but, unlike other forms of IIA, sets out a list of host state rights which appear to operate in a manner similar to exceptions (Arts. 25–8).

376 Canadian model FIPA, Arts. 9, 10, 16 and 17; US model BIT, Arts. 14, 18, 20 and 21. The COMESA Investment Agreement (2007) has a similar set of exceptions in Arts. 22–5.

377 See Section 4.5 (Scope of application).

378 The IISD model treaty adopts this approach.

379 One other possible approach discussed above is positive listing, meaning that the obligations apply to only those sectors of the host state economy that the host state lists in a schedule to the IIA. See Section 5.2 (Right of establishment) for a discussion of positive listing.

IIAs. Right to regulate provisions are not found in many IIAs and, as a consequence, such provisions have not had the benefit of extensive consideration in investor–state cases.[380]

Finally, there are a number of circumstances recognised under general customary international law that excuse a state from liability for actions that would otherwise be a breach of IIA obligations. Since these circumstances precluding liability are not based on IIA provisions, they will not be discussed in the Guide.[381]

5.12.1 IIA practice regarding exceptions

Exceptions in IIAs exempt a party state from obligations in the treaty in situations where compliance with the obligations would be inconsistent with the achievement of some public policy goal defined in the exception. In this way, exceptions are intended to ensure that the application of an IIA is balanced between protecting investors and achieving other policy goals. Exceptions may be general, in the sense that that they apply to all obligations in the treaty, or limited to specific obligations. In terms of treaty design, general exceptions and exceptions applicable to a number of specific obligations are typically set out in a separate provision while exceptions applying to single obligation are usually incorporated in the provision creating the obligation. In this section, IIA practice regarding different categories of exceptions is discussed.

Exceptions for health, the environment, public morals and law enforcement

Policy areas included in exceptions

The Canadian model treaty addresses some of the common categories of exceptions found in some existing IIAs. The Canadian model creates general exceptions which allow a party state to take measures necessary to: (i) protect human, animal or plant life or health; (ii) conserve living or non-living exhaustible natural resources; and (iii) ensure compliance with laws and regulations that are not inconsistent with the provisions of the Agreement.[382] The COMESA Investment Agreement has a similar

380 There has been some consideration of the right to regulate in the context of cases on indirect expropriation and state's police powers as well as cases considering fair and equitable treatment claims.

381 These include, for example, the defence of necessity. See, generally, A Newcombe and L Paradell (2009), *Law and Practice of Investment Treaties: Standards of Treatment*, Wolters Kluwer International, The Netherlands, at 510–28.

382 These exceptions were added to Canada's model investment treaty in 2004. The US model BIT has a broader provision dealing with environmental measures, but it does not create an exception (Art. 12.2). Bartels notes that states have used these types of clauses to increase their policy space in relation to environmental and cultural issues, as well as indigenous rights. However, these types of clauses have not addressed human rights or labour rights concerns. L Bartels (2009), 'Social Issues: Labour, Environment and Human Rights', in S Lester and B Mercurio (eds), *Bilateral and Regional Trade Agreements: Commentary, Analysis and Case Studies*, Cambridge University Press, Cambridge, at 6. With respect to exceptions to permit the enforcement of law, the ASEAN Agreement (Art. 17) and the India–Singapore CECA (Art. 6.11) go on to specify that this includes laws and regulations relating to:

set of exceptions, but lists measures to protect public morals as well,[383] a category also included in the India–Singapore CECA and the ASEAN Agreement.[384] The precise manner in which these categories are expressed is somewhat variable,[385] but these categories are common. In structure, they generally follow the well-known language of the exceptions in Article XX of the *GATT* (set out in Box 5.20).

Structure of exceptions – requirements for availability

There are several approaches to the structure of exceptions in this category. Typically, IIAs include requirements to prevent abuse of the exception by states. Often the exceptions adopt some or all of the requirements applicable to the exceptions in *GATT* Article XX. In the Canadian model, some of the exceptions follow the architecture of the exceptions in Article XX of the *GATT* closely and require that all the *GATT* requirements be met before the exception is available. The most stringent requirements under *GATT* Article XX are as follows.

- **A state measure has to be 'necessary' to achieve one of the identified goals.**[386] This requirement has been interpreted as meaning that there must not be an alternative measure reasonably available to the state to achieve the defined objective that is less restrictive of trade.[387]
- **A state measure cannot be applied in a manner that would constitute 'a means of arbitrary or unjustifiable discrimination between countries where the same conditions prevail,**[388] **or a disguised restriction on international trade'.**[389] These generally applicable requirements are sometimes referred to as the requirements of the 'chapeau' of *GATT* Article XX.[390]

---

i. The prevention of deceptive and fraudulent practices to deal with the effects of a default on a contract;
ii. The protection of privacy of individuals in relation to the processing and dissemination of personal data and the protection of the confidentiality of individual records and accounts;
iii. Safety.

These follow the exceptions provided in *GATS*, Art. XIV.

383 COMESA Investment Agreement (2007), Art. 22.

384 India–Singapore CECA (2005), Art. 6.11; ASEAN Agreement (2009), Art. 17.

385 The Australia–India BIT (1999) refers to the 'prevention of diseases or pests' as well (Art. 15).

386 Such a requirement is found in Switzerland–Mauritius, Agreement between the Swiss Confederation and the Republic of Mauritius on the Promotion and Reciprocal Protection of Investment, signed 26 November 1998, in force 21 April 2000, Art. 11.5.

387 *European Communities – Measures Affecting Asbestos and Products Containing Asbestos* (Complaint by Canada) (2001), WTO Doc. WT/DS135/AB/R (Appellate Body Report).

388 Such a requirement is found in the Australia–India BIT (1999), Art. 15. See also Argentina–New Zealand, Agreement between the Government of the Argentine Republic and the Government of New Zealand for the Promotion and Reciprocal Protection of Investments, signed 27 August 1999, not yet in force, which includes a proviso that the measure be 'not applied in a manner that would constitute a means of arbitrary or unjustified discrimination' (Art. 5).

389 Such a requirement is found in Canada–Armenia, Agreement between the Government of Canada and the Government of the Republic of Armenia for the Promotion and Protection of Investments, signed 8 May 1997, in force 29 March 1999, Art. XVII.

390 These chapeau requirements appear in the India–Singapore CECA (2005) (Art. 6.11) and the ASEAN Agreement (2009) (Art. 17).

Demonstrating that a measure is necessary has proved to be a high standard in WTO cases considering *GATT* Article XX. Instead of requiring that measures are 'necessary' to achieve the policy objective, the COMESA Investment Agreement requires only that a measure be 'designed and applied' to achieve the objective, an easier standard for host states to meet.[391]

The USA adopts a different approach to measures related to the environment in its model agreement. The importance of the protection of the environment is recognised. The provision then goes on to provide as follows:

> Nothing in this Treaty shall be construed to prevent a Party from adopting, maintaining or enforcing any measure *otherwise consistent with this Treaty* that it considers appropriate to ensure that investment activity is undertaken in a manner sensitive to environmental concerns.[392] (Emphasis added.)

A provision that requires that a measure be 'otherwise consistent' with the treaty, however, is not an exception at all. It is a guide to interpretation only.

Box 5.20 General exceptions in the *GATT*

Article XX
General Exceptions

Subject to the requirement that such measures are not applied in a manner which would constitute a means of arbitrary or unjustifiable discrimination between countries where the same conditions prevail, or a disguised restriction on international trade, nothing in this Agreement shall be construed to prevent the adoption or enforcement by any contracting party of measures:

a. Necessary to protect public morals;
b. Necessary to protect human, animal or plant life or health;
c. Relating to the importations or exportations of gold or silver;
d. Necessary to secure compliance with laws or regulations which are not inconsistent with the provisions of this Agreement, including those relating to customs enforcement, the enforcement of monopolies operated under paragraph 4 of Article II and Article XVII, the protection of patents, trademarks and copyrights, and the prevention of deceptive practices;
e. Relating to the products of prison labour;
f. Imposed for the protection of national treasures of artistic, historic or archaeological value;

(Continued)

391 COMESA Investment Agreement (2007), Art. 22.1. The agreement adopts a similar set of qualifications for reliance on the exceptions.
392 E.g. US–Uruguay BIT (2005), Art. 12.

(Continued)

g. Relating to the conservation of exhaustible natural resources if such measures are made effective in conjunction with restrictions on domestic production or consumption;

h. Undertaken in pursuance of obligations under any intergovernmental commodity agreement which conforms to criteria submitted to the CONTRACTING PARTIES and not disapproved by them or which is itself so submitted and not so disapproved;

i. Involving restrictions on exports of domestic materials necessary to ensure essential quantities of such materials to a domestic processing industry during periods when the domestic price of such materials is held below the world price as part of a governmental stabilisation plan; *Provided* that such restrictions shall not operate to increase the exports of or the protection afforded to such domestic industry, and shall not depart from the provisions of this Agreement relating to non-discrimination;

j. Essential to the acquisition or distribution of products in general or local short supply; *Provided* that any such measures shall be consistent with the principle that all contracting parties are entitled to an equitable share of the international supply of such products, and that any such measures, which are inconsistent with the other provisions of the Agreement shall be discontinued as soon as the conditions giving rise to them have ceased to exist. The CONTRACTING PARTIES shall review the need for this sub-paragraph not later than 30 June 1960.

Article XVI of the *GATS* contains a similar list of exceptions.

Exceptions for prudential measures

Another category of exception relates to the operation of a state's financial system. For example, Canada excludes from the application of investment treaty obligations reasonable state measures 'for prudential reasons,' including:

(g) the protection of investors, depositors, financial market participants, policy-holders, policy-claimants, or persons to whom a fiduciary duty is owed by a financial institution;

(h) the maintenance of the safety, soundness, integrity or financial responsibility of financial institutions; and

(i) ensuring the integrity and stability of a Party's financial system.[393]

This kind of exception provides states with significant flexibility to act to protect people who deal with financial institutions, the financial institutions themselves and

393 Canadian model FIPA, Arts. 10.2 and 10.3.

the financial system as a whole. The only requirement is that the measures must be reasonable. The Canadian exception further provides that nothing in an IIA applies to 'non-discriminatory measures of general application taken by any public entity in pursuit of monetary or credit policies or exchange rate policies'.[394] This kind of exception can be relied on with respect to measures relating to a financial crisis, but applies to a much broader range of circumstances. In the Canadian model, restrictions on the movement of funds out of the host state are also permitted under exceptions to the funds transfer obligation discussed above, including in balance of payments emergencies.[395]

Exceptions for prudential measures are not common in existing IIAs, but increasingly appear in new treaties and generally follow the approach in the Canadian model.[396] The US model treaty has a similar provision, but it also contains a procedure to address situations in which the exception is being relied on by a state in an investor–state arbitration. Essentially, the financial authorities in each jurisdiction will be asked to make a joint determination regarding whether the exception applies and, if they make a determination, it is binding on the arbitration tribunal.[397]

The ASEAN Agreement deals with this issue by adopting the prudential measures exception in the Annex on Financial Services to the *GATS*, which is similar in coverage and effect to the Canadian model exception described above.[398]

Security exceptions

In many IIAs, parties reserve the right to take any measure to protect their 'essential security interests'. Several IIAs go on to provide that a party state can invoke a general treaty exception in situations where a requirement to comply with the agreement would impede 'the fulfilment of its obligations with respect to the maintenance or restoration of international peace or security'.[399] This type of exception is found in the US and Canadian model agreements.[400] The US model agreement provides as follows:

> Nothing in this Treaty shall be construed:
>
> 1. to require a Party to furnish or allow access to any information the disclosure of which it determines to be contrary to its essential security interests; or
>
> 2. to preclude a Party from applying measures that it considers necessary for the fulfilment of its obligations with respect to the maintenance or restoration of international peace or security, or the protection of its own essential security interests.

---

394 The US model BIT does not require that measures be reasonable (Art. 20).

395 See Section 5.8 (Free transfer of funds).

396 UNCTAD (2007) *Treaties 1996-2006* op. cit., at 90–1.

397 US model BIT, Art. 20.

398 ASEAN Agreement (2009), Art. 17.2. The *GATS* prudential measures exception is described in Appendix 2.

399 E.g. US model BIT, Art. 18.

400 Canadian model FIPA, Art. 10.4; US model BIT, Art. 20. The Canadian model FIPA says that 'such obligations would be those derived from the Charter of the United Nations'. Similar language is in the Japan–Korea BIT (2002) (Art. 16).

The Canadian model is more limited. Rather than simply excluding all measures for the protection of its own essential security interests, Canada's exception is restricted to measures taken in time of war, or other emergency in international relations and those that relate to arms trafficking or the implementation of national policies or international agreements related to the non-proliferation of nuclear weapons.

Typically, IIAs do not define what is meant by 'essential security interests'.[401] The US and Canadian model treaties along with some others expressly allocate to the state the power to determine when this exception applies. The exception is available whenever the state 'considers [an action] necessary for the protection of its essential security interests'.[402] This approach would seem to prevent an investor–state tribunal from finding that a measure was not related to a state's essential security interests if the state claimed that it was and relied on the exception. It may be that the only issue a tribunal could consider is whether the state was acting in good faith in invoking the exception. Some other IIAs except only actions that are 'necessary' to protect essential security interests. In the Australia–India BIT, measures qualify for the exception only if they are applied 'reasonably and on a non-discriminatory basis'. With these kinds of words, arbitral tribunals would be able to assess whether the criteria for the availability of the exception are met.

Another limiting approach is to restrict the security exception to certain obligations, such as national treatment or MFN treatment.[403] It is also possible to impose procedural requirements as a condition of eligibility for the exception, such as prior notice of a measure relying on the exception and its purpose.[404]

A few IIAs deal with an exception for national security issues in the context of dispute settlement only. Instead of having an explicit exception for measures related to security in the treaty, these IIAs provide that investors cannot invoke the dispute settlement procedures of the agreement if a state justifies its action as based on national security considerations.[405]

---

401 Some treaties use different words. For example, Hong Kong–New Zealand, Agreement between the Government of Hong Kong and the Government of New Zealand for the Promotion and Protection of Investments, signed 6 July 1995, in force 5 August 1995, refers to 'essential interests' (Art. 8), while Caribbean Community–Cuba, Trade and Economic Cooperation Agreement between the Caribbean Community and the Government of the Republic of Cuba, signed 5 July 2000, not yet in force, refers to 'national security interests' (Art. XVII).

402 Canadian model FIPA, Art. 10.4. Similar language is in the Japan-Korea BIT (2002) (Art. 16). The COMESA Investment Agreement (2007) requires that the measure be 'designed and applied' to protect national security.

403 *Ad* Art. 3(a) of the Germany–Mexico BIT provides an exception that only applies to national treatment and MFN: 'The measures taken by reason of national security, public interest, public health or morality shall not be considered as a "less favourable treatment", according to Article 3'.

404 E.g., Japan–Vietnam, Agreement between Japan and the Socialist Republic of Vietnam for the Liberalization, Promotion and Protection of Investment, signed 14 November 2003, in force 19 December 2004, Art. 15.

405 Sweden–Mexico, Agreement between the Government of the Kingdom of Sweden and the Government of the United Mexican States concerning the Promotion and Reciprocal Protection of Investments, signed 3 October 2000, in force 1 July 2001, Art. 18. In an exchange of letters pursuant to Art. 6.12(4) of the India–Singapore CECA (2005), Singapore and India agreed that a state decision that it could rely on the national security exception in the agreement could not be reviewed by any tribunal.

Some security exceptions, such as Canada's, do not include measures to protect 'public order', though this is provided for in some other treaty models.[406] Protecting public order seems to contemplate measures needed to maintain peace and the rule of law in a state, rather than to deal with more serious threats of war or armed conflict which may threaten a state's essential security interests. Typically, because of its potentially broad application, an exception for measures to maintain the public order is subject to certain conditions that are based on the chapeau of *GATT* Article XX. An IIA might contain a proviso that such measures will not be applied in a manner that would constitute a means of arbitrary or unjustifiable discrimination in the party state, or a disguised restriction on investment. Also, measures may have to be necessary to be eligible for the exception.[407]

Exceptions for taxation

Domestic tax regimes often have discriminatory elements that favour domestic businesses. For this reason, some countries exclude taxation measures entirely from the scope of their IIAs.[408] The Canadian and US model treaties have a more nuanced approach that permits expropriation claims based on taxation measures, provided there is no agreement among the tax authorities of the party states that the expropriation claim should *not* proceed.[409] If the tax authorities agree that there is no expropriation then the claim cannot proceed. Claims related to tax measures cannot be made on the basis of other provisions of the treaty. The approach in the Canadian and US models provides limited protection for investors where the tax measure is so severe that at least one party state, probably the investor's state, thinks it is an expropriation. The approach in the Norwegian draft model APPI is similar, except that it contemplates that the competent tax authority of any treaty party can decide that a measure should be considered under the expropriation provision.[410] The COMESA Investment Agreement adopts a similar approach.[411]

Exceptions for culture

A number of states, including France, Canada and China, have included exceptions in their IIAs intended to protect their ability to enact measures to protect local culture. In its treaties, France has included a broad exception for measures 'in the

406 E.g. Norwegian draft model IPPA, Art. 24(i); Korea–Japan BIT (2002), Art. 16(1)(d); Finland–Kyrgyzstan, Agreement between the Government of Finland and the Government of the Kyrgyz Republic on the Promotion and Protection of Investments, signed 3 April 2003, in force 8 December 2004, Art. 14.2.

407 E.g. Korea–Japan BIT (2002), Art. 16(1)(d); Finland–Kyrgyzstan BIT (2003), Art. 14.2.

408 UK model IPPA (Art. 7) excludes all international and domestic measures related to taxation from the national treatment and MFN obligations. See, similarly, Argentina–New Zealand BIT (1999), Art. 5; Mexico–Germany BIT (1998), *Ad* Art. 3(b).

409 Canadian model FIPA, Art. 16; US model BIT, Art. 21. The Canadian model has a similar mechanism to permit claims that there has been a breach of an agreement between an investor and the host state by a tax measure unless the tax authorities determine that there is no breach of the agreement.

410 Norwegian draft model IPPA, Art. 28.

411 COMESA Investment Agreement (2007), Art. 23.

framework of policies designed to preserve and promote cultural and linguistic diversity'.[412] This exception would appear to be broad enough to protect measures directed at the production of culture, such as rules limiting the screening of foreign films, as well as any policies in other areas within 'the framework of policies' related to culture, which might include the manufacture and distribution of cultural products, however defined.[413] A few other states have included provisions that broadly exempt all measures that the state determines are designed to protect culture.[414]

Canada's model treaty contains an exception that applies to measures related to cultural industries.[415] This is a broad exclusion of entire sectors of activity related to cultural products, though it does have the benefit of being more specific and predictable than the French exception. Canada's definition of cultural industries is set out in Box 5.21.

Box 5.21 Definition of cultural industries in the Canadian model FIPA

Cultural industries means persons engaged in any of the following activities:

i. The publication, distribution, or sale of books, magazines, periodicals or newspapers in print or machine readable form but not including the sole activity of printing or typesetting any of the foregoing;

ii. The production, distribution, sale or exhibition of film or video recordings;

iii. The production, distribution, sale or exhibition of audio or video music recordings;

iv. The publication, distribution, sale or exhibition of music in print or machine readable form; or

v. Radio communications in which the transmissions are intended for direct reception by the general public, and all radio, television or cable broadcasting undertakings and all satellite programming and broadcast network services.

The ASEAN Agreement and the India–Singapore CECA adopt a narrower approach. These treaties simply include the language found in *GATT* Article XX – 'measures imposed for the protection of national treasures of artistic, historic or archaeological value' – and incorporate the requirements of the chapeau of Article XX.[416]

412 E.g. France–Uganda, Agreement between the Government of the Republic of France and the Government of the Republic of Uganda on the Reciprocal Promotion and Protection of Investments, signed 3 January 2003, in force 20 December 2004, Art. 1.

413 Ibid.

414 E.g. Norwegian draft model IPPA, Art. 27.

415 Canadian model FIPA, Art. 14.6.

416 *GATS*, has a similar chapeau limiting the availability of most exceptions in that agreement (GATS, Art. XIV).

Exceptions for non-disclosure of confidential information

As noted above, many countries have exceptions that allow them not to disclose confidential personal information.[417] Often the exception for confidential information is included in IIA transparency provisions. Canada's model includes a general exception to ensure that the agreement creates no requirement for disclosure of information that would impede law enforcement or run contrary to a state's domestic rules protecting government confidentiality and personal privacy. The extension of the exception to government confidentiality was included to address Canada's concern that it should not have to disclose confidential government information that it was ordered to disclose by investment arbitration tribunals in investor–state cases under NAFTA.[418]

Exceptions for government procurement and subsidies

One of the common ways in which many governments support local businesses is to give them preferences when the government buys goods and services, known as government procurement. Discriminatory procurement practices may affect the business of foreign investors who supply goods or services in competition with local suppliers. The Canadian and US model agreements create exceptions for procurement by governments and state enterprises that allow them to prefer local businesses.[419] These exceptions apply only to the national treatment and MFN obligations in the Canadian and US model agreements, as well as to the commitments regarding the entry of foreign personnel and prohibiting nationality requirements in these models. As discussed below, these are the obligations most likely to be breached by procurement practices.

Subsidies are another way in which many governments support national businesses. Both the Canadian and US models create exceptions for government subsidies, including government-supported loans, guarantees and insurance.[420] These exceptions are also limited to the national treatment and MFN obligations and the obligations regarding the entry of personnel and nationality requirements in the Canadian and US model agreements. The India–Singapore CECA exempts subsidies and grants from all obligations in its provision defining the scope of the agreement.[421] Few other agreements address subsidies.

Other exceptions

Ultimately, each state must decide for itself what policy areas need the benefit of exceptions. While the categories of exceptions discussed above are those that are currently found in some IIAs, it may be that for a particular state additional exceptions

---

417 See Section 5.10 (Transparency).

418 *United Parcel Service of America, Inc. v. Canada*, UNCITRAL, Decision of the Tribunal Relating to Canada's Claim of Cabinet Privilege, 8 October 2004, at para. 11; *Pope & Talbot v. Canada*, UNCITRAL, Decision by Tribunal on Privilege , 6 September 2000, at para. 1.4.

419 Canadian model FIPA, Art. 9.5(a); US model BIT, Art. 14.5(a).

420 Canadian model FIPA, Art. 9.5(b); US model BIT, Art. 14.5(b).

421 The India–Singapore CECA (2005), Art. 6.2(5).

are desirable. For example, an exception for development programmes was discussed above.[422] Equally, some of the categories listed above may not be necessary.

One further category of exception should be considered if an IIA contemplates investor obligations, such as obligations related to human rights, labour rights, indigenous peoples' rights and anti-corruption, or host state obligations in these areas, including obligations related to the enforcement of investor obligations. All of these kinds of obligations are discussed below in the Guide. Where such obligations are present in an IIA, it would be useful for the agreement to provide expressly that actions taken by a party state to give effect to obligations it undertakes or to enforce investor obligations are not breaches of the investor protection obligations in the agreement.

Scope of exceptions

In principle, exceptions may apply to all obligations in an IIA or only to specified obligations. The Canadian model provides examples of both. The general exceptions relating to health and the environment, prudential measures, cultural industries and security interests apply to all obligations. The exceptions for subsidies and procurement, however, apply only to national treatment, MFN and a few other obligations. In general, exceptions that apply to all obligations provide more flexibility to host states, while narrower exceptions provide greater certainty and predictability for investors. It is impossible to anticipate all policy measures that a state may want to adopt in a particular area, but some kinds of government measures are more likely to conflict with particular obligations. For example, as noted above, since government procurement policies are most likely to discriminate in favour of local suppliers, an exception from the national treatment obligation is most likely to be needed to protect government procurement measures. There may be little need to except government procurement from other obligations. For example, since procurement decisions are unlikely to constitute expropriation, an exception from an IIA obligation not to expropriate without compensation would not be needed. In each case, a state needs to consider what its actual policies are and identify the areas of domestic policy in which it wants to retain flexibility for the future. On this basis, a state can determine what exceptions it needs in an IIA. These exceptions will then have to be negotiated with the other party. As will be discussed below, for specific policies and policy areas that only one state wants to protect, reservations may be used instead of exceptions.

An additional issue arises in connection with the obligation not to expropriate without paying compensation and fair and equitable treatment. As discussed, these two IIA obligations reflect customary international law requirements, at least to some extent. While states may contract out of their customary law obligations through exceptions, it would undoubtedly seem anomalous to most capital-exporting countries that an IIA contained exception provisions that would give their investors less substantive protection than they would have had without the treaty. If an action of a host state that would be an expropriation or a breach of fair and equitable treatment fits within an exception, then there is no international liability for the

422 See Section 5.3 (National treatment).

state. For example, if the state were to expropriate land owned by a foreign investor to create a nature reserve for endangered species, such an action might fit within an exception for the protection of exhaustible natural resources in the IIA, so long as the expropriation did not discriminate between foreign and domestic landowners and met any other requirements for the availability of the exception. In this case, the state would have no obligation under the treaty to compensate any foreign investor who had been expropriated. By virtue of the exception, there would be no breach of the treaty. Such a result would be inconsistent with the customary international law obligation of states to provide compensation for expropriation and domestic legal requirements in most states.[423] The application of many exception provisions in IIAs to the expropriation and fair and equitable treatment obligations has never been tested. It may be that some other interpretation consistent with customary law would be adopted. Nevertheless, some states may object to treaty provisions that create exceptions to these basic customary international law obligations.

Safeguards and phase-ins

In addition to fairly broad exceptions, the COMESA Investment Agreement has a form of safeguard provision under which a member state that suffers or is threatened with any serious injury as a result of its commitments under the agreement may take such emergency measures 'as may be necessary to prevent or to remedy such injury'. A member state's use of such emergency measures is subject to review by the COMESA Common Investment Area Committee, composed of ministers of the member states.[424] Few other treaties contain such safeguard provisions in relation to investment.[425]

An alternative approach to facilitate a gradual adjustment to IIA commitments would be to have obligations phased in over time. This could be achieved through an IIA commitment to accept a particular obligation at some fixed date in the future or to progressively remove restrictions that a host state had excluded from its obligations through reservations.

Issues related to the use of exceptions

As noted in the previous section, there has been relatively little arbitral case law on the use of exceptions in investment agreements. Commentators have expressed a number of concerns about the effectiveness of exceptions.

---

423 This point was suggested to the authors by the work of Professor Andrew Newcombe.

424 COMESA Investment Agreement (2007), Art. 24.

425 The agreement between the member countries of the Caribbean Community contains a general emergency safeguard mechanism. In that agreement, a member state may impose restrictions on services trade which could include investment where the exercise of rights granted in the treaty creates 'serious difficulties in any sector of the economy of a member State or occasions economic hardships in a region of the Community' where that state has been adversely affected. See Caribbean Community, *Revised Treaty of Chaguaramas Establishing the Caribbean Community Including the* CARICOM *Single Market and Economy*, signed 5 July 2001, in force 5 February 2002, and subsequently revised, Art. 47. A sector-specific safeguard in financial services was created in NAFTA (1992), allowing Mexico to impose caps on market share if certain foreign ownership levels were surpassed after it removed existing restrictions at those levels. See NAFTA (1992), Annex VII, Schedule of Mexico, Part B.

- **Exceptions will be interpreted narrowly because they are inconsistent with the overall purpose of IIAs, which is to protect and promote investment.** This approach has been taken in a number of investor–state arbitration cases.[426] Though this approach has been criticised[427] and not universally applied,[428] it appears to be the dominant approach. In part, this approach could be avoided by changing the way in which the objectives of the agreement are described. How this might be done is discussed above.[429]

- **A state has the burden of proving that its measure falls within an exception.** A number of investor–state tribunals have adopted this approach.[430] In general, party states in investor–state arbitrations cases have to prove that they are entitled to rely on provisions of an IIA that they invoke.

- **Exceptions necessarily refer to a discrete list of policy areas in which state action is permitted despite being otherwise inconsistent with the IIA's investor protection obligations. Therefore they can never provide comprehensive protection for all future state regulation and may even provide less flexibility than is built into the substantive standards of investor protection.** In a number of cases, investor–state arbitration tribunals have interpreted investor protection obligations flexibly to permit non-discriminatory host state regulation without relying on exceptions. For example, as discussed above, cases interpreting when investments are 'in like circumstances' for the purposes of the national treatment obligation have permitted states to treat foreign investors less favourably than domestic investors if doing so is to achieve some legitimate non-discriminatory public policy goal. For the purposes of the measure, the foreign investor and the domestic investor were found not to be in like circumstances.[431] Unlike exceptions, the category of acceptable government policy is not closed under the national treatment obligation. Some commentators have suggested that there is far more flexibility under national treatment than would exist through exceptions, especially if exceptions are limited by the kinds of qualifications that are present in the chapeau of *GATT* Article XX.[432]

  Another example of flexibility built into a substantive investor protection obligation is the expropriation obligation. Many agreements now include a specification of what constitutes state regulation as opposed to expropriation that is not tied to any particular policy area.[433]

---

426 Newcombe, 'General Exceptions', op. cit., at 361–3.

427 Ibid. at 363–4.

428 *United Parcel Service of America, Inc. v. Canada*, op. cit. (dealing with the cultural exemption in NAFTA).

429 See Section 4.2.1 (The role of preambles in IIAs) and Section 4.4 (Statement of objectives).

430 Ibid., at 154.

431 See Section 5.3 (National treatment). The tribunal in *SD Myers*, op. cit., said that the national treatment enquiry was akin to the kind of analysis required in applying *GATT* Art. XX exceptions (at para. 29).

432 N DiMascio and J Pauwelyn (2008), 'Non-Discrimination in Trade and Investment Treaties: Worlds Apart or Two Sides of the Same Coin?', 102 *American Journal of International Law* 48, at 82–3; Newcombe, 'General Exceptions', op. cit., at 367–9.

433 See Section 5.6 (Limitations on expropriation and nationalisation).

- **Exceptions may be considered by investor–state arbitration tribunals to represent an exhaustive list of the policy areas in which the party states want flexibility to regulate. In some cases this will result in narrower protection than if the exceptions were not in the IIA.** Because the parties to an IIA expressly described the policy areas that are to be excluded from the application of the investor protection provisions in detailed exception provisions, an investor–state tribunal might conclude that states did not intend to protect their flexibility in any other area. This might encourage tribunals to abandon the approach to the application of investor-protection provisions described in the previous point and to interpret investor protection provisions in IIAs less flexibly than they have in the past.

These kinds of concerns discouraged the IISD from including general exceptions in its model agreement. Instead, a right to regulate was provided.

5.12.2 IIA practice regarding the right to regulate

Some IIA models seek to address concerns regarding whether states are free to regulate to achieve their development goals by including a provision setting out a positive right to regulate. For example, Article 25 of the IISD model treaty states:

> A. Host states have, in accordance with the general principles of international law, the right to pursue their own development objectives and priorities.
>
> B. In accordance with customary international law and other general principles of law, host states have the right to take regulatory or other measures to ensure that development in their territory is consistent with the goals and principles of sustainable development, and with other social and economic policy objectives...[434]

In addition, in order to address the uncertainties created by investor–state arbitration decisions with respect to the balancing of the host state's right to regulate and the rights of investors under IIAs,[435] the IISD model expressly provides that the right to regulate is to be considered 'within a balance of the rights and obligations' of investors and investments and host states.[436] The IISD model also seeks to ensure that non-discriminatory regulation introduced by the host state to comply with its international obligations is not a breach of the IIA.[437]

The inclusion of a positive right to regulate in an IIA is an attractive way to protect state regulatory flexibility. Because it is not tied to any particular policy

434 See also the European Free Trade Association–Ukraine Free Trade Agreement, signed 24 June 2010, in force 1 June 2012, and Art.12 of the Norwegian draft treaty, for more qualified statements of the right to regulate.

435 H Mann (2008), *International Investment Agreements, Business and Human Rights: Key Issues and Opportunities*, IISD Publication Centre, Winnipeg, at 20.

436 IISD model treaty, Art. 25.

437 IISD model treaty, Art. 25. The IISD model treaty provides for the implementation of the provisions of the IIA into domestic law for the purpose of allowing for its enforcement in host state courts. This would ensure that the right to regulate is recognized in this context as well.

area, it provides comprehensive cover for state regulatory actions in all areas, unlike exceptions that are limited to specific policy areas. In addition, asserting a right to regulate should avoid the problem of narrow interpretation that has limited the effective scope for relying on exceptions in investor–state cases. The right to regulate is given equal status with investor protection. Even though a general right to regulate has not been incorporated in IIAs, it is consistent with the police powers doctrine developed in expropriation cases under customary international law to define permitted state regulation that should not be considered an expropriation.

Nevertheless, a right to regulate raises several issues.

- **Because a general right to regulate is a novel type of provision not present in existing IIAs, it is not clear how such a right would be interpreted in investor–state arbitration.** One presumed benefit of preserving a state's regulatory flexibility through a right to regulate provision is that it lessens the burden on the state to demonstrate that a measure challenged by an investor is permitted. However, it is not obvious that this benefit would be realised in practice. To rely on an exception, the state has the burden of showing that its measure is within the exception. With a right to regulate, the investor would have the burden of demonstrating a breach of a substantive obligation, including, if raised by the state, demonstrating that the measure was not a legitimate exercise of the right to regulate, since the right qualifies and limits the state's obligation to the investor. Inevitably, however, the state would have to produce arguments that the measure was within its right to regulate to counter the arguments put forward by the investor, so the effect of creating a right as opposed to an exception or reservation may not be so different in practice in investor–state arbitration.
- **The scope of the right to regulate is unclear**. While states are entitled to regulate, it is difficult to know what kind of state activity falls within this right. In addition, it is not clear how a right to regulate should be applied in relation to the investor protection provisions in IIAs. If a state successfully argues that its action is within its right to regulate, does that mean that the investor protection provisions simply do not apply, or is a more nuanced balancing of investor protection and the state's right to regulate required in each case? For example, is it necessary for the regulatory action by the state to be proportional to the harm it addresses for it to be upheld when it violates one of the substantive investor protection provisions? Because of this uncertainty, reliance on a right to regulate approach would seem to leave significant discretion to investor–state tribunals to determine what it permits on particular facts and impair the predictability of IIA obligations.
- **Exceptions may be easier to negotiate than a right to regulate.** A final, more practical, reason to prefer seeking to preserve host state flexibility in an IIA through exceptions and reservations, rather than a right to regulate, is simply that exceptions – indeed increasingly broad exceptions – and specific reservations are more and more the norm in current IIA practice. This may make it easier to negotiate specific exceptions than an open-ended right to regulate.

5.12.3 IIA practice regarding reservations

A number of treaties contemplate that each party state will list reservations that exclude specific sectors or measures from the application of some or all of the obligations in the IIA.[438] This is a form of negative listing.[439] Reservations in an IIA allow parties to customise their obligations by carving out specific measures (sometimes referred to as 'non-conforming measures'), policy areas or sectors where they want to preserve their freedom to regulate without regard to the requirements of the agreement. For example, the Canadian and US model treaties contemplate that reservations may be taken for sectors and specific non-conforming measures listed in annexes to the agreement for each party state.[440] Reservations can be listed, however, only in relation to the obligations regarding national treatment, MFN, the prohibition on performance requirements and the prohibitions on nationality requirements for senior management and entry restrictions in those models.[441] Significantly, treaty requirements related to fair and equitable treatment, expropriation and the free transfer of funds are obligations against which reservations may not be taken under either the US or Canadian model. The reservations include the following:

- All existing non-conforming measure maintained by a:
    - Party state at the national level and listed in its schedule,
    - Sub-national government;
- The continuation or renewal of any such non-conforming measure and any amendment to any such non-conforming measure that *does not increase its non-conformity* with the IIA obligations regarding national treatment, MFN, the prohibition on performance requirements and the prohibition on nationality requirements for senior management and entry restrictions; and
- Any measure that a party state currently maintains *or adopts in the future* with respect to sectors, sub-sectors or activities set out in its schedule.

All these categories of measures are exempt from the listed obligations.[442]

This approach in the Canadian and US agreements combines specific listing of existing national measures with the exclusion of whole sectors and areas of policy-making. For example, the US typically 'reserves the right to adopt or maintain any measure according rights or preferences to socially or economically disadvantaged

438 Reservations in this context are not unilateral statements by a state at the time it signs or ratifies a treaty in which it purports to exclude or modify the effect of the treaty, but rather a provision in the treaty agreed to by all parties that limits the application of the treaty in some way for one party.

439 See Section 5.2 (Right of establishment).

440 Canadian model FIPA, Art. 9; US model BIT, Art. 14. See, similarly, China–Germany, Agreement between the People's Republic of China and the Federal Republic of Germany on the Encouragement and Reciprocal Protection of Investments, signed 1 December 2003, in force 11 November 2005.

441 The Canadian model FIPA also includes the prohibition on restrictions on entry in its list of obligations to which reservations apply.

442 A similar approach is taken in the ASEAN Agreement (2009), Art. 9.1.

minorities'.[443] Also, all existing measures by sub-national governments are excluded under the Canadian and US models. This means that it is not necessary to conduct a survey of sub-national measures to prepare a list of measures that are excluded from the identified obligations. From an investors' point of view, this approach is less transparent than the specific listing required for national level measures because it does not disclose the restrictions that are in place.

One important feature of the Canadian and US approaches is what has been referred to as a 'ratchet effect' associated with the reservations for specific measures. The exclusion for a listed non-conforming measure applies only to the measure in the form that it takes when the agreement comes into force and to any amendments that do not make the measure less consistent with the obligations in the agreement. As a result, if a party state changes a listed measure to, for example, remove a preference in favour of domestic businesses, then the reservation continues to apply to the amended measure. However, the party state cannot subsequently reinstate the preference or change the measure in any other way that makes it less consistent with its obligations under the IIA. In effect, once a party liberalises its regime, the new level of openness provided by the party immediately become part of the party's bound obligations in the sense that the obligations of the agreement apply to any subsequent change, other than one that further liberalises the party's regime. In this sense, liberalisation by a party ratchets up the level of the party's obligation.

An alternative approach would be to provide that a host state commits not to change its regime to make it less liberal than provided for in its list of reservations. This is the approach adopted in the *GATS*. Member states commit to accord services and services suppliers from other members treatment no less favourable than under the terms and conditions set out in their national schedule of commitments.[444] Under the agreement a state could liberalise its regime by, for example, removing a preference in favour of domestic businesses and subsequently reinstate the preference.

The COMESA Investment Agreement, the India-Singapore CECA and the ASEAN Agreement all contemplate reservations.[445] Only the COMESA Investment Agreement, however, provides for reservations from all treaty obligations. Nevertheless, even if some IIA obligations are not subject to reservations, the impact of an IIA for a country on its policy-making flexibility will be highly dependent on the depth and breadth of reservations included for its benefit.

An alternative to reservations that can have the same functional effect, but is administratively simpler to implement, is to limit the obligations undertaken in a treaty to specific sectors listed in an annex to the IIA. This approach, called positive listing, was discussed above.[446] It is typically less onerous for host states because it does not require an exhaustive inventory of non-conforming measures to be undertaken

443 E.g. NAFTA (1992) Annex II, Schedule of the United States.

444 *GATS*, Arts. XVI.1, XVII.1.

445 India–Singapore CECA (2005), Art. 6.16; ASEAN Agreement (2009), Art. 9; and COMESA Investment Agreement (2007), Art. 18.

446 See Section 5.2 (Right of establishment).

to ensure that they are excluded from an IIA by listing them. Such an inventory is required if a negative list approach is followed. As a practical matter, the burden associated with negative listing is significantly mitigated in relation to a particular negotiation where the state has undertaken an identical exercise in relation to a previous negotiation. A disadvantage of positive listing for investors is that the remaining restrictions in sectors that a state has not listed are not disclosed to them.

Box 5.22 Summary of options for exceptions, reservations and the right to regulate

1. *No exceptions or reservations*
2. *General right to regulate but no (or few) exceptions or reservations*
3. *Including exceptions for measures to achieve an identified policy objective*

   Exceptions may only be available if requirements like those in GATT Article XX have been satisfied. Under Article XX, for some exceptions to be available for a measure, the measure:

   i. Must be necessary to achieve the identified policy objective;

   ii. Must not be applied in a discriminatory manner;

   iii. Must not be applied in an arbitrary or unjustifiable manner, or so as to constitute a disguised restriction on international trade.
4. *Including reservations for specific measures or all measures in an identified policy area*

5.12.4 Discussion of options

1. *No exceptions or reservations*

Many IIAs contain few exceptions or none at all and do not contemplate reservations. This is especially true in relation to BITS. FTAs often have exceptions that apply to investment commitments. Some argue that, even in the absence of exceptions and reservations, the substantive investor protection obligations are inherently flexible enough to accommodate legitimate host state regulation. Unfortunately, investor–state arbitration tribunals have not consistently interpreted IIA obligations to provide such flexibility. To some extent, this can be addressed by adopting some of the provisions discussed elsewhere in the Guide that limit the scope of the investor protection provisions. As noted below, exceptions and reservations can provide more specific protection for government policy-making in specific areas, but are also subject to some limitations.

2. *General right to regulate but no (or few) exceptions or reservations*

A general right to regulate expressed in an IIA provides comprehensive cover for state regulatory actions in all policy areas because, unlike exceptions, it is not tied to any particular area. In addition, providing a right to regulate should avoid the problem of narrow interpretation of exceptions that has limited the effective scope for states to rely on exceptions in some investor–state cases. On the other hand, a right to regulate is a new and novel feature not common in existing IIAs. It is not clear how such a right would be interpreted in an investor–state arbitration case. Its presumed benefits over exceptions may not materialise in practice. In particular, it is not certain how a right to regulate would operate to protect a host state's action that would otherwise be a breach of a substantive investor protection obligation or what would be the burden on the host state to justify its action as falling within its right to regulate.

3. *Including exceptions for measures to achieve an identified policy objective*

Exceptions provide a clear expression of party states' intention to exclude certain areas of policy-making from the scope of IIA obligations. They are increasingly being used in IIAs for this purpose, though exceptions remain rare in BITS. Depending on the scope, number and content of exceptions, they may deter some investors by carving out areas of policy-making from the investor protection provisions in the agreement. Reliance on exceptions may be subject to some limits in practice.

- Exceptions may be interpreted narrowly where they are determined to be inconsistent with the overall purpose of an IIA that is intended to protect and promote investment. In part, this could be addressed by changing the way in which the objectives of the agreement are specified. How this might be done is discussed above.[447]
- A state has the burden of proving that its measure falls within an exception. A number of investor–state tribunals have adopted this approach.
- Exceptions necessarily refer to a discrete list of policy areas in which state action is permitted, even if it would otherwise be inconsistent with the IIA investor protection obligations. Therefore they can never provide comprehensive protection for all future state regulation and may provide less flexibility than is built into the substantive standards of investor protection.
- Exceptions may be considered by investor–state arbitration tribunals to represent an exhaustive list of the policy areas in which the party states want flexibility to regulate; in some cases this may result an interpretation of the substantive investor protection obligations in a manner that provides less flexibility for host states than if the exceptions were not in the IIA.

In addition to these possible limitations, the effectiveness of exceptions will depend on their form. To the extent that they are only available if the requirements of GATT Article XX have been satisfied, their availability in practice will be limited. At the same time, these limits on availability provide certainty and predictability

447 See Section 4.2.1 (The role of preambles in IIAs) and Section 4.4 (Statement of objectives).

for investors. Under Article XX, for exception to be available for a measure, in most cases, the measure:

i. Must be necessary to achieve the identified policy objective;

ii. Must not be applied in a discriminatory manner; and

iii. Must not be applied in an arbitrary or unjustifiable manner, or so as to constitute a disguised restriction on international trade.

In IIAs providing exceptions, the general exceptions for measures to protect health or the environment tend to be made subject to these requirements, whereas exceptions for measures related to prudential considerations, essential security interests, taxation, culture, non-disclosure of confidential information, subsidies and government procurement tend not to be. Indeed, in the case of some of these exceptions, including, in particular, the security exceptions, the host state often has the power to self-determine if the exception is available. This provides maximum flexibility for host states, but creates a lack of predictability that may be of concern to capital-exporting states and their investors. In the COMESA Agreement, the language 'designed and applied' to achieve a particular objective is used to define when an exception is available, instead of the requirement that a measure be necessary to achieve the objective in order to provide greater flexibility for host states. Another alternative would be to require only that the state action be proportional to the importance of the objective the state is seeking to achieve.

4. *Including reservations for specific measures or all measures in an identified policy area*

Reservations safeguard a state's freedom to act in a particular area to ensure the attainment of important public policy objectives but, unlike exceptions, they are separately listed for each party and typically are not symmetrical. They permit IIA obligations to be cut back to reflect national policies and priorities. Reservations can be used to permit the maintenance of specific legislation or programmes that would otherwise be contrary to the obligations in the treaty, or they can carve out entire sectors or policy areas. They may be general or, as is more common, limited to specific categories of treaty obligations.

The use of reservations is becoming more common in IIAs but can raise the same issues as discussed above with respect to exceptions. Their greater specificity and typically unqualified expression, however, increase the likelihood that states will be able to rely on them successfully, leading to increased predictability. Depending on the scope, number and content of reservations, they may deter some investors by carving out areas of policy-making from the investor protections in the agreement.

With respect to options 2, 3 and 4, it is possible that any more favourable IIA obligations that a state has entered into in another IIA would be incorporated into an IIA that contained an MFN clause. On this basis, an investor may argue that an exception or reservation in the IIA that does not appear in another IIA should not apply.[448]

448 See Section 5.4 (Most favoured nation).

5.12.5 Discussion of sample provisions

The introduction of much broader exceptions and reservations in the Canadian model treaty and some other IIAs suggests that there is an opportunity to adopt an approach to reservations and exceptions that is more nuanced, balanced and flexible than is common in most existing IIAs. In particular, exceptions and reservations may be used to preserve policy space in areas that are important for sustainable development. The sample provision incorporates an extensive pattern of reservations and exceptions, such as is found in the Canadian model agreement, the COMESA Investment Agreement and other IIAs, but adds several additional provisions designed to ensure that host states have adequate flexibility to make policy to achieve sustainable development.

Policy objectives of general exceptions: The policy objectives drawn from GATT Article XX and recited in the Canadian model have been included, but the list of objectives has been expanded to reflect IIA practice and sustainable development considerations. The policy areas in the sample provision are:

- Human, animal or plant life or health;
- Internationally and domestically recognised human rights, labour rights and the rights of indigenous peoples;
- The environment, including, but not limited to, the conservation of living or non-living exhaustible natural resources;
- Public order;
- Prudential measures;
- Essential security interests;
- Culture;
- Taxation;
- Subsidies;
- Government procurement;
- Disclosure of confidential information.

In addition, measures to ensure compliance with laws and regulations that are not inconsistent with the provisions of the IIA and measures to comply with international obligations are excluded.

Ultimately, each state must decide for itself what policy areas need the benefit of exceptions. The suggested list of areas may need to be adjusted. For example, if an IIA imposes investor obligations related to human rights, labour rights, indigenous peoples' rights and anti-corruption, or host state obligations in these areas, it would be useful to expressly provide that actions taken by the host state in order to give effect to these obligations or enforce them could not be considered breaches of the other obligations in the agreement.[449]

Requirements for availability of exceptions: The sample provisions adopt an approach to the availability of exceptions that builds on existing practices to create more space for states to regulate. Nevertheless, in some of the exception provisions, requirements for availability have been included in the interests of providing certainty to investors. The chapeau approach from *GATT* Article XX has been maintained with respect to measures taken to achieve the first three policy objectives listed above and measures to ensure compliance with laws and regulations that are not inconsistent with the provisions of the IIA, as has been done in the Canadian model and some other agreements. Such measures will be valid only if they do not constitute arbitrary or unjustifiable discrimination between investments or between investors and are not a disguised restriction on investment. These are common limitations that are intended to ensure that the exceptions will be relied on only where there is a genuine connection between the measure and the policy objective identified in the exception. The requirement that the measures be 'necessary' to achieve the listed objectives in the Canadian model has been replaced with a requirement that they be 'designed and applied' to achieve the indicated objectives, following the COMESA Investment Agreement. The requirement that a measure be 'necessary' to the achievement of the objectives was not used on the basis that it was unduly restrictive. To require the host state to demonstrate that a measure is 'necessary' to achieve its stated policy objective places an onerous burden on that state in light of WTO jurisprudence interpreting *GATT* Article XX, which might be applied to the interpretation of similarly worded IIA exceptions.

An exception for measures to maintain public order has been included. To allay fears that such an exception creates a very open-ended authorisation for government action, the exception extends only to actions 'necessary' for the maintenance of public order, as is found in a number of agreements.

The exception for essential security interests is expressly made self-determining. None of the other exceptions have language that limits their availability, except that measures to comply with international obligations under other treaties must be non-discriminatory.

With respect to the cultural exception, the more specific and predictable Canadian approach to the exception has been adopted. An exception is created for measures

449 Investor obligations related to human rights, labour rights, indigenous peoples' rights and anti-corruption are discussed below in Section 6.8 (Investor obligation to respect internationally recognised human rights and undertake human rights due diligence), Section 6.9 (Investor obligation to refrain from the commission of, or complicity in, grave violations of human rights), Section 6.10 (Investor obligation to comply with core labour standards), Section 6.11 (Investor obligation to refrain from acts, or complicity in acts, of bribery and corruption). State obligations relating to human rights, labour rights, indigenous peoples' rights, environmental protection and anti-corruption are discussed in Section 6.12 (Other rights and obligations of party states). State enforcement of investor obligations is discussed in Section 6.13 (Enforcement of investor obligations) and Sections 6.14–6.17.

related to cultural industries, which is defined in the sample provision on definitions.[450] This is broader than the exception for the protection of national treasures in *GATT* Article XX that is incorporated in some IIAs. Each country should consider whether the list of cultural industries in the definition of that term is sufficiently broad to include the domestic cultural activities that it wants to protect from the obligations of the IIA.

Taxation measures excluded except from expropriation obligation in some circumstances: Rather than excluding tax measures in their entirety as in the UK model agreement, the sample provision follows the approach in the US and Canadian models. Tax measures are excluded from all but the expropriation obligation, and expropriation claims can proceed in relation to taxation measures only if the competent authorities in both parties cannot agree that the measure was not an expropriation.[451] This gives the parties some control over such claims.

Government procurement and subsidies are excluded from the national treatment and MFN obligations: Limiting the exclusion in these two areas to the national treatment and MFN obligations follows the Canadian and US models and has been adopted on the basis that these are the obligations most likely to constrain domestic policy in these areas. These are areas in which states often discriminate.

In the sample provision, national treatment does not apply where a party state grants a financial institution an exclusive right to deliver activities or services forming part of a public retirement plan or statutory system of social security. States may prefer that such an institution carrying out such an important public function be domestically controlled.

Application to expropriation and FET: In light of the existence of a customary international law obligation regarding compensation for expropriation, none of the exceptions apply to the expropriation provision other than the exception for taxation measures described above. In accordance with the expropriation provision itself, however, measures designed to achieve legitimate public policy objectives cannot be indirect expropriations.[452] The exceptions do, however, apply to the fair and equitable treatment obligation. This was done because of the inherently broad and unpredictable scope of this obligation. In practice, the prospects for conflict between the FET obligation and actions that the host state may want to take under the enumerated exceptions may be small.

Confidential information not required to be disclosed: This kind of exclusion is found in IIAs. Such an exception could also be included in the transparency provision and an example is provided in the sample transparency provision.[453] The exclusion in the sample exception provision is broader. It permits states to refuse to disclose

---

450 See Section 4.3 (Definitions).

451 See Section 5.6 (Limitations on expropriation and nationalisation).

452 See Section 5.6 (Limitations on expropriation and nationalisation).

453 See Section 5.10 (Transparency).

information that would impede law enforcement or would be contrary to the host state's law protecting government confidences, personal privacy or the confidentiality of the financial affairs and accounts of individual customers of financial institutions.

Reservations: The extensive categories of reservations against the national treatment and MFN obligations contemplated in the Canadian and US model agreements are reproduced in the sample provision as an example.[454] It may be that other kinds of reservations will be preferable for some states where their domestic policies require exemption from other IIA obligations. In addition, if commitments related to performance requirements, entry of personnel or the prohibition of restrictions on nationality requirements are included in an IIA, consideration should be given to whether the reservations should apply to these obligations too. The sample provision contemplates two categories of reservations to be listed by each party state in schedules attached to an Annex to the agreement: Annex I schedules will set out specific measures that are excluded; Annex II schedules will set out entire sectors or areas of public policy that are excluded. In addition, all sub-national measures are excluded.

With respect to the Annex I reservations for specific measures, the sample provision contemplates that each party state will set out in their respective schedules to the annex limitations on the national treatment and/or MFN obligations as those obligations apply to them. The sample provision obliges each party to accord to investors of the other party and their investments treatment that is no less favourable than provided for in their schedules. This approach follows the model in the *GATS*. To the extent that a state sets out the restrictions that currently exist in its national regime, this commitment amounts to a standstill, meaning that it commits states not to introduce further restrictions that are inconsistent with national treatment or MFN. A state could, however, set out limitations on its obligations in its schedule that allow restrictions on investment that are more onerous than its existing regime. To the extent that states do so, they may introduce new restrictions so long as they are permitted by the limitations on their obligations in their schedules.

An alternative approach would be to follow the US and Canadian models and provide that listed measures are not subject to the national treatment or MFN obligations and then go on to provide that any continuation or renewal of a listed non-conforming measure and any amendment that does not make the measure less consistent with national treatment and MFN is excluded from the application of the national treatment and MFN obligations as well. Under this approach, however, if a host state amends a non-conforming measure to make it more liberal regime or removes it altogether, the reservation does not permit the state to return to the less liberal approach that it previously maintained. For example, if a party state had listed a restriction on foreign ownership in a particular sector, such as hotels, in its Annex I schedule and then unilaterally removed the restriction, the Annex I reservation would not operate to permit the state to reinstate the restriction on foreign ownership in the hotel sector. The state's regime as liberalised by removal of the foreign ownership restriction would be subject to all of the obligations in the agreement. In this example, the national

454 See Section 5.3 (National treatment) and Section 5.4 (Most favoured nation).

treatment obligation might prohibit the reinstatement of the foreign ownership restriction. This is an example of the ratchet effect described above. In order to have flexibility on an ongoing basis to liberalise the rules in a particular sector and then return to a less liberal regime under this approach, it would be necessary for a host state to list the sector in its Annex II reservation schedule. In the sample provision, however, there is no ratchet that operates to increase the level of obligation for a state beyond what is expressly set out in its schedule to the annex. If a state changes its domestic regime to remove some permitted measure that discriminates against foreign investment, it retains the right to reimpose the measure.

Other exceptions in other parts of the Guide: In a number of other places in the Guide, exceptions have been included in relation to specific provisions.

- MFN – exceptions for past and future agreements of various kinds and dispute settlement procedures. See Section 5.4 (Most favoured nation).
- Expropriation – exception for compulsory licences of intellectual property rights. See Section 5.6 (Limitations on expropriation and nationalisation).
- Funds transfer – exceptions for measures related to law enforcement in various areas, for prudential measures and for balance of payments emergencies. The prudential measures exception in the funds transfer provision overlaps with but does not fully duplicate the general prudential measures exception. See Section 5.8 (Free transfer of funds).
- Transparency – exception permitting non-disclosure of confidential information. This exception overlaps with the general exception for confidential information in this section. See Section 5.10 (Transparency).

5.12.6 Sample provision: reservations for non-conforming measures

Reservations for Non-Conforming Measures

1. With respect to each Party, its Schedule to Annex I sets out the terms, limitations and conditions of its obligations under [Guide sample provision in Section 5.3 (National treatment)] and [Guide sample provision in Section 5.4 (Most favoured nation)]. Each Party shall accord investors of the other Party and their investments treatment no less favourable than specified in its Schedule.
2. [Guide sample provision in Section 5.3 (National treatment)] and [Guide Section 5.4 (Most favoured nation)] shall not apply to treatment accorded by a Party with respect to sectors set out in its schedule to Annex II.
3. In respect of intellectual property rights, a Party may derogate from [Guide sample provision in Section 5.3 (National treatment)] and [Guide sample provision in Section 5.4 (Most favoured nation)] in a manner that is consistent with its international agreements on intellectual property rights.
4. The provisions of [Guide sample provision in Section 5.3 (National treatment)] and [Guide sample provision in Section 5.4 (Most favoured nation)] of this Agreement shall not apply to:

a. Procurement by a Party or state enterprise; and

b. Subsidies or grants provided by a Party or a state enterprise, including government-supported loans, guarantees and insurance.

5. For greater certainty, [Guide sample provision in Section 5.3 (National treatment)] of this Agreement shall not apply to the granting by a Party to a financial institution of an exclusive right to provide activities or services forming part of a public retirement plan or statutory system of social security.

5.12.7 Sample provision: general exceptions

General Exceptions

1. Subject to the requirement that such measures are not applied in a manner that would constitute arbitrary or unjustifiable discrimination between investments or between investors or a disguised restriction on investment, nothing in this Agreement shall be construed to prevent a Party from adopting or enforcing measures that are designed and applied:

   a. To protect human, animal or plant life or health;

   b. To protect internationally and domestically recognised human rights, labour rights or the rights of indigenous peoples;

   c. To ensure compliance with laws and regulations that are not inconsistent with the provisions of this Agreement; and

   d. To protect the environment, including but not limited to the conservation of living or non-living exhaustible natural resources.

2. Nothing in this Agreement shall be construed to prevent a Party from adopting or maintaining measures for prudential reasons, such as:

   a. the protection of investors, depositors, financial market participants, policy-holders, policy-claimants or persons to whom a fiduciary duty is owed by a financial institution;

   b. The maintenance of the safety, soundness, integrity or financial responsibility of financial institutions; and

   c. Ensuring the integrity and stability of the Party's financial system.

3. Nothing in this Agreement shall apply to non-discriminatory measures of general application taken by any public entity in pursuit of monetary and related credit policies or exchange rate policies.

4. Nothing in this Agreement shall be construed:

   a. To require any Party to furnish or allow access to any information the disclosure of which it determines to be contrary to its essential security interests;

   b. To prevent any Party from taking any actions that it considers necessary for the protection of its essential security interests:

i. relating to the traffic in arms, ammunition and implements of war and to such traffic and transactions in other goods, materials, services and technology undertaken directly or indirectly for the purpose of supplying a military or other security establishment,

ii. taken in time of war or other emergency in international relations, or

iii. relating to the implementation of national policies or international agreements respecting the non-proliferation of nuclear weapons or other nuclear explosive devices; or

a. To prevent any Party from taking action in pursuance of its obligations under the United Nations Charter for the maintenance of international peace and security;

b. To prevent any Party from taking any measure necessary for the maintenance of public order.

5. Nothing in this Agreement shall be construed to require a Party to furnish or allow access to information the disclosure of which would impede law enforcement or would be contrary to the Party's law protecting government confidences, personal privacy or the confidentiality of the financial affairs and accounts of individual customers of financial institutions.

6. Nothing in this Agreement shall be construed to prevent a Party from taking *bona fide*, non-discriminatory measures to comply with international obligations under other treaties.

7. Subject to section 8, the provisions of this Agreement shall not apply to investments in cultural industries or to matters relating to taxation.

8. Nothing in this article applies to [Guide sample provision in Section 5.6 (Limitations on expropriation and nationalisation)] of this agreement, except that where an investor claims that a taxation measure involves an expropriation the investor may submit a claim to arbitration under [Guide sample provisions in Section 7.1 (Investor–state dispute settlement)] of this Agreement only if:

   a. The investor has first referred to the competent tax authorities of both parties in writing the issue of whether that taxation measure involves an expropriation; and

   b. Within 180 days after the date of such referral, the competent tax authorities of both parties fail to agree that the taxation measure is not an expropriation.

Chapter 6

New Provisions Addressing Sustainable Development

Cross references

6.1 Making the link between investment and sustainable development

Foreign investment contributes to development in developing countries. However, increased investment inflows alone do not automatically lead to sustainable development. For this reason, the Guide explores various ways that states can channel increased investment into sustainable development.

The Guide discusses treaty provisions that a government can seek in its IIAs in order to support its ability to regulate foreign direct investment so that it contributes to sustainable development. The primary emphasis is on two policy tools. The first is adapting provisions typically found in IIAs, such as national treatment, MFN, FET and protection against expropriation without compensation, so that they are more protective of the state's ability to pursue its sustainable development policies. The discussion in Chapter 5 will help states to evaluate the challenges that their existing agreements represent for the pursuit of sustainable development, as well as help them to negotiate future agreements with provisions better adapted to their needs.

The second tool consists of new sustainable development provisions not found in existing IIAs. In this chapter, the Guide discusses various forms that such provisions can take, such as the inclusion of sustainability assessment processes in the treaty, the imposition of obligations on investors to respect human rights, labour rights, indigenous peoples' rights and the environment, prohibitions on bribery and other forms of corruption, the creation of civil and criminal liability for investors that harm the environment or violate human rights, the use of liability in the home state to hold investors accountable for harms caused in host states and various modifications to the investor–state dispute settlement process that can redress the imbalance between states and investors under current IIAs.

Each state will adopt its own definition of sustainable development and implement policies to achieve its development goals. In doing so, a state will have to address what approaches to regulating foreign investors can best achieve these goals or are most compatible with government policy. The discussion in this chapter of the Guide is intended to provide inspiration to policy-makers about how to build a robust link between investment policy and sustainable development policy.

In this chapter, we frequently refer to international human rights, including labour rights and the rights of indigenous peoples. We also refer to environmental sustainability and best practices for promoting environmentally friendly investment. These references are not meant to be prescriptive. Each developing country will necessarily adapt its pursuit of sustainable development to its social and political circumstances and to the interests of its people.

In particular, not all states have ratified and implemented the same international human rights and labour rights instruments. In consequence, each state will have to determine for itself which rights need to be reflected in its policies on foreign investment.

Finally, not all states will seek the same balance between environmental protection, the protection of human rights, labour rights and indigenous peoples' rights, on the one hand, and natural resource exploitation and other forms of investment on the other. For these reasons, no one set of domestic institutions, laws and regulations or one set of provisions in an IIA can meet the needs of every developing country.

However, if government policy-makers wish to use treaty-based mechanisms to bolster their domestic measures to promote human rights and environmental protection and prohibit corruption, they can draw on various mechanisms discussed in this section of the Guide. This discussion begins with an examination of the difficulties of effectively regulating foreign investors. Later, the Guide discusses the benefits of regulation, both for citizens of the host country, whose communities may benefit from investment, and for investors and domestic businesses, who will be attracted by a predictable regulatory framework based on the best practices of good governance.

6.2 The challenges of regulating foreign investors and holding transnational corporations accountable

Developed and developing countries often face challenges regulating foreign investors to ensure that their investments contribute to sustainable development. This is partly because of some fundamental weaknesses in international law as a tool to regulate foreign investors. It is also caused by ineffective regulation of investors by host and home states. A final contributing factor is the risk that international investment arbitrators will subordinate sustainable development considerations to the protection of investors' interests when they are interpreting a state's IIA obligations.

6.2.1 Weaknesses in international law

International law does not provide many effective ways of holding to account foreign investors who violate international human rights, labour rights[1] or norms for environmental protection. For example, international human rights law does not impose direct obligations on investors. Rather, it requires states to take steps – through legislation or administrative and other measures – to ensure that private actors such as investors do not violate the human rights of individuals within their territory and subject to their jurisdiction. Victims of human rights abuses committed by an investor or caused by an investment can seek redress from the investor or its investment only in the domestic courts or administrative institutions of the host state.[2] If this fails, the only avenue open to victims of human rights abuses is to bring a complaint against the host state before an international human rights tribunal for failing to take appropriate steps to prevent the investor from violating their rights.[3]

Another problem in holding investors legally accountable for violations of human rights, labour rights, the rights of indigenous peoples and environmental damage is the complex legal structure of many transnational businesses. Typically, they are made up of many distinct entities, including a parent corporation, multiple subsidiaries and joint-venture partners that are incorporated or organised under the laws of different countries. International law and most domestic laws treat each of these entities as a separate legal entity that is governed by the domestic laws of the state in which it is incorporated or organised.[4]

---

1 See, for example, B A Frey (1997), 'The Legal and Ethical Responsibilities of Transnational Corporations in the Protection of International Human Rights', 6 *Minnesota Journal of Global Trade* 153 at 163; S Joseph (1999), 'Taming the Leviathans: Multinational Enterprises and Human Rights', 46 *Netherlands International Law Review* 171 at 175; and R McCorquodale (2002), 'Human Rights and Global Business', in S Bottomley and D Kinley (eds), *Commercial Law and Human Rights*, Ashgate Publishing, Aldershot, 89 at 92–7.

2 JD Taillant and J Bonnitcha (2011), 'International Investment Law and Human Rights', in Cordonier Segger et al. (eds), *Sustainable Development in World Investment Law*, Kluwer Law International, The Hague, at 58–60, 73.

3 Ibid.

4 J Crawford and S Olleson (2003), 'The Nature and Forms of International Responsibility', in M D Evans (ed.), *International Law*, Oxford University Press, Oxford and New York, 445 at 448.

However, the reality is that these corporate groups operate as a complex integrated network of actors connected by links of ownership and contract. As result of this network, transnational businesses can allocate their assets within this network to minimise liability risk. For example, a transnational business may seek to minimise risk related to its activities in a host state by allocating few assets to its subsidiary carrying on business in that state.[5] Claimants in the host state who have proved that they were harmed by the transnational business may be able to make a legal claim only against the subsidiary, because the parent corporation and other components of the transnational business are distinct legal entities. Although there may be sufficient assets within the transnational business as a whole, the claimants may have recourse to only the inadequate assets of the subsidiary to satisfy their claims.

6.2.2 Weaknesses in domestic law in host states and investors' home states

Sometimes the domestic law of host states does not provide effective remedies that allow individuals to sue foreign investors for harms they have suffered as a consequence of the investor's activities.[6] In addition, the legal institutions of the host state may lack sufficient resources to follow up on complaints. Many developing countries do not possess the technical capacity or the physical and institutional infrastructure to regulate the environmental or the social effects of foreign investments effectively. The problem is sometimes political – industry lobby groups and various political interests may make it difficult for governments to regulate or control foreign investors.[7] It has been suggested that 'where [investors] set up foreign operations in locations characterized by weak, non-existent or corrupt governance, the prospect of effective local regulation is even more remote'.[8]

There is little that those located in the investor's home state or other states can do to support the host state government or citizens of the host state who wish to hold foreign investors accountable for their acts. For instance, there are a wide range of obstacles to bringing a civil suit against a parent corporation in the home state for the acts of its foreign subsidiaries that commit human rights and other violations in the host state, despite the fact that all the companies are linked. These kinds of claims have rarely been successful. Thus, concerned citizens or groups located in the investor's home state that advocate for citizens of a developing country harmed by a foreign investor have few options for obtaining redress for victims.

---

5 S Joseph (2012), 'Protracted Lawfare: The Tale of Chevron Texaco in the Amazon', 3 *Journal of Human Rights and the Environment*, 70 at 89.

6 Taillant and Bonnitcha, op. cit., at 74.

7 The California Global Corporate Accountability Project (2002), *Beyond Good Deeds: Case Studies and a New Policy Agenda for Corporate Accountability*, a collaboration of the Nautilus Institute for Security and Sustainable Development, the Natural Heritage Institute, and Human Rights Advocates, Berkeley, July, at xiv.

8 G Gagnon, A Macklin and P Simons (2003), 'Deconstructing Engagement: Corporate Self-Regulation in Conflict Zones: Implications for Human Rights and Canadian Public Policy', University of Toronto, Public Law Research Paper No. 04–07, Toronto at 11, available at: http://ssrn.com/abstract=557002 (accessed 28 May 2012).

A further problem is the potential for investors to use the protections provided to them by an IIA to evade their obligations under the domestic law of the host state. The actions of Chevron Corporation, an American multinational energy company, to avoid liability for severe environmental damage in the Ecuadorian Amazon illustrate this tactic. By means of a merger, Chevron acquired the Ecuador oil interests and liabilities of Texaco, another oil company. Chevron was then sued in Ecuador for harms caused by Texaco. To derail the suit in Ecuador, Chevron engaged in a number of tactics before the Ecuadorian court issued its judgment. One of them was to initiate a claim against Ecuador under the US–Ecuador BIT on the basis that the court proceedings in Ecuador were in breach of the obligation to guarantee fair and equitable treatment to Chevron.

The Ecuadorian court found against Chevron and awarded the plaintiffs US$9.4 billion and conditional punitive damages of US$8.4 billion.[9] This decision was affirmed by an appeals court in January 2012. Chevron has appealed that ruling to the Supreme Court of Ecuador.[10] The international investment arbitration panel then issued a number of interim rulings, one of which called on the Government of Ecuador to 'take all measures necessary to suspend or cause to be suspended the enforcement and recognition within and without Ecuador of the judgments'[11] against Chevron. The Ecuador court refused to do so.[12] The international investment arbitration panel then proceeded to find that it had jurisdiction over Chevron's claim under the BIT.[13] In consequence, Chevron's case against Ecuador for breach of the US–Ecuador BIT will now proceed to the merits. This case illustrates how a transnational corporation such as Chevron can try to use a BIT in order to attempt to nullify rulings of courts in the state where the investment is located.

6.2.3 Investor–state tribunals do not give priority to considerations other than investment protection

The decisions of investment tribunals have not been very helpful in asserting the obligations of foreign investors to respect human rights, labour rights or the rights of indigenous peoples. So far, they have not recognised that states can give priority to the protection of the human rights and other rights of their citizens over their obligations to investors under IIAs.

9 For a full discussion of the Chevron case, see Joseph (2012), op. cit.

10 Ibid., at 91.

11 *Chevron and Texaco v. Ecuador*, PCA Case No. 334877, Second Interim Award on Interim Measures, 16 February 2012, at para 3, available at: www.chevron.com/documents/pdf/ecuador/SecondTribunalInterimAward.pdf (accessed 29 May 2012).

12 E Garcia, 'Ecuador court rejects Chevron arbitration ruling' (*Reuters*, 20 February 2012), available at: www.reuters.com/article/2012/02/20/us-ecuador-chevron-idUSTRE81J17A20120220 (accessed 9 May 2012).

13 *Chevron and Texaco v. Ecuador*, PCA Case No. 334877, Third Interim Award on Jurisdiction and Admissibility, 17 February 2012, at para. 5.2, available at: www.chevron.com/documents/pdf/ecuador/PCA-Jurisdiction-Decision.pdf (accessed 9 May 2012).

Few cases have explored the relationship between human rights and IIAs. Some cases recognise that where an IIA contains a vague standard, human rights law can be used as an aid in interpreting them.[14] However, when states have argued that their IIA obligations conflict with their human rights obligations, tribunals have refused to give priority to the protection of human rights. This means that where a state enacts laws or acts to promote or protect human rights and these laws or actions harm foreign investors, states may have to respect their obligations to investors regardless of whether, in the eyes of the state, this renders their domestic human rights regime or their acts to promote and protect human rights less effective.[15]

Taillant and Bonnitcha summarise their view of the negative consequences of the current cases in stark terms:

> Foreign investment law makes no consideration for stakeholder impact [for example, the impact of investor actions on citizens of the host state]. Rather the rights of the investor are defended despite the impact defending those rights has on stakeholders and in absolute disregard for any obligations the State may have vis-à-vis those stakeholders. Further, vulnerable groups that are often-times adversely and disproportionately impacted by the externalities of such investments in times of turmoil must often bear the costs and burdens of upholding investment profit agreements. Put simply, individual and community stakeholders currently have no place at the dispute settlement table in [international] investment law, except to pay for the check when it comes at an awkward time.[16]

6.3 Different approaches to integrating foreign investment and sustainable development

There are many policy options for host states seeking to hold investors accountable for protecting and promoting human rights, good labour practices, the rights of indigenous peoples and the environment. This section of the Guide discusses the advantages and disadvantages of various methods for doing so.

---

14 In *Biwater v. Tanzania*, Tanzania cancelled a water concession contract with Biwater without following the termination procedure specified in the contract. Tanzania argued that the concession did not provide adequate water or sewage services, and a number of *amici curiae* argued that the human right to water thus justified the government's actions (*Biwater Gauf v. Tanzania*, ICSID Case No. ARB/05/22, Award, 24 July 2008, at paras. 380, 387. The tribunal interpreted the fair and equitable treatment obligation in the investment treaty in light of Tanzania's obligation to protect the right to water of its citizens (ibid., at para. 601).

15 In *Siemens v. Argentina*, Argentina argued that it was justified in not respecting its contractual obligations to Siemens because the country was facing an economic crisis and it was imperative to protect the human rights of its citizens. The tribunal held that Argentina's obligations to respect Siemen's contractual rights did not conflict with its obligations to protect human rights. In consequence, the tribunal refused to consider Argentina's human rights arguments when deciding whether it had violated its obligations to Siemens (*Siemens A.G. v. The Argentine Republic*, Award, 6 February 2007, at paras. 75, 79). For a summary of the legal consequences of the *Siemens* and *Biwater*, op. cit., cases, see Taillant and Bonnitcha, op. cit., at 77.

16 Ibid. at 78.

6.3.1 Using domestic laws, regulations and institutions to promote investor compliance with sustainable development policies

One way to ensure that foreign investors comply with human rights and other norms and implement policies that contribute to environmental protection is to enact domestic laws and regulations and create domestic institutions to implement the country's international legal obligations to respect human rights, labour rights and indigenous peoples' rights, to promote environmental sustainability and address corruption. Of course, different states are parties to different treaties in these areas and so it is necessary for each state to take an inventory of its international obligations and research best practices for implementing them. To the extent that foreign investors are subject to the domestic law of the host state, domestic mechanisms can be used to ensure investor accountability.

It is not possible for this Guide to survey all the best practices for implementing international obligations through domestic law. They extend from incorporating a robust bill of rights into a state's constitution to creating human rights commissions and environmental review boards. However, the Guide considers one mechanism that could be implemented in domestic law in some depth – sustainability assessments (SAs).[17] As will be explained below, this mechanism is explored because the assessment process is directly linked to the process of evaluating, admitting, monitoring and ensuring the ongoing accountability of foreign investments in the host state.

6.3.2 Integrating sustainable development into an IIA

In addition to enacting domestic legislation, IIAs could be used to promote sustainable investment. As most existing IIAs do not incorporate principles of sustainable development, few models exist for doing so. However, IIAs can provide several useful and practical mechanisms that enhance host state capacity to ensure that foreign investors operate in a manner consistent with sustainable development. These mechanisms can include:

1. Creating treaty-based standards for investors that require them to act in a manner consistent with sustainable development criteria;[18]
2. Providing ways to enforce those standards in the treaty[19] such as:
    a. requiring *host states* to allow civil and/or criminal suits in their courts against investors who fail to meet norms for sustainable development,

17 See Section 6.6 (Sustainability assessments).

18 See Section 6.7 (Investor obligation to comply with the laws of the host state), Section 6.8 (Investor obligation to respect internationally recognised human rights and undertake human rights due diligence), Section 6.9 (Investor obligation to refrain from the commission of, or complicity in, grave violations of human rights), Section 6.10 (Investor obligation to comply with core labour standards) and Section 6.11 (Investor obligations to refrain from acts, or complicity in acts, of bribery and corruption).

19 See Section 6.13 (Enforcement of investor obligations).

b. requiring investors' *home states* to allow civil and/or criminal suits in their courts against investors who fail to meet norms for sustainable development;

3. Creating incentives for investors to comply with obligations by limiting their access to treaty-based remedies against the state; and[20]

4. Requiring that investors' home states provide technical assistance to support host state development of more effective domestic regulatory schemes and the implementation of the agreement.[21]

In addition to including these new kinds of provisions, which will be addressed on an individual basis below, we have already discussed another approach: adapting IIA investor protection provisions to protecting the ability of the host state to regulate effectively.[22] As discussed in Chapter 5 (Substantive Obligations of Host States Regarding Investor Protection), some provisions traditionally included in IIAs have been interpreted by international arbitration panels so as to limit the ability of governments to enact new laws and regulations that adversely affect foreign investors.[23] This is of particular concern from the point of view of sustainable development if the host state is considering creating new legal mechanisms in the future for protecting the environment, protecting or promoting human rights, labour rights or the rights of indigenous peoples or addressing corruption. For example, if these mechanisms have an impact on foreign investors, there is a risk that these investors may claim that the mechanisms violate provisions of an IIA such as the obligation to provide fair and equitable treatment or to prohibit expropriation without compensation. The Guide discusses how these provisions may be adapted to better ensure that states have sufficient policy space to regulate to achieve sustainable development.

6.3.3 The elements of sustainable development addressed in the sample provisions

In this chapter of the Guide, examples of a variety of new kinds of provisions not found in existing IIAs are set out. These provisions are designed to facilitate the

20 See Section 7.1 (Investor–state dispute settlement).

21 See Chapter 8 (Investment Promotion and Technical Assistance).

22 See Section 5.2 (Right of establishment), Section 5.3 (National treatment), Section 5.4 (Most favoured nation), Section 5.5 (Fair and equitable treatment and the minimum standard of treatment), Section 5.6 (Limitations on expropriation and nationalisation), Section 5.7 (Compensation for losses), Section 5.8 (Free transfer of funds) and Section 5.10 (Transparency).

23 The line of ICSID cases involving Argentina's response to its financial crisis in the late 1990s and early part of the new millennium illustrate this. For example, in *CMS Gas Transmission Company v. The Argentine Republic*, ICSID Case No. ARB/01/8, Award, 21 May 2005, the tribunal found that Argentina had breached its obligations under the US–Argentina BIT by changing the way in which gas prices were calculated, eliminating the practice of pegging the value of the peso to the US dollar, failing to negotiate what CMS considered a more appropriate exchange rate for the gas industry, and failing to renegotiate gas licences in accordance with an arrangement used in other sectors. Argentina had justified these measures on the basis that the financial crisis it faced made them necessary. The tribunal's decision in effect limited the host state's right to regulate the gas industry in order to respond to a financial crisis.

achievement of sustainable development more positively and directly. It is useful to remember that in designing these sample provisions, it was necessary to make some choices about the meaning of 'sustainable development'. The nature and sources of this conception of sustainable development were discussed in some detail in Section 2.3.[24] The elements of the concept of sustainable development used to create the sample text are summarised here in order to remind host states to review the discussion and the sample provisions critically with an eye to identifying where the concept of sustainable development that they embody differs from a state's preferred approach.

As mentioned above,[25] the Guide uses a conception of sustainable development grounded in widely accepted international legal documents that include the following elements:

- Increased foreign investment can contribute to sustainable development;
- Sustainable development recognises the need to promote and protect human rights, labour rights, the rights of indigenous peoples, the environment and other development priorities consistent with both the home and host states' international obligations;
- To promote sustainable development, foreign investment must contribute to meeting the needs of people in the host country;
- Developing countries require adequate technical preparation and proper information when negotiating international investment agreements;
- Due regard must be had to the political and institutional challenges of developing countries, and IIA commitments should reflect an effort to overcome them;
- To ensure that international investment rules yield outcomes consistent with sustainable development, they should be developed through wide consultation with people in the host country, including local and indigenous communities, to permit them to play an active role in development;[26]
- The negotiation, application and interpretation of international investment agreements should be transparent and consistent;
- The achievement of sustainable development requires the co-operation of both developed and developing countries; and
- The achievement of sustainable development requires the recognition of the equality of all states and the need to overcome political, social and economic barriers to equal participation of all in a fair and just international investment regime.

---

24 An explanation of the nature and sources of this conception of sustainable development is provided in Section 2.3 (Links between foreign investment and sustainable development).

25 Section 2.3 (Links between foreign investment and sustainable development).

26 See *New Delhi Declaration of Principles of International Law Relating to Sustainable Development*, Res. 3/2002, 209 UN Doc. A/57/329, reprinted in International Law Association, *Report of the Seventieth Conference, New Delhi 2002*, at 211–16, Principle 5.1. See also, A Boyle and D Freestone (1999), eds., *International Law and Sustainable Development: Past Achievements and Future Challenges*, Oxford University Press, Oxford, at 15–16.

6.4 Overview of Guide sample provisions promoting sustainable development

6.4.1 Summary of the provisions

The Guide discusses policies in three related categories that may be effective in integrating sustainable development into an IIA.

Sustainability assessments

The Guide discusses a process called a 'sustainability assessment' (SA) for assessing environmental, social and human rights impacts.[27] It explains how such assessments can be applied both to investment provisions contained in an international agreement and to particular investments in order to ensure that foreign investment is compatible with a state's sustainable development policy.

The Guide also discusses how to integrate sustainability assessments into an IIA by making it a treaty requirement for some foreign investments that meet identified criteria. If such an approach is adopted, foreign investors would be required to submit investments of a substantial size or in sensitive sectors to an assessment of their social, environmental and human rights impact prior to making the investment. As a result of the assessment process described in the Guide, a management plan for the implementation of the investment would be created in negotiation with the host state. The management plan should demonstrate that the investment has put in place corporate management systems to ensure ongoing assessment, management and monitoring of the investment. The plan should include systems to ensure that the investment contributes to sustainable development.

The Guide also discusses how to use a grievance process to permit persons affected by the investment to make a complaint if they are harmed. In addition, the Guide discusses mechanisms for the host state to deal with a failure of the investor to prevent the harms identified in the sustainability assessment process or to live up to their obligations in the management plan resulting from the assessment, including through civil actions in the host state and the investor's home state.

The Guide discusses how to integrate sustainability assessments into both domestic law and an IIA. The principal difference between these two approaches is that integration of sustainability assessments into an IIA facilitates the use of treaty-based enforcement mechanisms.

Obligations on investors

The Guide discusses various ways of ensuring that investors respect human rights, including labour rights, the rights of indigenous peoples and principles of

27 See Section 6.6 (Sustainability assessments).

environmental sustainability.[28] The sample provisions demonstrate ways within the framework of an IIA to create standards that foreign investors must meet, including requirements to comply with the domestic law in the host state, to respect internationally recognised human rights and to meet core international labour standards. The provisions also illustrate how IIA provisions can be used to prohibit investors from engaging in grave violations of human rights, bribery and other forms of corruption.

Sanctions on investors who fail to comply with their obligations

As discussed, few sanctions are available in international law against investors who fail to protect human rights or the environment. Section 6.13 (Enforcement of investor obligations) discusses various ways of rectifying this failing.

The sample provisions focus on integrating a comprehensive system for sanctioning foreign investors into an IIA. Since investors are not party to the treaty, in order to make these standards for investor behaviour effective, the provisions contemplate that party states will take responsibility for creating legal institutions to sanction investors who fail to comply with their obligations.

For instance, the sample provisions provide examples of how both the host state and the investor's home state can be obliged to impose criminal liability for investors who commit or are complicit in grave violations of human rights and corrupt activities contrary to treaty obligations for investors in these areas. The sample provisions also show how to create an obligation on both party states to provide in their domestic law for investors to be held civilly liable both for violations of human rights and in situations in which an investor is in breach of IIA standards relating to core labour rights. Civil liability will also result if the investor does not comply with the host state's domestic laws or fails to take the steps set out in the management plan to mitigate the risks posed by its investment as identified in the sustainability assessment of its investment.[29]

Finally, the sample provisions contemplate a counterclaim mechanism[30] that would enable a state against which an investor has made a claim in investor–state arbitration to make a counterclaim for relief for injuries suffered as a result of the investor's failure to comply with the investor obligations set out in the agreement.

---

28 See Section 6.7 (Investor obligation to comply with the laws of the host state), Section 6.8 (Investor obligation to respect internationally recognised human rights and undertake human rights due diligence), Sections 6.9 (Investor obligation to refrain from the commission of, or complicity in, grave violations of human rights), Section 6.10 (Investor obligation to comply with core labour standards), and Section 6.11 (Investor obligation to refrain from acts, or complicity in acts, of bribery or corruption).

29 The process by which each state will implement its obligations in this regard will be determined by its domestic constitutional system.

30 See Sections 6.17 (Counterclaims by states in investor–state arbitration) and 7.1.7 (Sample provisions: investor–state dispute settlement, Article [W] (Counterclaims).

6.5 Assessing the costs and benefits of the sample provisions in the Guide

The sample provisions discussed in this chapter are novel and untested. For both these reasons, they may not be readily accepted by countries negotiating IIAs. From the point of view of foreign investors, the provisions may seem to impose additional onerous obligations not contained in existing IIAs. In consequence, they may make an IIA based on the sample provisions less attractive to them. For example, imposing obligations on investors to comply with human rights and protect the environment may discourage them from investing. This may be a concern for both capital-importing and capital-exporting states. In addition, host states may find the implementation and enforcement of these provisions burdensome and a strain on domestic capacity.

Conceptually, it might seem unwise to incorporate principles of sustainable development into a treaty to regulate foreign investment. After all, the agreement is about investment – human rights and environmental protection are addressed in separate international treaties. Furthermore, the meaning of human rights or the wisdom of promoting environmental protection may be politically contested. Some may argue that including sustainable development provisions in an IIA will make it far too long and complicated and may lead to uncertain interpretations of treaty obligations by investment arbitration panels.

This reasoning appears to be reflected in most existing IIAs. To date, few of them address sustainable development in any meaningful way. Those that do refer to sustainable development do not impose enforceable obligations to achieve it. Often, the only mention of sustainable development is a non-binding reference in the preamble of the agreement.[31] Despite the fact that there is no legal or structural barrier to the inclusion of provisions to address the environmental and social impacts of foreign investment,[32] few IIAs currently in force set standards for investors relating to the protection of labour rights,[33] indigenous peoples' rights, human rights or the protection of the environment. They also do not prohibit investor complicity in violations of human rights or acts of corruption.

Despite cogent arguments against doing so, however, there are also a variety of reasons for including provisions designed to promote sustainable development in IIAs:

1. **International law lacks effective mechanisms for holding investors accountable for the harms they cause:** Most international legal obligations to uphold human rights, to protect the environment and to address corruption are imposed on states, not individuals or corporations. Including obligations for an investor to promote and protect human rights and the environment and to avoid corrupt activities in an IIA can help to rectify this problem.

---

31 E.g. Canadian model FIPA, preamble; Norwegian draft APPI, preamble. The US Model BIT, the Indian Model BIPPA and the UK Model IPPI do not refer to sustainable development.

32 H. Mann (2008), *International Investment Agreements, Business and Human Rights: Key Issues and Opportunities*, IISD Publication Centre, Winnipeg, at 12–13.

33 Ibid. at 11.

2. **There is a need for more balanced agreements:** Including the kinds of provisions discussed in the Guide will create a more balanced agreement. Traditional IIAs focus primarily on the host state's obligations to investors and include few, if any, obligations that flow from investors towards states and their citizens. This imbalance could be redressed so that investors that benefit from profitable investments protected by IIAs are required in return to protect the communities and the natural environment in which they operate.
3. **Developed country investment partners increasingly recognise the importance of sustainable development:** Many developed countries, including the European Union (EU), Canada and the USA, now routinely seek commitments regarding at least labour and environmental standards in their trade and investment agreements.[34] This indicates that some developed country investment partners are becoming more interested in provisions that promote sustainable development.
4. **Developed countries recognise the need to regulate the behaviour of their investors operating abroad:** In some developed countries, there is increasing pressure on governments to develop legal oversight mechanisms to ensure that their investors operating in other states respect human rights, labour rights and environmental standards and do not engage in corruption. However, for a number of reasons, it can be difficult for the investor's home state to impose standards on investors investing abroad through extraterritorial application of its law. For instance, attempts to do so may be viewed by the host state as an intrusion on their sovereignty or even as neo-colonialist interference.[35] However, if states agree to impose obligations on foreign investors through an IIA, this perceived barrier is removed. Instead, home states and host states can work together to regulate foreign investors. In addition, home states may be encouraged to provide other mechanisms for holding their investors accountable. Consequently, there may be an interest in some home states in the kinds of provisions proposed in this section of the Guide, even though they impose additional obligations on their investors.
5. **It can be difficult to put in place a domestic legal regime to protect and promote human rights:** Implementation of human rights protections can be costly and time-consuming and requires significant expertise. Moreover, there may be political hurdles in identifying the rights that should be protected domestically and creating the institutions needed to protect them. However, fewer hurdles may exist for imposing obligations on *foreign* investors rather than on all investors, both foreign and domestic. Creating obligations in an IIA requiring foreign investors to respect human rights and comply with norms of environmental sustainability may be simpler than creating a comprehensive set of domestic institutions.

---

34 See for instance the recent Canada–Peru FTA (2008) and the US Model BIT.

35 S Seck, 'Home State Responsibility and Local Communities: The Case of Global Mining' (2008), 11 *Yale Human Rights and Development Law Journal at 177*. Seck describes, for example, how these considerations led to the defeat in 2001 of the Corporate Code of Conduct 2000, Australian legislation that would have imposed environmental, human rights, labour rights and health and safety standards on Australian corporations acting abroad.

6. **Current interpretations of traditional IIA provisions limit host states' ability to regulate foreign investors:** Some controversial decisions by international arbitrators suggest that it may be difficult for a host state to create new laws and institutions to protect human rights or promote environmental sustainability if these impair the investors' expectations about the conditions in which they will operate in the host state or if they are not sufficiently consulted about proposed changes. The introduction of investor obligations into an IIA will support a more balanced interpretation of the treaty that will take into account policy considerations beyond investor protection.

7. **Placing obligations on investors in an IIA allows states to create treaty-based remedies for harms created by foreign investors:** Foreign investors are often able to avoid compensating victims of human rights or environmental disasters because of a lack of robust domestic legal institutions in the host state. IIA provisions can be used to provide effective remedies for host states and their citizens seeking compensation from investors.

8. **Foreign investors may not be deterred by requirements to comply with human rights, prohibitions on corruption or requirements to protect the environment:** Sophisticated foreign investors are generally familiar with requirements to respect human rights and labour rights, to avoid corruption and to protect the environment as they must meet them in their home country. Requiring investors to plan and implement their investments in an environmentally friendly way, with due regard for the rights of the host state's residents, may not discourage investment substantially. Companies in industries with the potential to harm the environment or human rights are increasingly recognising that there is a demand among their investors and the public in their home states to make their foreign investments sustainable.[36]

---

36 For example, in November 2006, the Canadian government completed a series of national roundtables on corporate social responsibility (CSR) and the Canadian extractive sector in developing countries. The roundtables were held in response to a report of the Standing Committee on Foreign Affairs and International Trade calling on the federal government to initiate a multi-stakeholder process with the goal of strengthening existing CSR programmes and policies, and developing new programmes and policies for Canadian extractive industries operating outside Canada in developing countries. The roundtables advisory group, composed of members from the private sector, academia and NGOs, produced a consensus report released in March 2007 that recommended to the Canadian government the adoption of a comprehensive CSR framework, including voluntary standards, reporting guidelines and an accountability mechanism. See Parliament, 'Response of the government to the 14th Report of the Standing Committee on Foreign Affairs and International Trade (mining in developing countries – corporate social responsibility)', in Sessional Papers, No. 8512-381–179 (2005); and National Roundtables on Corporate Social Responsibility (CSR) and the Canadian Extractive Sector in Developing Countries, Advisory Group Report, Foreign Affairs and International Trade, Ottawa, Canada, 29 March 2007. However, see also the government response, Government of Canada (2009), 'Building the Canadian Advantage: A Corporate Social Responsibility (CSR) Strategy for the Canadian International Extractive Sector', Foreign Affairs and International Trade Canada, available at: www.international.gc.ca/trade-agreements-accords-commerciaux/ds/csr-strategy-rse-stategie.aspx (accessed 3 September 2011), which puts forward a voluntary self-regulation scheme for Canadian companies, with no reporting requirements or sanctions. It includes a complaints mechanism. However, the mechanism allows for investigation into allegations of human rights abuses by a Canadian company only in cases where the company consents.

Also, because of the adverse impact on their reputation and profitability, many businesses are interested in strategies to avoid the risks of violating human rights, labour rights or the rights of indigenous peoples, participating in corrupt activities or being implicated in environmental degradation. More and more, business associations and investors are developing voluntary standards to promote investment in ways that manage these risks.[37] The standards discussed in the sustainable development sections of the Guide reflect existing and emerging international norms that investors will already be familiar with and may have internalised in their operations in some countries, including in their home state.

9. **Specifying investor obligations in an IIA provides certainty to investors**: Often, these obligations are not clearly set out in the domestic law of the host state, especially if it is still in the process of developing its legal institutions. Clarity through the expression of standards in an IIA could be a benefit in attracting investors. Weak and uncertain standards may discourage reputable companies from investing in the host state.[38]

10. **Attracting desirable investors:** While some investment may be deterred from investing in a regime with a robust sustainable development policy and regulatory framework, these investors may be those unwilling to observe high standards for human and labour rights, avoidance of corruption and protection the environment.

For these and other reasons, the benefits of including provisions in an IIA to promote sustainable development may outweigh any dissuasive effect they might have on potential investors.

The sample provisions for promoting sustainable development contained in the Guide are based on best practices in the field. For instance, they reflect the principles set out in the UN Protect, Respect and Remedy policy framework and the UN Guiding Principles on Business and Human Rights developed by the Special Representative of the UN Secretary-General on the Issue of Human Rights and Transnational Corporations and other Business Enterprises. The framework and Guiding Principles focus on enhancing host state capacity to regulate foreign investors in a manner consistent with the state's international human rights

---

37 Examples include: AccountAbility 1000 Framework; AA1000 Assurance Standard; Business Principles for Countering Bribery; CERES Principles; Clean Clothes Campaign: Model Code; Eco-Management and Audit Scheme; Ethical Trading Initiative: Base Code; Fair Labor Association: Workplace Code of Conduct; UN Global Compact; Global Reporting Initiative; Global Sullivan Principles of Corporate Social Responsibility; ICC Business Charter for Sustainable Development; Marine Stewardship Council's Principles and Criteria for Sustainable Fishing; The Natural Step Principles; OECD Guidelines for Multinational Enterprises; Shell Business Principles; SIGMA: Sustainable Guidelines for Management; Voluntary Principles on Security and Human Rights; International Council on Mining and Metals Sustainable Development Framework.

38 D Franks (2012), *Social Impact Assessment of Resource Projects*, International Mining for Development Centre, Crawley, at 3.

obligations; they clarify and elaborate the responsibility of corporate actors to respect human rights and to engage in human rights due diligence; and they recommend the development of effective remedies for victims of corporate human rights violations and discuss the principles upon which complaint mechanisms should be based.[39] Both the policy framework and the Guiding Principles have been widely endorsed by states and businesses.[40]

Concerns regarding the burden of the obligations provided for in this section for host states may be met, in part, by technical assistance and investment promotion commitments to be undertaken by investors' home states, as is contemplated in Chapter 8 (Investment Promotion and Technical Assistance).

Each state must determine how best to accommodate investor protection and its freedom to regulate to achieve sustainable development. In addition, the contested and novel nature of the policy tools discussed in this section mean that each state's choices regarding them must be carefully weighed. States negotiating an IIA should adopt only those policy mechanisms that they determine best meet both their need for attracting foreign investment and their need to promote sustainable development in a manner consistent with domestic policy.

6.6 Sustainability assessments

Cross references

2.3 Links between foreign investment and sustainable development 18
6 New Provisions Addressing Sustainable Development 252

39 See UNHRC (2008), 'Protect Respect and Remedy: A Framework for Business and Human Rights: Report of the Special Representative of the Secretary-General on the Issue of Human Rights and Transnational Corporations and other Business Entities', UN Doc. A/HRC/8/5; and UNHRC (2011), Guiding Principles on Business and Human Rights: Implementing the United Nations 'Protect, Respect and Remedy' Framework: Report of the Special Representative of the Secretary-General on the Issue of Human Rights and Transnational Corporations and other Business Enterprises, John Ruggie, UN Doc A/HRC/17/31.

40 The Guiding Principles on Business and Human Rights were unanimously endorsed by the Human Rights Council (see *Human Rights and Transnational Corporations and Other Business Enterprises*, UNHRC, 17th Sess, UN Doc A/HRC/17/L.17/Rev.1, (2011). For business endorsement see, for example, the International Organization of Employers (2011), Address to the UN Human Rights Council, delivered at the Palais des Nations in Geneva, Switzerland, 31 May 2011, available at: www.un.org/webcast/unhrc/archive.asp?go=110531#pm1 (accessed 8 January 2013), which 'supports the approach taken in the principles to elaborate the implications of existing standards and practice into practical guidance rather than seeking to create new international legal obligations or seek to assign legal liability'. See also the range of letters from business actors endorsing the Guiding Principles, including Coca Cola, Statement by Edward Potter, personal communication, 26 May 2011, available at: www.global-business-initiative.org/SRSGpage/files/Guiding%20Principles%20Endorsement%20from%20Coke.pdf (accessed 29 May 2012); and Total, Statement by Peter Herbl, personal communication, 23 May 2011, available at: www.global-business-initiative.org/SRSGpage/files/Total%20S%20A%20letter%20to%20John%20Ruggie.pdf (accessed 29 May 2012).

Assessing the environmental, social and human rights impacts of foreign investments is an important way to ensure that investment is compatible with sustainable development. Assessments employ sound principles of risk management and evidence-based evaluation to achieve the goals of environmental protection, community participation and the protection of human rights. In addition, they enhance the benefits of an investment both for the investor and the community in which the investment is located.

Assessment is an essential tool to help states to implement their obligations to *protect* human rights, health, labour rights and the rights of indigenous peoples and to protect the environment. It is also useful for ensuring that investors fulfil their responsibility to *respect* human rights.[41] For instance, the UN Guiding Principles on Business and Human Rights state that business enterprises should '[a]void causing or contributing to adverse human rights impacts' and that they should '[s]eek to prevent or mitigate' such impacts.[42] To do this, the Guiding Principles suggest that business enterprises carry out 'human rights due diligence' by assessing 'actual and potential human rights impacts' of their activities.[43] Assessment is thus an important part of actualising the duty of states and investors to protect those affected by an investment.

Assessment can help attract sustainable foreign investment. It is more cost-effective for investors to identify in advance possible risks that their investment might create for environmental sustainability or human rights and adopt strategies to mitigate them than to deal with the damage after it materialises. Also, the assessment process builds a relationship between the investor and the government of the host state that can be beneficial should problems arise. Overall, assessment creates greater certainty for investors that their investment will succeed.[44]

41 UN Guiding Principles on Business and Human Rights, A/HRC/17/31, Principle 12.

42 UN Guiding Principles on Business and Human Rights, ibid., Principle 13. Principles 17–21 provide more detail on how business enterprises should go about doing this.

43 UN Guiding Principles on Business and Human Rights, ibid., Principle 17.

44 A M Esteves, D Franks and F Vanclay (2012), 'Social Impact Assessment: The State of the Art', 30 *Impact Assessment and Project Appraisal* 34 at 36.

Environmental Impact Assessments[45] (EIAs) have become commonplace both domestically and internationally.[46] Obtaining an EIA of an investment, reviewing this assessment and agreeing on a management plan for implementing the recommendations resulting from the assessment and review are all essential elements of a rational plan for ensuring environmental protection.[47] While not required in any existing IIA, Article 12 of the IISD model agreement provides for this kind of assessment of investment prior to its establishment. It also requires states to have in place an effective regulatory structure that sets standards for conducting the assessment and determines the scope of the assessment required of different classes of investors.[48]

As mentioned in Section 2.3 of the Guide (Links between foreign investment and sustainable development), sustainable development also has a social aspect that includes the alleviation of poverty, the protection of human and labour rights, and the rights of indigenous peoples. To eradicate poverty, protect the environment and respect, protect and fulfil economic, social, cultural, civil, political and other human rights in an integrated way, the principle of sustainable development also requires an *assessment of the social impact* of an investment prior to the investment being established.[49] In recognition of this, Article 12(B) of the IISD model treaty requires a social impact assessment of potential investments. The social impact of an investment includes its impact on human rights, and it also extends to

45 Defined as 'the process of identifying, predicting, evaluating and mitigating the biophysical, social, and other relevant effects of development proposals prior to major decisions being taken and commitments made' (International Association for Impact Assessment (2009), *What is Impact Assessment?* IAIA, Fargo). Earlier definitions focused almost exclusively on environmental impacts. For instance, the UNEP defined EIA as an 'assessment of the likely or potential environmental impacts of [a] proposed activity' (UNEP, Governing Council decision: Goals and Principles of Environmental Impact Assessment, Principle 4, UNEP/GC.14/17 Annex III, UNEP/BC/DEC/14/25 (17 June 1987).

46 R K Morgan (2012), 'Environmental Impact Assessment: The State of the Art', 30 *Impact Assessment and Project Appraisal* 5–14.

47 S A Atapattu (2006), *Emerging Principles of International Environmental Law,* Transnational Publishers, Ardsley, New York, at 130. See also J C Dernbach (2003), 'Achieving Sustainable Development: The Centrality and Multiple Facets of Integrated Decision-making', 10 *Indiana Journal of Global Legal Studies* 247; and *Report of the Expert Group Meeting on Identification of Principles of International Law for Sustainable Development*, Geneva, September 1995, prepared by the Division for Sustainable Development for the Commission on Sustainable Development, 4th session, 1996, available at: www.un.org/documents/ecosoc/cn17/1996/background/ecn171996-bp3.htm (accessed 29 May 2012).

48 Art. 21 of the IISD Model Treaty requires states to legislate and pass regulations to protect the environment including setting standards for environmental assessments and criteria for determining which investments should be required to undergo an assessment before they are approved. Art. 12(A) requires the state to apply screening criteria for determining the scope of the assessment required. The Agreement notes that the scope will vary based on the size of the investment and the nature of its inputs and outputs. Small enterprises and some service-related enterprises may be exempt from an environmental impact assessment. Other IIAs provide that party states may not reduce environmental protection and human rights to attract investment. For instance, see Art. 20 of the IISD Model Treaty, as well as provisions in the Canadian, US and draft Norwegian models (Canadian model FIPA, Art. 11; US model BIT, Art. 12; and Norwegian draft model APPI, Art. 11). There is no comparable provision in the Indian model BIPPA or the UK model IPPA.

49 Esteves et al., op. cit.

consideration of impacts on the host state's social policies more generally, including its sustainable development policies. The components of a social impact assessment are set out in Box 6.1.

Box 6.1 Components of a social impact assessment

An effective sustainability assessment includes an assessment of the social impacts of an investment. These can include the impact on the following.

1. Way of life
2. Culture
3. Community
4. Political systems
5. Environment
6. Health and well-being
7. Personal and property rights
8. People's fears and aspirations[50]

Recently, Human Rights Impact Assessments (HRIAs) have emerged. They are generally based on the work of the United Nations Special Representative on Human Rights and Business,[51] who has introduced the concept of human rights due diligence. 'Due diligence' refers to the responsibility of business enterprises to assess 'actual and potential human rights impacts', integrate and act on the findings, track responses and communicate to the public how they have addressed the impacts they identified.[52] An HRIA is defined as 'measuring the impact of policies, programmes, projects and interventions on human rights'.[53] This new tool can co-exist with social impact assessments. However, it differs from the social impact assessment (SIA) process because it is based on international legal standards of human rights rather than on the achievement of desirable social outcomes.[54] The relatively recent emergence of HRIAs means that methodologies for assessing human rights impacts are still in their infancy. However, the new emphasis placed on human rights due diligence by the

50 F Vanclay (2003), 'International Principles for Social Impact Assessment', 21 *Impact Assessment and Project Appraisal* 5 at 8.

51 Esteves et al., op. cit.

52 Guiding Principles on Business and Human Rights, op. cit., Principle 17.

53 Human Rights Impact Resource Centre, 'An Introduction to Human Rights Impact Assessment', available at: www.humanrightsimpact.org/hria-guide/overview (accessed 8 January 2013).

54 J Harrison (2011), 'Human Rights Measurement: Reflections on the Current Practice and Future Potential of Human Rights Impact Assessment', 3 *Journal of Human Rights Practice* 162 at 167.

UN Special Representative is likely to spur rapid development of effective assessment tools.

States may wish to integrate all three kinds of assessment into their investment assessment process, thus creating a comprehensive system for *Sustainability Assessment.*

6.6.1 Sustainability assessment in practice

Sustainability assessment and its various components – environmental impact assessments and social impact assessments – are well-established tools for the promotion of states' sustainable development goals. Human rights impact assessment, as already noted, is still in its infancy, although various methodologies are being developed.

Despite the general use of select elements of sustainability assessment in many states, assessment in general features little in investment agreements. Apart from model investment agreements such as the IISD model, no agreement requires states to enact domestic laws and regulations to implement SAs, nor do any impose obligations on investors to conduct such an assessment.

Nevertheless, various aspects of sustainability assessment such as environmental impact assessment are common in the domestic legislation of states.[55] EIA is also referred to in a number of international treaties and soft law documents.[56] This demonstrates that states acknowledge that assessment provisions are an effective way of implementing sustainable development policy. Such an effective tool can be transposed to international agreements as discussed below.

While they do not feature in IIAs, the use of EIA in other international agreements is evidence that states accept that 'international EIA commitments are well suited to integrate international environmental norms into decision-making processes and to promote outcomes that reflect prevailing international environmental norms'.[57] In other words, EIA requirements in treaties influence policy-makers to implement their international obligations under international environmental law.[58]

There may be a customary international legal obligation for states to conduct EIAs in some circumstances.[59] The notion that international law requires EIA stems from the duty of states to prevent harm to others beyond its territory and to co-operate with other states to prevent such harm.[60] However, despite this general obligation to prevent harm, international law does not specify what the content of assessments must be or the circumstances in which they are required.[61]

---

55 N Craik (2008), *The International Law of Environmental Impact Assessment: Process, Substance and Integration*, Cambridge University Press, Cambridge at 5.

56 Ibid.

57 Ibid. at 12.

58 Ibid. at 12 and 15.

59 See, for example, the separate opinion of Judge Weeramantry in the *Gabcikovo-Nagymaros Case* (Hungary/Slovakia), (1997) ICJ Rep 7 at 111–13. For a helpful interpretation, see Craik, op. cit., at 114–15.

60 Craik, ibid. at 121.

61 Ibid. at 90.

Most specific obligations to conduct EIAs are contained in environmental treaties. States should review their treaty commitments in international environmental treaties to determine if they have taken on any obligations to conduct EIAs that they interpret as applying to the assessment of the impact of IIAs or investments protected by them. For instance, treaties that apply to transboundary pollution may require parties to conduct EIAs to determine potential impacts on other parties of foreign investments located in their territory.[62]

International organisations such as the World Bank also require EIAs as part of their organisations' commitment to implement environmentally sound and sustainable projects.[63] These policies may have a direct impact on developing countries.

In general, the prevalence of EIA requirements in domestic and international legal instruments indicates a general willingness on the part of states to use assessment as a means of implementing their sustainable development policies. It is for this reason that the Guide discusses various ways of applying sustainability assessment to foreign investment in order to establish a strong link between each state's investment policy and its development goals.

6.6.2 Policy discussion

Why do a SA?

At first glance, it might seem that one of the competitive advantages of developing countries that makes them attractive to foreign investors is the lower cost of complying with a developing country's laws and regulations in comparison with the cost of compliance with the more complicated requirements in place in many developed countries. According to this logic, investors would prefer to operate in a country that does not require costly assessment and consideration of environmental, social or human rights as a precondition to investment. Putting in place a process for conducting such assessments will drive away potential foreign investors.

While some investors may be deterred, other competing concerns must be weighed against the possibility of losing investors when deciding whether to submit potential investments to an assessment process. Assessing an investment to determine the potential risk that it represents for citizens and the environment can fulfil many of the goals of the government's sustainable development policy.[64] In addition, assessment can help governments and investors to determine what community support activities could be useful to help integrate the investment into the

62 However, parties to such treaties as the *Convention on Environmental Impact Assessment in a Transboundary Context* (Espoo Convention), signed 25 February 1991, 1989 *United Nations Treaty Series* 309, 30 International Legal Materials 800, are mostly developed states (Craik, ibid., at 124).

63 Ibid. at 108–10.

64 OECD (2006), *Applying Strategic Environmental Assessment: Good Practice Guidance for Development Co-operation*, OECD, Paris, at 42. For a good overview of the benefits of conducting a sustainability impact assessment, see D Collins, (2010), 'Environmental Impact Statements and Public Participation in International Investment Law', 7 *Manchester Journal of International Economic Law*, 4.

community.[65] Assessment is thus one of the key ways of integrating foreign direct investment into a comprehensive sustainable development policy.

Conducting a SA allows for public participation in the investment approval process.[66] This participation is an important element of democracy, which underlies many of the human rights protected in international documents. Public participation also legitimises both the investment and the state's decision to approve it. Assessment of the impact of the investment will allow citizens to gain access to public decision-making processes and inform them about future investments in their community.[67] Investors who conduct a robust SA are likely to encounter less resistance to the investment from individuals and the community that may be affected by the investment.

Assessing the impacts of an investment can be a highly subjective process.[68] Different individuals and communities as well as different investors will identify different impacts depending on their circumstances. They will have differing views on the relative significance of various impacts. Furthermore, different individuals are comfortable with different levels of risk. Conducting an assessment of an investment allows both government agencies and investors to identify risks and impacts and understand how their attitudes towards these impacts may differ from those of the affected community and from each other. Parties can use the assessment process to identify possible conflicting interests between various stakeholders.

Sustainability assessment helps to uncover information about an investment of which the investor and the government were previously unaware. Governments will learn about new environmental protection measures employed by cutting-edge firms. They will be able to identify impacts that had not previously been in evidence, and develop policies, plans and programmes to deal with them.[69] Investors, too, benefit from sharing information about relevant regulatory standards and practices and the various dispute resolution mechanisms available to them should a problem arise.

SA helps the parties to determine the baseline for ongoing monitoring of the performance of investments.[70] The assessment outlines existing environmental and

65 Franks, op. cit., at 12.

66 Ibid. at 46. A number of international documents stress the importance of stakeholder participation in assessments, including *Rio Declaration on Environment and Development*, principles 10 and 17; *Convention on Access to Information, Public Participation in Decision-Making and Access to Justice in Environmental Matters*, signed on 25 June 2009 (Aarhus Convention), 38(3) *European Legal Materials* 517–533, in force 30 October 2001; Espoo Convention, e.g. Art. II.2; and UN Guiding Principles on Business and Human Rights,. op. cit.

67 Ibid.

68 Collins, op. cit.

69 Ibid. at 45.

70 The importance of ongoing monitoring is stressed in Principle 20 of the UN Guiding Principles on Business and Human Rights, op. cit.

social conditions that can be used to measure the benefits and harms of the investment as it proceeds.

Conducting an impact assessment can reduce the costs of doing business. The OECD points out that when investors do not conduct an EIA, they are likely to face increased business costs and will not have a feasible plan for avoiding or mitigating future conflicts.[71] Moreover, conducting an assessment helps the investor and the government to determine what technologies and policies will be appropriate for managing potential risks. Esteves et al. identify other benefits to business, including:

1. Greater certainty for project investments and increased chance of project success;
2. Avoidance and reduction of social and environmental risks and conflicts faced by industry and communities;
3. A process to inform and involve internal and external stakeholders and to assist in building trust and mutually beneficial futures;
4. Improved quality of life for employees and improved attraction and retention of skilled workers;
5. A positive legacy beyond the life of the project; and
6. Increased competitive advantage through enhanced social performance and corporate reputation.[72]

Having a SA process in place will attract responsible investors. Many multinational businesses have policies that require them to assess the impact of their activities on local communities.[73] Having a SA system in place will help these companies implement their assessment policies. Also, a well-managed SA process signals to socially and environmentally responsible investors that the jurisdiction they are entering has an effective governance regime in place.

Finally, obtaining investment financing is often conditional on conducting risk assessments, especially environmental impact assessments. The European Bank for Reconstruction and Development (EBRD) and the Asian Development Bank (ADB), for example, require environmental assessments prior to funding development-related projects. The Multilateral Investment Guarantee Agency (MIGA), which provides financial insurance against non-commercial risks, has a policy on environmental and social impact assessments. Likewise, the International Finance Corporation (IFC) has a similar policy for providing financing.[74]

71 Collins, op. cit., at 45.

72 Esteves et al., op. cit.

73 Ibid.

74 For a comprehensive review of the requirements of these different financing and insurance agencies, see Collins, op. cit.

Elements of an effective SA system

An SA can be conducted in a number of ways. However, best practices in the field of impact assessment identify certain essential elements for an effective process.[75] Generally, the costs of a SA are shared by the government, which sets up the impact assessment system, and the investor, which must conduct a review of its investment in accordance with the government system. However, there are various ways of distributing the costs of the actual assessment. For instance, the whole cost of conducting the assessment can be placed on the investor, or various cost-sharing measures between the host state and the investor can be put in place. The elements of an effective SA strategy are set out in Box 6.2.

Box 6.2 Elements of an effective SA strategy[76]

1. **Determine scope of assessment:** Initial work involves determining the appropriate scale, timing and focus of the assessment. This may involve identifying those who will be affected by the investment and what activities of the investment are likely to produce impacts.
2. **Produce a profile and conduct baseline studies:** Investors should gather information about the community in which they will invest and identify the important stakeholders. This can include identification of the different needs and interests of stakeholders and communities. Based on this information, a benchmark can be established against which change can be measured.
3. **Predictive assessment:** Once information is gathered and a baseline established, potential impacts can be identified and their likelihood assessed.
4. **Participation:** Civil society groups should be able to participate meaningfully in the assessment process (see UN Guiding Principles on Business and Human Rights, Principle 18(b)). To ensure this participation, investors must communicate with stakeholders about the risks posed by their investment and steps taken to mitigate this risk (see Principle 21). They should also provide stakeholders with an ongoing role in assessing, managing and monitoring the investment.
5. **Agreement-making process:** An SA should identify appropriate processes for arriving at agreements between investors and stakeholders. Especially in the case of indigenous peoples, free, prior and informed consent for major decisions relating to an investment should be obtained.

(Continued)

75 For best practices, see Vanclay, op. cit., and Franks, op. cit.

76 Ibid. For a summary of the classic EIA model, see Morgan, op. cit., at 9. Esteves et al., op. cit., also provide a summary of 'Current good practice' for social impact assessments.

(Continued)

6. **Planning:** The investor should have a management plan, approved by the host state, for protecting the environment, human rights, health, labour rights and the rights of indigenous peoples. The plan can be the basis for ongoing monitoring. It will ensure that the appropriate organisational systems and budget allocations are in place within the investment to address potential impacts (see UN Guiding Principles on Business and Human Rights, Principles 19(a)(i) and (ii)).
7. **Monitoring of harms:** An effective SA should include a system for the community to inform the investor and the government of potential harms at an early stage. This recognises that investors have an obligation to monitor the ongoing risk that their investment poses to the community (see UN Guiding Principles on Business and Human Rights, Principles 17(c) and 20). A 'cumulative effects' approach to monitoring harms should be taken. Isolated harms may be small taken individually, but cumulatively, their impact may be significant.[77]
8. **Monitoring of benefits:** Investments can provide many benefits to a community through procurement, employment and the provision of community support programmes. These should be part of the ongoing system of monitoring.
9. **Enforcement:** The assessment system should provide an effective enforcement mechanism if an investor fails to comply with a management plan. Enforcement mechanisms create incentives for compliance.
10. **Use best practices:** An effective SA system should be based on international best practices for environmental, social and human rights protection.

Assessing the sustainability of IIAs

One complementary approach to conducting SAs of investments that reflects international best practices is to conduct an assessment of IIAs themselves. While the assessment of individual projects will always have a central place in an effective sustainable development policy, the assessment literature increasingly recognises the importance of assessing the sustainability impacts of broad government policies and programmes.[78] Assessing the sustainability of IIAs is described in Box 6.3.

77 Morgan, op. cit.

78 Morgan, for instance, notes that strategic environmental assessment 'has been vigorously promoted as a way to extend impact assessment to higher level decision-making at policy, programme and plan levels, a reaction to the project orientation of most EIA applications', op. cit., at 7, citing B Sadler et al. (2011), 'Taking Stock of SEA', in B Sadler (ed.), *Handbook of Strategic Environmental Assessment*, Earthscan, London, 1.

Box 6.3 Submitting proposed IIAs or model IIAs to an assessment process

The *Guiding Principles on Human Rights Impact Assessments of Trade and Investment Agreements* affirm that all states ought to evaluate the human rights impact of both trade and investment agreements.[79]

The OECD has developed a comprehensive methodology for assessing the environmental impacts of international trade agreements.[80]

These assessments can influence negotiating positions. They can also inform parties about policies in areas outside the core disciplines of the IIA that can be developed to mitigate detrimental impacts.[81]

Various OECD members such as the USA, the EU and Canada have evaluated the environmental impacts of free trade agreements and even IIAs.[82]

How to set standards for SAs

In order to facilitate the conduct of sustainability assessments and to ensure consistency of outcomes, the assessment of environmental and social impacts has often been combined in international initiatives in this area. The IFC's performance standards are an example of a process for assessing social and environmental impacts of an investment in an integrated way.[83] ISO 14001 sets out another system for managing environmental assessments, while ISO 26000 represents a system for implementing best practices in the area of social responsibility.[84]

The starting point for a human rights impact assessment must be the international human rights obligations entered into by the parties to an IIA.[85] States should review these obligations and ensure that any human rights assessment process reflects them.

79 United Nations, 'Report of the Special Rapporteur on the Right to Food, Olivier De Schutter: Guiding Principles on Human Rights Impact Assessments of Trade and Investment Agreements', (19 December 2011, A/HRC/19/59/Add.5, Principle 1.

80 OECD (1994), *Methodologies for Environmental and Trade Reviews*, OCDE/GD(94)103, OECD, Paris.

81 M W Gehring (2011), 'Impact Assessments of Investment Treaties', in Cordonier Segger et al., op. cit., at 155.

82 Ibid. Gehring provides an overview of the processes used and the experience of the various OECD members in using them.

83 For the performance standards, see: www.ifc.org/ifcext/sustainability.nsf/Content/EnvSocStandards (accessed 29 May 2012). See also: International Business Leaders Forum and International Finance Corporation, *Draft* (June 2007), *Guide to Human Rights Impact Assessment and Management, Road-Testing*, available at: www.globalgovernancewatch.org/resources/guide-to-human-rights-impact-assessment-and-management-roadtesting-draft-june-2007 (accessed 29 May 2012).

84 See International Organization for Standardization (ISO) (2010), *Guidance on social responsibility*, ISO 26000:2010, available at www.iso.org/iso/iso26000 (accessed 24 June 2012).

85 UN, 'Guiding Principles on Human Rights Impact Assessments', op. cit., Principle 5.

The International Centre for Human Rights and Democratic Development provides standards for assessing the impact of an investment on human rights.[86] Harrison has produced a comprehensive catalogue of existing human rights assessment tools[87] that can be useful to states contemplating an expansion of their existing domestic assessment processes or the integration of a SA process into an IIA. Both he and the UN Special Rapporteur on the Right to Food have set out the various methodological steps involved in an effective human rights assessment process.[88]

An assessment process designed to promote sustainable development should also give effect to important principles of international environmental law.[89] These principles are:

1. The precautionary principle;
2. The principle of common but differentiated responsibilities; and
3. The polluter pays principle.

The precautionary principle

The precautionary principle reaffirms the ability of the host state to regulate investors and their investments in a way that avoids future environmental harms. Host states may wish to put in place measures to protect human health or the environment even where there is no consensus in the scientific community that the measures are necessary. A good example from the trade context is Europe's measures regarding genetically modified organisms (GMOs) – while there is no scientific consensus that foods incorporating GMOs are more harmful than other products, the EU has chosen to regulate GMOs based on a credible minority of scientific opinion.

The precautionary principle is well recognised in international legal regimes.[90] Increasingly, it is interpreted as placing the onus on the person who wants to engage in an activity, be it a private investor or a state, to demonstrate that its activities will not adversely affect the environment before the state grants it the right to carry out the proposed activity.[91]

---

86 E.g. International Centre for Human Rights and Democracy (2007), *Human Rights Impact Assessments for Foreign Investment Projects*, International Centre for Human Rights and Democracy, Montreal, available at: http://publications.gc.ca/collections/collection_2007/dd-rd/E84-21-2007E.pdf (accessed 8 January 2013).

87 J Harrison (2010), 'Measuring Human Rights: Reflections on the Practice of Human Rights Impact Assessment and Lessons for the Future', Warwick School of Law Research Paper No. 2010/26, Warwick, available at: http://papers.ssrn.com/sol3/papers.cfm?abstract_id=1706742 (accessed 29 May 2012). See also J Harrison and M-A Stephenson (2010), *Human Rights Impact Assessment: Review of Practice and Guidance for Future Assessments. Report for the Scottish Human Rights Commission*, available at: www.scottishhumanrights.com/ourwork/publications/article/HRIAresearchreport (accessed 29 May 2012).

88 J Harrison, 'Human Rights Measurement', op. cit.; UN, 'Guiding Principles on Human Rights Impact Assessments', op. cit., Principle 7.

89 Vanclay lists the precautionary principle and the polluter pays principle as guiding principles for social impact assessment, op. cit., at 10.

90 *EC-Measures Concerning Meat and Meat Products (Hormones)*, WT/DS48/AB/R, 16 January 1998.

91 P Sands (2003), *Principles of International Environmental Law*, 2d ed., Cambridge University Press, Cambridge, at 27.

The process of carrying out a SA is itself an application of the precautionary principle, as the goals of the assessment are to identify future risks and develop a plan to eliminate or mitigate them.[92]

Common but differentiated responsibilities

The principle of common but differentiated responsibilities recognises that states at different levels of economic, social and political development have different capacities to protect against environmental degradation and deal with social, economic and political instability.[93] The principle also recognises that environmental standards can apply in different ways to different states based on their capacity to respond to threats to the environment and the different contributions of developed and developing countries to environmental degradation.[94]

The principle is well known in international law, and it has been implemented in international legal regimes such as international trade law.[95] It is compatible with the well-recognised duty of states to co-operate in good faith.[96] In the domain of investment, the application of the principle of common but differentiated responsibilities requires that developed country parties to an IIA provide technical and financial assistance to developing country parties to implement the provisions of the agreement to the extent that they can.[97]

Reference to this principle in an IIA will help the parties and investment arbitrators to interpret the agreement taking into account sustainable development. For instance, a developed country that is party to an IIA might be held more strictly to deadlines for implementing the agreement than its developing country partner. Provisions requiring technical assistance for a developing country in putting in place various treaty-based mechanisms may also be interpreted in a way that acknowledges the importance of such measures for a country at a particular stage of development.

Polluter pays principle

The polluter pays principle requires that the polluter bear the cost of the pollution it causes. Although it is incorporated in a number of international treaties, it remains a contentious principle. The debate about its validity is articulated in the wording of Principle 16 of the Rio Declaration:[98]

---

92 Gehring, op. cit., at 150.

93 Ibid. at 286. See also Principle 7 of the *Rio Declaration on Environment and Development*, op. cit.

94 *New Delhi Declaration*, op. cit., at 3.4.

95 For instance, the *Agreement on Technical Barriers to Trade* (33 *International Legal Materials* 9 (1994)) and the *Agreement on Sanitary and Phytosanitary Measures*, both WTO agreements (33 *International Legal Materials* 9 (1994)), contain many such provisions, called 'special and differential treatment' provisions in WTO law.

96 Chapter IX of the UN Charter and the Declaration on Principles of International Law Concerning Friendly Relations and Co-operation among States in accordance with the Charter of the United Nations, UNGA Res. 2625 (XXV) (1970).

97 See Chapter 8 (Investment Promotion and Technical Assistance).

98 *Rio Declaration on Environment and Development*, op. cit.

> National authorities should endeavour to promote the internalization of environmental costs and the use of economic instruments, taking into account the approach that the polluter should, in principle, bear the costs of pollution, with due regard to the public interests and without distorting international trade and investment.

The polluter pays principle can be helpful to a host state seeking to enforce an investor's obligation to mitigate environmental harms and compensate victims of acts of environmental degradation.

Box 6.4 Summary of options for sustainability assessments

1. *Do not submit foreign investments to an assessment procedure prior to approving them*
2. *Use existing domestic laws and regulations to assess the environmental, social and human rights impacts of investments*
3. *Develop new domestic laws and regulations to assess the environmental, social and human rights impacts of an investment*
4. *Integrate SAs into IIAs*

SAs can be integrated into IIAs in the following ways:

a. Specify in the IIA that a SA does not violate the agreement;

b. Specify SA as a condition of investment: Here are some features of a SA process that could be required in an IIA:

   i. Ongoing monitoring,

   ii. Consultation, involvement and participation, or consent of stakeholders;

c. SA as a condition of investment plus effective enforcement mechanisms where an investor does not comply with SA obligations:

   i. Limit access to dispute resolution,

   ii. Create domestic complaint and investigation procedures,

   iii. Allow the host state and private parties to sue investors that harm the environment, human rights, labour rights and the rights of indigenous peoples in the host state, and

   iv. Allow investors' home state and private parties to sue investors for harm to the environment, human rights, labour rights and the rights of indigenous peoples in the home state.

6.6.3 Discussion of options

1. *Do not submit foreign investments to an assessment procedure prior to approving them*

The advantage of this approach is that it does not require the host state to devote any resources to assessment. In addition, investors may be attracted to a jurisdiction that does not have a complex assessment procedure in place, as this will lower its cost of doing business at the front end of the investment.

The disadvantage of this approach is that neither the home state nor the investor will have a clear idea of the magnitude of the risks that the investment represents. Without consulting with the local community, social risks in particular may be hard to foresee. It may also be difficult to put in place systems for avoiding or mitigating risks should they occur. The assessment procedure builds a relationship between the government and the investor, both of whom are involved in a comprehensive assessment. If no assessment takes place, this relationship may not be strong, and the response to pollution or other risks may be slow.

An assessment procedure that involves the public throughout the life of the investment promotes democratic participation and transparency. This transparency can build public support for an investment that can be useful when risks materialise. Also, investors may save money in the long term if they are able to put a risk mitigation plan in place that will be less costly than responding to risks in an ad hoc fashion after they materialise.

Finally, states have an obligation to prevent business enterprises from causing harm to those living in the state's territory.[99] Besides, business enterprises themselves have a responsibility 'to avoid causing or contributing to adverse human rights impacts.'[100] Putting in place an assessment process helps both states and investors fulfil their duties.

2. *Use existing domestic laws and regulations to assess the environmental, social and human rights impacts of investments*

The host state may apply existing domestic laws and regulations to assess investments, or it may update existing assessment provisions to provide a more comprehensive sustainability assessment process. The advantage of this approach is that it allows the use of existing assessment institutions and agencies and permits them to apply their expertise to assessing foreign investments. In dealing with sophisticated transnational corporations, host state personnel may learn about new practices employed by foreign investors to deal with environmental protection or the protection of labour rights, human rights and the rights of indigenous peoples. Using domestic legislation also ensures that there is a common assessment system for domestic and foreign investments that promote fairness and transparency. Finally, a domestic SA system implements the state's duty to protect its citizens and those living in its territory against human rights abuses by domestic and foreign businesses.[101]

A drawback to this approach is that foreign investors may be able to challenge some government actions as part of the assessment process by relying on investor protections in the IIA. For instance, investors may challenge administrative processes to which

99 UN Guiding Principles on Business and Human Rights, Principle 1.
100 UN Guiding Principles on Business and Human Rights, Principle 13.
101 UN Guiding Principles on Business and Human Rights, Principle 1.

they must submit as violating FET requirements. The risk of these actions will depend on the specific obligations in the IIA, including whether the IIA provides a right of establishment.

If a state uses a purely domestic system rather than including SA provisions in an IIA, it is more difficult for a state to use treaty-based enforcement mechanisms such as counterclaims, grievance procedures or state-to-state consultations to encourage investors to comply with their obligations to protect the environment, human rights, labour rights and the rights of indigenous peoples. Treaty-based enforcement mechanisms could be triggered by a failure to comply with domestic SA requirements, however.

3. *Develop new domestic laws and regulations to assess the environmental, social and human rights impacts of an investment*

States may not have existing laws or regulations that require a SA, or existing laws may not contemplate a comprehensive assessment of environmental, social and human rights impacts. One option is to develop such a system using best practices in other jurisdictions. The advantages of this approach are similar to those discussed in option 2 above.

There are a number of drawbacks to this approach. They include the following:

- The financial cost of developing and implementing a new assessment system;
- The political cost of developing and implementing a new assessment system;
- Running afoul of existing IIAs – implementing a new SA process may be challenged by foreign investors as a violation of FET or an expropriation requiring compensation; and
- Lack of access to treaty-based enforcement mechanisms to create incentives for foreign investors to comply with assessments and take steps to prevent or mitigate risks.

4. *Integrate SAs into IIAs*

SAs can be integrated into IIAs in the following ways:

a. **Specify in the IIA that a SA does not violate the agreement:** If this approach is taken, reservations and/or exceptions will be used to exempt existing or future domestic SA requirements from the investor protection provision in the treaty, including the prohibition on expropriation without compensation or the fair and equitable treatment obligation. In this way, the host state will have the regulatory space to apply existing SA processes or to create new ones.

   This approach has the advantage of protecting the state's right to regulate foreign investors by applying an existing domestic SA system or developing a new one. It has the disadvantage of not providing the host state with access to treaty-based enforcement mechanisms.

b. **SA as a condition of investment:** It is possible for the host state to make a SA a condition for both the approval of the investment and the applicability to an investor of the investment protection obligations. The framework for the SA could be spelt out in the treaty, or the treaty could require compliance with the SA process under host state law. An advantage of doing this is that the application of a SA system implements the state's duty to protect its citizens and those living in its territory against human rights abuses by domestic and foreign businesses. It also implements the state's obligation to protect the environment. In addition, if the SA procedure is combined with effective treaty-based remedies, it will create strong incentives for investors to comply with their obligations not to harm third parties.

The disadvantages are similar to those involved in setting up a new domestic SA system. However, if a host state sets up a system that applies solely to foreign investors pursuant to an IIA, it is likely to be less costly than establishing a comprehensive domestic evaluation system. On the other hand, if the standards that apply to foreign and domestic investors or to foreign investors from different countries are different, this may cause administrative difficulties and lead to perceptions of unfairness and differential treatment.

If the SA is made a condition of investment, the IIA will include a provision requiring investments of a certain size and/or in certain sectors to undergo an assessment. SAs can be more or less comprehensive. The following are some features of a SA process that could be required in an IIA:

i. **Ongoing monitoring:** The investor and the state regulatory body will develop a plan for ongoing monitoring of the investment. In this way, the government and local residents are kept informed about the ongoing impacts of an investment on the environment and the community.

ii. **Consultation, involvement and participation, or consent of stakeholders:** Requiring investors to consult with those affected by the investment and take into account the results of this consultation is a less onerous requirement than requiring them to involve stakeholders in decision-making or obtain the consent of those affected before allowing the investment to proceed. However, best practices, for example in the area of indigenous rights, point to consent as the most rights-protective standard.

c. **SA as a condition of investment plus effective enforcement mechanisms:** It is possible to complement a requirement that an investor conduct a SA as a condition of being permitted to make its investment by creating treaty-based enforcement mechanisms in the IIA to ensure that the investor complies with the plans to mitigate risks posed by the investment elaborated in the initial assessment and the management plan that results from it. Examples of enforcement mechanisms include the following:

i. **Limit access to dispute resolution:** If the investor fails to meet its obligations to comply with a SA in the treaty, it will not be able to access investor–state dispute resolution. This approach redresses the imbalance in most IIAs, which provide treaty remedies for harms against investors, but no mechanisms for ensuring that investors comply with their obligations. Making compliance with a SA a condition of accessing treaty-based investor–state dispute resolution creates incentives for the investor to come before an investment tribunal with clean hands.

ii. **Create domestic complaint and investigation procedures:** Allowing community members and those affected by the investment to bring to the state's attention harms to their community or to the environment is a more proactive way of ensuring the investor's ongoing compliance with standards for environmental protection, human rights, labour rights and indigenous peoples' rights than simply limiting access to dispute settlement if an investor is not in compliance with its post-SA management plan. However, there are financial, bureaucratic and political costs associated with establishing such procedures.

iii. **Allow the host state and private parties to sue investors that harm the environment, human rights labour rights or the rights of indigenous peoples:** This involves creating civil and criminal liability for investors when risks identified in the SA, such as violations of human rights or damage to the environment, materialise. There are obvious financial and administrative costs in taking this route. However, there are also many advantages. Most obviously, civil remedies create a process through which injured parties can seek relief. Civil and criminal liability will help deter investors from engaging in the conduct constituting the harm. Also, creating civil and criminal liability will help local administrative tribunals and courts develop expertise in the relevant areas of law. This may improve the quality of due process in the host state. It will also encourage foreign investors to engage with domestic law and domestic courts, integrating them more fully into the democratic life of the host state. Finally, it ensures that domestic decision-makers familiar with local circumstances, laws and norms, rather than an international arbitration panel or court, will adjudicate issues. This will ensure greater integration of the foreign investor into the local community.

iv. **Allow the investor's home state and private parties to sue investors for harm to the environment, human rights, labour rights or the rights of indigenous peoples:** Investors' home states can play a role when an IIA contains obligations relating to SAs. An IIA could include provisions requiring the home state to have similar forms of liability for their nationals investing abroad to ensure investor accountability for environmental harms or infringements of human rights in the host state. In addition to supporting enforcement in the host state, including a treaty provision requiring home state enforcement addresses possible concerns about infringing the host state's sovereignty that might discourage a home state from taking action. The application of the domestic law of the investor's home state in relation to actions in the host state might be seen as an invasion of the host state's sovereignty. However, providing for home state liability in the IIA should ensure that the parties accept the need for co-operation in protecting the environment and human rights. They will have balanced the costs and benefits of home state enforcement during the negotiation of the IIA, and the host state will have agreed to the outcome.

All of these enforcement mechanisms in an IIA could be tied to a SA process set out in the treaty or a SA process already established under the law of the host state. It is important to recognise, however, that at most, an IIA provision can provide a basic framework for an assessment process. Substantial investment in the development of domestic rules and administration will be required.

6.6.4 Discussion of the sample SA provisions

The Guide sample provisions on sustainability assessment aim at achieving the policy goals of sustainable development discussed above. They also take into account best practices in the area. Given the novelty of the provisions and the potential technical difficulties in integrating a SA requirement into an IIA, the sample provisions provide one example of how this can be done. Of course, states may choose to rely on existing domestic assessment regimes or adopt less comprehensive forms of assessment requirements in their IIAs. The main features of the sample SA provisions are summarised in Box 6.5.

Box 6.5 Key features of the SA system in the sample provisions

1. Recognises the right of each party state to establish its own level of domestic environmental protection and to pursue its own priorities in regard to sustainable development;
2. Acknowledges that party states will develop a SA system that reflects their international legal obligations in relation to human rights, labour rights and the rights of indigenous peoples, including, but not limited to, rights set out in the eight core ILO conventions,[102] the core UN human

(Continued)

102 *Convention (No. 100) concerning Equal Remuneration for Men and Women Workers for Work of Equal Value*, adopted 29 June 1951, in force 23 May 1953; *Convention (No. 111) concerning Discrimination in Respect of Employment and Occupation*, adopted 25 June 1958, in force 15 June 1960; *Convention (No. 87) concerning Freedom of Association and Protection of the Right to Organize*, adopted 9 July 1948, in force 4 July 1950; *Convention (No. 98) concerning the Application of the Principles of the Right to Organise and Collective Bargaining*, adopted 1 July 1949, in force 18 July 1951; *Convention (No. 138) concerning Minimum Age for Admission to Employment*, adopted 26 June 1973, in force 19 June 1976; *Convention (No. 182) concerning the Prohibition and Immediate Action for the Elimination of the Worst Forms of Child Labour*, adopted 17 June 1999, in force 19 November 2000; *Convention (No. 29) concerning Forced or Compulsory Labour*, adopted 28 June 1930, in force 1 May 1932; and *Convention (No. 105) concerning the Abolition of Forced Labour*, adopted 25 June 1957, in force 17 January 1959.

(Continued)

rights treaties,[103] the Universal Declaration of Human Rights 1948 and the UN Declaration on the Rights of Indigenous Peoples and customary international law;

3. Requires host states to develop standards to be applied in the assessment process through consultation with potentially affected groups;
4. Requires host states to determine the appropriate scope of the SA (i.e. decide what investments require assessment);
5. Requires investors to conduct SA of investments that fall within the scope;
6. Ensures that the assessment will be conducted in consultation with affected groups prior to the approval of the investment;
7. Ensures that the host state reviews the assessment;
8. Ensures that the host state and the investor agree to a management plan for implementing the assessment and the review;
9. Allows those affected by an investment to participate in the SA process and decision-making about investments;
10. Secures the free, prior and informed consent of affected communities before an investment proceeds;
11. Requires the parties to implement an effective system for monitoring the ongoing compliance of investors;
12. Ensures public access to the recommendations in the assessment and the review, and to the results of ongoing monitoring processes;
13. Gives parties the flexibility to revise assessment standards and the methods to achieve them as the circumstances of the state and the investment change;

(Continued)

103 These include the *International Convention on the Elimination of All Forms of Racial Discrimination*, adopted 21 December 1966, in force 4 January 1969; *International Covenant on Civil and Political Rights*, adopted 21 December 1965, in force 4 January 1969, 660 *United Nations Treaty Series* 195; *International Covenant on Economic Social and Cultural Rights*, signed 16 December 1966, in force 23 March 1976. *Convention on the Elimination of All Forms of Discrimination against Women*, adopted 18 December 1979, in force 3 September 1981, 1249 *United Nations Treaty Series* 13; *Convention against Torture and Other Cruel, Inhuman or Degrading Treatment*, adopted 10 December 1984, in force 26 June 1987, 1577 *United Nations Treaty Series* 3; *Convention on the Rights of the Child*, adopted 20 November 1989, in force 2 September 1990, 1577 *United Nations Treaty Series* 3; *International Convention on the Protection of the Rights of Migrant Workers and Their Families*, adopted 18 December 1990, in force 1 July 2003, 2220 *United Nations Treaty Series* 3; *International Convention on the Rights of Persons with Disabilities*, adopted 20 December 2006, in force 3 May 2008, 2515 *United Nations Treaty Series* 3.

(Continued)

14. Provides an effective and affordable grievance procedure for those affected by an investment; and
15. Provides effective remedies for those whose rights have been violated or who suffer harm as a result of an investment.

The Guide contains two provisions for integrating a SA system into an IIA.

Sample Provision 1: Creation of SA process

This sample provision (Section 6.6.5) requires that a party state put in place an effective system of laws and regulations for assessing the environmental, social and human rights impact of proposed investments.

The Guide does not prescribe the kind of detailed requirements found in the performance standards of the IFC, ISO 14001 or ISO 26000. Instead, it adopts a more streamlined and customised approach that requires that the standards for the assessment be developed in consultation with all parties potentially affected by them (subsection (2)). Parties may decide that only investments that are substantial or that involve substantial risks will be subject to assessment, while investments by small businesses or in sectors in which investments are unlikely to raise significant environmental, social or human rights issues, such as most services sectors, may be excluded or subject to a less onerous assessment process.

The sample assessment provision envisions that the standards used in the SA will reflect important principles of sustainable development (subsections (1)(a)(i)–(vii)). If parties wish to ensure that there is a mutual understanding of the principles that should underlie the SA system established under this provision, they could include a list of these principles in a similar fashion to the sample provision. Of course, the states negotiating an IIA will have to determine what these principles ought to be in order to best reflect their sustainable development policies and goals. The principles listed in subsections (1)(a)(i)–(vii) are only suggestive examples.

In its non-prescriptive list of sustainable development principles, the Guide sample provision includes the precautionary principle and the polluter pays principle (subsections (1)(a)(iii) and (iv)). The reference to the precautionary principle and the polluter pays principle aims to make clear that the host state can require the investor through the management plan to take measures to internalise the cost of environmental pollution and to protect against environmental harms about which there is scientific uncertainty, but which the host state has reasonable grounds to wish to prevent.

The non-prescriptive list also reflects the need for stakeholders to participate in decision-making (subsection (1)(a)(v)) and for investors to obtain the free, prior and informed consent of indigenous peoples before the investment is approved (subsection

(1)(a)(vi)). Finally, the investment and the assessment process must respect the rights of indigenous peoples recognised by the host state (subsection (1)(a)(vii)).

The IISD model treaty requires that environmental and social impact assessments apply the standards of the party that provides the highest level of protection for environment and human rights. The Guide sample provision 6.6.6 differs in that it requires the parties to determine the appropriate standards for the assessment and the screening criteria in consultation with individuals and communities that will be affected by the standards or their implementation, with the safeguard that these standards cannot be less protective than those of the party that provides the highest degree of protection (subsection (1)(c)).

There are two reasons for adopting this approach. First, consultation with individuals potentially affected by the investments ensures that the standards and screening criteria are appropriate to the type of industry in which the investor is involved as well as to the specific circumstances in the host state.

Second, practical problems arise in requiring the parties to adopt the domestic laws of the state providing the greatest level of protection. For instance, the states may not have in place domestic standards that are relevant to the particular kind of investment that is the subject of the assessment process. In addition, foreign investment may raise different concerns from domestic investment. The process for setting standards outlined in the sample provisions of the Guide ensures that the standards for SA are best adapted to the type of investment that foreign investors are making, as well as to the unique vulnerabilities of the individuals of a party that will be affected by the investment.

Although the sample provisions encourage host states to set standards for the SA in consultation with affected parties, they nonetheless specify that the standards arrived at through the consultative process should not be less protective of the environment or the rights of individuals or groups in the host state than the laws and regulations of the party state providing the highest standards. In other words, a party state should use the best standards available as the starting point for discussions regarding the appropriate standards for the assessment.

One of the challenges for host states associated with the assessment procedure contemplated in the sample provisions is what is frequently called 'ratcheting up'. The SA provisions in the Guide require that the SA process adopted by the parties is no less protective than that provided for in the laws of the party state with the highest standards. Once the host state has compared its regulations with those of other parties, it may find that the new standards it must put in place for foreign investors are higher than existing standards. Foreign investors may be subject to higher standards than those that must be met by domestic investors. The provision in the Guide will thus have the effect of 'ratcheting up' the lower standards of one party to the higher standards of the other.

As discussed earlier, the sample provisions in the Guide may require host states to create a new legal and regulatory framework for SA or expand existing domestic systems. This may be onerous for some because of limited resources or lack of suitable training.

6.6.5 Sample provision: standards for sustainability assessment of investments

Standards for Sustainability Assessment of Investments

1. Recognising the right of each Party to establish its own level of domestic environmental protection and its own policies and priorities in regard to sustainable development, each Party shall establish laws and regulations to create an effective and efficient system for sustainability assessment of all foreign investments in the Party by an investor of the other Party. These laws and regulations will incorporate standards in accordance with the Party's national and international obligations to promote sustainable development, including the protection of the human and natural environment, human health, the protection and promotion of human and labour rights, and the recognition and promotion of the rights of indigenous peoples.

   a. The standards must take into account:

      i. The promotion of sustainable development;

      ii. The need to respect national and international human rights, labour rights, the rights of indigenous peoples and environmental standards consistent with a Party's international obligations under treaty and customary international law;

      iii. The precautionary principle;

      iv. The principle that the polluter should bear the costs of pollution;

      v. The requirement that affected communities should fully participate in decisions regarding aspects of the investment that could potentially affect them;

      vi. The requirement that indigenous peoples give their free, prior and informed consent to the investment on issues that could potentially affect them;

      vii. The promotion of effective environmental, social and human rights performance of investors through the effective integration of risk prevention and mitigation strategies in the investor's management systems; and

      viii. Respect for and promotion of the dignity, human rights, cultures and livelihoods of indigenous peoples as recognised in the national law of the host state and international law, and other international instruments including but not limited to the *UN Declaration on the Rights of Indigenous Peoples* and ILO *Convention (No. 169) concerning Indigenous and Tribal Peoples in Independent Countries*, 1989.

   b. These standards must include screening criteria for determining the appropriate scope of the pre-establishment environmental, social and human rights impact assessment required under [Guide sample provision (Pre-Establishment

Sustainability Assessment Process)], including what investments are subject to review. The criteria will take into account factors including: the size of the investment; the nature of the investment and its potential for harming the environment or infringing the health, human and labour rights of persons of the Party or the rights of indigenous peoples within the territory of the Party; and the standards articulated in subsections (1)(a)(i)–(vii) above.

c. The standards and criteria established in accordance with this section shall not provide less protection than those applied by the Party that provides the highest degree of protection.

2. Before establishing the standards referred to in section 1, a Party shall consult with all persons of the Party potentially affected by the standards or their implementation and take into account the feedback from such persons.

3. The consultation process referred to in section 2 must be open, transparent and accessible to the public and to investors of the other Party and any other person of the Party affected by the standards and criteria.

Sample Provision 2: Requirement to carry out a SA before the investment is established

Subsection 1 of this sample provision (Provision 6.6.6) requires that investors carry out a SA, and subsection 2 ensures that the host state reviews this assessment. Section 3 requires that the host state and the investor agree to a management plan for implementing the assessment results. The plan must include an effective system for monitoring ongoing compliance of the investment. The plan must provide the public with access to the recommendations in the assessment and review, and access to the results of ongoing monitoring processes (Section 4 in sample provision 6.6.6). The sustainability assessment, review and management plan must all be completed before the host state approves the investment.

This sample provision in the Guide seeks to improve on the IISD model agreement[104] in various respects. The IISD model agreement does not require the host state to review the SA, nor does it require that a management plan be formulated to ensure that the investment complies with good environmental and social practices throughout the life of the investment. The inclusion of these requirements in the Guide orients the party states, investors and affected parties towards practical solutions for avoiding or mitigating potential harms.

6.6.6 Sample provision: pre-establishment sustainability assessment process

Pre-establishment Sustainability Assessment Process

Before a Party approves an investment in that Party by an investor of the other Party, the following must occur.

104 IISD model treaty, Art. 21.

1. Where required under the standards and screening criteria determined under [Guide sample provision 6.6.5 (Standards for sustainability assessment of investments)], the investor or its investment must conduct a sustainability assessment of the proposed investment in accordance with the laws and regulations established in accordance with that article.
2. The Party approving the investment shall review the assessment.
3. The investor and the investment and the Party approving the investment shall agree on a management plan in relation to the investment that is in accordance with the assessment as reviewed by the Party, and that provides steps to ensure that the investment achieves the assessment standards determined under [Guide sample provision 6.6.5 (Standards for sustainability assessment of investments)] and that it avoids, minimises, mitigates or compensates for adverse impacts of the investment on workers, affected communities and the environment.
4. Each Party shall make sustainability assessments, reviews and management plans relating to investments in its territory public and accessible to persons in the Party affected by them.

6.6.7 Technical assistance

In order to make it more feasible for host states to implement the SA scheme in the sample provisions, the Guide provides an example of a provision on technical assistance that requires parties to provide each other with the information necessary for them to comply with their obligations.[105] This provision also requires the parties to agree on technical and financial assistance to help developing country parties to create and implement the assessment framework. These provisions are based on the idea that the relationship between the parties is a partnership aimed at facilitating sustainable development in both states. It also recognises that the parties have common but differentiated responsibilities as a result of their different levels of development and that technical assistance should reflect these differences.

A variety of other sample provisions throughout the Guide are designed to ensure the effectiveness of the assessment process. One sample provision creates a grievance procedure under which affected individuals and groups may complain about actions by an investor that harms their interests.[106] The Guide also includes a sample provision that establishes a procedure for securing compliance with the management plan created through the assessment process.[107] Finally, another sample provision contemplates that in some circumstances of persistent non-compliance, damages or an order for compliance may be sought in the domestic courts of the host state or the investor's home state.[108]

---

105 See Section 8.2 (Technical assistance).

106 See Section 6.15 (Grievance procedure and other measures to enforce the management plan produced in the sustainability assessment).

107 See Section 6.15 (Grievance procedure and other measures to enforce the management plan produced in the sustainability assessment).

108 See Section 6.16 (Civil liability of investors).

6.7 Investor obligation to comply with the laws of the host state

Cross references

It is fundamentally important to all states that foreign investors operating in their territories comply with the requirements of their domestic laws. Otherwise, the achievement of state regulatory goals will be undermined. In addition, the principles of sustainable development require that investors comply with the domestic laws and regulations enacted by host states to protect the environment, human rights, labour rights and rights of indigenous peoples of the states in which they operate. IIA provisions can encourage compliance with domestic law by imposing requirements on foreign investors to do so. As discussed in Section 4.5 (Scope of application), many IIAs limit the application of the agreement to investments made in accordance with host state law. This section addresses obligations of investors to comply with host state law generally.

6.7.1 IIA practice

The *OECD Guidelines for Multinational Enterprises* state that compliance with the domestic laws of the states in which they operate is the first obligation of transnational corporations.[109] UNCTAD, in its *Investment Policy Framework for Sustainable Development*, has suggested that states could include a provision in their IIAs requiring investors to comply with domestic law at the entry and post-entry stages of investment.[110]

Some investment treaties incorporate requirements to comply with domestic law. For example, the COMESA Investment Agreement includes a provision requiring COMESA investors to comply with the domestic law of the host state.[111] The IISD model treaty incorporates a similar obligation, and also requires investors to strive to contribute to the host state and local government's development goals.[112] However, most IIAs, such as the Canadian model FIPA, the 2012 US model BIT, the UK model IPPA and the Indian model BIPPA, contain no such provision.

---

109 OECD (2011), 'The OECD Guidelines for Multinational Enterprises', 25 May ; OECD Declaration on International Investment and Multinational Enterprises (Ministerial Meeting) at 15.

110 UNCTAD (2012), *Investment Policy Framework for Sustainable Development*, United Nations, New York and Geneva, at 58.

111 COMESA Investment Agreement (2007), Art. 13.

112 IISD model treaty, Art. 11.

Box 6.6 Summary of options for obligation on investors to comply with the laws of the host state

1. No obligation on investors to comply with domestic law
2. Incorporate into an IIA an obligation on investors to comply with domestic law

6.7.2 Discussion of options

Failure by foreign investors to comply with domestic law challenges state governance and sovereignty[113] and can undermine the rule of law. There are important advantages for host states that wish to pursue sustainable development in incorporating a clear obligation into an IIA requiring investors to comply with domestic laws and regulations, including laws and regulations related to environmental protection, human rights, labour rights and indigenous peoples' rights.

Clarifies expectations and complements domestic law: A treaty obligation to comply with domestic law clarifies the expectations on investors and raises the obligation to the international level. It thus balances the requirement to obey the laws of the host state with investor protections in the IIA.[114]

Access to treaty-based compliance mechanisms: Host states may face difficulties in regulating the environmental, social and human rights impacts of investors' activities. Incorporating the investor's obligations to comply with domestic law into an IIA creates a straightforward way to use a menu of treaty-based enforcement options beyond the usual domestic mechanisms that may be available to the host state. The sample provisions of the Guide provide options for additional enforcement mechanisms, such as civil liability for investors who violate treaty obligations in both the host state and the investor's home state.[115] They also include the possibility for the host state to seek relief from the investor's non-compliance by way of counterclaim in any investor–state arbitration initiated by the investor.[116]

6.7.3 Discussion of sample provision

Drawing on both the COMESA Investment Agreement and the IISD model treaty,[117] the Guide sample provision reiterates the general obligation of investors to comply with domestic law, but also makes specific reference to human rights, labour rights, the rights of indigenous peoples and environmental laws, regulations and standards. This provision simply requires that all legal obligations be complied with. It may be

113 I Brownlie (2003), *Principles of Public International Law*, 6th ed., Oxford University Press, Oxford, at 106.

114 UNCTAD (2012), *Investment Policy Framework for Sustainable Development*, op. cit., at 7, 11, 12, 39, 58.

115 See Section 6.16 (Civil liability of investors).

116 See Sections 6.17 (Counterclaims by states in investor–state arbitrations) and 7.1.7 (Sample provisions: investor–state dispute settlement, Article [W] (Counterclaims)).

117 COMESA Investment Agreement (2007), Art. 13; IISD model treaty, Art. 11(A).

that an investor–state tribunal hearing a state counterclaim alleging that an investor had not complied with this obligation would not grant relief for every minor instance of non-compliance. A tribunal might establish some threshold of significance before it would award damages.

The sample provision includes an obligation on investors to orient their policies and practices so as to support and contribute to the development objectives of the state in which they operate.[118] In light of the inherently broad and uncertain content of development objectives, it must be recognised that this latter obligation is largely aspirational.

6.7.4 Sample provision: obligation to comply with the laws of the host state

Obligation to Comply with the Laws of the Host State

1. Investors of a Party and their investments are subject to and shall respect the laws and regulations of the other Party, including, but not limited to its laws, regulations and standards for the protection of human rights, labour rights, the rights of indigenous peoples and the environment, and they shall not be complicit or assist in the violation of such rights by others in the other Party, including by public authorities or during civil strife.
2. Investors of a Party and their investments shall strive, through their management policies and practices, to contribute to the development objectives of the other Party and of sub-national levels of government that govern the area where the investment is located.

6.8 Investor obligation to respect internationally recognised human rights and undertake human rights due diligence

Cross references

118 See IISD model treaty, Art. 11(C) for the equivalent provision.

The protection of human rights is a fundamental aspect of sustainable development, as discussed in Section 2.3 of the Guide.[119] An IIA that purports to support sustainable development must therefore support the protection of the human rights of individuals and communities affected by investment.

6.8.1 The impacts of foreign investment

The investment activities of investors may have both negative and positive impacts on the human rights of individuals in the host state. On the positive side, increased investment leads to economic growth and can provide a host state with economic resources to put in place programmes to fulfil human rights, particularly economic, social and cultural rights. Increased revenues from foreign investment can provide host states with resources to pay for primary, secondary and tertiary education and to create new jobs, for example.

On the negative side, investment does not, on its own, ensure that the human rights of individuals and communities are protected. The individuals most likely to suffer direct impacts of the foreign investment on their human rights (including labour rights and the rights of indigenous peoples) are local employees of the investor and the people in the communities living in and around the investment, as well of those who might be affected by environmental pollution to water sources, air and land that may spread beyond the immediate area of the investment site.

Not all investments will have the same impact on human rights. Such impacts will differ depending on the nature and size of the business, the location of the proposed investment and the social, political, legal and ecological context of its operations. For example, the risk of human rights impacts will be different and less serious in connection with the establishment of a bank in an urban centre than a gold mine or other extractive venture located on indigenous land or in an ecologically sensitive area.

For investment to contribute to sustainable development, and in particular to the protection of human rights, it must be effectively regulated to ensure that foreign investor activity does not violate human rights within the host state. Investment treaties can constrain the ability of states to regulate in the public interest, including laws and regulations aimed at protecting and promoting respect for human rights.[120] IIAs can be drafted to minimise this constraining effect as discussed below.

---

119 See Section 2.3 (Links between foreign investment and sustainable development).

120 UNHRC (2008), 'Protect Respect and Remedy', op. cit., at paras. 34–6. See also, for example, D Schneiderman (2000), 'Investment Rules and the New Constitutionalism', 25 *Law and Social Inquiry* 757 at 758; M Sornarajah (2010), *The International Law of Foreign Investment*, 3d ed., Cambridge University Press, Cambridge, at 227–9. See also K Miles (2010), 'International Investment Law: Origins, Imperialism and Conceptualizing the Environment', 21 *Colorado Journal of International Environmental Law and Policy* 1 at 40, 47, discussing the restraint on state capacity to regulate with respect to the environment.

6.8.2 The UN Guiding Principles on Business and Human Rights

The United Nations Special Representative of the Secretary-General on the Issue of Human Rights and Transnational Corporations and Other Business Enterprises (SRSG) has developed Guiding Principles on Business and Human Rights.[121] These principles clarify the international human rights obligation of states to exercise due diligence to protect individuals from violations of human rights caused by private actors, including investors. This is known as the obligation to *protect*. The Guiding Principles also recognise that business actors have a responsibility to respect human rights. The principles provide guidance for corporations on the substance and operational aspects of this responsibility. The Guiding Principles acknowledge that business activity can potentially affect 'virtually the entire spectrum of internationally-recognised human rights'. Business actors therefore have a responsibility to respect *all* human rights.[122]

The UN Human Rights Council unanimously endorsed the Guiding Principles in June 2011.[123] The latter have also been well received by the global business community.[124] These core principles on the responsibility to respect human rights have also been reiterated in the *OECD Guidelines for Multinational Enterprises*[125] and the ISO 26000 standards.[126] Both these instruments provide voluntary standards for socially responsible business behaviour. UNCTAD has also recognised these principles as standards of responsible investment, to which governments should encourage adherence.[127] The key principles relevant for investment are set out in Box 6.7. The rationale for a due diligence process that businesses should follow in relation to human rights is set out in Box 6.8.

Box 6.7 *Guiding Principles on Business and Human Rights:* Implementing the United Nations 'Protect, Respect and Remedy' framework

UN Doc. A/HRC/17/31 (2011)

II. The corporate responsibility to respect human rights

A. Foundational principles

Principle 11. Business enterprises should respect human rights. This means that they should avoid infringing on the human rights of others and should address adverse human rights impacts with which they are involved.

(Continued)

121 UN Guiding Principles on Business and Human Rights, op. cit.

122 Ibid. at Principle 12, commentary.

123 Human Rights and Transnational Corporations and Other Business Enterprises, UNHRC, 17th Sess, UN Doc A/HRC/17/L.17/Rev.1 (2011).

124 See, for example, the 'IOE Statement', op. cit. See also the range of letters from business actors endorsing the Guiding Principles, including 'Coca-Cola Statement', op. cit., and 'Total Statement', op. cit.

125 *OECD Guidelines*, op. cit.

126 ISO 26000:2010.

127 UNCTAD (2012), *Investment Policy Framework for Sustainable Development*, op. cit., at 29.

(Continued)

Principle 12. The responsibility of business enterprises to respect human rights refers to internationally recognized human rights – understood, at a minimum, as those expressed in the International Bill of Human Rights and the principles concerning fundamental rights set out in the International Labour Organization's Declaration on Fundamental Principles and Rights at Work.

Principle 13. The responsibility to respect human rights requires that business enterprises:

a. Avoid causing or contributing to adverse human rights impacts through their own activities, and address such impacts when they occur;

b. Seek to prevent or mitigate adverse human rights impacts that are directly linked to their operations, products or services by their business relationships, even if they have not contributed to those impacts.

Principle 14. The responsibility of business enterprises to respect human rights applies to all enterprises regardless of their size, sector, operational context, ownership and structure. Nevertheless, the scale and complexity of the means through which enterprises meet that responsibility may vary according to these factors and with the severity of the enterprise's adverse human rights impacts.

Principle 15. In order to meet their responsibility to respect human rights, business enterprises should have in place policies and processes appropriate to their size and circumstances, including:

a. A policy commitment to meet their responsibility to respect human rights;

b. A human rights due-diligence process to identify, prevent, mitigate and account for how they address their impacts on human rights;

c. Processes to enable the remediation of any adverse human rights impacts they cause or to which they contribute.

Box 6.8 What is human rights due diligence and why is it important?

- *Definition*. Due diligence refers to exhaustive processes undertaken by corporations or financial institutions, for example, when preparing a business transaction such as a merger or acquisition or when determining whether to lend money to a business entity for a specific project.
- *Purpose*. The aim of the due diligence process is:

  a. To ensure that the corporation has all of the information necessary to properly understand the full range potential liabilities of the entity it proposes to buy or to merge with;

(Continued)

(Continued)

b. To ensure that a financial institution providing a loan to a corporation is fully apprised of all potential liabilities regarding the project for which the loan is being sought;[128] and

c. To ensure that corporations and financial institutions discharge their legal responsibilities to fully assess the risk of the merger, acquisition or loan, as the case may be. Due diligence, therefore, has a legal dimension since it 'is part of the process of dealing with legal liability and so has to meet the standards set up in law to discharge a duty of care'.[129]

- *Human rights due diligence for the state.* States have an obligation under international human rights law to exercise due diligence to protect the human rights of individuals from the acts of private parties that may violate such rights.[130]
- *Human rights due diligence for business actors.* This is a new concept. A human rights due diligence process does not assess the risks of an investment to the corporation, but rather requires a corporation to fully apprise itself of the potential adverse impacts of its presence and activities on the human rights of individuals and communities in the country in which it plans to invest or in which it is already in the process of investing. It also requires the corporation to take steps to prevent, avoid and, if necessary, mitigate such impacts and report on the effectiveness of such measures.
- *Why human rights due diligence is important.*

a. *Puts human rights on the 'corporate radar'.* A duty to engage in human rights due diligence can help to internalise 'concerns over human rights impacts into corporate psyche and culture [and] [t]he due diligence process then allows this concern to be put into operation'.[131]

b. *Shows corporations take their duty to protect human rights seriously.* Human rights due diligence is also one of the means by which corporate actors can demonstrate that they are taking their obligation to respect human rights seriously.

c. *Limits legal liability of corporations.* Undertaking due diligence may help to mitigate potential legal liability. According to the SRSG:

> Conducting appropriate human rights due diligence should help business enterprises address the risk of legal claims against them by showing that they took every reasonable step to avoid involvement with an alleged human rights abuse. However, business enterprises conducting such due diligence should not assume that, by itself, this

(Continued)

128 P Muchlinski (2012), 'Implementing the New UN Corporate Human Rights Framework: Implications for Corporate Law, Governance, and Regulation', 22 *Business Ethics Quarterly* 145 at 156.

129 Ibid. at 157.

130 *Velásquez Rodriguez v. Honduras*, op. cit., at paras 172, 176.

131 Muchlinski, op. cit., at 156.

(Continued)

will automatically and fully absolve them from liability for causing or contributing to human rights abuses.[132]

d. *Human rights due diligence is a risk prevention tool.* Where a corporation engages in a robust human rights due diligence process, it should be possible to prevent most human rights abuses and mitigate adverse impacts that cannot be avoided or prevented. It may also identify situations in which the investment should not proceed.

- *Putting human rights due diligence into practice:* Human rights due diligence is defined in the Guiding Principles as a process in which corporations 'identify, prevent, mitigate and account for how they address their adverse human rights impacts', and it requires the corporation to determine both actual and potential human rights impacts, integrate and act on its findings, track responses and report on how the impacts are to be addressed.[133] Guiding Principle 17 states that:

  Human rights due diligence:

  a. Should cover adverse human rights impacts that the business enterprise may cause or contribute to through its own activities, or which may be directly linked to its operations, products or services by its business relationships;

  b. Will vary in complexity with the size of the business enterprise, the risk of severe human rights impacts, and the nature and context of its operations;

  c. Should be ongoing, recognizing that the human rights risks may change over time as the business enterprise's operations and operating context evolve.[134]

- *Due diligence includes consultation with, and involvement of, those affected by the investment.* The human rights due diligence process outlined in the Guiding Principles includes consultation with indigenous and other communities as well as other stakeholders in a manner that allows for their effective participation in such consultation. Where such consultation is not possible, corporations are encouraged to consult with human rights non-governmental organisations.[135]

The Guiding Principles lay out in Principles 17–21 the minimum requirements for such a due diligence process for a business:

- It must be initiated at the earliest possible stage of the project and be ongoing.
- It should include a human rights impact assessment (HRIA):[136]
  - The process should have input from an internal human rights expert or an external independent expert,

132 UN Guiding Principles on Business and Human Rights, op. cit., at Principle 17, commentary.

133 Ibid., at Principle 17.

134 Ibid.

135 Ibid., at Principle 18, commentary.

136 See Section 6.6 (Sustainability assessments).

  - The business should engage in 'meaningful consultation' with affected stakeholders, including indigenous and other communities and individuals; this means that the consultation should take into account language and other barriers to seeking such input.[137]
- The findings of the HRIA should be integrated into the business's management processes.
- The business must take appropriate action to prevent and/or mitigate adverse impacts. This may include ending relationships with contractors or suppliers.[138]
- The business must 'track the effectiveness of their response' to any potential or actual adverse impacts by drawing on internal and external feedback.[139]
- The business should report accurately and accessibly on how it addresses its human rights impacts, providing sufficient information to assess the adequacy of its response without posing risks to stakeholders or compromising confidential commercial information.[140]
- The business should provide or assist in providing remediation to victims, where the due diligence process reveals that the business has caused or contributed to adverse human rights impacts.[141]

The responsibility of investors to respect human rights as set out in the Guiding Principles is not legally binding since it has not been incorporated into a treaty or into the domestic laws of states. This means that the corporate responsibilities to respect human rights, engage in human rights due diligence and to provide remediation for adverse human rights impacts remain voluntary duties.

6.8.3 IIA practice

No existing IIA includes an obligation on investors to respect human rights and/or to engage in a process of human rights due diligence. However, a few IIAs do incorporate language on human rights. For example, the preamble of the draft Norwegian APPI, which has now been shelved,[142] reaffirms the parties' commitments to human rights and fundamental freedoms and references the principles set out in the UN Charter and the Universal Declaration of Human Rights.[143] In the EU–Russia Cooperation and Partnership Agreement, the parties commit in the body of the treaty to engage in regular political dialogue to ensure that they 'endeavour to cooperate on matters pertaining to the observance of the principles of democracy and human rights' and consult if necessary on implementation of such principles.[144]

---

137 UN Guiding Principles on Business and Human Rights, op. cit., at Principle 18, commentary.

138 Ibid., at Principle 19, commentary.

139 Ibid., at Principle 20, commentary.

140 Ibid., at Principle 21, commentary.

141 Ibid., at Principle 22, commentary.

142 See draft Norwegian APPI.

143 Draft Norwegian APPI, preamble. See also the European Free Trade Association–Singapore Free Trade Agreement, signed 26 June 2002, in force 1 January 2003, preamble.

144 European Union–Russia, Agreement on Partnership and Cooperation between the European Communities and the Russian Federation, signed 24 June 1994, in force 1 December 1997, Art. 6.

More recently, some states have begun to incorporate provisions into IIAs that deal with corporate social responsibility (CSR) and make reference to human rights or to standards that address human rights.[145] The Canada–Colombia FTA, for example, includes a non-binding recommendation that party states encourage foreign investors to 'voluntarily incorporate internationally recognized standards of corporate social responsibility in their internal policies' relating to human rights, labour rights, environmental issues, anti-corruption and community relations.[146] A similar provision can be found in the Canada–Peru FTA.[147] The draft Norwegian APPI includes an obligation on party states 'to encourage investors to conduct their investment activities in compliance with the OECD Guidelines for Multinational Enterprises and to participate in the United Nations Global Compact'.[148] Both the OECD Guidelines[149] and the Global Compact[150] are voluntary codes of conduct establishing ethical rules for corporate behaviour.

UNCTAD notes that CSR standards are increasingly being taken into account in states' investment policies. It suggests that these policies should encourage investors to adopt and comply with international corporate social responsibility standards, and that some states may wish to incorporate these standards, including the Guiding Principles on Business and Human Rights, into domestic laws and regulations.[151]

Box 6.9 Summary of options for investor obligation to respect human rights and undertake human rights due diligence

1. *Do not require foreign investors or their investments to respect human rights and undertake human rights due diligence prior to approving them*
2. *Use existing domestic laws to regulate the human rights impacts of investors and their investments*
3. *Incorporate into domestic law an obligation on investors to respect human rights and engage in human rights due diligence*
4. *Incorporate a provision in an IIA recommending that states encourage their investors to include internationally recognised CSR standards in their corporate policies*
5. *Integrate into IIAs an obligation on investors to respect human rights and engage in human rights due diligence*

145 J Hepburn and V Kuuya (2011), 'Corporate Social Responsibility and Investment Treaties', in Cordonier Segger et al., op. cit., 589 at 599ff.
146 Canada–Colombia FTA (2008), Art. 816.
147 Canada–Peru FTA (2008), Art. 810.
148 Draft Norwegian APPI, Art. 32.
149 OECD *Guidelines*, op. cit.
150 *UN Global Compact*, available at: www.unglobalcompact.org (accessed 8 January 2013).
151 UNCTAD (2012), *Investment Policy Framework for Sustainable Development*, op. cit., at 29.

6.8.4 Discussion of options

States will have to determine the most appropriate course of action for dealing with investor activities that may have adverse human rights impacts, taking into consideration the costs and benefits of the options outlined below.

1. *Do not require foreign investors or their investments to respect human rights and undertake human rights due diligence prior to approving them*

It is costly to develop a regulatory framework: States may decide, for instance, not to take any steps to require investors and their foreign investments to respect human rights and to undertake human rights due diligence prior to approval of the investment. This course of action has the advantage of not requiring the outlay of resources to develop and enforce a regulatory framework to ensure that businesses engage in a comprehensive human rights due diligence process, either as a part of a broader sustainability assessment or as a free-standing process. This will keep costs lower both for investors and for the host state from the pre-establishment phase throughout the life cycle of the investment.

Leaving investors to self-regulate does not protect human rights: Human rights due diligence is not currently required by most host states and only some investors in a few industries are beginning to assess stakeholder concerns as part of an overall social impact assessment.[152] This means that investors that currently carry out such assessments can pick and choose the standards that they apply. Experience has shown that self-regulation has failed to prevent business actors, in any consistent way, from violating human rights or becoming complicit in such violations.[153]

Lack of information can result in a failure to prevent and mitigate adverse human rights impacts: Where the investor fails to undertake human rights due diligence, neither the host state nor the investor will have a clear idea of the potential human rights impacts of the investment. In particular, without consultation of affected individuals and communities, the specific human rights impacts will be difficult to determine. This will make it challenging for the state and the investor to develop appropriate systems to prevent and mitigate adverse human rights impacts. The investor will also have no means to demonstrate that it and its investment are respecting human rights.

Human rights violations have social and financial costs: When deciding whether or not to regulate the human rights impacts of investor activity, states may wish to consider the less obvious social and financial costs of failing to require investors to engage in human rights due diligence.

---

152 R Davis and D M Franks, 'The Costs of Conflict with Local Communities in the Extractive Industry', in D Brereton, D Pesce and X Abogabir (eds), *Proceedings of the First International Seminar on Social Responsibility in Mining*, Santiago, Chile, 19–21 October 2011, at 5 (copy of full paper on file with the authors).

153 P Simons (2004), 'Corporate Voluntarism and Human Rights: The Adequacy and Effectiveness of Voluntary Self-Regulation Regimes', 59 *Relations industrielles/Industrial Relations* 101; P Simons and A Macklin (2013 forthcoming), *The Governance Gap: Extractive Industries, Human Rights, and the Home State Advantage*, Routledge London, at Chapter 3.

- *Social costs*. Abuses of human rights by investors can lead to increased discrimination, marginalisation of vulnerable populations, increased poverty[154] and civil unrest. In the most serious cases, human rights abuses can lead to deaths and conflict. In doing so, they undermine state goals of sustainable development and even economic development.
- *Impacts on investment*. Blume and Voigt's study of the economic effects of human rights found that strong human rights protections are beneficial for economic growth and welfare; they can influence productivity and the development of human capital.[155] States with robust human rights protections attract more investment than states with weak records of protecting human rights.[156] Therefore, host states that fail to protect human rights may lose foreign investment to other states that have stronger regulatory protection of human rights, undermining their ability to meet both their economic development and sustainable development goals.

States may be in breach of their human rights obligations: Finally, states have an obligation under international human rights law to protect human rights. This means they must take steps through legislative and other measures to ensure that investors do not violate the human rights of individuals and groups, consistent with the state's international human rights obligations. The SRSG notes in the *Guiding Principles* that '[w]hile States generally have discretion in deciding upon these steps, they should consider the full range of permissible preventative and remedial measures, including policies, legislation, regulations and adjudication'.[157] Requiring human rights due diligence by corporations is an important means to accomplish this end. The responsibility of businesses to conduct human rights due diligence as articulated in the Guiding Principles was unanimously endorsed by the UN Human Rights Council.[158] Therefore, by failing to require investors to engage in a robust due diligence process consistent with the nature, scope and location of the investment, states could be found to be in breach of their obligations by international human rights tribunals.

2. *Use existing law to regulate the human rights impact of investors and their investments*

States that have a robust regulatory system in place to protect the human rights of individuals and communities from the human rights impacts of foreign investors may not wish to put further resources into developing new laws and regulations on this issue. However, existing domestic laws are unlikely to include the requirement for investors to engage in human rights due diligence, since this is a new concept

154 M Sepúlveda and C Nyst (2012), 'The Human Rights Approach to Social Protection', Ministry for Foreign Affairs of Finland, available at: www.ohchr.org/Documents/Issues/EPoverty/HumanRightsApproachToSocialProtection.pdf, at 17.

155 L Blume and S Voigt (2004), 'The Economic Effects of Human Rights', University of Kassel Working Paper 66/04, University of Kassel, Kassel, at 3, 30, 37.

156 Ibid. at 35.

157 UN Guiding Principles on Business and Human Rights, op. cit., at Principle 1, commentary.

158 Human Rights and Transnational Corporations and Other Business Enterprises, UNHRC, op.cit.

developed and disseminated by the SRSG. The main disadvantages of not specifically requiring foreign investors to engage in such a due diligence process prior to investment are discussed in the preceding subsection. Additionally, even where good laws and regulations exist to protect human rights, states may still encounter challenges in enforcing such laws against foreign investors. All states face difficulties in regulating the conduct of transnational corporations.[159] These entities can restructure themselves or transfer assets to another jurisdiction in order to avoid liability under domestic law.

3. *Incorporate into domestic law an obligation on investors to respect human rights and engage in human rights due diligence*

Given the novelty of the concept of the business responsibility to respect human rights and engage in human rights due diligence, the impacts of incorporating such an obligation into domestic law are unknown. However, it is possible to identify some potential problems as well as benefits.

It is costly to develop a regulatory framework: Incorporating into domestic law a requirement on investors to respect human rights and to engage in human rights due diligence could be burdensome for host states. Both financial and human resources would have to be dedicated to developing the regulatory framework and institutions to facilitate and monitor such a process. While some industries, such as those in the extractive sector, are in the process of operationalising the requirements of the Guiding Principles, the concept of human rights due diligence is in its infancy and the specific modalities of such a process have not yet been fully developed. A further important point is that current practice of human rights impact assessment consists of privately undertaken assessments that are not publicly reported. There are few examples of human rights impact assessments of investments that have been publicly released.[160]

States will need to determine the appropriate human rights for any due diligence process based on their international obligations: In developing an appropriate regulatory framework, states will need to consider the range of human rights that investors will have to take into account in their due diligence process in light of the nature, size, location and context of the investment. As mentioned above, states have international human rights obligations to take steps to *protect* individuals from violations of human rights perpetrated by private actors, including investors. States will therefore have to ensure that the due diligence requirements reflect their international obligations. The United Nations core human rights treaties[161] include:

---

159 S Marks (2003), 'Empire's Law', 10 *Indiana Journal of Global Legal Studies* 449 at 461.

160 See, for example, the human rights impact assessment undertaken by a consultant for Goldcorp in relation to the controversial Marlin mine in Guatemala: On Common Ground Consultants Inc. (2010), 'Human Rights Assessment of Goldcorp's Marlin Mine', available at: www.hria-guatemala.com/en/MarlinHumanRights.htm (accessed 8 January 2013).

161 This excludes the optional protocols. See OHCHR, 'The Core International Human Rights Instruments and their Monitoring Bodies', available at: www2.ohchr.org/english/law/index.htm#core (accessed 8 January 2013).

- *International Convention on the Elimination of All Forms of Racial Discrimination* 1965 (ICERD);
- *International Covenant on Civil and Political Rights* 1966 (ICCPR);
- *International Covenant on Economic Social and Cultural Rights* 1966 (ICESCR);
- *Convention on the Elimination of All Forms of Discrimination against Women* 1979 (CEDAW);
- *Convention against Torture and Other Cruel, Inhuman or Degrading Treatment and Punishment* 1984 (CAT);
- *Convention on the Rights of the Child* 1989 (CRC);
- *International Convention on the Protection of the Rights of Migrant Workers and Their Families* 1990 (ICRMW);
- *International Convention for the Protection of All Persons from Enforced Disappearance* 2006 (CPED); and
- *Convention on the Rights of Persons with Disabilities* 2006 (CRPD).

Only 12 Commonwealth member countries have ratified the ICRMW and only two have ratified the CPED. However, 28 Commonwealth member countries have ratified the CRPD, and an overwhelming majority of Commonwealth member countries have ratified the other core treaties and therefore have obligations under them.

The Declaration on the Rights of Indigenous Peoples (UNDRIP) provides the most comprehensive articulation of indigenous peoples' rights and although it is a non-binding declaration, it has been endorsed by the UN General Assembly, including by 38 Commonwealth countries. In addition, some of the rights set out in the UNDRIP are entrenched in customary international law. These include the duty to consult indigenous peoples[162] and the obligation to obtain the free, prior and informed consent of indigenous peoples in three key situations:

- Where a proposal contemplates the removal of indigenous communities from their lands and territories;[163]
- Where a state is considering storing or disposing of hazardous waste on indigenous territory;[164] and

162 P Simons and L Collins (2010), 'Participatory Rights in the Ontario Mining Sector: An International Human Rights Perspective', 6 *McGill International Journal of Sustainable Development Law and Policy* 177 at 193–4.

163 A Perrault, K Herbertson and O J Lynch (2007), 'Partnerships for Success in Protected Areas: The Public Interest and Local Community Rights to Prior Informed Consent (PIC)', 19 *Georgetown International Environmental Law* Review 475 at 491; J Anaya (2005), 'Indigenous Peoples' Participatory Rights in Relation to Decisions about Natural Resource Extraction: The More Fundamental Issue of What Rights Indigenous Peoples Have in Lands and Resources', 22 *Arizona Journal of International and Comparative Law* 7 at 17.

164 Perrault et al., op. cit., at 491. *Declaration on the Rights of Indigenous Peoples*, GA Res 61/295, UNGAOR, 2007, 61st Sess, UN Doc A/ RES/61/295 (2007) Art. 29 (2): 'States shall take effective measures to ensure that no storage or disposal of hazardous materials shall take place in the lands or territories of indigenous peoples without their free, prior and informed consent'.

- According to a recent decision of the Inter-American Court on Human Rights, where large-scale projects may have a significant impact within indigenous territory.[165]

Where states wish to go beyond their customary international law obligations and incorporate into domestic law a general right of indigenous peoples to free, prior and informed consent, each state will have to consider the appropriate legislative, administrative and policy measures necessary to do so. This could include constitutional, legislative and regulatory amendments, as well as the establishment of institutions to ensure that indigenous title can be registered if necessary.

It could deter investment: There is a possibility that incorporating into domestic law an obligation on investors to respect human rights and engage in human rights due diligence could deter investment for a number of reasons. Investors may feel that it will be too costly to develop the internal management, tracking, response and reporting requirements. Investors may also be concerned that a legal obligation to engage in a human rights due diligence process may expose them to the risk of further legal liability. The requirement on investors to publicly undertake due diligence, including a human rights impact assessment, and report on how they are addressing any harmful human rights impacts of the investment may put into the public domain information about conduct that could be perceived by the investor to expose them to liability. Transnational human rights claims brought against investors in their home state for human rights abuses allegedly committed in the host state are becoming more frequent, as are civil actions brought in the host state. However, these suits have generally dealt with only the most egregious violations of human rights or environmental abuse.[166] Finally, investors may be reluctant to engage in human rights due diligence where such a process could also expose abusive practices by the host state.

Domestic laws can be difficult to enforce against a foreign investor: As discussed above, even where a state introduces laws and regulations requiring investors to respect human rights and engage in human rights due diligence, it may face considerable difficulties enforcing them against foreign investors.

Risk of investor challenge under an IIA: Another problem in introducing such an obligation into domestic law is the potential for investors to challenge such measures

165 *Case of the Saramaka People v. Suriname* (Preliminary Objections, Merits, Reparations, and Costs), (2007) Inter-American Commission on Human Rights, No. 172/5 at para. 134.

166 See, for example, *Recherches Internationales Quebec v. Cambior Inc.* [1998] QJ no 2554 (QL) (Qc Sup Ct). That case involved a claim concerning the rupture of Cambior's gold mine dam releasing 'some 2.3 billion litres of liquid containing cyanide, heavy metals and other pollutants spilled into two rivers, one of which is Guyana's main waterway'. See also *Association canadienne contre l'impunité (ACCI) c Anvil Mining Ltd*, 2011 QCCA 1035, in which the plaintiffs claimed that Anvil Mining was complicit in egregious violations of human rights perpetrated by the Congolese military in suppressing an uprising in the port town of Kilwa. Anvil provided logistical support to the troops, including transport, and the plaintiffs allege that the company also transported civilians to places where they were executed.

under an existing IIA as a violation of the FET provisions. A number of investment tribunals have defined FET obligations expansively to the effect that the introduction or amendment of domestic laws that are inconsistent with the reasonable expectations of investors is considered a breach of the fair and equitable treatment obligation.[167] If the investor were successful in an investor–state arbitration claim, the state would be required to pay compensation. The magnitude of this risk will depend on the scope and nature of the obligations in the treaty.

Implements the state's duty to protect human rights and sets a clear standard for investor behaviour: An advantage of incorporating such a requirement into domestic law is that it implements a state's international human rights obligations and clarifies expectations for the behaviour of foreign investors. Creating a legal obligation for investors to respect human rights and undertake human rights due diligence is an important step towards ensuring that investors and their investments contribute to, rather than detract from, sustainable development in a host state. Having a domestic law in place that specifically implements a human rights due diligence requirement and which is accompanied by administrative and legal compliance mechanisms would go a long way towards regulating the human rights behaviour of investors and domestic corporations, thereby better protecting human rights of individuals and communities within the host state.

There is a growing practice among investors of human rights due diligence: Although corporate due diligence processes are routine for most businesses, as discussed above, *human rights* due diligence is a new concept. Some foreign investors have begun to develop the necessary tools and internal processes and procedures for engaging in human rights due diligence processes, including a human rights impact assessment. The International Council on Mining and Metals, for instance, has developed a guide for mining companies on how to incorporate human rights due diligence (as recommended by the Guiding Principles on Business and Human Rights) into general corporate risk and management processes.[168] In addition, many extractive companies have begun to develop and undertake human rights impact assessments.[169] Other investors, however, may not be familiar with the term, let alone have developed a practice of undertaking human rights due diligence.

Respecting human rights can be cost-effective: As with a full sustainability assessment,[170] a human rights due diligence process creates transparency and accountability. It provides information and allows for public participation, and it therefore helps to establish a social licence to operate. An investor that does not assess and take action based on such an assessment to prevent, avoid, mitigate or

167 See Section 5.5 (Fair and equitable treatment and the minimum standard of treatment).

168 ICCM (2012), 'Integrating Human Rights Due Diligence into Corporate Risk Management Processes', ICCM, available at: www.icmm.com/page/75929/integrating-human-rights-due-diligence-into-corporate-risk-management-processes (accessed 8 January 2013).

169 R Boele and C Crispin, 'Should We Take the "Impact" Out of Human Rights Impact Assessment?' at 2 (copy on file with the authors).

170 See Section 6.6 (Sustainability assessments).

address human rights impacts could lose such a licence. In cases of severe human rights abuses, this could exacerbate local tensions and create conflict, which could put the investment at risk. A recent study examined the economic costs of clashes between extractive corporations and local communities. This included situations ranging from administrative proceedings and litigation to publicity campaigns, public protests, physical violence and deaths. It found that companies involved in such conflict suffered financial losses for employee time allocated to managing such issues, disruption to production, loss of property value, property damage, suspension of operations or development, and injury to, or death of, employees. For a major mining project, losses for delays in exploration or lost productivity alone were found to amount to US$10 million and US$20 million respectively per week.[171]

Reduces corporate risk and attracts socially responsible investment: Developing a domestic law that requires investors to respect human rights and engage in a human rights due diligence process may also help to attract socially responsible investors and investments, as well as investors concerned about their global reputations. More and more investors are interested in managing risks related to human rights liability and projecting a socially responsible image. Where a corporation engages in a robust human rights due diligence process, it should be possible to prevent most human rights abuses and mitigate adverse impacts that cannot be prevented. Such a process will also identify situations in which the potential human rights impacts are severe and cannot be prevented or mitigated, and therefore where the investment should not proceed. Identifying such situations will be beneficial both for investors, who may not want to risk the potential liability, and for states wishing to protect human rights and in particular to avoid approving investments that are likely to cause such serious harm.

4. *Incorporate a provision in an IIA recommending that states encourage their investors to include internationally recognised CSR standards into their corporate policies*

Highlights the need for socially responsible conduct: These types of provisions could be considered important for underlining the need for investors to operate in a socially responsible manner.

Does not protect human rights: However, such provisions are hortatory and do not require states to implement a policy on corporate social responsibility. Nor do they require investors to operate pursuant to best CSR practices. Rather, these provisions leave investors to self-regulate and, as noted above, self-regulation has not prevented investors, in any consistent way, from violating human rights. Nor has it ensured that investors operate in compliance with internationally accepted CSR standards.[172]

171 Davis and Franks, op. cit., at 3–8.
172 Simons and Macklin, op. cit.

5. *Integrate into IIAs an obligation on investors to respect human rights and engage in human rights due diligence*

There are a number of ways to integrate the due diligence requirement into an IIA; these are similar to those canvassed in the section on sustainability.[173]

The potential benefits and drawbacks of integrating an obligation to respect human rights and to engage in human rights due diligence into an IIA are similar to those identified above with respect to incorporating the obligation into domestic law. There are, however, several additional advantages to including such a provision in an IIA.

- **Supports domestic law.** Including such an obligation in an IIA will complement any domestic law in place requiring investors to respect human rights and conduct human rights due diligence. If included in an IIA, such an obligation would also need to be supplemented by domestic laws and regulations in order to further interpret the obligation and specify the required measures needed to fulfil it, as well as to create institutions to monitor corporate compliance.
- **Overcomes the problem of a potential investor challenge.** Including a provision requiring a human rights due process in an IIA overcomes the possibility of investor challenge in investor–state arbitration under the IIA. The imposition of such a requirement could be specifically authorised through a general exception[174] and/or qualifications to the core investor protections.[175]
- **Gives access to treaty-based enforcement mechanisms.** The most important benefit of including such a provision in an IIA, rather than relying exclusively on domestic law, is that it raises the obligation to the international level.[176] Host states can rely on treaty-based enforcement mechanisms that can support domestic enforcement mechanisms. These include grievance processes, obligations to comply with a management plan developed based on a sustainability assessment, civil liability and state counterclaims in dispute settlement, as discussed elsewhere in the Guide.[177]

An IIA could be drafted to provide that treaty-based enforcement mechanisms would apply to the failure by the investor to comply with domestic legal requirements regarding a human rights due diligence process. To the extent that such a process is required by domestic law, the treaty obligation to comply with domestic law discussed above has the effect of doing this.[178] Nevertheless, including the obligation in the treaty makes the requirements more transparent. Besides, since the concept of a

---

173 See Section 6.6 (Sustainability assessments).

174 See Section 5.12 (Reservations and exceptions).

175 See Section 5.3 (National treatment); Section 5.4 (Most favoured nation); Section 5.5 (Fair and equitable treatment and the minimum standard of treatment); and Section 5.6 (Limitations on expropriation and nationalisation). If applied to all foreign investors, there might be a risk of a challenge under another IIA entered into by the host state.

176 UNCTAD (2012), *Investment Policy Framework for Sustainable Development*, op. cit., at 12.

177 See Section 6.6 (Sustainability assessments): Section 6.15 (Grievance procedure and other measures to enforce the management plan produced in the sustainability assessment); Section 6.16 (Civil liability of investors); and Sections 6.17 (Counterclaims by states in investor–state arbitration) and 7.1.7 (Sample provisions: investor–state dispute settlement, Article [W] (Counterclaims)).

178 Section 6.7 (Investor obligation to comply with the laws of the host state).

human rights due diligence process is new, domestic laws will likely not provide for such a process.

6.8.5 Discussion of sample provision

The Guide sample provision requires investors to respect internationally recognised human rights by engaging in a due diligence process and sets out the principles for the due diligence process. As discussed above, corporate human rights due diligence is a new concept. States will need to determine, based on their own circumstances and their assessment of the costs and benefits discussed above, whether or not they wish to implement such an obligation into domestic law and/or incorporate it into an IIA. The sample provision in the Guide aims to provide a blueprint for states that wish to do so.

The Guide sample provision draws on the UN Guiding Principles and tracks some of the language. It establishes an obligation on investors to respect human rights. This includes an obligation to exercise due diligence to avoid committing or contributing to human rights abuses and to prevent or mitigate adverse human rights effects linked to their operations and supply chain, even where they have not directly contributed to the violations.

Investors must respect all human rights: The content of the responsibility to respect in the Guide sample provision goes beyond the definition in the Guiding Principles. The Guiding Principles define 'internationally recognized human rights', which are to be applicable to business actors in all circumstances, as those rights set out in the International Bill of Rights[179] and the principles set out in the ILO's *Declaration on Fundamental Principles and Rights at Work*.[180] Other rights, such as women's rights, indigenous peoples' rights, children's rights, rights of persons with disabilities and the rights of minorities, are relegated to the category of 'additional standards' that businesses may need to consider in particular circumstances.[181] An investor proposing to establish a bank in an urban centre may not have an impact on certain rights of indigenous peoples and may not need to consider the prohibitions against torture or enforced disappearance in such a context. However, the rights of vulnerable groups such as women, children, disabled persons and migrant workers, as well as rights relating to racial discrimination (including against indigenous peoples), will always be applicable.

As discussed above, where states decide to develop a domestic law or a provision in an IIA imposing an obligation on investors to respect human rights and conduct human rights due diligence, they may wish to ensure that they are in compliance with their obligation to protect human rights. This can be done by requiring investors, in conducting their due diligence, to consider the full range of human rights, consistent with the state's international human rights obligations under treaty and customary

179 This includes the *Universal Declaration on Human Rights*, GA Res 217(III), UNGAOR, 3d Sess, Supp No 13, UN Doc A/810 at 71 (1948) [UDHR], the ICCPR and the ICESCR.

180 37 *ILM* 1233 (1998); CIT/1998/PR20A.

181 *UN Guiding Principles on Business and Human Rights*, op. cit., at Principle 12, commentary.

international law, as well as any domestic constitutional rights or other legal or administrative measures aimed at protecting human rights.

The sample provision therefore goes beyond the Guiding Principles on Business and Human Rights by defining 'internationally recognized human rights' as including those rights set out:

- In *all* the UN human rights treaties (but excluding the optional protocols) that are designated by the UN as core human rights treaties;[182]
- The *Universal Declaration on Human Rights*;[183] and
- The *United Nations Declaration on the Rights of Indigenous Peoples* (UNDRIP).[184]

The sample provision does not deal with investor obligations to respect labour rights since those are dealt with in a separate sample provision.[185]

Principles of human rights due diligence: As noted, the Guide sample provision draws on the concept of human rights due diligence set out in the Guiding Principles and tracks some of the language contained in them. The sample provision specifies the following.

- The human rights due diligence process must start *prior* to investment.
- The human rights impact assessment aspect of the due diligence process must be incorporated into the pre-establishment sustainability assessment process where a party requires investors to conduct such a comprehensive assessment.[186]
- The investor must incorporate the relevant aspects of the human rights due diligence process into any agreed management plan arising out of a sustainability assessment. Sustainability assessments are discussed in Section 6.6 (Sustainability assessments).
- The minimum requirements for the human rights impact assessment should be either those established by the host state or the Guiding Principles, whichever are the most rigorous.
- The investor and its investment should seek input from international human rights experts.
- The investor must take feedback received in consultations with affected individuals and communities into account in making decisions regarding how and

182 See OHCHR, op. cit.

183 UDHR. Most of the provisions of the UDHR are considered to be customary international law (see H Hannum (1995), 'Status of the Universal Declaration of Human Rights in National and International Law', 25 *Georgia Journal of International and Comparative Law* 287 at 289; J H Currie, C Forcese and V Oosterveld (2007), *International Law: Doctrine, Practice and Theory*, Irwin Law, Toronto, at 553.

184 UNDRIP, op. cit..

185 See Section 6.10 (Investor obligation to comply with core labour standards).

186 See Section 6.6 (Sustainability assessments).

whether to proceed with the investment. This requirement aims to address the risk that investors may treat consultation as a 'box-ticking' exercise, acknowledging but not acting on vital feedback from stakeholders.

- The investor and its investment must develop appropriate systems for addressing human rights violations and ensuring the effectiveness of their response to abuses and develop a transparent reporting mechanism.
- There will be certain circumstances in which the potential violations of human rights are so egregious, such as where an investor is proposing to operate in a conflict zone, that the investment should not go ahead.

Investors must prevent, avoid or mitigate adverse human rights impacts and make reparation for such impacts: Where an investor:

- Violates human rights or is complicit in such violations; or
- Fails to exercise due diligence to prevent and avoid harmful human rights impacts directly linked to its operations, products or services, even if the investor or investment did not directly contribute to such impacts,

it must take steps to mitigate the negative impacts and provide reparations to victims.

The scope of the due diligence obligation will vary depending on the size of the investor and its investment, the risk of severe human rights violations associated with their operations, products or services, and the nature and contexts of the investor's or the investment's operations: The requirements of the human rights due diligence process to be carried out by an investor of a party will vary in a manner determined by the investor and approved by the party state in which the investment is to be established. This flexibility is incorporated in the sample provision and recognises that in relation to some investments the human rights risks are small. The range of risks will be related to the scope of investments protected under the treaty.[187] If, for example, loans to the host state are covered by the treaty, a state might determine that there is no need for a human rights due diligence process at all.

Reparations must be made in good faith. In order to ensure that reparations are made in good faith and are commensurate to the adverse human rights impacts, the provision also provides that any reparations made will not preclude victims of human rights abuses from bringing a civil claim where such reparations are grossly disproportionate to the damage suffered.

As noted at the outset, each state will have to consider, in light of its particular circumstances and the costs and benefits of the options discussed above, the appropriateness of these standards and whether such standards should be implemented into domestic law, or an IIA, or both. If a state decides to include a requirement for an investor to conduct a pre-establishment sustainability assessment in domestic law or an IIA, some of the components of the Guide's sample provision could be integrated into it. The state would have to decide what aspects would best be dealt with as part

187 See Section 4.3 (Definitions).

of a comprehensive sustainability assessment. Additionally, states will need to take into account the fact that for an IIA obligation on investors to respect human rights and undertake due diligence to be fully effective, it will need to take effect prior to the establishment of the investment.[188]

In situations where the host state has domestic legislation for an environmental impact assessment (or an environmental and social impact assessment) already in place, or has no legislation in place on impact assessments and does not contemplate introducing such legislation (including the requirement for an sustainability assessment into an IIA), the sample provision could also serve as the starting point for a stand-alone domestic law provision to deal specifically with preventing and minimising the human rights impacts of investors and their investments.

6.8.6 Sample provision: obligation to respect internationally recognised human rights and undertake human rights due diligence

Obligation to Respect Internationally Recognised Human Rights and Undertake Human Rights Due Diligence

1. Investors of a Party and their investments shall respect internationally recognised human rights in their operations in the other Party.
2. For greater certainty, the obligation to respect human rights means that:
   a. Investors of a Party and their investments have a legal obligation to exercise due diligence to avoid violating or contributing to the violation of the human rights of individuals and communities in the other Party;
   b. Investors of a Party and their investments shall exercise due diligence to prevent or mitigate adverse human rights impacts that are directly linked to their operations, products or services by their business relationships in the other Party, even if the investor or the investment has not contributed to those impacts;
   c. Where an investor of a Party or its investment violates the human rights or is complicit in the violations of human rights of individuals or groups of individuals in the other Party, the investor and/or its investment shall take measures to mitigate such adverse impacts and shall provide reparations to the victims, including restitution, compensation and satisfaction, as appropriate; and
   d. Where an investor of a Party or its investment fails to exercise due diligence to prevent or mitigate adverse human rights impacts that are directly linked to their operations, products or services by their business relationships in the other Party, even if the investor or the investment has not contributed to those impacts, the investor or its investment shall provide reparations to the victims, including restitution, compensation and satisfaction, as appropriate.

188 The time for the commencement of investor obligations is discussed in Section 5.2 (Right of establishment).

3. The responsibility to respect internationally recognised human rights requires investors of a Party and their investments to respect at a minimum and in all circumstances the rights set out in the following international human rights instruments:

   a. *Universal Declaration of Human Rights* 1948

   b. *International Convention on the Elimination of all Forms of Racial Discrimination* 1965

   c. *International Covenant on Civil and Political Rights* 1966

   d. *International Covenant on Economic Social and Cultural Rights* 1966

   e. *Convention on the Elimination of All Forms of Discrimination against Women* 1979

   f. *Convention against Torture and Other Cruel, Inhuman or Degrading Treatment* 1984

   g. *Convention on the Rights of the Child* 1989

   h. *International Convention on the Protection of the Rights of Migrant Workers and Their Families* 1990

   i. *Convention for the Protection of All Persons from Enforced Disappearance* 2006

   j. *International Convention on the Rights of Persons with Disabilities* 2006

   k. *United Nations Declaration on the Rights of Indigenous Peoples* 2007.

4. The investor of a Party or its investment shall have in place:

   a. A policy commitment to meet its obligation to respect human rights;

   b. A robust human rights due diligence process to identify, prevent, mitigate and account for how it addresses their human rights impacts in the other Party; and

   c. Processes to enable remediation and reparation of any human rights violations they commit or to which they contribute or which are directly linked to their operations in the other Party.

5. Subject to section 6, the human rights due diligence process to be carried out by an investor of a Party in relation to an investment in the other Party shall:

   a. Be initiated prior to the establishment of the investment in the other Party and be ongoing for the lifecycle of the investment;

   b. Include a human rights impact assessment and the minimum requirements for such impact assessment shall be those established by the other Party;

   c. Incorporate the human rights impact assessment into a pre-establishment sustainability assessment where such a comprehensive assessment has been established and is required by the other Party prior to the approval of an investor or an investment;

d. Incorporate the relevant aspects of the human rights due diligence process into any agreed management plan as required under [see Guide sample provision in Section 6.6 (Sustainability assessments)];

e. Include input from independent human rights experts, such as international and domestic human rights lawyers and local and international human rights non-governmental organisations;

f. Consult with potentially affected groups and other relevant stakeholders in the other Party and use that feedback to inform the decision-making process of the investor with respect to the investment;

g. Integrate the findings of the human rights impact assessment into its decision-making processes with respect to the investment by ensuring that:

   - responsibility for addressing human rights violations is assigned to the appropriate level of management within the investor or the investment, and

   - internal decision-making, budget allocations and oversight processes enable effective responses to such impacts;

h. Include systems to verify that the investor and/or the investment addresses any violations of human rights committed by the investor or investment or in which it is complicit, as well as systems to track the effectiveness of the response;

i. Include an accessible and effective reporting mechanism that:

   - provides sufficient information to allow stakeholders to evaluate the adequacy of an investor's and investment's response to each human rights violation, and

   - protects affected stakeholders and personnel, as well as confidential commercial information.

6. Notwithstanding Section 5, the requirements of the human rights due diligence process to be carried out by an investor of a Party may vary from those set out in Section 5 in a manner determined by the investor and approved by the Party in which the investment is to be established, taking into account the size of the investor and its investment, the risk of human rights violations associated with its operations, products or services, and the nature and contexts of the investor's or the investment's operations.

7. Where a human rights due diligence process shows that the investor and/or the investment cannot operate in the territory or a particular area of territory of a Party without committing or becoming complicit in grave violations of human rights, the investor shall not establish the investment in the Party or in the particular area of the territory of the Party.

8. For greater certainty, reparations by the investor or the investment for violations of, or complicity in violations of, human rights shall not prevent the victims of

such violations from bringing a civil claim against the investor or the investment in the courts of either Party, where there is reasonable cause to believe that the reparations made by the investor or the investment were grossly disproportionate to the damage or injury suffered.

6.9 Investor obligation to refrain from the commission of, or complicity in, grave violations of human rights

Cross references

Investors operating in host states may sometimes find themselves in zones of weak governance, including situations of armed conflict or civil strife. This is particularly true of investors in the extractive industries, whose decisions regarding where to operate are more constrained by the location of resources.[189]

In some cases, the presence of foreign investors can exacerbate minor local tensions, which then escalate into a situation of conflict or worsen an existing conflict. In such circumstances, and in other areas of weak governance,[190] investors may employ private security forces or may be required by the host state to use public security forces to protect their investments. In the course of protecting the investors or the investment, security forces may commit human rights abuses, including grave violations of human rights, some of which may constitute international crimes.[191]

---

189 See *Human Rights Principles for Transnational Corporations and Other Business Enterprises, Introduction*, ECOSOC, U.N. Doc. E/CN.4/Sub.2/2001/WG.2/WP.1/ Add.1 (February 2002 for discussion in July/August 2002) at 3.

190 The OECD defines weak governance zones as: 'investment environments in which governments cannot or will not assume their roles in protecting rights (including property rights), providing basic public services (e.g. social programmes, infrastructure development, law enforcement and prudential surveillance) and ensuring that public sector management is efficient and effective'. See OECD (2006), 'OECD Risk Awareness Tool for Multinational Enterprises in Weak Governance Zones', at 11.

191 For example, allegations of complicity in forced displacement, extrajudicial killings, disappearances, rape and abduction, the use of forced labour and violent repression of peaceful protests have been made against investors such as Premier Oil, Talisman Energy Inc, British Petroleum plc (BP) and, Royal Dutch/Shell Group. See Simons, op. cit., at 102–3. See also the cases being brought with respect to Anvil Mining's activities in the DRC (*Association canadienne contre l'impunité (ACCI) c Anvil Mining Ltd*, and Exxon Mobile's activities in Aceh, Indonesia (*John Doe VIII v. Exxon Mobil Corporation*, 654 *Federal Reporter* 3d 11 (DC Cir 8 July 2011)).

It is now widely accepted in international law that, like individuals, corporations and other business entities have an obligation not to commit, or be complicit in, such abuses and crimes.[192] The Guiding Principles on Business and Human Rights recommend that corporations '[t]reat the risk of causing or contributing to gross human rights abuses as a legal compliance issue'.[193] The obligations of corporations and other business entities are not clearly articulated in any treaty or in domestic laws, although there is a growing number of states in which investors can be prosecuted for acts, or complicity in acts, constituting international crimes under the principle of universal jurisdiction.[194] However, few states have initiated criminal prosecutions against investors for their participation in such crimes.[195] The result may be that investors operating outside their home state can commit, or become complicit in, such acts with impunity.[196] No existing IIA imposes an obligation on investors to refrain from the commission or complicity in grave violations of human rights.

Box 6.10 Options regarding investor obligations to refrain from the commission of, or complicity in, grave violations of human rights

1. *Do not prohibit foreign investors from committing, or being complicit in, grave violations of human rights*
2. *Use existing domestic laws to address investors committing, or being complicit in, grave violations of human rights*
3. *Incorporate into domestic law an obligation on investors not to commit, or be complicit in, grave violations of human rights*
4. *Integrate into an IIA an obligation on investors not to commit, or be complicit in, grave violations of human rights*

---

192 A Clapham (2004), 'State Responsibility, Corporate Responsibility, and Complicity in Human Rights Violations', in L Bomann-Larsen and O Wiggen (eds), *Responsibility in World Business: Managing Harmful Side-Effects of Corporate Activity*, United Nations University Press, Tokyo, 50 at 68. See also the recognition of such liability by the SRSG, *Report of the Special Representative of the Secretary-General on the Issue of Human Rights and Transnational Corporations and other Business Entities, John Ruggie*, UNHRC, UN Doc A/HRC/4/35, (2007) at paras. 19–32; M T Kamminga and S Zia-Zarifi (2000), 'Liability of Multinational Corporations under International Law: An Introduction', in M T Kamminga and S Zia-Zarifi (eds), *Liability of Multinational Corporations under International Law*, Kluwer Law International, The Hague, at 8.

193 *UN Guiding Principles on Business and Human Rights*, op. cit., at Principle 23.

194 Ibid. at Principle 23, commentary. See also A Ramasastry and R C Thompson (2006), 'Commerce, Crime and Conflict: Legal Remedies for Private Actor Liability for Grave Breaches of International Law – A Survey of Sixteen Countries', 536 Fafo-Report, Fafo, Oslo, available at: www.fafo.no/pub/rapp/536/536.pdf (accessed 8 January 2013). Fafo undertook surveys of the relevant laws of 16 countries: Argentina, Australia, Belgium, Canada, France, Germany, India, Indonesia, Japan, The Netherlands, Norway, South Africa, Spain, Ukraine, the UK and the USA.

195 See Simons and Macklin, op. cit., Chapter 4.

196 Gagnon et al., op. cit., at 3.

6.9.1 Discussion of options

1. *Do not prohibit foreign investors from committing, or being complicit in, grave violations of human rights*

States may be in violation of *jus cogens* norms and their international human rights obligations: States have an obligation under international human rights law to protect human rights. This means they must take steps through legislative and other measures to control, regulate, investigate and prosecute actions by investors that violate the human rights of those within their territory and subject to their jurisdiction. By failing to prohibit the most egregious violations of human rights, states will be in breach of this obligation. In addition, many grave violations of human rights amount to international crimes and their prohibition amounts to a *jus cogens* norm. These are peremptory customary international law norms from which no state may derogate.

A failure by the state to prohibit and punish egregious acts could deter investment: Impunity for grave violations of human rights can undermine the peace and stability of a state. Studies have shown a clear link between conflict escalation and grave violations of human rights such as extra judicial killings, torture, enforced disappearance and other violations of liberty and security rights.[197] Investors may perceive the failure of the host state to deal with such abuses as an indication of weak governance capacity and prefer to establish their investments in more stable and effective regulatory environments. Investors perceive host states in which actors have a licence to commit such egregious acts as difficult investment environments that pose increased risks to their investments.[198]

2. *Use existing domestic laws to address investors committing or being complicit in grave violations of human rights*

Existing domestic laws may not address grave human rights abuses or impose criminal liability on legal persons: It may be preferable for states that have robust criminal law provisions that address criminal liability of both legal and natural persons for international crimes and effective criminal law institutions to use existing domestic law to regulate such behaviour. There can be a strong deterrent factor in prosecuting both individuals and corporations responsible for the crime, particularly where criminal penalties for the corporation include significant fines or sanctions, such as revocation of a licence to operate. However, some states may not have domestic laws in place that specifically address these types of grave violations of human rights. In addition, some states do not have criminal law regimes that impose criminal liability on legal persons such as corporations, or significant resources to devote to enforcement.

197 O N T Thoms and J Ron (2007), 'Do Human Rights Violations Cause Internal Conflict?', 29 *Human Rights Quarterly* 674 at 694–5.

198 OECD (2006), 'OECD *Risk Awareness Tool*', op. cit.

Domestic laws can be difficult to enforce against a foreign investor: States may also encounter challenges in enforcing domestic laws against foreign investors. All states, even the most powerful, face difficulties in regulating the conduct of transnational business actors.[199] Transnational business groups may undercapitalise the entity that is operating the host state, restructure themselves or move assets between jurisdictions in order to avoid liability under domestic law.

3. *Incorporate into domestic law an obligation on investors not to commit or be complicit in grave violations of human rights*

It is costly to develop a regulatory framework: It can be burdensome for states to develop a new regulatory framework and oversight mechanisms to address grave violations of human rights. It will require host states to dedicate significant resources to developing the regulatory framework and institutions for investigating allegations, prosecuting investors and enforcing any sentence imposed.

Domestic laws can be difficult to enforce against a foreign investor: As noted above, even where a state introduces robust criminal laws to sanction egregious behaviour by foreign investors, it may be difficult to enforce such laws against them.

It implements states' international human rights and international law obligations: However, incorporating such a prohibition into domestic law implements the state's duty to protect human rights and sets a clear standard for investor behaviour. Prohibiting and enforcing a prohibition of the most egregious violations of international human rights is fundamental to sustainable development. Having a domestic law in place that specifically targets such grave abuses will help to protect vulnerable communities from the worst forms of violence.

It may be perceived as increasing potential liability of extractive industry investors: Investors engaged in resource extraction are more likely to become complicit in grave human rights violations than those in other industries, since the location of their operations is constrained by the location of the resources. This may mean that extraction projects will be situated on, or in close proximity to, indigenous lands or in zones of weak governance, including conflict zones. Investors routinely hire private security companies or use public forces to protect their investments in such locations and may become complicit in serious violations of human rights through the acts of such security forces. A domestic law targeting such violations may be seen by such investors as increasing their potential liability and may therefore deter investment in the natural resource sector.

It can help reduce corporate risk and attract socially responsible investment: Nevertheless, as discussed above, most investors prefer to invest in a stable rights-protective regulatory environment. Kofi Annan has emphasised that 'economic success depends in considerable measure on the quality of governance a country enjoys' and this includes ensuring respect for, and the protection of, human rights.[200]

199 Marks, op. cit., at 461.

200 We the Peoples: The Role of the United Nations in the Twenty-First Century, Report of the Secretary-General, UNGAOR, 54 Sess, UN doc A/54/2000, (2000), at para 84.

Thanks in part to the high-profile work of the SRSG, investors are becoming much more aware of the risks of violating human rights in the states in which they operate and are taking steps to avoid such risks. Having strong human rights obligations in place will reduce the risk that investors will become implicated in these types of abuses. As noted in Section 6.8 above, the majority of transnational litigation against corporate actors relates to allegations of grave violations of human rights. An effective prohibition on grave violations of human rights may help to attract more socially responsible investors, as well as those that wish to improve or protect their global reputations.

4. *Integrate into an IIA an obligation on investors not to commit or be complicit in grave violations of human rights*

The potential benefits and drawbacks of including such a prohibition in an IIA are similar to those identified above with respect to incorporating the obligation into domestic law. An IIA provision has other advantages.

Access to treaty-based compliance mechanisms: Another advantage of including such a provision in an IIA is that it raises the obligation to the international level and allows access to treaty-based enforcement mechanisms. The ability of a host state to use treaty-based enforcement mechanisms complements domestic enforcement measures and helps to address the difficulty of ensuring that foreign investors comply with domestic laws and regulations. Such treaty-based mechanisms include grievance processes (which could expose such conduct), civil and criminal liability in the host and home states for an investor in breach of treaty obligations, and state counterclaims in investor–state dispute settlement to recover compensation for losses resulting from an investor's breaches.[201]

It would also be possible to provide in an IIA that these treaty-based enforcement mechanisms could be used for breaches of domestic laws in the host state that prohibit grave violations of human rights. The treaty obligation to comply with domestic law discussed above has the effect of doing this to the extent that such violations are prohibited under domestic law.[202] Tying enforcement to standards expressed in the treaty has the benefit of making clear what the standards for investors are and can help ensure compatibility with international standards.

6.9.2 Discussion of sample provision

The Guide sample provision provides an example of an IIA obligation on investors not to commit or be complicit in grave violations of human rights. The aim of the Guide sample provision is to clarify the specific legal obligations of investors with respect to the commission of, or complicity in, grave violations of human rights. Drawing on a similar provision in the *UN Norms on the Responsibilities of Transnational*

201 See Section 6.14 (Criminal sanctions); Section 6.15 (Grievance procedure and other measures to enforce the management plan produced in the sustainability assessment); Section 6.16 (Civil liability of investors); and Sections 6.17 (Counterclaims by states in investor–state arbitration) and 7.1.7 (Sample provisions: investor–state dispute settlement, Article [W] (Counterclaims)).

202 Section 6.7 (Investor obligation to comply with the laws of the host state).

Corporations and Other Business Enterprises[203] and a legislative proposal for the regulation of corporate activity in conflict zones,[204] the sample provision incorporates an obligation on investors not to commit, or be complicit, in grave violations of human rights.

The Guide sample provision prohibits the commission of, or complicity in, a range of egregious acts, including genocide, crimes against humanity, war crimes and torture, among others. It also requires investors to take steps to ensure that their investments do not contribute directly or indirectly to, or benefit from, the commission of such acts. Investors must also ensure that any security providers, whether public or private, comply with the international human rights norms on the use of force in their protection of the assets and installations of the investment.

Relationship with preceding sample provisions: The sample provision deals with only the most egregious and violent violations of human rights. The preceding sample provision deals with the general obligation on investors and investments to respect human rights and the duty to exercise due diligence to avoid violating or contributing to the violation of human rights.[205] The first sample provision in this section requires investors to comply with the domestic law of a host state, including those laws relating to the protection of human rights.[206] There is, however, a relationship between the sample provision creating an obligation to respect human rights[207] and this sample provision prohibiting commission of, or complicity in, grave abuses of human rights.

- *A violation of this provision would also be a violation of the Obligation to Respect Internationally Recognised Human Rights and Undertake Human Rights Due Diligence*. In most situations, a robust human rights due diligence process would reveal the possibility of the investor and its investment committing, or becoming complicit in, grave violations of human rights in a particular host state or in a specific location within a host state. In such a case, strategies to avoid this risk could be developed and implemented.
- *This sample provision targets specific conduct requiring criminal sanctions*. A violation of the obligation to respect human rights and conduct due diligence triggers an obligation to make reparations to the victims of such abuses. The obligation to refrain from the commission of, or complicity in, grave violations of human rights differs from the preceding general obligation in that it prohibits specific conduct and may lead to criminal sanctions. The idea behind a separate provision is to

203 Norms on the Responsibilities of Transnational Corporations and Other Business Enterprises with Regard to Human Rights, ECOSOC, UN Doc E/CN.4/Sub.2/2003/12/Rev.2 (2003); Commentary on the Norms on the Responsibilities of Transnational Corporations and Other Business Enterprises with Regard to Human Rights, UN Doc. E/CN.4/Sub.2/2003/38/Rev.2, (2003).

204 Gagnon et al., op. cit.

205 See Section 6.8 (Investor obligation to respect internationally recognised human rights and undertake human rights due diligence).

206 See Section 6.7 (Investor obligation to comply with the laws of the host state).

207 See Section 6.8 (Investor obligation to respect internationally recognised human rights and undertake human rights due diligence).

target egregious behaviour which may violate international criminal law, and for which simple reparations would be wholly inadequate. In addition, it allows for different enforcement mechanisms to be used, in this case criminal liability.

The prohibition is not limited to situations of conflict: While egregious violations of human rights will usually occur during armed conflict or civil strife, the prohibition is not limited to such situations. It also applies in other zones of weak governance and would include, for example, the murder or disappearance of trade unionists.

6.9.3 Sample provision: obligation not to commit, be complicit in or benefit from grave violations of human rights

Obligation Not to Commit, Be Complicit in or Benefit from Grave Violations of Human Rights

1. Investors of a Party and their investments shall neither commit nor be complicit in grave violations of international human rights or violations of international humanitarian law committed by the other Party or by a non-state actor in the territory of the other Party. Such violations include, but are not limited to, genocide, war crimes, crimes against humanity, torture, enforced or involuntary disappearance, forced or compulsory labour, hostage-taking, extra judicial, summary or arbitrary executions, forced displacement or other international crimes against the human person as defined by international law, in particular international criminal law, international human rights law and international humanitarian law.

2. Investors of a Party and their investments shall ensure that their activities in the other Party do not contribute directly or indirectly to international crimes, grave violations of international human rights or violations of international humanitarian law as defined in Section 1 and that they do not benefit from such violations.

3. Investors of a Party and their investments shall ensure that any arrangement for the security of the investor or their investments shall observe international human rights norms on the use of force in the other Party, including the *UN Basic Principles on the Use of Force and Firearms by Law Enforcement Officials*, the *UN Code of Conduct for Law Enforcement Officials* and the laws and professional standards of the other Party.

4. For greater certainty, a security arrangement includes any public or private security force or other means of protecting an investor of a Party or its investment.

6.10 Investor obligation to comply with core labour standards

Cross references

Section 4.2.1 The role of preambles in IIAs 42
Section 5.3 National treatment 110

The imposition on investors by host states of a duty to respect core labour standards has traditionally been viewed as likely to discourage foreign investment.[208] This is because investors might be attracted to a state by its lower labour standards, which may translate into a lower cost of doing business. Contrary to this view, however, empirical studies over the last decade have shown that the maintenance of high labour standards does not in fact discourage foreign investment. As noted by the OECD:

> … any fear on the part of developing countries that better core standards would negatively affect either their economic performance or their competitive position in world markets has no economic rationale. On the contrary, it is conceivable that the observance of core standards would strengthen the long-term economic performance of all countries.[209]

These studies show that the level of local labour standards is not a significant factor in investment decision making.[210] Moreover, it appears that violations of labour rights actually have the effect of *discouraging* foreign investment, even where the host state is a small or poor developing country.[211]

Strong core labour laws are also a central aspect of sustainable development. For example, the reduction and eventual abolition of child labour will enhance a state's development by ensuring that children have the opportunity to go to school and gain

---

208 R Howse, B Langille and J Burda (2006), 'The World Trade Organization and Labour Rights: Man Bites Dog', in V A Leary and D Warner (eds), *Social Issues, Globalisation and International Institutions*, Martinus Nijoff, Leiden, 157 at 168.

209 OECD (1996), *Trade, Employment and Labour Standards: A Study of Core Workers' Rights and International Trade*, OECD, Paris, at 105.

210 Ibid.

211 M Busse, P Nunnenkamp and M Spatareanu (2011), 'Foreign Direct Investment and Labour Rights: A Panel Analysis of Bilateral FDI Flows', 18 *Applied Economics Letters* 149 (looking at the impact of fundamental labour rights on bilateral FDI flows in 82 developing countries).

the education and skills that will enable them to contribute as adults to economic growth and prosperity.[212]

6.10.1 IIA practice

A small but increasing number of IIAs, especially FTAs, now includes some language on labour standards.[213] There are a number of different approaches reflected in IIA practice. References to, or provisions on, labour protection may be included in the preamble or the body of a treaty in a separate provision, or in a side agreement, among other things.

Language in the preamble: Preambular language on labour protection does not create binding obligations and is not very protective of labour rights. A preamble sets out the overall goals of the party states in entering the treaty and provides part of the context for interpreting treaty obligations. For example, a preamble may articulate a desire of the parties for the objectives of the treaty to be accomplished in a manner consistent with certain values. The preamble in the US–Uruguay BIT, for instance, lists the protection of health, safety, the environment and international labour rights.[214] The EC–CARIFORUM EPA, on the other hand, articulates the need of the parties 'to promote economic and social progress for their people in a manner consistent with sustainable development by respecting basic labour rights … and by protecting the environment'. A preamble could be drafted to give precedence in the interpretation of the treaty to such non-investment norms. In the absence of a clear specification to this effect, however, it is likely that an interpreter of an IIA will give preference to investment protection and promotion.

Provisions in the body of the treaty: Three types of provisions are becoming common in IIAs. The first is a provision acknowledging that it is inappropriate for the parties to encourage investment by lowering domestic labour law standards and requiring parties not to waive or derogate from domestic labour laws and/or not to fail to effectively enforce such laws. This is the approach of the Economic Partnership

---

212 ILO (2002), 'A Future without Child Labour: Global Report under the Follow-Up to the ILO Declaration on Fundamental Principles and Rights at Work', International Labour Conference, 90th session, ILO, Geneva, at 1.

213 For a comprehensive comparison of the various labour provisions in US and EU agreements, see R Grynberg and V Qalo (2006), 'Labour Standards in US and EU Preferential Trading Arrangements', 40 *Journal of World Trade* 619; see also K Gordon (2008), 'International Investment Agreements: A Survey of Environmental, Labour and Anti-Corruption Issues', in OECD, *International Investment Law: Understanding Concepts and Tracking Innovations*, OECD, Paris, 135; L Bartels (2009), 'Social Issues: Labour, Environment and Human Rights', in S Lester and B Mercurio (eds), *Bilateral and Regional Trade Agreements: Commentary, Analysis and Case Studies*, Cambridge University Press, Cambridge, 342; and for an excellent critique of the concept of 'core labour standards', see P Alston (2004), 'Core Labour Standards and the Transformation of the International Labour Rights Regime', 15 *European Journal of International Law* 457 at 497–506.

214 See, for example, the preamble of the US–Uruguay BIT (2004).

Agreement between the EC and CARIFORUM,[215] the 2012 US model BIT[216] and several US FTAs,[217] the Austrian model BIT[218] and the EU–Korea FTA.[219]

In addition to a requirement not to relax domestic labour standards, some IIAs also contain provisions: (i) affirming the parties' commitments as ILO members and under the 1998 *ILO Declaration on Fundamental Principles and Rights at Work*, (ii) recognising the right of the parties to establish their own labour standards, (iii) requiring the parties to either maintain high levels of labour standards or endeavour to ensure that domestic labour standards are consistent with certain listed international labour standards, and (iv) requiring parties to strive to improve such standards. The listed standards often include the right of association, the right to organise and bargain collectively, prohibition of forced labour, minimum age for the employment of children, the prohibition of the worst forms of child labour, and the right to acceptable conditions of work with respect to minimum wages, hours of work, occupational safety and health.[220]

The EC–CARIFORUM EPA provides a variation of this type of provision. Like the provisions discussed above, it requires parties to ensure that their domestic laws 'provide for and encourage high levels of social and labour standards' in line with listed international labour standards. However, it also recognises the right of the parties 'to regulate in order to establish their own social regulations and labour standards in line with their own social development priorities and to adopt or modify accordingly their relevant laws and policies'.[221]

---

215 EC–CARIFORUM EPA (2008), Arts. 73 and 193.

216 Art. 13. See also the Canada–Colombia FTA (2008), Arts. 1601–4. That agreement also references the obligations between the parties set out in the Canada–Colombia Agreement on Labour Cooperation, signed 21 November 2008, in force 15 August 2011.

217 See, for example, Australia–US FTA (2004); United States–Dominican Republic Central America Free Trade Agreement, signed 5 August 2004, in force 1 January 2009, Art. 16.2; United States–Chile Free Trade Agreement, signed 6 June 2003, in force 1 January 2004, Art. 18.2; United States–Jordan Free Trade Agreement, signed 24 October 2000, in force 17 December 2001, Art. 6; United States–Morocco Free Trade Agreement, signed 15 June 2004, in force 1 January 2006, Art. 16.2.

218 Art 5. See also Art. 5 of both Austria–Tajikistan, Agreement for the Promotion and Protection of Investment between the Republic of Austria and the Republic of Tajikistan, signed 15 December 2010, not yet in force, and the Kosovo–Austria, Agreement between the Government of the Republic of Kosovo and the Republic of Austria on Promotion and Protection of Investments, signed 22 January 2010, not yet in force; as well as Art. 6 of Belgium–Luxembourg–Ethiopia, Agreement between the Belgium–Luxembourg Economic Union on the one hand, and the Federal Democratic Republic of Ethiopia, on the other hand, on the Reciprocal Promotion and Protection of Investments, signed 26 October 2006, not yet in force.

219 Arts. 13.4, 13.7.

220 Belgium–Luxembourg–Ethiopia BIT (2006), Arts. 6 and 1(6); US Model BIT, Art. 13; Australia–US FTA (2004) Arts. 18.1 and 18.7; US–CAFTA FTA (2004), Arts. 16.1 and 16.8; US–Chile FTA (2003), Arts. 18.1 and 18.8; US–Jordan FTA (2000), Art 6; and US–Morocco FTA (2004), Art. 16.1 and 16.7. The European Union–South Korea Free Trade Agreement, signed 15 October 2009, in force 1 July 2011, Art. 13.4, goes slightly further than the US Model BIT and other US FTAs and BITs by recognising the parties' commitments to the 2006 Ministerial Declaration of the UN Economic and Social Council on Full Employment and Decent Work and the importance of 'full and productive employment and decent work for all' for sustainable development.

221 Arts. 192 and 191.

The main aim of these various provisions is to prevent competition between states that will lead to a 'race to the bottom' of labour standards, rather than to ratchet up the level of labour protection. These types of provisions do not oblige party states to ensure minimum standards are met in their domestic law in compliance with their international labour obligations, and they target investor behaviour only indirectly and weakly.

Side accord: Another method states have adopted to address the problem of a 'race to the bottom' is to negotiate a side accord to an FTA. These side accords are generally based on the *North American Agreement on Labor Cooperation* (NAALC), the side accord to NAFTA. In that agreement, the parties are obliged to maintain high domestic labour standards and to strive to improve such standards.[222] In addition, party states are required to facilitate compliance with and enforce their labour laws through appropriate government measures and to ensure that judicial and non-judicial mechanisms and other procedures are available to individuals to enforce such laws.[223] These side agreements essentially do the same thing as IIAs with provisions requiring parties to enforce their labour laws.[224] Under the NAALC, states do not commit to upholding international core labour standards. Rather they agree to promote a list of principles,[225] subject to their respective law and with the proviso that such principles do not set common minimum standards.

Compliance mechanisms: Some IIAs, FTAs and side accords, such as the NAALC and the side accords to the Canada–Chile, Canada–Costa Rica and Canada–Colombia FTAs, incorporate compliance mechanisms and complaint mechanisms to ensure that states comply with their domestic labour standards or certain specified international labour standards. The NAALC, the Canadian agreements and some US FTAs establish a compliance system that includes a means for individuals to make complaints about a party's failure to enforce its labour laws and regulations.[226] These systems are primarily diplomatic, although in principle, under some side agreements

---

222 Canada–Mexico–United States, North American Agreement on Labour Cooperation, signed 14 September 1993, in force 1 January 1994, Art. 2.

223 NAALC (1993), Arts. 2 and 3.

224 One difference is that the side agreement commitments cannot be the subject of dispute settlement under the treaty. However, even where labour commitments are incorporated directly in an IIA, it is possible to carve these obligations out of the dispute settlement procedures in the treaty.

225 NAALC (1993), Annex 1. The principles are: freedom of association and protection of the right to organize; the right to bargain collectively; the right to strike; prohibition of forced labour; labour protections for children and young persons; minimum employment standards; elimination of employment discrimination; equal pay for women and men; prevention of occupational injuries and illnesses; compensation in cases of occupational injuries and illnesses; and the protection of migrant workers.

226 See Australia–US FTA (2004), Art. 18.4(2); US–CAFTA FTA (2004), Art 16.4(3); US–Chile FTA (2003), Art. 18.4(7): US–Morocco FTA (2004), Art. 18.4(1); United States–Singapore Free Trade Agreement, signed 6 May 2003, in force 1 January 2004, Art. 17.4(5).

and FTAs, certain disputes over labour issues could lead to the imposition of fines[227] or, in some cases, even sanctions.[228] The NAALC compliance procedure is discussed in more detail below in the section on minimum standards of human rights, labour rights, indigenous peoples' rights, and environmental protection and standards to address corruption.[229]

These types of provisions do not directly target investor behaviour and the IISD has observed that there is little evidence that these compliance mechanisms (including the complaint processes) have been effective in ensuring that states enforce their domestic labour laws and regulations against foreign investors.[230]

Exceptions: A few IIAs also include exception clauses that are aimed at ensuring that a state's labour laws will not be subject to investor challenge in investor–state arbitration. The US–Uruguay BIT includes a provision stating that:

> [n]othing in this Treaty shall be construed to prevent a Party from adopting or maintaining, or enforcing any measure *otherwise consistent with this Treaty* that it considers appropriate to ensure that investment activity in its territory is undertaken in a manner sensitive to labor concerns.[231] (Emphasis added.)

This provision, however, is likely to have limited legal effect since it requires any regulation on labour issues to be consistent with the core investor protections in the BIT. The section in the Guide on reservations and exceptions discusses this problem further and provides a discussion of approaches to using exceptions to carve out policy areas from the application of an IIA more effectively.[232]

Co-operation between parties on labour issues: Another approach states have taken in FTAs and side accords is to establish a mechanism to enhance co-operation between the party states on labour issues. The US FTAs discussed above, for example, all require the parties to designate a contact point within their ministry of labour and

227 See, for example, the Canada–Colombia Agreement on Labour Cooperation (2008), Art. 20; it allows for a Review Panel to determine whether a party has demonstrated a persistent pattern of failure to enforce its domestic laws, among other things, to impose a fine on the party to be paid into a fund and spent on appropriate labour-related initiatives in the territory of such a party. The annual amount of any such fines may not exceed US $15 million (see Annex 4). See also NAALC, Art. 39(4)(2) and Annex 39; Canada–Chile Agreement on Labour Cooperation, signed 6 February 1997, in force 5 July 1997, Art. 35(4)(b) and Art. 37, under which the parties may eventually seek enforcement and collection of fines through the domestic courts of the offending party state. The US FTAs discussed above provide for fines.

228 NAALC (2003), Arts. 28 and 29; Australia–US FTA (2004), Art. 21.12; US–CAFTA FTA (2004), Art. 20.17; US–Chile FTA (2003), Art. 18.6(7).

229 See Section 6.12 (Other rights and obligations of party states).

230 N Bernasconi-Osterwalder and L Johnson (2011), 'Commentary to the Austrian Model Investment Treaty', IISD Report at 27.

231 US–Uruguay BIT (2005), Art. 13(3).

232 See Section 5.12 (Reservations and exceptions).

establish an indicative list of co-operative activities on labour and the implementation of co-operative activities.[233] These provisions focus on exchange of information, educational activities and technical co-operation.

The EC–CARIFORUM EPA, on the other hand, requires co-operation on enforcement of labour standards against investors. It imposes an obligation on the party states both to co-operate and to take measures domestically to ensure that investors:

- Comply with the core labour standards set out in the ILO Declaration; and
- Do not manage or operate their investments in a manner that circumvents labour obligations arising from the international obligations of the parties.[234]

This approach is much more protective of labour rights than the other provisions discussed above. First, it goes beyond simply requiring parties to enforce their own domestic law. Second, it specifically requires parties to take action to ensure investor compliance with labour standards that are consistent with international core labour standards. Finally, the obligation of co-operation harnesses the regulatory capacity of the home state in addition to the host state in ensuring investor compliance.

Obligations on investors to comply with core labour standards: The most protective approach would be to adopt provisions in an IIA that impose obligations:

- *On parties* to maintain high levels of labour rights protection consistent with the parties' international obligations;
- *On parties* to co-operate and to take measures domestically to prevent investors from operating or managing their investments in a manner that circumvents labour rights consistent with the parties' international obligations; and
- *On investors* requiring them to respect domestic labour laws and to comply with international core labour standards.

None of the IIAs discussed above go this far. The EC–CARIFORUM provision is a step forward in its requirement on party states to ensure investor compliance with such standards. Only the IISD model treaty incorporates a provision that imposes obligations directly on investors to 'act in accordance with core labour standards as required by the *ILO Declaration on Fundamental Principles and Rights of Work, 1998*'.[235]

233 Australia–US FTA (2004), Art. 18.5; US–CAFTA FTA (2004), Art. 16.5 and Annex 16.5; US–Chile FTA (2003), Art. 18.5 and Annex 18.5: US–Morocco FTA (2004), Art. 16.5 and Annex 16-A; and US–Singapore FTA (2003), Art. 17.5 and Annex 17A. See also NAALC (2003), Arts. 8–19.

234 EU–CARIFORUM EPA (2008), Art. 72(b), and (c).

235 IISD Model IIA, Art. 14(C).

Box 6.11 Summary of options for investor obligation to comply with core labour standards

1. *Do not require foreign investors to comply with core labour standards*
2. *Use existing domestic labour laws to regulate investor activity*
3. *Introduce new stronger domestic labour laws, consistent with a state's international labour law obligations*
4. *Integrate language on labour rights into an IIA through:*
   a. Language in the preamble
   b. Provisions in an IIA or side agreement to address the problem of a 'race to the bottom' of labour standards
   c. An exception for labour laws and regulations
   d. An obligation on states to co-operate to ensure investor compliance with international core labour standards
   e. An obligation on investors to comply with core labour standards

6.10.2 Discussion of options

1. *Do not require foreign investors to comply with core labour standards*

It may deter investment: There are few advantages to not taking action to ensure that investors and their investments comply with domestic labour standards. Studies have shown that the level of local labour standards is not a key factor in investor decision-making about where to invest. In other words, investors will not necessarily choose to invest in a state with lower labour standards. In addition, studies have demonstrated that labour standard violations in the host state may actually discourage foreign investment. Therefore, having domestic laws that are not sufficiently protective of core labour rights and/or failing to enforce those laws may not be an effective strategy for attracting investment.

States may be in breach of their international labour rights obligations: Further, states that do not implement their international obligations into domestic law and require foreign investors to comply with such laws may be in breach of their international obligations. Most states have ratified the eight core ILO treaties[236] and therefore have obligations under those treaties to protect such standards under domestic law.

2. *Use existing domestic labour laws to regulate investor activity*

This approach may be attractive for states that have strong labour laws that protect international core labour rights. It would not require any further resources on the part

236 See the list of the ILO core conventions above.

of the state to be dedicated to developing a regulatory framework and enforcement institutions.

However, existing labour laws may not be sufficiently rigorous and/or may not be consistent with a state's international labour law obligations. Moreover, even where states do have a robust labour regulatory framework in place, they may face difficulties in enforcing such laws against foreign investors. All states, even the most economically powerful, confront challenges in regulating the behaviour of transnational business actors,[237] which can restructure or transfer assets out of a state in order to avoid liability.

3. *Introduce new stronger domestic labour laws, consistent with a state's international labour law obligations*

It is costly to develop a regulatory framework: As discussed above with respect to investor obligations to respect human rights, developing a robust regulatory framework to protect labour rights can be costly. It will require the host state to dedicate resources to strengthening its labour laws and regulations to meet its international standards.

It may increase the costs of doing business: The introduction and enforcement of domestic laws that protect labour rights could:

- Raise wages;
- Require investors to take steps to ensure that the work environment complies with health and safety standards;
- Require investors to have policies and processes in place to protect against discrimination in the workplace;
- Require investors to engage in collective bargaining; and
- Prohibit child labour or the worst forms of child labour.

Investors may feel that such requirements would be too costly for them to comply with and may choose to operate in states with lower standards. However, as noted above, empirical studies have shown that strong labour standards are not a significant factor in investment decision making and may therefore not act as a deterrent to investment.

Domestic laws can be difficult to enforce against a foreign investor: As discussed above, even where a state brings its domestic labour laws and regulations into line with its international obligations, it may be difficult to enforce them against foreign investors.

There is a risk of investor challenge under an IIA: As with implementing a new obligation on investors to respect human rights and undertake human rights due diligence, introducing more rigorous labour laws and regulations into domestic law

237 Marks, op. cit.

might trigger a challenge by an investor under an existing IIA. The investor might argue that the introduction of such measures is a violation of the FET provisions. Some, but not all, investment tribunals have interpreted FET obligations so broadly that host states may have little room to change the regulatory environment that persuaded the investor to invest.[238] The risk is greatest if a host state's action targets only foreign investors. If the investor is successful in an investor–state arbitration claim, the state will be required to pay compensation.

It implements the state's international labour law obligations and supports sustainable development: On the other hand, there are important benefits to introducing new domestic labour laws and regulations or amending existing laws and regulations. First, it allows states the opportunity to bring its laws into compliance, if they are not already, with their international labour law obligations. Creating a rigorous labour law framework will help ensure that investors contribute in a positive way to state development goals by supporting sustainable development in a host state. It will also more effectively protect the labour rights of individuals within the host state.

It attracts investment including, in particular, socially responsible investment: In addition, having a strong regulatory framework of labour protections sends a signal to investors, particularly socially responsible investors and investors concerned about their global reputations, that the state has a stable, rights-protective regulatory environment in which to conduct business.

It helps manage corporate risk: More and more investors are interested in managing risks related to labour rights issues. Corporations operating in a state with strong labour protections are less likely to face strikes or public protests that may disrupt operations. They are also less likely to be the target of non-governmental organisation (NGO) campaigns that can expose investors to reputational damage, or to be brought before administrative tribunals or courts for violations of labour rights.

4. *Integrate language on labour rights into an IIA*

There are a variety of different ways of incorporating labour rights protections into IIAs to promote conformity with a state's international obligations. The following are some examples.

Language in the preamble: The parties could negotiate a general statement in the preamble stating that the IIA is to be interpreted in accordance with the parties' international obligations in regard to labour rights. Such an approach can be stronger or weaker, depending on the wording:[239]

- *Stronger approach (more protective of labour rights)*: The preamble could state that the protection of labour rights is of the same level of importance as the investor protections included in the IIA. This will ensure that labour rights protection

238 See Section 5.5 (Fair and equitable treatment and the minimum standard of treatment).

239 See Section 4.2.1 (The role of preambles in IIAs).

is not subordinated to investment protection considerations in interpreting the treaty.

- *Weaker approach (less protective labour rights)*: The parties could specify that the IIA is to be interpreted in a way that is consistent with international labour rights. Such a statement leaves unspecified the priority of investment protection, compared with labour rights protection, although it may imply that norms relating to investment promotion and protection should be given precedence in interpreting the treaty.

As noted above, preambular language does not create any binding obligations on the parties or on investors and does not on its own provide effective protection of labour rights.

Provisions in an IIA or side agreement to address the problem of a 'race to the bottom' of labour standards: States can negotiate provisions in an IIA or in a side agreement that:

- Reaffirm their commitments to international labour law instruments;
- Establish an obligation on the parties not to relax domestic labour laws and regulations in order to attract or retain investment and not to fail to enforce such standards;
- Establish an obligation on the parties to either maintain high levels of labour standards or endeavour to ensure that domestic labour standards are consistent with certain listed international labour standards and require parties to strive to improve such standards.

These types of provisions are becoming more common in IIAs.

These provisions offer flexibility. These provisions might be attractive to states because of the latitude they offer. First, they allow states parties to pick and choose the labour standards that (for the purposes of the IIA) they intend to protect under domestic law. Second, they do not require states to ensure that domestic law is consistent with international labour standards and they impose only a 'best endeavours' obligation to improve standards of labour protection.

There is a risk of investor challenge for states wishing to strengthen labour protections. An important limitation of these provisions is that they provide no direct protection from an investor challenge under an IIA for states interested in strengthening existing laws and regulations or introducing new labour protection measures. As noted above, an investor could argue that the introduction or strengthening of such measures is a breach of its legitimate expectations under an FET provision in some circumstances.[240] However, the recognition in the IIA that a state should act to protect labour rights in the treaty would undermine an investor's claim that it had a legitimate expectation that a state would not act to provide such protection.

240 See Section 5.5 (Fair and equitable treatment and the minimum standard of treatment).

They do not allow for treaty-based enforcement mechanisms targeting investor conduct. Finally, states may have difficulty in ensuring that investors comply with domestic labour laws. Since these types of provisions do not impose specific standards on investor conduct, they do not allow for the use of treaty-based enforcement mechanisms to supplement domestic enforcement mechanisms.

An exception for labour laws and regulations: Negotiating an exception for labour measures would provide a clear expression of the parties' intention to carve out labour regulation from the application of investors' protections under an IIA. It would therefore give the host state the policy space to introduce new labour laws and regulations, or to strengthen such measures, without the fear of triggering an arbitral claim against the host state by an investor. A full discussion of the costs and benefits of using exceptions to exclude certain areas of policy making from the purview of an IIA is found in Section 5.12 (Reservations and exceptions).[241]

An obligation on states to co-operate to ensure investor compliance with international core labour standards:

This harnesses home state regulatory capacity and co-operation in regulating investor conduct. This option, which is the approach taken in the EC–CARIFORUM EPA discussed above, can help states to address some of the challenges to regulating effectively the behaviour of powerful foreign investors by requiring enforcement action on behalf of the home state, in addition to the host state, to ensure that investors do not evade compliance with international core labour standards. It also obliges co-operation between the parties in this regard.

There is a risk of investor challenge under an IIA. However, this approach does not avoid the problem, discussed above, faced by states that wish to introduce more rigorous labour laws and regulations, that changes to a state's domestic regime of this kind could potentially be challenged by an investor under the investor-protection provisions in an IIA. To avoid this issue with certainty, a treaty would also need to include provisions that protect the right of states to introduce or strengthen such laws and regulations. As noted above, one way to do this would be to include a general exception for labour laws and regulations. Another is to ensure that this kind of regulation is permitted under the investor protection obligations in the treaty, such as the national treatment, MFN, minimum standard of treatment and expropriation provisions. How states can retain the flexibility to regulate in areas such as labour rights is discussed in relation to each of the Guide's respective sample provisions.[242]

---

241 If a state had entered into other IIAs, it would have to determine whether there was a risk that any increase in labour standards for all businesses could be challenged under another treaty.

242 See Section 5.3 (National treatment); Section 5.4 (Most favoured nation); Section 5.5 (Fair and equitable treatment and the minimum standard of treatment); Section 5.6 (Limitations on expropriation and nationalisation); and Section 5.12 (Reservations and exceptions). As previously noted, if a state had entered into other IIAs, it would have to determine whether there was a risk that any increase in labour standards for all businesses could be challenged under another treaty.

An obligation on investors to comply with core labour standards: The potential costs and benefits of introducing a provision imposing an obligation directly on investors to comply with certain core labour standards are similar to those identified above regarding the introduction of new labour protection measures or amending existing domestic laws and regulations to strengthen labour rights protection. There are, however, two additional advantages to including such a provision in an IIA rather than simply relying on existing domestic laws or introducing more stringent labour requirements into domestic law.

Overcomes the problem of a potential investor challenge. As long as states comply with the core provisions of the IIA in their enforcement of core labour obligations in an IIA, incorporating the labour standards for investors' activities into the treaty would address the risk that the adoption and enforcement of those standards would be challenged through investor–state arbitration. States could also address this risk directly by excluding non-discriminatory labour regulation and enforcement of the identified standards from the purview of the treaty through an exception.[243]

Access to treaty-based enforcement mechanisms. The most important benefit of including such a provision in an IIA is that it raises the obligation to comply with core labour standards to the international level.[244] This not only helps balance investor rights with obligations in the treaty, but also allows states, if they wish, to complement domestic laws and enforcement mechanisms with treaty-based enforcement mechanisms. These can include grievance processes,[245] civil liability[246] and state counterclaims in dispute settlement[247] as discussed below.

An IIA could be drafted to provide that treaty-based enforcement mechanisms would apply to the failure by an investor to observe domestic labour standards. The treaty obligation to comply with domestic law discussed above has the effect of doing this.[248] Expressing standards in the treaty itself makes the requirements for investor more transparent.

6.10.3 Discussion of sample provision

The Guide includes a sample provision obliging investors to meet core international labour standards. The sample provision does not deal with state obligations. These are considered below in a separate section.[249]

States will have to determine, based on their international obligations, their particular circumstances and the costs and benefits discussed above, whether or not they wish to adopt or strengthen labour legislation and/or incorporate an obligation on investors into an IIA in the manner provided for in the sample provision. The

243 See Section 5.12 (Reservations and exceptions).

244 UNCTAD (2012), *Investment Policy Framework for Sustainable Development*, op. cit., at 12.

245 See Section 6.15 (Grievance procedure and other measures to enforce the management plan produced in the sustainability assessment).

246 See Section 6.16 (Civil liability of investors).

247 See Sections 6.17 (Counterclaims by states in investor–state arbitration) and 7.1.7 (Sample provisions: investor–state dispute settlement, Article [W] (Counterclaims)).

248 See Section 6.7 (Investor obligation to comply with the laws of the host state).

249 See 6.12 (Other rights and obligations of party states).

inclusion of core labour standards in an IIA may be acceptable to host states, investors and their home states for a number of reasons:

- As discussed above, the maintenance of strong core labour standards has been found not to be a deterrent to investment, while violations of labour rights can deter investment.
- Almost all states have accepted the *ILO Declaration*,[250] and the large majority of Commonwealth countries have ratified the key ILO Conventions underlying the principles set out in the *ILO Declaration*.[251]
- Many investors are likely to be familiar with the international standards imposed in this provision. Investors are represented in the tripartite ILO structure, and many large companies list the *ILO Declaration* in their corporate social responsibility policies. In addition, these obligations are all specifically recognised as corporate responsibilities in voluntary codes of conduct for investors such as the *Global Compact*[252] and the *OECD Guidelines for Multinational Enterprises*.[253] Moreover, the revised *Guidelines for International Investment* of the International Chamber of Commerce encourage investors to comply with domestic and international labour laws even where such laws are not enforced.[254] Many investors claim to have adapted their operations to meet these standards. Therefore, compliance with these standards should not be unduly burdensome for them.

The Guide sample provision goes further than the current practice in IIAs and side accords in relation to the protection of labour standards in several ways.

- **Imposes obligations on investors:** The most radical departure from current IIA practice is that it imposes a treaty obligation directly on investors to comply with core labour standards.
- **Lists core labour rights and references the eight core ILO treaties:** The sample provision spells out the core standards set out in the *ILO Declaration*, rather than simply referencing the non-binding *Declaration*. It also links the obligations to the relevant ILO Conventions. This goes some way to addressing one of the criticisms of the regime created by the *ILO Declaration*, namely that it obscures the precise relationship between the principles of the Declaration and the legal rights that are set out in the underlying ILO Conventions.[255]

---

250 H Mann, K von Moltke, LE Peterson and A Cosbey (2005), *IISD Model International Agreement on Investment for Sustainable Development*, International Institute for Sustainable Development, Winnipeg, available at: www.iisd.org/pdf/2005/investment_model_int_agreement.pdf (accessed 29 May 2012) at 26.

251 See ILO, Ratifications of the Fundamental Human Rights Conventions by Country, ILOLEX Database of International Labour Standards, available at: www.ilo.org/ilolex/english/docs/declprint.htm (accessed 8 January 2013).

252 UN Global Compact, op. cit.

253 *OECD Guidelines*, op. cit.

254 ICC (2012), 'ICC Guidelines for International Investment', ICC, Paris, available at: www.uscib.org/docs/2012_04_21_icc_investment_guidelines.pdf (accessed 8 January 2013), at 14.

255 For a full discussion of this and other criticisms of the Declaration regime, see Alston, op. cit. These conventions are: ILO Convention No. 29, 87, 98, 100, 105, 111, 138 and 182.

The obligations set out in the Guide provision elaborate on the minimum labour standards to which investors are bound, regardless of whether adherence to such standards is specifically required by domestic law. As a result, the article provides investors with clear benchmarks for conduct alongside domestic requirements. The provisions of the Guide draw extensively on the equivalent provisions in the *Draft UN Norms on the Responsibilities of Transnational Corporations*.[256]

- **Takes into account host state policies to address past discrimination against certain groups:** The obligation on investors and investments to ensure equality of opportunity and treatment in employment by eliminating discrimination is subject to the obligation to comply with host state requirements to hire and promote individuals from certain historically disadvantaged groups.[257]
- **Requires security providers to respect freedom of association:** The obligation to respect the right to freedom of association in the Guide sample provision goes beyond the IISD model treaty by requiring that investors exercise due diligence to ensure that their contractors, including security contractors, respect this right in connection with all work related to, or conducted for, the investment. The aim of this provision is to ensure that investors are not complicit in violations of this right and do not profit from violating it.
- **Protects the right to a healthy and safe work environment:** The Guide sample provision adds to the core labour rights listed in the *ILO Declaration* the obligation to provide a healthy and safe work environment. By doing so, the sample provision addresses a second important critique of the Declaration, that the selection of principles to be included in the Declaration was somewhat arbitrary and diluted by political compromise.[258] Commentators generally agree that the Declaration should have included the right to a healthy and safe work environment.[259]

  The obligation in the sample provision requires investors to comply with the health and safety standards of the home or host state, whichever standards are more rigorous for the particular industry in question. The rationale for choosing these more rigorous standards is that investors should be held to the highest standards of health and safety in all countries in which they operate and should not be able to provide less protection for their workers simply because they are operating in states with less rigorous standards. Ensuring high standards of health and safety in employment, as with other core labour rights, is an important aspect of sustainable development. The requirement to provide a healthy and safe work

256 Draft UN Norms, op.cit.

257 South Africa's Black Economic Empowerment (BEE) policy requires, among other measures, the hiring and promotion into management positions of blacks, Coloureds and Indians. For a critical discussion of the BEE policy and international investment law, see D Schneiderman (2009), 'Promoting Equality, Black Economic Empowerment, and the Future of Investment Rules', 25 *South African Journal on Human Rights* 246.

258 Alston, op. cit., at 485–6.

259 Ibid.

> environment is reflected in the *OECD Guidelines* and the *Draft UN Norms*. It is also recognised in the labour side accords to the Canadian FTAs with Chile, Costa Rica and Colombia, in the NAALC, in the Austrian model BIT, in the 2012 US model BIT and in the US FTAs discussed above, as well as the Austrian BITs noted above in this section, all of which impose obligations on party states to enforce their labour laws and regulations.

The prohibition against forced labour is not included in the Guide's core labour provisions because it is specifically dealt with in the sample provision setting out the prohibition against the commission of, or complicity in, grave violations of human rights.[260]

6.10.4 Sample provision: obligation to comply with core labour standards

Obligation to Comply with Core Labour Standards

In relation to all of their activities in the other Party, investors of a Party and their investments shall:

a. Ensure equality of opportunity and treatment in employment by eliminating discrimination based on race, colour, sex, language, religion, political opinion, national or social origin, social status, indigenous status, disability and age or other status of the individual unrelated to the inherent requirements to perform the job consistent with ILO *Convention (No. 100) concerning Equal Remuneration for Men and Women Workers for Work of Equal Value, 1951*, and ILO *Convention (No. 111) concerning Discrimination in Respect of Employment and Occupation, 1958*, and any other international obligation to which either Party is party on this subject;

b. Notwithstanding the obligations set out in paragraph (a), comply with all measures of the other Party designed to overcome past discrimination against identified groups;

c. Respect the right of individuals to freedom of association consistent with ILO *Convention (No. 87) concerning Freedom of Association and Protection of the Right to Organize, 1948*, and exercise due diligence to ensure that their contractors, including but not limited to their security contractors, respect this right in all work related to, or conducted for, the investor or the investment;

d. Respect the right of workers to organise and collectively bargain consistent with ILO *Convention (No. 98) concerning the Application of the Principles of the Right to Organise and Collective Bargaining, 1949*, not act in such a way as to impede this right and ensure that workers have access to information necessary to give effect to this right;

e. Respect the right of children to be protected from economic exploitation and support the efforts of the other Party to abolish child labour consistent with ILO *Convention (No. 138) concerning Minimum Age for Admission to*

260 See Section 6.9 (Investor obligation to refrain from the commission of, or complicity in, grave violations of human rights).

Employment 1973, ILO *Convention (No. 182) concerning the Prohibition and Immediate Action for the Elimination of the Worst Forms of Child Labour 1999*, and the *Convention on the Rights of the Child 1999*;

f. Respect other international obligations of either Party on subjects covered in sections a., c., d. and e.; and

g. Provide employees with a healthy and safe working environment in accordance with national laws of the Party or the other Party, whichever are more rigorous in relation to the investment in question.

6.11 Investor obligation to refrain from acts, or complicity in acts, of bribery and corruption

Cross references

Section 6.7	Investor obligation to comply with the laws of the host state	292
Section 6.8	Investor obligation to respect internationally recognised human rights and undertake human rights due diligence	294
Section 6.10	Investor obligation to comply with core labour standards	322
Section 6.12	Other rights and obligations of party states	345
Section 6.14	Criminal sanctions	373
Section 6.15	Grievance procedure and other measures to enforce the management plan produced in the sustainability assessment	381
Section 6.16	Civil liability of investors	387
Section 6.17	Counterclaims by states in investor–state arbitration	401
Section 7.1.7	Sample provisions: investor–state dispute settlement, Article [W] (Counterclaims)	478

Corruption can undermine sustainable development and its goals of environmental protection and the eradication of poverty. It discourages investment and reduces economic growth.[261] It can result in the diversion of aid and loss of tax revenue, directly affecting a state's ability to finance public goods, including education. It can also distort public procurement decisions, which in turn has an impact on the cost-effectiveness and quality of public infrastructure and government services.[262] Corruption can also distort competition, create inefficiencies and lead to human rights abuses and environmental and other damage, where procedures and substantive rules are waived or not enforced as a result of corrupt actions.[263] On the other hand,

261 P Mauro (1996), 'The Effects of Corruption on Growth, Investment, and Government Expenditure', No 96/98 IMF Working Paper at 7–8. See also R S Igwike, M E Hussain and A Noman (2012), 'The Impact of Corruption on Economic Development: A Panel Data Analysis', available at: http://ssrn.com/abstract=2003061, at 5 (accessed 8 January 2013); S Rose-Ackerman (2010), 'The Law and Economics of Bribery and Extortion', 6 *Annual Review of Law and Social Science* 217 at 219 (noting the social costs of bribery); and C R Kumar (2006), 'Corruption as a Human Rights Issue in South Asia: Law, Development and Governance', Paper delivered at Human Rights 2006: The Year in Review Conference, Castan Centre for Human Rights Law, Monash University, available at: www.law.monash.edu.au/castancentre/events/2006/conf-06-kumar-paper.html (accessed 8 January 2013).

262 Mauro, ibid.

263 P Eigen and J Moberg (2007), 'Transparency and Accountability as a Driver for Growth', in *The State of Responsible Competitiveness 2007: Making Sustainable Development Count in Global Markets*, AccountAbility, London, 71 at 71–2. See also L Pellegrini (2011), *Corruption, Development and the Environment*, Springer, Dordrecht, at 149–50.

it has been shown that protecting and realising economic, social and cultural rights, which target poverty and economic inequality, increases the state's ability to control corruption and to operate in a manner that is transparent and consistent with the rule of law, as well as strengthening the ethics of private business behaviour.[264]

Corruption can also have negative impacts on investors. Agreements reached through bribery are legally unenforceable.[265] In addition, an increasing number of states have introduced laws prohibiting individuals and corporations from engaging in bribery and other forms of corruption in other states, and have begun to investigate and prosecute offenders.[266] Allegations of corruption and, especially, prosecution can cause significant reputational damage to corporations, and defending against criminal charges can be costly.

Five Commonwealth countries[267] are parties to the OECD *Convention on Combating Bribery of Foreign Public Officials in International Business Transactions*,[268] which imposes obligations on parties to establish criminal sanctions for acts of bribery of foreign public officials. Moreover, 16 Commonwealth states are party to the *African Union Convention on Preventing and Combatting Corruption*[269] and thus have obligations to take steps to eliminate corruption domestically and to exercise jurisdiction over nationals engaging in corrupt activities in another state. In addition, 44 Commonwealth countries[270] are party to the *UN Convention against Corruption*,[271]

---

264 D Kaufmann (2005), 'Human Rights and Governance: The Empirical Challenge' in P Alston and M Robinson, (eds), *Human Rights and Development: Towards Mutual Reinforcement*, OUP, Oxford and New York, 352, at 382–383.

265 Pellegrini, op. cit., at 61.

266 See, for example, the UK case of *Corner House Research and Campaign Against Arms Trade v. The Director of the Serious Fraud Office and BAE Systems PLC*, [2008] EWHC 714 (Admin). See also the US cases, *US v. Siemens Aktiengesellschaft*, No 08-367 (DDC Filed Dec 15, 2008); *SEC v. Siemens Aktiengesellschaft*, No 1:08-cv-02167 (DDC Filed Dec 15, 2008); *US v. ABB Inc*, No 4:10-cr-00664 (SD Tex 2010). In Canada, Niko Resources pleaded guilty to charges of corruption in relation to its operations in Bangladesh. See *R v. Niko Resources Ltd*, (23 June 2011) (AB QB) Agreed Statement of Facts, available at: www.osler.com/uploadedFiles/Agreed%20statement%20of%20facts.pdf (accessed 8 January 2013). In addition there is an ongoing investigation of SNC Lavalin for corruption in its operations in Libya and Bangladesh. See Andrew Chung (2012), 'RCMP Raids SNC-Lavalin's Montreal Headquarters', *Toronto Star*, 13 April, available at: www.thestar.com/news/canada/article/1161146–rcmp-raids-snc-lavalin-s-montreal-headquarters (accessed 8 January 2013).

267 Australia, Canada, New Zealand, South Africa and the UK.

268 OECD *Convention on Combating Bribery of Foreign Public Officials in International Business Transactions*, adopted 21 November 1997, in force 15 February 1999, OECD Doc DAFFE/IME/BR(97)20. As of 2004, all parties to the OECD Convention had enacted legislation to implement the treaty, see OECD, 'OECD Convention on Combating Bribery of Foreign Public Officials in International Business Transactions, Ratification Status as of April 2012'.

269 *African Union Convention on Preventing and Combatting Corruption*, adopted 11 July 2003, in force 5 August 2006, 43 *International Legal Materials* 5 (2004), Art. 4.

270 Antigua and Barbuda, Australia, The Bahamas, Bangladesh, Brunei Darussalam, Cameroon, Canada, Cyprus, Dominica, Fiji, Ghana, Guyana, India, Jamaica, Kenya, Lesotho, Malawi, Malaysia, Maldives, Malta, Mauritius, Mozambique, Namibia, Nauru, New Zealand, Nigeria, Pakistan, Papua New Guinea, Rwanda, St. Lucia, Samoa, Seychelles, Sierra Leone, Singapore, Solomon Islands, South Africa, Sri Lanka, Swaziland, United Republic of Trinidad and Tobago, Uganda, United Kingdom, United Republic of Tanzania, Vanuatu and Zambia.

271 *UN Convention against Corruption*, adopted 31 October 2003, in force 14 December 2005, GA Res 58/4, UN Doc A/58/422 (2003), 43 *International Legal Materials* 37 (2004).

and 12 are party to the *Inter-American Convention Against Corruption*.[272] Both these latter conventions require states to take measures to address corruption domestically and permit states to exercise jurisdiction over nationals that engage in corruption abroad. Where states have fully implemented their obligations under these treaties, their nationals may have obligations not to engage in acts of corruption, including bribery, in any state in which they operate. In addition, both the *OECD Guidelines for Multinational Enterprises*[273] and the *Global Compact*[274] strongly discourage acts of corruption, including bribery, as a core principle of corporate social responsibility.

6.11.1 IIA practice

A few existing IIAs address corruption. The preambles of the Austria–Kosovo BIT and the Austria–Tajikistan BIT, for instance, make reference to 'the necessity for all governments and civil actors alike to adhere to UN and OECD anti-corruption efforts, most notably the UN Convention against Corruption (2003)'.[275]

Other IIAs impose obligations on the states parties to implement legislative and other measures to prohibit and sanction corruption. The EU–Korea FTA, for example, recalls the obligations of the parties under the OECD Convention and requires each party to adopt or maintain appropriate measures to prohibit and punish bribery and corruption in the pharmaceutical and health care sectors, and to bring to the attention of the other party situations of bribery in these sectors.[276]

The EC–CARIFORUM EPA has a provision that is more broadly focused. The parties agree to 'take the necessary legislative and administrative measures to comply with international standards, including those laid down in the United Nations Convention against Corruption' and to co-operate and take domestic measures, including legislation, to prohibit and punish bribery or corruption.[277]

A stronger approach, going beyond imposing obligations on party states to address bribery and other forms of corruption, would be to target investor conduct directly by imposing obligations on investors. The IISD model treaty departs from IIA practice by establishing an obligation on investors to refrain from acts of bribery and corruption. The obligation tracks the wording of the OECD and UN conventions, but it also includes language to ensure that bribes directly given to an official's family or close associates are within the scope of proscribed activity.[278]

---

272 *Inter-American Convention Against Corruption*, adopted 29 March 1996, in force 6 March 1997, Art. 7.

273 *OECD Guidelines*, op. cit.

274 *UN Global Compact*, op. cit.

275 See Kosovo–Austria BIT (2010), preamble; Austria–Tajikistan BIT, preamble.

276 See preamble and Annex 2-D, Art. 4, European Union–South Korea Free Trade Agreement, signed 15 October 2009, in force 1 July 2011.

277 EC–CARIFORUM EPA (2008), Arts. 237 and 72.

278 IISD Model Treaty, Art. 13.

Box 6.12 Summary of options for investor obligations to refrain from acts or complicity in bribery and corruption

1. *Do not require foreign investors to refrain from acts or complicity in acts of bribery and corruption*
2. *Use existing domestic laws to regulate and sanction bribery and corruption*
3. *Introduce new legislation to prohibit and punish bribery and corruption consistent with a state's international obligations*
4. *Integrate provisions on corruption into an IIA through:*
   a. Language in the preamble
   b. Provisions in the agreement requiring parties to prohibit corruption in a particular industry, enforce appropriate penalties and notify the other party of situations of corruption
   c. An obligation on states to co-operate to ensure investors are prohibited from, and effectively sanctioned for, engaging in corruption
   d. Obligation on investors to refrain from acts or complicity in acts of bribery and corruption

6.11.2 Discussion of options

1. *Do not require foreign investors to refrain from acts or complicity in acts of bribery and corruption*

This may deter investment: Not taking any action to prevent and punish acts of bribery or corruption is likely to discourage foreign investment. Investors generally prefer to invest in open, stable states with strong, transparent regulatory frameworks.

It undermines sustainable development: Corruption can undermine the ability of government to pursue its sustainable development goals. It can result in a loss of government revenues, illegitimate and inefficient government procurement decisions, and distorted competition, as well as leading to human rights and environmental abuses.

States may be in breach of their international obligations: Many Commonwealth countries have ratified the *UN Convention against Corruption*, the African Union convention or the *Inter-American Convention against Corruption* and some are parties to the OECD anti-bribery convention. Thus they have obligations under those treaties to prohibit and punish acts of bribery and other forms of corruption. Failure to enact such laws would put them in breach of these obligations.

2. *Use existing domestic laws to regulate and sanction bribery and corruption*

This option may be attractive to states because it would not require any further expenditure of resources on the part of the state. However, existing laws may not be sufficiently robust or may not target all corrupt activities. In addition, some states may have limited resources to devote to enforcement and many states encounter difficulties in regulating the behaviour of powerful foreign investors.

3. *Introduce new legislation to prohibit and punish bribery and corruption, consistent with a state's international obligations*

It is costly to develop a regulatory framework: Adopting new legislation will require states to dedicate resources to developing a robust anti-corruption framework to meet their international obligations. This may require establishing new institutions to enforce the laws and will be onerous for some states.

Domestic laws can be difficult to enforce against foreign investors: As noted above,[279] all states face challenges in enforcing domestic laws against powerful business actors. Thus, even where a state enacts or strengthens existing anti-corruption laws, it may be unable to effectively enforce such laws against foreign investors in some cases.

This implements the states' international obligations and supports sustainable development: Conversely, there are significant advantages to introducing a strong anti-corruption regulatory framework. It will bring states that have international obligations under the OECD Convention, the UN Convention or other instruments into compliance with such commitments, if they are not already. It will also help ensure that investors and their investments support, rather than undermine, the sustainable development goals of the host state.

It may decrease the costs of doing business: Reducing bribery and corrupt activities will increase transparency and predictability regarding the payments investors are required to make to host state governments and in their relations with host state governments generally. This may decrease the cost of doing business in the host state.

It attracts investment and in particular socially responsible investment: Studies have shown that corruption deters investment. Having strong anti-corruption laws indicates to potential investors, particularly to socially responsible investors and investors concerned with maintaining their global reputation, that the state has a stable, transparent and predictable regulatory environment.

It helps manage corporate risk: Where a contract is concluded through bribery or other corrupt activities, it can be unenforceable. In many situations, investors can be prosecuted under the laws of their home states for engaging in bribery or other forms of corruption in other states. Investors that come under investigation for corruption, even where they are not convicted, can suffer significant reputational damage, which can lead to a decrease in share value. Operating in a state with strong anti-corruption legislation can reduce the risk that investors will get caught up in corrupt activities.

---

279 See Section 6.8 (Investor obligation to respect internationally recognised human rights and undertake human rights due diligence) and Section 6.10 (Investor obligation to comply with core labour standards).

4. *Integrate provisions on corruption into an IIA*

There are several options for integrating provisions that address bribery and other forms of corruption into an IIA. The following are a few examples.

Language in the preamble: As discussed in the preceding section,[280] preambular language does not create binding obligations for party states or investors. The language may be used to interpret states' obligations under the IIA, but will not on its own provide a means of effectively addressing corruption.

Provisions in the agreement requiring parties to prohibit corruption in a particular industry, enforce appropriate penalties and notify the other party of situations of corruption: This type of provision is used in the EU–Korea FTA.

Is less costly. This option will be less onerous for some host states with scarce resources, allowing them to focus their enforcement measures on a particular industry or on the most corrupt sectors.

Requires states to share information on corruption. Requiring parties to exchange information of any corrupt activities in a particular sector may aid states in investigating and prosecuting investors that engage in corrupt practices or activities.

Does not fully implement states' international obligations. Focusing on a few industry sectors, however, does not fulfil states' obligations under the OECD, UN, AU or Inter-American conventions. If the commitment is not limited to particular sectors, however, this problem can be avoided.

May deter investment. This option may not sufficiently address corrupt activities among investors and may discourage investors that are seeking transparent and predictable business environments.

An obligation on states to co-operate to ensure investors are prohibited from, and effectively sanctioned for, engaging in corruption.

Harnesses home state regulatory capacity and co-operation in regulating investor conduct. As discussed above with respect to labour rights, this type of provision can also help states to address the challenges of regulating foreign investors that might otherwise be able to evade compliance with domestic law of the host state. It requires both states to take domestic measures and to co-operate in their enforcement to ensure that corruption is prohibited and sanctioned under domestic law.

Is more cost-intensive. This approach, which has been adopted in the EC–CARIFORUM EPA, will require more state resources than the preceding option. States will need to develop an effective anti-corruption regulatory and institutional framework and devote resources to co-operative enforcement measures to fulfil such an obligation.

Obligation on investors to refrain from acts, or complicity in acts, of bribery and corruption: The potential benefits and drawbacks of incorporating into an IIA an obligation on investors to refrain from acts, or complicity in acts, of bribery and corruption are similar to those identified above with respect to incorporating such an obligation into domestic law.

280 See Section 6.10 (Investor obligation to comply with core labour standards).

There is, however, an additional significant advantage to including such a provision in an IIA. It makes the obligation to refrain from bribery and corruption a treaty obligation. This means that states can support domestic enforcement mechanisms with treaty-based enforcement mechanisms. These mechanisms could include criminal enforcement in both the host state and the investor's home state, grievance processes (which can reveal information on bribery and corruption), civil liability and state counterclaims in dispute settlement, all of which are considered below.[281]

An IIA could be drafted to provide that treaty-based enforcement mechanisms would apply to the failure by an investor to comply with domestic laws on bribery and corruption. The treaty obligation to comply with domestic law discussed above has the effect of doing this.[282] Expressing standards in the treaty itself makes the requirements for investor more transparent and can help ensure compatibility with international standards.

6.11.3 Discussion of sample provision

The aim of the sample provision is to prohibit investors from engaging in corrupt activities directly. States will have to determine, based on their international obligations, their particular circumstances and the costs and benefits discussed above, whether or not they wish to adopt or strengthen anti-corruption legislation and/or incorporate an obligation on investors into an IIA in the manner provided for in the sample provision.

The Guide sample provision departs from current IIA practice and adopts a modified version of the IISD provision imposing direct obligations on investors not to commit, or be complicit in, bribery or other acts of corruption in relation to their investment. It does not address state co-operation because this is addressed in a separate section on state obligations.[283]

It includes the IISD provision's language prohibiting bribery of an 'official's family, business associate or other person in close proximity to an official'. In doing so, it provides a higher standard than in the OECD, UN, AU or Inter-American conventions. Drawing on the UN Convention, the sample provision also includes in the prohibited outcomes of an act of bribery or corruption '[o]btaining or retaining any other business or other undue advantage in relation to such investment'.[284]

In order for the obligation in the sample provision to be fully effective and capable of being addressed in a counterclaim by states, it will need to take effect prior to the investment being approved by the state. Otherwise, bribery and corruption in

281 See Section 6.14 (Criminal sanctions); Section 6.15 (Grievance procedure and other measures to enforce the management plan produced in the sustainability assessment); Section 6.16 (Civil liability of investors); and Sections 6.17 (Counterclaims by states in investor–state arbitration) and 7.1.7 (Sample provisions: investor–state dispute settlement, Article [W] (Counterclaims)).

282 See Section 6.7 (Investor obligation to comply with the laws of the host state).

283 See Section 6.12 (Other rights and obligations of party states).

284 *UN Convention against Corruption*, Art 16.

connection with investment approvals would not be caught. The time for the commencement of investor obligations is discussed above.[285]

Other sample provisions in the Guide impose consequences for investors who breach the obligations relating to corruption. These provisions, if included in an IIA, would require party states to impose criminal sanctions for such behaviour and permit civil actions for relief for injuries that such behaviour may cause.[286] In addition, investors in breach of these obligations may be subject to a counterclaim by states in investor–state arbitration cases that they initiate.[287]

6.11.4 Sample provision: obligation to refrain from acts, or complicity in acts, of bribery and corruption

Obligation to Refrain from Acts, or Complicity in Acts, of Bribery or Corruption

1. Investors of a Party and their investments shall not, either prior to or after the establishment of an investment, offer, promise, or give any undue pecuniary or other advantage, whether directly or indirectly, to a public official of the other Party, or to a member of such an official's family or such official's business associate or other person in close proximity to such official, in order that the official or third party act or refrain from acting in relation to the performance of official duties, or use his or her influence to:
   a. Obtain any favour in relation to a proposed or actual investment;
   b. Obtain or renew any licences, permits, contracts or other rights in relation to a proposed or actual investment; or
   c. Obtain or retain any other business or other undue advantage in relation to such investment.
2. Investors of a Party and their investments shall not be complicit in any act described in Section 1, including incitement, aiding and abetting, conspiracy to commit or the authorisation of such acts.

6.12 Other rights and obligations of party states

Cross references

Section 2.3	Links between foreign investment and sustainable development	18
Section 4.2.1	The role of preambles in IIAs	42
Section 5.3	National treatment	110
Section 5.4	Most favoured nation	124
Section 5.5	Fair and equitable treatment and the minimum standard treatment	138
Section 5.6	Limitations on expropriation and nationalisation	152

285 See Sections 4.4 (Statement of objectives) and 5.2 (Right of establishment).

286 See Section 6.14 (Criminal sanctions) and Section 6.16 (Civil liability of investors).

287 See Sections 6.17 (Counterclaims by states in investor–state arbitration) and 7.1.7 (Sample provisions: investor–state dispute settlement, Article [W] (Counterclaims)).

As discussed above,[288] international human rights law imposes a three-part obligation on states to respect, protect and fulfil human rights[289] with respect to individuals within their territory and subject to their jurisdiction. The *obligation to protect* is an obligation of due diligence.[290] International human rights law requires a state to take measures, such as enacting legislation and adopting administrative practices, to control, regulate, investigate and prosecute actions by non-state actors that violate the human rights of those within the territory, and subject to the jurisdiction, of that state.[291]

States have been found by international human rights treaty monitoring bodies to be in breach of the obligation to protect in a variety of situations, including where corporate actors have violated labour rights,[292] where the activities of companies have polluted both air and land,[293] and for failures by the state to protect indigenous peoples' land from harm caused by business activities or from commercial development.[294]

---

288 See Section 6.8 (Investor obligation to respect internationally recognised human rights and undertake human rights due diligence).

289 See, for example, the analysis by the UN Committee on Economic, Social and Cultural Rights in *General Comment No 13: The Right to Education*, UNCESCR, UN Doc E/C.12/1999/10, (1999) at para. 46, where the Committee states: 'The right to education, like all human rights, imposes three types or levels of obligations on states parties: the obligations to respect, protect and fulfill. In turn, the obligation to fulfill incorporates both an obligation to facilitate and an obligation to provide'.

290 See generally A Clapham (1993), *Human Rights in the Private Sphere*, Clarendon Press, Oxford; A Clapham (2001), 'Revisiting Human Rights in the Private Sphere: Using the European Convention on Human Rights to Protect the Right of Access to the Civil Courts', in C Scott (ed.), *Torture as Tort: Comparative Perspectives on the Development of Transnational Human Rights Litigation*, Hart Publishing, Oxford, 513 at 513.

291 See, for example, *Velásquez Rodriguez v. Honduras*, op. cit., 294; *Herra Rubio v. Colombia* (161/1983), (1988) HRC Report, GAOR, 43rd Sess., Supp. 40, 190 [11]; *Ergi v. Turkey* (App. 23818/94) (1998) 32 EHRR 388; *Timurtas v. Turkey* (App. no. 23531/94) (2000) ECHR 13 June 2000; and *A v. UK* (App. no. 25599/94) (1999) 27 EHRR 611.

292 See, for example, *Young, James and Webster v. UK*, (1981) 44 ECHR (Ser A), 4 EHRR 38.

293 See, for example, *Lopez Ostra v. Spain*, (1994) 303C ECHR (Ser A), 20 EHRR 277; *Guerra v. Italy*, (1998) 7 ECHR, 26 EHRR 357. See *Social and Economic Rights Action Centre for Economic and Social Rights v. Nigeria*, (2001) Communication No 155/96 African Commission.

294 See, for example, *Yanomani v. Brazil*, (1985) Inter-Am Ct HR (Ser L) No 12/85; *The Mayagna (Sumo) Awas Tingni Community v. Nicaragua*, (2001) Inter-Am Ct HR (Ser C) No 79; *Hopu and Bessert v. France*, HRC, UN Doc CCPR/C/60/D/549/1993/Rev.1, (1997) at para 10.3; *Saramaka People v. Suriname*, op cit.

An important criticism of current IIAs, which has been discussed in various sections of the Guide, is that they can restrict the capacity of host states to implement laws, regulations and policies to comply with their environmental obligations and their international human rights obligations, including their duties under international labour law and their international obligations with respect to indigenous peoples, as well as their obligations to prevent and punish bribery and corruption.[295] An IIA that aims to promote foreign investment that supports and facilitates sustainable development should not unduly restrict the host state's capacity to comply with these international legal duties. The agreement must therefore protect the state's right to introduce laws and regulations for this purpose. The UN Special Representative of the Secretary-General on the Issue of Human Rights and Transnational Corporations and other Business Enterprises (SRSG) has urged states that are in the process of, or considering, reviewing their policy with respect to IIAs 'to ensure that the new model BITs combine robust investor protection with adequate allowances for *bona fide* public interest measures, including human rights, applied in a non-discriminatory manner'.[296]

These concerns are addressed by the sample provisions on investor protection standards, as well as the provisions dealing with reservations and exceptions discussed above.[297] The following section of the Guide addresses states' implementation and enforcement of their international obligations.

In order to realise the overall goal of promoting sustainable development, party states must play an important role in promoting and protecting human rights (including labour rights and indigenous peoples' rights), protecting the environment, and preventing and punishing bribery and corruption, as well as addressing other development priorities. To achieve these goals, states should take the necessary steps to bring their domestic laws into compliance with their international obligations.[298] The obligations on investors set out in the Guide will be most effective if they are supported by host states through legislative, administrative and other measures to ensure that foreign investment supports, rather than undermines, sustainable development. Introducing such domestic laws and regulations is a first and fundamental step in this regard. Negotiating a provision in an IIA requiring states to adopt standards in their domestic law would complement and reinforce such domestic measures.

295 See UNHRC (2008), 'Protect Respect and Remedy', op. cit.; Sornarajah, op. cit.; Schneiderman, op. cit., and Miles, op. cit.

296 'Report of the Special Representative of the Secretary-General on the Issue of Human Rights and Transnational Corporations and Other Business Enterprises, John Ruggie. Business and Human Rights: Further Steps toward the Operationalization of the "Protect, Respect and Remedy" Framework', UNHRC, UN Doc A/HRC/14/27, (2010) at para 23. See also *UN Guiding Principles on Business and Human Rights*, op. cit., at Principle 9 and commentary.

297 See Section 5.12 (Reservations and exceptions).

298 See, for example, the rights set out the core UN human rights treaties (as well as their optional protocols) including, *ICCPR* and *ICESCR*; *ICERD*; *CAT*; *CEDAW*: *CRC*; *ICRMW*; *CPED*; *CRPD*. In addition, see the ILO Conventions 29, 87, 98, 100, 105, 111, 138 and 182.

This section builds on the discussion in previous sections by considering in more detail the costs and benefits of introducing new domestic laws setting minimum standards for human rights, labour rights, indigenous peoples' rights, and environmental protection as well as anti-corruption measures as a means to help achieve sustainable development. It also considers a range of alternative a means for states to incorporate an obligation to meet minimum standards for their domestic laws in these areas into an IIA. In the consultations undertaken in developing the Guide some state representatives articulated a strong concern that IIA provisions creating obligations for states with respect to minimum standards in these areas would represent an inappropriate intrusion into state sovereignty. In particular, some were concerned that such provisions would create opportunities for other party states to put pressure on a state with respect to the design and enforcement of its domestic laws in these complex and sensitive areas. In light of the controversial nature of IIA provisions that impose minimum standards in these areas, no sample provision of this kind has been included in the Guide. Nevertheless, there are potential benefits that could flow from this kind of provision from a sustainable development point of view. These benefits as well as the costs are discussed below. For states that wish to consider ways of incorporating such an obligation into an IIA, the discussion of IIA practice in this section makes reference to a range of examples and options that are drawn from state practice.

6.12.1 IIA practice

A growing number of IIAs include obligations on states regarding standards to be reflected in their domestic laws. The sections on investor obligations have canvassed IIA practice with respect to human rights, labour rights, and bribery and corruption.[299] This section focuses on obligations relating to environmental protection.

Language on protecting the environment is becoming more commonplace in IIAs, with about 50 per cent of new treaties each year including provisions on environmental protection.[300] States have taken a variety of approaches to addressing environmental concerns associated with foreign investment. Gordon and Pohl, in a survey of 1,623 IIAs, identify a range of provisions that are increasingly found in IIAs.[301] Examples of these different types of provisions are discussed below, together with other types of provisions not identified in that study. Such provisions include language on environmental protection in the preamble, references to environmental standards in

---

299 See Section 6.8 (Investor obligation to respect internationally recognised human rights and undertake human rights due diligence); Section 6.9 (Investor obligation to refrain from the commission of, or complicity in, grave violations of human rights); Section 6.10 (Investor obligation to comply with core labour standards); Section 6.11 (Investor obligation to refrain from acts, or complicity in acts, of bribery and corruption).

300 K Gordon and J Pohl (2011), 'Environmental Concerns in International Investment Agreements: A Survey', 2011/1 OECD Working Papers on International Investment at 7, available at: www.oecd.org/dataoecd/50/12/48083618.pdf (accessed 8 January 2013).

301 Ibid. at 13–25.

separate provisions in the body of the treaty text or in a side agreement, exceptions, CSR provisions and provisions on co-operation regarding investor compliance with environmental standards.

Language in the preamble: Language in the preamble on environmental protection does not create binding obligations on states or, on its own, provide effective protection of the environment. As discussed above,[302] the aim of the preamble is to describe the overall goals of the parties in entering the treaty and to set out the context for interpreting treaty obligations. A preamble might, for instance, express the desire that the objectives of the treaty be accomplished in a manner consistent with certain principles, such as environmental protection or sustainable development. For example, the preamble of the EC–CARIFORUM EPA considers the need of the parties 'to promote economic and social progress for their people in a manner consistent with sustainable development by respecting basic labour rights ... and by protecting the environment'.[303] Similarly, the preamble of the US–Morocco FTA expresses the desire of the parties 'to strengthen the development and enforcement of ... environmental policies ... promote sustainable development, and implement this Agreement in a manner consistent with environmental protection and conservation'.[304] States can draft a preamble so as to give precedence in the interpretation of the treaty to environmental or other non-investment norms. However, if such precedence is not clearly specified in an investment treaty, a person or an investment tribunal interpreting the treaty will be likely to give preference to investment protection and promotion over other norms.

Obligation not to relax domestic environmental standards to encourage investment: Some IIAs include a provision recognising that it is inappropriate for parties to lower or waive environmental standards in order to attract investment. The Canadian model FIPA, for example, incorporates a provision in which the parties recognise that it is inappropriate to encourage investment 'by relaxing domestic health, safety or environmental measures.'[305] The Austrian model BIT includes a similarly worded provision, but it also provides for consultations where a party considers that the other party is attempting to encourage investment by lowering such standards.[306] The US model BIT goes somewhat further by specifically prohibiting waiving or derogating from environmental laws so as to lower the protections provided by such laws or consistently failing to apply such laws to encourage investment.[307]

302 Section 4.2.1 (The role of preambles in IIAs).
303 EC–CARIFORUM EPA (2008), preamble.
304 US–Morocco FTA (2004), preamble.
305 Art 11.
306 Austria Model BIT. See also NAFTA (1992), Art. 1114(2);
307 2012 US Model BIT, Art. 12. See also EC–CARICOM EPA (2008), Arts. 73, 188.1(a),(b); EU–Korea FTA (2009), Art. 13.7; US–Chile FTA (2003), Art. 19.2; US–Singapore FTA (2003), Art. 18.2; Australia–US FTA (2004), Art. 19.2.

Obligation to strengthen domestic laws on environmental protection: In addition to an obligation not to relax domestic environmental laws and regulations, a few IIAs also contain provisions that:

- Recognise the right of the parties to establish their own environmental standards;
- Oblige the parties to maintain high levels of environmental protection; and
- Require the parties to strive to improve such standards.[308]

Some IIAs, such as the Belgium–Luxemburg model BIT, also reaffirm the parties' international commitments under environmental treaties and impose an obligation on the parties to strive to ensure that these international environmental law obligations are implemented in domestic law.[309]

The EC–CARIFORUM EPA provides a variation of this type of provision. It highlights the need for developing countries to take into account their development priorities and their level of development:

> 1. Recognising the right of the Parties and the Signatory CARIFORUM States to regulate in order to achieve their own level of domestic environmental and public health protection and their own sustainable development priorities, and to adopt or modify accordingly their environmental laws and policies, each Party and Signatory CARIFORUM State shall seek to ensure that its own environmental and public health laws and policies provide for and encourage high levels of environmental and public health protection and shall strive to continue to improve those laws and policies.
> 2. The Parties agree that the special needs and requirements of CARIFORUM States shall be taken into account in the design and implementation of measures aimed at protecting environment and public health that affect trade between the Parties.[310]

The goal of these various types of provisions is not so much to improve the level of environmental protection, but to prevent competition for investment between states that will lead to a 'race to the bottom' of environmental standards. These provisions do not oblige party states to ensure that their domestic laws and regulations reflect minimum environmental standards consistent with their international environmental obligations.

Side accords: As with labour rights protections, some states have opted to negotiate side accords to free trade agreements to address the problem of a potential 'race to the bottom' of environmental standards. The North American Agreement on Environmental Cooperation (NAAEC), for example, includes provisions on environmental protection that mirror the NAALC provisions on labour rights protection.[311] The NAAEC recognises the right of parties to establish their own

---

308 See Australia–US FTA (2004), Art. 19.1; US–Chile FTA (2003), Art. 19.1; US–Singapore FTA (2003), Art. 18.1.

309 Art. 5(3). See also the Belgium–Luxembourg–Ethiopia BIT (2006), Art. 5(3).

310 EC–CARIFORUM EPA (2008), Art. 184.1

311 See Section 6.10 (Investor obligation to comply with core labour standards).

domestic environmental standards, policies and priorities, and to adopt or modify such laws and regulations. It also requires parties to ensure that their domestic laws and regulations 'provide high levels of environmental protection' and to 'strive' to improve domestic standards.[312]

In addition, party states are required to facilitate compliance with and enforce their environmental laws through appropriate government measures and to ensure that judicial and non-judicial mechanisms and other procedures are available to individuals to enforce such laws.[313] The provisions in the NAAEC aim to accomplish the same thing as the provisions of IIAs, discussed above, which merely require parties to enforce their environmental laws. There is no requirement on the parties to bring their domestic laws into compliance with their international obligations or to continuously improve such standards.

Compliance mechanisms: Some IIAs, including FTAs and side accords, incorporate mechanisms intended to ensure that states enforce their domestic environmental standards. The NAAEC and certain US FTAs establish a compliance system that includes a means for individuals and organisations to make complaints about a party's failure to enforce its environmental laws and regulations.[314] These systems are analogues of those in place to enforce labour standards, discussed above.[315] They rely primarily on consultations between the party states.[316] However, in principle, under some side agreements and FTAs, a narrow set of disputes can go on to be settled through arbitration[317] and could lead to the imposition of fines[318] or, in some cases, even sanctions to enforce such fines.[319]

Like the equivalent labour compliance mechanisms, these types of provisions do not directly target investor behaviour. According to the IISD, these compliance mechanisms are relatively new and have not to date played any significant role. In addition, there is little evidence that these compliance mechanisms, together with their complaint processes, have been effective in preventing a 'race to the bottom' by ensuring that states enforce their domestic environmental standards against foreign investors.[320]

---

312 Canada–Mexico–United States, North American Agreement on Environmental Cooperation, signed 1 January 1994, in force 1 January 1994, Art. 2.

313 NAAEC, Arts. 4–7.

314 See NAAEC (1994), Art 14. The Australia–US FTA (2004), US–Chile FTA (2003) and US–Singapore FTA (2003) only provide for members of the public to make 'communications' on environmental enforcement. The parties in each case are only under a 'best efforts' obligation 'to respond favorably to requests for consultations by such persons or organizations'. See Arts. 19.5, 19.5, 19.18.5, respectively.

315 See 6.10 (Investor obligation to comply with core labour standards).

316 See NAAEC (1994), Arts. 22–23; US–Australia FTA (2004), Art. 18.7; US–Chile FTA (2003), Art.19.5; and US–Singapore FTA (2003), Art. 18.7.

317 See NAAEC (1994), Arts. 24–36; Australia–US FTA (2004), Chapter 21; US–Chile FTA (2003), Chapter 22; US–Singapore FTA (2003), Chapter 20.

318 See NAAEC (1994), Art. 34(4)(b); Australia FTA–US (2004), Art. 21.11(1); US–Chile FTA (2003), Art. 22.15(1); US–Singapore FTA (2003), Art. 20.6(1).

319 See NAAEC (1994), Art. 36; Australia–US FTA (2004), Art. 21.11(2); US–Chile FTA (2003), Art. 22.15(2); US–Singapore FTA (2003), Art. 20.6(2).

320 Bernasconi-Osterwalder and Johnson, op. cit., at 27.

General exceptions: Some IIAs include exceptions with language that relates to environmental protection even where such provisions do not specifically use the terms 'environment' or 'environmental protection'. IIA exception provisions commonly reference 'human, animal and plant life or health, or the protection of natural resources'.[321] The Canadian model treaty includes in its exception provision the right to take measures necessary to protect, among other things, human, animal or plant life or health, and the conservation of living or non-living exhaustible resources.[322] There are a range of problems with how exceptions are commonly worded and how they are interpreted by investment tribunals.

The US–Singapore FTA includes a provision stating that:

> Nothing in this Chapter shall be construed to prevent a Party from adopting, maintaining, or enforcing any measure *otherwise consistent with this Chapter* that it considers appropriate to ensure that investment activity in its territory is undertaken in a manner sensitive to environmental concerns.[323] (Emphasis added.)

This type of provision is likely to be quite limited in its legal effect, since it requires any regulation on environmental protection to be consistent with the core investor protection provisions in the FTA. It is more in the nature of a guide to interpretation.

The section of the Guide that deals with reservations and exceptions considers the use of exceptions in more detail and discusses approaches to excluding policy areas from the application of an IIA.[324]

Exceptions excluding regulation as a basis for claims of indirect expropriation: A small number of IIAs incorporate provisions that aim to specifically preclude environmental regulation from becoming the basis for an investor to claim that such regulation constitutes indirect expropriation.[325] For instance, Canada's model FIPA includes a provision stating:

> Except in rare circumstances, such as when a measure or series of measures are so severe in the light of their purpose that they cannot be reasonably viewed as having been adopted and applied in good faith, non-discriminatory measures of a Party that are designed and applied to protect legitimate public welfare objectives, such as health, safety and the environment, do not constitute indirect expropriation.[326]

---

321 Ibid. at 17.

322 Canadian Model FIPA, Art. 10.

323 US–Singapore FTA (2003), Art. 15.10. See also, the Australia–US FTA (2004), Art. 11.11, for example.

324 See Section 5.12 (Reservations and exceptions).

325 Ibid. at 22.

326 Annex B.13(1)(c).

Similar provisions can be found in the US model BIT,[327] some US FTAs[328] and the Austrian model BIT.[329] The aim of these provisions is to ensure that *bona fide*, non-discriminatory regulation in certain policy areas will not be found by an investment tribunal to indirectly expropriate an investment and thus require the host state to pay compensation. The problem of indirect expropriation is discussed at length in Section 5.6 (Limitations on expropriation and nationalisation).

Obligation to encourage compliance with voluntary mechanisms on environmental performance: Some IIAs include general provisions on CSR relating to human rights, the environment and corruption, and they may reference CSR instruments such as the *OECD Guidelines* or the *Global Compact*.[330] These provisions are discussed in more detail above.[331] Certain US FTAs include CSR provisions that specifically target the environment. For example, the Australia–US FTA incorporates an obligation on the parties to promote 'as appropriate' the development of voluntary, market-based mechanisms that 'encourage the protection of natural resources and the environment'.[332] The US–Singapore and the US–Chile FTAs include a non-binding recommendation that parties 'encourage enterprises operating within [their] territory or subject to [their] jurisdiction to voluntarily incorporate sound principles of corporate stewardship in their internal policies, such as those principles or agreements that have been endorsed by the Parties'.[333] While these provisions raise awareness of the need for environmentally responsible conduct by investors, they have no binding effect. They do not impose obligations on states to implement laws or policies on CSR. Nor do they require investors to operate in accordance with internationally accepted CSR norms. Thus, such provisions are not directly protective of the environment.

Co-operation between parties on environmental issues: Another approach states have taken in FTAs and side accords is to establish a mechanism to enhance co-operation between the parties on environmental issues. The three US FTAs discussed in this section recognise the importance of capacity building for the purpose of environmental protection and incorporate provisions on the sharing of information relating to the environmental effects of trade agreements and policies.[334] The environmental co-operation provisions in the US–Chile FTA are more expansive and resemble the labour provisions found in some US FTAs, which provide an indicative list of co-operative activities and the implementation of such activities.[335] The US–Chile

327 Annex B, Art. 4(b).

328 See, for example, Australia–US FTA (2004), Annex 11-B, Art 4(b); US–Chile FTA (2003), Annex 10-D, Art. 4(b); US–Morocco FTA (2004), Annex 10-B, Art. 4(b).

329 Art. 7(4).

330 Canada–Colombia FTA (2008), Art. 816; Canada–Peru FTA (2008), Art. 810; Norwegian draft APPI, Art. 32.

331 See Section 6.8 (Investor obligation to respect internationally recognised human rights and undertake human rights due diligence).

332 See Australia–US FTA (2004), Art. 19.4.

333 See US–Singapore FTA (2003), Art. 18.9; US–Chile FTA (2003), Art. 19.10.

334 See the Australia–US FTA (2004), Art. 19.6; US–Singapore FTA (2003), Art. 18.6.

335 See Section 6.10 (Investor obligation to comply with core labour standards).

FTA includes such provisions[336] but goes further to require the parties to pursue certain 'cooperative projects'. These include, for example, developing a public database of chemicals that have been released into the environment, reducing the pollution from mining projects, protecting wildlife and reducing ozone-depleting substances.[337]

In contrast, the EC–CARIFORUM EPA co-operation provision focuses on the enforcement of environmental protection standards against investors. It imposes an obligation on the states parties both to co-operate and to take measures domestically to ensure that investors do not manage or operate their investments in a manner that circumvents international environmental obligations consistent with the international obligations of the parties.[338]

This provision (which is the same provision discussed with respect to labour and bribery and corruption in preceding sections of the Guide)[339] is more protective of the environment than some of the other provisions discussed in this section. First, it goes beyond simply requiring parties not to lower their domestic standards and to enforce their domestic environmental protection laws. Second, it specifically requires both parties to take action to ensure investor compliance with international environmental standards. It thus obliges the *home state* to exercise its regulatory power to ensure investor compliance with environmental norms consistent with the parties' international obligations. Finally, it requires the home state and the host state to co-operate on these issues.

No existing IIA contains specific provisions requiring states to bring their laws into compliance with their international obligations with respect to human rights, labour rights, indigenous peoples' rights, environmental protection, and bribery and corruption, or even requires parties to provide minimum levels of protection in each of these policy areas and to strive to improve such protections.

The IISD model treaty goes the furthest in this regard. It affirms state obligations under international human rights and environmental agreements.[340] According to the IISD, the aim of this provision is to put the parties on notice that these 'obligations are not superseded by the present Agreement'.[341] The IISD model treaty also includes a provision that tracks some of the language from the EC–CARIFORUM EPA. It recognises the right of parties to establish their own levels of environmental protection and requires the parties to establish high levels of human rights, labour rights and environmental protection appropriate to their level of development, to strive to improve such protection, and to bring their labour laws into compliance with international core labour standards as set out in the ILO Declaration.[342]

---

336 See the US–Chile FTA (2003), Annex 19.3, Art. 2.

337 US–Chile FTA (2003), Annex 19.3, Art. 1.

338 EC–CARIFORUM EPA (2008), Art. 72(b), (c).

339 See Section 6.10 (Investor obligation to comply with core labour standards); and Section 6.11 (Investor obligation to refrain from acts, or complicity in acts, of bribery and corruption).

340 IISD model treaty, Art. 34.

341 Mann et al., op. cit., at 47.

342 IISD Model Treaty, Art. 21.

Box 6.13 Summary of options for party state obligations relating to minimum standards of human rights, labour rights, indigenous peoples' rights and environmental protection and standards to address corruption

1. Do not establish domestic laws and administrative measures to protect human rights, labour rights, indigenous peoples' rights and environmental protection or to address bribery and corruption
2. Use existing laws to protect human rights, labour rights, indigenous peoples' rights and environmental protection and to address bribery and corruption
3. Introduce stronger domestic laws to entrench minimum standards of human rights, labour rights, indigenous peoples' rights and environmental protection and to address bribery and corruption, consistent with a state's international obligations
4. Integrate into an IIA the obligation on states to enact and enforce legislation to protect human rights, labour rights, indigenous peoples' rights and the environment, and to address bribery and corruption by including:
   a. Language in the preamble
   b. Provisions in the body of the treaty or side agreement to address the problem of a 'race to the bottom'
   c. Exceptions for human rights, labour rights, indigenous peoples' rights, anti-corruption and environmental protection measures
   d. Provisions excluding regulation on human rights, labour rights, indigenous peoples' rights, anti-corruption measures and environmental protection as a basis for indirect expropriation
   e. Provisions recommending that the parties encourage investors to comply with voluntary CSR standards
   f. Obligations on states to co-operate to ensure that investors do not circumvent compliance with international human rights, labour rights, indigenous peoples' rights, international environmental protection obligations and anti-corruption obligations

6.12.2 Discussion of options

1. *Do not establish domestic laws and administrative measures to protect human rights, labour rights, indigenous peoples' rights and environmental protection or to address bribery and corruption*

This may deter investment: As discussed in the investor obligation sections,[343] there are few advantages that flow from failing to enact minimum standards of protection

343 See Section 6.8 (Investor obligation to respect internationally recognised human rights and undertake human rights due diligence); Section 6.9 (Investor obligation to refrain from the

for human rights (including labour rights and indigenous peoples' rights), and to prevent and punish corruption. Studies have shown that violations of labour rights even in small poor developing countries can deter investment, as can corruption.[344] Research has also shown that states with robust human rights protections attract more investment than those with weak protections and that strong human rights protection is beneficial for economic growth and general welfare.[345] This may also be true for environmental standards. Therefore, deciding not to provide such minimum protections or failing to enforce the laws and regulations that exist may not be a helpful strategy for attracting investment.

States may be in breach of their international obligations: In addition, states that do not implement their international obligations in domestic law and enforce such laws against foreign investors and other businesses may be in breach of their international obligations. These are discussed in the investor obligation sections[346] and in more detail below.

2. *Use existing laws to protect human rights, labour rights, indigenous peoples' rights and environmental protection and to address bribery and corruption*

This is less costly for states: This approach may be attractive for states that already have robust laws and regulations in place to address bribery and corruption, environmental protection and human rights, including labour rights and indigenous peoples' rights. The advantage of this approach is that host states will not have to commit further resources to developing a stronger regulatory framework and establishing or strengthening enforcement institutions.

Existing laws may not be consistent with states' international obligations: However, current domestic laws may not be sufficiently rigorous and/or may not be consistent with a state's international obligations. In addition, as discussed in the investor obligation sections, even where states have a strong regulatory framework in place, they may have difficulty enforcing such laws against foreign investors. All states, even those with robust laws and enforcement institutions, can face challenges in regulating the behaviour of transnational businesses. These corporate groups are able to restructure or to transfer assets from one state to another to avoid liability in the host state.

---

commission of, or complicity in, grave violations of human rights); Section 6.10 (Investor obligation to comply with core labour standards); and Section 6.11 (Investor obligation to refrain from acts, or complicity in acts, of bribery and corruption).

344 See OECD, Standards, op. cit.; P Busse et al. (February 2008), 'FDI Promotion through Bilateral Investment Treaties: More than a BIT?', Kiel Working Paper No. 1403, Kiel Institute for the World Economy, Kiel.

345 See Blume and Voigt, op. cit.

346 See Section 6.8 (Investor obligation to respect internationally recognised human rights and undertake human rights due diligence); Section 6.9 (Investor obligation to refrain from the commission of, or complicity in, grave violations of human rights); Section 6.10 (Investor obligation to comply with core labour standards); and Section 6.11 (Investor obligation to refrain from acts, or complicity in acts, of bribery and corruption).

3. *Introduce stronger domestic laws to entrench minimum standards of human rights, labour rights, indigenous peoples' rights and environmental protection and to address bribery and corruption consistent with a state's international obligations*

It is costly to develop a regulatory framework: As discussed in the preceding sections on investor obligations, developing strong laws, regulations and enforcement institutions can be burdensome for many states. States will need to dedicate what may be scarce resources to strengthening laws, regulations, administrative measures, the judiciary and the court system to meet their international obligations.

It may increase the costs of doing business and deter investment: Enacting and enforcing laws consistent with a host state's international obligations with respect to human rights, labour rights, indigenous peoples' rights, environmental protection and corruption may deter some investors. This is especially likely to be true where other states have not given effect to their international obligations in these areas. Investors may feel that it is too costly to comply with such standards.

Domestic laws can be difficult to enforce against foreign investors: As noted above in this section, even where states bring domestic laws and regulations into line with their international obligations, they may face significant challenges enforcing them against foreign investors.

There is a risk of investor challenge under an IIA: As discussed in the investor obligation sections, the introduction or amendment of laws and regulations on human rights, labour rights, indigenous peoples' rights and environmental protection might expose a host state to a challenge by a foreign investor under an existing IIA. The investor might argue, for example, that the introduction of such measures is a violation of the FET provisions. A number of investment tribunals have interpreted FET obligations so expansively that the capacity of host states to change the regulatory environment that induced the investor to invest may be significantly restricted.[347] The risk of such a challenge is greatest in situations where the action of the host state is directed only at foreign investors. In addition, in some circumstances an investor might argue that the introduction of environmental laws and regulations amounts to indirect expropriation.[348] Where an investor is successful in an investor–state arbitration claim, the state would be required to pay compensation. In some cases, awards of hundreds of millions of dollars have been made.[349]

It attracts investment and in particular socially responsible investment: On the other hand, there are important advantages in introducing stronger domestic standards for environmental protection, the protection of human rights, labour rights and indigenous peoples' rights and to address bribery and corruption. Having a robust regulatory framework indicates to investors, particularly investors that have

---

347 See Section 5.5 (Fair and equitable treatment and the minimum standard of treatment).

348 See Section 5.6 (Limitations on expropriation and nationalisation).

349 JA VanDuzer, P Simons and G Mayeda (2008) 'Modeling International Investment Agreements for Economic Development', in V Qalo (ed) *Bilateralism and Development: Emerging Trade Patterns*, Cameron May, London, 359, at 390.

developed socially responsible business practices, and other investors concerned about protecting their global reputations, that the state has a stable, transparent, rights-protective regulatory environment in which to conduct business. As noted above, in the case of labour rights, studies have shown that strong labour standards are not a significant factor in investment decision making.[350] Corruption can increase business costs unpredictably and has been shown to deter investment.[351] Investors prefer to invest in open stable states with strong, transparent regulatory frameworks.[352]

It helps manage corporate risk: Increasingly, investors are concerned with avoiding and managing the risks associated with potential rights violations and environmental impacts. In addition, regulating the human rights and environmental impacts of investors by requiring them to undertake impact assessments and engage in human rights due diligence prior to their investment and to prevent, avoid and mitigate harmful impacts, can reduce costs for investors and the risk of liability. As noted in the section on sustainability assessments, investors that fail to conduct an impact assessment and therefore have no plan in place to deal effectively with future conflicts may face higher and unexpected costs with their operations.[353] The financial costs of conflict between investors and communities can be significant.[354] Foreign investors operating in a state with a robust regulatory environment are less likely to face strikes or public protests that may disrupt operations. They are also less likely to be the target of NGO campaigns that can expose them to reputational damage, or to be the subject of civil or administrative claims for violations of rights or environmental harm. In addition, investors are also increasingly concerned with avoiding corruption in connection with their investments. Not only may contracts procured through bribery and other forms of corruption be unenforceable, but investors also risk being prosecuted in the host state, their home state or both. As discussed in the preceding section,[355] even where investors are not convicted, an investigation and the media attention that accompanies a prosecution can result in reputational damage, which in turn can result in a decrease in share value. Operating in a state with strong anti-corruption legislation can reduce the risk that investors will get caught up in corrupt activities.

It implements states' international obligations and supports sustainable development: Introducing new stronger domestic laws and regulations, or amending existing laws and regulations in the areas of human rights (including labour rights and indigenous

---

350 See OECD, Trade, Employment and Labour Standards, op. cit. See Section 6.10 (Investor obligation to comply with core labour standards).

351 Busse et al. (2008), op. cit.

352 See Section 6.11 (Investor obligation to refrain from acts, or complicity in acts, of bribery and corruption).

353 See Section 6.6 (Sustainability assessments).

354 Davis and Franks, op. cit. See Section 6.8 (Investor obligation to respect internationally recognised human rights and undertake human rights due diligence).

355 See Section 6.11 (Investor obligation to refrain from acts, or complicity in acts, of bribery and corruption).

peoples' rights), anti-corruption and environmental protection, allows states the opportunity to bring their laws into compliance (where they are not already) with their international obligations. The most widely accepted international obligations in these areas are surveyed below.

Anti-corruption and environmental protection obligations

As discussed in the previous section, most Commonwealth countries are parties to one or more anti-corruption treaties.[356] In addition, most states have ratified the following major international environmental treaties, and may be parties to a range of others, and therefore have obligations under such agreements:

- *Convention on International Trade in Endangered Species of Wild Fauna and Flora*, 1973[357]
- *Framework Convention on Climate Change*, 1992[358]
- *Kyoto Protocol to the Framework Convention on Climate Change*, 1997[359]
- *Convention on Biological Diversity*, 1992[360]
- *Cartagena Protocol on Biosafety*, 2000[361]
- *Vienna Convention for the Protection of the Ozone Layer*, 1988[362]
- *Montreal Protocol on Substances that Deplete the Ozone Layer*, 1987[363]
- *Stockholm Convention on Persistent Organic Pollutants*, 2001[364]

---

356 See Section 6.11 (Investor obligation to refrain from acts, or complicity in acts, of bribery and corruption).

357 *Convention on International Trade in Endangered Species of Wild Fauna and Flora*, adopted 3 March 1973, in force 1 July 1975, 27 UST 1087; 993 *United Nations Treaty Series* 243.

358 *United Nations Framework Convention on Climate Change*, adopted 9 May 1992, in force 21 March 1994, 1771 *United Nations Treaty Series* 107, 31 *International Legal Materials* 849 (1992).

359 *Kyoto Protocol to the United Nations Framework Convention on Climate Change*, adopted 11 December 1997, in force 16 February 2005, 2303 *United Nations Treaty Series* 148, 37 *International Legal Materials* 22 (1998).

360 *Convention on Biological Diversity*, adopted 5 June 1992, in force 29 December 1993, 1760 *United Nations Treaty Series* 79, 31 *International Legal Materials* 818 (1992).

361 *Cartagena Protocol on Biosafety to the Convention on Biological Diversity*, adopted 29 January 2000, in force 11 September 2003, 2251 *United Nations Treaty Series* 205, 39 *International Legal Materials* 1027 (2000).

362 *Vienna Convention for the Protection of the Ozone Layer*, adopted 22 March 1985, in force 22 September 1988, 1513 *United Nations Treaty Series* 293, 26 *International Legal Materials* 1516 (1987).

363 *Montreal Protocol on Substances that Deplete the Ozone Layer*, adopted 16 September 1987, in force 1 January 1989, 1522 *United Nations Treaty Series* 3, 26 *International Legal Materials* 1541 (1987).

364 *Stockholm Convention on Persistent Organic Pollutants*, adopted 22 May 2001, in force 17 May 2004, 2256 *United Nations Treaty Series* 119, 40 *International Legal Materials* 532 (2001).

- *Convention on the Law of the Sea*, 1982[365]
- *Convention to Combat Desertification*, 1994[366]

Only three Commonwealth member countries are parties to the Convention on Long-Range Transboundary Air Pollution, 1979,[367] and the Convention on Access to Information, Public Participation in Decision-making and Access to Justice in Environmental Matters, 1998 (Aarhus Convention).[368] However, states may wish to consider the standards set out in these instruments. In particular, the norms set out in the Aarhus Convention are relevant to states interested in pursuing sustainable development. This treaty recognises, among other things, the importance of protecting the environment as necessary for human well-being and the enjoyment of human rights and to protect the interest of future generations.[369] It provides rights and protections regarding access to environmental information,[370] meaningful participation in environmental decision making,[371] and rights to challenge environmental decisions in both judicial and non-judicial fora.[372]

Human rights standards

In determining the adequacy of existing domestic law, states should consider their human rights obligations under customary international law and under the core UN human rights treaties discussed above.[373] They may also wish to refer to the measures proposed in the section on investors' human rights obligations,[374] which if implemented in domestic law would go some way to satisfying the international human rights law obligation to protect human rights.

Labour rights standards

States' labour rights obligations include those entrenched in customary international law and the following obligations:

---

365 *United Nations Convention on the Law of the Sea*, adopted 10 December 1982, in force 16 November 1994, 1833 *United Nations Treaty Series* 3, 21 *International Legal Materials* 1261 (1982).

366 *United Nations Convention to Combat Desertification in those Countries Experiencing Serious Drought and/or Desertification, Particularly in Africa*, adopted 14 October 1994, in force 26 December 1996, 1954 *United Nations Treaty Series* 3, 33 *International Legal Materials* 1332 (1994).

367 *Convention on Long-Range Transboundary Air Pollution*, adopted 13 November 1979, in force 16 March 1983, 1302 *United Nations Treaty Series* 217, 18 *International Legal Materials* 1442 (1979).

368 *Convention on Access to Information, Public Participation in Decision-making and Access to Justice in Environmental Matters*, adopted 25 June 1998, in force 30 October 2001, 2161 *United Nations Treaty Series* 447, 38 *International Legal Materials* 517 (1999).

369 Ibid., preamble.

370 Ibid., Arts. 4, 5.

371 Ibid., Arts. 6, 7, 8.

372 Ibid., Art. 9.

373 See Section 6.8 (Investor obligation to respect internationally recognised human rights and undertake human rights due diligence).

374 See Section 6.8 (Investor obligation to respect internationally recognised human rights and undertake human rights due diligence).

- The ILO conventions to which states are parties;[375] and
- Other relevant international instruments, including general human rights treaties which protect labour rights to which states are parties, such as the *ICERD, ICCPR, ICESCR, CEDAW, CRC, ICRMW, CPED and CPRD.*

In addition, the labour protections put in place by states that are members of the ILO[376] should also reflect the principles of ILO Declaration on Social Justice for a Fair Globalization, 2008.[377] Together with the ILO Constitution, 1919, the Philadelphia Declaration, 1944, and the Declaration on Fundamental Principles and Rights at Work, 1998, the *Declaration on Social Justice for a Fair Globalization* provides the basis and method of implementation for the constitutional objectives of the ILO.[378] The 2008 Declaration institutionalises the Decent Work Agenda, and requires that ILO member states 'place full and productive employment and decent work at the centre of economic and social policies' pursuant to four 'inseparable, interrelated and mutually supportive' strategic objectives. These are set out in Box 6.14.

Box 6.14 Objectives of the ILO Declaration on Social Justice for a Fair Globalization

i. Promoting employment by creating a sustainable institutional and economic environment in which:
    - Individuals can develop and update the necessary capacities and skills they need to enable them to be productively occupied for their personal fulfilment and the common well-being;
    - All enterprises, public or private, are sustainable to enable growth and the generation of greater employment and income opportunities and prospects for all; and
    - Societies can achieve their goals of economic development, good living standards and social progress;

(Continued)

375 See, for example, the eight core ILO conventions.

376 All Commonwealth member states, except Nauru and Tonga, are members of the ILO.

377 10 June 2008, 97th Session, ILC Conference.

378 ILO, *Director General's Announcement, IGDS No. 36 (Version 1)*, 13 August 2008 at para. 2. According to Maupain, while the Declaration is not a normative instrument, it has a distinct legal nature. Although it does 'not modify or formally interpret the [ILO's] Constitution ... [it] nevertheless entails important legal consequences vis-à-vis the Organization and its members ... it imparts legal meaning to the concept of "decent work" within the ILO. Its unanimous adoption by all members would make it difficult – if not formally impossible – to challenge the restatement of the ILO's objectives contained therein on grounds of variance with the provisions of the Constitution or the Declaration of Philadelphia' (see F Maupain (2009), 'New Foundation or New Façade? The ILO and the 2008 Declaration on Social Justice for a Fair Globalization', 20 *European Journal of International Law* 823 at 832.

(Continued)

ii. Developing and enhancing measures of social protection – social security and labour protection – which are sustainable and adapted to national circumstances, including:

- The extension of social security to all, including measures to provide basic income to all in need of such protection, and adapting its scope and coverage to meet the new needs and uncertainties generated by the rapidity of technological, societal, demographic and economic changes;
- Healthy and safe working conditions; and
- Policies in regard to wages and earnings, hours and other conditions of work, designed to ensure a just share of the fruits of progress to all and a minimum living wage to all employed and in need of such protection;

iii. Promoting social dialogue and tripartism as the most appropriate methods for:

- Adapting the implementation of the strategic objectives to the needs and circumstances of each country;
- Translating economic development into social progress, and social progress into economic development;
- Facilitating consensus building on relevant national and international policies that impact on employment and decent work strategies and programmes; and
- Making labour law and institutions effective, including in respect of the recognition of the employment relationship, the promotion of good industrial relations and the building of effective labour inspection systems; and

iv. Respecting, promoting and realising the fundamental principles and rights at work, which are of particular significance, as both rights and enabling conditions that are necessary for the full realisation of all of the strategic objectives, noting:

- That freedom of association and the effective recognition of the right to collective bargaining are particularly important to enable the attainment of the four strategic objectives; and
- That the violation of fundamental principles and rights at work cannot be invoked or otherwise used as a legitimate comparative advantage and that labour standards should not be used for protectionist trade purposes.[379]

379 *Declaration on Social Justice for Fair Globalization*, 10 June 2008, 97th Session, ILC Conference at Section I, subsections A and B.

The *Declaration* emphasises that how states attain these objectives is a matter to be determined by each state, taking into account its international obligations and the fundamental principles and rights at work, and in light of international labour standards, a state's circumstances and priorities and the co-operation among ILO member states.[380]

Rights of indigenous peoples

No international instrument currently exists that specifically articulates the rights of indigenous peoples and the corresponding responsibilities of states, corporations or individuals in relation to investment. However, relevant rights and their related responsibilities can be extracted from international instruments pertaining to indigenous peoples, including the UN Declaration on the Rights of Indigenous Peoples (UNDRIP) and the ILO Convention (No. 169) Concerning Indigenous and Tribal Peoples in Independent Countries, 1989.[381] To date, 38 Commonwealth countries have endorsed the non-binding UN Declaration, while only two Commonwealth member countries are parties to the ILO Convention.

The primary concern that arises regarding IIAs from the perspective of indigenous peoples is ensuring that none of the state's obligations in relation to investors limits the state's ability to adopt and enforce laws, regulations or policies that implement its international obligations towards indigenous peoples or that secure their rights. In particular, states that have endorsed the UNDRIP have committed to protect the rights set out in Box 6.15 below, among others.

Box 6.15 Overview of key provisions of the *United Nations Declaration on the Rights of Indigenous Peoples*

- The right to the full enjoyment, as a collective or individuals of all human rights and fundamental freedoms recognised in the UN Charter, the Universal Declaration on Human Rights and international human rights law (Article 1);
- The right to be free from discrimination (Article 2);
- The right to self-determination (Article 3);
- The right to autonomy or self-government in matters relating to their internal and local affairs (Article 4);
- The right to life, physical and mental integrity, liberty and security of the person and the right not to be subjected to any act of genocide or violence (Article 7);

(Continued)

380 Ibid. at Section I, subsection C.

381 *Convention (No. 169) concerning Indigenous and Tribal Peoples in Independent Countries*, adopted 27 June 1989, 7 in force 5 September 1991.

(Continued)

- The right not to be forcibly removed from their lands or territories or relocated without free, prior and informed consent (Article 10);
- The right to restitution of cultural, intellectual, religious and spiritual property taken without their free and informed consent (Article 11);
- The right to practice and revitalise their cultural traditions and customs, including maintaining and protecting past, present and future archaeological and historical sites, artefacts, designs, ceremonies, technologies, visual and performing arts and literature (Article 11);
- The labour rights established in international and national law (Article 17);
- The right to full participation at all levels of decision making in matters that affect them and their rights and to good faith consultation to obtain their free prior and informed consent before adoption and implementation of laws and administrative measures that may affect them (Articles 18 and 19);
- The right to develop their political, economic and social systems or institutions, to be secure in the enjoyment of their own means of subsistence and development, and to engage freely in all their traditional and other economic activities (Article 20);
- The right to determine, develop and administer health, housing and other economic and social programmes affecting them (Article 23);
- The right to protection of traditional medicines and health practices, including the protection of vital medicinal plants, animals and minerals, to access to all social and health services and to the highest standard of physical and mental health (Article 24);
- The right to own, use, develop and control the lands they have traditionally owned or otherwise occupied or used (Article 26);
- The right to conservation and protection of the environment and the productive capacity of their lands or territories and resources (Article 29);
- The right to maintain, control and protect their cultural heritage, traditional knowledge, traditional cultural expressions and their intellectual property over such cultural heritage, traditional knowledge and traditional cultural expressions (Article 31);
- The right to determine and develop priorities and strategies for the development or use of their lands or territories and other resources, and the right to free and informed consent prior to the approval of projects affecting their lands, territories and other resources (Article 32);
- The right to recognition, observance and enforcement of treaties, agreements and other arrangements between states and indigenous peoples (Article 37); and
- The right to access financial and technical assistance in the realisation of these rights (Article 39).

States should be aware that laws, regulations and policies relating to investors and their investments have the potential to affect indigenous populations in their territory. As discussed in the section on investor human rights obligations,[382] states have a duty under international law to seek the free, prior and informed consent of indigenous peoples in certain limited circumstances.[383] These situations include the following:

- Where proposals to remove indigenous communities from their lands and territories are being considered;[384]
- Where the storage and disposal of hazardous waste on indigenous territory is being contemplated;[385]
- Cases where large-scale projects may have a significant impact within indigenous territory.[386]

In all other situations states have, at a minimum, an obligation to consult indigenous peoples. According to the Inter-American Court of Human Rights such consultation must meet the following criteria:

- Be undertaken in good faith;
- Be pursued through culturally appropriate procedures;
- Be undertaken in accordance with the traditions of the particular indigenous group;
- Have the goal of reaching an agreement;
- Provide clear information to the indigenous group of the possible risks of a particular development or investment plan; and
- Result in a plan that is accepted by the indigenous group knowingly and voluntarily.[387]

Moreover, the state should require an independent environmental and social impact assessment and guarantee reasonable benefit sharing[388] where this is appropriate, such as in situations of resource exploration and/or extraction on indigenous lands.

Where investment activity could negatively affect the property rights of indigenous peoples, there is an emerging obligation on states to seek the consent of the indigenous community in question for this activity. In situations where consent is not given, 'there is a strong presumption that the project should not go forward'.[389] If the investment is

---

382 See Section 6.8 (Investor obligation to respect internationally recognised human rights and undertake human rights due diligence).
383 See Section 6.8 (Investor obligation to respect internationally recognised human rights and undertake human rights due diligence).
384 Perrault et al., op. cit., at 491; Anaya, op. cit., at 17.
385 Perrault et al., ibid. UNDRIP, Art. 29 (2): 'States shall take effective measures to ensure that no storage or disposal of hazardous materials shall take place in the lands or territories of indigenous peoples without their free, prior and informed consent'.
386 *Saramaka v. Suriname*, op. cit., at para. 134.
387 Ibid. at para. 133.
388 Ibid. at para. 129.
389 Anaya, op. cit., at 17.

pursued, the state must take steps to ensure that the indigenous group in question benefits from the investment and it must also take effective measures to mitigate any negative effects.[390] States may also wish to provide a further level of protection to indigenous peoples by requiring that their free and informed consent be obtained before the state enacts any laws or regulations in regard to foreign investment that may affect such groups.

The relationship between foreign investment and sustainable development is discussed earlier in the Guide.[391] For foreign investment to promote sustainable development or even economic development, the inhabitants of the host state must be able to reap some of its benefits. Creating a strong, transparent, rights-protective regulatory framework addressing these important policy areas would help to ensure that investors and their investments make a positive contribution to sustainable development in a host state. It would also better protect the rights of individuals and groups, as well as the host state's environment. States that enact and enforce such laws will contribute substantially to these goals.

4. *Integrate into an IIA the obligation on states to enact and enforce legislation to protect human rights, labour rights, indigenous peoples' rights and the environment, and to address bribery and corruption*

There are a variety of different approaches that could be used in IIAs to promote conformity with international obligations relating to human rights, labour rights, indigenous peoples' rights, environmental protection and anti-corruption standards that impose varying levels of obligation on party states. These approaches were discussed above in relation to human rights, labour rights, anti-corruption and environmental standards and are summarised here.[392]

Language in the preamble: The parties could negotiate a general statement in the preamble clarifying that the IIA is to be interpreted in accordance with the parties' international obligations in identified non-investment policy areas. States would want to ensure that in the preamble, human rights, labour rights, indigenous peoples' rights and environmental protection, as well as anti-corruption measures, are described as having the same level of importance as the investor protections included in an IIA. This would ensure that in interpreting the treaty, these norms are not subordinated to investment protection considerations. States that are serious about protecting these areas of policy concern, however, should incorporate other provisions addressing these issues in addition to such language in the preamble since statements in a preamble do not create binding obligations.[393]

---

390 Ibid.

391 See Section 2.3 (Links between foreign investment and sustainable development).

392 See Section 6.8 (Investor obligation to respect internationally recognised human rights and undertake human rights due diligence), Section 6.9 (Investor obligation to refrain from the commission of, or complicity in, grave violations of human rights), Section 6.10 (Investor obligation to comply with core labour standards), Section 6.11 (Investor obligation to refrain from acts, or complicity in acts, of bribery and corruption) and Section 6.12 (Other rights and obligations of party states).

393 It would also be useful to include statements according priority to these policy objectives in a statement of objectives of the agreement. See Section 4.4 (Statement of objectives).

Provisions in the body of the treaty or side agreement to address the problem of a 'race to the bottom': States could negotiate provisions in an IIA or in a side agreement that:

- Reaffirm their commitments under international human rights, labour rights, indigenous peoples' rights treaties and other instruments, environmental protection treaties and anti-corruption conventions;
- Establish obligations not to relax domestic laws and regulations for the purpose or attracting or retaining investment, and not to fail to enforce domestic standards;
- Establish an obligation on the parties to strive to maintain high levels of human rights, labour rights, indigenous peoples' rights protection, environmental protection and robust anti-corruption laws, and require parties to strive to improve such standards.

States may prefer to adopt the approach of the EC–CARIFORUM EPA for the latter type of provision. As discussed in the subsection on IIA practice, the EPA qualifies the obligation to establish high levels of domestic protection and to strive to improve such standards by recognising the right of the parties to enact regulation to achieve their own domestic health and environmental standards and sustainable development priorities and to adopt and modify such standards and priorities.[394]

These types of provisions are increasingly used. The provisions described above are becoming more common in relation to labour and environmental protection standards.

These provisions offer flexibility. Under these types of provisions, states have significant flexibility. The provisions do not require states to bring their domestic laws into compliance with international standards and there is no obligation to raise the level of domestic protection; only a requirement *to strive* to do so.

There is a risk of investor challenge for states seeking to strengthen their domestic laws. A key shortcoming of these provisions, of which states should be aware, is that they do not directly protect states that introduce new or amended domestic laws from an investor challenge under an IIA. An investor might claim that the introduction or amendment of domestic laws or regulations is a breach of its legitimate expectations under an FET provision.[395] The risk of such a claim is small, however. It would be hard for an investor to claim that it did not expect a state to act pursuant to the provision expressed in the treaty. This problem could be addressed more directly by introducing a general exception and/or a provision that excluded measures in these areas from the obligations of the treaty.[396]

A party could potentially use state-to-state dispute resolution to enforce these provisions against another party. Where the provision is included in the body of the treaty, such as the obligation not to fail to enforce certain domestic laws, a party could potentially

394 EC–CARIFORUM EPA (2008), Art. 184.1.

395 See Section 5.5 (Fair and equitable treatment and the minimum standard of treatment).

396 See Section 5.6 (Limitations on expropriation and nationalisation); and Section 5.12 (Reservations and exceptions).

use the state-to-state dispute settlement process[397] to pressure another party to comply with such obligations. States may see this as a violation of their sovereignty and may not want to create obligations that would allow the IIA to become an indirect mechanism for enforcing standards in complex and sensitive areas such as human rights protection.

One way to deal with this problem is to specifically exclude such obligations from enforcement under the state-to-state dispute settlement process.[398] Another approach, which is the approach used in some US FTAs with respect to labour rights, is to include a provision clarifying and limiting the scope of a party's obligations:

> ... each Party retains the right to exercise discretion with respect to investigatory, prosecutorial, regulatory, and compliance matters and to make decisions regarding the allocation of resources to enforcement with respect to other labour matters determined to have higher priorities. Accordingly, the Parties understand that a Party is in compliance with [the obligation not to persistently fail to enforce its labour laws] where a course of action or inaction reflects a reasonable exercise of such discretion, or results from a *bona fide* decision regarding allocation of resources.[399]

Such a provision would probably make it difficult to find a state in breach of its obligation not to persistently fail to enforce its domestic laws in a particular policy area.

Compliance provisions: There are a number of options available for states that do wish to provide for some form of mechanism in an IIA to encourage parties to enforce their domestic laws, even if they do not agree to state-to-state dispute settlement in connection with their obligations. Two of these are considered below.

Complaint mechanism and enforcement mechanism to encourage states to enforce domestic law. Parties to an IIA could negotiate provisions that provide for a means to receive complaints about non-enforcement of domestic laws and provide a consultative procedure for states to deal with a party's persistent pattern of non-enforcement of human rights, labour rights or indigenous peoples' rights, or environmental or anti-corruption laws.

The *North American Agreement on Labour Cooperation* (NAALC) provides an example of this type of soft enforcement mechanism. Complaints under NAALC regarding non-enforcement of a party state's labour laws are initially dealt with through consultations between National Administrative Offices (NAOs)[400] or government ministers.[401] Where the matter is not resolved through ministerial consultations, a party state may request that an Evaluation Committee of Experts (ECE) be created

---

397 The Guide provides a discussion of state-to-state dispute settlement. See Section 7.2 (State-to-state dispute settlement).
398 See Section 7.2 (State-to-state dispute settlement).
399 US–Singapore FTA (2003), Art. 17.2(b).
400 *NAALC* (1994), Art. 21.
401 *NAALC* (1994), Art. 22.

to investigate and report on the matter.[402] This latter procedure is restricted to non-enforcement of occupational health and safety laws and 'other technical labor standards'[403] that are trade related and recognised in the laws of both states.[404] Where the issue concerns an 'alleged persistent pattern' of failure to enforce 'occupational health and safety, child labor or minimum wage technical standards' that is not resolved by the ECE, recommendations can, in principle, lead to the creation of an arbitral panel and sanctions, but this is by no means automatic and has never been done.[405]

This type of mechanism has not been very effective in ensuring that states comply with their domestic standards and does not prevent a 'race to the bottom' of labour and environmental standards.[406] Its advantage is that it provides a means for public participation by allowing members of the public to bring complaints and thus to exert some pressure on governments to enforce their domestic laws against foreign investors as well as domestic businesses.

Ministerial consultations. Another weaker option is simply to provide for issues of persistent non-enforcement of domestic laws to be addressed through ministerial consultations co-ordinated by a body established by the IIA.[407]

Exceptions for measures related to human rights, labour rights, indigenous peoples' rights, anti-corruption and environmental protection: Including an exception for regulatory measures relating to human rights, labour rights, indigenous peoples' rights, anti-corruption and environmental protection would provide a clear expression of the intention of the parties to remove these areas of regulation from the application of the investor protections under an IIA. This means that the host state would retain the flexibility to introduce new regulatory measures or to strengthen existing ones without breaching its investor protection obligations. The advantages and drawbacks

402 *NAALC* (1994), Art. 23(1).

403 *NAALC* (1994), Art. 23(2).

404 *NAALC* (1994), Art. 23(3)(1).

405 See *NAALC* (1994), Arts. 28, 29. Under Art. 29(1) an arbitral panel can be convened by written request of a party state to the Council of the Commission for Labor Cooperation and following a two-thirds vote in the Council in favour of such action.

406 Bernasconi-Osterwalder and Johnson, op. cit., at 27. See also Maquila Solidarity Network (2004), 'NAFTA Ten Years Later: Why the Labour Side Agreement Doesn't Work for Workers', 1 January, available at: http://en.maquilasolidarity.org/issues/trade/nafta/naalc/critique?SESS89c5db41a82abcd7da7c9ac60e04ca5f=unvlgtie, which states that in 2004: 'After 10 years of NAFTA, not one of the 28 complaints made under the NAALC has resulted in any significant improvements in labour law enforcement or in workers' lives. This is not the rosy future Mexican workers were promised by NAFTA's signatories'. On the NAAEC, see L J Allen (2012), 'The North American Agreement on Environmental Cooperation: Has It Fulfilled Its Promises and Potential? An Empirical Study of Policy', 23 *Colorado Journal of International Environmental Law and Policy* 122 at 190, noting that the Commission on Environmental Cooperation 'has been the most effective in facilitating cooperation between the three NAFTA countries, somewhat less effective in improving the enforcement of environmental laws through the citizen submission process, minimally effective in undertaking independent reporting of environmental issues of regional significance, and not effective in integrating trade and environment in support of the goals of NAFTA'.

407 See Section 9.2 (Commission).

of using exceptions to carve out certain areas of regulation from the purview of an IIA are discussed in detail in the section above on reservations and exceptions.[408]

Provisions excluding from indirect expropriation regulation to promote or protect on human rights, labour rights, indigenous peoples' rights, for environmental protection or to address corruption measures: These kinds of provisions are an important tool for states in protecting their right to regulate. In removing certain areas of regulation from being considered indirect expropriation, states preserve their policy space and protect themselves from having to compensate investors for introducing new laws and regulations or strengthening existing ones. Approaches to preserving regulatory space in the drafting of substantive investor protection provisions in an IIA are discussed in the sections above on investor protections.[409]

Provisions recommending that the parties encourage investors to comply with voluntary CSR standards: These types of provisions recognise the need for investors to operate in a socially responsible manner. On the other hand, they do not require states to implement and enforce laws on CSR. Nor do they require investors to comport themselves in a manner consistent with international CSR standards. On the contrary, investors are left to self-regulate. As discussed in the section on investor human rights obligations,[410] voluntary self-regulation has not consistently prevented investors from violating human rights. Nor has it ensured that investors comply with internationally accepted CSR standards, such as the *OECD Guidelines* or the *Global Compact*.[411]

Obligations on states to co-operate to ensure that investors do not circumvent compliance with international human rights, labour rights, indigenous peoples' rights, international environmental protection obligations and anti-corruption obligations: This type of provision has been discussed above in the sections on core labour standards,[412] bribery and corruption,[413] and in the subsection on IIA practice in relation to provisions on environmental protection. The EC–CARIFORUM EPA includes such a provision.

It harnesses home state regulatory capacity and co-operation in regulating investor conduct. This option can assist states in addressing some of the difficulties in regulating the behaviour of foreign investors by requiring investors' home state to take domestic measures *to complement* actions by the host state to ensure that investors do not evade compliance with identified international norms consistent with the parties' international obligations. It also requires each party to co-operate with the other by providing assistance with the party's enforcement efforts.

408 See Section 5.12 (Reservations and exceptions).

409 E.g. Section 5.6 (Limitations on expropriation and nationalisation).

410 See Section 6.8 (Investor obligation to respect internationally recognised human rights and undertake human rights due diligence).

411 See Simons and Macklin, op. cit.

412 See Section 6.10 (Investor obligation to comply with core labour standards).

413 See Section 6.11 (Investor obligation to refrain from acts, or complicity in acts, of bribery and corruption).

There is a risk of investor challenge under an IIA. A limitation of this approach is that it does not directly avoid the problem for states that wish to introduce more rigorous domestic laws to promote sustainable development of having such measures challenged by an investor in investment arbitration. As noted above, an investor might claim that the introduction or amendment of domestic laws or regulations is a breach of their legitimate expectations under an FET provision.[414] It would be difficult, however, for an investor to claim that it did not expect a state to act pursuant to the provision expressed in the treaty. This problem could be addressed more directly through a general exception and/or a provision that excluded measures in these areas from the obligations in the treaty.[415] In addition, states could negotiate qualifications to the national treatment, MFN, fair and equitable treatment and other investor protection standards, such as those discussed in the Guide.[416]

6.12.3 Summary

As discussed at the beginning of this section, in light of the political sensitivity of these types of provisions, the Guide does not provide a sample provision imposing obligations on party states relating to the implementation and enforcement of minimum standards for human rights, labour rights, indigenous peoples' rights, and environmental protection and standards to address corruption. States will have varying views on the extent to which provisions of this kind are desirable and what form they should take. States' views may also depend on the context in which an IIA is being negotiated. Each state must determine for itself, based on its own particular circumstances and taking into account the costs and benefits of the various options described above, whether it wishes to include provisions in an IIA regarding these areas of regulation and, if so, whether they should be made subject to dispute settlement under the treaty.

However, because these types of provisions can be useful from a sustainable development perspective, some states may wish to incorporate a minimum standards provision into an IIA. The subsection on IIA practice, above, considers a range of different ways in which states have included language or minimum standard obligations on environmental protection. These, and similar provisions on labour rights and anti-corruption measures discussed in earlier sections,[417] can provide guidance for states on the development of more comprehensive minimum standards obligations. In particular, the EC–CARIFORUM EPA provides a useful example of a minimum standards provision that provides states with leeway to enact environmental standards appropriate to their level of development.[418] It also establishes an obligation for party states to co-operate to ensure investor compliance with domestic labour,

414 See Section 5.5 (Fair and equitable treatment and the minimum standard of treatment).

415 See Section 5.6 (Limitations on expropriation and nationalisation); and Section 5.12 (Reservations and exceptions).

416 See Section 5.3 (National treatment); Section 5.4 (Most favoured nation); Section 5.5 (Fair and equitable treatment and the minimum standard of treatment).

417 See Section 6.10 (Investor obligation to comply with core labour standards); and Section 6.11 (Investor obligation to refrain from acts, or complicity in acts, of bribery and corruption).

418 EC–CARIFORUM EPA, Art. 184.1.

environmental and anti-corruption laws.[419] States could adapt this latter provision to address a wider range of concerns such as human rights and indigenous peoples' rights. It is possible to avoid the concern that the IIA could be used as a general mechanism for enforcing domestic law in these sensitive policy areas. Any minimum standards provision could be specifically excluded from enforcement under the state-to-state dispute settlement process.[420]

6.13 Enforcement of investor obligations

Many developing country host states face significant challenges in seeking to regulate the activities of foreign investors.[421] This lack of capacity can create a governance gap that undermines the achievement of sustainable development generally. As a result of this gap, investors may remain unaccountable for corrupt practices, for acts that violate human and labour rights or the rights of indigenous peoples or for damage to the environment. Those injured by the acts of investors may be without an effective means of redress.

Few IIAs contain investor obligations or enforcement mechanisms for such obligations. In order to deal with this issue, the Guide includes a variety of sample provisions that provide examples of enforcement mechanisms that correspond to the standards to be met by investors set out in the investor obligation sections above. These sample provisions are designed to ensure investor compliance with IIA obligations and support host states' efforts to regulate them. They include the following:

- Criminal sanctions;
- A grievance procedure;
- A process to deal with non-compliance with a management plan produced as result of a sustainability assessment;
- Civil liability; and
- Counterclaims by states in investor–state arbitration.

Developed states and some developing states have the power, resources and legal capacity to exercise some form of oversight over the transnational activities of their investors. Accordingly, the sample provisions in this section oblige investors' home states to provide for criminal and civil enforcement in their domestic courts of treaty standards in relation to the extraterritorial activities of their investors.[422] These enforcement mechanisms supplement the domestic enforcement mechanisms in the host state.

---

419 EC–CARIFORUM EPA, Art. 72 (a)-(c).

420 See Section 7.2 (State-to-state dispute settlement) for discussion of the costs and benefits of excluding certain provisions from the state-to-state dispute settlement process.

421 See M Ssenyonjo (2007), 'Non-State Actors and Economic, Social and Cultural Rights', in M A Baderin and R McCorquodale (eds), *Economic, Social and Cultural Rights in Action*, Oxford University Press, Oxford, 109 at 121–2, who notes that 'states where protection of human rights against violations by [non-state actors] is most needed are often those least able to enforce them against [non-state actors] such as international financial institutions and TNCs – the main driving agents of the global economy, exercising control over global trade, investment and technology transfers – who possess much desired investment capital or technology'.

422 See Section 6.14 (Criminal sanctions); and Section 6.16 (Civil liability of investors).

Other sample provisions in this section require party states to put in place grievance and compliance procedures to support compliance with the sustainability assessment process discussed in Section 6.6 (Sustainability assessments) and the obligation to respect human rights and conduct human rights due diligence discussed in Section 6.8 (Investor obligation to respect internationally recognised human rights and undertake human rights due diligence).[423] Finally, states that are the subject of investor claims in investor–state arbitration may counterclaim against investors for injuries suffered as a consequence of the investor not complying with its obligations under the agreement.[424]

The particular scope of these enforcement obligations will be defined by which investor obligations states decide to include in their investment treaties. If all the investor obligations contained in the Guide's sample provisions are not included in an IIA, then the sample provisions on enforcement would have to be adjusted accordingly.

The enforcement mechanisms, like the standards for investors themselves, are novel and untested. They may be onerous for particular states to implement. Because they impose enforcement commitments on investors' home states, they may be especially difficult to negotiate. Further, because they are designed to make investor obligations more effective, they may have the effect of deterring some investment.

On the other hand, including these types of enforcement mechanisms in an IIA will assist the host state in ensuring that foreign investment under the treaty supports sustainable development. Each state must therefore weigh the potential costs and benefits of such provisions, taking into consideration its particular circumstances, and determine whether the enforcement mechanisms discussed are appropriate and, if so, whether they should simply be incorporated into domestic law and/or included in a treaty. If states include these enforcement provisions in an IIA, they will have to decide whether these provisions should be subject to the state-to-state dispute settlement mechanism. The costs and benefits of such a decision are considered below in the section on state-to-state dispute settlement.[425]

6.14 Criminal sanctions

Cross references

Section 6.2	The challenges of regulating foreign investors and holding transnational corporations accountable	254
Section 6.3	Different approaches to integrating foreign investment and sustainable development	257
Section 6.8	Investor obligation to respect internationally recognised human rights and undertake human rights due diligence	294
Section 6.9	Investor obligation to refrain from the commission of, or complicity in, grave violations of human rights	316

423 See Section 6.15 (Grievance procedure and other measures to enforce the management plan produced in the sustainability assessment).

424 See Sections 6.17 (Counterclaims by states in investor–state arbitration) and 7.1.7 (Sample provisions: investor–state dispute settlement, Article [W] (Counterclaims)).

425 See Section 7.2 (State-to-state dispute settlement).

The obligations on investors not to commit or be complicit in grave violations of human rights or to engage in acts of corruption, including bribery, may be supported by corresponding duties on states to criminalise and prosecute such actions. All states have jurisdiction under international law to prosecute those who have committed war crimes, crimes against humanity or genocide. States that have ratified the UN *Convention against Torture* are obliged to criminalise torture and to extradite or prosecute individuals suspected of committing acts of torture.[426] States have obligations under other international human rights treaties to protect human rights. As discussed above,[427] states must therefore exercise due diligence to prevent, and take action with respect to, violations of human rights committed by private actors. States must, in addition to implementing legislative and administrative measures, investigate and prosecute private actors that commit grave violations of human rights that constitute crimes.

In relation to corruption, including bribery, the UN, African Union and Inter-American conventions require party states to establish criminal liability for domestic acts of corruption.[428] In addition, the UN, African Union, OECD and Inter-American conventions require home states to establish criminal liability for acts of bribery of a foreign public official.[429] The UN and OECD treaties specifically oblige states to establish liability for acts committed by both natural and legal persons and require the imposition of effective, appropriate criminal penalties.[430] In addition, the UN convention requires states to impose criminal sanctions for other acts of corruption, including trading in influence, abuse of function, money laundering, concealment

426 *CAT*, Arts. 4 and 7.

427 See Section 6.8 (Investor obligation to respect internationally recognised human rights and undertake human rights due diligence).

428 See *UN Convention against Corruption*, Art. 15; *AU Convention on Preventing and Combatting Corruption*, Art. 5(1). The AU Convention only requires parties to establish 'offences' but does not specify criminal offences and thus could include administrative offences.

429 *UN Convention against Corruption*, Art. 16; *OECD Anti-Bribery Convention*, Art. 1; and the *AU Convention on Preventing and Combatting Corruption*, Arts. 5(1), 13; and *Inter-American Convention against Corruption*, Art. 8. Note that the *UN Convention against Corruption* and *Inter-American Convention against Corruption* only permit but do not require states to assume jurisdiction over acts of their nationals committed outside their territories. See *UN Convention against Corruption*, Art. 42(2)(b); and the *Inter-American Convention against Corruption* Art. 5(2). However, both conventions require states to assume jurisdiction where an alleged offender is present in their territory and the state does not extradite that person to another country because he/she is a national.

430 *UN Convention against Corruption*, Arts. 26, 30; *OECD Anti-Bribery Convention*, Arts. 2, 3.

and obstruction of justice.[431] Finally, all of these treaties mandate co-operation between the party states in the investigation and prosecution of the proscribed acts of corruption.[432]

Grave violations of human rights and bribery and corruption by foreign investors are a transnational issue. To date, home states have not taken effective steps to regulate the transnational activity of their investors with respect to human rights.[433] However, as noted above, they have been relatively more diligent in prosecuting bribery and corruption pursuant to their international treaty obligations.[434]

6.14.1 IIA practice

No existing IIA includes an obligation on the parties to prosecute grave violations of human rights and few IIAs specifically oblige parties to prosecute corruption. As discussed above,[435] the EU–Korea FTA obliges party states to adopt or maintain appropriate measures to prohibit and punish bribery and corruption in the pharmaceutical and health care sectors.[436] Also, the EC–CARIFORUM EPA requires the parties to implement their international obligations, including those under the *UN Convention against Corruption*, and to co-operate and take domestic measures, including legislation, to prohibit and punish bribery or corruption.[437] It also obliges states to co-operate and take measures domestically to prevent investors from circumventing labour obligations arising from the international obligations of the parties,[438] including the prohibition against forced labour, which is a *jus cogens* norm.

The IISD model treaty includes a provision requiring the party states to impose criminal sanctions for acts of bribery and other forms of corruption and for complicity in such acts.[439] In addition, it requires investors' home states to ensure that fiscal and

---

431 Ibid., Arts. 18, 19, 23–5. See also the *Inter-American Convention against Corruption* and the *AU Convention on Preventing and Combatting Corruption*, which cover certain other acts of corruption.

432 *Inter-American Convention against Corruption*, Art. 16; *AU Convention on Preventing and Combatting Corruption*, Arts. 18, 19; *UN Convention against Corruption*, Arts. 37, 38; and *OECD Anti-Bribery Convention*, Art. 9.

433 To date no state has enacted specific legislation directly regulating the human rights impacts of transnational corporate actors (see P Simons (2012), 'International Law's Invisible Hand and the Future of Corporate Accountability for Human Rights', 3 *Journal of Human Rights and the Environment* 5 at 31). A number of legislatures have considered such legislation. The most recent attempt was the Canadian Bill C-300, dubbed the 'Responsible Mining Bill', that survived to its third reading, but it was defeated by six votes on 27 October 2010. Had it been enacted it would have imposed obligations on Canadian extractive corporations to comply with certain human rights and environmental standards when operating in developing countries (see Bill C-300, *An Act Respecting Corporate Accountability for the Activities of Mining, Oil or Gas in Developing Countries*, 3rd Sess, 40th Parl, 2010–11).

434 See 6.11 (Investor obligation to refrain from acts, or complicity in acts, of bribery and corruption).

435 See Section 6.11 (Investor obligation to refrain from acts, or complicity in acts, of bribery and corruption).

436 EU–Korea FTA (2009), Annex 2-D, Art. 4.

437 EC–CARIFORUM EPA (2008), Arts. 72, 172.

438 EC–CARIFORUM EPA (2008), Art. 72(b)(c).

439 IISD model treaty, Arts. 22, 32.

tax laws, regulations and policies do not allow investors to recover or deduct monies paid or benefits given as bribes or obtained through other forms of corruption.[440]

Box 6.16 Summary of options for criminal sanctions against bribery and corruption and grave violations of human rights

1. *Do not provide sanctions against bribery and corruption or grave violations of human rights*
2. *Use existing domestic criminal law to address bribery and corruption or grave violations of human rights*
3. *Develop domestic laws and regulations that provide more effective criminal sanctions for bribery and corruption and grave violations of human rights*
4. *Integrate into an IIA an obligation on states to co-operate and to provide for criminal enforcement of prohibitions on bribery and corruption and grave violations of human rights and to co-operate with respect to enforcement*

6.14.2 Discussion of options

1. *Do not provide sanctions against bribery and corruption or grave violations of human rights*

States may be in breach of their international obligations: States that do not have effective laws and institutions in place to prohibit and prosecute grave violations of human rights or bribery and other forms of corruption will be in violation of their international human rights obligations and their obligations under the anti-corruption treaties to which they are parties. As noted above, the international human rights obligation to protect requires states not only to take legislative and administrative measures to ensure that private actors, including investors, do not violate the human rights of others, but also to investigate and punish such violations. Equally, the UN and OECD conventions require states to introduce appropriate criminal sanctions and to investigate and punish actors that engage in corruption.

This may deter investment: Empirical studies have shown that corruption deters investment. Investors prefer to invest in states with stable, transparent regulatory environments. Creating a robust legislative framework to impose criminal sanctions on those actors that engage in grave violations of human rights or corruption sends a clear signal to investors that the host state supports the rule of law.

2. *Use existing domestic criminal law to address bribery and corruption or grave violations of human rights*

There are costs and benefits to using existing domestic laws to sanction these acts.

440 IISD model treaty, Art. 32(B).

It is a low-cost option: Using existing law may be attractive to states, as they will not have to develop new laws or institutions to sanction bribery and corruption or grave violations of human rights. Enforcement resources may be limited. However, even though a state has international obligations in these areas, in some cases its existing laws may not be well adapted to address bribery and corruption or grave violations of human rights.

It may be difficult to prosecute foreign investors: As discussed above,[441] all states can face difficulties in enforcing domestic law against powerful foreign investors. These entities are often able to restructure to avoid liability or to transfer assets outside the host state to avoid criminal fines.

3. *Develop domestic laws and regulations that provide more effective criminal sanctions for bribery and corruption and grave violations of human rights*

It is costly to develop a regulatory framework: A potential disadvantage of this option is the cost. States would need to dedicate resources to developing robust criminal law sanctions, enforcement mechanisms and institutions to meet their international obligations.

It may be difficult to prosecute foreign investors: Even where states have robust criminal laws and institutions in place, they may still face challenges in enforcing such laws against foreign investors, particularly powerful transnational business actors.

It implements states' international obligations and supports sustainable development: On the positive side, creating strong criminal sanctions and institutions to deal with grave violations of human rights and corruption brings states into compliance with their international obligations. It would also help to ensure that investors and their investments support sustainable development in a host state.

It may decrease the costs of doing business: Another potential benefit of introducing criminal sanctions is that it may deter bribery and other corrupt activities. This will increase transparency and predictability in commercial transactions and dealings with government. Having robust anti-corruption laws can potentially decrease the cost of doing business for both domestic and foreign businesses.

It attracts investment and in particular socially responsible investment: Studies have shown that corruption deters investment. It may also be true that incidents of egregious violations of human rights that go unpunished will deter investment. Establishing and enforcing criminal laws targeting corruption and grave violations of human rights indicates to socially responsible investors and investors wishing to maintain their global reputations that the state has a stable, transparent, rights-protective and lower-risk regulatory environment in which to conduct business.

It helps manage corporate risk: As discussed above,[442] in many situations investors can be prosecuted under the laws of their home states for engaging in bribery or other

441 See Section 6.8 (Investor obligation to respect internationally recognised human rights and undertake human rights due diligence).

442 See Section 6.11 (Investor obligation to refrain from acts, or complicity in acts, of bribery and corruption).

forms of corruption in other states. Many states also have laws in place to prosecute investors for extraterritorial commission of or complicity in egregious human rights abuses.[443] Operating in a state that prosecutes such activities can reduce the incidence of such crimes and decrease the risk that investors will get caught up in corrupt or human rights-violating behaviour. This also means that investors will be less likely to be the subject of NGO campaigns and that institutional investors, concerned about the behaviour of the businesses in which they invest, will be less likely to withdraw their investments.

4. *Integrate into an IIA an obligation on states to provide for criminal enforcement of prohibitions on bribery and corruption and grave violations of human rights and to co-operate with respect to enforcement*

The potential costs and benefits of integrating into an IIA an obligation on states to criminalise such behaviour and prosecute investors engaged in such activities are similar to those identified above with respect to incorporating the obligation into domestic law.

There are, however, other significant benefits to including such a provision in an IIA, rather than simply relying on existing domestic laws or introducing more stringent anti-corruption legislation and other measures.

Host state criminal enforcement is complemented by criminal enforcement in the investor's home state and by state co-operation: Perhaps the most important benefit of including such a provision in an IIA is that it requires *both* parties, home and host state, to create criminal sanctions and to co-operate with respect to their enforcement. Home state actions would complement and supplement host state efforts to investigate and prosecute this type of behaviour. Home state assistance and home state prosecution will help to address some of the difficulties faced by host states in holding foreign investors accountable for egregious acts.

Supported by other treaty-based enforcement mechanisms: Criminal sanctions for investor complicity in bribery and corruption and grave violations of human rights criminal liability of investors, whether required in an IIA or not, can be complemented by several other kinds of IIA enforcement commitments that are discussed below. One is a grievance procedure that has the potential to produce information that could provide the basis for a criminal investigation.[444] The sample provisions also provide an example of a requirement for both parties to establish civil liability for, among other things, harms arising from grave abuses of human rights and corrupt activities.[445] Criminal responsibility can also be complemented by a

443 Ramasastry and Thompson, op. cit.

444 See Section 6.15 (Grievance procedure and other measures to enforce the management plan produced in the sustainability assessment).

445 See Section 6.16 (Civil liability of investors).

counterclaim mechanism, which allows host states to counterclaim in investor–state proceedings where the investor has violated its obligations under the treaty.[446]

Including an obligation to provide for criminal enforcement in an IIA also means that, unless excluded from state-to-state dispute settlement, one state could initiate this process for the purpose of ensuring that the other state was in compliance with its enforcement obligations. Access to such a process may assist host states to have home states act on their commitments with respect to enforcement. It could also be used by home states to put pressure on host states to take more rigorous enforcement action.

6.14.3 Discussion of sample provision

The aim of the Guide sample provision is to require party states to criminalise and punish grave abuses of human rights and corruption. The sample provision obliges party states to impose criminal sanctions on:

- Investors to punish them for committing, or being complicit in, grave violations of human rights and corruption, including bribery;
- Public officials for soliciting bribes or other undue advantage for the purpose of performing or not performing an official duty, or for the purpose of using influence to obtain a favour, licence or other undue advantage in order to obtain or retain an investment; and
- Investors for complicity in such acts of corruption by a public official.

Requires effective and dissuasive enforcements and sanctions: The sample provision also obliges parties to implement appropriate enforcement measures and sanctions for these acts.

Targets both legal and natural persons: Concerns have been raised by the OECD Working Group on Bribery regarding the lack of liability of *legal* persons for acts of bribery in domestic legal systems, which, as mentioned above,[447] is required by both the OECD and UN conventions.[448] Accordingly, the Guide sample provision specifically provides for the criminal liability of legal persons for acts of bribery and corruption and, drawing on the language of the UN Convention, provides for the prosecution of natural and legal persons for the same act.

Requires parties to make every effort to prosecute: The provision imposes a 'best endeavours' obligation on parties to prosecute grave violations of human rights and corrupt activities related to investment in order to encourage state action on these commitments.

---

446 See Sections 6.17 (Counterclaims by states in investor–state arbitration) and 7.1.7 (Sample provisions: investor–state dispute settlement, Article [W] (Counterclaims)).

447 See Section 6.11 (Investor obligation to refrain from acts, or complicity in acts, of bribery and corruption).

448 OECD (2008), 'OECD Working Group on Bribery Annual Report 2007', available at: www.oecd.org/dataoecd/21/15/40896091.pdf (accessed 8 January 2013).

Obligates parties to co-operate in enforcement: Finally, the sample provision requires states to co-operate with each other in the enforcement of criminal laws prohibiting investors from committing, or being complicit, in grave violations of human rights and acts of bribery or corruption.

6.14.4 Sample provision: obligation to provide criminal offences, enforcement and sanctions for grave violations of human rights and corruption

Obligation to Provide Criminal Offences, Enforcement and Sanctions for Grave Violations of Human Rights and Corruption

1. Each Party shall make it a criminal offence:

    a. For an investor of the other Party or its investment to violate the obligations set out in [Guide sample provision in Section 6.9 (Investor obligation to refrain from the commission of, or complicity in, grave violations of human rights)] and [Guide sample provision in Section 6.11 (Investor obligation to refrain from acts, or complicity in acts, of bribery and corruption)];

    b. For a public official to solicit or accept any pecuniary or other undue advantage, directly or indirectly, whether on his or her own behalf or on behalf of a third party, in order that the official or third party perform or refrain from performing an official duty or use his or her influence for the purpose of obtaining or retaining for the investor or investment

        i. a favour in relation to a proposed or actual investment,

        ii. a licence, permit, contract, or other rights in relation to a proposed or actual investment, or

        iii. any other business or other undue advantage in relation to such investment;

    c. For an investor or its investment to be complicit in any act described in subsection b., including incitement, aiding and abetting, conspiracy to commit or authorisation of such an act.

2. The offences created under Section 1, whether committed by a natural person or an enterprise or both, shall include provision for appropriate, effective, proportionate and dissuasive criminal enforcement of and sanctions for commission of those offences.

3. The criminal liability of enterprises in relation to the offences created under Section 1 shall be without prejudice to the criminal liability of the natural persons who have committed an offence.

4. Each Party shall make every effort to prosecute the offences created under Section 1 in accordance with its domestic law.

5. Each Party shall co-operate with the other Party in measures taken by the other Party to enforce the criminal offences created under Section 1.

6.15 Grievance procedure and other measures to enforce the management plan produced in the sustainability assessment

Cross references

The UN Guiding Principles on Business and Human Rights recommend that states 'provide effective and appropriate non-judicial grievance mechanisms, alongside judicial mechanisms, as part of a comprehensive State-based system for the remedy of business-related human rights abuse'.[449] According to the UN Special Representative on Business and Human Rights (SRSG), such mechanisms are crucial to supplement judicial mechanisms, which are unable to deal with all human rights-related complaints.[450] This is similarly true with respect to complaints about an investment relating to labour rights, indigenous peoples' rights or environmental abuses. The court system of the host state will not be able to address all such concerns. Many complaints will not translate into legally actionable issues. In addition, courts may be inaccessible to many individuals in the host state because of factors such as cost, distance, lack of knowledge, cultural barriers or lack of legal aid programmes.

One of the key functions of a grievance procedure is to provide information about harms caused by an investment's activities, including, but not limited to, harms caused by the failure of the investor to comply with its obligations. A grievance procedure provides a means through which affected individuals and communities can bring complaints about the harms caused by the investment that they may have suffered. It can serve as a forum for settling disputes and providing adequate reparations.

Non-judicial grievance mechanisms can function as alternative dispute resolution (ADR) processes providing mediation and/or adjudication and should be conceived so as to be culturally appropriate, and able to deal with rights-related issues[451] and environmental complaints. The UN Guiding Principles on Business and Human Rights suggest that such grievance mechanisms should be based on principles of legitimacy, accessibility, predictability, equity and transparency, and that they should be rights-compatible and a source of continuous learning.[452]

---

449 UN Guiding Principles on Business and Human Rights, op. cit., at Principle 27.

450 Ibid., at Principle 27, commentary.

451 Ibid.

452 Ibid., at Principle 31.

The Guide contains sample provisions that contemplate that:

- States will establish a sustainability assessment process;[453]
- Investors will undertake a pre-establishment sustainability assessment and develop a management plan to implement the assessment and outline how the investor will prevent, avoid, minimise, mitigate or compensate for their adverse impacts and, in appropriate circumstances, provide for benefit sharing with indigenous peoples;[454] and
- States will establish a consultative process for dealing in the first instance with non-compliance with the management plan by an investor.

A grievance procedure may be used to ensure that the benefits of a management plan are realised and, more generally, to address harms caused by the investment.

Box 6.17 Summary of options for grievance mechanism and other measures to enforce the management plan

1. *Do not create a grievance mechanism or other measures to enforce a management plan*
2. *Enact a domestic law establishing a grievance mechanism and process for enforcing a management plan*
3. *Integrate into an IIA an obligation on party states to establish a grievance mechanism and a compliance process for a management plan*

6.15.1 Discussion of options

1. *Do not create a grievance mechanism or other measures to enforce a management plan*

Low-cost option: This may be attractive to states with few resources to dedicate to such an endeavour. Financial and human resources will be needed to develop and operate a grievance mechanism. If it is to be effective, additional resources will probably be required to ensure that affected communities are aware of the mechanism and know how to make use of it. In addition, it could be costly to ensure that the mechanism is culturally appropriate where the affected individuals and community are, for example, indigenous peoples or minority groups.

No forum for victims and no compliance procedure for a management plan: If states do not create a grievance mechanism for investment-related disputes, many individuals and communities affected by the investment will have no access to a non-judicial forum for bringing complaints about alleged harms caused by an investor or its investment, and to seek redress or settle disputes related to the investor or investment in a non-adversarial and cost-effective manner.

453 See Section 6.6 (Sustainability assessments).

454 See Section 6.6 (Sustainability assessments).

In terms of compliance with the management plan, the state will have no procedure in place that provides clear expectations as to how it will deal with non-compliance by the investor. Further, there will be no consultative process to bring the investor into compliance before ratcheting up sanctions to more adversarial forms of enforcement, such as civil actions in domestic courts and counterclaims in investor–state dispute settlement. This could lead to a breakdown in the relationship between the investor and the host state.

2. *Enact a domestic law establishing a grievance mechanism and process for enforcing a management plan*

May be onerous for some states to establish and resource these mechanisms: A potential disadvantage of this option is that states will have to dedicate financial and human resources to develop and administer a grievance mechanism. A less costly option would be to require the establishment of a grievance mechanism only for investments in the extractive industry and other similar sectors, where there is the greatest potential for significant impacts on human rights, labour rights, indigenous peoples' rights and the environment.

May discourage investment: The grievance process could create a repository of information accessible to the public and media. Such information could be damaging to some investors or even to the state. It could be used by the media and NGOs to target both the state and investor conduct and to provide the basis for claims by affected stakeholders against an investor for relief. Some investors may consequently be discouraged from investing.

Implements the state's international obligations and supports sustainable development: On the other hand, establishing this type of complaint mechanism and process to enforce a management plan would demonstrate that a state is complying with its international obligations to protect human rights, labour rights, indigenous peoples' rights and the environment. As discussed above, states have obligations to protect human rights by taking administrative, legislative and enforcement measures to ensure that investors do not violate the human rights of individuals and certain groups within the territory or subject to the jurisdiction of the state. Providing a non-judicial complaint mechanism for settling disputes and addressing harms of those affected by an investment helps to fulfil the obligation to protect human rights. Equally, providing a process to help bring an investor back into compliance with a management plan which deals with prevention, avoidance and mitigation of, and reparation for, human rights violations also fulfils a component of this duty.

May decrease the costs of doing business and promote goodwill: As noted above, clashes between investors and the local community can result in significant costs to the investor through disrupted production, delayed operations, loss of property value, property damage, injuries to employees or worse.[455] A non-judicial grievance

455 Section 6.8 (Investor obligation to respect internationally recognised human rights and undertake human rights due diligence). See Davis and Franks, op. cit., at 3–8.

mechanism under which problems can be aired, disputes settled and reparations made could diffuse tensions, help to protect the investor's social licence to operate and save companies millions of dollars.

In addition, dealing with complaints about an investment outside the court system is less expensive and may reduce the investor's cost of doing business in the host state. Similarly, having a non-judicial, non-adversarial process for initially dealing with investor non-compliance with a management plan will be less expensive for both the investor and the state, and will facilitate the maintenance of a good relationship between them.

Helps manage corporate risk: Where investors participate in a non-judicial grievance process in good faith and provide adequate reparations for harm, they are less likely to be sued in either the host or the home state for harms caused by the investment. They are also less likely to be targeted by NGOs for unethical and rights-violating behaviour or to become the subject of a divestment campaign.

Supports sustainable development: As discussed above in the section on the relationship between investment and sustainable development,[456] foreign investment will be successful in promoting sustainable development – even a concept of sustainable development restricted to economic development – only if citizens of the host state benefit from such investment. Creating a low-cost, non-judicial grievance mechanism will provide an accessible, culturally appropriate forum to deal with adverse impacts in a rights-protective manner and ensure that any necessary reparations are made to affected individuals and communities. In this way, it will help to ensure that investors and their investments play a part in achieving sustainable development in a host state. Likewise, states and individuals will benefit from a consultative process between the state and investor to bring the investor back into compliance with the management plan, which aims to prevent or reduce adverse impacts on human rights and the environment.

3. *Integrate into an IIA an obligation on party states to establish a grievance mechanism and a compliance process for a management plan*

The potential benefits and drawbacks of integrating into an IIA an obligation on states to establish a grievance mechanism and a process to enforce a management plan are similar to those canvassed above with respect to establishing such a mechanism and process through domestic law. There is, however, an important added benefit of including such a provision in an IIA. A grievance mechanism and management plan enforcement process can be complemented by other treaty-based enforcement mechanisms, including criminal[457] and civil liability[458] and counterclaims in dispute settlement.[459]

---

456 See Section 2.3 (Links between foreign investment and sustainable development).

457 See Section 6.14 (Criminal sanctions).

458 See Section 6.16 (Civil liability of investors).

459 See Sections 6.17 (Counterclaims by states in investor–state arbitration) and 7.1.7 (Sample provisions: investor–state dispute settlement, Article [W] (Counterclaims)).

6.15.2 Discussion of sample provisions

Based on the discussion of costs and benefits above, a state may decide to include a grievance mechanism in its IIAs. The sample provisions discussed below provide examples of how this could be done.

Grievance mechanism: The first sample provision below imposes an obligation on states to establish a non-judicial grievance mechanism. It must be available to individuals or groups of individuals who allege that they have suffered violations of their human rights, labour rights or indigenous peoples' rights or harmful environmental impacts caused by the investment. It also sets out the principles on which the procedure is to be based.

In the context of investment, this type of grievance mechanism could be used by individuals or communities in the host state or by host state civil society groups to:

- Raise concerns regarding the impact of a foreign investment on their health, safety or social welfare;
- Report instances of unacceptable environmental degradation resulting from the investment;
- Report instances of a failure by the investor or investment to respect human rights, labour rights or indigenous peoples' rights;
- Report instances of the host state's failure to protect the environment affected by the investment;
- Report and address an investors' failure to abide by the management plan developed through the sustainability assessment process; or
- Seek reparation for abuses or harm caused by the investment.

Procedure to ensure investor compliance with a management plan: In the case of an alleged failure to comply with a management plan, a separate sample provision creates a process to deal with such non-compliance as follows:

- The host state notifies the investor of such failure;
- The investor then has six months to remedy its non-compliance in consultation with the host state and persons of the host state who are affected by the investor's non-compliance;
- Where the investor has not complied with the management plan within six months, consultations involving the investor, the host state and the investor's home state are required;
- Where consultations fail, a host state, private person or organisation may commence an action against the investor in the domestic courts of the host state or the home state to seek an order directing compliance with the management plan and/or to obtain compensation for losses suffered as a result of non-compliance; [460] and

460 See 6.16 (Civil liability of investors).

- A state may also bring a counterclaim in any investor–state arbitration initiated by the investor where consultations have not resulted in compliance or in an agreement for a reasonable and appropriate modification of the plan.[461]

6.15.3 Sample provision: obligation to establish a grievance procedure

Obligation to Establish a Grievance Procedure

1. Each Party, in consultation with anyone potentially affected by investments of investors of the other Party, shall establish an effective grievance procedure for individuals and groups of individuals who claim that their human rights, labour rights, rights as indigenous peoples, or health, safety or social welfare are affected by an investor of the other Party or its investment, or who wish to report instances of unacceptable environmental degradation resulting from the investment or from the Party's failure to protect the environment affected by the investment. Such grievance procedure must be legitimate, accessible, predictable, equitable, transparent and compatible with the rights and interests sought to be protected.
2. Where it is determined that the investment has affected the rights of such individuals or groups of individuals or caused environmental damage, the investor shall make reparations to such persons and groups commensurate with the severity of the violations or damage caused.
3. For greater certainty, reparations under Section 2 shall include restitution, compensation and satisfaction.

6.15.4 Sample provision: compliance with management plan

Compliance with Management Plan

1. If an investor of a Party or its investment fails to implement a management plan developed in accordance with [see Guide sample provision in Section 6.6 (Sustainability assessments)] relating to an investment in the other Party, the other Party shall give notice to the investor or investment of such non-compliance. The investor or investment shall re-establish compliance with the plan in a timely manner having regard to the harms resulting from non-compliance. In the process of doing so, the investor or investment shall consult in good faith with the other Party and with persons affected by the failure to comply.
2. Failure of the investor or investment to comply with the management plan within 180 days of notice having been given under Section 1 shall result in consultation between the other Party, the investor and affected persons in order to re-establish compliance or modify the management plan in a reasonable and appropriate way and in a timely manner having regard to the harms resulting from non-compliance.

461 See 6.17 (Counterclaims by states in investor–state arbitration).

6.16 Civil liability of investors

Cross references

Imposing civil liability on investors and their investments for breaches of their treaty obligations is another way to facilitate compliance in the host state with standards set out in the treaty. Civil suits brought against corporate actors for their acts or complicity in acts that violate human rights, labour rights and indigenous peoples' rights, or for harm caused by corruption or environmental damage may provide the sole avenue for redress for victims, given the current lack of other mechanisms and processes for addressing the adverse impacts of investment. Litigation can expose unscrupulous investor conduct and investors may have to expend significant amounts in legal fees, even where such litigation is unsuccessful. Given this, the potential high reputational and financial costs of even an unsuccessful suit may deter similar future conduct by investors.[462] In addition, a decision in favour of the plaintiffs would help to deter future abusive conduct on behalf of investors operating in host states. However, there are a number of significant jurisdictional, procedural, evidentiary and other legal hurdles to bringing successful civil suits against an investor in the host state and the investor's home state. Three important ones are discussed below.

No legal cause of action in the home state: In many common law jurisdictions such as Australia, Canada and the UK there is no specific cause of action for violations of human rights, labour rights or indigenous peoples' rights that may result from an investment in other countries. Such claims must be framed as torts, such as

462 See B Stephens (2007), 'U.S. Litigation against Corporations for Gross Violation of Human Rights', written for the ICJ Expert Legal Panel on Corporate Complicity in International Crimes, at 23 (copy on file with the authors), who notes that '[t]o the extent that well-publicized cases influence the many corporations that learn about them and fear becoming targets, the cases can have an impact on corporate culture and business practices'.

assault, battery, false imprisonment, intentional or negligent infliction of emotional distress, wrongful death or negligence, and then proved according to the tort laws of the particular jurisdiction. The USA, on the other hand, has specific legislation that facilitates suits for egregious extraterritorial violations of certain human rights. In addition to claims made under ordinary tort laws, plaintiffs are able to file such claims under the *Alien Torts Claims Act* (ATCA),[463] and a number of other statutes. However, some US courts have ruled that corporations can no longer be sued under the ATCA in certain US jurisdictions and one such decision has been appealed to the US Supreme Court.[464] The Supreme Court decision will probably determine once and for all whether corporate liability is actionable under the ATCA.

Home state judicial doctrines such as *forum non conveniens*: One of the challenges to bringing a claim in an investor's home state for acts committed by the investor or its investment in a host state is the domestic judicial doctrine of *forum non conveniens*. This, and other doctrines relating to jurisdiction, may discourage a home state court from hearing a matter if an investor objects to the jurisdiction of the court on the basis that it would be more convenient to hear the matter elsewhere. Some national courts are unwilling to assert jurisdiction over actions that take place outside a state's borders on this basis. The application of these kinds of judicial doctrines to refuse to hear the case severely undermines the effectiveness of requiring civil liability in home states, since the subject matter of the claim in each case will relate to actions in the host state.[465]

Complex organisation of transnational businesses: Another problem faced by plaintiffs suing investors in the investor's home state (and by home states seeking to criminally prosecute investors)[466] for acts committed in the host state is the separate legal personality of the different entities that make up many transnational businesses. Many investors are organised as corporate groups composed of multiple related legal entities. An investor that is a legal person may legitimately use a subsidiary incorporated in the host state that it controls to carry on its operations there or use other arrangements that shelter the parent company and other members of a corporate group from liability for activities carried out for the benefit of the group.[467] Courts are reticent to 'pierce the veil' of corporate groups to impose liability on parent companies

463 27 USC, §1350.

464 Petition for Writ of Certiorari, *Kiobel v. Royal Dutch Petroleum*, (2011) 565 US (No 10–1491). In *Mohamad v. Palestinian Authority*, no 11–88 (18 April 2012), affd 634 F 3d 604 (DC Cir 2011), available at: www.supremecourt.gov/opinions/11pdf/11-88.pdf (accessed 8 January 2013), the US Supreme Court confirmed that the *Torture Victim Protection Act* applies only to natural persons and does not therefore impose liability on organisations.

465 For a full discussion of the barriers to bringing these types of claims, see International Commission of Jurists (2008), 'Corporate Complicity and Legal Accountability: Volume 3 – Civil Remedies: Report of the International Commission of Jurists Expert Legal Panel on Corporate Complicity in International Crimes', International Commission of Jurists, available at: www.icjcanada.org/fr/document/doc_2008-10_vol3.pdf (accessed 8 January 2013).

466 See Section 6.14 (Criminal sanctions).

467 R Nicolson and E Howie (2008), 'The Impact of the Corporate Form on Corporate Liability for International Crimes: Separate Legal Personality, Limited Liability and the Corporate Veil – An Australian Law Perspective', Paper written for the ICJ Expert Legal Panel on Corporate Complicity in International Crimes at 11, available at: www.hrlrc.org.au/files/icj-paper-e-howie-and-r-nicolson-final-0207.pdf (accessed 8 January 2013).

for acts of their subsidiaries.[468] Home state courts will be more reluctant to assume jurisdiction over a claim that can be pursued only against a subsidiary incorporated and operating in a the host state.

Attaching liability to the appropriate entity becomes more problematic when a number of subsidiaries incorporated in a variety of states are interposed between the parent and the subsidiary that committed the impugned acts in the host state, and where the local subsidiary has insufficient assets to satisfy claims for injuries caused. In such a case, liability of the subsidiary in the host state will not result in relief being provided. The challenge is to hold liable an appropriate entity in a corporate group that has sufficient assets. This challenge is often further complicated by the wide variety of ownership and contractual relationships that can exist between members of a related group that together make up a transnational business.

There are a number of ways to attempt to address this issue, including:

- States can establish *enterprise liability* for investors and their investments;
- States can impose an obligation on investors to take out liability insurance for violations of human rights, labour rights, indigenous peoples' rights and environmental damage, as a condition of permitting the investment; and
- States can impose an obligation on investors to post a bond as a condition of permitting the investment to supplement liability insurance for potential liabilities in the host state. Such a requirement could be restricted to investments that are more likely to have significant unforeseen harmful social and environmental impacts.

6.16.1 Enterprise liability

To date, no generally accepted solution has been found for the problem of establishing liability of appropriate legal persons in complex transnational businesses composed of multiple distinct legal entities. As discussed above, the traditional approach of states has been to treat parent, subsidiaries, affiliates, joint venture partners and other entities in a transnational business (or corporate group) as separate legal entities with liability attaching only to the entity whose agents directly participated in the action giving rise to liability.

Some states have, however, employed enterprise law – treating corporate groups as a single juridical unit[469] – in areas of tax law, competition law, bankruptcy law, labour law, administrative law and discrimination law. Under corporate law in most jurisdictions, courts may 'pierce the corporate veil' (look behind the separate legal existence) of a corporation in certain limited circumstances to impose liability on shareholders, including parent corporations. Enterprise law goes beyond the piercing of the corporate veil, in that it allows a court not only to find a parent corporation liable for the acts of a subsidiary, but also to find a sister subsidiary (a corporation that

468 Subsidiary means a corporation under the control of a parent corporation through the parent's ownership of all or a majority of the voting shares of the subsidiary.

469 G Wright (2010), 'Risky Business: The Case for Enterprise Analysis at the Intersection of Corporate Groups and Torts', available at: http://papers.ssrn.com/sol3/papers.cfm?abstract_id=1966777, at 5. (accessed 8 January 2013).

is under the common control of the parent) liable, because the entire corporate group is regarded as a single entity.[470]

The application of enterprise liability in the case of third party victims of actions by an undercapitalised entity within a corporate group can be justified on two grounds. It reflects the economic reality of transnational business groups, which often operate as an integrated whole; and it reallocates the liability risk to the business group, which has the choice to refrain from the activities that would cause harm or to ensure that the entity directly responsible for the harmful acts has sufficient assets to compensate people injured by those activities.[471]

A range of countries, including the USA, Germany, India and Albania, has developed laws that impose enterprise liability in certain circumstances. These laws employ some form of legal or factual test (or both) for control to determine whether two entities are affiliated. Dine argues that Albanian company law contains state-of-the-art provisions on enterprise liability that go beyond the laws in other jurisdictions. For example, it focuses on the flow of money, rather than legal control, and in so doing, it creates the prospect of attaching liability to the whole corporate group and not simply the parent company.[472] According to Dine this 'concept is also broad enough ... to include relationships such as franchising or other kinds of supply or distribution, outsourcing of certain enterprise functions or quality-assurance systems'.[473] Box 6.18 reproduces the provisions of the Albanian law related to parents and subsidiaries.

Box 6.18 ***Law No. 9901, 14 April 2008, on Entrepreneurs and Companies***

Article 207 Parents and Subsidiaries

1. A parent–subsidiary relationship shall be deemed to exist where one company regularly behaves and acts subject to the directions or instructions of another company. That control shall be called [the] control group.
2. If a company, based on its capital share in another company or based on an agreement with that company, has the right to appoint at least 30 per cent of members of the Board of Administration or Supervisory Board or of the administrators of that company, or if it has at least 30 per cent of votes at the General Meeting, it shall be considered a parent of the other company and the other company as its subsidiary. That control shall be called an equity group.
3. The parent's rights over the subsidiary as specified in Paragraph 2 of the present Article shall be considered such even where those rights are exercised

(Continued)

470 Ibid. at 5.
471 Ibid. at 10.
472 J Dine (2012), 'Jurisdictional Arbitrage by Multinational Companies: A National Law Solution?', 3 *Journal of Human Rights and the Environment* 44 at 66–67.
473 Ibid.

(Continued)

through another company, controlled by the parent or a third party acting on account of that other company or the parent itself.

Article 208 Legal Consequences of Control Group

1. Where there is a parent–subsidiary relationship as defined in Article 207 Paragraph 1 of the present Law, the parent shall have a duty to compensate the subsidiary for its annual losses.
2. …
3. Creditors of the subsidiary shall at any time have the right to require the parent to offer adequate security for their claims owed by the subsidiary.
4. Creditors of the subsidiary shall include persons who have incurred damage due to a subsidiary's actions wherever the subsidiary is registered.[474]

Albanian company law could provide a useful template for ensuring enterprise liability for victims of investor abuses of human rights, core labour rights and indigenous peoples' rights and environmental harm or harm caused by bribery or other forms of corruption. It provides a basis for such victims to enforce any judgment in their favour against the parent of a corporate group. It also defines such victims as creditors of the corporate group. Dine notes, however, that these provisions need further refinement and development, in particular with respect to the concept of control and in order to address partnerships, which are another business form commonly used by transnational businesses.[475]

In the transnational context, the use of enterprise liability with respect to a transnational business can be problematic since it can lead to a conflict between the domestic laws of two states.[476] The imposition of enterprise liability by one state on an investor that affects an affiliated entity in another state could also be viewed by the other state as a violation of sovereignty. An agreement in an IIA to the imposition of enterprise liability would address this sovereignty concern.

6.16.2 Liability insurance

Liability insurance is a less challenging tool that might be used to address the problem of a foreign investor evading civil liability for the acts of its subsidiary, affiliate or joint venture partnership in the host state in some cases. For example, in addition to establishing civil liability for investors, a state could require the foreign investor to

474 Ibid. at 62–4.

475 Ibid. at 67.

476 P I Blumberg (1993), *The Multinational Challenge to Corporation Law: The Search for a New Corporate Personality*, Oxford University Press, New York, at 153–4.

obtain third party liability insurance for its activities in the host state as a condition of being allowed to establish its investment.

Investors routinely take out political risk insurance from export credit agencies and other financial institutions for operations in jurisdictions deemed to be politically unstable. Such insurance provides protection from the risk of actions by the state, such as a breach of contract, expropriation, political violence, restrictions on currency conversion or transfer, repossession of physical assets, and non-payment by a government of loans or a financial guarantee.[477] Third party liability insurance could cover investor liability for some kinds of negligent acts that may violate the human rights, labour rights, indigenous peoples' rights or cause environmental damage.

The amount of insurance required could be determined having regard to the outcome of a sustainability assessment. The insurance would need to be purchased by the investor for the benefit of the subsidiary, joint venture partner or other legal entity through which the investor is operating the investment in the host state. The proceeds of the insurance would form a pool of money held by the subsidiary that could be used for the purpose of satisfying any judgments against the subsidiary or other entity in a civil claim or in counterclaim in investor–state dispute settlement or to satisfy any reparations that are determined to be required through a grievance process. Alternatively, the host state itself could be made the beneficiary of such insurance.

6.16.3 Posting a bond or guarantee

A further option to address the problem of transnational businesses evading civil liability for adverse impacts is to require the investor to post a bond or obtain a guarantee from either a public or private financial institution for such liability that may arise in the host state. Bonds and guarantees are a routine part of international business transactions and the International Chamber of Commerce has developed a widely used set of rules for bonds and guarantees that could be adapted for this purpose.[478] The bond would have to be posted or the guarantee would have to be made for the benefit of the host state. The host state would then be responsible for distributing the proceeds to individuals with claims against the investor.

6.16.4 IIA practice

There appear to be no existing IIAs that include provisions requiring parties to establish civil liability for investor violations of human rights, labour rights or indigenous peoples' rights, for environmental damage or for harm caused by corruption. The IISD model treaty contemplates such a provision. It provides a right for host states, individuals and organisations to bring a civil action in the host state and recover damages for breach by an investor or investment of their obligations under the IISD model treaty.[479]

---

477 See, for example, Export Development Canada, 'Political Risk Insurance', available at: www.edc.ca/EN/Our-Solutions/Insurance/Pages/political-risk-insurance.aspx (accessed 8 January 2013).

478 ICC (1978), *ICC Uniform Rules for Contract Guarantees*, International Chamber of Commerce, Paris.

479 IISD model treaty, Art. 17.

The IISD model treaty also provides that investors may be held civilly liable in the investors' home state.[480] This provision creates an additional means of redress for those whose rights have been violated or who have suffered harm caused by an investor or its investment in situations where remedies within the host state may be limited or ineffective. It also allows victims in the host state to pursue a claim in the state where the investor is likely to hold more assets, such as the home state.

Finally, the IISD model treaty further attempts to address the jurisdictional obstacles of bringing a claim in the home state for acts that were perpetrated in the host state. It imposes an obligation on home states to ensure that bringing such actions is not prevented just because the impugned acts occurred in the host state. This means that a claim for compensation is more likely to be heard and an award of damages has more chance of being effectively enforced. The IISD provision does not address the problem posed by separate legal personality of the different entities in a corporate group with different nationalities.

Box 6.19 Summary of options for obligation on states to establish civil liability for investors

1. Do not establish civil liability for harm caused by investors
2. Use existing domestic law in relation to civil liability for harm caused by investors
3. Enact a domestic law establishing civil liability for investors
4. Integrate into an IIA an obligation on both party states to establish civil liability for investors

6.16.5 Discussion of options

1. *Do not establish civil liability for harm caused by investors*

States may not be in compliance with their international human rights obligations: As discussed above, states have an obligation to protect human rights. This means they must take action through legislative, administrative and other measures to protect individuals from violations of human rights caused by private actors, including investors. Providing a means for victims of human rights abuses to bring a claim for such harm is one way of fulfilling this duty. In addition, the right to an effective remedy is a fundamental human right that is explicitly protected under a range of human rights treaties, including most of the core UN human rights treaties discussed above,[481] as well as regional instruments. The majority of international universal

480 IISD model treaty, Art 31.

481 See Section 6.8 (Investor obligation to respect internationally recognised human rights and undertake human rights due diligence). See *ICERD*, Art. 6; *ICCPR*, Art 2(3); *CEDAW*, Art 2(c); *CAT*, Art. 14; *ICRMW*, Art. 83; *CPED*, Arts. 8(2), 20(2).

and regional human rights instruments require 'both the procedural right of effective access to a fair hearing and the substantive right to a remedy'.[482]

This can undermine the rule of law and deter investment: Remedies are a key feature of the rule of law. They can deter future violations of human rights and they provide redress to victims of such abuses.[483] Failing to provide for effective remedies for abuses of human rights, labour rights, indigenous peoples' rights and environmental damage and harm caused by corrupt practices could weaken the rule of law in the host state. This in turn may discourage investment.

2. *Use existing domestic law in relation to civil liability for harm caused by investors*

Low-cost option: This option may be attractive to states with few resources to dedicate to developing new judicial remedies and the institutions necessary to make them effective. Many host states will already have in place a means through which individuals and communities adversely affected by an investment can sue the investor in domestic courts.

No specific cause of action for violations of human rights, labour rights, indigenous peoples' rights, environmental harm or corruption: Existing laws in a host state may not provide a specific legal basis for claims regarding violations of human rights, labour rights or indigenous peoples' rights, environmental damage or injuries resulting from corrupt activities. This means such abuses will have to be based on other legal grounds, which may not properly address the harms caused. It may also be the case that certain abuses will not be actionable.

Possible difficulty in enforcing a judgment against a foreign investor: As discussed in the sections above,[484] states may have difficulty in enforcing domestic laws against foreign investors, including judgments. Foreign investors can structure themselves so as to avoid exposure to liability. Investors may purposely undercapitalise the subsidiary, affiliate or joint venture partner through which they are operating in the host state or transfer assets to another entity within the corporate group to avoid successful enforcement of any judgment against it.

3. *Enact a domestic law establishing civil liability for investors*

States could implement legislation specifically establishing civil liability for violations of human rights, labour rights, indigenous peoples' rights and environmental damage caused, or contributed to, by foreign investors, as well as for harms caused by corrupt activities of foreign investors.

---

482 D Shelton (2005), *Remedies in International Human Rights Law*, 2d ed, Oxford University Press, Oxford, at 115.

483 Ibid.

484 See, for example, Section 6.2 (The challenges of regulating foreign investors and holding transnational corporations accountable); Section 6.3 (Different approaches to integrating foreign investment and sustainable development); Section 6.7 (Investor obligation to comply with the laws of the host state); and Section 6.8 (Investor obligation to respect internationally recognised human rights and undertake human rights due diligence).

It may be onerous for some states to establish a new basis for a civil claim: The development of a new cause of action for violations of human rights, labour rights, indigenous peoples' rights, environmental damage caused by foreign investors or for harm resulting from corrupt practices will require financial and human resources. It may be necessary to engage in consultations with experts and previously affected communities in developing such a law. States will need to ensure that the judiciary and the legal profession, among others, are sufficiently informed and trained on the international law standards underlying such a cause of action.

Investors may challenge a new law under existing IIAs: Investors could potentially challenge such a new law, or even a claim brought under such a new law, as a violation of FET under an existing IIA. This is particularly true where such a new law allows for the host state to address harms caused by the investor. Some investment tribunals have interpreted FET so broadly as to significantly restrict the capacity of states to change the regulatory environment that existed at the time the investment was established.[485] The risk of these types of investor–state claims is greater where the host state acts to permit suits against only foreign, and not domestic, investors. If the investor is successful in an investor–state arbitration claim, the host state could be required to pay significant damages.

It may be difficult to enforce a judgment against a foreign investor: As noted above with respect to using existing domestic law, investors may be able to avoid liability for damages awarded against them in a civil case under any new law.

It implements the state's international obligations and supports sustainable development: On the other hand, establishing such a cause of action would demonstrate that a state has taken steps, in compliance with its international obligations, to protect human rights (including the right to an effective remedy), labour rights, indigenous peoples' rights, and the environment and to address corruption. Creating civil liability for such adverse impacts of foreign investment may deter egregious investor conduct and allow for redress for victims and the host state. This will help to ensure that investors and their investments play a positive role and contribute to sustainable development in a host state.

It may deter investors from engaging in hazardous activities or incentivise investors to prevent and mitigate adverse impacts: The creation of civil liability for adverse impacts on human rights, labour rights, indigenous peoples' rights and for environmental damages may push investors to more thoroughly assess their potential impacts, seek to prevent the most severe effects and mitigate others in compliance with a management plan developed as a result of such an assessment. Investors may also have an incentive to deal with complaints arising from their activities through a non-judicial grievance process and to provide adequate reparations where necessary to avoid drawn-out and costly legal proceedings.

It reallocates risk: Providing civil liability for violations of human rights (including labour rights and indigenous peoples' rights) and environmental damage by foreign investors

---

485 See Section 5.5 (Fair and equitable treatment and the minimum standard of treatment).

and their investments, as well as harm caused by corrupt practices, can help to reallocate risk. If individuals have no access to effective judicial remedies where non-judicial remedies fail to provide effective redress, they bear the risk of such harms. Similarly, if a host state cannot take legal action against an investor for adverse impacts of the investment, then it also bears the social and financial risk of harm. For example, abuses of human rights can lead to increased levels of discrimination, greater marginalisation of certain groups, increased poverty[486] and even conflict.[487] Environmental damage can lead to problems such as the pollution of water supplies and arable land, and the consequent social impacts on health and quality of life. Civil liability is a mechanism to allocate the risks of these losses to the investor who caused them.

4. *Integrate into an IIA an obligation on both party states to establish civil liability for investors*

The potential benefits and drawbacks of integrating into an IIA an obligation on states to establish civil liability for investors are similar to those identified above with respect to developing and implementing a new domestic law allowing for such claims. However, including an obligation in an IIA requiring party states to establish civil liability for investors has several additional important advantages.

It helps to overcome the problem of a potential investor challenge to domestic law implementing such a cause of action: Including such a provision in an IIA diminishes the likelihood of investor challenge. As long as states comply with the core investor protections in an IIA in bringing such claims, and do not solely target foreign investors, investor claims based on the introduction and use of a civil liability regime are unlikely to be successful. An express exception for civil liability measures could also be included.

It harnesses the regulatory capacity of the home state: Requiring the home state to establish a civil liability regime under an IIA can complement civil liability in the host state. Home state civil actions allow victims of abuse to bring a claim in the jurisdiction in which the investor is likely to hold its assets and which may have more plaintiff-friendly laws, such as laws that permit class actions, provide legal aid to poor claimants or allow fee-paying arrangements where lawyers representing claimants can agree that they will be paid only if the claim is successful.[488]

Investors can be required to obtain liability insurance and/or post a bond: An obligation could also be imposed on an investor to obtain insurance for the benefit of the entity through which it is operating in the host state for the sole purpose of satisfying any judgment in a civil claim. This would ensure that the investor could not evade liability by transferring assets out of, or undercapitalising, the entity. Another option is to oblige investors, particularly those engaged in hazardous activities, such as extractive and major infrastructure projects, to post a bond in favour of the host state. This addresses the higher risk of major unanticipated liability typical of these

486 See Sepúlveda and Nyst, op. cit.
487 See Thoms and Ron, op. cit.
488 This is sometimes referred to as a 'contingency fee' payment arrangement.

kinds of investments. It would ensure that insurance coverage could be supplemented where it would be insufficient to cover a judgment for harm caused in violation of the investor obligations.

It can be complemented with other treaty-based enforcement mechanisms: Establishing civil remedies for investor violations of human rights, labour rights, indigenous peoples' rights, environmental harm, complicity in bribery and corruption, failure to comply with a management plan resulting from a sustainability assessment and any obligation under domestic law can be complemented by several other kinds of IIA enforcement commitments discussed in the Guide. A grievance procedure required under an IIA could produce information that may provide the basis for a civil claim.[489] An IIA requirement to provide for the criminal prosecution of investors complicit in corruption or grave violations of human rights may lead to criminal prosecutions that could also provide information and decisions that could be useful in a civil claim.[490] Civil responsibility is also complemented by a counterclaim mechanism, which allows host states to counterclaim in investor–state proceedings where the investor has allegedly violated its obligations under the treaty.[491]

Including an obligation in an IIA to provide for civil enforcement also means that, unless this is excluded from state-to-state dispute settlement, one state could initiate this process for the purpose of ensuring that the other state was in compliance with its obligations to provide for civil liability. Access to such a process may assist host states in ensuring that home states act on their commitments with respect to civil liability. It could also be used by home states to pressure host states to take action with respect to the IIA requirements for the host state's civil liability regime.

6.16.6 Discussion of sample provision

The Guide sample provision requires both the host state and the investor's home state to create a regime permitting individuals and the host state to sue for civil relief for acts, decisions or omissions of the investor or its investment that violate the investor obligations in the IIA between the home and host state.[492] The sample provision has the following additional features.

Imposes civil liability for failure to comply with a management plan after six months: Civil liability is imposed where the consultative process to ensure the investor is brought back into compliance with a management plan (developed pursuant to a

489 See Section 6.15 (Grievance procedure and other measures to enforce the management plan produced in the sustainability assessment).

490 See Section 6.14 (Criminal sanctions).

491 See Sections 6.17 (Counterclaims by states in investor–state arbitration) and 7.1.7 (Sample provisions: investor–state dispute settlement, Article [W] (Counterclaims)).

492 See Section 6.7 (Investor obligation to comply with the laws of the host state); Section 6.8 (Investor obligation to respect internationally recognised human rights and undertake human rights due diligence); Section 6.9 (Investor obligation to refrain from the commission of, or complicity in, grave violations of human rights); Section 6.10 (Investor obligation to comply with core labour standards); and Section 6.11 (Investor obligation to refrain from acts, or complicity in acts, of bribery and corruption).

sustainability assessment) has failed to yield such compliance.[493] No civil liability or other recourse is available in circumstances where a management plan itself does not conform to the criteria identified in Section 6.6 (Sustainability assessments). In some cases, however, such non-conformity may be a violation of some other obligation in the investment treaty for which civil liability or other remedies are provided.

Requires states to remove jurisdictional barriers to transnational claims: In order to minimise the impact of domestic judicial doctrines, such as *forum non conveniens*, the Guide sample provision imposes an obligation on each party state to remove these kinds of barriers to civil actions.[494] If states include such a provision in their treaty, concerns sometimes expressed by home states and their courts about avoiding extraterritorial application of their laws and encroaching on the sovereignty of the host state are avoided. By including this type of provision, the host state is agreeing to the home state's assertion of jurisdiction in these kinds of cases.

Addresses problems of enforcement against transnational businesses: The sample provision aims to address the problem of transnational business groups being able to structure themselves so as to avoid liability in the host state by under capitalising the subsidiary, affiliate or joint venture partner through which the investor operates the investment in the host state or transferring assets out of the host state to another entity within the corporate group in another state to avoid paying any judgment against its entity operating in the host state. The sample provision does not require party states to create enterprise liability for investors since it is not apparent that a single solution would work in every jurisdiction, given the range of different legal constructs and liabilities.

Instead, the sample provision imposes an obligation on party states to require investors, as a condition of the investment to do the following:

- To purchase liability insurance on behalf of the subsidiary, affiliate or joint venture partner. The amount of the insurance will be determined through the sustainability assessment process.[495]
- To post a bond in favour of the host state in situations where the sustainability assessment reveals that potential adverse impacts on human rights, labour rights, indigenous peoples' rights or the environment are sufficiently serious to require extra funds to satisfy any judgment against the investor for breach of the investor's obligations under the treaty. The amount of the bond will be determined through the sustainability assessment process.[496] The aim of the bond is to supplement liability insurance that may be insufficient or unavailable. It will be required

493 See Section 6.6 (Sustainability assessments).

494 While such jurisdictional hurdles exist mainly in common law states, the courts of European states parties to the Brussels Convention are now prevented from objecting to the jurisdiction of a claim relating to acts that occurred in another state. See *Group Josi Reinsurance Company SA v. Universal General Insurance Company*, C-412/98, [2000] ECR I-5925; *Owusu v. Jackson*, C-281/02, [2005] ECR I–1383.

495 See Section 6.6 (Sustainability assessments).

496 See Section 6.6 (Sustainability assessments).

only in situations where the investment poses a risk of significant harms, such as extractive industry activities or large infrastructure projects.

Limitation to breaches that cause a loss to the party state or persons of the party state: Civil liability arises only where a violation by an investor of a treaty obligation causes a loss or injury to a party state or a person of a party state. This should help to limit the use of civil actions to harass investors on the basis of trivial violations of treaty standards. The risk of such actions may be most significant in relation to an obligation of an investor to comply with domestic law in the host state as is discussed above.[497] With such an obligation, there is a risk that civil liability would be imposed even for relatively minor or technical violations by the investor. It would be possible to limit civil claims based on violations of domestic law by establishing a minimum threshold of seriousness for an investor's liability. An IIA could provide that only breaches that are 'substantial' or 'material' could be the basis of a civil claim. In the absence of such qualifying language, it would be up to the court hearing the case to determine whether to hold an investor liable for a minor or technical violation, and if so, what should be the appropriate level of damages for such violations. Since the sample provision contemplates civil liability only where a loss or injury has been suffered as a result of the breach and domestic courts typically have the power to deal with any abuse of their civil process, no such limitation has been included in the sample provision.

6.16.7 Sample provision: obligation to provide for civil liability of investors

Obligation to Provide for Civil Liability of Investors

1. Each Party shall take such measures as may be necessary to permit the Party or a person of the Party to initiate an action against an investor of the other Party or its investment in the first Party's domestic courts for compensation for losses of or injuries to the Party or a person of the Party arising from an alleged breach by the investor or its investment of the standards set out in:

   a. [see Guide sample provision in Section 6.7 (Investor obligation to comply with the laws of the host state)];

   b. [see Guide sample provision in Section 6.8 (Investor obligation to respect internationally recognised human rights and undertake human rights due diligence)];

   c. [see Guide sample provision in Section 6.9 (Investor obligation to refrain from the commission of, or complicity in, grave violations of human rights)];

   d. [see Guide sample provision in Section 6.10 (Investor obligation to comply with core labour standards)]; and

   e. [see Guide sample provision in Section 6.11 (Investor obligation to refrain from acts, or complicity in acts, of bribery and corruption)]

of this Agreement.

497 See Section 6.7 (Investor obligation to comply with the laws of the host state).

2. Each Party shall take such measures as may be necessary to permit the Party or a person of the Party to initiate an action against an investor of the other Party or its investment in the first Party's domestic courts for compensation for losses of or injury to the Party or a person of the Party arising from non-compliance with an management plan in relation to the investor's investment, where consultation has not resulted in compliance with the management plan or the reasonable and appropriate modification of the plan in accordance with [see Guide sample provision in Section 6.15 (Grievance procedure and other measures to enforce the management plan produced in the sustainability assessment)] within 180 days of the commencement of such consultations.

3. Each Party shall take such measures as may be necessary to permit the other Party or a person of the other Party to initiate an action against an investor of the Party or its investment in the Party's domestic courts for damages arising from an alleged breach by the investor or its investment of the obligations listed in Sections 1 and 2.

4. Each Party shall take such measures as may be necessary to ensure that its domestic courts have jurisdiction to hear actions contemplated under this Article, notwithstanding that the non-compliance complained of may occur partially or wholly outside the Party. For greater certainty, each Party shall ensure that its domestic courts shall not decline to hear such actions based on *forum non conveniens* or any similar judicial or statutory rule in the Party.

5. In connection with any action against an investor or other persons in the circumstances contemplated in this Article, each Party shall empower its domestic courts to order that the investor or other person shall comply with their obligations under this Agreement and that damages be paid in accordance with its domestic law to the injured Party or person where the investor or other person is found not to be in compliance with its obligations under this Agreement.

6. Each Party shall require an investor to obtain liability insurance as a condition of making an investment as determined to be appropriate in accordance with the results of the sustainability assessment conducted in accordance with [see Guide sample provision in Section 6.6 (Sustainability assessments)].

7. Each Party shall require an investor to post a bond in favour of the Party in which it is making investment where the sustainability assessment process conducted in accordance with [Guide sample provision in Section 6.6 (Sustainability assessments)] determines that the potential adverse impacts of the investment on human rights, labour rights, indigenous peoples' rights or the environment are sufficiently severe to require such a bond to be posted.

8. For greater certainty:

   a. The requirement to post a bond shall be in addition to the requirement to obtain liability insurance;

   b. The amount of such a bond shall be determined by the Party in which the investment is to be made on the basis of the results of the sustainability assessment conducted in accordance with [Guide sample provision in Section 6.6 (Sustainability assessments)];

c. The proceeds of any bond posted in favour of the Party in which the investment is made shall be distributed to:

   i. the individuals affected by the investment, or

   ii. a Party, where such Party has brought a civil action for breach of an investor obligation,

   Pursuant to a judgment of the court of a Party awarding damages in favour of such individuals or the Party on the basis of a breach by the investor or its investment of obligations listed in Section 1 or 2.

9. For greater certainty, any bond posted in favour of a Party shall be distributed only where the liability insurance referred to in Section 6 is insufficient to cover the full amount awarded in the judgment referred to in Subsection 8c.

6.17 Counterclaims by states in investor–state arbitration

Cross references

Section 6.7	Investor obligation to comply with the laws of the host state	292
Section 6.8	Investor obligation to respect internationally recognised human rights and undertake human rights due diligence	294
Section 6.9	Investor obligation to refrain from the commission of, or complicity in, grave violations of human rights	316
Section 6.10	Investor obligation to comply with core labour standards	322
Section 6.11	Investor obligation to refrain from acts, or complicity in acts, of bribery and corruption	338
Section 6.15	Grievance procedure and other measures to enforce the management plan produced in the sustainability assessment	381
Section 6.16	Civil liability of investors	387
Section 7.1	Investor–state dispute settlement	408

Another means of enforcing investor obligations under an IIA is through the establishment of a counterclaim mechanism. A counterclaim would allow a host state to bring a claim in investor–state arbitration proceedings for violations of investor obligations under the treaty. If such a claim were successful, the state would be able to offset any award in favour of the investor by the amount of any award in favour of the state for investor misconduct, or, if the investor's claim is unsuccessful, the state would be entitled to an award of damages enforceable against the investor.

6.17.1 IIA practice

Both the arbitration rules under the ICSID Convention and the UNCITRAL Arbitration Rules provide for counterclaims. These are the arbitral rules applicable to most investor–state arbitrations. However, under the ICSID rules, counterclaims must arise 'directly out of the subject matter of dispute' that is the basis of the claim brought by the investor.[498] No counterclaim would be permitted that arose out of facts unrelated to the investor's claim. Also, in order for an ICSID tribunal to have jurisdiction the counterclaim must relate to a 'legal dispute arising directly out of an investment.'[499] The UNCITRAL rules in place prior to 2010 permitted counterclaims in an even narrower set of circumstances. A counterclaim could be made only if it arose 'out of the same contract' that was the subject of the investor's claim.[500]

Not surprisingly, under these strict requirements counterclaims have been rare in investor–state arbitration and typically not successful. ICSID tribunals have determined that counterclaims must have a close connection to the investor's claim in order for jurisdiction to be established.[501] For example, in an arbitration involving an investor's claim regarding a state's actions in reorganising its banking sector that resulted in the forced administration of a financial institution owned by the investor, the tribunal decided that the state's counterclaims for taxes owed by the investor and for violations of the state's domestic commercial and banking laws were not within its jurisdiction.[502] In one case, a state's counterclaim was allowed where it was based on one of three contracts that together were an 'indivisible whole' of the investment transaction.[503]

In 2010, the UNCITRAL rules were amended to provide that a counterclaim is permitted any time the tribunal has jurisdiction over it.[504] This change expands the circumstances in which counterclaims may be made. In each case, however, counterclaims are available only if they are within the consent of the parties, which defines the tribunal's jurisdiction.[505] Consent to counterclaims in accordance with the ICSID or some other arbitral rules applicable to the dispute may be found in the parties' consent to arbitrate under these rules in the IIA. However, the IIA itself may impose limitations on the tribunal's jurisdiction. For example, if the treaty provides that only breaches of the investor protection obligations in the treaty may be the subject of a claim, a state's counterclaim based on domestic law would be precluded as outside the parties' consent.[506] If a treaty provided for obligations on investors related to areas such as

---

498 ICSID Convention, Art. 46.

499 ICSID Convention, Art. 25(1) defining the jurisdiction of ICSID arbitration tribunals.

500 UNCITRAL Arbitration Rules, Art. 19.3.

501 *Sergei Paushok, CJSC Golden East Company and CJSC Vostokneftegaz Company v. Mongolia*, UNCITRAL, Award on Jurisdiction and Liability of 28 April 2011 (no jurisdiction over any of the counterclaims).

502 *Saluka Investments BV v. Czech Republic*, Decision in Jurisdiction over the Czech Republic's Counterclaim, PCA IIC, 7 May 2004 (Respondent state's counterclaim based on violations of domestic tax law rejected). See Y Kryvoi (2011), 'Counterclaims in Investor–state Arbitration', 8/2011 LSE Working Papers, available at: http://papers.ssrn.com/sol3/papers.cfm?abstract_id=1891935 (accessed 8 January 2013), at 11.

503 *Klochner v. Cameroon*, ICSID Reports, vol. 2, Award, 21 October 1983. This was an arbitration related to a contract not an alleged breach of an investment treaty.

504 UNCITRAL Arbitration Rules, Art. 21.3.

505 This is expressly provided for in ICSID Convention, Art. 46.

506 *Spyridon Roussalis v. Romania*, ICSID Case No. ARB/06/1, Decision on Respondent's Counterclaim (not public), 31 March 2009. If there is a governing law clause in the treaty, it may limit the jurisdiction of the tribunal with respect to counterclaims.

human rights labour rights and anti-corruption, as discussed in the Guide counterclaims based on these obligations would have to be made the subject of the parties, consent to arbitrate for them to be the basis of a counterclaim. Such a consent would likely satisfy the requirement under the UNCITRAL rules that the counterclaim be within the jurisdiction of the tribunal. Even with a consent in the IIA, the counterclaim might not be permitted in an arbitration under the ICSID rules if it did not relate to an investment and arise 'directly out of the subject matter of dispute'.[507]

Few existing IIAs explicitly address the right of counterclaim by the host state. The COMESA Investment Agreement permits a state to bring a counterclaim for breaches of the investor obligations contemplated in that treaty, and permits a state to raise non-fulfilment by the investor of its obligations as a defence or set-off.[508] The IISD model treaty also provides for a right of counterclaim[509] and a right of a set-off where an investor persistently fails to comply with certain investor obligations under the treaty and the breach is determined to be materially relevant to the issues before the arbitral panel.[510] A counterclaim or set-off under these treaty provisions would allow a state to bring a claim in investor–state arbitration against the investor that is independent of the claim made by the investor against the state based on the failure by the investor to comply with its treaty obligations.

There are several important distinctions between a set-off and a counterclaim. A set-off is a form of defence. In investor–state arbitration, a set-off would be an argument by the state that any amount to be paid on the investor's claim should be reduced based on some claim to compensation that is owed by the investor to the state. A set-off defence is linked to the investor's claim in that it can only reduce the amount of any award in favour of the investor. If the investor's claim is unsuccessful for any reason, nothing can be awarded to the state as a set-off. For example, if a state was held responsible for expropriating an investor's assets, the state might claim a set-off based on a claim that the investor had breached an obligation to the state that caused the state to expropriate the investor. The set-off claim might relate to expenses the state had incurred. In contrast, any award under a counterclaim can be applied against any award in favour of the investor. Also, unlike a set-off defence, if the amount of the award to the investor is less than the amount of the counterclaim, the investor would be responsible for paying the difference to the state. If the investor were unsuccessful in its claim, it would still be responsible for paying the award in favour of the state under the counterclaim.[511]

507 A counterclaim based on the investment authorisation that was the basis of the investor's claim was allowed in *Goetz v. Burundi*, ICSID Case No. ARB/01/2, Award, 21 June 2012.

508 COMESA Investment Agreement (2007), Art. 28.9.

509 IISD model treaty, Art. 18(E).

510 IISD model treaty, Art. 18(D).

511 V Pavic (2006), 'Counterclaim and Set-off in International Commercial Arbitration', *1 Annals of the Faculty of Law in Belgrade - Belgrade Law Review, International Edition*, 101.

Box 6.20 Summary of options for a counterclaim in investor–state arbitration

1. *Do not introduce counterclaim mechanism into an IIA*
2. *Deny investors the right to pursue an investor–state claim where they have failed to comply with their obligations under an IIA*
3. *Integrate the right of counterclaim for party states into an IIA*

6.17.2 Discussion of options

1. *Do not introduce counterclaim mechanism in an IIA*

Maintains the status quo: Having no right to counterclaim in an IIA maintains the existing state of affairs in which the host state may only defend itself against a claim brought by the investor, but has no explicit basis within the context of investor–state arbitral proceedings to bring a separate claim against an investor for investor misconduct, apart from the limited rights that may be available under the applicable arbitral rules as discussed above.

2. *Deny investors the right to pursue an investor–state claim where they have failed to comply with their obligations under an IIA*

Provides no basis for relief for host state and denies investor the right to make an otherwise valid claim: An alternative to providing for a counterclaim would be to limit access to investor–state arbitration where investors are not in compliance with the standards set in the treaty. While permitting host states to avoid liability in this way would undoubtedly create an additional incentive for investors to comply, an investor would inevitably challenge a state's assertion that the investor was not in compliance, and the result would be that the issue of the investor's compliance would have to be adjudicated before the tribunal. In these circumstances, substantial costs would be incurred without any compensation being payable to the state for losses suffered. In addition, the state would be relieved of liability for a possibly unrelated breach of its obligations under the treaty. On balance, it seems appropriate to permit a state to claim compensation for losses caused by the investor's non-compliance through a counterclaim, as well as to bear responsibility for a breach of its own obligations.

3. *Integrate the right of counterclaim for party states into an IIA*

This redresses the balance of power in investor–state arbitration: Where the investor has caused harm to individuals, communities or the environment or engaged in corruption or breached obligations to the state, such as failing to perform a contract or pay taxes, having the right of counterclaim for any losses caused helps to balance the power in investor–state proceedings more equitably between the host state and the foreign investor. Where investor obligations are included in an IIA, the availability of a counterclaim is particularly important because, in some circumstances, there may be no other forum in which a state could make its claim. For example, a state may not provide a civil right of action in its domestic law that could be used to seek damage awards for breaches of human rights standards, corrupt activities or environmental degradation. Having an effective right of counterclaim enhances the effectiveness of any investor obligations in an IIA. Also, the possibility to resolve both the investor's claim and the state's counterclaim in one proceeding is more efficient than having two separate proceedings, especially where the claims are related, such as because they arise out of the same facts.

It may deter investment: Investors may be deterred from investing in a state where that state has the capacity to seek relief from investor conduct within investor–state proceedings. One of the important benefits of an IIA has been the right of investors to bring states to binding international arbitration for violation of the investor protection provisions of the treaty. Under existing IIAs, states have no way of challenging investor misconduct. The introduction of a counterclaim mechanism may be viewed by investors as too great a limitation of these traditional benefits of investment treaties.

Counterclaim awards may be more easily enforced than court judgments: An award of damages by counterclaim will be enforceable by the host state as an arbitral award. By virtue of several international treaties, arbitral awards are readily enforced in most countries in the world.[512] By contrast, court judgments of one country are often not enforceable outside that country.

It may deter investors from bringing or threatening investor–state claims: Another important advantage of the right of counterclaim is that it may provide a disincentive for investors to resort to investor–state arbitration or to threaten investor–state arbitration in situations where such investors do not come to the dispute settlement process with clean hands, in the sense that they have breached obligations to the state under domestic law or standards set out in the treaty.

It reallocates risk and supports sustainable development: Providing the right of counterclaim in an IIA can help to reallocate the risks of the investment to the investors, rather than allowing the risks to be borne by the host state and the individuals residing in that state. Where investor obligations are included in an IIA, the availability of a counterclaim empowers the state to hold investors accountable for violations of human rights or labour rights or indigenous peoples' rights, environmental damage and harm caused by corrupt practices and to offset any amount awarded by such a counterclaim against any damages awarded in favour of the investor. In doing so, it can help to ensure that foreign investment contributes to sustainable development.

It may discourage investors from engaging in hazardous activities and incentivise investors to prevent and mitigate adverse impacts: The introduction of a state right of counterclaim into an IIA for breaches by the investor of its obligations under the treaty with respect to human rights, labour rights, indigenous peoples' rights and for environmental damage or breaches of its obligation to refrain from acts of corruptions may provide a strong incentive for investors to assess their potential impacts in these

512 These treaties are discussed in Section 7.1 (Investor–state dispute settlement).

areas more thoroughly, prior to making their investment, to seek to prevent the most severe effects and to mitigate others in compliance with a management plan. Investors may be more motivated to deal with complaints arising from their impacts through a non-judicial grievance process and to provide adequate reparations where necessary to avoid a counterclaim.

Right to counterclaim can be complementary to other treaty-based enforcement mechanisms: The right to counterclaim can supplement other enforcement mechanisms mandated by an investment treaty. As discussed above, the preceding sample provision contemplates that states can sue investors civilly both in their domestic courts and in the courts of the investor's home state where the investor has breached a domestic law obligation in the host state.[513] A counterclaim can be used like civil liability as a last resort where consultation and grievance processes fail. It may provide an incentive to the investor to ensure that consultations and grievance processes are successful.[514]

Transnational businesses have complex structures: States bringing a counterclaim will encounter the same problems with enforcing any award against an investor discussed in the preceding section on civil liability, though, as noted, international arbitration awards are typically more easily enforced than domestic court judgments.[515] Many foreign investors are able to restructure or to transfer assets out of the host state to avoid liability. As discussed above, one way to address this problem is to require investors to take out liability insurance for the benefit of the entity through which it is operating in the host state to ensure that sufficient funds are available to satisfy a counterclaim award. Where the investor proposes to engage in hazardous activities in the host state, the host state may also wish to request that the investor post a bond or obtain a guarantee from a financial institution, or even from the home state, to satisfy any excess liability that the insurance will not cover. This will help to ensure that the host state will not be left without the ability to enforce its counterclaim for significant social and financial costs due to severe abuse of rights, environmental damage or harm caused by corrupt practices of the investor in violation of investor obligations.

6.17.3 Discussion of sample provision

The Guide sample provision, which is found in the section on dispute settlement,[516] creates a right on the part of the host state to bring an independent claim against an investor in the context of investor–state arbitral proceedings. Thus, if an investor brings an investor–state claim against the host state on the basis that the state has violated its obligations under the agreement or domestic law, the host state may counterclaim for damages that it or its nationals have suffered on the basis that:

513 See Section 6.16 (Civil liability of investors).

514 See Section 6.15 (Grievance procedure and other measures to enforce the management plan produced in the sustainability assessment).

515 See Section 6.16 (Civil liability of investors).

516 See 7.1.7 (Sample provisions: investor–state dispute settlement, Article [W] (Counterclaims)).

i. The investor has failed to comply with the management plan resulting from the sustainability assessment and review;[517]
ii. The investor has failed to comply with any other standard for investor behaviour in the investment treaty;[518] or
iii. The investor is liable to the state for any other reason.

The sample provisions expressly provide that, in submitting its claim, the investor consents to counterclaims based on investor obligations under domestic law or the treaty. An issue that may arise in practice is whether a counterclaim should be available even for relatively minor or technical violations by the investor. As discussed above in the section on civil liability, it would be possible to qualify an investor's liability by establishing a minimum threshold of seriousness. An IIA could provide that only violations that are 'substantial' or 'material' could be the basis of a counterclaim. In the absence of such qualifying language, it would be up to the tribunal to determine whether to hold an investor liable for a minor or technical violation, and if so, what should be the appropriate level of damages. In some investor–state cases, arbitral tribunals have required such a minimum threshold for investor claims based on fair and equitable treatment.[519] In the interests of certainty and to ensure that the counterclaim mechanism is not used for insignificant breaches of domestic law, the sample provision restricts counterclaims to violations of domestic law by the investor that the Tribunal determines are sufficiently serious to justify an award of damages. This language parallels language that imposes an identical limit on the award of damages to investors.[520]

The sample provision also expressly permits the tribunal hearing a case to award damages to the host state where the investor's claim is unsuccessful or results in an award of damages that is less than the award of damages to the host state under the counterclaim.

Note: The sample counterclaim provision is set out in Section 7.1.7 (Sample provisions: investor–state dispute settlement, Article [W] (Counterclaims)).

517 See Section 6.6 (Sustainability assessments).

518 See Section 6.7 (Investor obligation to comply with the laws of the host state); Section 6.8 (Investor obligation to respect internationally recognised human rights and undertake human rights due diligence); Section 6.9 (Investor obligation to refrain from the commission of, or complicity in, grave violations of human rights); Section 6.10 (Investor obligation to comply with core labour standards); and Section 6.11 (Investor obligation to refrain from acts, or complicity in acts, of bribery and corruption).

519 See Section 5.5 (Fair and equitable treatment and the minimum standard of treatment).

520 See Section 7.1.7 (Sample provisions: investor–state dispute settlement), Article [V] (Final Award)).

Chapter 7

Dispute Settlement

7.1 Investor–state dispute settlement

Cross references

Historically, only a party state had standing to make a claim that another party state had not complied with its obligations under an IIA, even if it was the state's investor that had suffered a loss as a result. Often, the only direct recourse that foreign investors had when they were unhappy about something a host state had done was through domestic courts or other institutions in the host state under domestic law or, if the dispute related to a contract between the investor and the host state, through any dispute settlement procedure provided in the contract. Most IIAs now give an investor of one party state the right to claim compensation directly against the other party state in binding arbitration if the other party state breaches the substantive standards of investor protection set out in the agreement and cause a loss to the investor.[1,2] While investor–state arbitration has some benefits for investors and host states, it also raises a number of serious concerns for host states.

7.1.1 Costs and benefits of investor–state arbitration

Investor–state dispute settlement was developed at the initiative of developed capital-exporting states because it offers significant benefits for their investors.

1 Some IIAs contemplate a broader scope of application of the investor–state dispute settlement process (UNCTAD (2007), *Bilateral Investment Treaties 1995–2006: Trends in Investment Rulemaking*, UN publication, Sales No. E.06.II.D.16 at 23, United Nations, New York and Geneva, at 101–4). Most treaties now provide for investor–state dispute settlement in some form (ibid. at 100).

2 Most Caribbean and Pacific BITs provide for investor–state arbitration (M Malik (2009), *Report on Bilateral Investment Treaties*, Commonwealth Secretariat, London, at 31, 60).

- **Seeking redress in the host country's domestic courts or through administrative remedies may be unattractive to foreign investors because of the weakness of local institutions.** Investor–state arbitration removes the investor's exposure to any uncertainties, delays and other problems with the host state's judicial and administrative systems. Investors may be concerned that local judicial or administrative procedures are slow and that local judges are unsophisticated, will be prejudiced towards foreigners or lack independence from the government whose actions are being challenged by them.[3]
- **Investor–state arbitration allows foreign investors to claim relief for the violation of standards of state behaviour set out in the IIA.** Such standards may permit claims for relief under a much wider range of circumstances than is possible under the domestic law of the host state. As noted, investor–state cases have produced some surprisingly broad interpretations of these obligations.
- **Investor–state arbitration can be initiated at the discretion of the investor.** If an investor is forced to rely on its home state to pursue claims against a host state on its behalf, the investor has to lobby its home government to take up its claim. The willingness of the investor's home state to pursue a private claim may ultimately depend on a range of political considerations that are beyond the control of the investor and unrelated to the merits of the investor's claim. The relative political power of the home and host states and the political sensitivities related to the investment in the host state and to the measure challenged will also play a role. Replacing reliance on state espousal of an investor's claim with binding investor–state arbitration that can be initiated by the investor ensures that an investor has access to a process for seeking relief if a state breaches its IIA obligations. In addition, the investor will be in control of how to pursue its claim in the dispute resolution process, making its own decisions about how to argue its case, whether to settle and so on.
- **Investor–state arbitration can lead to awards of compensation directly to the investor.** Where an investor's home state initiates and pursues a claim against a host state for breach of an international obligation, there is no guarantee that any relief will ultimately be received by the investor. In investor–state arbitration, where a breach by a host state is found, the tribunal orders compensation to be paid to the investor and, typically, the investor has certain rights to enforce the arbitral award under the IIA or the domestic laws of the host state if the host state does not pay.

From the point of view of a host state, agreeing to submit to investor–state arbitration can also have certain benefits.

- **Committing to investor–state arbitration in an IIA demonstrates a strong commitment to the investor protection obligations set out in the agreement and so may help to encourage investment in the host state.**

---

3 UNCTAD (2003), *World Investment Report 2003: FDI Policies for Development: National and International Perspectives*, United Nations, New York and Geneva, at 114–18.

- **Committing to investor–state arbitration in an IIA can help to lock in investment-liberalising reforms to the host state's domestic regime.** The possibility of investor claims based on broad treaty standards for investor protection through investor–state arbitration in an IIA may make it difficult for future host state governments to change the domestic regime affecting foreign investors. This may be attractive to a host state government interested in ensuring that future governments do not back away from reforms it has adopted to open markets to foreign investors.
- **Investor–state disputes settlement depoliticises disputes with investors**. In the past, state-to-state disputes were sometimes resolved through the exertion of political pressure by developed states on developing states. Investor–state arbitration requires disputes to be resolved based on the application of the legal standards in the IIA to the state's conduct, rather than on the relative power of the states.[4]

At the same time, experience with investor–state arbitration has shown that it can impose a variety of costs on host states and can constrain their ability to legislate to achieve sustainable development.

- **Investor–state arbitration is initiated by investors solely to pursue commercial interests (e.g. profit) and may be used to challenge actions by host states to achieve their public policy goals.** The intergovernmental and other factors that tend to limit the claims brought on behalf of investors by their home states do not operate under an IIA regime that permits investor–state arbitration.
- **Exposure to investor–state arbitration may create 'regulatory chill'.** Especially because the obligations in IIAs are broadly worded and so far the subject of limited and sometimes inconsistent interpretation, investors and their counsel have an incentive to bring a wide variety of claims on novel and sometimes outlandish theories. This is not to say, of course, that all such claims will be successful. Nevertheless, the existence of investor–state dispute settlement increases the risk that claims may be brought and that states will be held responsible to investors for their actions. Generally, a state cannot be required to change its investment regime by an arbitral tribunal. The relief available to investors through investor–state arbitration in existing IIAs is normally limited to monetary compensation.[5] Some argue, however, that the threat of investor–state arbitration has a chilling effect on domestic legislators, discouraging them from actions that are, or that even might be, contrary to investment obligations.[6]

---

4 It is argued that because inequalities of power continue, treaty making and dispute settlement are not really neutral or depoliticised: e.g. M Sattorova (2012), 'Return to the Local Remedies Rule in European BITSs? Power (Inequalities), Dispute Settlement, and Change in Investment Treaty Law', 39 *Legal Issues of Economic Integration* 223.

5 See, generally, M Endicott (2007), 'Remedies in Investor–state Arbitration: Restitution, Specific Performance and Declaratory Awards', in P Kahn and T Wälde (eds), *New Aspects of International Investment Law*, Martinus Nijhoff, The Hague, at 517.

6 H Mann and K von Moltke (1999), *NAFTA's Chapter 11 and the Environment*, International Institute for Sustainable Development, Winnipeg.

- **Committing to investor–state arbitration exposes host states to a process that is very costly.** The awards obtained in some investor–state cases to date have been large. In 2012, almost US$1.9 billion was awarded to a US investor against Ecuador.[7] This is one of the largest investor–state awards ever made. For small states, even one large award like this could be catastrophic. Even if a host successfully defends a claim, the cost of defending the claim is typically significant. Usually, the parties split the cost of the arbitration tribunal and any institutional fees, and pay their own costs. The OECD recently reported that the average cost of participating in an investor–state dispute for both parties is around US$8 million, but that it can be much higher.[8] The defence of claims by small states tends to be more expensive if they lack internal capacity to carry on the defence and have to hire private sector lawyers.
- **Investor–state arbitration raises legitimacy and democracy concerns.** In many investor–state arbitration cases, the investor is seeking relief from the actions of a host state that have been taken by the state with a view to fulfilling its responsibility to regulate in the public interest. For the adjudication of challenges to such public acts to be regarded as legitimate, the process should meet certain standards for openness and accountability. In addition, sustainable development requires rule-making that ensures the fair representation of all affected stakeholders. Although some improvements have been made over time, in many respects investor–state dispute settlement is not open and accountable in the way that domestic courts are in most countries. Specific concerns include the following:
  - Domestic laws and policies of host states are subject to interpretation by international arbitrators who may have no background in host state law;
  - There is limited transparency regarding the proceedings. Except in a few IIAs, there are no guarantees regarding public access to documents submitted to or issued by tribunals. Not all final awards are made public;
  - While public access to investor–state arbitration hearings is sometimes permitted in investor–state arbitration, there are no guarantees that hearings will be open to the public, except in a few IIAs; and
  - Civil society groups lack effective access to investor–state proceedings, although there has been some progress in allowing limited participation through *amicus curiae* submissions.[9]

7 *Occidental Petroleum v. Ecuador*, ICSID Case No. ARB06/11, Award, 5 October 2012. Previously, one of the largest awards had been US$867 million against the Slovak Republic in *SCOB* v. *Slovak Republic*, ICSID Case No. Arb/97/4, Final Award, 29 December 2004.

8 OECD, *Investor–state Dispute Settlement, Public Consultation*: 16 May–23 July 2012, available at: www.oecd.org/dataoecd/61/29/50291642.pdf (accessed 24 June 2012), at 19. S Franck (2011), 'Rationalizing Costs in Investment Treaty Arbitration,' 88 *Washington University Law Review* 279, discusses the complexity of measuring costs.

9 J A VanDuzer (2007), 'Enhancing the Procedural Legitimacy of Investor–state Arbitration through Transparency and *Amicus Curiae* Participation', 52 *McGill Law Journal* 681.

- **Investment arbitrators are not subject to the same requirements for independence and accountability as judges.** While arbitral rules and some IIAs have requirements for arbitrator independence, as well as procedures to challenge arbitrators, investment arbitrators are not subject to the same independence standards as domestic judges. Arbitrators are appointed on an ad hoc basis for a particular case. Usually each party selects one arbitrator and the parties agree on a third. It is the parties who pay them. Unlike judges in domestic and some international tribunals, arbitrators do not have security of tenure or financial independence and are not prohibited from undertaking other remunerative work. As a result, it is argued that arbitrators have an incentive to try to make decisions that will result in their reappointment. They may have other kinds of interests that could affect their decision making. For example, unlike judges, some arbitrators act as counsel in investment arbitrations. Their interest in getting work as advocates could affect their independence as decision-makers.[10]
- **Investment arbitrators often have no expertise in non-investment-related matters and are alleged to have a pro-investor bias**. Most IIAs contain no requirement for arbitrators to be competent in relation to any particular subject matter. Those who are appointed tend to be experienced international investment law experts. They often lack familiarity with non-investment issues that may be important considerations in determining the legality of state actions. For a particular case, expertise related to host state law, the rights of indigenous peoples, environmental protection or human rights may be needed to make a proper assessment of a claim. The result, some argue, is that tribunals tend to be biased in favour of investors' interests.[11]
- **Investor–state awards have lacked consistency, impairing the predictability of IIA obligations.** While investment arbitrators often refer to prior arbitral decisions in their awards, prior awards are not binding and tribunals have not always followed prior decisions. UNCTAD recently concluded that the awards issued in 2011 demonstrated continued disagreement on the meaning of core IIA provisions,[12] though there are contrary views regarding the pervasiveness and significance of inconsistent awards.[13] Inconsistency undermines predictability for

---

10 J Wouters and N Hachez (2011), 'Institutionalization of Investment Arbitration and Sustainable Development', in M-C Cordonier Segger, A Newcombe and M Gehring (eds), *Sustainable Development in World Investment Law*, Kluwer Law International, The Hague, at 627–9.

11 A related concern that has been expressed by some commentators is that if the Secretary-General of ICSID is the person who appoints arbitrators where the parties fail to do so, there may be a perception that the process may be affected by the interests of the World Bank. The empirical research on the question of whether arbitrators have a pro-investor bias is mixed. Susan Franck found that there is no correlation between developing country status of respondent states or the developing country origin were not related to the outcome of arbitrations: S Franck (2009), 'Development and Outcomes of Investment Treaty Arbitration', 50 *Harvard Law Review* 435.

12 See UNCTAD (2012), *Latest Developments in Investor–state Dispute Settlement*, IIA Issues Note No. 1, United Nations, New York and Geneva.

13 C Schreuer and Weinigar (2008), 'A Doctrine of Precedent', in P Muchlinski, F Ortino and C Schreuer (eds), *The Oxford Handbook of International Investment Law*, Oxford University Press, Oxford and New York, at 1188.

all parties and aggravates the challenge of compliance for host states, as well as exacerbating the regulatory chill effect noted above.

- **Definitions of investors of a state in IIAs that are based solely on the state in which an investor is incorporated or organised permit increased use of investor–state arbitration through treaty shopping.** In the Section of the Guide dealing with the definition of investor, the problem of treaty shopping was discussed.[14] Where a person can qualify as an investor under an IIA that a state has with another state simply by incorporating a subsidiary in the state, it is relatively easy for investors to structure their affairs so as to be able to acquire treaty protection and become eligible to bring investor–state claims.
- **Some investor–state state disputes have become politicised.** As noted, one of the anticipated benefits of investor–state arbitration is that it helps to ensure that disputes between investors and host states are resolved on the basis of law, not power. Recently, a couple of developments have revealed ways in which investor–state disputes may still be subject to the exercise of political power. Argentina has taken the position that investors with awards against it should seek to enforce them in Argentinian courts. Rather than do this, some US investors lobbied the US government to put pressure on Argentina to pay. In 2012, the US government suspended trade concessions granted to Argentina under its Generalized System of Preferences until Argentina pays the awards against it.[15] In another development, Ecuador initiated state-to-state dispute settlement proceedings under the Ecuador–US BIT to, in effect, overturn an interpretation adopted by an investor–state tribunal in a case against it.[16]

7.1.2 Statistics show increasing use of investor–state arbitration

One measure of the growing significance of investor–state arbitration is the dramatic increase in the number of investor–state cases. It is impossible to obtain a reliable estimate of all investor–state cases or to find out about the disposition of all cases, because there is no complete public record. Nevertheless, UNCTAD recently reported that at the end of 2011 450 known treaty-based investment arbitration claims had been initiated, most by developed country investors against developing countries.[17]

---

14 See Section 4.3 (Definitions).

15 UNCTAD (2012), *World Investment Report 2012: Towards a New Generation of Investment Policies*, United Nations, New York and Geneva, at 87, citing United States, Presidential Proclamation, 'To Modify Duty-Free Treatment under the Generalized System of Preferences and for Other Purposes', *Federal Register*, 26 March 2012.

16 UNCTAD (2012), *World Investment Report 2012*, ibid. at 87. The interpretation challenged was that adopted by the tribunal in *Chevron Corporation (USA) and Texaco Petroleum Company (USA) v. The Republic of Ecuador*, UNCITRAL, PCA Case No. 34877, Partial Award on the Merits, 30 March 2010.

17 See UNCTAD (2012), *Latest Developments in Investor–state Dispute Settlement*, op. cit. This statistic includes only claims that have actually been submitted to arbitration. It does not include cases in which only a notice of an intention to submit a claim to arbitration has been filed. It also includes only known arbitrations.

While this may seem a relatively modest total, there has been a significant increase in investor–state claims in the past few years. More than 85 per cent of treaty-based investor–state claims have been filed since 2000. Forty-six new claims were filed in 2011, the highest single-year total and more than 10 per cent of all claims ever filed. Overall, 89 states have been the subject of treaty-based claims. Argentina has been named in the largest number of claims (51), followed by Venezuela (25), Ecuador (23), Mexico (19) and the Czech Republic (18). Canada has been the subject of 17 claims, while the USA, Egypt, Poland and Ukraine have all been named in 14 claims.[18] Out of 220 concluded cases, 40 per cent were decided in favour of the state, 30 per cent were decided in favour of the investor and the remaining 30 per cent were settled by the parties.

The growth in claims is undoubtedly the result of the increasingly dense international network of IIAs providing for investor–state arbitration, combined with growth in international investment activity.[19] Increased awareness regarding the existence and nature of investor–state proceedings resulting, in part, from increased transparency and a few large high-profile awards may also be factors.

7.1.3 Dissatisfaction with investor–state arbitration

While the inclusion of investor–state arbitration procedures is typically sought by developed countries in the IIAs that they negotiate because of the advantages that these procedures offer to their investors, recent experience with investor–state arbitration starkly illustrates the costs and challenges for host states that may be associated with investors' use of these procedures, as discussed above. In response, some states have adjusted their IIA models to ensure a better balance between the interests of states and investors and sought to clarify IIA provisions to avoid undesired interpretations. Others have rejected investor–state dispute settlement entirely. In 2011, the Australian government broke ranks with all other developed countries and announced that it would no longer seek investor–state arbitration in the IIAs it negotiates.[20] India has announced that it will not agree to investor–state arbitration in its ongoing negotiations for a free trade agreement with the EU. Venezuela, Bolivia and Ecuador have denounced the ICSID Convention,[21] which

18 Ibid. at 1–2.

19 UNCTAD (2007), *Treaties 1996–2006*, op. cit., at 16.

20 Gillard Government Trade Policy Statement, available at: www.dfat.gov.au/publications/trade/trading-our-way-to-more-jobs-and-prosperity.html (accessed 29 May 2012). South Africa issued a policy statement in 2010 declaring that it 'will only enter into BITs in future on the basis of compelling economic or political reasons' (Republic of South Africa, Department of Trade and Industry (2010), Policy Statement: The South African Government's Approach to Future International Investment Treaties, available at: www.jadafa.co.za/LinkClick.aspx?fileticket=9A6eXZstRl0%3D&tabid=432 (accessed 8 January 2013).).

21 The ICSID Rules are contained in the Convention on the Settlement of Investment Disputes between States and Nationals of Other States, done at Washington 18 March 1965, 575 *United Nations Treaty Series* 159, reprinted in 4 *International Law Materials* 532 (1965) and the rules created by the Administrative Council of ICSID under Arts. 6(1)(a)–(c) of the ICSID Convention, published in *ICSID Basic Documents*, ICSID, Washington, 2006.

establishes the arbitral procedure used in approximately two-thirds of investor–state arbitrations. Recently, Ecuador and some other countries have gone so far as to terminate some of their IIAs altogether.[22] In August 2010, more than 50 academics from around the world signed a public statement of concern about the harm done to public welfare by international investment agreements. The statement asserts that international investment agreements hamper the ability of governments to act for their people in response to concerns regarding human development and environmental sustainability.[23]

These expressions of dissatisfaction make clear that each state must carefully consider, as a threshold question, whether to agree to investor–state arbitration in its IIAs at all. To the extent that a state has already agreed to investor–state arbitration in an IIA, the commitments undertaken should be reviewed. Nevertheless, states, including developing countries, continue to negotiate IIAs with investor–state arbitration provisions. Fifty-four new IIAs were negotiated in 2011. Most of them include investor–state arbitration provisions. Where a state does agree to investor–state dispute settlement, close attention must be paid to the precise terms that are included in investor–state procedures. The Guide discusses the costs and benefits of some of the options.

7.1.4 Features of investor–state dispute settlement procedures

The features of investor–state dispute settlement procedures in IIAs vary widely in their scope, content and level of detail. Some model agreements set out few details.[24] Others, including the Canadian and US models, the ASEAN Agreement and the COMESA Investment Agreement, set out much more comprehensive schemes dealing precisely with many aspects of the process.

Typically, investor–state proceedings take place under a set of international arbitration rules chosen by the investor from several permitted under the treaty, as modified by the provisions of the treaty itself. The typical procedural steps in investor–state arbitration are set out in Box 7.1.

---

22 In 2008, Ecuador terminated nine BITs. A few other BITS have been denounced: Bolivia had denounced its BIT with the United States, Nicaragua has denounced its BIT with El Salvador and the Bolivarian Republic of Venezuela has renounced its BIT with the Netherlands. In 2010, Ecuador's Constitutional Court declared arbitration provisions of six more BITs unconstitutional (UNCTAD (2010), *Denunciation of the ICSID Convention and BITS: Impact on Investor–state Claims*, IIA Issues Note No. 2, December 2010).

23 Public Statement on the International Investment regime, available at: www.osgoode.yorku.ca/public_statement (accessed 24 June 2012).

24 E.g., UK model IPPA; Indian model BIPPA. Few Caribbean BITs have detailed rules governing investor–state dispute settlement (Malik, op. cit., at 32). The same is true for the India–Singapore CECA (Art. 6.21). An UNCTAD study came to the same conclusion: UNCTAD (2007), *Treaties 1996–2006*, op. cit., at 101. The rules in the COMESA Investment Agreement are much more detailed (Arts. 28–31, Annex A).

Box 7.1 Overview of possible steps in the process of an investor–state arbitration

(Note: steps in brackets do not occur in every case)

- Request for consultations by investor to host state – disclosing legal and factual basis of claim (may be followed or accompanied by notice of intent to submit a claim if required under the IIA);
- Consultations between the investor and the state;
- Submission of claim by investor if no resolution within some specified time after request for consultations, including the investor's choice of arbitral rules;
- Arbitrators appointed – tribunal constituted and arbitration formally commenced;
- Preliminary motions by parties and orders by tribunal on various issues, including:
  - Challenges based on the tribunal lacking jurisdiction to hear the investor's claim,
  - Disclosure of documents and protection of confidentiality,
  - Scheduling filing of written submissions and oral hearing;
- Written submissions of parties filed with tribunal and each other, including responses to the other party's submissions;
- Oral hearing;
- Award by tribunal;
- (Judicial review or, in an ICSID arbitration, ICSID annulment proceeding regarding award may be initiated possibly leading to award being set aside);
- (Payment of damages in award, if any); and
- (Enforcement proceedings if award of damages not paid).

The content of the investor–state procedures in IIAs varies. An overview of the following key issues and approaches is provided below:

- Scope of application of investor–state dispute settlement;
- Initiation of investor–state claims;
- Dealing with jurisdictional challenges and frivolous claims;
- Alternative dispute resolution;
- Applicable arbitral rules;
- Selection of arbitrators;

- Governing law;
- Interpretation of IIAs by the parties;
- Subrogation of political risk insurers;
- Third party funding;
- Consolidation of claims based on identical or similar issues of fact or law;
- Transparency of proceedings and civil society participation in investor–state arbitration;
- Enforcement of awards;
- Dealing with inconsistent arbitration awards and other problems with investor–state arbitration through improved dispute settlement institutions; and
- Remedies issues.

Scope of application of investor–state dispute settlement

An important feature of investor–state arbitration procedures is what claims they allow to be brought. There are a variety of questions related to the scope of investor–state procedures including the following.

- Who is entitled to bring a claim?
- What substantive obligations may be the basis of a claim?
    - Do they include some or all of the substantive obligations set out in the treaty?
    - Do they include other claims that an investor may have against the state on other legal grounds through a so-called 'umbrella clause'?
- What are the time limits on claims?

Who is entitled to bring a claim?

In general, a legal or natural person satisfying the definition in an IIA of 'investor' of one party state who has made an investment in another party state is eligible to make a claim under the IIA against the other party state. An issue that arises is whether a corporation *incorporated under the laws of the host state* that is controlled by a foreign investor of the other party state (a *subsidiary*) should be able to make a claim. Based on its incorporation in the host state, under general principles of international law, the subsidiary has the nationality of the host state and so would not be able to make a claim against the host state. Nevertheless, some IIAs permit a claim to be made on behalf of the subsidiary so long as it is controlled by investors of the other party to the IIA.[25] Many other IIAs do not include such a provision, with the result that claims can be made by investors only on their own behalf.[26]

25 E.g. Canadian model FIPA, Art. 23; US model BIT, Art. 24.1(b).

26 E.g. ASEAN Agreement, Art. 32; COMESA Investment Agreement; India–Singapore CECA. Under the ASEAN–Australia–New Zealand FTA Investment Chapter, only investors can make claims, but they can claim for loss or damage suffered by them or by a covered investment, which would include a subsidiary (Art. 20(b)).

In an investor–state arbitration under the ICSID Convention, the requirements of the convention must be met as well as the requirements under an IIA. As discussed above,[27] the ICSID Convention generally permits arbitration under its rules only where the investor's state and the state complained against are different and both states are parties to the Convention. The Convention permits a subsidiary incorporated in the host state to bring a claim against the host state only if it is foreign controlled and the parties to the dispute both agree that the subsidiary should be treated as a national of another ICSID party state.[28] Some IIAs specifically provide this consent on behalf of the host state.[29] The investor consents by bringing the claim. If both parties consent, an investor of an IIA party state with a subsidiary in the host party state that is affected by a measure can cause the subsidiary to bring the claim under the ICSID Convention. For a treaty-based claim, however, the treaty would have to permit claims by the subsidiary as well. The investor can always claim on its own behalf for losses that it has suffered in relation to its investment in the subsidiary.

Whether or not the subsidiary can bring a claim may have important practical consequences. In some cases, the damages recoverable may vary depending on whether a claim is made for compensation by the subsidiary (or on behalf of the subsidiary) or by the foreign investor on its own behalf.[30] In general terms, if a host state measure affects a subsidiary of a foreign investor, the subsidiary can claim all the losses that it experiences, but the investor claiming on its own behalf can claim only for losses related to its investment in the subsidiary. In a variety of circumstances, the losses to the investor will be less than the losses of the subsidiary, such as where the investor does not own 100 per cent of the subsidiary.[31]

The ASEAN Agreement deals with one other problem related to nationality where a person is a dual national. Under the Agreement, a natural person who is a national of a party state cannot bring a claim against that state, even if they are also a national of the other treaty party.[32] This provision ensures that the requirement under the ICSID Convention for the investor to have a different nationality from the host state is satisfied. This issue can also be addressed by defining 'investor' of a party state to exclude nationals of the other party state. This latter approach not only denies such a person access to dispute settlement, but denies all the protections of the agreement to them.[33]

What substantive obligations may be the basis of a claim?

Many IIAs apply to all disputes related to investments that fall within the definition of 'investment' in the IIA.[34] Some provisions of this type are so broadly worded that

---

27 See Section 4.3 (Definitions) 'investor' and Box 4.4.

28 ICSID Convention, Art. 25(2).

29 E.g. Ethiopia–Malaysia BIT (1998), Art. 7.

30 S Ripinsky with K Williams (2008), *Damages in International Investment Law*, British Institute of Comparative Law, London, at 158.

31 This distinction was noted by the tribunal in *United Parcel Service of America, Inc.* v. *Canada*, UNCITRAL, Award on the Merits, 24 May 2007, at para. 35.

32 ASEAN Agreement (2009), Art. 29.2.

33 See Section 4.3 (Definitions) 'investor'.

34 UNCTAD (2007), *Treaties 1995–2006*, op. cit., at 102. E.g. India–Singapore CECA (2005), Art. 6.21.1; Indian model BIPPA, Art. 9(1).

they may extend to obligations owed by the state to the investor outside those in the IIA in relation to such investments. Other IIAs specifically restrict the process to breaches of obligations in the agreement.[35]

A provision in an IIA that obliges a party state to respect obligations it has towards investors from the other party state in addition to those obligations specifically set out in the treaty is called an *umbrella clause*. UNCTAD estimates that approximately 40 per cent of BITs have such a provision.[36] While the scope of these provisions varies, sometimes they are interpreted as extending to contractual commitments undertaken by a state to an investor, with the result that compensation for a host state breach of obligations under the contract can be pursued using the investor–state procedures in the treaty.[37] This may be so even in cases where the contract specifically requires the investor to use some other dispute settlement procedure for such disputes, such as litigation in domestic courts.[38]

Some agreements deal with obligations outside the substantive investor protection obligations in the IIA more specifically. The US model agreement, for example, provides that the investor–state procedures may be used to deal with a claim by an investor that a state has breached:

- An investor protection obligation under the treaty;
- A state authorisation to the investor to make an investment; or
- An investment agreement between the investor and the state that the investor has relied on in making the investment.[39]

There are few benefits of umbrella clauses and similar provisions for host states. The range of possible liability for states is wide and hard to define specifically, making it difficult for states to manage their liability risk. The possibility for an investor to bring a claim under the investor–state procedures in an IIA with a generally worded umbrella clause, when some other procedure has been agreed to in a contract governing the specific transaction between the investor and the state, seems to fly in the face of the parties' intentions expressed in the contract and raises the prospect of multiple claims in relation to the same dispute. In these circumstances, it would seem preferable for the state and the investor to be required to use whatever dispute settlement procedures they had agreed would govern their relationship in the context of the contract negotiation. In addition, to the extent that umbrella clauses operate to give rights to investors who are already engaged in contracts with the host state, they do not encourage new investment. In general, however, by broadening

35 Some IIAs are broader in that disputes need not relate to a *breach* of an IIA provision but could relate to other issues regarding the provisions. Some IIAs refer to any dispute 'concerning an obligation', e.g. China–Guyana, Agreement between the Government of the People's Republic of China and the Government of the Republic of Guyana on the Promotion and Protection of Investments, signed 27 March 2003, in force 26 October 2004, Art. 9.

36 UNCTAD (2007), *Treaties 1995–2006*, op. cit., at 73–5.

37 Ibid. See, for example, the China–New Zealand BIT (2008), Art. 10.

38 Malik, op. cit., at 14.

39 US model BIT, Arts. 1, 24.

the scope of possible investor–state claims for investors, it is possible that umbrella clauses could encourage investment.

Limiting investor–state dispute settlement to specific IIA obligations

The narrowest approach to the scope of investor–state arbitration provisions in IIAs is to limit their application to some subset of the obligations in the treaty. One approach is to limit investor–state arbitration to disputes about the amount of compensation for an expropriation.[40] Such a narrow scope for investor–state dispute settlement is rare. Many agreements limit access to investor–state arbitration to claims related to the main investor protection obligations in the IIA. The ASEAN–Australia–New Zealand FTA Investment Chapter, for example, permits claims only in relation to alleged breaches of the following provisions:

- National treatment;
- Fair and equitable treatment;
- Compensation for losses due to armed conflict, civil strife or state of emergency;
- Transfer of funds; and
- Expropriation without compensation.

The investor's claim must also relate to the 'management, conduct, operation or sale or other disposition' of a covered investment.[41] The US model agreement limits claims to a longer list of substantive investor protection obligations (national treatment, MFN, fair and equitable treatment, compensation for losses, expropriation, transfer of funds, and prohibitions on performance requirements and nationality restrictions) and adds the obligation compelling disclosure of existing laws and regulations in that model.[42] Unlike the ASEAN–Australia–New Zealand FTA Investment Chapter, the US model does not restrict the activities to which the breach must relate.

While it is not a common approach in IIAs, a state may want to exclude the interpretation of certain exceptions that deal with sensitive areas of policy, such as national security, from the scope of investor–state arbitration procedures altogether. A more flexible approach where a state seeks to rely on an exception would be to require a binding interpretation from the party states with respect to whether the exception is available to protect a measure that an investor is complaining is a breach of an IIA provision. If the parties decide that the exception is available, then an investor could not pursue the claim. A procedure for having the parties make binding interpretations is discussed below. An alternative, which gives even more flexibility to a state, would

---

40 E.g. China–Jamaica BIT (1994); Mauritius–Swaziland, Agreement between the Government of the Republic of Mauritius and the Government of the Kingdom of Swaziland for the Promotion and Reciprocal Protection of Investments, signed 15 May 2000, not yet in force.

41 ASEAN–Australia–New Zealand FTA (2009) Investment Chapter, Art. 20. See the similar approach taken in the ASEAN Agreement (2009) (Art. 32(a)) (the list in that agreement also includes the MFN obligation and the prohibition on nationality restrictions) and COMESA Investment Agreement (2007) (Art. 28.1).

42 US model BIT, Art. 24.1(a)(i)(A).

be to allow the state to declare unilaterally that an exception is available. While, as discussed above, some exceptions, such as national security exceptions, are often drafted to be self-defining in this way, most are not. Investors would probably be concerned that leaving it up to the state complained against to determine if an exception is available would provide too much flexibility for states and not enough certainty for investors.

Recent IIAs have adopted another limitation on access to investor–state arbitration. Both the Canadian and US model agreements require that a claimant must have suffered loss or damage by reason of, or arising out of, the breach.[43] The same approach is followed in recent BITs of other countries.[44] Such a requirement may go some way towards avoiding frivolous claims.

Finally, where investor obligations are contemplated in an IIA, several issues arise regarding the scope for the investor–state arbitration process to address host state claims that an investor must have not complied with its obligations. These issues are discussed above.[45]

What are the time limits on claims?

Claims that relate to events occurring before the treaty comes into force are often excluded from the scope of investor–state arbitration.[46] However, many IIAs are not specific in this regard. Claims based on a breach of the treaty may be limited by a scope provision in the treaty. If the treaty does not apply to measures enacted prior to the treaty coming into force, then no claim can be made that such a measure is a breach of the treaty, even if the measure continues to operate after the treaty comes into force.[47]

Some investor–state procedures also set maximum time periods after which no claim can be brought. In the Canadian model treaty and some other treaties, for example, claims can be made only within three years after the investor became aware of the events giving rise to the claim. In the draft Norwegian model treaty, the limitation period is ten years. Limitation periods provide certainty and finality for states regarding their liability risk.[48] Restrictions on claims that arise following termination of the IIA are discussed below.[49]

Initiation of investor–state claims

General requirements

IIAs impose a variety of preliminary requirements on investors that must be satisfied before they can initiate investor–state arbitration. Typically, the state and the

43 Canadian model FIPA, Art. 23, NAFTA (1992), Art. 1118, US model BIT, Art. 24.

44 UNCTAD (2007), *Treaties 1995–2006*, op. cit., at 104, identifying Austria, Japan and Mexico, as well as the US and Canada. See also ASEAN Agreement (2009), Art. 29; India–Singapore CECA (2005), Art. 6.21.1; COMESA Investment Agreement (2007), Art. 28.1.

45 See Section 6.13 (Enforcement of investor obligations).

46 E.g. ASEAN Agreement (2009), Art. 20(3); AALCC model Agreements, Art. 10.

47 See Section 4.5 (Scope of application).

48 E.g. Canadian model FIPA, Art. 26, COMESA Investment Agreement (2007), Art. 28.2.

49 See Section 9.3 (Termination of IIAs).

investor must consult prior to the formal commencement of an arbitration.[50] In many IIAs, this is facilitated by a requirement for the investor to file a notice of intent to bring a claim 90 days prior to the submission of the claim itself.[51] The notice of intent provides some basic information to the state to permit it to make a preliminary assessment of the claim and engage in consultations with the investor on a more informed basis.

Most agreements impose a requirement for investors to wait between three and six months after the events giving rise to the claim before filing their claim.[52] IIA practice seems to be converging on a six-month delay.[53] Under the COMESA Investment Agreement, during this six-month 'cooling off' period before a claim may be filed, the parties must participate in mediation with a view to resolving the dispute.[54] In addition, each set of arbitral rules that may govern an investor–state arbitration has its own specific requirements for initiating an arbitration.[55]

Exhaustion of local remedies

IIA practice One significant design issue in relation to an IIA's prerequisites to allowing an investor to initiate investor–state arbitration is determining whether it is appropriate to require investors to seek relief through domestic dispute resolution mechanisms prior to making a claim in investor–state arbitration. While many IIAs give investors the right to make claims to compensation against states in binding arbitration, in a few, access to international arbitration is subject to requirements for the investor to seek local remedies first.

One option is to require that an investor exhaust all remedial possibilities under domestic law before being able to make a claim for relief through investor–state

50 Canadian model FIPA, Art. 25; US model BIT, Art. 23; COMESA Investment Agreement (2007), Art. 26.3; ASEAN Agreement (2009), Art. 31; India–Singapore CECA (2005), Art. 6.21(2); NAFTA (1992), Art. 1118.

51 E.g. Canadian model FIPA, Arts. 24–6; US model BIT, Art. 24; ASEAN Agreement (2009), Art. 34.1(b); COMESA Investment Agreement (2007), Art. 26; India–Singapore CECA (2005), Art. 6.21(4)(b); ASEAN–Australia–New Zealand FTA (2009) Investment Chapter, Art. 22.1(b). The Colombian model agreement requires 180 days, notice of an intention to file a claim (Art. IX.5).

52 Canadian model FIPA, Arts. 24–6; US model BIT, Art. 24. The COMESA Investment Agreement (2007) has a similar provision (Arts. 26.1, 28) as does the ASEAN Agreement (2009) (Arts. 31, 34.1) and the India–Singapore CECA (2005) (Art. 6.21(3)). Caribbean and Pacific BITS typically require between 3 and 6 months to have elapsed prior to a claim being filed (Malik, op. cit., at 32, 60). The Colombian model agreement requires 12 months to have expired before a claim can be filed (Art. IX.4).

53 UNCTAD (2007), *Treaties 1995–2006*, op. cit., at 105. Some IIAs do not have a time limit, e.g. Australia–India BIT (1999), Art. 12.

54 COMESA Investment Agreement (2007), Arts. 26.3–26.6.

55 E.g. *Arbitration Rules of the United Nations Commission on International Trade Law*, approved by the United Nations General Assembly on 15 December 1976, UN GAOR, 31st Session, Supp. No. 17 at 46, Chapter V, Section C, UN Doc. A/31/17, 1976, as revised in 2010 approved by the United Nations General Assembly on 6 December 2010, UN GAOR, 65th Session, No. 17, Chap. III, U.N. Doc. A/Res/65/2, Art. 3; ICSID Convention, Art. 36.

dispute settlement under an IIA. Such a provision prevents investors from initiating an investor–state claim if they have not pursued domestic remedies diligently. Most IIAs, however, do not mention exhaustion of local remedies. Neither the Canadian model treaty nor the US model, for example, contains an exhaustion of local remedies requirement. In the absence of a specific requirement to exhaust local remedies, arbitral cases have confirmed that IIAs do not require exhaustion of local remedies. By contrast, the IISD model treaty requires all domestic remedies to be exhausted before international investor–state dispute settlement mechanisms are engaged.[56]

The draft Norwegian treaty adopted a compromise approach. It requires investors to exhaust their domestic remedies, but imposes a time limit for doing so. If the dispute cannot be resolved within 36 months from the date of the submission of the dispute to a local court, the investor can proceed directly to investor–state arbitration.[57] An investor is not required to exhaust local remedies, however, if there is no reasonable possibility of local remedies providing redress for the injury to the investor. Some existing treaties similarly provide requirements for investors to seek to exhaust local remedies, but for limited time periods.[58]

Another approach adopted in some IIAs is to require investors to have recourse to domestic administrative review procedures, as opposed to the exhaustion of all local remedies, as a condition of being able to commence investor–state arbitration.[59]

Costs and benefits of exhaustion of local remedies requirements A requirement to exhaust local remedies prior to resorting to relief before international tribunals is consistent with the approach taken generally under international law. In addition, there are several advantages to having investors submit to domestic law and domestic procedures, as listed in Box 7.2.

56 IISD model treaty, Art. 45(B). Article 26 of the ICSID Convention specifically contemplates that states may require exhaustion of local remedies as a condition of consenting to arbitration.

57 Norwegian draft APPI, Art. 15.3. The Colombian model agreement requires the exhaustion of local administrative remedies if required by the domestic law of the host state but only up to 6 months (Art. IX.1).

58 E.g. China–Côte d'Ivoire, Agreement between the Government of the People's Republic of China and the Government of the Republic of Côte d'Ivoire on the Promotion and Protection of Investments, signed 23 September 2002, not yet in force, Art. 9 (6 months); Italy–Jamaica, Agreement between the Government of the Italian Republic and the Government of Jamaica for the Promotion and Protection of Investments, signed 29 September 1993, in force 9 November 1995 (18 months).

59 E.g. Protocol to China–Latvia, Agreement between the Government of the People's Republic of China and the Government of the Republic of Latvia on the Promotion and Protection of Investments, signed 15 April 2004, in force 1 February 2006; and Belgium–Luxembourg–Colombia, Agreement between the Belgium–Luxembourg Economic Union and the Republic of Colombia for the Reciprocal Promotion and Protection of Investments, signed 4 February 2009, not yet in force.

Box 7.2 Advantages of an IIA requirement to exhaust local remedies

- Domestic tribunals have an opportunity to correct mistakes made by states by providing relief in obvious cases.
- Domestic tribunals can screen out claims with no obvious merit.
- Domestic dispute resolution may be less costly.
- Forcing disputes to be addressed first under domestic law and by domestic tribunals creates incentives for foreign investors, domestic investors and the host state to further develop domestic investment rules and contribute to the development of domestic institutions.
- Domestic dispute resolution contributes to a perception that the outcome to a dispute is more legitimate, since it has been decided in accordance with democratically determined domestic laws and is consistent with domestic constitutional requirements.
- If investor–state arbitration tribunals are subsequently required to interpret domestic law for the purpose of settling a dispute, they will have access to interpretations of these laws made by domestic courts, which have more expertise in domestic law.

The question of legitimacy of investor state arbitration decisions noted in Box 7.2 is an important one. For instance, in the CMS *Gas* case, the ICSID tribunal took it upon itself to interpret the Argentine Constitution,[60] an approach that raised concerns about the legitimacy of the ICSID decision in Argentina and other developing countries.

However, there are also potential drawbacks to insisting on the exhaustion of domestic dispute resolution mechanisms. The main drawback is that such a requirement could discourage potential investors from investing as a result of the difficulties that could arise if they must use domestic courts. As discussed, avoiding domestic courts is one of the essential reasons that motivate investors to seek treaty-based investor–state arbitration. A concern for host states is that an exhaustion of local remedies requirement creates the possibility that a host state may spend some period of time defending an investor's claim in its domestic courts and then be forced to defend essentially the same claim in investor–state arbitration. This issue of dealing with multiple claims is discussed in the next section.

Issues related to multiple remedial possibilities for investors

Even where exhaustion of local remedies is not required, many IIAs have other provisions that address the interaction between investor–state arbitration and remedies

60 CMS *Gas Transmission Company v. The Argentine Republic*, ICSID Case No. ARB/01/8, Award, 21 May 2005, at paras. 119–20.

in the host state. One of the challenges for host states is finding ways to manage the risk that investors may pursue multiple litigation strategies in different venues in connection with a particular host state action. For example, where an investor has a contract with the host state, the contract itself may contemplate a particular dispute resolution procedure, such as commercial arbitration, which, depending on the terms of the dispute resolution clause, may be pursued in parallel with domestic court action. A claim under an IIA may also be possible, depending on the scope of the dispute resolution provisions in the treaty. A broadly worded umbrella clause may permit a treaty-based claim in addition to the others. Finally, the foreign investor may be organised as a related group of entities with different nationalities and this may permit it to initiate multiple investor–state arbitration claims under different IIAs that the host state has entered into. Some IIAs have tried to address these kinds of problems in limited ways, as discussed below.

Waiver Some IIAs provide that a choice by an investor to initiate investor–state arbitration means that the investor must give up all other claims to relief. Both the US and Canadian models require that investors waive their rights to initiate or continue any other dispute settlement procedure relating to the measure for which the investor is seeking relief as a condition of the investor being permitted to pursue its claim in investor–state arbitration. This waiver does not extend to claims for relief other than monetary compensation, since these claims may not be pursued in investor–state arbitration.[61] Waivers are also required under the ASEAN Agreement and the India–Singapore CECA.[62] The ASEAN Agreement and the India–Singapore CECA go on to provide that once a claim has been made, relief cannot be sought through diplomatic negotiations between states.[63] The COMESA Investment Agreement simply provides that after a claim is made, the investor may not pursue relief in other fora.[64] Sometimes the approach taken in these treaties is described as a 'no U-turn' model. Waiver requirements are not a barrier to pursuing investor–state arbitration. Nor do they prevent an investor from seeking local remedies until they prove unsuccessful and then initiating an investor–state arbitration.[65] Once the investor–state claim is made, however, recourse to other remedies is precluded, even if the investor–state claim is ultimately unsuccessful.

Waiver provisions are consistent with Article 26 of the ICSID Convention, which provides that the consent of the parties to arbitration under the Convention is deemed, in the absence of any agreement to the contrary, to mean that parties have agreed to arbitrate 'to the exclusion of any other remedy'. Article 27 of the Convention stipulates that no party state can pursue a diplomatic solution or bring an

61 Canadian model FIPA, Art. 27; US model BIT, Art. 26.

62 The ASEAN Agreement (2009) (Art. 34.1(c)) and the India–Singapore CECA (2005) (Art. 6.21) do not carve out injunctive relief.

63 ASEAN Agreement (2009), Art. 34.3, and the India–Singapore CECA (2005), Art. 6.21(4).

64 The COMESA Investment Agreement (2007), Art. 28.3.

65 An investor would have to initiate the claim before the expiry of any maximum time period in the treaty. See above 'General requirements'.

international claim with respect to a dispute which one of its nationals and another party state have agreed to arbitrate under the Convention. The only exception to this limitation is if the other party state fails to abide by and comply with an award rendered in the dispute. Some IIAs contain similar provisions.

'Fork in the road' Some treaties provide that an investor must choose to pursue its claim either in domestic courts or through investor–state arbitration under an IIA and that, once that choice is made, it is final and irrevocable. This means that the investor cannot pursue relief in any other forum. Such a provision is known as a 'fork in the road provision' and is intended to ensure that states have to defend investors' claims in only one forum. The Colombia model agreement provides this fork in the road provision:

> Once the investor has submitted the dispute to either a competent tribunal of the Contracting Party in whose territory the investment has been admitted or any of the arbitration mechanisms stated above, the choice of the procedure shall be final.[66]

A fork in the road provision is not a barrier to investor–state claims. In fact it may encourage them where seeking domestic relief is unattractive for any reason. An investor will not want to risk losing an opportunity to pursue relief in investor–state arbitration by pursuing a risky domestic claim.

Other approaches to the risk of multiple claims States can also seek to avoid multiple claims in other ways. Where a host state and an investor have entered into a contract, a state may seek to include a term in the contract that commits the investor to deal with disputes under the agreed dispute resolution mechanism in the contract to the exclusion of all other procedures, including those provided for in IIAs. In their IIAs, states may wish to confirm that investors who have entered into such a commitment cannot make a claim under IIA investor–state arbitration in relation to any dispute that is subject to the contractual dispute settlement mechanism. Such an approach, under which an investor waives their right to investor–state arbitration, is not currently part of IIA practice. States may also consider not entering into IIAs that have umbrella clauses to limit their exposure to multiple claims. If an IIA does not contain an umbrella clause, an investor can only bring an investor–state claim based on a breach of an IIA provision, not on a simple a breach of a contract with the host state or other obligation owed to the investor by the state.[67] States should review their existing treaties and contracts to determine their exposure to multiple claims.

State consent and prerequisites to making a claim

The consent of both parties is required to create the jurisdiction of an arbitration tribunal. The state's consent is typically provided in the treaty to all claims that are

66 Colombian model agreement, Art. IX.7.

67 Some breaches of contract might amount to a breach of an IIA in some circumstances.

made in accordance with the treaty,[68] though some IIAs do not expressly mention the state's consent. The investor's consent is given at the time it initiates the arbitration. A small number of treaties provide that the state must separately give its consent in each case.[69] This allows a host state to decide whether it wants to arbitrate with an investor, based on the facts of a specific case. While this provides maximum flexibility to the host state, it renders the possibility of investor–state arbitration much less certain for investors.

An issue that has arisen in investor–state arbitrations under NAFTA is whether preliminary requirements that an IIA requires be satisfied prior to a claim being filed, such as filing a waiver of other claims, are merely procedural or should be interpreted as conditions of the state's consent to arbitration.[70] The Canadian model FIPA adopted in 2004 and the new US model BIT adopted in 2012 expressly identify satisfaction of all pre-arbitration requirements in these agreements as conditions of the state's consent.[71] As a result, the failure by an investor to satisfy any one of them deprives the tribunal of jurisdiction and the investor is forced to recommence its arbitration after satisfying the condition.[72]

Dealing with jurisdictional challenges and frivolous claims

Jurisdictional challenges by states are common in investor–state arbitration. In an IIA, the state gives its consent in advance to arbitrate with an unlimited class of investors who satisfy the requirements of the treaty for standing to bring a claim. Often, whether an investor meets one of these requirements is challenged by the host state. A state may dispute, for example, whether the person making the claim is an investor of the other party to the IIA within the meaning of the IIA's definition of investor. As noted in the previous section, if one of the conditions of the state's consent to arbitrate has not been satisfied, an arbitral tribunal has no jurisdiction to hear the claim.

Jurisdictional challenges are typically raised by the host state early in an investor–state case. In some cases, however, tribunals have declined to deal with a jurisdictional issue at an early stage in the arbitration because they have determined that they needed all of the evidence and submissions of the parties on the merits of the claim to be provided before they could render a decision on the issue.[73] In these cases, the tribunals made their decision on the jurisdictional issues at the same time as their decisions on the

---

68 E.g. Canadian model FIPA, Art. 25; US model BIT, Art. 25; COMESA Investment Agreement (2007), Art. 28.4; India–Singapore CECA (2005), Art. 6.21(4).

69 E.g. Argentina–New Zealand BIT (1999), Art. 12; Sweden–Malaysia, Agreement between the Government of Sweden and the Government of Malaysia concerning the Mutual Protection of Investments, signed 3 March 1979, in force 6 July 1979, Art. 6.

70 *Waste Management, Inc.* v. *United Mexican States*, ARB (AF)/98/2, Award, 2 June 2000.

71 Canadian model FIPA, Art. 27; US model BIT, Art. 26.

72 The same approach is taken in the draft Norwegian APPI (Art. 15.4) and the ASEAN Agreement (2009) (Art. 34).

73 Tribunals are expressly empowered to decide to do either under the ICSID Convention (Art. 41).

merits. This practice has caused concerns for some states that cases that were outside the jurisdiction of the tribunal were not being terminated until considerable expense had been incurred in connection with the case, including costs related to extensive argument on procedural matters, the preparation of lengthy submissions on the merits and an oral hearing.

Some states have been similarly concerned that investors' claims with little merit were not being disposed of at an early stage. As a result, states have been forced to incur substantial unnecessary costs.[74]

One response to these concerns has been to adopt IIA provisions that require tribunals to deal with preliminary challenges, including challenges that the investor's claim or part of it is either frivolous or outside the competence of the arbitral tribunal, at the earliest opportunity. The ASEAN Agreement, for example, requires that where a party state makes a preliminary objection that the investor's claim is outside the competence of the tribunal or 'manifestly without merit', the tribunal must deal with the objection before proceeding to the merits.[75] The tribunal assumes, for the purposes of such a preliminary objection, that that the facts alleged by the investor are true and then decides if the claim (or part of the claim) is one that it has jurisdiction to adjudicate or if the claim has enough merit to proceed.

In order to protect against both frivolous claims and frivolous objections to claims, it would be possible to provide in an IIA that a tribunal that rejects a frivolous claim or objection could award the costs associated with the claim or objection against the losing party. No IIA has addressed this issue specifically.

Alternative dispute resolution

Experience with investor–state arbitration has demonstrated its costs to host states. As a consequence, there has been increasing interest in approaches to the resolution of disputes other than through binding adjudication by arbitral tribunals. In addition to cost savings, alternative dispute resolution (ADR) procedures are more likely to preserve the relationship between the investor and the state, compared with investor–state arbitration, which has proved to be protracted and contentious. ADR creates the possibility of faster and more flexible solutions agreed to by the parties that are not available in arbitration, where there must be a winner and a loser. In arbitration, an award of compensation is made or the investor gets nothing. ADR may also be a useful way to deal effectively with frivolous claims.[76] Typical ADR procedures are described in Box 7.3.

74 UNCTAD (2007), *Treaties 1996–2006*, op. cit., at 122–3.

75 ASEAN Agreement (2009), Arts. 36.1–36.4. The Canadian model FIPA (all preliminary objections, no procedure specified) and the US model BIT (objections to jurisdiction only, detailed procedure specified) contain a similar process for dealing with preliminary objections.

76 UNCTAD (2010), *Investor–state Disputes: Prevention and Alternatives to Arbitration*, United Nations, Geneva and New York, at 4–7, 16–20.

Box 7.3 Examples of alternative dispute resolution procedures

There is significant variation within categories of ADR procedures and the categories themselves overlap. Nevertheless, it is possible to identify the general characteristics of the following major categories of ADR procedures.

- **Negotiation:** The parties to the dispute meet to exchange information about their interests, arguments about their legal positions and proposals for resolution of the dispute with the goal of agreeing on a particular resolution. No third party is involved.
- **Mediation (or assisted negotiation):** At the request of the parties to the dispute, a third party assists the parties to negotiate a solution by:
  - Seeking to ensure a constructive process of communication and interaction between the parties, including, in some cases, acting as the communications conduit;
  - Helping parties to identify their real interests in the dispute (as opposed to their legal positions) and reframing issues with a view to facilitating agreement;
  - Providing advice on substantive issues;
  - Identifying possible solutions; or
  - On request, giving an opinion regarding the likely legal outcome of the dispute.
- **Fact finding:** Where the facts in a dispute are contested, the parties agree to each submit factual information to a neutral expert, who makes a non-binding assessment of what the facts are. The goal is to obtain an independent assessment of the facts to facilitate the settlement of the dispute. The fact finder does not make recommendations to the parties regarding how the dispute should be resolved.
- **Early neutral evaluation:** The parties agree to submit their dispute to a lawyer or other expert, often someone with specific knowledge of the dispute, for a confidential assessment of the likely outcome of the case, should it go to arbitration. At a meeting with the expert, the parties present their arguments and evidence and the expert provides the assessment. The goal is to facilitate settlement by providing an early evaluation of the likely outcome of an arbitration. The expert may play a continuing role in trying to assist the parties to settle following the assessment.
- **Conciliation:** This is the most formal ADR method. At the request of the parties to the dispute and in accordance with specific rules, a third party (the conciliator or a panel of conciliators) encourages the parties to settle by:
  - Seeking to ensure a constructive process of communication and interaction between the parties;

(Continued)

(Continued)

- Providing advice on substantive issues;
- Suggesting possible solutions; or
- Producing a non-binding written report on how the issue may be resolved.[77]

IIA practice

As noted above, IIAs require a period of time to elapse prior to the initiation of an investor–state arbitration claim to permit the host state and the investor to consult with a view to negotiating a solution. Also, IIAs often mandate the investor and the host state to try to settle the dispute amicably.[78] To assist in the process, many IIAs identify ADR methods, especially conciliation, as alternative approaches to the resolution of disputes that the parties may agree to pursue.[79] In a few agreements, participation in ADR is mandatory. Under the COMESA Investment Agreement, during the six-month period before a claim may be filed, the parties must participate in mediation with a view to resolving the dispute.[80]

The ICSID Convention permits conciliation, as well as fact finding, to be used as alternatives to arbitration with the agreement of the parties. Under the ICSID rules, the role of the conciliation commission set up under the Convention is 'to clarify the issues in dispute between the parties and to endeavour to bring about agreement between them upon mutually acceptable terms'.[81] If the parties reach agreement, the conciliation commission draws up a report noting the issues in dispute and recording that the parties have reached agreement. If the parties do not agree, the commission draws up a report recording its failure to bring the parties to agreement.[82] Under the ICSID fact-finding rules, an independent committee is established to provide an impartial and non-binding assessment of the facts. No conclusions are reached regarding the application of the law and no recommendations to the parties are made.[83]

77 These categories are discussed at length, ibid., at 25–30.

78 E.g. Canadian model FIPA, Art. 25.1; US model BIT, Art. 23; Indian model BIPPA, Art. 9; ASEAN–Australia–New Zealand FTA (2009), Investment Chapter, Art. 19.1; India–Singapore CECA (2005), Art. 6.21.1.

79 E.g. Indian model BIPPA, Art. 9(2) (conciliation under the UNCITRAL Conciliation Rules); UK–Jamaica BIT (1987) (ICSID conciliation). Some treaties simply identify the possibility of the use of non-binding third party procedures, e.g. ASEAN–Australia–New Zealand FTA (2009) Investment Chapter, Art. 19.1.

80 COMESA Investment Agreement (2007), Arts. 26.3–26.6.

81 ICSID Convention, Art. 34(1).

82 ICSID Convention, Art. 34(2).

83 ICSID Additional Facility Rules, Schedule A – Fact Finding (Additional Facility) Rules.

Challenges and limitations of requiring ADR in IIAs

Despite its availability and advantages over investor–state arbitration, use of ADR has been rare in investor–state disputes.[84] This may be because there are specific challenges that impede the use of ADR procedures by states:

- **States' flexibility to find solutions to disputes with investors may be limited by requirements to act through laws and regulations that involve more or less complex and time-consuming procedures and multiple stakeholders;**
- **Government officials may not have appropriate authority to take decisions in the context of ADR procedures to propose or agree to solutions;** [85] **and**
- **ADR procedures may not be well known to government officials or investors.** Since ADR procedures typically require the consent of the parties, a lack of familiarity may discourage their use.

Dispute prevention policies are another useful alternative approach to dealing with conflicts between investors and host states. These host state policies seek to identify and address developing conflicts with investors at an early stage to prevent them from developing into disputes. There is increasing discussion of such policies and they undoubtedly have a role to play. Since, in most cases, however, they do not involve IIA provisions, they will not be further addressed in this section of the Guide.[86] Technical assistance to support the development and implementation of dispute prevention policies is discussed briefly in Section 8.2 (Technical assistance).

Applicable arbitral rules

Under most recent BITs, proceedings take place under a set of international arbitration rules chosen by the investor from a list of alternatives set out in the treaty, as modified by the provisions of the treaty itself.[87] NAFTA is an example of a treaty that provides this option.[88]

Usually, where both the investor's state and the state complained against are parties to the ICSID Convention, arbitration may take place under the arbitration rules of the Convention.[89] The ICSID Convention came into force in 1965 with the

84 Ibid. at xxvi.

85 Gantz concludes that it is difficult for government officials to settle claims without a binding award. See D Gantz (2011), 'Resolution of Investor–state Controversies in Developing Countries', Arizona Legal Studies Discussion Paper No. 11–29, University of Arizona, Tucson.

86 UNCTAD (2010), *Investor–State Disputes*, op. cit.; R Echandi (2011), 'Toward a New Approach to Address Investor–state Conflict: Developing a Conceptual Framework', NCCR Trade Regulation Working Paper No. 2011/46, Bern.

87 Some treaties specify a single forum for dispute settlement, e.g. Saudi Arabia–Malaysia, Agreement between the Government of the Kingdom of Saudi Arabia and the Government of Malaysia concerning the Promotion and Reciprocal Protection of Investments, signed 25 October 2000, in force 14 August 2001.

88 NAFTA (1992), Art. 1120.

89 E.g. US model BIT; Indian model BIPPA; Canadian model FIPA. The UK model IPPA also contemplates arbitration under the rules of the Court of Arbitration of the International Chamber of Commerce and the investor and the state must agree on the applicable rules (Art. 8).

sponsorship of the World Bank and now has 148 parties. Its main goal is to create a set of rules specifically designed to govern disputes between private investors and states and to provide institutional support for arbitrations under those rules through the International Center for the Settlement of Investment Disputes (also known as ICSID). Where the investor's state and the state complained against are not both parties to the Convention, arbitration under the ICSID Convention is not available. To address this situation, ICSID's Administrative Council adopted the Additional Facility rules in 1973.[90] These rules, which are similar to the rules under the ICSID Convention, are routinely provided as an alternative in IIAs where one party to the IIA is not a party to the ICSID Convention.

In most recent IIAs, investors may also choose to arbitrate under the arbitration rules of the UN Commission on International Trade Law (UNCITRAL Arbitration Rules). These are general rules designed to govern private international commercial arbitrations. They are not specifically adapted to investor–state arbitration and do not have the support of an institution like ICSID. In Norway's draft treaty, UNCITRAL arbitration was not included as an option. The rationale expressed by the drafters was that the ICSID rules are preferable because they are designed to be used in investor–state dispute settlement and provide greater predictability. Some IIAs contemplate the use of other rules, such as those of the International Chamber of Commerce and the Stockholm Chamber of Commerce[91] or any rules that the parties may agree on.[92] ICSID arbitration has been preferred by investors in almost two-thirds of arbitrations to date.[93] Some states and commentators have expressed concerns about the fairness of the ICSID process for host states.[94]

Selection of arbitrators

Basic rules

Many IIAs do not address the selection of arbitrators, leaving this issue to be governed by the arbitral rules applicable to the investor–state arbitration.[95] Normally, IIAs that

---

90 The International Center for the Settlement of Investment Disputes Additional Facility for the Administration of Conciliation, Arbitration and Fact-Finding Proceedings was created by the Administrative Council of ICSID on 27 September 1978, reprinted in Document ICSID/11 (June 1979). Schedule C to the Additional Facility sets out the Arbitration (Additional Facility) Rules, as amended.

91 E.g. Korea–Trinidad and Tobago BIT (2002), Art. 8. The ASEAN Agreement (2009) allows the investor to choose to arbitrate at the Regional Centre for Arbitration in Kuala Lumpur or any other regional arbitration centre in ASEAN (Art. 33.1). Investor–state disputes under the COMESA Investment Agreement (2007) can be initiated before the COMESA Court of Justice, a regional institution established in accordance with the Treaty establishing the Common Market for Eastern and Southern Africa (Art. 28.1(b)).

92 E.g. Hong Kong–UK BIT (1998), Art. 8. Under this BIT, if the parties do not agree, the arbitration takes place under the UNCITRAL Arbitration Rules.

93 UNCTAD (2010), *Investor-state Disputes*, op. cit., at 1.

94 G van Harten (2010), 'Investment Treaty Arbitration, Procedural Fairness, and the Rule of Law', in S Schill (ed.), *International Investment Law and Comparative Public Law*, Oxford University Press, Oxford.

95 E.g. India–Singapore CECA (2005).

address the appointment of arbitrators provide that there should be three arbitrators, one appointed by each party and the third selected by the other two or agreed by the parties. These IIAs also provide an appointment procedure that applies if a party fails to appoint an arbitrator within the time specified in the treaty. Appointing authority might, for example, be given to the President of the International Court of Justice or the Secretary-General of ICSID.

This is the approach under the Indian model agreement. Each party must appoint an arbitrator within two months of the commencement of the arbitration and the arbitrators choose a presiding arbitrator. If the parties or arbitrators fail to appoint an arbitrator, an appointment is made by 'the President, the Vice-President or the next senior Judge of the International Court of Justice, who is not a national of either Contracting Party'.[96] The ASEAN–Australia–New Zealand FTA Investment Chapter provides similar, but more detailed, rules. A different feature of this agreement is that the parties themselves must agree on the third arbitrator, who cannot be a national of either party to the IIA. This approach is also followed in the US and Canadian model agreements and gives the parties more control over the identity of the arbitrators.[97]

Standards for arbitrators

An issue that arises in investor–state practice is the independence, impartiality and expertise of arbitrators. A few IIAs prescribe standards for arbitrators. For example, the Canadian model provides as follows:

> 2. Arbitrators shall
>
>   a. have expertise or experience in public international law, international trade or international investment rules, or the resolution of disputes arising under international trade or international investment agreements;
>   b. be independent of, and not be affiliated with or take instructions from, either Party or the disputing party [i.e. the host state, the investor's home state or the investor]; and
>   c. comply with any Code of Conduct for Dispute Settlement as agreed by the Commission.[98]

Where the arbitration relates to financial institutions, and the parties agree, the arbitrators are required to have expertise or experience in financial services law or practice. If they do not agree, then each party can appoint arbitrators with these qualifications.

The applicable arbitral rules may also provide some basic standards,[99] as well as procedures to challenge arbitrators where it is alleged that these standards are not

96 Indian model BIPPA, Art. 9(3)(c).

97 US model BIT, Art. 27; Canadian model FIPA, Art. 29.

98 Canadian model FIPA, Art. 29(2). The Commission is a committee composed of ministerial-level appointments from each party state. No roster has been established. The ASEAN–Australia–New Zealand FTA (2009) Investment Chapter has a similar provision (Art. 23.2).

99 E.g. UNCITRAL Arbitration Rules, Arts. 9, 10; ICSID Convention, Art. 14.

met.[100] These procedures have been used on a number of occasions in investor–state cases, though such challenges have rarely succeeded.[101] Neither the arbitration rules nor most IIAs address the standards for independence and impartiality in any detail. There are, however, other useful sources of rules.

Under NAFTA, a code of conduct has been agreed to by the party states for members of panels deciding state-to-state cases.[102] It contains the following elements:

- Standards for independence of panel members;
- Detailed requirements regarding disclosure of financial and personal relationships between a prospective arbitrator and the parties or the matter in dispute, including relationships through the prospective arbitrator's employer, partner, business, associate or family member;
- Standards for the conduct of panel members during the dispute and after its termination related to confidentiality; and
- A restriction on representing any participant in the dispute for one year following the termination of the dispute.

Some or all of these requirements, with any adjustments desired by the parties, could be adopted by parties in an IIA or a separate code of conduct.

In addition, the International Bar Association has developed a set of very specific guidelines regarding conflicts of interest for commercial arbitrators. The guidelines have been applied in a number of investor–state arbitrations considering challenges to arbitrators.[103] One award referred to the guidelines as representing 'international best practices.'[104] The guidelines set standards for arbitrator independence and for disclosure by arbitrators. They also deal with specific fact situations, such as an arbitrator previously having been retained to give advice or an expert opinion to one of the parties to the dispute. The guidelines assign conflicts to categories, depending on the seriousness of the risk of a conflict of interest, identifying which conflicts should be prohibited, as well as those that are less serious. While the guidelines are not specifically drafted for investor–state arbitration, they address issues that can arise in all arbitrations and could be referred to in an IIA to ensure that they are applied in investor–state arbitrations. Alternatively, key rules from the guidelines could be incorporated directly in an IIA to set specific mandatory standards for arbitrator independence.

---

100 E.g. UNCITRAL Arbitration Rules, Arts. 9, 10; ICSID Convention, Art. 12, 13.

101 E.g. *EDF International S.A., SAUR International S.A. and León Participaciones Argentinas S.A. v. Argentine Republic*, ICSID Case No. ARB/03/23 (BLEU/Argentina and France/Argentina BIT), Challenge Decision Regarding Professor Gabrielle Kaufmann-Kohler, 25 June 2008; *ICS Inspection and Control Services Limited (United Kingdom) v. Republic of Argentina*, UNCITRAL, PCA Case No. 2010-9 (UK/Argentina BIT), Decision on Challenge to Arbitrator, 17 December 2009.

102 Code of Conduct for Dispute Settlement Procedures under Chapters 19 and 20, available at: www.nafta-sec-alena.org/en/view.aspx?conID=658 (accessed 25 June 2012).

103 The IBA Guidelines on Conflicts of Interest in International Arbitration (adopted by the IBA Council 22 May 2004) were referred to in *EDF v. Argentina, Arbitrator Challenge*, op. cit., at para. 69.

104 *ICS v. Argentina*, Arbitrator Challenge, op. cit.

A second set of issues relates to the competence of arbitrators. Often, investor–state disputes require expertise not only in international investment law, but also in international law generally, especially if other areas are implicated in the dispute outside international investment law, such as international environmental law. In many cases, the domestic law of the host state must also be addressed. It may be difficult to find arbitrators with adequate expertise and who have the necessary independence. This is particularly true in developing countries. While the representation of developing countries on arbitral tribunals is desirable, there are often few people with the requisite expertise who are not associated with the state against which a claim is being made.

Existing IIAs do not address competence issues in a significant way. The US and Canadian models provide an option for arbitral tribunals to seek the advice of an expert, either on its own initiative or at the request of a party on any factual issue, concerning environmental, health, safety or other matters raised by the disputing party.[105]

One proposed solution to the challenge of ensuring that arbitrators have the necessary expertise is to create some kind of permanent decision-making institution to which the most competent persons would be appointed.[106] The challenges involved in establishing permanent institutions are discussed below in this section.[107]

The COMESA Investment Agreement adopts an approach that may address the problem of expertise in a modest way. It requires that a roster of qualified arbitrators be maintained by the party states from which parties to investor–state dispute can select arbitrators.[108] No specific qualifications are specified for roster members, however. Creating a roster and requiring that arbitrators be chosen from the roster is another way for the party states to exert more control over who decides the dispute and ensures that arbitrators have the competence or other characteristics desired by the party states. A roster may include, for example, developing country representatives or people with particular expertise beyond investment law.

A roster system could be made more effective by IIA commitments on technical assistance to support the training of competent developing country arbitrators who could become members of the roster. This would be likely to work most effectively in the context of a regional IIA. Within a region there would be more eligible candidates with expertise and the costs of training could be spread among more countries. Also, a regional training initiative could produce competent arbitrators, some of whom would not have the nationality of the state complained against and would not face conflicts of interest in arbitrations involving that state or its investors.[109]

---

105 Canadian model FIPA, Art. 42; US model BIT, Art. 32.

106 F Marshall (2009), 'Defining New Institutional Options for Investor–state Dispute Settlement', International Institute for Sustainable Development, Winnipeg.

107 See below in this section 'Dealing with inconsistent arbitration awards and other problems in investor–state arbitration through improved institutions'.

108 COMESA Investment Agreement (2007), Art. 30.

109 Technical assistance provisions in IIAs are discussed below. See Section 8.2 (Technical assistance).

Governing law

As noted above, the substantive legal basis for investor claims under an IIA is typically defined as a breach of the investor protection provisions of the treaty.[110] Beyond defining what can be the basis of a claim, many IIAs do not indicate specifically what is to be the governing law. For treaties that address the issue, the most common formulation is to say that the investor–state tribunal is to decide the claim 'in accordance with the treaty and applicable rules of international law'.[111] Applicable rules of international law include, for example, generally accepted principles of international law codified in the *Vienna Convention on the Law of Treaties*, which are typically used to interpret IIAs.[112] Also, in practice, in order to determine whether a domestic measure of the host state is consistent with the treaty provisions, often it will be necessary for the tribunal to consider the operation of the applicable domestic law.

Where there is no direction regarding governing law in the treaty, the applicable arbitral rules will apply. Article 42(1) of the ICSID Convention provides that in the absence of an agreement between the parties on the governing law, an arbitral tribunal shall apply the law of the host state and such rules of international law as may be applicable. Under the UNCITRAL Arbitration Rules, the tribunal is to determine the governing law by reference to whatever conflicts of law rules it determines are applicable.[113] In the interests of certainty, it is preferable for treaties to specify the governing law, rather than leaving it to arbitral tribunals.

Interpretation of IIAs by the parties

Some IIAs provide a mechanism by which the party states may adopt interpretations of the agreement that are binding on investor–state arbitration tribunals.[114] Such a mechanism provides a way for party states to correct interpretations of the agreement by investor–state tribunals that are unduly broad, inconsistent or otherwise objectionable to them. This mechanism has been used by Canada, the USA and Mexico in NAFTA and is provided for in the Canadian and US model treaties.[115] Under the ASEAN Agreement, tribunals may request interpretation on their own

---

110 Some existing IIAs further limit the scope of what may be the subject of an investor–state claim, e.g. ASEAN Agreement (2009), Art. 32.

111 E.g. US model BIT, Art. 30; Canadian model FIPA, Art. 40; draft Norwegian APPI, Art. 15(1); ASEAN–Australia–New Zealand FTA (2009) Investment Chapter, Art. 27 (also refers specifically to any applicable agreements between the parties). The UK model IPPA and the Indian model BIPPA do not expressly address governing law but investor–state dispute settlement is limited to disputes regarding the interpretation or application of the agreement (UK model IPPA, Art. 9; Indian model BIPPA, Art. 9).

112 For a discussion of the *Vienna Convention*, see Section 4.2.1 (The role of preambles in IIAs).

113 UNCITRAL Arbitration Rules, Art. 33.1.

114 E.g. US model BIT, Art. 30; Canadian model FIPA, Art. 40.2; draft Norwegian APPI, Art. 23; ASEAN Agreement (2009), Art. 40(2); ASEAN–Australia–New Zealand FTA (2009) Investment Chapter, Art. 27(2).

115 NAFTA (1992), Art. 1131; US model BIT, Art. 30; Canadian model FIPA, Art. 40. A similar provision is contained in the ASEAN Agreement (2009), Art. 40.3, and ASEAN–Australia–New Zealand FTA (2009) Investment Chapter, Art. 27.3.

account and must request an interpretation if one of the parties to an arbitration, typically the host state, asks for one.[116]

Subrogation of political risk insurers

Most developed countries, and an increasing number of developing countries, have state insurance programmes that protect their investors against political risks in connection with their investments abroad. These risks include, for example, the risk of expropriation by the host state without compensation. Some recent IIAs contain a subrogation provision that allows a state insurance company or other state agency that makes a payment to an investor to compensate for some act of a host state to assume any rights the investor may have to pursue an investor–state claim against the host state in relation to the act.[117] Some of these IIAs also allow an investor to pursue an investor–state claim even when they have received or may receive such compensation.[118] This reflects the view that the liability for host state action belongs to the host state and that the investor and the insurer can sort out who is entitled to any compensation that the host state is required to pay by an arbitral tribunal.

Allowing subrogation may promote investment. Giving insurers access to a mechanism that will permit them to recover benefits they have paid out should encourage them to issue insurance against political risk to foreign investors. In turn, the availability of such insurance should encourage investment.

Third party funding of investor–state arbitration

A relatively recent concern raised with respect to investor–state arbitration is investors being funded by third parties to pursue claims.[119] Third party funders typically have no interest in the investor's claim, but provide funds simply in return for a share of any eventual award. Third party funding permits some investors that have valid claims, but who would be deterred from pursuing them by the high costs of lengthy arbitration proceedings, to pursue their claims. Some argue that funders will fund only strong claims that have a relatively high chance of success.[120] However, at the same time, third party funding enhances the likelihood of more claims against states, with potentially large financial implications. The other main concern of host states is that

---

116 ASEAN Agreement (2009), Art. 40.2. The ASEAN–Australia–New Zealand FTA (2009) Investment Chapter has a similar provision (Art. 27.2). Both the Canadian and US models provide that tribunals shall request an interpretation when a host state relies on a reservation to the treaty as a defence and requests an interpretation. US model BIT, Art. 31; Canadian model FIPA, Art. 41.

117 UNCTAD (2007), *Treaties 1995–2006*, op. cit., at 114.

118 E.g. UK model IPPA, Art. 16; ASEAN–Australia–New Zealand FTA (2009) Investment Chapter, Art. 10. In the ASEAN–Australia–New Zealand FTA (2009), Investment Chapter, if an insurer has made a payment to the investor and taken over all the investor's rights, the investor cannot make a claim based on those rights without the permission of the insurer (Art. 22.3).

119 The incidence of third party funding is discussed in E de Brabandere and J Lepeltak (2012), 'Third-Party Funding in International Investment Arbitration', Grotius Centre Working Paper No. 2012/1, The Hague.

120 Ibid. at 7.

the interests of third party funders will influence the claim and the arbitration. Claims may be inflated to ensure that enough is awarded to satisfy both the funder and the investor. Settlement may be discouraged and proceedings delayed. Indeed, it is argued that in some cases the financial interests of third party funders result in an 'abuse of process', where they prolong or otherwise affect arbitral proceedings in ways that are inconsistent with the interests of the parties to the arbitration.[121]

No IIA addresses third party funding and only a few investor–state cases have considered its significance. In those cases, the issue has typically been whether the fact that an investor has its costs covered by a third party should be relevant to an allocation of costs in the final award. So far, tribunals have declined to take the existence of third party funding into account.[122]

IIA provisions could address third party funding by requiring investors to disclose the existence of any third party funding arrangement. Transparency in this regard would allow a tribunal to be on the watch for and address any possible abuse of process. It would also permit there to be an enquiry into whether the arbitrators were independent of the funders, as well as the parties to the dispute.

Consolidation of investor claims based on identical or similar issues of law or fact

In order to achieve the fair and efficient resolution of claims, some IIAs provide for the consolidation of claims where investors have initiated separate investor–state arbitrations raising identical or similar issues of law or fact. Where a government has enacted a measure that affects a number of investors in exactly the same way and more than one of the investors is making an investor–state claim against the host state in relation to the measure on the same legal basis it may be desirable to consolidate the claims into a single arbitration. Host states benefit from consolidation because combining arbitrations initiated by a number of investors should reduce the costs of defending the claims.[123] Consolidation also eliminates the risk of inconsistent decisions being made by tribunals on the same issues.[124]

---

121 This issue was raised unsuccessfully in the Australian High Court: *Campbells Cash and Carry Pty Ltd v. Fostif Pty Limited*, [2006] *High Court of Australia* 41.

122 See, for example, *ATA Construction, Industrial and Trading Company v. Hashemite Kingdom of Jordan*, ICSID Case No. ARB/08/2, Order Taking Note of the Discontinuance of the Proceeding, 11 July 2011.

123 E.g. US model BIT, Art. 33; Canadian model FIPA, Art. 32; ASEAN Agreement (2009), Art. 37.

124 Inconsistent investor–state arbitration decisions in relation to the same government measure occurred in three cases under NAFTA (*Archer Daniels Midland Company and Tate and Lyle Ingredients Americas, Inc. v. United Mexican States*, ICSID Case No. ARB (AF)/04/5 (NAFTA). Award (Redacted Version), 21 November 2007; *Cargill, Incorporated v. United Mexican States*, ICSID Case No. ARB(AF)/05/2 (NAFTA), Award (redacted version), 18 September 2009; *Corn Products International, Inc. v. United Mexican States*, ICSID Case No. ARB (AF)/04/1 (NAFTA), Decision on Responsibility (redacted version), 15 January 2008). A request for consolidation by Mexico of the *Archer Daniels* and *Corn Products* cases was refused on the basis that the parties were competitors and, in a consolidated case there was a risk of disclosure of confidential information (Order of the Consolidation Tribunal, 20 May 2005).

However, consolidation may increase the costs of proceedings for investors by enlarging their scope and the number of parties involved. In a consolidated proceeding, individual investors lose control of how the claim is argued. In addition, investors making the same claim will often be competitors, since investors affected by a host state measure will often be carrying on business in the same economic sector. In such a situation, consolidation may create the risk that an investor's confidential business information will be disclosed to a competitor.

NAFTA contains a consolidation procedure.[125] There have been several consolidation proceedings under NAFTA, but consolidation has been ordered in only one case.[126]

Transparency and civil society participation in investor–state arbitration

Until recently, most IIAs did not impose any requirements regarding the transparency of investor–state arbitration proceedings and, with some exceptions, there was limited public disclosure regarding such proceedings.[127] A large majority of agreements do not provide any mechanism for civil society to participate in investor–state arbitration. Since state measures intended to fulfil the state's responsibility to protect the public interest are often the subject of investor–state cases, this lack of openness has been strongly criticised.[128]

Transparency

Most IIAs that have incorporated transparency provisions related to dispute settlement procedures impose only limited requirements. For example, the ASEAN–Australia–New Zealand FTA Investment Chapter provides only that the host state *may* make publicly available all awards and decisions of an investor–state tribunal.[129] Transparency requirements in NAFTA are similar.[130] In investor–state arbitrations under NAFTA, however, much greater transparency has been provided in practice. Public access to documents submitted to and issued by arbitration tribunals (subject to the redaction of proprietary confidential information) and publicly accessible hearings have now become commonplace. Greater openness is beginning to occur in other investor–state procedures as well.[131] Public access to hearings is now expressly

---

125 NAFTA (1992), Art. 1126.

126 A consolidation tribunal ordered the stay of the individual arbitrations in *Canfor Corporation v. United States of America*, *Tembec Inc., et al. v. United States of America* and *Terminal Forest Products Ltd. v. United States of America*, UNCITRAL, Order of the Consolidation Tribunal, 7 September 2005, at paras. 3–17.

127 There are no transparency requirements in most Caribbean and Pacific BITS (Malik, op. cit., at 32, 61) or in the India–Singapore CECA (2005).

128 UNCTAD (2011), *Transparency in IIAs*, United Nations, New York and Geneva.

129 ASEAN–Australia–New Zealand FTA (2009) Investment Chapter, Art. 26.1.

130 In addition to disclosure of awards (NAFTA (1992), Art. 1137.4), a record must be kept of claims (NAFTA (1992), Art. 1126.13).

131 The NAFTA parties confirmed their commitment to such disclosure in NAFTA Free Trade Commission, 'Notes of Interpretation of Certain NAFTA Chapter 11 Provisions' (31 July 2001), available at: www.international.gc.ca/trade-agreements-accords-commerciaux/disp-diff/NAFTA-Interpr.aspx?lang=en (accessed 29 May 2012). They subsequently committed to public hearings. These developments are discussed in VanDuzer, op. cit., at 681–723.

permitted based on amendments to the ICSID arbitration rules and the Additional Facility rules adopted in 2006[132] and are mandatory under the Canadian and US model treaties, as well as the COMESA Investment Agreement.[133] The Canadian and US model agreements have detailed requirements relating to transparency of documents filed by the parties and issued by tribunals. Under the US model, the host state must make available to the public:

(a) The notice of intent [filed by the investor],

(b) The notice of arbitration [filed by the investor],

(c) Pleadings, memorials, and briefs submitted by a disputing party, …

(d) Minutes or transcripts of hearings of the tribunal, where available, and

(e) Orders, awards, and decisions of the tribunal.[134]

Disclosure of settlement terms is not addressed in any IIA. In the approximately 30 per cent of investor–state cases that are settled, typically there has been no disclosure regarding the terms of the settlement.

Participation by non-disputing party states and amici curiae

A few years ago, NAFTA tribunals began to permit NGOs to submit briefs as 'friends of the court' or *amici curiae* in investor–state cases. Subsequently, this practice has

132 Proposals for reform were made initially by the ICSID Secretariat in 'Possible Improvements of the Framework for ICSID Arbitration: ICSID Secretariat Discussion Paper,' released on 22 October 2004. The proposals were amended in March 2005 following comments from various constituencies and a revised working paper was issued 12 May 2005: 'Suggested Changes to the ICSID Rules and Regulations', available at: http://icsid.worldbank.org/ICSID/FrontServlet?requestType=CasesRH&actionVal=OpenPage&PageType=AnnouncementsFrame&FromPage=NewsReleases&pageName=Archive_%20Announcement22 (accessed 29 May 2012). Revised proposals were submitted to the Administrative Council of ICSID in autumn 2005. On 5 April 2006, the Administrative Council approved amendments of the ICSID Arbitration Rules (ICSID Arbitration Rules are contained in the *ICSID Convention*, and the arbitration rules created by the Administrative Council of ICSID under Arts. 6(1)(a)–(c) of the ICSID Convention and published by ICSID in ICSID Basic Documents (2006), ICSID, Washington, DC: *Administrative and Financial Regulations*; *Rules of Procedure for the Institution of Conciliation and Arbitration Proceedings (Institution Rules)*, and the *Rules of Procedure for Arbitration Proceedings (Arbitration Rules)*, as amended) and the Additional Facility Rules. Schedule C to the Additional Facility sets out the Arbitration (Additional Facility) Rules, as amended. These amendments to Arts. 32 and 48 of the ICSID Arbitration Rules and Arts. 39 and 53(3) (formerly 54(3)) of the Additional Facility Rules came into effect on 10 April 2006. Pursuant to Art. 44 of the ICSID Convention, unless otherwise agreed by the parties, an ICSID arbitration proceeding is conducted in accordance with the arbitration rules in effect on the date on which the parties consented to arbitration.

133 Canadian model FIPA, Art. 38; US model BIT, Art. 29; COMESA Investment Agreement (2007), Art. 28. The ASEAN Agreement (2009) permits (but does not require) a member state to disclose documents but contains no commitments regarding the openness of hearings and does not address *amicus curiae* participation (Art. 39). Other member states can obtain a copy of the notice of arbitration (Art. 39.6).

134 The Australia–Chile FTA (2008) (Art. 10) is similar.

been followed in a few ICSID cases under other IIAs. *Amicus curiae* submissions may provide relevant information to investor–state tribunals that is not available from the disputing parties and may represent interests affected by the dispute that are distinct from the general public interest. For example, in one recent claim by a Canadian mining company against the USA, an *amicus curiae* submission from a local Native American tribe was accepted because it provided unique information regarding the cultural and spiritual significance of the land that was the subject of the dispute.[135]

Both the Canadian and US model agreements confirm that tribunals have the authority to admit *amicus curiae* submissions.[136] The Canadian model goes on to establish detailed procedures for dealing with *amicus curiae* submissions. These address the process of submission, the criteria to be applied in deciding whether to accept a submission and the weight to be accorded to it. The provisions are intended to ensure that *amicus curiae* submissions assist, rather than encumber, the decision-making process. Tribunals have to consider:

- Whether the submission would assist the tribunal to deal with a factual or legal issue by bringing insights or information that are different from that provided by the disputing parties; and
- Whether there is a public interest in the subject matter of the arbitration.

Tribunals must also ensure that an *amicus curiae* submission does not disrupt the proceedings or unduly burden or prejudice either of the parties. Tribunals are not required to address *amicus curiae* submissions, even if they admit them.

The 2006 amendments to the ICSID rules also gave tribunals the power to allow a 'non-disputing' party to make a written submission after consulting with the parties.[137] Such non-disputing parties are just like *amici curiae* and the ICSID rules address some of the same issues as the rules for *amici curiae* in the Canadian model treaty.

The effectiveness of *amicus curiae* participation will be directly affected by their access to information regarding the dispute.[138] In this way, transparency requirements and the utility of *amicus curiae* submissions are linked.

As a practical matter, *amicus curiae* submissions are filed most often by NGOs in support of host state measures being challenged by investors. This is not necessarily the case, however. In a NAFTA claim brought by a US investor against Canada, the American Chamber of Commerce, a pro-business organisation, filed an *amicus curiae* brief challenging Canada's arguments regarding the interpretation of the national treatment obligation in NAFTA.[139]

---

135 *Glamis Gold Ltd. v. United States*, UNCITRAL, Application for Leave to File a Non-Party Submission, 19 August 2005.

136 Canadian model FIPA, Art. 39; US model BIT, Art. 28.3.

137 ICSID Arbitration Rules, Rule 37(2).

138 N Bernasconi-Osterwalder (2011), 'Transparency and *Amicus Curiae* in ICSID Arbitration' in Cordonier Segger et al., op. cit., at 201–206.

139 *United Parcel Service of America, Inc. v. Canada*, Application for *Amicus Curiae* Status by Chamber of Commerce of the United States, 20 October 2005.

Another feature of some investor–state procedures is that a IIA party state other than the one complained against is entitled to participate in the arbitration, at least in relation to issues associated with the interpretation of the investment treaty.[140] Such a right has been routinely exercised in NAFTA cases and provides party states with a right to have a say in the development of treaty norms that affect them.[141]

Costs and benefits of greater transparency and *amicus curiae* participation Greater transparency and the prospect of responding to *amicus curiae* submissions impose additional burdens on investors participating in investor–state dispute settlement, and may therefore reduce the attractiveness of dispute settlement procedures to them. Host states may have other reservations regarding transparency and *amicus curiae* submissions. Making documents and proceedings publicly accessible is not required under the domestic legal systems of all states to the same extent. In some cases, states may prefer proceedings to be conducted without public scrutiny. The involvement of *amicus curiae* in investor–state cases, in particular, remains controversial.[142] Many states do not permit participation by non-parties in domestic legal proceedings.

Nevertheless, greater transparency and involvement of civil society contributes to public understanding of the arbitration process and enhances the democratic accountability of states for what occurs in dispute settlement.[143] Civil society participation may also help to improve the sensitivity of arbitration tribunals to policy considerations other than the protection and promotion of investment. For these reasons, many consider that greater openness is important to the legitimacy of the investor–state dispute settlement procedures and to a process that contributes to sustainable development.[144]

Enforcement of awards

Most IIAs provide that investor–state arbitration decisions are final and binding[145] and many go on to state that a host state against which an award had been made will comply with it. Only a few address enforcement in any further detail. Commitments regarding enforcement in IIAs do not bind non-party states, but other international treaties addressing the enforcement of arbitral awards may apply to them, as well as to the party states to the IIA under which an award was made.

- **United Nations Convention on the Recognition and Enforcement of Foreign Arbitral Awards** (known as the *New York Convention*): This treaty requires that each party state recognise and enforce foreign arbitral awards, which include

140 E.g. Canadian model FIPA, Arts. 33–6. A similar right is provided for in the Norwegian draft APPI (Art. 18). No such right is provided for in the UK model IPPA, the US model BIT or the Indian model BIPPA.

141 NAFTA (1992), Art. 1128.

142 UNCTAD (2011), *Transparency*, op. cit., at 71.

143 Soloway describes the problem as follows: '[The] lack of transparency seems to run counter to "the values and views" integral to the post-war trading system and indeed democratic principles, where transparency of legal process is a fundamental norm' (J Soloway (1999), 'NAFTA's Chapter 11, the Challenge of Private Party Participation', 16 *Journal of International Arbitration*, 8 at 10).

144 VanDuzer, op. cit.

145 E.g. Indian model BIPPA, Art. 9(3)(c)(iii).

investor–state awards. Normally this is done through domestic courts in the party state.[146] There are very limited grounds upon which a domestic court in a New York Convention state can refuse enforcement of an arbitral award under the treaty. Grounds include the arbitral tribunal exceeding its jurisdiction and fundamental procedural errors in the conduct of the arbitration.[147] Some states have filed a reservation permitted under the New York Convention, which provides that they are required to respect the requirements of the treaty in relation only to arbitral awards made in other New York Convention party states.[148] States are also permitted to file reservations that limit their convention obligations to foreign arbitral awards that arise out of 'commercial' disputes. One hundred and forty-six countries are parties to the New York Convention and more than half have filed a reservation limiting their obligations to awards made in other party states. More than 40 have filed a reservation limiting their obligation to awards arising out of commercial disputes.[149]

- **ICSID Convention:** The ICSID Convention has its own enforcement scheme for awards made under the Convention. ICSID provides a procedure in which a party to an arbitration may seek to have an award annulled. It is not an appeal and an award may only be annulled on limited grounds, including the arbitral process being tainted by serious procedural problems and the tribunal manifestly exceeding its jurisdiction.[150] The grounds for annulment are set out in Box 7.4. Subject to the successful annulment of an award, which is relatively rare, each party to the ICSID Convention must ensure that the award is enforced in its territory as if it were a final judgment of a court in that state. There is no basis to refuse enforcement, but execution of the award is governed by the same rules that govern the execution of domestic court judgments.[151] As noted, 148 states are parties to the ICSID Convention.[152]

Box 7.4 ICSID annulment proceedings

Under Article 52 of the ICSID Convention, a party to an investor–state arbitration under the ICSID rules may request that an arbitration award be annulled on any of the following grounds:

(Continued)

146 *United Nations Convention on the Recognition and Enforcement of Foreign Arbitral Awards*, signed 6 July 1958, in force 7 June 1959 (called the *New York Convention*), Art. III.

147 *New York Convention*, Art. V. Awards may be set aside by a court in the place of arbitration on similar grounds.

148 *New York Convention*, Art. I.

149 See status table maintained by UNCITRAL, available at: www.uncitral.org/uncitral/en/uncitral_texts/arbitration/NYConvention_status.html (accessed 22 May 2012).

150 ICSID Convention, Art. 54. Some other grounds for annulment are provided for in Art. 54.

151 ICSID Convention, Art. 54. Domestic rules in the state in which enforcement is sought regarding the sovereign immunity from execution of foreign state assets still apply (Art. 55)

152 See ICSID list of contracting states, available at: www.uncitral.org/uncitral/en/uncitral_texts/arbitration/NYConvention_status.html (accessed 22 May 2012).

(Continued)

a. The tribunal was not properly constituted;

b. The tribunal has manifestly exceeded its powers;

c. There was corruption on the part of a member of the tribunal;

d. There has been a serious departure from a fundamental rule of procedure; or

e. The award has failed to state the reasons on which it is based.

When the Secretary-General of ICSID receives a request, the Chairman of the ICSID Administrative Council is required to appoint an ad hoc committee of three persons, none of whom served on the original tribunal or have the same nationality of the parties or any of the arbitrators on the original tribunal. The procedure followed by an annulment committee is essentially the same as for regular ICSID arbitrations.

While the grounds for annulment are narrow, annulments have been granted in a number of cases. Annulment decisions have not been consistent, even in cases that have the same issues of fact or law, resulting in substantial criticism of the process.[153]

Some IIAs include provisions to ensure that that investor–state awards benefit from these enforcement obligations. One approach is to require that an award be made in a state that is party to the New York Convention and to include a provision deeming the award to be 'commercial' for the purposes of the Convention.[154]

Where a party state fails to comply with an award, it is usually possible for the investor's home state to initiate state-to-state procedures under the IIA to seek compliance. Some IIAs expressly provide for this.[155] Effective enforcement measures may be an important feature of IIAs for investors, though they have not been used frequently in practice.

---

153 D Kim (2011), 'The Annulment Committee's Role in Multiplying Inconsistency in ICSID Arbitration: The Need to Move Away from an Annulment-Based System', 86 *New York University Law Review* 242.

154 E.g. Canadian model FIPA, Arts. 36, 45.7; US model BIT, Arts. 28.1, 34.10; ASEAN Agreement (2009), Art. 34.3. No such provision is included in the UK model IPPA, the ASEAN–Australia–New Zealand FTA (2009) Investment Chapter, the COMESA Investment Agreement (2007) or the Indian model BIPPA. Enforcement may occur in similar circumstances under the *Inter-American Convention on International Commercial Arbitration*, signed 30 January 1975, in force 16 June 1976, to which many states in the Americas are party.

155 E.g. Canadian model FIPA, Art. 45.5; US model BIT, Art. 34.8. A similar right is provided for in the India–Singapore CECA (2005) (Art. 6.21.6) and the Australia–India BIT (1999) (Art. 12). No such provision is found in the UK model IPPA, the Indian model BIPPA, the COMESA Investment Agreement (2007) or the ASEAN–Australia–New Zealand FTA (2009) Investment Chapter.

Dealing with inconsistent arbitration decisions and other problems with investor–state arbitration through improved dispute settlement institutions

As noted, one concern regarding investor–state arbitration is inconsistency between arbitral decisions that are interpreting the same or similar IIA provisions. Some inconsistency is an inevitable result of decisions made by tribunals appointed on an ad hoc basis for a particular case and tasked with interpreting provisions in different treaties that are not identical. In addition, while arbitral awards frequently rely on previous decisions for guidance, there is no requirement in investor–state arbitration that a decision in one case must be consistent with that in another, unlike in some domestic legal systems. The likelihood of inconsistent decisions is compounded by the fact that most arbitrations have taken place in the last few years, and that submissions of parties and awards of arbitrators cannot take into account arguments and awards in other cases that are being argued and decided at the same time. While there is disagreement about the magnitude and seriousness of the problem of inconsistent decisions, there is no doubt that new and different interpretations by international tribunals of an obligation in one IIA that is similar or identical to provisions in other existing agreements force states to revise their understanding of the effective scope of their obligations. Inconsistent interpretation also reduces the predictability of IIA obligations for investors and, more importantly, for states.[156] Predictability is further impaired by the increasing frequency of dissenting opinions, in which one of the arbitrators expresses different conclusions regarding the interpretation of IIA provisions from the others.

Concerns about inconsistent decisions have produced a number of proposals for reform of investor–state arbitration procedures, though very little has been done in IIAs to date.[157] Most proposals involve the creation of permanent institutions in order to ensure greater consistency, predictability and quality in decisions interpreting IIA obligations. For example, the IISD model treaty tries to address the problem of inconsistent decisions by establishing a permanent dispute resolution body, whose decisions are binding precedents for future decisions. The model contemplates a roster of 35 experts, three of whom will be selected for each case, who must meet high standards for independence and expertise.[158] The IISD model also contemplates a standing appellate body with nine full-time members appointed for seven-year terms (renewable once). All proceedings are to be open to the public.[159] The aim

156 In some circumstances there may also be a risk of parallel claims under: (i) an IIA and domestic law in local courts; (ii) an IIA and a contractually agreed dispute settlement procedure; and (iii) multiple IIAs. States may wish to clearly stipulate in an IIA that an investor's commitment to an exclusive dispute settlement clause in an investment contract precludes resort to IIA investor–state arbitration in any dispute that is subject to the contractual dispute settlement mechanism. Likewise, in relation to such disputes, states may wish to incorporate a clause in their IIAs that an investor may by contract waive its right to bring a claim under the IIA.

157 US–Uruguay BIT (2005) obliges the parties to discuss the desirability of an appellate body (Annex E).

158 A roster of presiding arbitrators is contemplated under NAFTA (1992) (Art. 1124) but has never been established.

159 IISD model treaty, Art. 46(D).

of these provisions is to promote both procedural fairness and greater accountability to the public in both host and home states[160] as well as to eliminate the problem of inconsistencies in decisions of arbitration tribunals.[161]

A permanent dispute resolution body or appellate review by a standing appellate body can also address another problem arising out of the ad hoc nature of investor–state arbitration. As noted, the institutional safeguards that guarantee the independence of judges in national and international judicial systems, such as security of tenure and a prohibition on accepting outside remuneration, do not exist in investor–state arbitration. A permanent dispute resolution body and/or appellate review by a standing appellate body would help to ensure that decisions are ultimately taken by people whose independence is protected by such safeguards.

A standing permanent dispute resolution body or appellate body could, however, have significant resource implications for party states. Resources would be needed to identify and appoint judges and support the operation of permanent bodies. If appointees were to be full time and not pursue other remunerative activities, the cost would be greater. In a bilateral treaty context, there may be too few disputes to justify such expenditures. Where a dispute resolution body is charged with dealing with disputes under multiple agreements, the resource implications may be more manageable. The resource constraints will be reduced, for example, if a regional body is set up to deal with disputes between investors and all the states in a region, either under a regional agreement or under multiple IIAs.[162]

Another approach, discussed above, would be to have a roster of experts selected by the party states that constitutes a pool of people from which arbitrators would be appointed for a particular dispute. Such a solution does not deliver the institutional safeguards of a permanent institution, but may go some way to improving consistency and quality in decisions. It also gives parties more control over who the arbitrators will be. As discussed above, finding appropriate qualified people for the roster may prove challenging for some states. Some strategies for dealing with this problem are discussed above.[163]

As noted, another approach in existing IIAs to addressing the problem of inconsistent decisions is to permit the party states to issue authoritative interpretations. Unlike an appellate process, however, interpretations are not capable of correcting the result

---

160 IISD model treaty, Art. 40. See also Annex A.

161 IISD model treaty, Annex A, Art. 14. On the advisability of establishing a permanent dispute resolution body, see N Blackaby (2003), 'Public Interest and Investment Treaty Arbitration', in A J van den Berg (ed.), *International Commercial Arbitration: Important Contemporary Questions*, Kluwer International, New York; see also W M Reisman (1994), 'Control Mechanisms in International Dispute Resolution,' 2 *United States–Mexico Law Journal* 129.

162 The COMESA Investment Agreement (2007) is one of the few existing IIAs that provide for an appellate process. In state-to-state disputes, member states may appeal to the COMESA Court of Justice (COMESA Investment Agreement (2007), Annex A, Art. 13).

163 See above 'Selection of arbitrators'. See also Section 8.2 (Technical assistance).

in a particular case decided before the interpretation was issued. In addition, an interpretation power does not address the other problems noted above that flow from ad hoc arbitration.

Remedies issues

The remedies available in IIAs are generally limited to restitution of property or monetary damages.[164] Except with respect to compensation for expropriation, most IIAs provide no guidance regarding the assessment of damages. A few IIAs exclude the possibility of punitive damages.[165] As discussed above, investor–state tribunals have determined that it is not appropriate to award punitive damages.[166] The basis of damage awards should be compensation for loss.

There are several ways that damage awards could be limited to address some of the challenges associated with broad and unclear IIA standards for investor protection, as well as other situations in which an argument can be made that damages should be reduced or limited:

- **Reduce damages where the investor's own conduct has contributed to the loss suffered by the investor:** The notion of contributory fault is recognised in international law generally and has been applied in some investor–state cases.[167] The COMESA Investment Agreement provides that a state may assert as a 'defence, counterclaim or set-off' that an investor has not fulfilled its obligations under the agreement, which suggests the possibility of reducing damages where the investor bears some fault.[168] The COMESA Investment Agreement requires that investors comply with the domestic law of the host state. A failure to do so could be a basis for reducing damages paid to the investor in some cases where the breach by the investor was what caused the state to act. The expression and application of a principle of contributory fault, however, is complex. Investor–state tribunals would have significant discretion to determine whether an investor's conduct forced the state to act or otherwise contributed to the harm suffered and to what extent damages should be reduced as a result.
- **Reduce damages where the state's action has breached rules that the tribunal determines were unclear or subject to conflicting interpretation in some way that is relevant to the finding of liability:** Some tribunals have taken uncertainty of IIA standards into account in their awards, though there is no accepted practice in this regard.[169]

164 E.g. US model BIT, Art. 34.1; Canadian model FIPA, Art. 44.1; ASEAN–Australia–New Zealand FTA (2009) Investment Chapter, Art. 28.1; ASEAN Agreement (2009), Art. 41.2. Typically a state may elect to pay damages instead of giving restitution.

165 E.g. US model BIT, Art. 34.3; ASEAN–Australia–New Zealand FTA (2009) Investment Chapter, Art. 28.3; ASEAN Agreement (2009), Art. 41.4; NAFTA (1992), Art. 1135(3).

166 See Section 5.6 (Limitations on expropriation and nationalisation).

167 Ripinsky with Williams, op. cit., at 314–19.

168 Arguably, this provision also refers to unrelated breaches by the investor of its obligations.

169 E.g. *Ethyl Corporation v. Canada*, UNCITRAL, Decision on Jurisdiction, 24 June 1998 (regarding costs).

- **Reduce damages to the extent that the investor has not taken reasonable steps to mitigate its losses:** This principle is accepted in most domestic legal systems[170] and major international commercial instruments.[171] It is specifically provided for in the COMESA Investment Agreement.[172]
- **Preclude damages where the breach by the state does not surpass some minimum threshold of seriousness:** This approach has been taken by the European Court of Justice in some cases regarding claims that there has been a breach of Community law.[173] In some investor–state arbitration cases dealing with the fair and equitable treatment standard a minimum threshold of seriousness has been required as a condition of granting relief.[174]

To some extent, the incorporation of express provisions to address these issues would direct tribunals to do what some tribunals are doing already. In particular, taking into account contributory fault and a failure to mitigate damages are well-accepted principles for the assessment of damages, and their express inclusion in an IIA should be uncontroversial. Expressing these principles in the treaty has the benefit of ensuring that tribunals will consider them. The application of these principles may lessen the burden of investor–state arbitration for states. Damage awards may be smaller in some cases, and fewer cases may be brought as a result. At the same time, expressing these requirements in an IIA may affect investors' perception of the likely benefits of investor–state arbitration.

Some other limitations on damages, discussed in relation to compensation for expropriation, could also be adopted in relation to the assessment and payment of damages for breaches of other obligations.[175] These were the following:

- **Limiting compensation to direct losses, not including loss of future profits, and prohibiting the calculation of compensation based on the discounted value of future cash flows:** The main purpose of this limitation is to avoid damages based on unreliable speculation regarding the profits an investment would have made in the future. However, such a blanket limitation would extend to situations in which lost future profits could be ascertained with reasonable certainty, such as where a business has made consistent profits for a period of years.
- **Prohibit awards of moral damages to compensate for non-economic losses, such as for mental suffering and injury to reputation:** As discussed,[176] these kinds of damages have been sought and, in at least one investor–state case, awarded. Nevertheless, they are likely to be rarely appropriate in investor–state cases,

170 Ripinsky with Williams, op. cit., at 319.

171 E.g. United Nations Convention on Contracts for the International Sale of Goods (1980), Art. 77. There is evidence that it is becoming accepted as a general principle of law (Ripinsky with Williams, op. cit., at 321–2).

172 COMESA Investment Agreement (2007), Art. 28.9.

173 *Brasserie du Pecheur v. Germany*, [1996] All ER (EC) 301 CASE C-46/93.

174 See Section 5.5 (Fair and equitable treatment and the minimum standard of treatment).

175 See Section 5.6 (Limitations on expropriation and nationalisation).

176 See Section 5.6 (Limitations on expropriation and nationalisation).

which are fundamentally about the protection of economic interests, and are inherently unpredictable. Prohibiting moral damages would make damage awards more predictable. On the other hand, mental suffering and other kinds of non-economic losses can be suffered by investors in some cases. Moral damages may be useful to deter states from mistreating investors and their personnel.

Neither of these is expressed as a general rule related to the award of damages in existing IIAs, but consideration could be given to including them in a treaty.

Two other procedural devices were discussed in the section on expropriation that would help host states to deal with their liability in a manner that is responsive to their particular circumstances:[177]

- **Giving the state and the investor a period of time to negotiate compensation prior to an award of damages by the tribunal after a finding of state liability; and**
- **Providing for situations in which payment of compensation by the state may be delayed, including, for example, a financial crisis.**

While IIA provisions according these procedural options are not generally found, the second option does appear in the COMESA Investment Agreement.[178]

One other clarification of the manner in which damages are to be established may be helpful in an IIA. A treaty could expressly indicate that the investor has an obligation to prove all elements of its claim, including damages suffered, and to show that the losses were sustained by reason of the host state's breach of its IIA obligations. Such a requirement is consistent with general principles of law applicable to international arbitration and is included in some IIAs.[179]

Counterclaims

Counterclaims were discussed above in Section 6.17 (Counterclaims by states in investor–state arbitration).

Box 7.5 Summary of options for investor–state dispute settlement provisions

1. *No investor–state arbitration*
2. *Agree to investor–state arbitration but subject to one or more of the following limitations*

(Continued)

177 See Section 5.6 (Limitations on expropriation and nationalisation).

178 COMESA Investment Agreement (2007), Art. 20(5). See the same provision in the IISD model treaty (Art. 8(F)).

179 E.g. US–Uruguay BIT (2005), Protocol, Art. 2.

(Continued)

a. Limitations on the scope of protection, such as permitting only claims by investors that the state has breached listed investor-protection obligations in the IIA and not including an umbrella clause.

b. Limitations in the form of prerequisites that must be satisfied for the investor to obtain access to investor–state arbitration:

   i. Exhaustion of local remedies or a fork in the road;

   ii. Waivers of other claims;

   iii. Consultations and ADR procedures;

   iv. Limitation periods.

c. Limitations in the form of additional institutional requirements to ensure the fairness and quality of the process:

   i. Specify arbitral rules;

   ii. Require tribunals to rule on challenges to jurisdiction and objections that an investor's claim is frivolous before proceeding to the merits;

   iii. Set standards for arbitrators and their appointment;

   iv. Create a permanent dispute settlement body and/or appellate body;

   v. Establish requirements for transparency and *amicus curiae* participation;

   vi. Permit consolidation of multiple claims based on the same or similar issues of fact or law;

d. Limitations on the damage awards:

   i. Reducing damage awards where:

      - The investor's conduct contributed the losses suffered;

      - The state's action breached rules that the tribunal determines were unclear or subject to conflicting interpretation;

      - The investor did not take reasonable steps to mitigate its losses;

   ii. The breach by the state does not surpass some minimum threshold of seriousness;

   iii. Limiting compensation to direct losses not including loss of future profits and prohibiting the calculation of compensation based on the discounted value of future cash flows;

   iv. Requiring a period of time following a finding of state liability to negotiate the amount of damages;

(Continued)

(Continued)

v. Permitting payment of damages to be delayed in some circumstances based on hardship to the host state;

vi. Prohibiting punitive or moral damages; and

vii. Imposing requirements that damages be proved.

3. *Permit counterclaims by states and limitations on access to dispute settlement for investors that have breached their obligations under an IIA*

4. *Agree to investor–state arbitration for all claims by an investor against a host state through an umbrella clause with or without the other limitations in options 2 and 3*

7.1.5 Discussion of options

1. *No investor–state arbitration*

Given the concerns that states and others have expressed regarding the cost of investor–state arbitration, the uncertainty and unpredictability of the results and the lack of institutional guarantees regarding independence of the decision-makers, some states may decide that they should not agree to include investor–state arbitration procedures in their IIAs. This would be a marked shift from historical IIA practice. Until recently, investor–state arbitration has been universally sought by developed countries and many developing countries because of the benefits that it provides to their investors. However, in light of states' experience with investor–state arbitration and the concerns it has produced, some countries, including Australia, are no longer willing to accept this mode of dispute resolution. Consequently, not including investor–state arbitration may be more feasible than ever before in some negotiating contexts. If it was excluded, it is possible that any investment-enhancing effect of the IIA would be reduced.

In the absence of an IIA commitment to investor–state arbitration, a state could still agree to investor–state arbitration in a particular case where it chose to do so. Without a state's agreement to investor–state arbitration, the investor often would be limited to seeking relief in the domestic courts of the host state under host state law, or through commercial arbitration, if provided for in a contract with the host state, or lobbying its home state to espouse its claim through the state-to-state dispute settlement procedures in the IIA or in some other way. Under the constitutional laws of some host states, IIA investor-protection standards will be incorporated into domestic law and may form the basis of a claim in domestic courts. Under some other constitutional systems, however, such a claim is impossible because treaty obligations are not part of domestic law.[180]

180 Some treaties specifically address treaty-based claims in domestic law. Such claims are prohibited under NAFTA (1992) (Art. 2031).

Even if investor–state dispute settlement is not included in an IIA, it is possible that an obligation to give investors from the other party state the benefit of such a procedure would be incorporated into the IIA if it contained an MFN clause and the state had entered into another IIA that provided for investor–state arbitration. As discussed in Section 5.4 (Most favoured nation), a number of investor–state cases have allowed the importation of more favourable investor–state procedures from other treaties. As yet, no case has permitted the wholesale importation of investor–state arbitration where the parties have not agreed to the procedure.

2. *Agree to investor–state arbitration but subject to one or more of the following limitations*

   a. Limitations on the scope of protection, such as permitting only claims by investors that the state has breached listed investor-protection obligations in the IIA and not including an umbrella clause

      As noted, many treaties now specify that an investor's claim can be based only on alleged breaches of listed investor protection obligations in the IIA that have resulted in a loss to the investor. This approach reflects the view that some IIA provisions are intended to commit the host state to creating a generally supportive environment for investment, but where a failure by the host state to comply does not cause any direct loss to the investor. As a result, these obligations should not be subject to investor–state dispute settlement. General transparency obligations to publish laws are one example.

      Specification of the provisions that can be the basis for a claim enhances certainty regarding the scope and effect of investor–state procedures. By comparison, umbrella clauses that treat all obligations owed by the state to an investor as obligations under the treaty, and subject to claims under treaty-based investor–state arbitration, broadly expand the scope of access to the investor–state procedures in unpredictable ways and create the prospect of investors pursuing claims in different fora: domestic courts and dispute settlement procedures agreed to in contracts with the state, as well as treaty-based investor–state dispute settlement. A specific list of provisions that may be the basis of an investor–state claim is used in a number of treaties and in Canada's treaty model. Restricting the scope of potential claims to breaches of identified provisions may be viewed negatively by some capital-exporting states, especially those that have umbrella clauses in their model treaties.

   b. Limitations in the form of prerequisites that must be satisfied for the investor to obtain access to investor–state arbitration

      i. Exhaustion of local remedies or a fork in the road

         Relatively few IIAs impose a requirement to exhaust local remedies. In large part, this is because a significant objective of developed countries and their investors in seeking investor–state arbitration in IIAs was to avoid having to rely on domestic courts in the host state for relief.

Including an exhaustion of local remedies requirement may be perceived negatively by capital-exporting states and their investors as a result. Nevertheless, as indicated, there are a significant number of possible benefits associated with forcing investors to seek relief in the host state, including early resolution of many claims, resort to a process in which the decision-makers have expertise in local law and local conditions, and giving investors a stake in the improvement of host state institutions. A possible compromise position adopted in some treaties is to limit the time that an investor must pursue local remedies before they can make an investor–state claim.

A disadvantage of an exhaustion of local remedies requirement from a host state's point of view is that it sets up the possibility that the state will have to defend itself in domestic courts for some time, and then find itself re-litigating the investor's claim in investor–state arbitration. To avoid this possibility, some IIAs include a 'fork in the road' provision, under which an investor must choose to pursue investor–state arbitration or domestic relief. Once the choice is made, the investor can never pursue relief through another procedure. While this does not create any impediment to investor–state arbitration, it does eliminate the prospect of multiple sequential claims by an investor using different procedures.

ii. Waivers of other claims

Another approach to limiting the risk of multiple claims by investors is to require that they waive their right to pursue other relief in other fora as a condition of being able to make an investor–state claim. This approach is found in many IIAs, including the Canadian and US models.

Another issue relating to the risk of multiple claims is the possibility of claims under other investment treaties entered into by the host state by entities that are affiliated with an investor that is making a claim. This might occur, for example, where an investment is ultimately controlled by a parent corporation incorporated in one state through a series of intermediate subsidiaries incorporated in other states. It is possible that, under IIAs between the host state and the country of each of these entities, each entity could bring a claim based on the same host state measure. While an investor–state tribunal might consider that bringing multiple claims under multiple treaties was an abuse of process, it may be reluctant to strike out the claim it is hearing, since it only has jurisdiction over that claim. A provision could be included in an IIA that contains a waiver of claims by affiliated corporations related to the same measure.

iii. Consultations and ADR procedures

Virtually all agreements provide that some period, usually six months, must expire after the events giving rise to a claim before an investor can file an investor–state claim. Most agreements provide that this is a period in which the parties should attempt to settle their dispute amicably.

Some IIAs contemplate that the parties may agree to try to resolve their dispute through mediation, conciliation or an undefined category of third party assisted negotiation. For the most part, these ADR procedures have not been used. There are some inherent impediments to the use of ADR procedures to reach a settlement with an investor, especially where the investor is complaining about a measure put in place to achieve an important public policy objective through legislation or some other formal government procedure that may be difficult for the host state to change. Another barrier is a lack of knowledge and experience regarding ADR procedures among host states and investors.

The nature of many ADR procedures is that both parties must agree to their use if they are to be effective. Their desirability and feasibility are likely to vary with the circumstances. As a consequence, while it is possible to contemplate the possibility of the parties using ADR procedures in an IIA, it may not be helpful to make them mandatory.

Undoubtedly, in practice, ADR procedures, as well as dispute prevention policies, can play a useful role in reducing the duration, cost and frequency of disputes between investors and host states and providing ways to deal with disputes that are more likely to preserve the relationship between an investor and the host state. In order to make use of these strategies, however, states will have to develop capacity and expertise related to them.

iv. Limitation periods

Many treaties now contain time limits after which an investor is prohibited from bringing a claim. Limitation periods provide certainty and finality for states regarding their liability risk.

c. Limitations in the form of additional institutional requirements to ensure the fairness and quality of the process.

i. Specify arbitral rules

Most treaties provide that the investor may choose from a list of arbitral rules, usually including the rules under ICSID Convention and the UNCITRAL Arbitration Rules. While this has become accepted in IIA practice, some treaties provide a single set of rules. Such an approach may make the process somewhat more predictable for states, since they will know in advance what rules will apply. More important, however, a state should provide in the treaty itself any procedural requirement that it views as necessary and that is not adequately addressed in the possibly applicable arbitral rules.

ii. Require tribunals to rule on challenges to jurisdiction and objections that an investor's claim is frivolous before proceeding to the merits

In order to avoid the costs associated with written arguments and hearings on an investor–state claim that a tribunal ultimately finds to be frivolous or outside its jurisdiction, a few recent IIAs require that tribunals address both kinds of preliminary objection before proceeding to the merits of the claim. In principle, there is no obvious objection to the early resolution of these issues. Both parties may benefit. In practice, however, it may be hard for tribunals to make these assessments without the benefit of extensive submissions by the parties in some cases. In these cases, some of the expected cost savings may be reduced.

iii. Set standards for arbitrators and their appointment

Few IIAs create standards to be met by arbitrators in terms of competence or independence. While most arbitral rules impose some standards for independence as well as procedures to challenge arbitrators who do not meet them, the Canadian model agreement goes farther than most treaties to describe such standards. The Canadian treaty model, however, refers only to independence and general competence in international investment law and, in the case of issues related to financial services, in financial services. Given the various other kinds of policy issues that have to be addressed in investor–state cases, it may be that other kinds of expertise should be provided for as well. IIA provisions could also incorporate more specific standards for independence and requirements related to disclosure of interests by arbitrators; requirements for arbitrator protection of confidentiality during and after the arbitration; and restrictions on arbitrators representing the parties to a dispute for a period of time after the completion of an arbitration. Such provisions could draw on the code of conduct for members of state-to-state dispute settlement panels established under NAFTA and the International Bar Association Guidelines on Conflicts of Interest in International Arbitration.

Another approach to ensuring the quality of arbitrators is to establish a roster from which arbitrators are to be selected. The party states may agree on members of the roster or, as in some other contexts, each party could provide a set number of nominees. Such a pre-approved roster would contribute to consistency in decision making as well as ensuring that arbitrators have the qualities that the parties desire. To address the shortage of arbitrators from developing countries, IIAs could require the provision of technical assistance for arbitrator training.

None of these kinds of provisions should raise concerns among capital-exporting states or their investors.

iv. Create a permanent dispute settlement body and/or appellate body

Even with standards for arbitrators, ad hoc investment arbitration does not provide the significant institutional guarantees of independence that are found in domestic judicial systems. In order to establish these kinds of guarantees, it would be necessary to provide for a permanent dispute settlement body and/or a permanent appellate body with the authority to overturn tribunal decisions, the members of which have the benefit of such guarantees. The appointment of permanent decision-makers would help to improve the consistency and quality of investor–state decisions as well.

Investors are unlikely to be greatly concerned about creating such permanent institutions, except to the extent that it results in delays and increased expense in obtaining a final disposition of their claim. There are resource implications for states related to establishing permanent institutions that would have to be considered by states. These will be greatest where bodies are established for the purpose of a single bilateral IIA, but might be mitigated in regional institutions with responsibilities for disputes under multiple IIAs.

v. Establish requirements for transparency and *amicus curiae* participation

Greater transparency and involvement of civil society in investor–state arbitration as *amici curiae* enhance the democratic accountability of states for what occurs in dispute settlement. Participation of *amici curiae* may also help to improve the awareness of arbitration tribunals regarding policy considerations beyond the protection and promotion of investment. For these reasons, transparency and *amicus curiae* participation contribute to the legitimacy of the investor–state dispute settlement procedures and to ensuring that it is a process that promotes sustainable development.

At the same time, greater transparency and the prospect of responding to *amicus curiae* submissions impose additional burdens on investors participating in investor–state arbitration and, as a consequence, may reduce the attractiveness of the process to them. Some states may be hesitant about committing to transparency because making documents and proceedings publicly accessible is not required in their domestic legal systems. Even fewer states provide for *amicus curiae* participation in domestic judicial proceedings. While there appears to be a growing willingness to undertake transparency commitments, the involvement of *amici curiae* in investor–state cases remains controversial.

Only a few IIAs, including the Canadian and US models, contain explicit requirements for transparency and *amicus curiae* participation. Even these models, however, do not require disclosure of agreements to settle investor–state cases.

vi. Permit consolidation of multiple claims based on the same or similar issues of fact or law

A procedure for the consolidation of claims based on the same or similar issues of fact or law appears in some recent IIAs. It can have benefits for states. Multiple claims raising the same issues can be dealt with more efficiently in a single arbitration and the prospect of inconsistent results in similar or identical cases is avoided. In practice, investors may object to losing control of their case by having to co-ordinate their claim with other similarly situated investors. Nevertheless, the NAFTA experience suggests that consolidation will be used infrequently in practice and the inclusion of consolidation in an IIA is unlikely to be a significant concern for investors or capital-exporting states.

d. Limitations on the damages that can be awarded

Damages in investor–state arbitration are generally intended to compensate the investor for the loss that they have suffered as a consequence of the breach of an IIA provision. Nevertheless, there are several rules that may be adopted to reduce the burden of damage awards:

i. Reducing damage awards where
   - The investor's conduct contributed to the losses suffered;
   - The investor did not take reasonable steps to mitigate its losses;
   - The state's action breached rules that the tribunal determines were unclear or subject to conflicting interpretation;

ii. Declining to award damages where the breach by the state does not surpass some minimum threshold of seriousness;

iii. Limiting compensation to direct losses, not including loss of future profits, and prohibiting the calculation of compensation based on the discounted value of future cash flows to avoid the risk of speculative damages being awarded;

iv. Requiring a period following a finding of state liability to permit the parties to negotiate the amount of damages;

v. Permitting payment of damages to be delayed in some circumstances based on hardship to the host state;

vi. Prohibiting punitive or moral damages; and

vii. Imposing requirements that damages be proved.

Reducing damages on the basis of contributory fault and a failure to mitigate damages are general principles recognised in international law that have been applied in some investor–state cases. Nevertheless, neither is identified specifically as a principle to govern the award of compensation in IIAs, with the exception of the COMESA Investment Agreement. While these principles may often be applied in any case by investor–state tribunals, referring to them specifically ensures that every tribunal will take them into account.

Reducing damages where the applicable IIA standard is uncertain, excluding damages unless some minimum threshold of seriousness is met and limiting compensation to direct losses are not accepted international principles that have been endorsed in investor–state cases or the expression of these limitations on damages in an IIA, though both have some basis in investor–state practice. Imposing vague and untested threshold requirements for the seriousness of the breach by the state and the certainty of the IIA standard violated may be seen by capital-exporting states and their investors as leaving too much discretion in the hands of an investor–state tribunal.

Limiting compensation to direct losses removes the prospect that a host state will be held liable for speculative future profits, but investors may view a blanket exclusion as arbitrary, since it would extend to situations where a state measure made impossible the continued operation of a business with a demonstrated and consistent record of earning profits or caused a reduction from well-established profit levels. In such a situation, investors would undoubtedly view the present value of those certain future profits as a part of their loss that should be compensated.

Prohibiting awards of punitive damages, as is done in some treaties, may be justified on under general principles of international law that require damages for breaches of international law to be compensatory. Prohibiting awards of moral damages to compensate for non-economic losses, by contrast, is not supported under international law. Moral damages have been sought and, in at least one investor–state case, awarded. While they may be rarely appropriate in investor–state cases and unpredictable, mental suffering and other kinds of non-economic losses will be suffered by investors in some cases. Capital-exporting states and their investors may value the possibility of awards of moral damages to discourage states from mistreating investors and their personnel.

An IIA could provide that the state and the investor should have a period of time to negotiate compensation prior to an award of damages by the tribunal. Though this could occur in practice in any case, an express provision ensures that a tribunal delays its assessment of damages following a finding of state liability to permit the state to negotiate the compensation to be paid. It may also be useful to provide for situations in which payment of compensation by the state may be delayed, including, for example, a financial crisis. A delay in this specific situation may be permitted based on exceptions in the agreement in some circumstances, such as a prudential exception.

It may be useful to expressly indicate that the investor has an obligation to prove all elements of its claim, including damages suffered, and to show that the losses were sustained by reason of the host state's breach of its IIA obligations. Such a requirement is consistent with general principles of law applicable to international arbitration and is included in some IIAs.

Where any of the limitations discussed above are incorporated into an IIA, it is possible that a host state obligation to give investors from the other party state the benefit of a more favourable procedure would be incorporated into the IIA if (i) the treaty contained an MFN clause and (ii) the host state had entered into another IIA that provided more favourable investor–state procedures.[181]

3. *Permit counterclaims by states and limitations on access to dispute settlement for investors that have breached their obligations under an IIA*

Where an IIA imposes obligations on investors, access to investor–state arbitration could be denied where an investor has failed to comply with its obligations. Alternatively, a host state against which a claim has been made could be given the right to make a counterclaim for losses suffered by it or its people as a consequence of the investor's failure to comply. Counterclaims may be used in other circumstances to the extent permitted by the IIA and the applicable arbitral rules. Counterclaims were discussed above.[182]

Counterclaim awards may be set off against any damages awarded to an investor in an investor–state case, but if the investor is not successful a counterclaim award must still be paid. There are a variety of situations in which investors may avoid paying damages awarded to a state under a counterclaim. This will be especially likely if the investor's claim is unsuccessful and the investor must find funds to pay the counterclaim award. In some cases, the investor may have few assets. This is a real risk since transnational businesses often have complex structures where multiple entities together carry on business. Within the group, the entity making the claim may not have been allocated significant assets. This might have been done for the purpose of limiting its ability to pay damages claimed by the state. This problem is discussed in detail above.[183] In addition to the options discussed, another way to address this problem might be to make the investor's state responsible for paying the damages if the investor is unable to pay after some period of time. No treaty has adopted this approach.

4. *Agree to investor–state arbitration for all claims by an investor against a host state through an umbrella clause, with or without the other limitations in options 2 and 3*

This is the broadest protection for investors, but creates a serious risk that investors will be able to pursue claims in multiple fora, including domestic courts and dispute settlement procedures agreed to in contracts with the state as well as treaty-based investor–state dispute settlement. To some extent, the risk of multiple claims can be reduced by fork in the road, waiver and other provisions.

A state's exposure to liability under an umbrella clause is broad and unpredictable. In most cases, an investor will have other remedial options to address state actions and may not require the additional option of treaty-based investor–state arbitration. As a result, the benefits to investors may be marginal, while the costs to host states may be substantial.

181 See Section 5.4 (Most favoured nation).

182 See Section 6.17 (Counterclaims by states in investor–state arbitration).

183 See Sections 6.13 (Enforcement of investor obligations) and 6.16 (Civil liability of investors).

7.1.6 Discussion of sample provisions

Some form of investor–state dispute settlement is included in most IIAs. Agreements that include investor–state procedures demonstrate a strong commitment to a pro-investment environment. Increasing dissatisfaction with investor–state arbitration, however, has caused a few states to reject it and many others to reconsider IIA provisions that establish and govern such procedures. Some states may decide that not committing to investor–state arbitration is the best choice. Other states may continue to agree to investor–state arbitration because of the protection afforded to its investors, in the hope of attracting more investment or as a concession to negotiating partners. The sample provision provides an example of a set of investor–state arbitration provisions that incorporate existing or emerging best practices from a sustainable development perspective and some new provisions that attempt to address some of the concerns that have been raised above.

Detailed specification of obligations

As noted, in overall design, investor–state dispute settlement procedures vary significantly in terms of the amount of detail in which the procedures are specified. In the UK and Indian models, relatively few details are provided. By comparison, the Canadian and US models are much more comprehensive.[184] In recent treaties, such as the COMESA Investment Agreement, the ASEAN–Australia–New Zealand FTA Investment Chapter and the ASEAN Agreement, more detailed rules are provided. The approach taken in the Guide sample provisions has been to provide detailed and specific procedures to give greater certainty and to put more control of the process into the hands of party states.[185] In addition, strict and specific time limits govern the dispute resolution process to help to ensure that it proceeds expeditiously.

Claims only permitted on the basis of listed investor protection provisions in the IIA

With a view to avoiding multiple investor claims in different fora arising out of the same facts and adding certainty to the scope of host state responsibility, the sample provisions provide that investors can seek relief only on the basis that the host state has breached identified investor protection provisions in the IIA and the investor has suffered a loss as a result. An umbrella clause permitting an investor to use the investor–state process in the treaty in relation to any dispute that the investor may have with the host state has not been included.

In accordance with the practice in most IIAs, claims by enterprises incorporated or organised under the laws of the host state and controlled by investors eligible for IIA protection cannot be brought under the investor–state procedure. Only claims by investors for losses that they have suffered themselves can be made.

---

184 Compare Canadian model FIPA, Arts. 20–47, and US model BIT, Arts. 23–36, with UK model IPPA, Art., 8 and Indian model BIPPA, Art. 9. The draft Norwegian APPI provides more details than the UK and Indian models but fewer than the models of Canada and the United States (draft Norwegian APPI, Art. 15.3).

185 UNCTAD (2007), *Treaties 1996–2006*, op. cit., identifies this as a trend, at 120.

Limits on access to investor–state arbitration through procedural prerequisites

The sample provisions impose limits on investor access to investor–state arbitration:

- **Access to investor–state dispute settlement is conditional on the exhaustion of local remedies, but this requirement is subject to a time limit of three years, following the approach in the draft Norwegian model agreement:**[186] After three years have expired since the investor first filed its claim in a domestic court, if the investor is still not satisfied with the result, it may make an investor–state claim. An exception to this three-year period is provided where there is no reasonably available domestic remedy. This approach reflects investors' interest in having access to an alternative to domestic litigation in the host state, but requires a substantial prior effort to seek relief in domestic courts. A fork in the road provision is a possible alternative that creates no barrier to investor–state claims, but ensures that an investor will be able to pursue only either a domestic remedy or an investor–state claim.
- **The investor must waive all rights to pursue a claim based on the same facts in any other forum:** This provision goes some way to reducing the incidence of multiple claims and follows the approach in the Canadian and US model agreements.
- **Investor claims are subject to a five-year limitation period:** A limitation on the period within which an investor may bring a claim provides certainty and finality for states regarding their liability risk. The five-year period in the sample provision is longer than the three-year period adopted in the Canadian and IISD models in order to accommodate the requirement that investors must seek to exhaust local remedies for at least three years.

Consultations are also required. ADR is permitted but not mandatory because most ADR procedures require the consent and co-operation of both parties to be successful. All of these requirements for the initiation of an investor–state claim are characterised as conditions of the jurisdiction of an arbitral tribunal.

Early decisions on jurisdictional challenges and a host state's objection that investor's claim is frivolous are required

The sample provision requires investor–state tribunals to make preliminary rulings on issues of jurisdiction raised by host states and on host state objections that an investor's claim is frivolous prior to addressing the substantive merits of an investor's claim in order to ensure that cases are terminated at the earliest possible stage at the least cost. This approach is followed in a number of existing IIAs.

Consolidation of multiple investor claims permitted

A sample provision creating a process for the consolidation of claims, which is found in the Canadian and US model treaties, as well as some other IIAs, is included because

186 Draft Norwegian APPI, Art. 15.3.

of the potential cost-saving benefits for host states and the desirability of avoiding the risk of conflicting decisions. Consolidation is not mandatory, however, and may be ordered by a tribunal only if it is satisfied that the benefits exceed the costs.

Transparency required and amicus curiae participation permitted

As noted, the newest models for IIAs, including the draft Norwegian agreement, the COMESA Investment Agreement and the Canadian and American model agreements, contain extensive provisions requiring transparency in investor–state proceedings and rules permitting, on certain conditions, the submission of *amicus curiae* briefs by interested parties. The Guide sample provisions include requirements for transparency and a procedure for tribunals to consider applications from interested persons to make *amicus curiae* submissions in the interests of ensuring public accountability.

In most cases, *amicus curiae* submissions will be in support of the state and could complicate and delay the resolution of an investor's claim. Nevertheless, experience under NAFTA suggests that permitting *amicus curiae* participation does not fundamentally undermine the benefits of investor–state dispute settlement for investors. The Guide sample provisions also contain clauses designed to ensure that the investor's interest in a speedy and efficient resolution of its claim is not abused by *amicus curiae* participation, such as a requirement to obtain leave of the tribunal and limits on the length of submissions.

Arbitrator qualifications

In order to ensure that arbitrators have the appropriate independence and expertise, requirements for both are specified in the sample provisions. The party states are also permitted to adopt a code of conduct for arbitrators and to make rules to govern investor–state arbitration. Requirements for arbitrators (i) to disclose conflicts of interest, (ii) to protect confidentiality during and after the arbitration and (iii) not to represent either of the parties for one year after the completion of the arbitration are included in the sample provision. These requirements are based on the NAFTA code of conduct for panellists in state-to-state dispute settlement proceedings.

In addition, it is provided that a roster is to be appointed by the party states, from which arbitrators are to be chosen. This will help to ensure that arbitrators have the characteristics that the party states desire. The number of members of the roster is set at 40, with each party entitled to appoint 20. While these numbers are somewhat arbitrary and may be changed to suit the views of particular negotiating parties, they are consistent with the approach taken in some other agreements.[187] The discussion of technical assistance below addresses the use of such assistance to provide training to developing country arbitrators to help create a pool from which roster members may be chosen.[188]

187 NAFTA (1992) contemplates a roster of 45 (15 appointed by each party state) for investor–state dispute settlement (Art. 1125.4).

188 See Section 8.2 (Technical assistance).

Limits on damages

Damages may be reduced where the investor was partly responsible for the losses it suffered or failed to take reasonable steps to mitigate the losses that it suffered: Consistent with general principles of law and some investor–state tribunal practice, the sample provisions provide that damages awarded to an investor may be reduced where the investor was partly responsible for the losses it suffered or failed to take reasonable steps to mitigate the losses that it suffered.

Damages are limited to an investor's direct losses: A limitation on damages to those needed to compensate the investor for direct losses, excluding loss of future profits and prohibiting the calculation of compensation based on the discounted value of future cash flows, is also included in the sample provisions. This limitation has some basis in the investor–state jurisprudence on expropriation and there will be cases in which it would be appropriate to apply such a limitation to breaches of other obligations. Nevertheless, there will be cases where an investor's actual loss will reasonably include future profits.[189]

No punitive or moral damages may be awarded: These categories of damages typically have not been awarded in investor–state cases to date. Punitive damages are generally not awarded for violations of international law.

Damages are awarded only where a state's breach of its obligations exceeds a minimum threshold for seriousness: An investor may not recover damages where the breach does not meet a minimum threshold for seriousness as determined by the tribunal. The last requirement is not well established in investor–state tribunal practice, but is based on practice before the European Court of Justice.

An obligation for tribunals to reduce damages where, in the tribunal's view, the liability of the host state is based on an obligation that was not certain and predictable at the time that the state acted was not included. It has no clear basis in principle or arbitral decisions. The discussion of the substantive investor protection obligations elsewhere in the Guide provides some suggestions for making these obligations more certain and their application more predictable.

Tribunals have discretion to delay obligation to pay damages: The sample provision gives a tribunal discretion to permit a delay in payment in situations where payment would be a significant hardship for the state. This may be especially important for small and vulnerable countries. An opportunity to negotiate compensation following an arbitral tribunal's determination of state liability and prior to an assessment of damages is also provided.

Investor has burden of proving damages: The sample provision clarifies that an investor that makes a claim has the burden of proving all elements of its claim,

---

189 This limitation on damages and the previous one were included in the sample expropriation provision. If they were incorporated in a damages provision relating to all investor–state arbitrations, there would be no need to duplicate these provisions in the expropriation provision. See Section 5.6 (Limitations on expropriation and nationalisation).

including the damages that it alleges were sustained as a consequence of the alleged breach. This reflects the approach taken in investor–state cases and general principles of international arbitration.

No permanent dispute resolution body

A permanent dispute resolution body and/or a permanent appellate body would help to improve the consistency and quality of investor–state decisions, as well as providing a way of putting in place institutional guarantees of independence that are lacking in the current system of investor–state arbitration. Investors are unlikely to be greatly concerned about creating permanent institutions, except to the extent that doing so results in delays and increased expense in obtaining a final disposition of their claims. Nevertheless, the Guide does not contain sample provisions establishing a permanent dispute settlement body or appellate review. This is because the resource implications for states related to establishing and maintaining permanent institutions are likely to make it infeasible, except in particular circumstances, such as in the context of a regional integration agreement where it would be possible to create institutions with responsibilities for disputes under multiple IIAs. The COMESA Investment Agreement provides an example of a regional institution, the COMESA Court of Justice, which may provide a model.[190] The IISD model treaty also has a well-developed model for a permanent dispute resolution body and an appellate body.[191]

Parties can issue binding interpretations

Consistency in decision making can be addressed to some extent by allowing a body established under the IIA to provide authoritative interpretations of the agreement. The power to issue binding interpretations gives the party states more direct control over the development of the standards in the agreement without the resource commitments associated with creating a standing dispute resolution or appellate body. The Guide sample provision provides an example of how this can be done.[192] The use of a roster may also assist in promoting high-quality, consistent decisions.

Counterclaims by states in investor–state arbitration are provided for

The considerations relevant to counterclaims were discussed above in Section 6.17 (Counterclaims by states in investor–state arbitrations). In the interests of consistency, the same rules for the assessment of damages that apply to awards of damages to investors apply to awards of damages in counterclaims, except that moral damages may be awarded. This difference is to address the fact that violations of some home state laws or treaty requirements related to areas such as human rights and labour rights will often be associated with the kinds of non-economic losses that moral damages compensate.

As well, the sample provision includes a requirement that the investor's host state will pay damages awarded in a counterclaim to the extent that the investor has not paid

190 COMESA Investment Agreement (2007), Art. 28.
191 IISD model treaty, Art. 40.
192 See also Section 9.2 (Commission).

them within 12 months of the award. While undoubtedly such a state guarantee will be resisted strongly by capital-exporting states, it does provide a strong incentive for investors' home states to encourage their investors operating abroad to comply with their obligations, including paying any counterclaim award made against them.

Other features of the sample provisions

Several other features have been included in the sample provisions to make the dispute resolution process more predictable and effective:

- Investor's claims can relate only to state actions that occur after the IIA comes into force;
- A form is provided for notices of intent to file a claim to ensure that host states receive adequate information regarding the nature of the claim;
- The identity of any third party funders of an investor's claim must be identified by the investor;
- Home state insurers are subrogated to the rights of investors where they have paid compensation to the investor for a host state's action;
- Arbitral tribunals may seek advice from experts;
- Party states, other than the one responding to a claim, are permitted to make submissions on issues raised by the claim that are related to the interpretation of the agreement; and
- The Commission (a ministerial level body composed of representatives of both party states)[193] can cap the level of arbitrators' fees.[194]

Some other provisions have been included to ensure that the dispute settlement provisions are consistent with applicable arbitral rules.

7.1.7 Sample provisions: investor–state dispute settlement

[Note: All references to other sample provisions from the Guide in these sample provisions are for convenience and illustrative purposes only and not recommendations that any particular provision be included in an IIA.]

Part [X]

Settlement of Disputes between an Investor and a Party[195]

---

193 See also Section 9.2 (Commission).

194 Capping fees at the ICSID maximum of US$3,000 per day was recently recommended by the European Union.

195 For the purposes of these provisions '*Party*' means a state party to the treaty, '*disputing Party*' means a party state against which a claim has been made by an investor, '*disputing party*' or '*disputing investor*' means an investor that has filed a claim, '*disputing parties*' means both the investor making the claim and the state against which a claim has been made, '*non-disputing Party*' means the state party to the treaty other than the state against which a clam has been made and '*non-disputing party*' means a person who has been given permission to file a non-disputing party submission.

Article [A]

Purpose

Without prejudice to the rights and obligations of the Parties under [Guide sample provision in Section 7.2 (State-to-state dispute settlement)], this Part establishes a mechanism for the settlement of investment disputes.

Article [B]

Claim by an Investor of a Party

An investor of a Party may submit to arbitration under this Part a claim that the other Party has breached an obligation under [Guide sample provision in Section 5.3 (National treatment)], [Guide sample provision in Section 5.4 (Most favoured nation)], [Guide sample provision in Section 5.5 (Fair and equitable treatment and the minimum standard of treatment)], [Guide sample provision in Section 5.6 (Limitations on expropriation and nationalisation)], [Guide sample provision in Section 5.7 (Compensation for losses)] and [Guide sample provision in Section 5.8 (Free transfer of funds)] by a measure that becomes effective after this agreement has come into force and that the investor has incurred loss or damage by reason of, or arising out of, that breach.

Article [C]

Notice of Intent to Submit a Claim to Arbitration

1. The disputing investor shall deliver to the disputing Party written notice of its intent to submit a claim to arbitration at least 90 days before the claim is submitted, which notice shall specify:
    a. The name and address of the disputing investor;
    b. The provisions of this Agreement alleged to have been breached and any other relevant provisions;
    c. The issues and the factual basis for the claim, including the measures at issue; and
    d. The relief sought and the approximate amount of damages claimed.
2. The disputing investor shall also deliver, with its Notice of Intent to Submit a Claim to Arbitration, evidence establishing that it is an investor of the other Party.

Article [D]

Settlement of a Claim through Consultation

1. Before a disputing investor may submit a claim to arbitration under this Part, the disputing parties shall first hold consultations in an attempt to settle the claim amicably.
2. Consultations shall be held within 30 days of the submission of the Notice of Intent to Submit a Claim to Arbitration, unless the disputing parties otherwise agree.

3. The place of consultation shall be the capital of the disputing Party, unless the disputing parties otherwise agree.

4. At any time, the disputing parties may agree to use any non-binding dispute resolution procedures, including mediation, fact finding and conciliation, with a view to settling a dispute.

Article [E]

Conditions Precedent to Submission of a Claim to Arbitration

1. A disputing investor may submit a claim to arbitration under Article [B] (claim by an investor of a Party) only if:

    a. The investor consents to arbitration in accordance with the procedures set out in this Agreement, including to arbitration of any counterclaim by the disputing Party under Article [W] (counterclaims);

    b. At least six months have elapsed since the events giving rise to the claim;

    c. Not more than five years have elapsed from the date on which the investor first acquired, or should have first acquired, knowledge of the alleged breach and knowledge that the investor has incurred loss or damage thereby;

    d. The investor can demonstrate that local remedies in the disputing Party have been exhausted, provided that the investor does not need to satisfy this requirement if the investor can demonstrate that there are no reasonably available local remedies to provide effective redress to the investor for losses resulting from the alleged breach referred to in Article [B] (claim by an investor of a Party); or more than 36 months have passed since the investor has made a claim in a local court in the disputing Party in relation to the measure that is the basis of the alleged breach, after having exhausted any administrative remedies in the disputing Party;

    e. The investor has delivered the Notice of Intent to Submit a Claim to Arbitration required under Article [C] (notice of intent to submit a claim to arbitration) in accordance with the requirements of that Article at least 90 days prior to submitting the claim;

    f. The investor and, where the claim is for loss or damage to an interest in an enterprise of the other Party that is a juridical person that the investor owns or controls directly or indirectly, the enterprise waive their right to initiate or continue before any administrative tribunal or court under the law of any Party, or other dispute settlement procedures, any proceedings with respect to the measure of the disputing Party that is alleged to be a breach referred to in Article [B] (claim by an investor of a party), except for proceedings for injunctive, declaratory or other extraordinary relief not involving the payment of damages, before an administrative tribunal or court under the law of the disputing Party; and

    g. It identifies any government, person or organisation (a 'third party funder') that has provided or agreed to provide any financial or other assistance to the investor in connection with the claim or has an interest in the outcome of the claim, including the following information:

i. its membership and legal status (e.g. company, trade association or other non-governmental organisation), its general objectives, the nature of its activities, and any parent organisation (including any organisation that directly or indirectly controls the third party funder);

ii. whether the third party funder has any affiliation, direct or indirect, with any disputing party; and

iii. the nature of the interest that the third party funder has in the arbitration.

2. A consent and waiver required by this Article shall be delivered to the disputing Party and shall be included in the submission of a claim to arbitration.

3. A waiver under section 1f. from the enterprise owned or controlled by the investor shall not be required only where a disputing Party has deprived a disputing investor of control of the enterprise.

4. Failure to meet any of the conditions precedent provided for in sections 1 through 3 shall nullify the consent of the Parties given in Article [G] (consent to arbitration).

Article [F]

Submission of a Claim to Arbitration

1. A disputing investor of a Party who meets the conditions precedent provided for in Article [E] (conditions precedent to submission of a claim to arbitration) may submit a claim to arbitration under:

a. The ICSID Convention provided that both the disputing Party and the Party of the disputing investor are parties to the Convention;

b. The Additional Facility Rules of ICSID provided that either the disputing Party or the Party of the disputing investor, but not both, is a party to the ICSID Convention;

c. The UNCITRAL Arbitration Rules as they exist at the time the investor submits its claim; or

d. Any other body of rules approved by the Commission as available for arbitrations under this Part.

2. The Commission shall have the power to make rules supplementing the applicable arbitral rules and may amend any rules of its own making. Such rules shall be binding on a Tribunal established under this Part and on individual arbitrators serving on such Tribunals.

3. The applicable arbitration rules shall govern the arbitration except to the extent modified by this Part and supplemented by any rules adopted by the Commission under this Part.

Article [G]

Consent to Arbitration

1. Each Party consents to the submission of a claim to arbitration in accordance with the procedures set out in this Agreement, including Article [W] (counterclaims).
2. The consent given in section 1 and the submission by a disputing investor of a claim to arbitration shall satisfy the requirement of:
   a. Chapter II of the ICSID Convention (Jurisdiction of the Centre) and the Additional Facility Rules for written consent of the parties; and
   b. Article II of the New York Convention for an agreement in writing.

Article [H]

Arbitrators

1. Except in respect of a Tribunal established under Article [K] (consolidation), and unless the disputing parties agree otherwise, the Tribunal shall comprise three arbitrators, one arbitrator appointed by each of the disputing parties and the third, who shall be the presiding arbitrator, appointed by agreement of the disputing parties.
2. Arbitrators shall:
   a. Have expertise or experience in public international law, international trade or international investment rules, or the resolution of disputes arising under international trade or international investment agreements;
   b. Be independent of, and not be affiliated with or take instructions from, either Party or the disputing party;
   c. Comply with Annex [H].1 and any Code of Conduct for Dispute Settlement adopted by the Commission; and
   d. Be chosen from the roster established under this article.
3. Where a disputing investor claims that a dispute involves measures adopted or maintained by a Party relating to financial institutions of the other Party, or investors of the other Party and investments of such investors, in financial institutions in a Party's territory, then:
   a. Where the disputing parties are in agreement, the arbitrators shall, in addition to meeting the criteria set out in section 2, have expertise or experience in financial services law or practice, which may include the regulation of financial institutions; or
   b. Where the disputing parties are not in agreement,
      i. each disputing party may select arbitrators who meet the qualifications set out in subsection 3a., and
      ii. if the Party complained against invokes [Guide sample provision in Section 5.8 (Free transfer of funds)] or [prudential measures exception in Guide

sample provision in Section 5.12 (Reservations and exceptions)], the chair of the panel shall meet the qualifications set out in subsection (a).

4. Where a Party claims that a dispute (including a counterclaim under Article [W] (counterclaims)) involves measures relating to the protection of human rights, labour rights or the rights of indigenous peoples or the environment or the interpretation of the domestic law of a Party:

   a. Where the disputing parties are in agreement, the arbitrators shall, in addition to meeting the criteria set out in section 2, have expertise or experience in the relevant area of law or practice; or

   b. Where the disputing parties are not in agreement, each disputing party may select arbitrators who meet the qualifications set out in subsection 4a.

5. The Parties shall establish a roster of [40] arbitrators for the purposes of conducting arbitrations under the Agreement. Each Party shall nominate [20] individuals to the roster who shall meet the requirements of subsections 2a., b. and c.

6. The disputing parties should agree upon the arbitrators' remuneration. If the disputing parties do not agree on such remuneration before the constitution of the Tribunal, the prevailing ICSID rate for arbitrators shall apply.

7. The Commission may establish rules relating to expenses incurred by the Tribunal and maximum fees that may be paid to arbitrators.

Article [I]

Constitution of a Tribunal When a Party Fails to Appoint an Arbitrator or the Disputing Parties Are Unable to Agree on a Presiding Arbitrator

1. The President of the International Court of Justice shall serve as appointing authority for an arbitration under this section. If the President is a national of either Party or is otherwise prevented from discharging the appointment function, the Vice-President of the International Court of Justice shall be invited to make the necessary appointments. If the Vice-President is a national of either Party or is otherwise prevented from discharging the appointment function, the member of the International Court of Justice next in seniority who is not a national of either Party shall be invited to make the necessary appointments.

2. If a Tribunal, other than a Tribunal established under Article [K] (consolidation), has not been constituted within 90 days from the date that a claim is submitted to arbitration, the President of the International Court of Justice, on the request of either disputing party, shall appoint, in his or her discretion, the arbitrator or arbitrators not yet appointed from the roster established under Article [H] (arbitrators), except that the presiding arbitrator shall not be a national of either Party. In making any such appointment, the President of the International Court of Justice shall ensure that any agreement of the disputing parties or any preference expressed by either of the disputing parties under Article [H] (arbitrators) in relation to the expertise, experience or independence of the arbitrators is given effect.

3. If no roster has been established under Article [H] (arbitrators) or no person on the roster is available to be appointed in accordance with the requirements of this Article, the President shall appoint another person who meets the requirements of subsections 2a., b. and c. of Article [H] (arbitrators) and this Article.

Article [J]

Agreement to Appointment of Arbitrators

For purposes of Article 39 of the ICSID Convention and Article 7 of Schedule C to the ICSID Additional Facility Rules, and without prejudice to an objection to an arbitrator based on a ground other than citizenship or permanent residence:

a. The disputing Party agrees to the appointment of each individual member of a Tribunal established under the ICSID Convention or the ICSID Additional Facility Rules; and

b. A disputing investor referred to in Article [B] (claim by an investor of a Party) may submit a claim to arbitration, or continue a claim, under the ICSID Convention or the ICSID Additional Facility Rules, only on condition that the disputing investor agrees in writing to the appointment of each individual member of the Tribunal.

Article [K]

Consolidation

1. A Tribunal established under this Article shall be established under the UNCITRAL Arbitration Rules and shall conduct its proceedings in accordance with those Rules, except as modified by this Part.

2. Where a Tribunal established under this Article is satisfied that claims submitted to arbitration under Article [F] (submission of a claim to arbitration) have a question of law or fact in common, the Tribunal may, in the interests of the fair and efficient resolution of the claims, and after hearing the disputing parties, by order:

   a. Assume jurisdiction over, and hear and determine together, all or part of the claims; or

   b. Assume jurisdiction over, and hear and determine one or more of the claims, the determination of which it believes would assist in the resolution of the others.

3. A disputing party that seeks an order under section 2 shall request the President of the International Court of Justice to establish a Tribunal and shall specify in the request:

   a. The name of the disputing Party and/or disputing investors against which the order is sought;

   b. The nature of the order sought; and

   c. The grounds on which the order is sought.

4. The disputing party shall deliver to the disputing Party and/or disputing investors against which the order is sought a copy of the request.

5. Within 60 days of receipt of the request, the President of the International Court of Justice shall establish a Tribunal comprising three arbitrators. The President shall appoint the presiding arbitrator from the roster of arbitrators established under Article [H] (arbitrators) who shall not be a national of any of the Parties. The President shall appoint the two other members of the Tribunal from the roster within the same time period. One member of the Tribunal shall be a national of the disputing Party and one member shall be a national of the Party of the disputing investors.

   If the President is a national of either Party or is otherwise prevented from discharging the appointment function, the Vice-President of the International Court of Justice shall be invited to make the necessary appointments. If the Vice-President is a national of either Party or is otherwise prevented from discharging the appointment function, the member of the International Court of Justice next in seniority who is not a national of either Party shall be invited to make the necessary appointments.

6. Where a Tribunal has been established under this Article, a disputing investor that has submitted a claim to arbitration under Article [F] (submission of a claim to arbitration) and that has not been named in a request made under section 3 may make a written request to the Tribunal that it be included in an order made under section 2, and shall specify in the request:

   a. The name and address of the disputing investor;

   b. The nature of the order sought; and

   c. The grounds on which the order is sought.

7. A disputing investor referred to in section 6 shall deliver a copy of its request to the disputing parties named in a request made under section 3.

8. A Tribunal established under Article [F] (submission of a claim to arbitration) shall not have jurisdiction to decide a claim, or a part of a claim, over which a Tribunal established under this Article has assumed jurisdiction.

9. On application of a disputing Party, a Tribunal established under this Article, pending its decision under section 2, may order that the proceedings of a Tribunal established under Article [F] (submission of a claim to arbitration) be stayed, unless the latter Tribunal has already adjourned its proceedings.

Article [L]

Notice to the Non-Disputing Party

A disputing Party shall deliver to the other Party a copy of the Notice of Intent to Submit a Claim to Arbitration and other documents, such as a Notice of Arbitration and Statement of Claim filed under this Part, no later than 30 days after the date that such documents have been delivered to the disputing Party.

Article [M]

Documents

1. The non-disputing Party shall be entitled, at its cost, to receive from the disputing Party in relation to a claim under this Part a copy of:
   a. The evidence that has been tendered to the Tribunal;
   b. Copies of all pleadings filed in the arbitration; and
   c. The written argument of the disputing parties.
2. The Party receiving information pursuant to section 1 shall treat the information as if it were a disputing Party.

Article [N]

Participation by the Non-Disputing Party

1. On written notice to the disputing parties, the non-disputing Party may make submissions to a Tribunal on a question of interpretation of this Agreement in an arbitration under this Part.
2. The non-disputing Party shall have the right to attend any hearings held under this Part, whether or not it makes submissions to the Tribunal.

Article [O]

Place of Arbitration

Unless the disputing parties agree otherwise, a Tribunal shall hold an arbitration in the territory of a state that is a party to the New York Convention, selected in accordance with:

a. The ICSID Arbitration Rules, if the arbitration is under the ICSID Convention;
b. The ICSID Additional Facility Rules, if the arbitration is under those Rules;
c. The UNCITRAL Arbitration Rules, if the arbitration is under those Rules; and
d. Any other rules governing the arbitration in accordance with this Part.

Article [P]

Preliminary Objections to Jurisdiction or Admissibility or that a Claim is Manifestly without Merit

1. Where an issue relating to jurisdiction or admissibility of a claim is raised as a preliminary objection by a disputing Party or a preliminary objection is made that a claim is manifestly without merit, a Tribunal shall decide on the objection before proceeding to the merits.
2. For greater certainty, the grounds for a preliminary objection include the following:

a. The investor is not an investor within the meaning of this Agreement;

b. The investor has not made or is not making an investment within the meaning of this Agreement; and

c. The investor has not fulfilled one of the conditions precedent to the submission of a claim to arbitration under Article [E] (conditions precedent to submission of a claim to arbitration).

Article [Q]

Public Access to Hearings and Documents

1. Hearings held under this Part shall be open to the public. To the extent necessary to ensure the protection of confidential information, including business confidential information, the Tribunal may hold portions of hearings *in camera*.

2. The Tribunal shall establish procedures for the protection of confidential information and appropriate logistical arrangements for open hearings in consultation with the disputing parties. Where a hearing has been closed to the public, transcripts of the hearings shall be prepared, and all aspects of those transcripts that are not protected from disclosure pursuant to this article shall be made available to the public. The disputing Party shall make public transcripts of hearings in the form and in the language in which it receives them from the Tribunal.

3. All Notices of Intent to Submit a Claim to Arbitration under Article [C] (notice of intent to submit a claim to arbitration) and claims to arbitration under Article [B] (claim by an investor of a Party) shall be made publicly available by the disputing Party in a timely manner, in the form and in the language in which it receives them, subject to the deletion of confidential information.

4. All documents submitted to, or issued by, the Tribunal shall be made publicly available by the disputing Party in a timely manner, in the form and in the language in which it receives them, subject to the deletion of confidential information.

5. Any Tribunal award under this Part shall be made publicly available by the disputing Party, subject to the deletion of confidential information, immediately upon its issue to the disputing parties.

6. If there is a dispute regarding designation of confidential information in documents referred to in section 2, 3, 4 or 5, the Tribunal, once constituted, shall promptly resolve that dispute and make an order regarding what must be disclosed.

7. For the purposes of this article, confidential information is information that is protected against disclosure by this Agreement or applicable law, confidential business information and information that may be designated as confidential by the Tribunal. A disputing party that provides information shall clearly designate whether it contends that the information is confidential at the time it submits the information to the disputing Party, in the case of information in documents referred to in section 3, or at the time it submits information to the Tribunal

in all other cases and shall, at the time it submits a document containing such information, submit a redacted version of the document that does not contain the information. Where the other disputing party disputes that any or all of such information is confidential, it shall so indicate within 30 days of receipt of the redacted document from the other party, identifying with precision the portions of the document that it contends ought not to be redacted. The arbitral tribunal shall then rule on any such objection to the designation or redaction of confidential information.

8. A disputing party may disclose to other persons in connection with the arbitral proceedings such unredacted documents referred to in section 2, 3, 4 or 5 as it considers necessary for the preparation of its case, but it shall ensure that those persons protect the confidential information in such documents.

9. The Parties may share with officials of their respective federal and sub-national governments all relevant unredacted documents referred to in section 2, 3, 4 or 5 in the course of dispute settlement under this Agreement, but they shall ensure that those persons protect any confidential information in such documents.

10. As provided under [Guide sample provision in Section 5.12 (Reservations and exceptions)], a Tribunal shall not require a Party to furnish or allow access to information the disclosure of which would impede law enforcement or would be contrary to the Party's law protecting government confidences, personal privacy or the financial affairs and accounts of individual customers of financial institutions, or which the Party determines to be contrary to its essential security interests.

11. To the extent that a Tribunal's confidentiality order designates information as confidential and a Party's law on access to information requires public access to that information, the Party's law on access to information shall prevail. However, a Party should endeavour to apply its law on access to information so as to protect information designated as confidential by the Tribunal.

12. Requirements for disclosure under this Article shall be satisfied by each Party establishing a publicly accessible web site and posting on that site all documents required to be disclosed under sections 2, 3, 4 and 5 of this Article in connection with any dispute with respect to which it is the disputing Party as required in those articles.

Article [R]

Submissions by a Non-Disputing Party

1. Any non-disputing party that is a person of a Party that wishes to file a written submission with a Tribunal (the 'Applicant') may apply for leave from the Tribunal to file such a submission, in accordance with Annex [R].1. The Applicant shall attach the submission to the application.

2. The Applicant shall serve the application for leave to file a non-disputing party submission and the submission on all disputing parties and the Tribunal.

3. The Tribunal shall set an appropriate date for the disputing parties to comment on the application for leave to file a non-disputing party submission.

4. In determining whether to grant leave to file an Applicant's submission, the Tribunal shall consider, among other things, the extent to which:

   a. The Applicant's submission would assist the Tribunal in the determination of a factual or legal issue related to the arbitration by bringing a perspective, particular knowledge or insight that is different from that of the disputing parties;

   b. The Applicant's submission would address a matter within the scope of the dispute;

   c. The Applicant has a significant interest in the arbitration; and

   d. The subject matter of the arbitration affects a public interest.

5. The Tribunal shall ensure that:

   a. Any Applicant's submission does not disrupt the proceedings; and

   b. Neither disputing party is unduly burdened or unfairly prejudiced by such submissions.

6. The Tribunal shall decide whether to grant leave to file a non-disputing party submission. If leave to file a non-disputing party submission is granted, the Tribunal shall set an appropriate date for the disputing parties to respond in writing to the non-disputing party submission. By that date, the non-disputing Party may, pursuant to Article [N] (participation by the non-disputing Party), address any issues of interpretation of this Agreement presented in the non-disputing party submission.

7. A Tribunal that grants leave to file a non-disputing party submission is not required to address the submission at any point in the arbitration or in the reasons for its decision, nor is the non-disputing party that files the submission entitled to make further submissions in the arbitration.

8. Access to hearings and documents by non-disputing parties that file applications under these procedures shall be governed by the provisions pertaining to public access to hearings and documents under Article [Q] (public access to hearings and documents).

Article [S]

Governing Law

1. A Tribunal established under this Part shall decide the issues in dispute in accordance with this Agreement and applicable rules of international law and the domestic law of the disputing Party.

2. Where a disputing Party requests an interpretation of a provision of this Agreement, the Tribunal shall request the interpretation of the Commission[196] on

196 See Section 9.2 (Commission)

the issue. The Commission, within 60 days of delivery of the request, shall submit in writing its interpretation to the Tribunal. If the Commission fails to submit an interpretation within 60 days, the Tribunal shall decide the issue.

3. An interpretation by the Commission of a provision of this Agreement shall be binding on a Tribunal established under this Part and any award under this Part shall be consistent with such interpretation.

Article [T]

Expert Reports

Without prejudice to the appointment of other kinds of experts where authorised by the applicable arbitration rules, a Tribunal, at the request of a disputing party or, unless the disputing parties disagree, on its own initiative, may appoint one or more experts to report to it in writing on any factual issue concerning environmental, health, safety or other matters raised by a disputing party in a proceeding, subject to such terms and conditions as the disputing parties may agree.

Article [U]

Interim Measures of Protection

A Tribunal may order an interim measure of protection to preserve the rights of a disputing party, or to ensure that the Tribunal's jurisdiction is made fully effective, including an order to preserve evidence in the possession or control of a disputing party. A Tribunal may not order attachment or enjoin the application of the measure alleged to constitute a breach referred to in Article [B] (claim by an investor of a party).

Article [V]

Final Award

1. Subject to Article [W] (counterclaims), where a Tribunal makes a final award against the disputing Party, the Tribunal may award, separately or in combination, only:

   a. Monetary damages and any applicable interest;

   b. Restitution of property, in which case the award shall provide that the disputing Party may pay monetary damages and any applicable interest in lieu of restitution.

   After making a finding of liability against a disputing Party but prior to making an award of damages under this Section, the Tribunal shall provide a reasonable time for the disputing parties to agree on the compensation to be paid by the disputing Party to the disputing party.

2. Where a Tribunal makes an award under Article [W] (counterclaim) against a disputing party, the Tribunal shall deduct the amount of any damages to be paid to the disputing Party under that award from any damages to be paid to the disputing party under this Section.

3. The Tribunal may also award costs in accordance with the applicable arbitration rules.

4. In assessing damages to be paid by a disputing Party, the Tribunal shall take into account the following principles:

   a. The investor shall take reasonable steps to mitigate its losses, and damages shall be reduced to the extent that it has not;

   b. Damages shall be reduced to the extent that the loss to the investor is attributable to the conduct of the investor;

   c. No punitive or moral damages shall be awarded;

   d. Damages shall be limited to direct losses of the investor and shall not include any amount for loss of future profits or be calculated on the basis of the discounted value of future cash flows; and

   e. No damages shall be awarded unless the breach of an obligation listed in Article [B] (claim by an investor of a Party) is sufficiently serious, in the Tribunal's discretion, to justify an award of damages.

5. The Parties confirm their shared understanding that when a disputing investor submits a claim to arbitration under this Part, it has the burden of proving all elements of its claim, including the damages that it alleges were sustained by reason of, or arising out of, the measures that are the basis of the claim.

6. Notwithstanding Article [X] (finality and enforcement of award), a Tribunal shall have a discretion to make an order that any payment of damages by a disputing Party be delayed where it determines that the payment would be a serious hardship for the Party. If the Tribunal determines that payment may be delayed, it shall establish a schedule for the payment of damages taking into account the ability of the disputing Party to make payments.

Article [W]

Counterclaims

1. Where an investor has submitted a claim under Article [F] (submission of a claim to arbitration), the disputing Party may counterclaim against the investor before the Tribunal established under this Agreement to hear the investor's claim that the investor has breached an obligation under [Guide sample provision in Section 6.7 (Investor obligation to comply with the laws of the host state)], [Guide sample provision in Section 6.8 (Investor obligation to respect internationally recognised human rights and undertake human rights due diligence)], [Guide sample provision in Section 6.9 (Investor obligation to refrain from the commission of, or complicity in, grave violations of human rights)], [Guide sample provision in Section 6.10 (Investor obligation to comply with core labour standards)] or [Guide sample provision in Section 6.11 (Investor obligation to refrain from acts, or complicity in acts, of bribery and corruption)], or non-compliance with a management plan in relation to the investor's investment where consultation

has not resulted in compliance with the management plan or the reasonable and appropriate modification of the plan in accordance with [Guide sample provision in Section 6.16 (Civil liability of investors)] or any other obligation owed to the disputing Party and the disputing Party or a person of the Party has suffered loss or damage by reason of, or arising out of, that breach.

2. Where a Tribunal makes a final award against the disputing party under this article, the Tribunal may award monetary damages and any applicable interest.

3. Where a disputing Party counterclaims against an investor under section 1, on the basis that the investor has breached an obligation under [Guide sample provision in Section 6.7 (Investor obligation to comply with the laws of the host state)], the Tribunal can only award damages if it determines that the breach is sufficiently serious, in the Tribunal's discretion, to justify an award of damages.

4. The Tribunal may also award costs in accordance with the applicable arbitration rules.

5. In assessing damages to be paid by a disputing party, the Tribunal shall take into account the following principles:

    a. The disputing Party shall take reasonable steps to mitigate its losses and damages shall be reduced to the extent that it has not;

    b. Damages shall be reduced to the extent that the loss to the disputing Party is attributable to the conduct of the disputing Party; and

    c. No punitive damages shall be awarded.

6. The Parties confirm their shared understanding that when a Party submits a counterclaim under this Part, it has the burden of proving all elements of its claim, including the damages that it alleges were sustained by reason of, or arising out of, the alleged actions which are the basis of the counterclaim.

Article [X]

Finality and Enforcement of an Award

1. An award, including any award made under Article [W] (counterclaims), made by a Tribunal shall have no binding force except between the disputing parties and in respect of that particular case.

2. Subject to Article [V] (final award), section 3 and any applicable review procedure for an interim award, a disputing investor and a disputing Party shall abide by and comply with an award without delay.

3. A disputing investor or a disputing Party may not seek enforcement of a final award, including any award made under Article [W] (counterclaims), until:

    a. In the case of a final award made under the ICSID Convention

        i. 120 days have elapsed from the date the award was rendered and no disputing party has requested revision or annulment of the award, or

ii. revision or annulment proceedings have been completed and the award has not been annulled; and

b. In the case of a final award under the ICSID Additional Facility Rules, the UNCITRAL Arbitration Rules or any other rules agreed to by the disputing parties

i. 90 days have elapsed from the date the award was rendered and no disputing party has commenced a proceeding to revise, set aside or annul the award, or

ii. a court has dismissed or allowed an application to revise, set aside or annul the award and no further appeal is available.

4. Each Party shall provide for the enforcement of an award, including any award made under Article [W] (counterclaims), in its territory.

5. If the disputing Party fails to abide by or comply with a final award, the Commission, on delivery of a request by the Party of the disputing investor, shall establish an arbitral panel under [Guide sample provision in Section 7.2 (State-to-state dispute settlement)]. The requesting Party may seek in such proceedings:

a. A determination that the failure to comply with the final award is inconsistent with the obligations of this Agreement; and

b. A recommendation that the disputing Party abide by or comply with the final award.

6. A disputing investor or a disputing Party may seek enforcement of an award, including any award made under Article [W] (counterclaims), under the ICSID Convention, or the New York Convention regardless of whether proceedings have been taken under section 5.

7. A claim that is submitted to arbitration under this Part shall be considered to arise out of a commercial relationship or transaction for purposes of Article I of the New York Convention.

8. If a disputing party against which an award of damages by counterclaim has been made under Article [W] (counterclaim) fails to satisfy the award in full within 12 months of the date of the award, the non-disputing Party of the investor shall pay any outstanding amount to the disputing Party.

Article [Y]

General

Time when a Claim is Submitted to Arbitration

1. A claim is submitted to arbitration under this Part when:

a. The request for arbitration under paragraph (1) of Article 36 of the ICSID Convention is received by the Secretary-General of ICSID;

b. The notice of arbitration under Article 2 of Schedule C of the ICSID Additional Facility Rules is received by the Secretary-General of ICSID;

c. The notice of arbitration given under the UNCITRAL Arbitration Rules is received by the disputing Party; or

d. The requirements for the initiation of an arbitration under any other rules governing the arbitration in accordance with this Part have been satisfied.

Service of Documents

2. Delivery of notice and other documents on a Party shall be made to the place named for that Party below.

For ____________ ....

For ____________ ....

Annex [H].1

Rules for Arbitrator Conduct

1. Every arbitrator shall avoid impropriety and the appearance of impropriety and shall observe high standards of conduct so that the integrity and impartiality of the dispute settlement process under this Agreement is preserved. Without limiting the generality of the foregoing, arbitrators shall meet the following requirements during an arbitration under this Part:

   a. An arbitrator shall be independent and impartial. An arbitrator shall act in a fair manner and shall avoid creating an appearance of impropriety or an apprehension of bias;

   b. An arbitrator shall not be influenced by self-interest, outside pressure, political considerations, public clamour, loyalty to a disputing party or fear of criticism;

   c. An arbitrator shall not, directly or indirectly, incur any obligation or accept any benefit that would in any way interfere, or appear to interfere, with the proper performance of the arbitrator's duties;

   d. An arbitrator shall not use the arbitrator's position on the Tribunal to advance any personal or private interests. An arbitrator shall avoid actions that may create the impression that others are in a special position to influence the arbitrator. An arbitrator shall make every effort to prevent or discourage others from representing themselves as being in such a position;

   e. An arbitrator shall not allow past or existing financial, business, professional, family or social relationships or responsibilities to influence the arbitrator's conduct or judgment; and

   f. An arbitrator shall avoid entering into any relationship, or acquiring any financial interest, that is likely to affect the arbitrator's impartiality or that might reasonably create an appearance of impropriety or an apprehension of bias.

2. For a period of one year after the completion of an arbitration under the Agreement, a former arbitrator shall not personally advise or represent either of the disputing parties.

3. An arbitrator shall disclose any interest, relationship or matter that is likely to affect the arbitrator's independence or impartiality or that might reasonably create an appearance of impropriety or an apprehension of bias in the arbitration to the disputing parties in writing prior to the arbitrator's appointment, taking into account the International Bar Association Guidelines on Conflicts of Interest for International Arbitrations. To this end, a candidate shall make all reasonable efforts to become aware of any such interests, relationships and matters, including:

   a. Any past or existing financial, business, professional, family or social relationship with either of the disputing parties, or their counsel, or any such relationship involving a candidate's employer, partner, business associate or family member; and

   b. Public advocacy or legal or other representation concerning an issue in dispute in the arbitration.

4. Once appointed, an arbitrator shall continue to make all reasonable efforts to become aware of any interests, relationships or matters referred to in section 3 and shall disclose them to the disputing parties in writing immediately upon becoming aware of them.

5. An arbitrator or former arbitrator shall not at any time disclose or use any non-public information concerning the dispute or acquired during the arbitration except for the purposes of the arbitration and shall not, in any case, disclose or use any such information to gain personal advantage or advantage for others or to affect adversely the interest of another.

Annex [R].1

Submissions by Non-Disputing Parties

1. An application for leave to file a non-disputing party submission shall:

   a. Be made in writing, dated and signed by the person filing the application, and include the address and other contact details of the applicant;

   b. Be no longer than five (5) typed pages;

   c. Describe the applicant, including, where relevant, its membership and legal status (e.g. company, trade association or other non-governmental organisation), its general objectives, the nature of its activities, and any parent organisation (including any organisation that directly or indirectly controls the applicant);

   d. Disclose whether the applicant has any affiliation, direct or indirect, with any disputing party;

   e. Identify any government, person or organisation that has provided any financial or other assistance in preparing the submission;

f. Specify the nature of the interest that the applicant has in the arbitration;

g. Identify the specific issues of fact or law in the arbitration that the applicant has addressed in its written submission;

h. Explain, by reference to the factors specified in Article [R](4) (submissions by non-disputing party), why the Tribunal should accept the submission; and

i. Be made in a language of the arbitration.

2. The submission filed by a non-disputing party shall:

a. Be dated and signed by the person filing the submission;

b. Be concise, and in no case longer than 20 typed pages, including any appendices;

c. Set out a precise statement supporting the applicant's position on the issues; and

d. Address only matters within the scope of the dispute.

7.2 State-to-state dispute settlement

Cross references

Section 6.6	Sustainability assessments	267
Section 6.12	Other rights and obligations of host states	345
Section 6.13	Enforcement of investor obligations	372
Section 7.1	Investor–state dispute settlement	408

Most IIAs contain some procedure to be followed for the resolution of any dispute between the party states to the treaty. Such disputes have been rare in practice. Perhaps for this reason, unlike investor–state dispute settlement and state-to-state dispute settlement under the WTO Dispute Settlement Understanding (DSU), state-to-state dispute settlement procedures in IIAs have received relatively little attention and there has been much less development in state-to-state dispute settlement provisions.[197] The content of state-to-state dispute settlement provisions is likely to be of little interest to investors, at least where IIAs provide for investor–state arbitration.

7.2.1 IIA practice

Most IIAs devote a single provision to state-to-state procedures[198] though some provisions are more detailed than others. Procedures typically (i) address the scope of application of the procedures, (ii) impose an obligation to consult prior to the establishment of an arbitral tribunal, and (iii) establish rules for the conduct of the arbitral procedure. A few go on to deal with transparency of the process and enforcement of decisions.

---

197 UNCTAD (2007), *Treaties 1996–2006*, op. cit., at 126.

198 E.g. Indian model BIPPA, Art. 10; US model BIT, Art. 37.

Comprehensive trade and investment agreements often contain more elaborate state-to-state procedures.[199] Under the COMESA Investment Agreement, disputes can be referred to a regional institution, the COMESA Court of Justice, or an independent arbitral tribunal.[200] The COMESA Investment Agreement sets out a detailed set of rules for state-to-state arbitration that are similar to the rules for investor–state dispute settlement.[201] Within ASEAN, disputes can be dealt with under the ASEAN Protocol on Enhanced Dispute Settlement Mechanism, which follows the WTO model.[202]

Scope

Virtually all IIAs define the scope of state-to-state dispute settlement as 'the interpretation and application' of the agreement.[203] 'Interpretation' refers to what provisions mean in particular situations, while 'application' refers to whether particular state actions comply with the agreement. In practice, there will be considerable overlap between the two. Under such a provision, all obligations that are imposed on either party state in the IIA may be the subject of these procedures. In some IIAs, resort to state-to-state procedures is precluded in relation to any dispute that an investor has submitted to investor–state arbitration. Typically, these kinds of provisions permit state-to-state dispute settlement where an award has been issued in favour of an investor but not paid by the host state.[204] Another caveat is that the manner in which particular provisions are drafted may make it difficult to address them in state-to-state dispute settlement. For example, if an exception for essential security issues in an IIA allows a state to define what it considers to be an essential security interest, then there is little scope for a dispute about whether a particular measure that a state says is needed to protect its essential security interests is covered by the exception.[205]

Specific IIA obligations can be carved out of state-to-state dispute settlement. There are likely to be few obligations in conventional IIAs that a state will wish to exclude. However, some obligations, such as host state obligations related to environmental protection, human rights, labour rights and the rights of indigenous peoples of the kind that are discussed above, may be so sensitive that a state may want to exclude them,[206] so that the other party state cannot initiate state-to-state dispute settlement claiming that the state has not complied with these obligations. Under the US model

---

199 E.g. Chapter 20 of NAFTA (1992).
200 COMESA Investment Agreement (2007), Art. 27.
201 COMESA Investment Agreement (2007), Annex A.
202 ASEAN Agreement (2009), Art. 27. Neither this procedure nor its predecessor has ever been used.
203 E.g. UK model IPPA, Art. 9; Indian model BIPPA, Art. 10; US model BIT, Art. 37; Canadian model FIPA, Art. 48.
204 See Section 7.1 (Investor–state dispute settlement).
205 Some agreements specifically exclude security exceptions from dispute settlement.
206 See 6.12 (Other rights and obligations of party states); Section 6.13 (Enforcement of investor obligations).

agreement, the limited obligations regarding the protection of labour rights and the environment are excluded from state-to-state dispute settlement.[207]

Consultations

Most IIAs require consultations between the party states for a period of time. If consultations are not successful by the expiry of the period, either state may submit the dispute to an arbitral tribunal.[208] Typically, the period for consultations is six months.[209] IIAs may also require or permit the parties to resort to alternative dispute resolution procedures. These were discussed above.[210]

Arbitration procedures

Many IIAs provide that each party state chooses one arbitrator and the two appointed arbitrators select the third member of the panel.[211] Alternatively, the third arbitrator may be chosen by agreement of the parties. [212] Typically, the third arbitrator cannot be a national of either party state and is the presiding arbitrator or chair of the panel. If appointments are not made within the time limit set in the IIA, most IIAs provide that someone, often the Secretary-General of ICSID or the President of the International Court of Justice, will appoint any arbitrator not appointed on the request of a party.

Few IIAs set standards for arbitrators in state-to-state dispute settlement. The Canadian model is an exception and sets the same standards for expertise and independence as it does for arbitrators in investor–state arbitration.

5. Arbitrators shall:

   a. have expertise or experience in public international law, international trade or international investment rules, or the resolution of disputes arising under international trade or international investment agreements;

   b. be independent of, and not be affiliated with or take instructions from, either Party; and

   c. comply with any Code of Conduct for Dispute Settlement as agreed by the Commission.

As with investor–state arbitrations, the Canadian model contemplates that if a party state claims that a dispute involves measures relating to financial institutions, or to investors or investments of investors in financial institutions, the parties can agree

207 US model BIT, Art. 37.

208 E.g. UK model IPPA, Art. 9; Indian model BIPPA, Art. 10; US model BIT, Art. 37; Canadian model FIPA, Art. 48.

209 UNCTAD (2003), *Dispute Settlement: State-to-State*, United Nations, New York and Geneva. Some treaties do not provide a time limit (e.g. Canadian model FIPA, Art. 48.2).

210 See Section 7.1 (Investor–state dispute settlement).

211 This approach is followed in the Canadian model FIPA, Art. 48.3, UK model IPPA, Art. 9(3), Indian model BIPPA, Art. 10(3), and Australia–India BIT (1999), Art. 13.3.

212 This approach is followed in the US model BIT, Art. 37.2.

that arbitrators must have expertise in financial services law and practice or the regulation of financial institutions.[213]

In terms of the procedure to be followed, some IIAs provide that the UNCITRAL rules shall be followed unless the parties agree to some other procedure.[214] Most provide simply that the panel established under the treaty shall decide on its own procedure.[215]

Each party state in a state-to-state dispute normally bears its own costs, while the fees and expenses of the tribunal are split between the parties. The Canadian model permits a panel to direct that a higher proportion of the costs be borne by one of the parties.[216] Such a rule would permit a panel to order that the loser pay a higher proportion of the costs.

The concerns that have been raised in connection with arbitrators in investor–state arbitration, including the absence of institutional guarantees of independence, have not been raised in relation to state-to-state dispute resolution. Undoubtedly, this is, in part, because of the very limited recourse to these procedures and the weak or non-existent enforcement procedures for state-to-state awards.

Transparency

Another design issue in relation to state-to-state dispute settlement is the degree to which the proceedings should be open and transparent. On this issue, there is significant variation among IIAs. The Canadian model, like most IIAs, does not address the issue, even though it has extensive provisions guaranteeing transparency in investor–state procedures, while the US model, the draft Norwegian model and the IISD model require essentially the same level of transparency and openness to the participation of *amici curiae* that they require for investor–state disputes be provided in state-to-state disputes.[217]

At the WTO, the general rule is that proceedings are confidential, but some parties now routinely provide public access to their submissions. *Amicus curiae* submissions have been accepted at the WTO. There is no evidence of such openness under state-to-state procedures in other contexts. In the three state-to-state disputes under NAFTA, for example, only the final awards have been disclosed. Greater openness in state-to-state dispute settlement may make it more difficult for the parties to

---

213 Canadian model FIPA, Art. 48.6. The US–Uruguay BIT (2005) contains a similar provision (Art. 20) but goes on to provide that the competent financial authorities from each party state shall consult with a view to finding an agreement prior to submitting the dispute to arbitration.

214 E.g. US model BIT, Art. 37.1. NAFTA (1992) Chapter 20 has its own procedural rules: Model Rules of Procedure for Chapter 20 of NAFTA.

215 E.g. Canadian model FIPA, Art. 48.7. The Indian model BIPPA and the UK model IPPA do not refer to what the arbitral rules should be or how they will be determined.

216 Canadian model FIPA, Art. 48.8.

217 US model BIT, Art. 37(4); IISD model treaty, Art. 43; draft Norwegian model APPI, Art. 21. See sample Article [Q] (public access to hearings and documents) in Section 7.1 (Investor–state dispute settlement).

negotiate a solution to the dispute, but may nevertheless be desirable to ensure public accountability for state actions.

Enforcement

Like most IIAs, under the Canadian, US, UK and Indian models, decisions of state-to-state tribunals are binding. Few IIAs, however, address what happens if a state fails to comply with a decision that its regime is not in compliance with the treaty. The Canadian model provides that if the parties cannot agree on how to resolve the dispute, which normally would require implementation of the panel decision, the other party state is entitled to receive compensation from the non-complying state or to suspend benefits to be accorded to the non-complying party that are of 'equivalent value to those awarded by the panel'. A number of questions would arise if this were ever to be used in practice, including the following:

- What benefits could be suspended?
- Would benefits be limited to the obligations owed to the party in breach under the IIA?
- What does it mean to limit the benefits suspended to benefits of 'equivalent value to those awarded by the panel', when there is no requirement for a panel to assess the costs of non-compliance?
- How would a suspension of benefits be valued?

To illustrate the last issue, consider the suspension of, for example, an IIA obligation to pay compensation for expropriation by a party in retaliation for the failure by the other party to change a measure that had been found by a state-to-state panel to be inconsistent with an IIA obligation. Such a suspension might create an incentive for compliance by the other party, but it is not obvious how one would value such a suspension. In any case, this kind of retaliation would undermine the overall objectives of the IIA.

Box 7.6 Summary of options for state-to-state dispute settlement provisions

1. *No reference to state-to-state dispute settlement*
2. *Include state-to-state dispute settlement possibly with:*
    a. Limitations on the scope of dispute settlement
    b. Requirements for transparency and *amicus curiae* participation

7.2.2 Discussion of options

1. *No reference to state-to-state dispute settlement*

    This option is not typically found in IIAs. State-to-state dispute settlement complements the establishment of legal standards in the IIA by providing a process to resolve differences regarding the interpretation of the treaty or its application to specific state actions. It also allows parties to know in advance how disputes will be addressed where consultation fails. State-to-state procedures also provide a mandatory process by which one party state can engage the other in addressing problems that arise. This may be particularly important for developing countries that are capital importers. For capital-exporting states, investor–state dispute settlement may be sufficient to deal with most problems.

2. *Include state-to-state dispute settlement*

   Once a decision to include state-to-state dispute settlement has been taken, there are few issues regarding the design of such a provision. The basic architecture of IIA provisions is the same in most agreements, and is not controversial. Investors are unlikely to take into account arrangements for state-to-state dispute settlement in their investment decisions. Two issues, however, should be addressed.

   a. Limitations on scope of dispute settlement

      IIAs typically define the scope of state-to-state dispute settlement as any issue related to the interpretation or application of the agreement. One issue is whether anything should be excluded from the scope of state-to-state dispute settlement. Where sensitive obligations regarding environmental protection, human rights, labour rights and the rights of indigenous peoples, such as those that are discussed in the Guide are being undertaken by states, they may decide to exclude them. This is the approach followed under the US model agreement for the obligations regarding the protection of labour rights and the environment.

   b. Requirements for transparency and *amicus curiae* participation

      Few IIAs create transparency requirements related to state-to-state arbitration. Subjecting state-to-state dispute settlement to requirements to make publicly available the submissions of the parties and panel decisions, to have open hearings and to permit *amici curiae* to participate, if certain conditions are met, as required for investor–state arbitration in some IIAs, may impede the parties from agreeing to a solution to their dispute. Frank discussion of positions and possible solutions may be inhibited. On the other hand, transparency and *amicus curiae* participation may be desirable to ensure public accountability for state actions. Some of the offsetting considerations that are relied on to argue in favour of limiting transparency and openness in investor–state arbitration, such as the burden on the investor and possible disincentives to invest, are not relevant in the state-to-state context.

7.2.3 Discussion of sample provision

State-to-state dispute settlement procedures exist in almost all IIAs. The Guide sample provision for a state-to-state dispute settlement procedure is relatively detailed, in the interests of providing greater certainty regarding how the process works.

Exclusions from scope: IIAs define the scope of state-to-state dispute settlement as an issue related to the interpretation or application of the agreement. The sample provisions adopt this approach but, following the approach in the US model agreement, any state obligations regarding environmental protection, human rights, labour rights and the rights of indigenous peoples[218] are excluded. States may want to consider whether other obligations should be excluded. If, for example, the novel enforcement provisions described above[219] for obligations on investors and state obligations related to sustainability assessments are included in an agreement, party states will need to consider whether they are comfortable with the prospect of these obligations being the subject of state-to-state dispute settlement.[220]

Arbitrator standards: The sample provision incorporates the same standards related to competence and independence for members of state-to-state dispute settlement panels as apply to arbitrators under the sample provisions on investor–state arbitration.[221]

Transparency: In the interests of public accountability and the trend towards transparency evident in international economic law generally, the sample provision provides for fully open hearings, public access to documents and the possibility of *amicus curiae* participation on the same basis as in investor–state proceedings.[222]

Enforcement: As in most existing IIAs, decisions are binding. However, no compensation or suspension of benefits provision has been included. The Canadian model is one of the few that provides for compensation to be paid and permits retaliation in circumstances where the parties cannot agree on the resolution of a dispute following the decision of a state-to-state dispute settlement panel. The Canadian model, however, does not provide adequate detail regarding how such a system of compensation and suspension would work, and it is not clear how a system of compensation or retaliation could be made to work. Also, experience to date does not suggest that such an enforcement provision is necessary or desirable.

7.2.4 Sample provisions: state-to-state dispute settlement procedure

State-to-State Dispute Settlement Procedure

1. Either Party may request consultations on the interpretation or application of this Agreement. The other Party shall give sympathetic consideration to the request. Any dispute between the Parties concerning the interpretation or application of this Agreement shall, whenever possible, be settled amicably through consultations.

2. If a dispute cannot be settled through consultations within 180 days of the submission of the request under section 1, it shall, at the request of either Party, be submitted to an arbitral panel for decision.

218 See Section 6.12 (Other rights and obligations of party states).
219 See Section 6.13 (Enforcement of investor obligations) and Sections 6.14 to 6.16.
220 See Section 6.6 (Sustainability assessments).
221 Sample provision Annex B.[H] in Section 7.1 (Investor–state dispute settlement).
222 The same approach is adopted in the COMESA Investment Agreement (2007), Art. 27.

3. Within two months after receipt through diplomatic channels of the request for arbitration, each Party shall appoint one member to the arbitral panel. The two members shall then select a national of a third state who, upon approval by the two Parties, shall be appointed Chair of the arbitral panel. The Chair shall be appointed within two months from the date of appointment of the other two members of the arbitral panel.

4. If within the periods specified in section 3 of this article the necessary appointments have not been made, either Party may invite the President of the International Court of Justice to make the necessary appointments. If the President is a national of either Party or is otherwise prevented from discharging the appointment function, the Vice-President shall be invited to make the necessary appointments. If the Vice-President is a national of either Party or is otherwise prevented from discharging the appointment function, the member of the International Court of Justice next in seniority who is not a national of either Party shall be invited to make the necessary appointments.

5. Panel members shall:

   a. Have expertise or experience in public international law, international trade or international investment rules, or the resolution of disputes arising under international trade or international investment agreements;

   b. Be independent of, and not be affiliated with or take instructions from, either Party; and

   c. Comply with the Annex to this Section and any code of conduct for dispute settlement agreed by the Commission.

6. Where a Party claims that a dispute involves measures relating to financial institutions, or to investors or investments of such investors in financial institutions, then:

   a. Where the disputing Parties are in agreement, the panel members shall, in addition to meeting the criteria set out in section 5, have expertise or experience in financial services law or practice, which may include the regulation of financial institutions; or

   b. Where the disputing Parties are not in agreement, each disputing Party may select arbitrators who meet the qualifications set out in subsection 6a.

7. Where a Party claims that a dispute involves measures relating to the protection of labour rights, human rights, the rights of indigenous peoples or the environment, or the interpretation of the domestic law of a Party:

   a. Where the disputing Parties are in agreement, the arbitrators shall, in addition to meeting the criteria set out in section 5, have expertise or experience in the relevant area of law or practice; or

   b. Where the disputing Parties are not in agreement, each disputing Party may select members who meet the qualifications set out in subsection 7a.

8. The arbitral panel shall determine its own procedure. The arbitral panel shall reach its decision by a majority of votes. Such decision shall be binding on both Parties. Unless otherwise agreed, the decision of the arbitral panel shall be rendered within 180 days of the appointment of the Chair in accordance with sections 3 or 4 of this article.

9. Each Party shall bear the costs of its own member of the panel and of its representation in the arbitral proceedings; the costs related to the Chair and any remaining costs shall be borne equally by the Parties. However, the arbitral panel may in its decision direct that a higher proportion of costs be borne by one of the two Parties, and this award shall be binding on both Parties.

10. The Parties shall, within 60 days of the decision of a panel, reach agreement on the manner in which to resolve their dispute. Such agreement shall implement the decision of the panel.

11. Articles [Q] (public access to hearings and documents), [R] (submissions by a non-disputing party) and [S] (governing law) shall apply, *mutatis mutandis*, to dispute settlement proceedings under this Article. [See Guide sample provisions in Section 7.1 (Investor–state dispute settlement).]

12. Paragraphs 1 through 11 shall not apply to a matter arising under [see possible sample provisions discussed under Guide Sections 6.7–6.11 (obligations of investors)] or [Guide sample provisions in Section 6.6 (Sustainability assessments)].

Annex

Rules for Panel Member Conduct

1. Every panel member shall avoid impropriety and the appearance of impropriety and shall observe high standards of conduct so that the integrity and impartiality of the dispute settlement process is preserved. Without limiting the generality of the foregoing, panel members shall meet the following requirements.

   a. A panel member shall be independent and impartial. A panel member shall act in a fair manner and shall avoid creating an appearance of impropriety or an apprehension of bias.

   b. A panel member shall not be influenced by self-interest, outside pressure, political considerations, public clamour, loyalty to a Party or fear of criticism.

   c. A panel member shall not, directly or indirectly, incur any obligation or accept any benefit that would in any way interfere, or appear to interfere, with the proper performance of the panel member's duties.

   d. A panel member shall not use the panel member's position on the tribunal to advance any personal or private interests. A panel member shall avoid actions that may create the impression that others are in a special position to influence the panel member. A panel member shall make every effort to prevent or discourage others from representing themselves as being in such a position.

e. A panel member shall not allow past or existing financial, business, professional, family or social relationships or responsibilities to influence the member's conduct or judgment.

f. A panel member shall avoid entering into any relationship, or acquiring any financial interest, that is likely to affect the panel member's impartiality or that might reasonably create an appearance of impropriety or an apprehension of bias.

2. For a period of one year after the completion of an arbitration under the agreement, a former panel member shall not personally advise or represent either of the Parties.

3. A panel member shall disclose any interest, relationship or matter that is likely to affect the panel member's independence or impartiality or that might reasonably create an appearance of impropriety or an apprehension of bias in the arbitration to the Parties in writing prior to the panel member's appointment taking into account the International Bar Association Guidelines on Conflicts of Interest for International Arbitrations. To this end, a candidate to be a panel member shall make all reasonable efforts to become aware of any such interests, relationships and matters, including:

   a. Any past or existing financial, business, professional, family or social relationship with either of the Parties, or their counsel, or any such relationship involving a candidate's employer, partner, business associate or family member; and

   b. Public advocacy or legal or other representation concerning an issue in dispute in the arbitration.

4. Once appointed, a panel member shall continue to make all reasonable efforts to become aware of any interests, relationships or matters referred to in section 3 and shall disclose them to the Parties in writing immediately upon becoming aware of them.

5. A panel member or former panel member shall not at any time disclose or use any non-public information concerning the dispute or acquired during the arbitration except for the purposes of the arbitration and shall not, in any case, disclose or use any such information to gain personal advantage or advantage for others or to affect adversely the interest of another.

Chapter 8

Investment Promotion and Technical Assistance

8.1 Investment promotion

Cross references

As noted in the review of the empirical literature,[1] evidence of the impact of IIAs on increasing investment flows into party states is weak. It may seem surprising, therefore, that a recent study by UNCTAD found that only a small minority of existing IIAs contain specific investment promotion provisions.[2] Agreements addressing the promotion of investment do so in a variety of ways, including committing parties to some of the categories of measures listed in Box 8.1. In general terms, investment promotion efforts involve some combination of measures to: (i) improve the host state's regulatory framework by making it more transparent and efficient, and less burdensome for investors; and (ii) facilitate investment by means such as incentives, information dissemination and the activities of investment promotion agencies.[3]

Box 8.1 Categories of investment promotion measures

- Improve the overall policy framework for investment in the host state, possibly with the support of technical assistance from the home state;
- Provide financial or fiscal incentives from either the home or host state to investors, including investment guarantees and insurance;

(Continued)

1 See Section 2.2 (Links between signing IIAs and attracting increased foreign investment) and the review of empirical studies in Appendix 1.

2 UNCTAD (2008), *Investment Promotion Provisions in International Investment Agreements*, UNCTAD, Geneva, UNCTAD/ITE/IIT/2007/7.

3 On the effectiveness of investment promotion activities see T Harding and B Javorcik (2012), 'Roll Out the Red Carpet and They Will Come: Investment Promotion and FDI Inflows', 72 *Columbia FDI Perspectives*.

(Continued)

- Give preferential market access to the host state market for goods and services that investors want to import;
- Reduce host state barriers to investment;
- Create an investment promotion agency in the host state;
- Commit to discrete investment promotion activities in the home state or the host state, such as workshops or fairs on investment opportunities, or the creation of information points either jointly or separately by the party states;
- Require the exchange of information between party states on:
  - Host state investment rules and opportunities,
  - The host state's legal regime, macroeconomic policies and characteristics, sectoral conditions and other factors related to the broad political and socio-economic context for investment,
  - Foreign investment promotion programmes in the home state;
- Promote linkages between foreign investors from the home state and domestic businesses in the host state;
- Encourage transfer of technology from investors of the home state to investors of the host state;
- Create an institutional framework for co-operation on investment promotion;
- Commit the investor's home state to provide the host state with technical assistance with the implementation of investment promotion programmes in the host state.[4]

8.1.1 IIA practice

Investment promotion provisions may require actions to be taken by investors' home states to promote investment in host states, but they most often contemplate activities that will be engaged in by the host state, the direct beneficiary of investment promotion. Investment promotion provisions may be voluntary, best efforts or mandatory. In most cases, investment promotion provisions in existing IIAs contain vague, non-binding commitments or merely confirm the continuation of existing programmes.[5] Often the

4 Among the most detailed and specific provisions dealing with investment promotion are those in the COMESA Investment Agreement (2007) (Schedules I and II).

5 E.g. UK model IPPA, Art. 2(1); European Union-Russian Federation, Agreement on Partnership and Cooperation between the European Communities and the Russian Federation, signed 24 June 1994, in force 1 December 1997, Art. 58; Colombian model agreement, Art. III.1. The AALCC Draft has a slightly stronger general commitment (Art. 2(i)). See also Art. IV of GATS.

obligation is expressed to apply only to the host state. For example, the UK model treaty provides that:

> Each Contracting Party shall encourage and create favourable conditions for nationals or companies of the other Contracting Party to invest capital in its territory ...

Some agreements, especially those that form part of regional economic integration initiatives, contain more detailed provisions. The ASEAN Agreement, for example, sets out both a series of investment promotion co-operation objectives and an indicative list of co-operation activities in relation to investment within the ASEAN region.[6] The COMESA Investment Agreement also sets out a detailed list of co-operation activities, including both country-level commitments and regional commitments, such as the creation of a regional database of suppliers and investment opportunities.[7] It would be possible to target investment promotion at categories of investment that promote sustainable development objectives or that meet certain standards for corporate social responsibility, though this is not typically done.

8.1.2 Possible costs and benefits of investment promotion commitments

Investment promotion provisions in IIAs may assist in encouraging increased investment into host countries more effectively than investor protection obligations alone. Providing a commitment to promote investment in the treaty text should increase the likelihood that party states will actually engage in promotion activities. Ultimately, of course, there can be no guarantee that investment will actually increase as a result of such activities. Because investment promotion provisions are relatively rare, successfully negotiating such commitments may give a host country an advantage in the competition with other states to attract investment.

Implementing investment promotion provisions may involve costs to the home state, the host state or both. States must take these costs into account in evaluating the desirability and content of investment promotion commitments. Capacity constraints in some host developing countries may prevent them from designing a coherent investment promotion strategy, setting up an investment promotion agency or even improving transparency regarding investment opportunities and rules. Host state commitments to engage in these investment promotion activities may have little effect in the absence of technical assistance from the other state to support their implementation. In addition, IIA commitments regarding investment promotion can restrict party state flexibility regarding the design and operation of investment promotion programmes. For example, commitments to provide incentives through generally available tax holidays may limit the funds available to a host state to adopt

6 ASEAN Agreement (2009), Arts. 24, 25 and 26.

7 COMESA Investment Agreement (2007), Schedule I and II. Precedents for investment promotion commitments may be found in a wide variety of agreements outside IIAs. See UNCTAD (2001), *Home Country Measures*, United Nations, New York and Geneva.

subsidy programmes targeting the promotion of investment in specific sectors or regions.[8]

8.1.3 Other issues in the design of investment promotion commitments

Other considerations relevant to the specific kinds of investment promotion activities to which states may wish to commit in an IIA include a host state's openness to foreign investment and, more generally, its orientation to the market. Countries that favour free markets as the best way to encourage development may want investment promotion to be directed to improving their general institutional framework and policy environment for investment. Countries that favour intervention to guide economic activity as the best approach to encouraging development may prefer investment promotion that is targeted at channelling investment to specific sectors or activities.

8.1.4 A role for investors' home state in investment promotion

From a home state point of view, the benefits associated with programmes and activities to promote investment in host states may not be obvious. Judging from existing practice, home states are satisfied with IIAs that promote investment only indirectly by providing protection to their investors. Nevertheless, there may be advantages to particular kinds of investment promotion activities. For example, efforts to improve the transparency and reduce the burden of domestic regulation in a host state support the operation of home state investors in the host state by reducing the burden of regulation and making its operation more predictable. Support for market-opening reforms in a host state that may be helpful to a home state's investors may also help other home state businesses. Commitments to reduce host state tariffs and other restrictions on inputs that home state investors want to import into the host state from businesses in the home state provide one example. Home states are most likely to be willing to support investment promotion commitments that further their interests.[9] A home state's interest in, and capacity to deliver on, investment promotion commitments will also be affected by its level of development. A final reason that a home state may be willing to make commitments related to the promotion of investment in the host state is that the home state's support for investment promotion may be used as a bargaining chip in exchange for the host state's agreement to protect the home state's investors through an IIA.

Finally, the provision of support to a developing country host state gives effect to exhortations in documents on sustainable development that co-operation between developed and developing countries in partnership is essential for the achievement of sustainable development. Moreover, this kind of support recognises the common but differentiated responsibilities of countries at different levels of development to help each other achieve the goals of sustainable development.

---

8 The use of incentives to target investment to specific sectors or regions may have investment distorting effects. UNCTAD (2007), *Development Implications of International Investment Agreements*, IIA Monitor No. 2, United Nations, New York and Geneva, at 2.

9 UNCTAD (2001), *Home Country Measures*, op. cit., at 7.

8.1.5 Relationship between investment promotion and other IIA provisions

In designing investment promotion commitments and programmes, it is necessary to consider their compatibility with other IIA commitments:

- **Some kinds of incentives that are conditioned on investors doing certain things, such as transferring technology, may be inconsistent with IIA performance requirement prohibitions, in the absence of an applicable exception in the agreement**;[10]
- **Using subsidies and other forms of incentives that discriminate in favour of investors from a particular home state may be contrary to an MFN obligation in an IIA with another state, in the absence of an applicable exception in that agreement**; and[11]
- **Transparency regarding a host state's regime guaranteed by commitments in an IIA may be useful to promote investment.** Transparency obligations in an IIA need to be consistent with investment promotion obligations and designed with investment promotion in mind.[12]

Box 8.2 Options for investment promotion provisions

1. *No reference to investment promotion*
2. *Including an investment promotion provision*

   There are two main variations in the form of investment promotion provisions:

   a. A provision that says simply that a party state shall endeavour to encourage investment from the other party state

   b. A provision that commits both parties to undertake specific investment promotion activities to encourage investment in a party state

8.1.6 Discussion of options

1. *No reference to investment promotion*

This is the most common approach in existing IIAs. It means that the only IIA commitments that may promote investment are the investor protection obligations and transparency commitments in the agreement. In addition, it may be that some other IIA obligations, such as commitments related to performance requirements, may limit a state's ability to engage in some kinds of investment promotion activities.

10 See Section 5.9 (Performance requirements).

11 See Section 5.4 (Most favoured nation).

12 See Section 5.10 (Transparency).

2. *Including an investment promotion provision*

   a. A provision that says simply that a party state shall endeavour to encourage investment from the other party state

This kind of provision does not create a commitment to any investment promotion activity, but rather creates a very vague non-binding best efforts undertaking by host states to create favourable conditions for investment. It does not impose any obligation at all on home states with respect to investment in the host state.

Nevertheless, a provision that expresses a non-binding intention of *both parties* that they will seek to promote investment may have some benefits. The negotiation of this kind of provision provides an opportunity for the party states to discuss (i) what needs the host state has with respect to investment promotion, (ii) what kinds of investment promotion activities are consistent with the policies of the host state and within its capacity to deliver, (iii) what opportunities exist for the home state to co-operate with the host state in the delivery of investment promotion activities consistent with the capacity of the home state and the needs and priorities of the host state, and (iv) how to ensure investment promotion activities generally are consistent with the other obligations agreed to in the IIA. Specific priority areas for investment promotion can be identified in such a provision.

If investment promotion is not provided as contemplated, a non-binding treaty provision still provides a basis for the host state to raise the issue with the home state. Such a provision may be complemented by obligations to monitor and/or periodically review what states have done to assess whether investment promotion activities are being carried out as contemplated in the treaty.

   b. A provision that commits parties to undertake specific investment promotion activities to encourage investment in the host state

As with option 2a., this option provides an opportunity to identify and articulate specific investment promotion commitments consistent with the host state's needs and priorities and the other party's capacity. Because these obligations are made specific and binding, however, performance is more likely and the dispute settlement provisions in the treaty could be used to seek compliance if consultations do not lead to a satisfactory solution.

Investment promotion activities pursuant to specific commitments may result in higher levels of investment in the host state, though in some cases they may involve costs that states will have to take into account.

8.1.7 Discussion of sample provision

In light of the diverse nature of investment promotion activities and the various factors that may influence party state choices regarding the priority to be attached to different sorts of investment promotion activities, the Guide includes a sample provision that directs party states to develop a programme of investment promotion rather than committing them to specific investment promotion activities. Similar to the ASEAN Investment Agreement, the provision identifies various possible activities that the party states should consider in determining what they will commit to. Each pair of negotiating states will have to determine the appropriate mix of investment promotion activities based on their needs, capacity and policy orientation. To help ensure the effectiveness of agreed activities, regular follow-up meetings of the party states are contemplated to review the implementation of the investment promotion commitments.

8.1.8 Sample provision: assistance and facilitation of foreign investment

Assistance and Facilitation of Foreign Investment

1. In accordance with the principle of common but differentiated responsibilities, a Party with the capacity to do so shall assist the other Party in the promotion and facilitation of foreign investment into the other Party, in particular by its own investors. Such assistance shall be consistent with the development goals and priorities of the other Party.
2. Such assistance may include but is not limited to:
    a. Provision of information to a Party's investors on the other Party's measures to promote investment in the other Party and information on the other Party's investment regime;
    b. Programmes based on commercial principles that provide insurance to its investors in connection with risks related to their activities in the other Party;
    c. Direct financial assistance and fiscal incentives to a Party's investors in support of their investments in the other Party or of feasibility studies prior to an investment in the other Party being established;
    d. Establishing links between a Party's research and training centres, specialised agencies and business organisations and those in the other Party; and
    e. Periodic trade missions, support for joint business councils and other co-operative efforts to promote sustainable development in the other Party.

The amount, type and duration of the assistance provided under section 1 will be determined by the Commission.[13] At least once per year, the Commission will review the implementation and operation of this Article and report on its findings to the Parties.

8.2 Technical assistance

Cross references

Section 5.10 Transparency 204
Section 6.6 Sustainability assessments 267

13 See Section 9.2 (Commission).

Few existing IIAs create specific obligations to provide technical assistance. In part, this is because traditional BITs only impose obligations on host states to refrain from actions that cause injury to investors. More recent agreements impose a more complex set of requirements for host states, including transparency obligations and commitments to ensure that domestic administrative procedures meet certain standards.[14] Some more recent IIAs, especially those in which investment obligations are combined with comprehensive trade commitments, such as free trade agreements and economic partnership commitments, contain positive obligations for host states to maintain and enforce standards in areas such as environmental protection, labour rights and bribery and corruption.[15] Some of these agreements also embrace a conception of the relationship between home and host states that is based on a partnership to contribute to sustainable development in the host state.[16] Agreements of this kind are more likely to contain technical assistance commitments to support the host state's implementation of its obligations, as well as to support the creation of robust and effective regulatory regimes in the host state to achieve its development goals and investment promotion programmes.[17]

The Guide discusses provisions that impose obligations on host states to ensure that their domestic regimes meet international standards for human rights, health and safety standards, and the protection of workers, indigenous peoples and the environment. The sample provisions in the Guide also provide examples of obligations that impose requirements for host states to:

- Establish standards and a process for sustainability assessments, including a grievance procedure and compliance process;
- Impose criminal sanctions against investors committing grave violations of human rights or being complicit in corruption; and
- Create a civil liability regime for non-compliance with standards imposed on investors under the treaty.[18]

All these obligations may be difficult to comply with if technical assistance by the other party state supported by adequate funding is not provided.

14 See Section 5.10 (Transparency).

15 E.g. EC–CARIFORUM, Economic Partnership Agreement, signed 15 October 2008, in force 29 December 2008, Part II, Title III, Investment Trade in Services and E-Commerce, Art. 11.

16 E.g. EC–CARIFORUM EPA (2008), Part I, Trade Partnership for Development.

17 E.g. EC–CARIFORUM EPA (2008), Part I, Art. 6–8, Part II, Title III, Investment, Trade in Services and E-Commerce, Arts. 56 and 57 (tourism), Art. 60 (e-commerce), Chapter 7 (Cooperation); SADC Investment Protocol (2006); Agreement on Trade-related Aspects of Intellectual Property Rights, Art. 66. See, generally, UNCTAD (2001), *Home Country Measures*, op.cit.

18 See Section 6.6 (Sustainability assessments); Section 6.16 (Civil liability of investors).

8.2.1 IIA practice

Technical assistance commitments in IIAs range from no commitment to hortatory statements to detailed and specific commitments backed up by funding obligations. No commitment is by far the most common approach. Technical assistance commitments can be made more effective if they are supported by institutions established under the treaty responsible for planning and co-ordinating delivery of technical assistance and monitoring compliance with commitments.[19] The EC–CARIFORUM EPA provides an example of an attempt to address the technical assistance challenge in specific ways related to the comprehensive relationship established between the parties under that agreement. Its main features are set out in Box 8.3.

Box 8.3 Key elements of EC–CARIFORUM EPA technical assistance provisions

- A general commitment to development co-operation with the identification of the following specific priorities.
  - i. The provision of technical assistance to build human, legal and institutional capacity in the CARIFORUM States so as to facilitate their ability to comply with the commitments set out in this Agreement;
  - ii. The provision of assistance for capacity and institution building for fiscal reform in order to strengthen tax administration and improve the collection of tax revenues with a view to shifting dependence from tariffs and other duties and charges to other forms of indirect taxation;
  - iii. The provision of support measures aimed at promoting private sector and enterprise development, in particular small economic operators, and enhancing the international competitiveness of CARIFORUM firms and diversification of the CARIFORUM economies;
  - iv. The diversification of CARIFORUM exports of goods and services through new investment and the development of new sectors;
  - v. Enhancing the technological and research capabilities of the CARIFORUM States so as to facilitate development of, and compliance with, internationally recognised sanitary and phytosanitary measures and technical standards and internationally recognised labour and environmental standards;

(Continued)

19 The IISD model treaty creates a technical assistance committee that is charged with organising the provision of technical assistance to the party states relating to the implementation of the agreement and with administering a special fund to be set up by the party states for the provision of technical assistance. See IISD model treaty, Art. 37. Precedents for technical assistance commitments may be found in a wide variety of agreements outside IIAs and home country programmes. See UNCTAD (2001), *Home Country Measures*, op. cit.

(Continued)

vi. The development of CARIFORUM innovation systems, including the development of technological capacity; and

vii. Support for the development of infrastructure in CARIFORUM States necessary for the conduct of trade.

- Additional more specific commitments to provide technical assistance in the following areas.

  i. Improving the ability of service suppliers of the Signatory CARIFORUM States to gather information on and to meet regulations and standards of the EC Party at European Community, national and sub-national levels;

  ii. Improving the export capacity of service suppliers of the Signatory CARIFORUM States, with particular attention to the marketing of tourism and cultural services, the needs of small and medium-sized enterprises, franchising and the negotiation of mutual recognition agreements;

  iii. Facilitating interaction and dialogue between service suppliers of the EC Party and of the Signatory CARIFORUM States;

  iv. Addressing quality and standards needs in those sectors where the Signatory CARIFORUM States have undertaken commitments under this Agreement and with respect to their domestic and regional markets as well as trade between the Parties, and in order to ensure participation in the development and adoption of sustainable tourism standards;

  v. Developing and implementing regulatory regimes for specific service sectors at CARIFORUM regional level and in Signatory CARIFORUM States in those sectors where they have undertaken commitments under this Agreement; and

  vi. Establishing mechanisms for promoting investment and joint ventures between service suppliers of the EC Party and of the Signatory CARIFORUM States, and enhancing the capacities of investment promotion agencies in Signatory CARIFORUM States.

- Additional sector-specific co-operation commitments related to tourism and ecommerce.
- Establishment of a regional development fund by both parties to mobilise and direct development funding.

The IISD model contains a specialised technical assistance commitment not found in any existing IIA. It provides for the establishment of a 'Legal Assistance Centre' to provide support for developing countries defending investor–state claims.

Modelled on the Advisory Centre on WTO Law, the Centre is to be independent of other institutions created under the agreement and provide: (i) legal advice in connection with specific cases; (ii) capacity building on legal issues; and (iii) support for implementation of the agreement. Financing is to come from a variety of sources.[20]

In addition to these recommendations, it would be prudent to consider the potential benefits of technical assistance in developing dispute avoidance policies and practices in host states as well as support for the development of expertise in ADR. The potential benefits of ADR in terms of maintaining relationships between investors and host states and increasing prospects for early, cost-effective and mutually satisfying resolution of disputes suggest that technical assistance in these areas would be useful for states and investors. Other possible targets for technical assistance related to dispute settlement might include the development of regional arbitration centres and training for arbitrators, with the goal of enhancing local competence to adjudicate investor–state and other disputes.

8.2.2 Challenges in drafting a technical assistance provision

It is not possible to specify in the abstract what assistance or what level of funding will be required in an IIA. The determination of what is appropriate must be left to each pair of negotiating states in light of the needs and priorities of the host developing country party and the capacity, resources and political will of the other party to the treaty. It is likely to be easier to negotiate technical assistance commitments in the context of regional integration initiatives and broad-based economic partnership agreements whose purposes go far beyond investor protection. In addition, like investment promotion, it will be easiest to negotiate technical assistance commitments that advance home state interests. For example, supporting improvements in the transparency and efficiency of host state regulation may be something that the home states would be interested in funding because such improvements facilitate the operation of their investors in the host state by reducing their costs and increasing the predictability of host state rules.[21]

Box 8.4 Summary of options for technical assistance provisions

1. *No technical assistance provision*
2. *A hortatory or best efforts technical assistance obligation*
3. *Binding obligation to provide technical assistance*
    a. Establish a body under the treaty with representation from both parties to identify technical assistance activities, develop a technical assistance plan and periodically review its achievements
    b. Establish a dedicated fund for the delivery of technical assistance

20 IISD model treaty, Art. 41.
21 IISD model treaty, Art. 41.

8.2.3 Discussion of options

1. *No technical assistance provision*

   If, as in most existing IIAs, there is no provision dealing with technical assistance, technical assistance will be provided only on the basis of ad hoc arrangements between the parties.

2. *A hortatory or best efforts technical assistance obligation*

   A provision that expresses a non-binding intention of the parties that one party will provide technical assistance creates no legal commitment, but may have some benefits. Its inclusion in an IIA means that the negotiating parties have directed their minds to the need for such assistance. Such a provision may set out a detailed elaboration of specific objectives or activities that the parties agree should be part of the non-binding commitment to provide technical assistance. The parties have an opportunity to discuss (i) the host state's needs for assistance, (ii) the kinds of technical assistance activities that are consistent with the policies of the host state, and (iii) the opportunities that exist for the home state to co-operate with the host state in the delivery of technical assistance, consistent with the capacity of the home state and the needs and priorities of the host state.

   If technical assistance is not provided as contemplated, a hortatory or best efforts treaty provision provides a basis for the host state to raise the issue with the home state. A hortatory or best efforts undertaking may be the subject of monitoring and/or an obligation to review periodically whether technical assistance is being provided as contemplated in the treaty.

3. *Binding obligation to provide technical assistance*

   This is the strongest form of obligation. As with option 2, this option provides an opportunity to identify and articulate specific technical assistance commitments. In addition, it could be the subject of dispute settlement where commitments were not being complied with. Such a provision can be made more effective by the following complementary provisions:

   a. Establish a body under the treaty with representation from both parties to identify technical assistance activities, develop a technical assistance plan and periodically review its achievements;

   b. Establish a dedicated fund for the delivery of technical assistance.

   In general, technical assistance commitments that are expressed in very specific terms will be easier to enforce. Agreement on technical assistance commitments is more likely in broad-based economic partnership agreements.

8.2.4 Discussion of sample provision

In recognition of the impossibility of enumerating specific technical assistance commitments in the abstract, the Guide sample provision simply contemplates that a technical assistance committee will be established by the parties acting through the Commission.[22] The committee will be responsible for developing a technical assistance plan. The purpose of the plan is to identify specific activities that support the implementation of the agreement and party states' compliance with their obligations. Assistance may also be directed towards a variety of other goals to be identified by the committee that may include improved domestic regulation, technology transfer, investment promotion and capacity building in relation to IIA dispute settlement and prevention, including training for arbitrators. The committee will also be responsible for administering a technical assistance fund to be set up by the party states. Each year, the committee will be charged with reporting to the Commission on the achievement of the milestones in the technical assistance plan and the expenditures from the fund. In the interests of transparency and accountability, the committee's report must be made public.

The sample provision also requires each party state to provide the other with information necessary to fulfil its obligations under the IIA. This may include information regarding standards employed by a party in its domestic sustainability assessment process, which would be needed by a host state in connection with the implementation of a provision like the Guide sample provision on sustainability assessments.[23]

8.2.5 Sample provision: technical assistance

Technical Assistance

1. The Commission shall establish a technical assistance committee with equal representation from both Parties composed of individuals with expertise in the promotion of sustainable development.
2. The technical assistance committee shall be responsible for developing a technical assistance plan that provides for:
    a. Actions designed to support the implementation of this Agreement and the compliance by Parties with their obligations under this Agreement, including obligations to:
        i. develop sustainability assessment standards and an assessment process [see Guide Section 6.6 (Sustainability assessments)];
        ii. develop a grievance procedure and compliance process related to environmental and social impact assessments in accordance with [Guide sample provision in Section 6.15 (Grievance procedure and other measures to enforce the management plan produced in the sustainability assessment)];
        iii. create a civil liability regime for non-compliance with this Agreement by investors in accordance with [Guide sample provision in Section 6.16 (Civil liability of investors)]; and

22 See Section 9.2 (Commission). This is a body composed of ministerial-level members of the executive branch of the governments of both party states.

23 See Section 6.6 (Sustainability assessments).

iv. impose criminal sanctions against investors of either Party for the commission of or complicity in grave violations of human rights or for the commission of or complicity in corruption in accordance with [Guide sample provision in Section 6.14 (Criminal sanctions)], and

b. Such other matters as the members of the committee or the Commission determine, which may include assistance by a Party to:

i. develop transparent and effective regimes for the facilitation, admission and regulation of foreign investment in the other Party;

ii. build human, legal and institutional capacity in the other Party so as to facilitate its ability to comply with the commitments set out in this Agreement;

iii. provide support aimed at promoting private sector and enterprise development, in particular small economic operators, and enhancing the international competitiveness of the other Party's firms and diversification of the other Party's economy;

iv. enhance the technological and research capabilities of the other Party so as to facilitate development of, and compliance with, internationally recognised technical, and labour and environmental standards;

v. support for the development of infrastructure in the other Party necessary for the conduct of economic development;

vi. build capacity with respect to the other Party's agencies responsible for and programmes on investment promotion and facilitation;

vii. provide technical or financial support for sustainability assessments of potential investments in the other Party;

viii. encourage technology transfer and exchange of expertise on entrepreneurship, management research and management centres, quality and production standards to the other Party;

ix. develop regional arbitration centres in the other Party and provide training of arbitrators in the other Party;

x. support the development of policies and procedures in the other Party designed to avoid disputes and manage conflicts with investors; and

xi. build capacity in the other Party state to engage in alternative dispute resolution procedures in connection with investor–state disputes.

c. Administering the technical assistance fund established under section 3; and

d. Reviewing the technical assistance plan on an annual basis and preparing a report to the Commission on the use of funds from the technical assistance fund and the implementation of the technical assistance plan.

The report of the Commission shall be made available to the public by the Commission.

3. The Parties shall establish a technical assistance fund to provide support for institutional development and capacity building in a Party and the achievement of the technical assistance plan. The amount of funds to be allocated to the technical assistance fund shall be determined annually by the Commission.

4. On request by the other Party, a Party shall, in a timely manner, provide to the other Party such information as is requested and available for the purposes of assisting that Party to meet its obligations and perform its duties under this Agreement. Parties shall protect confidential business information in fulfilling the obligations in this Article.

5. For greater certainty, the obligation of a Party under subsection 4 includes an obligation to provide information regarding the standards that would apply in that Party to investors in that Party in circumstances similar to those of an investment proposed by an investor of that Party in the other Party, including but not limited to standards employed in that Party's sustainability assessment process.

Chapter 9

Final Provisions: Commission, Entry into Force and Termination

9.1 Introduction

The Guide provides two final sample provisions. Versions of these provisions are found in most treaties:

- A provision establishing an institution responsible for the ongoing administration of the treaty;
- A provision describing the process by which the treaty, once adopted, enters into force and the rules applicable to the termination of the agreement.

9.2 Commission

Cross references

Section 6.13	Enforcement of investor obligations	372
Section 7.1	Investor–state dispute settlement	408
Section 7.2	State-to-state dispute settlement	483
Section 8.1	Investment promotion	493
Section 8.2	Technical assistance	499

Depending on the scope and nature of the obligations in an IIA, it is usually useful to have some kind of institution with representatives from both parties that are responsible for various tasks associated with the administration of the treaty. Only some IIAs provide for such an institution. Provisions for institutions are rare in BITs but more common in regional trade and investment treaties, such as FTAs.

9.2.1 IIA practice and options for institutional arrangements

Many traditional IIAs do not contemplate any form of institution.[1] In large part, this is because agreements did not contemplate ongoing co-operative activities by the parties. The Canadian model agreement is an exception in this regard. It provides for the establishment of a commission of ministerial-level representatives from both parties to supervise the implementation of the agreement, deal with disputes regarding its interpretation and adopt a code of conduct for arbitrators.[2] It may be desirable to add more elaborate provisions in an IIA regarding institutions. What institutions are needed, however, will depend on the obligations under the IIA, as

1 E.g. US model BIT, UK model IPPA, Indian model BIPPA.
2 Canadian model FIPA, Art. 51.

well as the resources of the parties and the nature and extent of their relationship. Where substantial ongoing co-operative activities of the kind contemplated in the sample provisions in the Guide are included in an IIA, a more elaborate institutional structure will be appropriate. In a broad-based regional integration arrangement, even more institutions will be needed. In COMESA,[3] for example, the member states have agreed to put in place a wide range of supportive institutions.[4]

9.2.2 Discussion of sample provision

The sample provision in the Guide contemplates the creation of a Commission charged with various responsibilities in connection with the administration of an IIA, including issuing authoritative interpretations of the agreement and performing other functions that have been referred to in the sample provisions in the Guide.[5] Each party state must appoint a ministerial-level person to the Commission. The scope of the Commission's responsibilities and the possible need for other institutions will vary depending on the nature of obligations in the IIA.

9.2.3 Sample provision: commission

Commission

1. The Parties hereby agree to establish a Commission, comprising ministerial-level representatives of the Parties or their designees.
2. The Commission shall:
   a. Supervise the implementation of this Agreement;
   b. Resolve disputes that may arise regarding its interpretation or application in accordance with [Guide sample provisions in Section 7.2 (State-to-state dispute settlement)];
   c. Determine the amount, type and duration of assistance to be provided by the Parties under [Guide sample provision in Section 8.1 (Investment promotion)];
   d. Establish a technical assistance committee in accordance with [Guide sample provision in Section 8.2 (Technical assistance)];
   e. Establish a code of conduct for dispute settlement in accordance with [Guide sample provision [H] (arbitrators) in Section 7.1 (Investor–state dispute

3 The COMESA Investment Agreement (2007) is part of a broad-based process of economic integration of the member states of the Common Market for Eastern and Southern Africa (Burundi, Comoros, Democratic Republic of Congo, Djibouti, Egypt, Eritrea, Ethiopia, Kenya, Libya, Madagascar, Malawi, Mauritius, Rwanda, Seychelles, Sudan, Swaziland, Uganda, Zambia and Zimbabwe).

4 Similarly, the ASEAN Agreement (2009) contemplates a number of institutions (Art. 42), as does the SADC Investment Protocol (2006).

5 See Sample Art. [S] (Governing Law) in Section 7.1 (Investor–state dispute settlement); Section 6.15 (Grievance procedure and other measures to enforce the management plan produced in the sustainability assessment); Section 8.1 (Investment promotion); Section 8.2 (Technical assistance).

settlement)] and [Guide sample provision in Section 7.2 (State-to-state dispute settlement)]; and

f. Consider any other matter that may affect the operation of this Agreement.

3. The Commission may take such other action in the exercise of its functions as the Parties may agree, including amendment of the code of conduct for arbitrators.

4. The Commission shall establish its rules and procedures.

9.3 Termination of IIAs

Cross reference

Section 4.5 Scope of application 94

The burden of obligations imposed under an IIA is defined in part by how long such obligations remain in force. The term and termination provisions in IIAs vary to some extent. Investors seeking certainty with respect to their investments will prefer longer guaranteed terms. For host states, committing to a longer term in an IIA provides a stronger signal of its commitment to the obligations in the treaty. However, in light of the unexpected costs and other concerns that have arisen in connection with the application of IIA standards in investor–state dispute arbitration, states may prefer shorter minimum terms, so that if IIA obligations prove to be too burdensome, earlier termination is possible.

Another issue that is frequently the subject of IIA provisions is whether obligations to investors who have made investments in the host state while the treaty was in force should continue for some period of time after termination of the treaty. Investors will favour such commitments, but they mean that even after a state has decided to terminate an IIA, it will continue to be bound to its obligations in relation to all investors whose investments were in place at the time of termination for the period specified in the treaty.

9.3.1 IIA practice

While almost all IIAs address termination and the post-termination continuation of obligations, the approach varies. The US and Canadian model treaties both contemplate indefinite duration in the absence of some action to terminate by one of the parties. The Canadian model treaty allows termination at any time, with 12 months' notice to the other party, but remains in force for another 15 years for investments or commitments to invest made before termination.[6] The US model BIT

6 Canadian model FIPA, Art. 52; Canada–Peru, Agreement between the Government of Canada and The Government of the Republic of Peru for the Promotion and Protection of Investments, signed 14 November 2006, in force 20 June 2007, Art. 52(3); Canada–Ecuador, Agreement between the Government of Canada and the Government of the Republic of Ecuador for the Promotion and Reciprocal Protection of Investments, signed 29 April 1996, in force 6 June 1997, Art. XVIII(2). The provisions in the Indian model BIPPA are the same (Art. 15(a)).

allows termination only after ten years on one year's written notice. However, the provisions remain in force for investments established or acquired prior to termination for a further ten years.[7] Under the UK model treaty, the agreement remains in force for 10 years and thereafter may be terminated on 12 months' notice, as under the US model, but for investments made while the agreement was in force, the obligations continue for 20 years after the date of termination.[8]

Similar provisions are found in developing country agreements. For example, in the COMESA Investment Agreement, the agreement remains in force for ten years and continues in force for a further ten years unless the member states agree by consensus to terminate the agreement.[9] The agreement continues to apply to investments of investors from member states established or acquired prior to termination for ten years after termination. Individual members may withdraw on notice to the COMESA Secretary-General, but the agreement continues in force for another twelve months and, for investments of investors of other member states made prior to withdrawal, the obligations of the withdrawing member continue for five years after the date of withdrawal.[10] The India–Singapore CECA continues in effect for 15 years after termination in relation to investments made prior to termination, though no termination mechanism is specified.[11]

UNCTAD found that the average IIA term was ten years and after the expiry of that period most IIAs may be terminated on one year's notice.[12] UNCTAD also found that since 1995 the dominant approach in IIAs has been to have an indefinite term and to include clauses providing for survival of obligations for between five and twenty years for investment made prior to the termination of the treaty.[13] The IISD model seeks to provide more flexibility for host states. It allows a host state to protect its non-investment interests by permitting a party to terminate the treaty 180 days after giving written notice. For investments in place at the time of the termination, the rights and obligations under the IISD model remain in force for a further five years.[14]

---

7 US model BIT, Art. 22.

8 UK model IPPA, Art. 14. Under United Kingdom–Mexico, Agreement between the Government of the United Kingdom of Great Britain and Northern Ireland and the Government of the United Mexican States, signed 12 May 2006, in force 25 July 2007, Art. 27 allows termination after 10 years with 1 year's notice, with the provisions remaining in effect for investments made prior to the date of termination for a further 15 years. Under Art. 13 of Barbados–Germany, Agreement between Barbados and the Federal Republic of Germany for the Promotion and Protection of Investments, signed 2 December 1994, in force 11 May 2002, termination is permitted after 10 years or thereafter following a 1-year notice period in both cases. For investments made before termination, the treaty continues to be effective for a further 20 years.

9 COMESA Investment Agreement (2007), Art. 39.1 and 39.2. The same approach is taken in the Colombian model agreement (Art. XIII).

10 COMESA Investment Agreement (2007), Art. 39.3.

11 India–Singapore CECA (2005), Art. 6.24.

12 UNCTAD (2007), *Treaties 1996–2006*, op. cit., at 20.

13 UNCTAD (2010), *Denunciation of the ICSID Convention and BITS: Impact on Investor–State Claims*, IIA Issues Note No. 2, December 2010, United Nations, New York and Geneva, at 3.

14 IISD model treaty, Art. 57.

Box 9.1 Summary of options for termination provisions

1. *No fixed term*
2. *Fixed term*
3. *Continuation of obligations after termination of IIA for pre-termination investments*

9.3.2 Discussion of options

1. *No fixed term*

Without any fixed term, an IIA may be terminated at any time in accordance with whatever termination provision is included in the treaty, such as on 12 months' notice by one party. This provides limited certainty to investors and maximum flexibility for the host state. This flexibility may be curtailed in relation to existing investments at the time of termination, if the IIA provides that its obligations continue to apply to these investments for some specified period after termination.

2. *Fixed term*

A minimum fixed term provides less flexibility for host states, but more certainty for investors, though the certainty for investors diminishes every year as the end of the term approaches. Long term commitments to protect investors under IIAs limit the extent to which host states can avoid the treaty's restrictions on their ability to regulate foreign investor activity consistent with their other international obligations and development objectives. If the IIA has a long term of application, host states that find, over time, that the provisions of the IIA are not compatible with their development objectives and human rights and other obligations may not be able to simply withdraw and terminate their obligations under them within a reasonable time frame.[15]

One other consideration regarding fixed terms is what happens following the end of the term. Most IIAs provide that they continue subject to some right for each party to terminate with some period of advance notice. An IIA may also provide for termination at the end of the term or that that treaty continues in force only if both parties agree based on a joint review of the agreement and its effects.

3. *Continuation of obligations after termination of IIA for pre-termination investments*

Providing protection for existing investments after termination provides significant security for investors but substantially restricts the ability of host states to avoid obligations that they have found unacceptable. Long survival periods reduce the

15 Schneiderman has compared the investor rights created by these treaties to constitution-like rights D Schneiderman (2000), 'Investment Rules and the New Constitutionalism', 25 *Law and Social Inquiry*, 757, at 771.

benefits to host states of IIA provisions that do not have a fixed term and can be terminated unilaterally by the host state.

9.3.3 Discussion of sample provision

Host states and investors sometimes have conflicting priorities in relation to term and termination provisions. Investors will generally want the longest guaranteed terms and lengthy post-termination protection for investments in place at the time of termination. States have an interest in attracting investment be agreeing to such provisions but, in light of concerns about IIAs, may also want flexibility to terminate without significant continuing obligations. The Guide sample termination provision takes a compromise approach. It follows recent IIA practice and provides for an indefinite term with a guaranteed minimum term of five years. After the expiry of the minimum term, termination by a party is possible at any time upon 180 days notice to the other party. Obligations in relation to investments in place at the time of termination continue for five years after termination. The periods for the term of the agreement, notice of termination and the survival of obligations in relation to investments in place at the time of termination are shorter than is common in current practice. States that decide that different terms and/or post-termination commitments better suit their needs can simply insert different time periods in the sample provision.

The sample provision also addresses when the treaty comes into force and provides that the annexes to the agreement are part of the parties' obligations under the treaty.

9.3.4 Sample provision: application and entry into force and termination

Application and Entry into Force and Termination

1. The Annexes hereto shall form integral parts of this Agreement.
2. Each Party shall notify the other Party in writing of the completion of the procedures required in its territory for the entry into force of this Agreement. This Agreement shall enter into force on the date of the later of the two notifications.
3. This Agreement shall remain in force for a term of five (5) years from the date it enters into force. After the expiry of that term, this Agreement will remain in force unless either Party notifies the other Party in writing of its intention to terminate it. The termination of this Agreement shall become effective 180 days after notice of termination has been received by the other Party. In respect of investments made prior to the date when the termination of this Agreement becomes effective, the provisions of the Agreement shall remain in force for a period of five (5) years from the date of termination.

Appendix 1. Review of Evidence Regarding Whether IIAs Encourage Investment Inflows to Signatory Countries

Introduction and overview

The views of those who have written about the anticipated effects of international investment obligations on FDI flows vary widely. Some, such as Sornarajah, suggest that 'in reality attracting foreign investment depends more on the political and economic climate for its existence rather than on the creation of a legal structure for its protection'.[1] Many others simply assume that international investment obligations will promote FDI inflows.[2] Proponents of IIAs as strategies to promote inward investment, however, have had to confront the fact that some developing countries, of which Brazil is the best example, have been extremely successful in attracting FDI from countries with which they do not have IIAs.[3] Other countries have signed IIAs and attracted little investment. Recently, researchers have tried to determine empirically whether international investment agreements actually result in increased foreign investment flows into signatory countries. Unfortunately, the empirical studies that have been done to date have not come to consistent conclusions regarding the effects of IIAs on investment flows.

Studies have looked at two main expected effects of signing IIAs on investment flows:

- **Commitment effect**: Signing an IIA creates an international commitment by a host country to comply with investor protection obligations in the treaty in relation to investors from the other party state. The anticipated effect is increased investment by investors from that other party state.
- **Signalling effect**: Signing an IIA sends a signal generally to foreign investors that a country is serious about protecting the rights and interests of foreign investors. The anticipated effect is increased investment from all countries.

To determine whether there is a commitment effect in practice, studies have looked at investment flows between pairs of countries that have signed a bilateral investment treaty. Some of these studies show a significant positive correlation between a developing country signing a BIT with a developed country and increased

1 M Sornarajah (2010), *The International Law of Foreign Investment*, 3d ed., Cambridge University Press, Cambridge, at 82.

2 A Guzman (1998), 'Why LDCs Sign Treaties that Hurt Them: Explaining the Popularity of Bilateral Investment Treaties', 38 *Virginia Journal of International Law* 639.

3 M Hallward-Driemeier (2003), 'Do Bilateral Investment Treaties Attract FDI? Only a Bit … and They Could Bite', World Bank Policy Research Paper WPS 3121, World Bank, Washington, DC; J W Salacuse and N P Sullivan (2005), 'Do BITs Really Work? An Evaluation of Bilateral Investment Treaties and Their Grand Bargain', 46 *Harvard International Law Journal* 67.

foreign investment from that developed country.[4] Other studies have found little or no evidence of such an effect. A similar inconsistency exists in studies seeking to determine if a signalling effect exists. Some studies have found a positive effect on total investment inflows into a country from all countries as a result of signing a BIT, while others have not. Most studies have found that other forms of IIA, such as preferential trade and investment agreements, have had a positive effect on investment inflows.

In some of the studies that found a positive relationship between signing an IIA and investment inflows, the results varied depending on particular circumstances. For example, several studies have found that the relationship between IIAs signed by a country and investment inflows to that country vary with the number of agreements entered into. At some point, signing an additional agreement was found to have little marginal effect.

Commentators have suggested that the inconsistency in results of studies looking at the relationship between signing an IIA and investment inflows is due to problems with data and econometric modelling techniques. For example, most studies do not attempt to control for the effect of investment-liberalising changes made by a host state to its domestic regime that often are contemporaneous with entering into a BIT. Where a study shows a positive relationship between signing a BIT and investment inflows, but does not try to eliminate the effects of pro-investment domestic reform, it may overstate the investment-inducing effect. Some of the new investment may be attributable to the changes to the domestic regime. While the impact of the changes to the domestic regime on the results is uncertain, the failure to control for such an impact in an empirical study of the effects of signing a BIT makes the results unreliable.

Attempts to use alternative empirical approaches to find evidence of the impact of the existence of investment agreements on investment flows, such as surveys of corporate decision-makers regarding the factors that they take into account in deciding whether to invest in a country, have been similarly inconclusive.

Review of empirical studies[5]

BITs

Studies of the commitment effect on bilateral investment flows

The first major empirical study of the relationship between IIAs and investment flows was completed by UNCTAD in 1998. It looked at the impact of signing a BIT between pairs of countries on bilateral FDI flows between the parties over the period 1971–94.

4 Ibid.

5 General surveys of the empirical work to date are provided in UNCTAD (2009), *The Role of International Investment Agreements in Attracting Foreign Direct Investment to Developing Countries*, United Nations, New York and Geneva, discussing the methodological problems with the empirical studies (at 56–8), and K P Sauvant, and L E Sachs (eds) (2009), *The Effect of Treaties on Foreign Direct Investment: Bilateral Investment Treaties, Double Taxation Treaties and Investment Flows*, Oxford University Press, Oxford.

The study showed that there was evidence of a positive relationship, but that the role of signing a BIT in attracting FDI was likely to be minor and of secondary importance. The prime explanatory variables for investment flows into the host state were the host state's GDP and population, and the level of domestic investment in the host state compared with the host country's GDP. The authors suggest that one possible explanation for this result was that the main political reason for a developed country to push for the conclusion of a BIT with a particular developing country was pressure from investors lobbying their governments to enter into treaties with countries in which they had already invested as a way of protecting their assets. Another suggested explanation was that some positive investment effects may lag behind the signing of a treaty by many years.

In 2003, Hallward-Driemeier completed a study for the World Bank that looked at annual flows between pairs of countries consisting of 31 host developing countries and 20 OECD countries over the period 1980–2000. It found that the relationship between FDI flows and BITs was not statistically significant, with a few exceptions.[6] Hallward-Driemeier also found that, in general, a country with a stronger institutional capacity (in terms of rule of law, the protection of property rights, lack of corruption, government effectiveness and regulatory quality) that had entered into a BIT was more likely to attract investment than a country that had entered into a BIT but was lacking such capacity. A BIT was seen as an effective complement to strong domestic institutions, but not a substitute. As discussed below, a study by Tobin and Rose-Ackerman reached a similar conclusion, based on aggregate investment flows into host countries that had signed BITs.[7] This is a significant finding for developing countries that might seek to rely on BIT commitments, rather than undertaking the more difficult challenge of reforming its domestic regimes, though, as noted below, other studies have concluded that BIT commitments can be a substitute for domestic reform.

Several studies of the effects of BITs have come to more positive conclusions about the relationship between signing a BIT and attracting foreign investment, though the results are far from uniform. Salacuse and Sullivan attempted to examine the possibility that BITs with different levels of investor protection might have different effects on FDI.[8] Their study looked at annual investment flows from the USA to 31 developing countries in the period 1991–2000. In general, US BITs provide higher levels of investor protection than the forms of agreement employed by some other countries. For example, US BITs provide prospective investors with a right to establish in a host state, impose restrictions on host state use of performance requirements, and include

6 Hallward-Driemeier, op. cit., at 2. Significantly, one of the exceptions was the North American Free Trade Agreement (signed 17 December 1992, in force 1 January 1994, reprinted in (1993) 32 *International Legal Materials* 605). The author acknowledged, however, that it was difficult to distinguish the impact of the NAFTA investment chapter from the effect of the other elements of the agreement.

7 J Tobin and S Rose-Ackerman (2003), 'Foreign Direct Investment and the Business Environment in Developing Countries: The Impact of Bilateral Investment Treaties', William Davidson Institute Working Paper No. 587, Michigan: The University of Michigan Business School, Ann Arbour.

8 Salacuse and Sullivan, op. cit.

a robust investor-state dispute settlement mechanism. Some of these provisions are lacking in other models. Salacuse and Sullivan found that there was a strong positive relationship between a developing country entering into a BIT with the USA and increased US FDI into the developing country, as well as with greater FDI from other OECD countries. They estimated that an annual increase of between 77 and 85 per cent in investment inflows from the USA resulted from signing a BIT with the USA. BITs with other OECD members also had a positive impact. The positive effect of a US BIT in this regard, however, was much more significant than the investment effects associated with weaker BITs negotiated by other OECD member countries. The authors concluded that the higher levels of investor protection in the US model BIT contributed to a stronger FDI stimulus from the signing of a BIT. They also found that the impact for a developing country entering into a US BIT was larger if the country's overall number of BITs was below the mean number of BITs entered into by developing countries with other OECD countries (7.3). Above the mean, the correlation between US BITs and increased FDI was very weak and statistically insignificant. The authors suggest that this could be because the US investment could get crowded out in situations where a developing country has strong investment relationships with a significant number of other OECD countries.

Subsequent studies have come to inconsistent conclusions regarding the impact of US BITs. In their study of 24 Latin American countries, Gallagher and Birch found no positive correlation between a US BIT with a country and US FDI into that country.[9] Some other studies have come to similar conclusions regarding the effect of US BITs,[10] while others have agreed with Salacuse and Sullivan.[11]

Surprisingly, Salacuse and Sullivan found that BITs entered into between developing countries had a negative impact on FDI flows between them. Some other studies have found that agreements between developing countries have no effect, even though BITs between developed and developing countries were found to have a positive effect.[12]

Studies of the signalling effect on total investment flows

Neumayer and Spess[13] reached some conclusions that are similar to those of Salacuse and Sullivan, but looking at the relationship between total investment flows into a

9 K P Gallagher and M B L Birch (2006), 'Do Investment Agreements Attract Investment? Evidence from Latin America', *Journal of World Investment Law and Trade* 7 at 961.

10 Tobin and Rose-Ackerman, op. cit.; P Busse et al. (February 2008), 'FDI Promotion through Bilateral Investment Treaties: More than a BIT?', Kiel Working Paper No. 1403, Kiel Institute for the World Economy, Kiel, at 25.

11 Y Z Haftel (2010), 'Ratification Counts: US Investment Treaties and FDI Flows into Developing Countries', 17 *Review of International Political Economy* 248 (explaining the different result from Gallagher and Birch by looking at BITs that were ratified, not just signed); and T Siegmann (2007), 'The Impact of Bilateral Investment Treaties and Double Taxation Treaties on Foreign Direct Investment', University of St. Gallen Law and Economics Research Paper Series, Working Paper No. 2008–22, St. Gallen, (adopting a similar explanation).

12 E.g. R Banga (2006), 'Do Investment Agreements Matter?', 21 *Journal of Economic Integration* 40 (comparing BITs between APEC members and those between ASEAN members).

13 E Neumayer and L Spess (2005), 'Do Bilateral Investment Treaties Increase Foreign Direct Investment in Developing Countries?', 33 *World Development* 1567. Egger and Merlo found that signing a BIT had a positive effect on FDI stocks in a study of BITS involving OECD countries and

country and signing a BIT.[14] Unlike Salacuse and Sullivan and Hallward-Driemeier, Neumayer and Spess used a very broad sample of 119 countries. Also, instead of using data from single years over a period of time, they looked at aggregate flows over a long period using a dataset running from 1970–2001.[15] They found a positive relationship between signing BITs and foreign investment inflows. In addition, Neumayer and Spess found evidence that the positive impact was more significant for countries with riskier domestic environments. They concluded that such countries would be more likely to experience an increase in inward investment as a result of signing a BIT on the basis that BITs function as substitutes for institutional quality in host countries. This conclusion conflicts directly with Hallward-Driemeier's conclusion that developing countries cannot expect BITs to substitute for domestic institutional quality.[16]

A number of other studies have found a positive relationship between signing a BIT and total inward investment.[17] Tobin and Rose-Ackerman did a new study in 2006 with an even larger sample, including 137 countries and using five-year averages of total FDI flows over the period 1980–2003.[18] They found a positive correlation between signing BITs and inward FDI in developing countries. They also found that the positive effect of signing a BIT decreased as the number of BITs worldwide increased. More recently, however, Büthe and Milner found that the more BITs a country signed, the more positive was the effect on aggregate investment inflows.[19]

In a 2007 study, Yackee[20] sought to replicate the results obtained by Neumayer and Spess, but used a dataset that included a longer time period, and a broader measure of investment agreements that included BITs, free trade agreements and other agreements containing investment provisions that are substantially similar to those found in a BIT. He also incorporated some other minor adjustments to the Neumayer and Spess model. In contrast to the results of Neumayer and Spess, Yackee's results

---

transition economies (P Egger and V Merlo (2007), 'The Impact of Bilateral Investment Treaties on FDI Dynamics', 30 *World Economy* 1536). Significantly, Egger and Merlo found that while there was a significant contemporaneous effect associated with entering into a BIT, the long-run impact was larger. See, similarly, P Egger and M Pfaffermayr (2004), 'The impact of bilateral investment treaties on foreign direct investment', 73 *Journal of Comparative Economics* 788, at 790.

14 Ibid.

15 Salacuse and Sullivan, op. cit., and Hallward-Driemeier, op. cit., used cross-sectional data for single years.

16 Two recent studies reached the same conclusion as Hallward-Driemeier regarding complementarity: Siegmann, op. cit., at 76; and Busse et al. (2008), op. cit., at 15.

17 Aggregate investment flows (T Büthe and H V Milner, 'Bilateral Investment Treaties and Foreign Direct Investment: A Political Analysis', in Sauvant and Sachs, op. cit.; R Grosse and L J Trevino (2005), 'New Institutional Economics and FDI Location in Central and Eastern Europe', 45 *Management International Review* 123; Banga, op. cit.; Siegmann, op. cit., at 76).

18 Tobin and Rose-Ackerman (2006), op. cit.

19 Büthe and Milner, op. cit., at 213.

20 J W Yackee (2007), 'Do BITs Really Work? Revisiting the Empirical Link between Investment Treaties and Foreign Direct Investment', Legal Studies Research Paper No. 1054, University of Wisconsin Law School, Madison.

showed no statistically significant positive relationship between BITs and FDI for a large minority of his observations. While he found some evidence of a positive relationship in relation to developing countries that had low levels of political risk, he found no evidence to support Neumayer and Spess's conclusion that the benefits of BIT signing were greater for countries with higher political risk. Indeed, his observations supported the conclusion that the opposite was true. In other words, the magnitude of the positive effect of BIT signing on investment increases as political risk declines. Yackee re-ran the analysis looking only at strong BITs, which he defined as those having binding investor state arbitration. The results obtained with this more limited dataset were consistent with his general findings. Significantly, he found that all his results were sensitive to various modelling choices. A similar conclusion was reached by Tobin and Rose-Ackerman.

Other forms of IIAs

There is stronger evidence that preferential trade and investment agreements (PTIAs) lead to increased inward FDI for party states, both from within the countries that are party to the agreement and from other countries seeking a platform for serving the countries that are parties to the PTIA.[21] In one recent study, researchers suggested a qualification to this result, based on their analysis of FDI flows between 1978 and 2004. They found that FDI is positively associated with a PTIA only if it creates commitments regarding the admission of investment. The presence of dispute settlement procedures in PTIAs, such as investor-state arbitration, was found to be less significant. The study also found that PTIAs without strong investment provisions may even discourage FDI by encouraging businesses from other party states to export to the host state, rather than investing in the host state to serve its market.[22]

Challenges associated with empirical studies of investment flows

In summary, there is some evidence that IIA obligations have a positive effect on FDI flows, though the empirical record is relatively thin and not entirely consistent. Overall, our understanding of the effects of IIAs on investment flows through the use of studies that use investment flow data to determine if there is an investment-inducing effect associated with signing an IIA is limited by several factors.

Problems with empirical models

Most studies looked simply at the correlation between IIAs and investment inflows and assumed that if the relationship was positive over time, that is signing an IIA

21 UNCTAD (2007), *Bilateral Investment Treaties 1995–2006: Trends in Investment Rulemaking*, UN publication, Sales No. E.06.II.D.16, United Nations, New York and Geneva, at 105–6, describes this conclusion as based on a consensus of the literature.

22 A Berger et al. (2010), 'Do Trade and Investment Agreements Lead to More FDI? Accounting for Key Provisions Inside the Black Box', Kiel Working Papers, No. 1647, Kiel Institute for the World Economy, Kiel, at 25.

was associated with increased investment, either from an IIA partner or generally from all countries, then it was the IIA that caused the increased investment. It is possible, however, that higher levels of bilateral investment encourage countries to negotiate IIAs, rather than the other way around.[23] This might occur, for example, where investors in a host state sought the protection of an IIA between their home state and the host state after making their investment and then their home state government negotiated a treaty. Alternatively, there may be variables that the model has left out that may affect investment flows. Most significantly, few studies to date have sought to separate the effects of IIAs from domestic policy changes liberalising the environment for FDI or otherwise promoting FDI.[24] In one of the few studies that have rigorously controlled for these kinds of problems, Aisbett concluded that it is impossible to say that IIAs caused increased investment flows.[25] In her view, the results found by Salacuse and Sullivan and by Neumayer and Spess are unreliable because they do not deal adequately with the possibility of reverse causation or other potential causes for the results observed, such as pro-investment domestic reform.[26]

Problems with data

There are a number of problems with using existing data to explain the relationship between FDI flows and signing investment treaties. One of the problems is that the data on investment flows for certain sectors, such as services, and for some countries, particularly least developed countries, are not always comparable or reliable.[27] This is particularly true regarding data on bilateral flows.[28] Investment flow data are also plagued by other problems associated with the complex organisation of transnational businesses. For example, sometimes investments may be identified as coming from a particular foreign country in which the entity making the investment is organised, but the real source of capital is another country. A national of one state may make an investment in that state through a wholly owned subsidiary corporation organised under the laws of another state. This kind of 'round-tripping' investment could be recorded as a foreign investment from the other state, even though it is really a domestic investment. Similarly, an investment that originates in one state may be identified as originating in another state if it has been flowed through a subsidiary organised under the laws of that other state. Such a structure might be adopted for

23 This problem is an example of what is referred to as 'endogeneity'. It arises where there are various possible interactions between what the researcher is trying to observe (in this case changes in investment flows) and other variables used in regression analysis to explain what is observed (in this case, the conclusion or number of IIAs).

24 Yackee (2007), op. cit. Studies have tried to address trade openness in their models. One study that did try to control for this found a positive correlation between IIAs and investment inflows (Busse et al. (2008), op. cit.).

25 E Aisbett (2009), 'Bilateral Investment Treaties and Foreign Direct Investment: Correlation versus Causation', in Sauvant and Sachs, op. cit.

26 Ibid.

27 J W Yackee (2010), 'Do Bilateral Investment Treaties Promote Foreign Direct Investment? Some Hints from Alternative Evidence', 51 *Virginia Law Review* 397 at 410.

28 Ibid. at 410–11.

various reasons, including seeking to take advantage of a low tax rate in the state in which the subsidiary is incorporated and the existence of an IIA between the state of incorporation of the subsidiary and the state in which the investment is made. In connection with these kinds of investments, investment flow statistics may not accurately reflect the true source of an investment.

The use of aggregate investment data may mask possible variations in the investment effects of IIAs from sector to sector. Different kinds of investments are likely to be affected by IIA commitments in different ways, though it is not clear what the effect will be. For example, it might be that investments in sectors where the international movement of capital is relatively easy, such as services, may be greatly affected by IIAs, while investments in sectors such as natural resources may not be affected by IIAs signed by a country that does not possess resources available for exploitation.[29] An alternative and opposite analysis is also possible. Investments with more sunk costs benefit more from the protections in an IIA. Thus investments in sectors such as natural resources, where there are substantial sunk costs that cannot be recovered unless the investment earns income for many years, may be more affected by IIAs. Other sectors, such as financial services, which do not involve significant sunk costs and where returns start to be earned earlier in its life cycle, may be little affected by IIA protection. Also, it may be that small and medium-sized businesses value IIA protection more highly, since large transnational corporations are often in a position to negotiate for commitments directly from the state.[30] As a result, IIA protection may have a greater effect on small and medium-sized investors. None of these kinds of considerations have been accounted for in the models used to date.

It may be that the sensitivity of investment flows to signing an IIA varies by the mode of investment entry. Perhaps investments in a country by foreign investors on their own are more likely to be affected by the country signing an IIA than investments in the form of joint ventures involving foreign and local partners, because the involvement of local partners may mitigate local political risk.

Finally, looking only at FDI inflows may not fully capture the FDI effects of IIAs. Such an approach does not measure investments that would have moved to another country in the absence of the IIA.[31]

IIAs with different strengths

Studies that use long-term data lump together many treaties signed by states over an extended period of time that may have varying terms providing quite different levels of protection for investors.[32] In particular, as noted, many early treaties did not provide

29 This is suggested by D L Swenson (2005), 'Why Do Developing Countries Sign BITs?' 12 *University of California Davis Journal of International Law & Policy* 131; Busse et al. (2008), op. cit., come to the opposite conclusion in their study (at 23).

30 UNCTAD (2007), *Treaties 1995–2006*, op. cit., at 52–3.

31 Swenson (2005), op. cit.

32 Ibid. Swenson developed a model that looked at the investment effects of signing a BIT, including effects occurring not only after the BIT was signed, but also for a period prior to signing during which

for investor-state arbitration, which significantly increases the effectiveness of the investor-protection provisions.[33] Few empirical studies control for the relative strength of IIA obligations. It may be that a more significant positive effect on investment inflows would be associated with IIAs incorporating stronger commitments. As noted above, however, those studies that looked only at the effects of strong US BITs have come to conflicting results.

Alternative evidence

In an attempt to address some of the methodological and data problems associated with the empirical studies discussed above, some researchers have surveyed investors to try to get a sense of the relative importance to them of the presence of an IIA in making decisions about where to invest. In a 2007 survey of transnational corporations for UNCTAD, more than 70 per cent of the respondents reported that the existence of an IIA with a country from which they would benefit did play a role in their decision about whether to invest in that country. Fewer than 25 per cent of the respondents, however, said that IIAs were relevant 'to a very great extent'. Only 23 per cent did not consider them 'at all'. Nine per cent of respondents answered 'don't know'.[34] Out of 33 factors, the existence of an investment treaty ranked about in the middle in terms of its relative importance. It ranked higher in relation to investments in transition economies.

In a recent study, Yackee used several alternative measures to try to understand the effect of BITs on investment and concluded that there is little evidence that BITs are likely to have a significant effect on investors' decision making.[35] First, he investigated whether the existence of BITs is correlated with a reduction in political risk. His hypothesis was that if BITs reduce political risk, then investment will be encouraged. Using data from two political risk-rating agencies, he tried to determine if signing BITs was correlated with lower political risk ratings. He found little evidence that signing BITs resulted in lower risk ratings for signatory countries. Second, Yackee looked at whether political risk insurers take into account the existence of a BIT in deciding whether and on what terms to issue insurance. If risk insurers take BITs into account, then investors are also likely to do so. He conducted an original survey of 56 insurers, both public and private, around the world. Nine of the fourteen political risk insurers that responded to his survey do not take BITs into account in assessing what premiums to charge, and eight said it was not their practice even to ask if a BIT was in place to protect the investor. Some of the others indicated that the existence of a BIT

---

investment might be stimulated by the anticipated signing of the agreement. She also attached more weight to lag effects than some other models. She found that new BIT signings in the early 1990s were not positively related to increased FDI, but that signing BITs in the late 1990s were positively related. In contrast, Siegmann, op. cit., found that BITs from 1985 to 1995 had a significant effect on investment flows, which treaties signed after 1995 did not.

33 Yackee (2007), op. cit., at 413.

34 L Kekic and K P Sauvant (2007), *World Investment Prospects to 2011: Foreign Direct Investment and the Challenge of Political Risk*, Economist Intelligence Unit and the Columbia Program on International Investment, London and New York, 96.

35 Yackee (2007), op. cit.

was an important consideration. Yackee concludes that there is little evidence from his survey to suggest that insurance underwriters, in general, consider BITs, and so it is unlikely that investors do either. Third, Yackee surveyed corporate counsel at major US corporations. Seventy-five (37%) of those surveyed responded. Even though awareness of BITs is probably increasing, with the growing number of high-profile investor-state arbitration claims, most respondents reported that they were fairly unfamiliar with them. With respect to their effectiveness, most of the respondents did not view the existence of a BIT as a significant factor in reducing the risk of adverse regulatory change. Only 5 per cent of respondents indicated that they viewed the existence of a BIT as very important to a decision to invest in a country.

Conclusion

While a majority of studies to date have found a positive relationship between a country signing an IIA and increased investment into that country, other studies dispute those results on a variety of grounds.

Taking a step back from technical critiques of the empirical analyses, there is another reason to question the reliability of some of the studies showing a strong positive relationship between IIAs and investment flows. The magnitude of the positive correlation between signing an IIA and increased investment found in some studies, such as the near doubling of investment inflows predicted by Salacuse and Sullivan, seems implausibly large. IIAs will always be only one factor relevant to investor decision making. Depending on the investor and its business objectives, other host state factors will be much more significant, including: (i) the size of and rate of growth of the domestic market; (ii) per capita income; (iii) geographical proximity to investors' home states; and (iv) the ease of investing in a market, including the availability, cost, reliability and quality of inputs into production such as labour, electricity, telecommunications and transport infrastructure. It does not accord with the experience of host countries that BITs would have such a large independent effect, given the obvious importance of these various other factors. Consequently, very strong positive results, such as those in Salacuse and Sullivan, may themselves suggest that the various identified problems with empirical analysis of investment flows must be playing a significant role, and that the reliability of the results is suspect. This is not, however, the same thing as saying that IIAs do not attract investment. Nevertheless, the work of Yackee and others looking at alternative sources of evidence suggest that if there is a role, it is relatively small.

In addition, whatever the evidence of benefits associated with concluding IIAs in the form of increased FDI inflows, it is not clear that they are higher than the substantial costs developing countries incur in negotiating, signing, ratifying and complying with the obligations typically contained in such treaties. This concern regarding the net benefits of IIAs is shared by some of those researchers who found that FDI inflows did result from signing IIAs.[36]

---

36 E.g. Neumayer and Spess, op. cit., at 1583; Büthe and Milner, op. cit., at 214.

Appendix 2. Overview of the *General Agreement on Trade in Services*

General introduction

The General Agreement on Trade in Services (*GATS*)[1] is one of the agreements entered into as part of the Uruguay Round of multilateral trade negotiations that resulted in the formation of the WTO. It was the first multilateral agreement on trade in services, though services are dealt with in many regional and bilateral trade and investment agreements. *GATS* applies to all measures of a WTO member that affect trade in services, including services supplied through a commercial presence, which includes some forms of investment.

GATS comprises both a general framework of obligations for WTO members that apply to all services and a negotiated set of additional specific commitments regarding the treatment of identified services activities that each member lists in a national schedule of commitments. *GATS* incorporates key principles from the General Agreement on Tariffs and Trade (*GATT*),[2] including most favoured nation (MFN) treatment, national treatment and transparency, though the application of these principles to services trade is substantially attenuated.

The most important general rule is the obligation to grant MFN treatment to foreign services and services suppliers. This means that members must treat services suppliers from other member states no less favourably than those from any other country. Members were permitted to list specified exceptions to their MFN obligation at the time they joined the WTO (*GATS* Art. II.2; Annex on Article II Exemptions).

For sectors listed in its national schedule, a member becomes subject to a higher level of obligation. Members must grant foreign services suppliers in these sectors national treatment (meaning treatment no less favourable than the treatment of domestic suppliers) (*GATS*, Art. XVII) and cannot impose certain restrictions on market access, such as limiting the total number of service providers in a sector and limiting the percentage of foreign ownership of a service supplier (*GATS*, Art. XVI). For listed sectors, the member's regulatory scheme must meet specified standards, including a requirement that measures affecting trade in services be administered in a reasonable, objective and impartial manner (*GATS*, Art. VI.I).

---

1 *General Agreement on Trade in Services*, signed 15 April 1994, in force 1 January 1995, Marrakesh Agreement Establishing the World Trade Organization, Final Act Embodying the Results of the Uruguay Round of Multilateral Trade Negotiations, GATT Doc. MTN/FA, Annex 1B, 1869 *United Nations Treaty Series* 183, 33 *International Legal Materials* 1167.

2 *General Agreement on Tariffs and Trade 1994*, signed 15 April 1994, in force 1 January 1995, Marrakesh Agreement Establishing the World Trade Organization, Final Act Embodying the Results of the Uruguay Round of Multilateral Trade Negotiations, GATT Doc. MTN/FA, Annex 1A, 1867 *United Nations Treaty Series* 187, 33 *International Legal Materials* 1153.

Listing a sector does not necessarily mean that foreign services suppliers from WTO members have an unrestricted right to enter the national market. The national treatment and market access obligations for listed sectors can be circumscribed by limitations inscribed in the schedule itself.

GATS commitments for the WTO's 159 member states interact with their IIA obligations in a variety of complex ways. Because each member's obligations are customised in its national schedule of commitments and MFN exemption list, IIAs and *GATS* do not interact in the same way for every country. This note on *GATS* provides a general overview of the provisions in *GATS* that are most relevant in relation to investment and IIA obligations.

Scope of application

Introduction

GATS applies to all measures taken by WTO member states that affect trade in services. Services are not defined. Instead, *GATS* simply states that trade in services means services supplied through any of four modes of supply:

- Mode 1: Cross-border supply – a service is supplied by a service supplier of a WTO member in the territory of the WTO member to a service consumer in the territory of any other member such as over the telephone or the internet;
- Mode 2: Consumption abroad – a service is supplied by a service supplier of a WTO member in the territory of the member to a service consumer of any other member where the service consumer travels to the supplier's country to consume the service;
- Mode 3: Commercial presence – a service is supplied by a service supplier of one member through a commercial presence in the territory of any other member; and
- Mode 4: Presence of natural persons – a service is supplied by a service supplier of one member through the presence of natural persons of that member in the territory of any other member (*GATS*, Art. 1.2).

GATS obligations apply to the measures of central, regional and local governments and to those of non-governmental bodies in the exercise of powers delegated by central, regional or local governments (*GATS* Art. 1.3(a)). For this purpose, non-governmental bodies include independent agencies and commissions exercising powers delegated by the state.

Services 'supplied in the exercise of governmental authority' are excluded from the disciplines of *GATS* provided two conditions are met: the service is not supplied on a commercial basis or in competition with other services providers (*GATS*, Art. 1.3(c)).[3]

3 The scope of the exclusion is extensively discussed in J A VanDuzer (2004), 'Health, Education and Social Services in Canada: The Impact of the GATS', in J M Curtis and D Curiak (eds), *Trade Policy Research 2004*, International Trade Canada, Ottawa, 287 at 367–407.

Supply of services through a commercial presence – a form of investment

Mode 3, commercial presence, includes some kinds of investments. In general, a service supplier of one WTO member is supplying a service through a commercial presence in the territory of another WTO member if:

- The supplier has a subsidiary (usually a corporation) or an unincorporated branch of its operation within the territory of that other member for the purpose of supplying the service; and
- The subsidiary or branch is owned or controlled by natural persons that are nationals of the first member or legal persons (usually corporations) organised under the laws of the first member.

A bank incorporated in the UK that is supplying banking services through a locally incorporated subsidiary in South Africa that it controls is an example of a UK service supplier supplying services in South Africa through a commercial presence.

Commercial presence under *GATS* does not include all of the forms of investor and investment that are eligible for protection under existing IIAs. Most obviously, commercial presence for the purposes of *GATS* does not include investments that do not involve the supply of a service, such as an investment to operate a local mine. Even in relation to services businesses, such as accounting or construction services, commercial presence does not include many forms of investment protected under an IIA. For instance, it does not include investments that do not give the foreign investor control over the local business such as a minority shareholding in a business. This kind of investment is often protected in IIAs.

Supply of services through the presence of natural persons

Mode 4, the presence of natural persons, can also be relevant with respect to the activities of foreign investors. In general, the obligations of the *GATS* apply to the supply of services by individuals, though the obligations are very limited. *GATS* obligations do not apply to natural persons seeking access to the employment market in a member state or measures regarding citizenship, residence, or employment on a permanent basis. Members are not obliged to give up measures to regulate entry, such as visas. However, each member can make commitments in its national schedule of commitments relating to the movement of natural persons. Many developed countries but few developing countries did so.[4] In some cases, these commitments relate to individuals who work at the operations of foreign investors in the host state.

Members who made commitments for mode 4 typically grant rights of temporary entry into their territory for specific categories of persons who have technical or managerial expertise subject to requirements set out in their national schedules. In its national schedule, for example, Canada committed to granting temporary entry into Canada

4 *GATS Annex on Movement of Natural Persons Supplying Services under the Agreement.*

to a number of categories of individuals, including 'Intra-corporate transferees', who are individuals of one member who go to work at an investment in another member. Intra-corporate transferees are granted entry for up to three years. In Canada's national schedule of commitments, intra-corporate transferees include senior executives and managers of a foreign service supplier, and specialists with some particular expertise related to the business of the supplier.[5]

Key obligations applying to all sectors

Most favoured nation

As noted, *GATS* Article II obliges members to provide MFN treatment. Under *GATS*, members can record one-time exemptions from the MFN obligation in their national schedules of commitments. Exemptions listed by members include existing bilateral and regional preferential arrangements of various kinds. Some members have listed exemptions that appear to extend to future preferential arrangements as well.[6]

The *GATS* MFN requirement is qualified by the agreement's Article V, which permits member countries to enter preferential regional and bilateral agreements to liberalise trade in services under prescribed conditions. Such agreements do not have to be set out in a member's MFN exemption list. To qualify for the Article V exemption, regional and bilateral agreements must meet conditions analogous to those in *GATT* Article XXIV, which provides a similar exemption in relation to trade in goods. Qualifying agreements must have 'substantial' sectoral coverage, in terms of the number of services sectors, volume of trade and modes of supply covered[7] and must provide for the elimination of substantially all discrimination in the trade of the parties. Few IIAs, apart from some comprehensive PTIAs, will meet these requirements. Consequently, the *GATS* MFN obligation could apply to preferences to particular countries granted under IIAs.

Transparency

Some of the transparency requirements in IIA models can be found in the *GATS* and other WTO Agreements. Article III of *GATS* requires WTO members to publish promptly all relevant measures of general application that pertain to, or would affect the operation of, *GATS*. A 'measure' is defined as 'any measure by a Member, whether in the form of a law, regulation, rule, procedure, decision, administrative action or any other form' (*GATS* Art. XXVIII(a)). Bilateral or plurilateral agreements on services must also be published. WTO members are obliged to respond to requests for information regarding their measures and agreements.[8]

---

5 See Box 5.18 for more details on Canada's commitments.

6 The MFN exemption list filed by Mauritius, for example, may be interpreted in this way (GATS/SC/55), available at: http://docsonline.wto.org (accessed 8 January 2013).

7 In order to meet this condition, agreements should not provide for the a priori exclusion of any mode of supply.

8 See Box 5.15 for more details on GATS transparency obligations.

Key sector-specific obligations

Structure of market access and national treatment commitments

As discussed above, by listing a service sector or activity in its national schedule, a member commits itself to another set of obligations under *GATS*, including commitments to provide market access and national treatment.[9] Market access has a specific meaning under *GATS*. For services sectors listed in national schedules, market access means that members must not impose the following specific market access restrictions (*GATS* Art. XVI:1):

- Limitations on the number of service suppliers, whether in the form of numerical quotas, monopolies, exclusive service suppliers or the requirement for an economic needs test;
- Limitations on the total value of service transactions or assets in the form of numerical quotas or the requirement for an economic needs test;
- Limitations on the total number of service operations or on the total quantity of service output expressed in terms of designated numerical units, whether in the form of quotas or the requirement for an economic needs test;
- Limitations on the number of natural persons that may be employed in a particular specified sector or activity or that a service supplier may employ who are necessary for, and directly related to, the supply of a specific service, whether in the form of numerical quotas or the requirement for an economic needs test;
- Measures which restrict or require specific types of legal entity or joint venture through which a service supplier may supply a service; and
- Limitations on the participation of foreign capital in terms of a maximum percentage limit on foreign shareholding or the total value of individual or aggregate foreign investment.

Each member may customise the precise level of market access and national treatment to which it is committed. Where a member wishes to maintain or be able to adopt a domestic measure inconsistent with the market access or national treatment obligations in relation to a listed sector or activity, the member must describe the measure or use other language preserving this flexibility in its national schedule of commitments. Limitations are listed separately in relation to each of the four modes of services supply. Limitations may take the form of a total exclusion of any obligation for one or more modes of supply. Alternatively, limitations may describe discrete conditions qualifying the extent of the member's commitment regarding a particular

9 *GATS* schedules are based on a sectoral classification developed by the WTO Secretariat, which divides services into 12 sectors, which, in turn, are broken down into 54 sub-sectors. Sub-sectors are further disaggregated into 161 activities. GATT Secretariat (1991), *Services Sectoral Classification List: Note by the Secretariat*, MTN.GNS/W/120, 10 July, available at: http://docsonline.wto.org (accessed 8 January 2013), which is based on United Nations (1991), *Statistical Paper Series M No. 77*, *Provisional Central Product Classification*, Department of International Economic and Social Affairs, Statistical Office of the United Nations, New York. Subsequently, the UN classification system has been revised.

mode of delivery in specific ways. In sum, the listing of a service activity in its schedule commits a member to accord in relation to that activity, and to suppliers of that service, both market access and national treatment with respect to each of the four modes of service supply, but subject to any limitation recorded in the schedule itself.

Most states, other than those that have joined the WTO since it was formed in 1994, have made weak commitments in their services schedules that, at most, oblige them to maintain the degree of openness that they provided to their domestic markets when *GATS* came into force in 1995. Negotiations are ongoing, however, and it is possible that stronger liberalising commitments will be a feature of a successful conclusion of the current Doha round of negotiations.

Domestic regulation requirements

GATS imposes a variety of additional obligations on members in relation to sectors listed in their national schedules. As noted, each member must ensure that all measures of general application are administered in a reasonable, objective and impartial manner. More importantly, under Art. V.5, measures relating to licensing and qualification requirements and technical standards cannot nullify or impair any specific commitment undertaken by a member in its national schedule of commitments by imposing requirements or standards not based on objective and transparent criteria, such as competence and ability to provide the service, or that are more burdensome than necessary to ensure the quality of the service. In the case of licensing procedures, the procedures themselves must not be restrictions on the supply of a service. These obligations are qualified by the caveat that the nullification and impairment 'could not reasonably have been expected of that member at the time the specific commitments in those sectors were made' (*GATS*, Art. VI.5(a)(ii)). In effect, this means that these domestic regulation commitments are 'standstill' obligations. Nullification or impairment can occur only as a result of new measures adopted after *GATS* came into force.[10] Also, where authorisation is required to provide a service in an activity subject to a member's specific commitments, each member must inform applicants regarding whether authorisation has been granted within a reasonable time (*GATS*, Art. VI.3).

Transfer of funds

GATS contains a transfer of funds obligation for all members. *GATS* prohibits members from restricting international transfers and payments for current transactions related to services that are listed in its national schedule of specific commitments and from restricting capital transactions in a manner that would be inconsistent with its commitments in its schedule (*GATS*, Art. XI). This obligation is, however, subject to an exception that permits a member to restrict trade in services and any related

10 *GATS*, Art. VI.4, 5. See J Trachtman (2005), 'Negotiations on Domestic Regulation and Trade in Services: (GATS Art. VI): A Legal Analysis of Selected Issues', in E U Petersmann (ed.), *Reforming the World Trading System: Legitimacy, Efficiency and Democratic Governance*, Oxford University Press, Oxford, at 205.

payment, even in sectors that it has listed in its national schedule of commitments, '[i]n the event of serious balance-of-payments and external financial difficulties or threat thereof' (*GATS*, Art. XII). *GATS* specifically recognises that 'particular pressures on the balance of payments' of a member that is a developing country or a transition economy may require the use of restrictions to ensure the maintenance of a level of financial reserves adequate for the implementation of its programme of economic development or economic transition.

Any restrictions on transfers under this exception must meet certain requirements. They:

(a) Shall not discriminate among members;

(b) Shall be consistent with the Articles of Agreement of the International Monetary Fund;

(c) Shall avoid unnecessary damage to the commercial, economic and financial interests of any other member;

(d) Shall not exceed those necessary to deal with [serious balance-of-payments and external financial difficulties or the threat thereof]; and

(e) Shall be temporary and be phased out progressively as the [serious balance-of-payments and external financial difficulties or the threat thereof] improves.

Any restrictions adopted by a member must be promptly notified to the WTO General Council. Any member applying restrictions must consult promptly with the Committee on Balance-of-Payments Restrictions on restrictions established under *GATS*.

Enhanced transparency obligations

There are enhanced transparency obligations for sectors in relation to which a member has undertaken specific commitments, which means that the member has listed the sector in the member's national schedule of commitments. In addition to the general publication obligation described above, each member must establish one or more enquiry points to provide specific information to other members regarding its services regime (*GATS*, Art. III.4). *GATS* does not oblige members to disclose confidential information the publication of which would impede law enforcement or otherwise conflict with the public interest, or which would prejudice legitimate commercial interests (*GATS*, Art. III*bis*).[11]

Monopoly services suppliers

Where a member authorises a monopoly service supplier to operate, such as a single provider of telecommunications services, and the services supplier competes in the

11 A similar proviso regarding confidential information is contained in the India–Singapore CECA (Art. 6.14(2)), the ASEAN Agreement (Art. 21.2) and the COMESA Investment Agreement (Art. 4.4). See Box 5.15 for more details on GATS transparency obligations.

supply of a service that is outside the scope of its monopoly rights and in a sector listed in the member's schedule, the member must ensure that the monopoly supplier does not abuse its monopoly position (*GATS*, Art. VIII). Abuse would include, for example, subsidising its activities in the competitive market with its monopoly profits.[12]

Exceptions

GATS Article XIV allow members to impose measures otherwise inconsistent with the *GATS* that are necessary to protect important national interests, including measures necessary to protect public morals, public order and human, plant or animal health. These exemptions are analogous to those found in *GATT* Article XX. *GATS* goes on to provide that measures necessary to ensure compliance with laws protecting privacy of personal data and safety and to prevent deceptive and fraudulent practices or the effects of defaults in services contracts are also exempt from the obligations in the agreement, so long as the laws themselves are not inconsistent with the *GATS*. Certain tax measures are exempt from national treatment, and measures related to international agreements on the avoidance of double taxation are exempt from MFN. All of these obligations are subject to a chapeau requirement, which provides that to qualify for the exception, a measure must not be 'applied in a manner which would constitute a means of arbitrary or unjustifiable discrimination between countries where like conditions prevail, or a disguised restriction on trade in services'.

GATS Article XIV(bis) contains a national security exception that is similar to that contained in *GATT* XXI. Nothing in *GATS* can be construed:

a. To require any member to furnish any information, the disclosure of which it considers contrary to its essential security interests; or

b. To prevent any member from taking any action which it considers necessary for the protection of its essential security interests:

    i. relating to the supply of services as carried out directly or indirectly for the purpose of provisioning a military establishment;

    ii. relating to fissionable and fusionable materials or the materials from which they are derived;

    iii. taken in time of war or other emergency in international relations; or

c. To prevent any member from taking any action in pursuance of its obligations under the United Nations Charter for the maintenance of international peace and security.

Because the exception is available any time a member 'considers' that its essential security interests are at risk, each member has a broad discretion to determine when it will rely on the exception. It is not clear to what extent it is possible to challenge the availability of the exception if a member claims to rely on it. If a member takes

12 Members are also obliged (GATS Art. VIII.1) to ensure that monopoly service suppliers do not undermine access commitments undertaken in national schedules of concessions.

a measure in reliance on the exception, the member is obliged to give notice to the WTO Council on Trade in Services.

GATS also excludes prudential measures in its Annex on Financial Services (s. 2). A member can take measures for prudential reasons, which are defined to include the protection of investors, depositors, policy holders or persons to whom a fiduciary duty is owed by a financial service supplier, or to ensure the integrity and stability of the financial system.

To the extent that such prudential measures do not conform with *GATS*, they are not to be used as a means of avoiding the member's obligations under the Agreement. The Annex goes on to provide that a member is not obliged to disclose any information relating to the affairs and accounts of individual customers or any confidential or proprietary information in the possession of public entities.

GATS built-in agenda

GATS requires WTO members to recommence negotiations on a number of aspects of the treaty with a view to increasing the level of members' commitments. Article XIX requires new negotiations with a view to achieving greater liberalisation of obligations in national schedules of commitments. These negotiations are now incorporated into the Doha Round of multilateral trade negotiations, which are ongoing.

Also, as part the built-in agenda of the *GATS*, members are required to negotiate rules to avoid trade-distorting effects caused by subsidies in services (*GATS*, Art. XV). *GATS*' MFN, national treatment and market access obligations do not apply to government procurement, but *GATS* requires that the members engage in negotiations on procurement commitments (Art. XIII). *GATS* also commits members to negotiate disciplines on the use emergency safeguard measures to address the effects of services liberalisation (*GATS*, Art. X). Finally *GATS* obliges members to negotiate rules that will ensure that measures relating to qualification requirements and procedures, technical standards and licensing requirements relating to services do not constitute unnecessary barriers to trade in services (*GATS*, Art. V.4). All of these negotiations are ongoing as part of the Doha Round.

Glossary

N.B. Many of the definitions of terms in this Glossary are based on definitions to be found in John Currie (2001), *Public International Law*, Irwin Law, Toronto.

Admission clause A provision in an IIA that limits the scope of the agreement's obligations to investments that have been admitted by a Party in accordance with its domestic law.

Alternative dispute resolution Processes for resolving disputes that do not involve litigation. Mediation, conciliation and negotiation are all forms of alternative dispute resolution.

Amicus curiae Latin. Literally, 'friend of the court.' Refers to a person (a 'non-disputing party') that presents arguments (written or oral) to a tribunal about the legal issues involved in the case in order to assist the tribunal in its decision.

Annulment The setting aside of an award made by a lower-level tribunal. In arbitrations under the ICSID rules, annulment refers to an annulment committee setting aside a decision of an ICSID arbitration tribunal.

Arbitration A method for resolving a dispute in which the disputing parties agree to submit the dispute to one or more persons (called 'arbitrators'). The parties agree to be bound by the arbitrator's decision. In most cases, arbitration decisions are based on the application of legal standards to the dispute.

Balance of payments accounts An accounting of monetary transactions between a state and all other states. The accounting includes payments for exports and imports of all goods, services, capital and financial transfers.

Bilateral investment treaty An international investment agreement between two states. Often referred to by its acronym 'BIT'.

Capital exporter An investor making an investment in a state of which the investor is not a national. The investor is said to be 'exporting' investment to the recipient state.

Capital-exporting state A state whose nationals are making investments in other states.

Capital flight Capital flight occurs when investors rapidly reduce their investments in the host state.

Capital-importing state A state that receives investments in the state from nationals of other states.

CARICOM An organisation of 15 Caribbean nations and dependencies. CARICOM's main purposes are to promote economic integration and co-operation among its members, to ensure that the benefits of integration are equitably shared, and to co-ordinate foreign policy. Its members are Antigua and Barbuda, The Bahamas,

Barbados, Belize, Dominica, Grenada, Guyana, Haiti, Jamaica, Montserrat, Lucia, St Kitts and Nevis, St Vincent and the Grenadines, Suriname, and Trinidad and Tobago.

CARIFORUM The Forum of the Caribbean Group of African, Caribbean and Pacific (ACP) States, the body that comprises Caribbean states for the purpose of promoting and co-ordinating policy dialogue, co-operation and regional integration, including within the framework of the CARIFORUM–European Community Economic Partnership Agreement (EPA). Its participants are The Bahamas, Barbados, Belize, Cuba, Dominica, Dominican Republic, Grenada, Guyana, Haiti, Jamaica, St Lucia, St Kitts and Nevis, St Vincent and the Grenadines, Suriname, and Trinidad and Tobago.

Commercial presence A mode of services delivery under the WTO *General Agreement on Trade in Services* that includes certain types of investments. In general, a service supplier of one WTO member is supplying a service through a commercial presence in the territory of another WTO member if (i) the supplier has a subsidiary or branch within the territory of that other member for the purpose of supplying that service, and (ii) the subsidiary or branch is owned or controlled by natural persons that are nationals of the first member or legal persons organised under the laws of the first member.

Common but differentiated responsibilities A principle in international law that recognises that states at different levels of economic, social and political development have different capacities to implement international legal obligations.

Compensation In the case of an award by a tribunal, the financial compensation that a person recovers for a breach of its legal rights by another who was under a duty to respect those rights.

Compulsory licence A licence granted by the state to a person that entitles that person to use a patent without requiring permission from the patent holder. The patent holder is usually paid a set fee for use of the patent. Compulsory licences are most frequently used in relation to patented medicines.

Conciliation A form of alternative dispute resolution in which the parties to the dispute request, in accordance with specific rules, a third party to facilitate the settlement of a dispute. While similar to mediation, it is more formal.

Counterclaim A claim made by the defending party in a lawsuit or arbitration that the complaining party has violated the defending party's rights. In an investor–state dispute settlement case, the term may refer to a claim by the state that the investor has not fulfilled its obligations under the applicable international agreement (e.g. a BIT or IIA).

Customary international law International law that exists independent of treaty law. It consists of rules of law that are derived from the consistent conduct of states in which the conduct is believed by the states to be required by law (Shabtai Rosenne (1984), *Practice and Methods of International Law*, Oceana, New York, at 55).

De facto Latin. 'In fact'. Distinguished from *de jure*. For instance, *de facto* discrimination by a state refers to a law, regulation or administrative act that *in fact* differentiates between one or more entities even if this differentiation is not expressly provided for in the law, regulation or administrative act (i.e., *de jure* discrimination).

De jure Latin. 'Legally' or 'in law'. For instance, *de jure* discrimination by a state is discrimination by a law, regulation or administrative act of the state that, on its face, treats two groups differently.

Denial of benefits clause A clause in an international investment agreement that allows the host state to deny the benefits of the agreement to an investor or investment in specific circumstances. For instance, some agreements permit the host state to deny benefits to an investment if the investor does not have substantial business operations in the other party state to the IIA and it is controlled by persons that are not nationals or legal persons of that state.

Discounted cash flow A method of valuation of losses for the purposes of assessing damages for a breach of an IIA provision that is based on the present value of the estimated cash receipts expected from the investment in each future year of its expected economic life less each year's expected cash expenditures to obtain those receipts. These present value of these net cash flows is calculated by discounting the cash flow for each year by a discount rate which reflects the expected rate of return on invested funds, taking into account expected inflation and the risk associated with the cash flows. The discount rate may be estimated based on the rate of return available in the same market on alternative investments of comparable risk. Discounted cash flow valuation is sometimes used in assessing the damages suffered by an investor whose investment has been expropriated.

Domicile of a corporation The state in which the corporation has its principal place of business.

Due diligence A person that is duly diligent is one that takes reasonable steps to fulfil its legal obligations. In the context of international human rights law, a duly diligent state is one that takes reasonable steps to protect the human rights of individuals from the acts of private parties that may violate such rights. In the same context, a duly diligent business actor is one that (i) takes reasonable steps to ensure that it is fully apprised of the potential adverse impacts of its presence and activities on the human rights of individuals and communities in the country in which it plans to invest or in which it is already in the process of investing, and (ii) takes reasonable steps to prevent, avoid and, if necessary, mitigate such impacts and reports on the effectiveness of such measures.

Due process The procedural safeguards that exist in law to ensure that a legal person is treated fairly and that its legal rights are respected.

Dynamic inconsistency Refers to the inconsistency between the policy preferences that a host state has before an investor has made an investment and those that it has after the investment has been made. For example, prior to an investment being made, a state that wants to attract investors has an incentive to create an attractive policy environment for investors with the goal of encouraging them to invest. A state may try to attract investment by providing financial incentives to investors such as low tax rates. Once an investor has sunk its capital into the investment, however, the host country no longer needs to offer benefits to attract investment. It only has to offer benefits sufficient to keep the investment from leaving. These benefits are typically less than those needed to attract the investment because the investor often has sunk costs that cannot be recovered if it divested. The host state can take advantage of this situation by changing the policy regime after the investment has been made to confer fewer benefits on the investor, such as by raising taxes.

Enterprise liability The liability of a business enterprise as a whole. It is distinguished from the liability of a specific legal entity in a group of related entities whose agents directly participated in a legally wrongful act. Enterprise liability treats related entities (e.g. subsidiaries, affiliates and joint-venture partners) as a single unit for the purposes of imposing liability for a wrongful act.

Equity In law, equity refers to the legal principles that apply to a person to ensure that this person is treated fairly and justly. It can act to mitigate the sometimes harsh application of legal rules by taking into account contextual and background factors relevant to a fair and just decision.

Exception (to an international agreement) An exception in an international agreement exempts a party state to the agreement from the commitment to comply with an obligation set out in the agreement in relation to a particular state measure if the measure meets the requirements for the application of the exception. For example, general exceptions relating to health, the environment, public morals or law enforcement would allow a party to take some action otherwise forbidden by the agreement if that action met the requirements of the exception, including the promotion of one of these policy objectives.

Exhaustion of local remedies A requirement that a national of another state fully exploit all legal remedies available under the national law of the host state before that national (or, if the national's claim is espoused by his or her state of nationality, the national's state) may assert a claim under international law against the host state.

Expropriation The act of a state that takes away the property of the owner or substantially deprives the owner of the benefits of the property. In the case of international investment law, it generally refers to the taking of benefits of an investment from a foreign investor. The state may or may not appropriate the expropriated benefits for itself. A **direct expropriation** involves the state taking property from the investor, generally by assuming title to the property, for instance through a seizure. An **indirect expropriation** involves the state taking actions short of acquiring title to the property where the actions interfere in a substantial way with the investor's enjoyment of the benefits of the investment.

Fair and equitable treatment A legal requirement contained in many international investment agreements that the host state not seriously abuse investors or their investments or treat them in an arbitrary or discriminatory manner.

Foreign direct investment Investment by an investor of one state in another state in which the investor obtains a lasting interest in some entity in the host country economy over which the investor exercises a significant degree of control.

Fork in the road provision A provision in an international investment agreement that provides that once a party has chosen one remedy it is barred from pursuing other remedies. For instance, the agreement may give an investor the option of pursuing relief in the domestic courts of the host state or relief through investor–state arbitration, but forbid it to pursue both forms of relief. Once the investor chooses to seek relief in domestic courts or through investor–state arbitration, the choice is irrevocable and precludes resort to the other remedy.

Forum non conveniens Latin. Specifically, the term means that the forum before which parties to a legal dispute have appeared is not the appropriate forum for the resolution of the dispute. More generally, the law of *forum non conveniens* is the set of domestic legal rules that regulate the jurisdiction of a tribunal to deal with a dispute brought before it.

Free transfer of funds obligation An obligation in an international investment agreement for the host state not to restrict an investor's ability to transfer funds out of the host state. Free transfer of funds obligations may be unqualified, in which case no limitations are permitted, or qualified, in which case the state may put in place limitations on transfers for certain specified purposes.

Government procurement The purchasing of goods and services by a government or public authority (for instance by a government agency).

Hard law International legal rules that states consider binding.

Home state The state of an investor.

Host state The state in which an investment is made. The state is said to 'host' the investment.

Human rights The fundamental rights enjoyed by a human being simply by virtue of his or her humanity.

ICSID arbitration rules The arbitration rules under the Convention for the Settlement of Investment Disputes between States and Nationals of Other States that are contained partly in the Convention and partly in the Rules of Procedure for Arbitration Proceedings (Arbitration Rules). These rules have been used in approximately two-thirds of investor–state arbitrations.

Implementation (e.g. of an international agreement) The process by means of which a state gives effect in its domestic law to its international legal obligations in accordance with its domestic constitutional system.

Indigenous peoples Ethnic groups that existed in a territory prior to colonisation.

Intellectual property Intangible property (as opposed to physical property such as land or chattels) that can include copyrights, patents, industrial designs, trademarks, trade names, geographical indications, trade and business secrets, technical processes, know-how and goodwill.

International agreement An agreement between two or more states in which each state is bound by the terms of the agreement under international law. Also known as a treaty.

International human rights law The international legal rules relating to the protection of the basic human rights of all human beings. See 'human rights' above.

International humanitarian law The international legal rules that restrict the means and methods of warfare and protect non-combatants and other persons not participating in the conflict.

International instrument International agreements and non-binding international documents. The former create rights and duties for the parties and, sometimes, for third parties. The latter may express existing obligations and/or non-binding norms or principles.

International investment agreement An international agreement whose subject matter is foreign investment. It is an umbrella term that can refer to provisions relating to investment found in many types of international agreements, including bilateral investment treaties, regional investment agreements, and investment chapters of bilateral and regional free trade agreements. Often referred to by its abbreviation 'IIA'.

International minimum standard of treatment The minimum standard in accordance with which a foreign national must be treated by the host state under customary international law.

International treaty See 'international agreement'.

Investment A broad term including assets and interests held by an investor in an asset or enterprise. For the purposes of an international investment treaty, 'investment' is a term defined in the agreement that sets out the kinds of assets and interests held by an investor to which the agreement applies. A definition of 'investment' can be 'open' if it includes every kind of asset, or 'closed' if it is limited to specific forms of assets identified in the agreement.

Investment contract A contract between a state and an investor in regard to an investment. It specifies the commitments and obligations of both the state and the investor towards each other in respect of an investment. Investment contracts are a common alternative or complement to an international investment agreement.

Investor A person that acquires assets (equity, debt securities, real estate, etc.) with the expectation of a financial return on those assets. For the purposes of an international investment treaty, 'investor' is a term defined in the agreement that sets out the kinds of persons whose investments are protected under the agreement.

Investor–state arbitration Arbitration under an international investment treaty between an investor and the state in which the investment is located with the purpose of settling an investor–state claim. See 'arbitration' above.

Investor–state claim A complaint by a foreign investor that it or its investment has suffered a loss as a result of conduct of the state in which the investment is located that is a legal wrong under an international investment agreement between that state and the investor's state. Typically the investor's claim is to receive compensation for the loss it has suffered as result of the wrong.

Juridical person See 'legal person' below.

Jus cogens Latin. A rule of international law that is recognised as being so fundamental to the maintenance of the international legal order that it cannot be set aside or suspended even on the consent of states. Sometimes called 'peremptory norms' or 'non-derogable norms' of international law.

Legal person Also 'juridical person.' An entity subject to the law. For the purposes of international investment agreements, a 'legal person' typically includes any entity constituted or organised under the law of a state, such as a corporation, trust or partnership, whether publicly or privately owned, and includes a state or a sub-state entity (such as a region, province or municipality).

Mediation An alternative dispute resolution process whereby two parties consent to assistance by a third party in negotiating a solution to the dispute.

Most favoured nation treatment The obligation under an international investment treaty requiring a party state to treat investors of the other party state and their investments no less favourably than it treats investors of any other state and their investments. Also called the 'most favoured nation obligation' or 'most favoured nation protection'. Often referred to by its abbreviation 'MFN'.

Multinational enterprise See 'transnational corporation' below.

National schedule of commitments A list forming part of the *General Agreement on Trade in Services* that sets out for a WTO member the services activities with respect to which it commits to grant national treatment and market access subject to any limitations written into the schedule.

National treatment The obligation under an international investment treaty requiring a party state to treat investors of the other party state and their investments no less favourably than it treats its own investors and their investments.

Natural person A human being. It is distinguished from a 'legal person'.

Negative list An approach to drafting an IIA whereby a state creates a list of measures, sectors or policy areas to which some or all of the provisions of the agreement do not apply. Anything not listed is subject to the obligations in the agreement.

Negotiation An alternative dispute resolution process whereby the parties to a dispute meet to exchange information about their interests, set out their legal positions, and propose various resolutions of the dispute. No third party is involved in this process.

Non-conforming measure See 'reservation' below.

Obligation to protect In international human rights law, it is the obligation of the state to exercise due diligence to protect individuals within its territory and subject to its jurisdiction from violations of human rights caused by third parties, including investors.

Obsolescing bargain See 'dynamic inconsistency' above.

Party (to a treaty or international agreement) A state that is bound by the terms of an international agreement.

Party state See 'party' above.

Performance requirement An obligation imposed on an investor by the host state that obliges the investor to take some specific action in order to achieve the state's policy objectives. For example, a host state may specify that a foreign investor may import capital into the host state only if it hires local workers.

Polluter pays principle The principle in environmental law that the person causing pollution must bear the costs associated with it.

Portfolio investment An investment in debt and equity securities that is intended only for financial gain and that does not create a lasting interest in or control over an enterprise.

Positive list An approach to drafting an IIA whereby a state creates a list of measures, sectors or policy areas to which specific provisions of the agreement apply. Anything not listed is not subject to those provisions in the agreement.

Preamble The preamble of an international agreement is the portion of the agreement in which the party states express their general intentions and goals in entering into the treaty. The preamble is distinguished from the substantive provisions, which set out the parties' specific rights and duties and does not create binding obligations.

Precautionary principle A principle in international environmental law that a state is entitled to regulate the activities of nationals and foreign nationals operating in its territory with a view to avoiding future harms, even in the absence of scientific certainty about the risk of the harm or the effectiveness of the measures put in place to prevent it.

Pre-establishment rights The rights of an investor under an international investment agreement that exist prior to the investment being admitted into the host state market. These rights protect their investors interests before they establish their business in the host state.

Preferential trading arrangement An arrangement, often in the form of an international agreement, between two or more states, in which each state promises to give more favourable treatment to goods and services imported from the other state(s) party to the agreement than it gives to imports from non-party states.

Prudential measures Measures taken by states to preserve the soundness and integrity of their financial institutions, to protect investors, insurance policy holders, policy claimants, depositors and other financial market participants or to ensure the integrity and stability of their financial system as a whole.

Punitive damages Compensation awarded to a plaintiff or complainant to punish the defendant for its actions and to dissuade it and others from taking similar actions in future. Punitive damages are distinguished from compensatory damages, which are intended to provide the plaintiff with compensation for the violation of its legal rights. While the value of compensatory damage awards is determined by the magnitude of the loss resulting from the violation of the right, the amount of punitive damages may not be related to the loss.

Race to the bottom A situation in which states, provinces or territories are in competition, for instance, to attract investors, with the result that these entities seek a competitive advantage by lowering or dismantling currently existing regulatory standards. In a race to the bottom, the result is generally an overall lowering of regulatory standards.

Ratification The process in which a state consents to be bound by an international agreement that has been negotiated and adopted by it and the other negotiating party states.

Regulatory chill The discouragement of domestic legislators from enacting laws and regulations for fear of the negative repercussions (perceived or real) of doing so, such as the risk of investor–state arbitration claims.

Reparations The remedy under which a party that has been found to have committed an internationally wrongful act must eliminate, as far as possible, the consequence of that wrongful act. It can include restitution, compensation and satisfaction.

Reservation A statement by a party to an international agreement that either modifies the legal effect of one or more of the agreement's provisions as it applies to that state or excludes the application of that provision to it. Reservations are not generally symmetrical, i.e. they are typically different for each party to an international agreement. Reservations may also be described as provisions addressing 'non-conforming measures'.

Responsibility to respect Under the legally non-binding Guiding Principles on Business and Human Rights, the moral duty of private actors, including investors, to respect human rights.

Restitution A remedy for a legally wrongful act that involves restoring the state of affairs that existed prior to that act.

Right of establishment In the context of international investment law, a right set out in an international agreement in which the host state commits to allowing a foreign investor to enter its market and carry on business.

Right to development As defined in the *UN Declaration on the Right to Development*, the right to development is 'an inalienable human right by virtue of which every human person and all peoples are entitled to participate in, contribute to, and enjoy economic, social, cultural and political development, in which all human rights and fundamental freedoms can be fully realized.'

Right to regulate The right asserted by a state to use domestic laws and regulations to control the activities of those operating in its territory. A right to regulate may be set out in the provisions of an international agreement. Some states believe that the right to regulate is implicit in the sovereignty of the state, and so need not be specifically identified in an international agreement in order to be exercised.

Satisfaction A remedy for a legally wrongful act that aims to address moral, non-material damage suffered by the victim of that act. For example, an apology may be a form of satisfaction for a legal wrong.

Schedule (to an international agreement) An appendix to a treaty that typically defines the obligations of a party to the treaty in a specific way. A schedule may list specific commitments made by a state to comply with some or all the obligations of an IIA in listed sectors of activity or policy areas. Such a positive list of commitments may be accompanied by reservations that cut back the scope of the obligations undertaken. See 'positive list' above. Alternatively, a schedule could list specific state measures, sectors of activity or policy areas that are excluded from some or all of the obligations in an IIA. This is a 'negative list'. For example, a negative list could set out specific measures to which a state is not obliged to extend national treatment, such as existing measures that discriminate between its domestic investors and foreign investors. See 'negative list' above.

Seat of a corporation The state in which the effective management of a corporation is located.

Soft law Rules of international conduct that are considered non-binding though they may be emerging as binding rules.

Spill over The effect, usually of economic activity such as an investment, that goes beyond the specific effects which the activity was intended to achieve. For instance, an investment may be intended to generate profit for the investor but it may also have a 'spill over' by improving the level of technical knowledge in the region in which the investment is made. Spill overs can be negative or positive.

Stabilisation clause A clause contained in an international investment agreement or investment contract whereby the host state promises not to change the rules, regulations and laws that govern an investment while the agreement or contract is in force.

State A 'stable, independent political community comprising a government exercising exclusive, sovereign jurisdiction over a given territory and population and capable of entering into international legal relations with other states' (Currie, op. cit.).

State espousal Action by a state to pursue (or 'espouse') the claim of its national against another state and seek a remedy, where the national has been injured by that other state.

State immunity The immunity of a state from the jurisdiction of a court located in a different state. Immunity may extend to liability for wrongful acts or for execution against its assets or both.

State sovereignty The ability of the state to exercise its powers and privileges over its territory and population without interference from other states but subject to international law.

Sub-national government Regional or local levels of government within a state. Contrasted with 'national government', which refers to the government of the state as a whole.

Subrogation The process whereby an insurer, in return for compensating the injured party for losses caused by another's actions, assumes any rights the injured party has to pursue legal claims against the other person. For instance, an IIA may contain a subrogation provision that allows a state insurance company or other state agency that compensates an investor for an injury caused by the host state to pursue an investor–state claim against the host state to which the investor would have been entitled in relation to the act that caused the injury.

Sustainability assessment A system for determining the impact of an investment on the environment, society and social institutions, and human rights.

Sustainable development A broad concept that includes economic, cultural, political and social development as well as environmental protection; the goal(s) set by the government of a state to achieve these forms of development and protect the environment.

Transnational corporation A corporate enterprise that produces goods or delivers services in more than one state. It is a synonym for 'multinational enterprise' and is sometimes referred to by the abbreviation 'TNC' or 'MNE'.

Treaty See 'international agreement' above.

Treaty shopping The process by which a person structures its business affairs in various states in order to take advantage of an international agreement whose terms are favourable to it. In the investment context, an investor may structure its investment through a legal entity it controls that is incorporated in a party state to an IIA if that would make its investment in the other party state to the IIA eligible for protection under the treaty.

Umbrella clause A clause in an international investment agreement that obliges a party state to respect obligations it has undertaken toward investors from the other party state that go beyond those obligations specifically set out in the treaty. For instance, an umbrella clause might oblige a party state to respect contractual commitments undertaken with regard to an investor even though these obligations are contractual and not based in the treaty.

UNCITRAL Arbitration Rules The general arbitration rules adopted by the United Nations Commission on International Trade Law in 1976 and most recently revised in 2010. The UNCITRAL Rules are the arbitration rules most frequently used in investor–state arbitration after the ICSID Arbitration Rules. In some IIAs, obligations benefiting from an umbrella clause may be the basis for an investor–state claim under the treaty.

Waiver The situation in which a party agrees to give up a claim to relief.

Bibliography

Adlung, R and M Molinuevo (2008), 'Bilateralism in Services Trade: Is There Fire Behind the (BIT-) Smoke', *Journal of International Economic Law*, Vol. 10, 1.

Aisbett, E (2009), 'Bilateral Investment Treaties and Foreign Direct Investment: Correlation versus Causation', in Sauvant, KP and LE Sachs (Eds), *The Effect of Treaties on Foreign Direct Investment: Bilateral Investment Treaties, Double Taxation Treaties and Investment Flows*, Oxford University Press, Oxford.

Allen, LJ (2012), 'The North American Agreement on Environmental Cooperation: Has It Fulfilled Its Promises and Potential? An Empirical Study of Policy', *Colorado Journal of International Environmental Law and Policy*, Vol. 23, 122.

Alston, P (2004), 'Core Labour Standards and the Transformation of the International Labour Rights Regime', *European Journal of International Law*, Vol. 15, 457, 497–506.

Anaya, J (2005), 'Indigenous Peoples' Participatory Rights in Relation to Decisions About Natural Resource Extraction: The More Fundamental Issue of What Rights Indigenous Peoples Have in Lands and Resources', *Arizona Journal of International and Comparative Law*, Vol. 22, 7.

Andreassen, BA and SP Marks (Eds) (2006), *Development as a Human Right*, Harvard University Press, Cambridge, MA.

Anghie, A (2005), *Imperialism, Sovereignty, and the Making of International Law* Cambridge University Press, Cambridge.

Asian-African Legal Consultative Committee (AALCC) (1983), 'Promotion and Protection of Investments', adopted at the 23rd Session, available at: www.aalco.int/PROMOTION%20AND%20PROTECTION%20OF%20INVESTMENTS.pdf (accessed 26 April 2012).

Atapattu, SA (2006), *Emerging Principles of International Environmental Law*, Transnational Publishers, Ardsley, NY.

Baderin, MA and R McCorquodale (Eds) (2007), *Economic, Social and Cultural Rights in Action*, Oxford University Press, Oxford.

Bartels, L (2009), 'Social Issues: Labour, Environment and Human Rights', in Lester, S and B Mercurio (Eds), *Bilateral and Regional Trade Agreements: Commentary, Analysis and Case Studies*, Cambridge University Press, Cambridge.

Banga, R (2006), 'Do Investment Agreements Matter?', *Journal of Economic Integration*, Vol. 21, 40.

Berger, A, M Busse, P Nunnenkamp and M Roy (2010), 'Do Trade and Investment Agreements Lead to More FDI? Accounting for Key Provisions Inside the Black Box', Kiel Working Papers, No. 1647, Kiel Institute for the World Economy, Kiel.

Bernasconi-Osterwalder, N (2011), 'Transparency and *Amicus Curiae* in ICSID Arbitrations' in Cordonier Segger M-C et al. (Eds), *Sustainable Development in World Investment Law*, Kluwer Law International, The Hague.

Bernasconi-Osterwalder, N and L Johnson (2011), 'Commentary to the Austrian Model Investment Treaty', International Institute for Sustainable Development, Winnipeg.

Bishop, RD, J Crawford and WM Reisman (2005), *Foreign Investment Disputes: Cases, Materials and Commentary*, Kluwer Law International, The Hague.

Blumberg, PI (1993), *The Multinational Challenge to Corporation Law: The Search for a New Corporate Personality*, Oxford University Press, New York.

Blume, L and S Voigt (2004), 'The Economic Effects of Human Rights', University of Kassel Working Paper 66/04, University of Kassel, Kassel.

Boele, R and C Crispin, 'Should We Take the "Impact" Out of Human Rights Impact Assessment?' (copy on file with the authors).

Bomann-Larsen, L and O Wiggen (Eds) (2004), *Responsibility in World Business: Managing Harmful Side-Effects of Corporate Activity*, United Nations University Press, Tokyo.

Bottomley, S and D Kinley (Eds) (2002), *Commercial Law and Human Rights*, Ashgate Publishing, Aldershot and Burlington, VT.

Boyle, A and D Freestone (Eds) (1999), *International Law and Sustainable Development: Past Achievements and Future Challenges*, Oxford University Press, Oxford.

Brereton, D, D Pesce and X Abogabir (Eds) (2001), Proceedings of the First International Seminar on Social Responsibility in Mining, Santiago, Chile.

Brownlie, I (2003), *Principles of Public International Law*, 6th ed., Oxford University Press, Oxford.

Busse, P, J Königer and P Nunnenkamp (2008), 'FDI Promotion through Bilateral Investment Treaties: More than a BIT?', Kiel Working Paper No. 1403, Kiel Institute for the World Economy, Kiel.

Busse, M, P Nunnenkamp and M Spatareanu (2011), 'Foreign Direct Investment and Labour Rights: A Panel Analysis of Bilateral FDI Flows', *Applied Economics Letters* Vol. 18, 149.

Büthe, T and HV Milner (2009), 'Bilateral Investment Treaties and Foreign Direct Investment: A Political Analysis', in Sauvant, KP and LE Sachs (Eds), *The Effect of Treaties on Foreign Direct Investment: Bilateral Investment Treaties, Double Taxation Treaties and Investment Flows*, Oxford University Press, Oxford.

California Global Corporate Accountability Project (2002), *Beyond Good Deeds: Case Studies and a New Policy Agenda for Corporate Accountability*, a collaboration of the Nautilus Institute for Security and Sustainable Development, the Natural Heritage Institute, and Human Rights Advocates, Berkeley.

Chung, Andrew (2012), 'RCMP Raids SNC-Lavalin's Montreal Headquarters', *Toronto Star*, 13 April, available at: www.thestar.com/news/canada/article/1161146–rcmp-raids-snc-lavalin-s-montreal-headquarters (accessed 8 January 2013).

Clapham, A (1993), *Human Rights in the Private Sphere*, Clarendon Press, Oxford.

Clapham, A (2001), 'Revisiting Human Rights in the Private Sphere: Using the European Convention on Human Rights to Protect the Right of Access to the Civil Courts', in Scott, C (Ed.), *Torture as Tort: Comparative Perspectives on the Development of Transnational Human Rights Litigation*, Hart Publishing, Oxford.

Clapham, A (2004), 'State Responsibility, Corporate Responsibility, and Complicity in Human Rights Violations', in Bomann-Larsen, L and O Wiggen (Eds), *Responsibility in World Business: Managing Harmful Side-Effects of Corporate Activity*, United Nations University Press, Tokyo.

Coca Cola (2011), Statement by Edward Potter, personal communication, 26 May 2011, available at: www.global-business-initiative.org/SRSGpage/files/Guiding%20Principles%20Endorsement%20from%20Coke.pdf (accessed 29 May 2012).

Collins, D (2010), 'Environmental Impact Statements and Public Participation in International Investment Law', *Manchester Journal of International Economic Law*, Vol. 7, 4.

Commonwealth Secretariat (2008), *Commonwealth Finance Ministers Reference Report 2008*, Commonwealth Secretariat, London.

Cordonier Segger, M-C, A Newcombe and M Gehring (Eds) (2011), *Sustainable Development in World Investment Law*, Kluwer Law International, The Hague.

Correa, CM (2004), 'Bilateral Investment Agreements: Agents of New Global Standards for the Protection of Intellectual Property Rights?', available at: www.grain.org/briefings_files/correa-bits-august-2004.pdf (accessed 29 May 2012).

Craik, N (2008), *The International Law of Environmental Impact Assessment: Process, Substance and Integration*, Cambridge University Press, Cambridge.

Crawford, J and S Olleson (2003), 'The Nature and Forms of International Responsibility', in Evans, MD (Ed.), *International Law*, Oxford University Press, Oxford and New York.

Currie, JH, C Forcese and V Oosterveld (2007), *International Law: Doctrine, Practice and Theory*, Irwin Law, Toronto.

Davis, R and DM Franks (2011), 'The Costs of Conflict with Local Communities in the Extractive Industry', in Brereton, D, D Pesce, and X Abogabir (Eds), *Proceedings of the First International Seminar on Social Responsibility in Mining*, Santiago, Chile.

de Brabandere, E and J Lepeltak (2012), 'Third-Party Funding in International Investment Arbitration', Grotius Centre Working Paper No. 2012/1, The Hague.

Dernbach, JC (2003), 'Achieving Sustainable Development: The Centrality and Multiple Facets of Integrated Decision-making', *Indiana Journal of Global Legal Studies*, Vol. 10, 247.

DiMascio, N and J Pauwelyn (2008), 'Non-Discrimination in Trade and Investment Treaties: Worlds Apart or Two Sides of the Same Coin?', *American Journal of International Law*, Vol. 102, No. 82.

Dine, J (2012), 'Jurisdictional Arbitrage By Multinational Companies: A National Law Solution?', *Journal of Human Rights and the Environment*, Vol. 3, 44.

Division for Sustainable Development for the Commission on Sustainable Development (1996), *Report of the Expert Group Meeting on Identification of Principles of International Law for Sustainable Development*, Geneva, September 1995, Division for Sustainable Development for the Commission on Sustainable Development, 4th session, 1996, available at: www.un.org/documents/ecosoc/cn17/1996/background/ecn 171996-bp3.htm (accessed 29 May 2012).

Dolzer, R (2006), 'The Impact of International Investment Treaties on Domestic Administrative Law', *NYU Journal of International Law and Politics*, Vol. 37, 953.

Dolzer, R and C Schreuer (2008), *Principles of International Investment Law*, Oxford University Press, Oxford.

Dumberry, P (2010), 'Compensation for Moral Damages in Investor-State Arbitration Disputes,' *Journal of International Arbitration*, Vol. 27, 247.

ECOSOC (2003), *Commentary on the Norms on the Responsibilities of Transnational Corporations and Other Business Enterprises with Regard to Human Rights*, UN Doc. E/CN.4/Sub.2/2003/38/Rev.2.

ECOSOC (2003), *Norms on the Responsibilities of Transnational Corporations and Other Business Enterprises with Regard to Human Rights*, UN Doc E/CN.4/Sub.2/2003/12/Rev.2.

Echandi, R (2011), 'Toward a New Approach to Address Investor-State Conflict: Developing a Conceptual Framework', NCCR Trade Regulation Working Paper No 2011/46, World Trade Institute, Bern.

Echandi, R and P Sauvé (Eds) (forthcoming), *Prospects in International Investment Law and Policy*, Cambridge University Press, Cambridge.

Economic and Social Council (ECOSOC) (1995), *The Realization of Economic, Social and Cultural Rights: The Relationship between the Enjoyment of Human Rights, in particular, International Labour and Trade Union Rights, and the Working Methods and Activities of Transnational Corporations*, UN Doc. E/CN.4/Sub.2/1995/11.

Egger, P and V Merlo (2007), 'The Impact of Bilateral Investment Treaties on FDI Dynamics', *World Economy*, Vol. 30, 1536).

Egger, P and M Pfaffermayr (2004), 'The impact of bilateral investment treaties on foreign direct investment', 73 *Journal of Comparative Economics* 788.

Eigen, P and J Moberg (2007), 'Transparency and Accountability as a Driver for Growth', in *The State of Responsible Competitiveness 2007: Making Sustainable Development Count in Global Markets*, AccountAbility, London.

Elkins, Z, A Guzman and B Simmons (2006), 'Competing for Capital: The Diffusion of Bilateral Investment Treaties, 1960–2000', *International Organization*, Vol. 60, 811.

Endicott, M (2007), 'Remedies in Investor-State Arbitration: Restitution, Specific Performance and Declaratory Awards', in Kahn, P and T Wälde (Eds), *New Aspects of International Investment Law*, Martinus Nijhoff, The Hague.

Escobar, A (1995), *Encountering Development: The Making and Unmaking of the Third World*, Princeton University Press, Princeton, NJ.

Esteves, AM, D Franks and F Vanclay (2012), 'Social Impact Assessment: The State of the Art', *Impact Assessment and Project Appraisal*, Vol. 30, 34.

Evans, MD (Ed.) (2003), *International Law*, Oxford University Press, Oxford and New York.

Export Development Canada (nd), 'Political Risk Insurance', available at: www.edc.ca/EN/Our-Solutions/Insurance/Pages/political-risk-insurance.aspx (accessed 8 January 2013).

Fink, C and M Molinuevo (2008), 'East Asian Free Trade Agreements in Services: Key Architectural Elements,' *Journal of International Economic Law*, Vol. 11, 263.

Franck, S (2009), 'Development and Outcomes of Investment Treaty Arbitration', *Harvard Law Review*, Vol. 50, 435.

Franck, S (2011), 'Rationalizing Costs in Investment Treaty Arbitration,' *Washington University Law Review*, Vol. 88, 279.

Franks, D (2012), *Social Impact Assessment of Resource Projects*, International Mining for Development Centre, Crawley.

Frey, BA (1997), 'The Legal and Ethical Responsibilities of Transnational Corporations in the Protection of International Human Rights', *Minnesota Journal of Global Trade*, Vol. 6, 153.

Gagnon, G, A Macklin and P Simons (2003), 'Deconstructing Engagement: Corporate Self-Regulation in Conflict Zones: Implications for Human Rights and Canadian Public Policy', University of Toronto, Public Law Research Paper No. 04–07, Toronto, available at: http://ssrn.com/abstract=557002 (accessed 28 May 2012).

Gallagher, KP and MBL Birch (2006), 'Do Investment Agreements Attract Investment? Evidence from Latin America', *Journal of World Investment Law and Trade*, Vol. 7, 961.

Gallagher, KP and L Zarsky (2005), 'No Miracle Drug: Foreign Direct Investment and Sustainable Development', in Zarsky, L (Ed.) *International Investment for Sustainable Development: Balancing Rights and Rewards*, Earthscan, London.

Gantz, D (2011), 'Resolution of Investor-State Controversies in Developing Countries', Arizona Legal Studies Discussion Paper No. 11–29, University of Arizona, Tucson.

Garcia, E (2012), 'Ecuador Court Rejects Chevron Arbitration Ruling', Reuters, 20 February, available at: www.reuters.com/article/2012/02/20/us-ecuador-chevron-idUSTRE81J17A20120220 (accessed 9 May 2012).

Garcia Amador, FV (1959), *Special Rapporteur's Report, Yearbook of the International Law Commission 1959*, Vol. 2.

Gehring, MW (2011), 'Impact Assessments of Investment Treaties', in Cordonier Segger M-C et al. (Eds), *Sustainable Development in World Investment Law*, Kluwer Law International, The Hague.

Gordon, K (2008), 'International Investment Agreements: A Survey of Environmental, Labour and Anti-Corruption Issues', in *International Investment Law: Understanding Concepts and Tracking Innovations*, OECD, Paris.

Gordon, K and J Pohl (2011), 'Environmental Concerns in International Investment Agreements: A Survey', 2011/1 OECD Working Papers on International Investment, available at: www.oecd.org/dataoecd/50/12/48083618.pdf (accessed 8 January 2013).

Government of Australia (2011), 'Trading Our Way to More Jobs and Prosperity', Gillard Government Trade Policy Statement, Department of Foreign Affairs and Trade, available at: www.dfat.gov.au/publications/trade/trading-our-way-to-more-jobs-and-prosperity.html (accessed 29 May 2012).

Government of Canada (2002), 'Canada's Foreign Investment Protection and Promotion Agreements (FIPAs) Negotiating Programme 2002', available at: www.bilaterals.org/spip.php?page=print&id_article=497 (accessed 25 May 2012).

Government of Canada (2004), 'Canada's New Model Foreign Investment Protection Agreement, Adopted in 2004', Foreign Affairs and International Trade Canada, available at: www.international.gc.ca/trade-agreements-accords-commerciaux/assets/pdfs/2004-FIPA-model-en.pdf (accessed 29 May 2012).

Government of Canada (2005), 'Response of the Government to the 14th Report of the Standing Committee on Foreign Affairs and International Trade (Mining in Developing Countries – Corporate Social Responsibility)', in Sessional Papers, No. 8512-381-179.

Government of Canada (2007), 'National Roundtables on Corporate Social Responsibility (CSR) and the Canadian Extractive Sector in Developing Countries', Advisory Group Report, Foreign Affairs and International Trade, Ottawa, Canada.

Government of Canada (2009), 'Building the Canadian Advantage: A Corporate Social Responsibility (CSR) Strategy for the Canadian International Extractive Sector', Foreign Affairs and International Trade Canada, available at: www.international.gc.ca/trade-agreements-accords-commerciaux/ds/csr-strategy-rse-stategie.aspx (accessed 3 September 2012).

Government of India (nd), 'Indian Model Text of Bilateral Investment Promotion and Protection Agreement (BIPA)', Department of Economic Affairs, available at: http://finmin.nic.in/the_ministry/dept_eco_affairs/icsection/Indian%20Model%20Text%20BIPA.asp (accessed 29 May 2012).

Government of Norway (2007), Norwegian draft model APPI (19 December), copy on file with the authors.

Government of the United States (2012), '2012 US Model Bilateral Investment Treaty', available at: www.ustr.gov/sites/default/files/BIT%20text%20for%20ACIEP%20Meeting.pdf (accessed 29 May 2012).

Grosse, R and LJ Trevino (2005), 'New Institutional Economics and FDI Location in Central and Eastern Europe', *Management International Review*, Vol. 45, 123.

Grynberg, R and V Qalo (2006), 'Labour Standards in US and EU Preferential Trading Arrangements', *Journal of World Trade*, Vol. 40, 619.

Guha Roy, T (1961), 'Is the Law of Responsibility of States for Injuries to Aliens a Part of Universal International Law?', *American Journal of International Law*, Vol. 55, 863.

Guzman, A (1998), 'Why LDCs Sign Treaties that Hurt Them: Explaining the Popularity of Bilateral Investment Treaties', *Virginia Journal of International Law*, Vol. 38, 639.

Häberli, C (2012), 'Foreign Direct Investment in Agriculture: Land Grab or Food Security Improvement', presented at Third Biennial Global Conference of the Society of International Economic Law, National University of Singapore.

Haftel, YZ (2010), 'Ratification Counts: US Investment Treaties and FDI Flows into Developing Countries', *Review of International Political Economy*, Vol. 17, 248.

Hannum, H (1995), 'Status of the Universal Declaration of Human Rights in National and International Law', *Georgia Journal of International and Comparative Law*, Vol. 25, 287.

Hallward-Driemeier, M (2003), 'Do Bilateral Investment Treaties Attract FDI? Only a Bit… and They Could Bite', World Bank Policy Research Paper, WPS 3121, World Bank, Washington, DC.

Harding, T and B Javorcik (2012), 'Roll Out the Red Carpet and They Will Come: Investment Promotion and FDI Inflows', *Columbia FDI Perspectives*, Vol. 72.

Harrison, J (2010), 'Measuring Human Rights: Reflections on the Practice of Human Rights Impact Assessment and Lessons for the Future', Warwick School of Law Research Paper No. 2010/26, Warwick, available at: http://papers.ssrn.com/sol3/papers.cfm?abstract_id=1706742 (accessed 29 May 2012).

Harrison, J (2011), 'Human Rights Measurement: Reflections on the Current Practice and Future Potential of Human Rights Impact Assessment', *Journal of Human Rights Practice*, Vol. 3, 162.

Harrison, J and M-A Stephenson (2010), *Human Rights Impact Assessment: Review of Practice and Guidance for Future Assessments. Report for the Scottish Human Rights Commission*, available at: www.scottishhumanrights.com/ourwork/publications/article/HRIAresearchreport (accessed 29 May 2012).

Hoekman, B and R Newfarmer (2005), 'Preferential Trade Agreements, Investment Disciplines and Investment Flows', *Journal of World Trade*, Vol. 39, 949.

Hoffman, AK (2008), 'Indirect Expropriation', in Reinisch, A (Ed.), *Standards of Investment Protection*, Oxford University Press, Oxford, 165.

Howse, R, B Langille and J Burda (2006), 'The World Trade Organization and Labour Rights: Man Bites Dog', in Leary, VA and D Warner (Eds), *Social Issues, Globalisation and International Institutions*, Martinus Nijoff, Leiden.

Human Rights Council (2011), *Human Rights and Transnational Corporations and Other Business Enterprises*, UNHRC, 17th Sess, UN Doc A/HRC/17/L.17/Rev.1, 15 June.

Human Rights Impact Resource Centre (HRIRC) (nd), 'An Introduction to Human Rights Impact Assessment', available at: www.humanrightsimpact.org/hria-guide/overview (accessed 8 January 2013).

ICSID Basic Documents (2006), *Administrative and Financial Regulations; Rules of Procedure for the Institution of Conciliation and Arbitration Proceedings (Institution Rules), and the Rules of Procedure for Arbitration Proceedings (Arbitration Rules)*, ICSID, Washington, DC.

Igwike, RS, ME Hussain and A Noman (2012), 'The Impact of Corruption on Economic Development: A Panel Data Analysis', available at: http://ssrn.com/abstract=2003061 (accessed 8 January 2013).

International Association for Impact Assessment (IAIA) (2009), *What is Impact Assessment?*, IAIA, Fargo, available at: www.iaia.org/publicdocuments/special-publications/What%20is%20IA_web.pdf (accessed 8 January 2013).

International Business Leaders Forum and International Finance Corporation (2007), *Guide to Human Rights Impact Assessment and Management, Road-Testing Draft, June 2007*, available at: www.ifc.org/ifcext/enviro.nsf/AttachmentsByTitle/p_SocialResponsibility_HRIARoadTesting/$FILE/Final+HRIA+road-testing+draft.pdf (accessed 29 May 2012).

International Centre for Human Rights and Democracy (2007), *Human Rights Impact Assessments for Foreign Investment Projects*, International Centre for Human Rights and Democracy, Montreal, available at: http://publications.gc.ca/collections/collection_2007/dd-rd/E84-21-2007E.pdf (accessed 8 January 2013).

International Centre for Settlement of Investment Disputes (ICSID) (1965), *1965 Convention on the Settlement of Investment Disputes between States and Nationals of Other States*, signed 18 March 1965, 575 *United Nations Treaty Series* 159, reprinted in *International Legal Materials*, Vol. 4, 532.

International Chamber of Commerce (ICC) (2012), 'ICC Guidelines for International Investment', ICC, Paris, available at: www.uscib.org/docs/2012_04_21_icc_investment_guidelines.pdf (accessed 8 January 2013).

International Commission of Jurists (2008), 'Corporate Complicity and Legal Accountability: Volume 3 – Civil Remedies: Report of the International Commission of Jurists Expert Legal Panel on Corporate Complicity in International Crimes', International Commission of Jurists, available at: www.icjcanada.org/fr/document/doc_2008-10_vol3.pdf (accessed 8 January 2013).

International Council on Mining and Metals (ICMM) (2012), 'Integrating Human Rights Due Diligence into Corporate Risk Management Processes', ICCM, available at: www.icmm.com/page/75929/integrating-human-rights-due-diligence-into-corporate-risk-management-processes (accessed 8 January 2013).

International Institute for Sustainable Development (2001), *Private Rights, Public Problems: A Guide to NAFTA's Controversial Investment Chapter*, International Institute for Sustainable Development, Winnipeg.

International Labour Organization (ILO) (2002), 'A Future without Child Labour: Global Report under the Follow-Up to the ILO Declaration on Fundamental Principles and Rights at Work', International Labour Conference, 90th session, ILO, Geneva.

International Labour Organization (ILO) (2008), *Director General's Announcement, IGDS No. 36 (Version 1)*, 13 August.

International Law Association (2002), *Report of the Seventieth Conference, New Delhi*, ILA, London.

ILO (nd), Ratifications of the Fundamental Human Rights Conventions by Country, ILOLEX Database of International Labour Standards, available at: www.ilo.org/ilolex/english/docs/declprint.htm (accessed 8 January 2013).

International Monetary Fund (IMF) (1992), 'Amended Articles of Agreement of the International Monetary Fund', *International Legal Materials*, Vol. 31, 1309.

IMF (2007), *IMF's Balance of Payments and International Investment Position Manual*, 6th ed., IMF, Washington, DC.

International Organization for Standardization (ISO) (2010), *Guidance on social responsibility*, ISO 26000:2010, available at www.iso.org/iso/iso26000 (accessed 24 June 2012).

International Organization of Employers (2011), Address to the UN Human Rights Council, delivered at the Palais des Nations in Geneva, Switzerland, 31 May, available at: www.un.org/webcast/unhrc/archive.asp?go=110531#pm1 (accessed 8 January 2013).

Joseph, S (1999), 'Taming the Leviathans: Multinational Enterprises and Human Rights', *Netherlands International Law Review*, Vol. 46, 171.

Joseph, S (2012), 'Protracted Lawfare: The Tale of Chevron Texaco in the Amazon', *Journal of Human Rights and the Environment*, Vol. 3, 70.

Joubin-Bret, A (2008), 'Admission and Establishment in the Context of Investment Protection', in Reinisch, A (Ed.), *Standards of Investment Protection*, Oxford University Press, Oxford, 25.

Kamminga, MT and S Zia-Zarifi (2000), 'Liability of Multinational Corporations under International Law: An Introduction', in Kamminga, MT and S Zia-Zarifi (Eds), *Liability of Multinational Corporations under International Law*, Kluwer Law International, The Hague.

Kekic, L and KP Sauvant (2007), *World Investment Prospects to 2011: Foreign Direct Investment and the Challenge of Political Risk*, Economist Intelligence Unit and the Columbia Program on International Investment, London and New York.

Kaufmann, P and T Wälde (Eds) (2007), *New Aspects of International Investment Law*, Martinus Nijhoff, The Hague.

Kaufmann, D (2005), 'Human Rights and Governance: The Empirical Challenge' in Alston P and M Robinson, (Eds), *Human Rights and Development: Towards Mutual Reinforcement*, Oxford University Press, Oxford and New York, 352.

Kim, D (2011), 'The Annulment Committee's Role in Multiplying Inconsistency in ICSID Arbitration: The Need to Move Away from an Annulment-Based System', *New York University Law Review*, Vol. 86, 242.

Kläger, R (2011), 'Fair and Equitable Treatment and Sustainable Development', in Cordonier Segger M-C et al. (Eds), *Sustainable Development in World Investment Law*, Kluwer Law International, The Hague.

Koh, JK (1982), 'Reservations to Multilateral Treaties', *Harvard International Law Journal*, Vol. 23, 71.

Kolo, A and T Wälde (2008), 'Capital Transfers under Modern Investment Treaties', in Reinisch, A (Ed.), *Standards of Investment Protection*, Oxford University Press, Oxford, 227.

Kryvoi, Y (2011), 'Counterclaims in Investor-State Arbitration', 8/2011 LSE Working Papers, London School of Economics, London, available at: http://papers.ssrn.com/sol3/papers.cfm?abstract_id=1891935 (accessed 8 January 2013).

Kumar, CR, 'Corruption as a Human Rights Issue in South Asia: Law, Development and Governance', Paper delivered at Human Rights 2006: The Year in Review Conference, Castan Centre for Human Rights Law, Monash University, available at: www.law.monash.edu.au/castancentre/events/2006/conf-06-kumar-paper.html (accessed 8 January 2013).

Lauterpacht, E (1962), 'The Drafting of Treaties for the Protection of Investment,' *International and Comparative Law Quarterly* (Supp. Publ. No. 3), 18.

Leary, VA and D Warner (Eds) (2006), *Social Issues, Globalisation and International Institutions*, Martinus Nijoff, Leiden.

Lester, S and B Mercurio (Eds) (2009), *Bilateral and Regional Trade Agreements: Commentary, Analysis and Case Studies*, Cambridge University Press, Cambridge.

Malik, M (2009), *Report on Bilateral Investment Treaties*, Commonwealth Secretariat, London.

Mann, H (2008), *International Investment Agreements, Business and Human Rights: Key Issues and Opportunities*, International Institute for Sustainable Development, Winnipeg.

Mann, H and K von Moltke (1999), *NAFTA's Chapter 11 and the Environment*, International Institute for Sustainable Development, Winnipeg.

Mann, H, K von Moltke, L E Peterson and A Cosbey (2005), *IISD Model International Agreement on Investment for Sustainable Development*, International Institute for Sustainable Development, Winnipeg, available at: www.iisd.org/pdf/2005/investment_model_int_agreement.pdf (accessed 29 May 2012).

Manning-Cabrol, D (1995), 'The Imminent Death of the Calvo Clause and the Rebirth of the Calvo Principle: Equality of Foreign and National Investors', *Law and Policy in International Business*, Vol. 26, 1169.

Maquila Solidarity Network (2004), 'NAFTA Ten Years Later: Why the Labour Side Agreement Doesn't Work for Workers', 1 January, available at: http://en.maquilasolidarity.org/issues/trade/nafta/naalc/critique?SESS89c5db41a82abcd7da7c9ac60e04ca5f=unvlgtie (accessed 8 January 2013).

Marks, S (2003), 'Empire's Law', *Indiana Journal of Global Legal Studies*, Vol. 10, 449.

Marshall, F (2009), 'Defining New Institutional Options for Investor-State Dispute Settlement', International Institute for Sustainable Development, Winnipeg.

Mattoo, A and P Sauvé (2010), 'The Preferential Liberalization of Services Trade', NCCR Working Paper No. 2010/13, World Trade Institute, Bern.

Maupain, F (2009), 'New Foundation or New Façade? The ILO and the 2008 Declaration on Social Justice for a Fair Globalization', *European Journal of International Law*, Vol. 20, 823.

Mauro, P (1996), 'The Effects of Corruption on Growth, Investment, and Government Expenditure', No. 96/98 IMF Working Paper, IMF, Washington, D.C.

Mayeda, G (2007), 'Playing Fair: The Meaning of Fair and Equitable Treatment in Bilateral Investment Treaties (BITs)', *Journal of World Trade*, Vol. 41, 273.

McCorquodale, R (2002), 'Human Rights and Global Business', in Bottomley, S and D Kinley (Eds), *Commercial Law and Human Rights*, Ashgate Publishing, Aldershot and Burlington, VT.

McLachlan, C, L Shore and M Weiniger (2007), *International Investment Arbitration, Substantive Principles*, Oxford University Press, Oxford.

Mercurio, B (2010), 'Reconceptualizing the Debate on Intellectual Property Rights and Economic Development', *Law and Development Review*, Vol. 3, 64.

Miles, K (2010), 'International Investment Law: Origins, Imperialism and Conceptualizing the Environment', *Colorado Journal of International Environmental Law and Policy*, Vol. 21, 1.

Miles, K (2011), 'Sustainable Development, National Treatment and Like Circumstances in Investment Law', in Cordonier Segger M-C et al. (Eds), *Sustainable Development in World Investment Law*, Kluwer Law International, The Hague.

Morgan, RK (2012), 'Environmental Impact Assessment: The State of the Art', *Impact Assessment and Project Appraisal*, Vol. 30, 5–14.

Muchlinski, P (2012), 'Implementing the New UN Corporate Human Rights Framework: Implications for Corporate Law, Governance, and Regulation', *Business Ethics Quarterly*, Vol. 22, 145.

NAFTA Secretariat (nd), 'Code of Conduct for Dispute Settlement Procedures under Chapters 19 and 20', available at: www.nafta-sec-alena.org/en/view.aspx?conID=658 (accessed 25 June 2012).

Neumayer, E and L Spess (2005), 'Do Bilateral Investment Treaties Increase Foreign Direct Investment in Developing Countries?', *World Development*, Vol. 33, 1567.

Newcombe, A (2011), 'General Exceptions in International Investment Agreements', in Cordonier Segger M-C et al. (Eds), *Sustainable Development in World Investment Law*, Kluwer Law International, The Hague.

Newcombe, A and L Paradell (2009), *Law and Practice of Investment Treaties: Standards of Treatment*, Wolters Kluwer Law International, The Netherlands.

Nicolson, R and E Howie (2008), 'The Impact of the Corporate Form on Corporate Liability for International Crimes: Separate Legal Personality, Limited Liability and the Corporate Veil – An Australian Law Perspective', Paper written for the ICJ Expert Legal Panel on Corporate Complicity in International Crimes, available at: www.hrlrc.org.au/files/icj-paper-e-howie-and-r-nicolson-final-0207.pdf (accessed 8 January 2013).

Organisation for Economic Co-operation and Development (OECD) (1993), *Declaration on National Treatment for Foreign-Controlled Enterprises*, OECD, Paris.

OECD (1994), *Methodologies for Environmental and Trade Reviews*, OCDE/GD(94)103, OECD, Paris.

OECD (1996), *OECD Detailed Benchmark Definition of Foreign Direct Investment*, 3rd ed. OECD, Paris, available at: www.oecd.org/investment/investmentpolicy/2090148.pdf (accessed 8 January 2013).

OECD (1996), *Trade, Employment and Labour Standards: A Study of Core Workers' Rights and International Trade*, OECD, Paris.

OECD (2004), 'Fair and Equitable Treatment Standard in International Investment Law', Working Papers on International Investment No. 2004/3, OECD, Paris.

OECD (2006), *Applying Strategic Environmental Assessment: Good Practice Guidance for Development Co-operation*, OECD, Paris.

OECD (2006), *OECD Risk Awareness Tool for Multinational Enterprises in Weak Governance Zones*, OECD, Paris.

OECD (2008), *OECD Benchmark Definition of Foreign Direct Investment*, 4th ed., OECD, Paris.

OECD (2008), 'OECD Working Group on Bribery Annual Report 2007', available at: www.oecd.org/dataoecd/21/15/40896091.pdf (accessed 8 January 2013).

OECD (2011), 'The OECD Guidelines for Multinational Enterprises', OECD Declaration on International Investment and Multinational Enterprises (Ministerial Meeting), OECD, Paris.

OECD (2012), *Investor-State Dispute Settlement, Public Consultation*: 16 May–23 July, available at: www.oecd.org/dataoecd/61/29/50291642.pdf (accessed 24 June 2012).

On Common Ground Consultants Inc. (2010), 'Human Rights Assessment of Goldcorp's Marlin Mine', available at: www.hria-guatemala.com/en/MarlinHumanRights.htm (accessed 8 January 2013).

Osgoode Hall Law School, York University (2010), 'Public Statement on the International Investment Regime, 31 August 2010', available at: www.osgoode.yorku.ca/public_statement (accessed 24 June 2013).

Oxfam International (2003), *The Emperor's New Clothes: Why Rich Countries Want a WTO Investment Agreement*, Oxfam International Briefing Paper 46, Oxford.

Pavic, V (2006), 'Counterclaim and Set-Off in International Commercial Arbitration', 1 *Annals of the Faculty of Law in Belgrade - Belgrade Law Review, International Edition*, 101.

Pellegrini, L (2011), *Corruption, Development and the Environment*, Springer, Dordrecht.

Perrault, A, K Herbertson and O J Lynch (2007), 'Partnerships for Success in Protected Areas: The Public Interest and Local Community Rights to Prior Informed Consent (PIC)', *Georgetown International Environmental Law Review*, Vol. 19, 475.

Peterson, LE (2004), *Bilateral Investment Treaties and Development Policy Making*, International Institute for Sustainable Development, Winnipeg.

Prasad, ES, RG Rajan and A Subramanian (November 2007), 'Foreign Capital and Economic Growth', NBER Working Paper, No. W13619, National Bureau of Economic Research, Cambridge, Massachusetts.

Ramasastry, A and RC Thompson (2006), 'Commerce, Crime and Conflict: Legal Remedies for Private Actor Liability for Grave Breaches of International Law – a Survey of Sixteen Countries', 536 Fafo-Report, Fafo, Oslo, available at: www.fafo.no/pub/rapp/536/536.pdf (accessed 8 January 2013).

Reinisch, A (2008) 'Legality of Expropriations,' in Reinisch, A (Ed.), *Standards of Investment Protection*, Oxford University Press, Oxford, 197.

Reinisch, A (Ed.) (2008), *Standards of Investment Protection*, Oxford University Press, Oxford.

Reisman, W M (1994), 'Control Mechanisms in International Dispute Resolution', *United States–Mexico Law Journal*, Vol. 2, 129.

Republic of South Africa, Department of Trade and Industry (2010), 'Policy Statement: The South African Government's Approach to Future International Investment Treaties', available at: www.jadafa.co.za/LinkClick.aspx?fileticket=9A6eXZstR10%3D&tabid=432 (accessed 8 January 2013).

Ripinsky, S with K Williams (2008), *Damages in International Investment Law*, British Institute of Comparative Law, London.

Rose-Ackerman, S (2010), 'The Law and Economics of Bribery and Extortion', *Annual Review of Law and Social Science*, Vol. 6, 217.

Sabahi, B (2011), *Compensation and Restitution in Investor-State Arbitration: Principles and Practice*, Oxford University Press, Oxford.

Sadler, B (Ed.) (2011), *Handbook of Strategic Environmental Assessment*, Earthscan, London.

Salacuse, JW and NP Sullivan (2005), 'Do BITs Really Work? An Evaluation of Bilateral Investment Treaties and Their Grand Bargain', *Harvard International Law Journal*, Vol. 46, 67.

Sands, P (2003), *Principles of International Environmental Law*, 2d ed., Cambridge University Press, Cambridge.

Sattorova, M (2012), 'Return to the Local Remedies Rule in European BITs? Power (Inequalities), Dispute Settlement, and Change in Investment Treaty Law', *Legal Issues of Economic Integration*, Vol. 39, 223.

Sauvant, K P and L E Sachs (2009), 'BITs, DTTs, and FDI Flows: An Overview', in Sauvant, K P and L E Sachs (Eds), *The Effect of Treaties on Foreign Direct Investment: Bilateral Investment Treaties, Double Taxation Treaties and Investment Flows*, Oxford University Press, Oxford.

Sauvant, K P and L E Sachs (Eds) (2009), *The Effect of Treaties on Foreign Direct Investment: Bilateral Investment Treaties, Double Taxation Treaties and Investment Flows*, Oxford University Press, Oxford.

Schneiderman, D (2000), 'Investment Rules and the New Constitutionalism', *Law and Social Inquiry*, Vol. 25, 757.

Schneiderman, D (2009), 'Promoting Equality, Black Economic Empowerment, and the Future of Investment Rules', *South African Journal on Human Rights*, Vol. 25, 246.

Schreuer, C (2007), 'Fair and Equitable Treatment: Interactions with Other Standards', *Transnational Dispute Management*, Vol. 4, 17.

Schreuer, C and M Weinigar (2008), 'A Doctrine of Precedent', in Muchlinski, P, F Ortino and C Schreuer (Eds), *The Oxford Handbook of International Investment Law*, Oxford University Press, Oxford and New York.

Seck, S (2008), 'Home State Responsibility and Local Communities: The Case of Global Mining', *Yale Human Rights and Development Law Journal*, Vol. 11, 177.

Sepúlveda, M and C Nyst (2012), 'The Human Rights Approach to Social Protection', Ministry for Foreign Affairs of Finland, available at: www.ohchr.org/Documents/Issues/EPoverty/HumanRightsApproachToSocialProtection.pdf (accessed 8 January 2013).

Scott, C (Ed.) (2004), *Torture as Tort: Comparative Perspectives on the Development of Transnational Human Rights Litigation*, Hart Publishing, Oxford.

Sen, A (1999), *Development as Freedom*, Anchor Books, New York.

Sengupta, A (2006) 'The Human Right to Development', in Andreassen, BA and SP Marks (Eds), *Development as a Human Right*, Harvard University Press, Cambridge, MA.

Shabtai, R (1984), *Practice and Methods of International Law*, Oceana, New York.

Shea, D (1955), *The Calvo Clause: A Problem of Inter-American and International Law and Diplomacy*, University of Minnesota Press, Minneapolis.

Shelton, D (2005), *Remedies in International Human Rights Law*, 2d ed., Oxford University Press, Oxford.

Siegmann, T (2007), 'The Impact of Bilateral Investment Treaties and Double Taxation Treaties on Foreign Direct Investment', University of St Gallen Law and Economics Research Paper Series, Working Paper No. 2008–22, St. Gallen.

Simons, P (2004), 'Corporate Voluntarism and Human Rights: The Adequacy and Effectiveness of Voluntary Self-Regulation Regimes', *Relations Industrielles/ Industrial Relations*, Vol. 59, 101.

Simons, P (2012), 'International Law's Invisible Hand and the Future of Corporate Accountability for Human Rights', *Journal of Human Rights and the Environment*, Vol. 3, 5.

Simons, P and L Collins (2010), 'Participatory Rights in the Ontario Mining Sector: an International Human Rights Perspective', *McGill International Journal of Sustainable Development Law and Policy*, Vol. 6, 177.

Simons, P and A Macklin (2013 forthcoming), *The Governance Gap: Extractive Industries, Human Rights, and the Home State Advantage*, Routledge, London.

Skovgaard Poulsen, L (forthcoming), 'Investment Treaties and the Globalisation of State Capitalism: Opportunities and Constraints for Host States', in Echandi R and P Sauvé (Eds), *Prospects in International Investment Law and Policy*, Cambridge University Press, Cambridge.

Smith, F (2012), 'Food Security, Foreign Direct Investment and Multilevel Governance in Weak States', presented at Third Biennial Global Conference of the Society of International Economic Law, National University of Singapore.

Soloway, J (1999), 'NAFTA's Chapter 11, The Challenge of Private Party Participation', *Journal of International Arbitration*, Vol. 16, 1.

Sornarajah, M (2010), *The International Law of Foreign Investment*, 3d ed., Cambridge University Press, Cambridge.

Ssenyonjo, M (2007), 'Non-State Actors and Economic, Social and Cultural Rights', in Baderin, MA and R McCorquodale (Eds), *Economic, Social and Cultural Rights in Action*, Oxford University Press, Oxford,

Stephens, B (2007), 'U.S. Litigation against Corporations for Gross Violation of Human Rights', written for the ICJ Expert Legal Panel on Corporate Complicity in International Crimes (copy on file with the authors).

Swenson, DL (2005), 'Why Do Developing Countries Sign BITs?', *University of California Davis Journal of International Law & Policy*, Vol. 12, 131.

Taillant, JD and J Bonnitcha (2011), 'International Investment Law and Human Rights', in Cordonier Segger et al. (Eds.), *Sustainable Development in World Investment Law*, Kluwer Law International, The Hague.

Tamanaha, B (1995), 'The Lessons of Law and Development Studies', *American Journal of International Law*, Vol. 89, 470.

Thoms, ONT and J Ron (2007), 'Do Human Rights Violations Cause Internal Conflict?', *Human Rights Quarterly*, Vol. 29, 674.

Thornton, J (2012), 'Divining the Content of the Customary International Law Minimum Standard Treatment from the Jurisprudence of the US–Mexico General Claims Commission', *World Arbitration and Mediation Review* (forthcoming).

Tobin, J and M Busch (2010), 'A BIT is Better than a Lot: Bilateral Investment Treaties and Preferential Trading Agreements', *World Politics*, Vol. 62, 1.

Tobin, J and S Rose-Ackerman (2003), 'Foreign Direct Investment and the Business Environment in Developing Countries: The Impact of Bilateral Investment Treaties', William Davidson Institute Working Paper No. 587, The University of Michigan Business School, Michigan.

Total (2011), Statement by Peter Herbl, personal communication, 23 May, available at: www.global-business-initiative.org/SRSGpage/files/Total%20S%20A%20letter%20to%20John%20Ruggie.pdf (accessed 29 May 2012).

Trachtman, J (2005), 'Negotiations on Domestic Regulation and Trade in Services: (GATS Art. VI): A Legal Analysis of Selected Issues', in Petersmann, EU (Ed.), *Reforming the World Trading System: Legitimacy, Efficiency and Democratic Governance*, Oxford University Press, Oxford.

UN (1992) *Rio Declaration on Environment and Development*, UN Doc. A/CONF.151/26 (Vol. I).

UN (1995), *Copenhagen Declaration on Social Development*, UN Doc.A/CONF.166/Res./1, United Nations.

UN (2000), *UN Millennium Declaration*, A/RES/55/2, adopted 18 September 2000, United Nations.

UN (2001), Report of the International Law Commission, Fifty-third session (23 April–1 June and 2 July–10 August 2001), UN Doc A/56/10, United Nations.

UN (2002), *Johannesburg Declaration on Sustainable Development: From Our Origins to the Future: Plan of Implementation of the World Summit on Sustainable Development*, UN Doc. A/CONF.199/20.

UN (2002), *New Delhi Declaration of Principles of International Law Relating to Sustainable Development*, Res. 3/2002, 209 UN Doc. A/57/329, United Nations, reprinted in International Law Association (2002), *Report of the Seventieth Conference, New Delhi*, ILA, London.

UN (2007), 'Report of the Special Representative of the Secretary-General on the Issue of Human Rights and Transnational Corporations and Other Business Enterprises (John Ruggie)', UNHRC, UN Doc A/HRC/4/35.

UN (2011), 'Report of the Special Rapporteur on the Right to Food, Olivier De Schutter: Guiding Principles on Human Rights Impact Assessments of Trade and Investment Agreements' (19 December), A/HRC/19/59/Add.5, Principle 1.

UN (nd), *UN Global Compact*, available at: www.unglobalcompact.org (accessed 8 January 2013).

UN Committee on Economic, Social and Cultural Rights (UNCESCR) (1999), *General Comment No 13: The Right to Education*, UNCESCR, UN Doc E/C.12/1999/10.

UN Conference on Trade and Development (UNCTAD) (1996), *World Investment Report 1996: Investment, Trade and International Policy Arrangements*, United Nations, New York and Geneva.

UNCTAD (1998), *Bilateral Treaties in the Mid-1990s*, United Nations, New York and Geneva.

UNCTAD (1999), *National Treatment*, United Nations, New York and Geneva.

UNCTAD (2001), *Home Country Measures*, United Nations, New York and Geneva.

UNCTAD (2003), *Dispute Settlement: State-to-State*, United Nations, New York and Geneva.

UNCTAD (2003), *World Investment Report 2003: FDI Policies for Development: National and International Perspectives*, United Nations, New York and Geneva.

UNCTAD (2007), *Bilateral Investment Treaties 1995–2006: Trends in Investment Rulemaking*, United Nations, New York and Geneva.

UNCTAD (2009), *The Role of International Investment Agreements in Attracting Foreign Direct Investment to Developing Countries*, United Nations, New York and Geneva.

UNCTAD (2010), *Denunciation of the ICSID Convention and BITS: Impact on Investor-State Claims*, IIA Issues Note No. 2, December 2010, United Nations, New York and Geneva.

UNCTAD (2010), *Investor-State Disputes: Prevention and Alternatives to Arbitration*, United Nations, Geneva and New York.

UNCTAD (2010), *Most Favoured Nation Treatment: A Sequel*, United Nations, New York and Geneva.

UNCTAD (2011), *Expropriation: A Sequel*, United Nations, New York and Geneva.

UNCTAD (2011), *Most Favoured Nation: A Sequel*, United Nations, New York and Geneva.

UNCTAD (2011), *Scope and Definition: A Sequel*, United Nations, New York and Geneva.

UNCTAD (2011), *Transparency in IIAs*, United Nations, New York and Geneva.

UNCTAD (2012), *A Review of Fair and Equitable Treatment: A Sequel*, United Nations, New York and Geneva.

UNCTAD (2012), *Investment Policy Framework for Sustainable Development*, United Nations, New York and Geneva, available at: http://unctad.org/en/PublicationsLibrary/webdiaepcb2012d6_en.pdf (accessed 8 January 2013).

UNCTAD (2012), *Latest Developments in Investor-State Dispute Settlement*, IIA Issues Note No. 1, United Nations, New York and Geneva, available at: http://unctad.org/en/PublicationsLibrary/webdiaeia2012d10_en.pdf (accessed 8 January 2013).

UNCTAD (2012), *World Investment Report 2012: Towards a New Generation of Investment Policies*, United Nations, New York and Geneva.

UN Environment Programme (UNEP) (1987), Governing Council decision: Goals and Principles of Environmental Impact Assessment, Principle 4, UNEP/GC.14/17 Annex III, UNEP/BC/DEC/14/25 (17 June 1987).

UN General Assembly Official Records (UNGAOR) (2000), 'We the Peoples: The Role of the United Nations in the Twenty-First Century', Report of the Secretary-General, UNGAOR, 54 Sess, UN Doc A/54/2000.

UN Human Rights Council (UNHRC) (2008), 'Protect Respect and Remedy: A Framework for Business and Human Rights: Report of the Special Representative of the Secretary-General on the Issue of Human Rights and Transnational Corporations and other Business Entities', UN Doc A/HRC/8/5.

UNHRC (2010), 'Report of the Special Representative of the Secretary-General on the Issue of Human Rights and Transnational Corporations and Other Business Enterprises, Business and Human Rights: Further Steps toward the Operationalization of the "Protect, Respect and Remedy" Framework', John Ruggie, UN Doc A/HRC/14/27.

UNHRC (2011), 'Guiding Principles on Business and Human Rights: Implementing the United Nations "Protect, Respect and Remedy" Framework: Report of the Special Representative of the Secretary-General on the Issue of Human Rights and Transnational Corporations and other Business Enterprises, John Ruggie', UN Doc A/HRC/17/31.

UN Millennium Project (2005), *Investing in Development: A Practical Plan to Achieve the Millennium Development Goals*, Routledge, London.

UN Secretary General (2008), *The Latest Developments Related to the Review Process on Financing for Development and the Implementation of the Monterrey Consensus*, UN Doc. A/63/179.

van den Berg, AJ (Ed.) (2003), *International Commercial Arbitration: Important Contemporary Questions*, Kluwer International, New York.

van Harten, G (2010), 'Investment Treaty Arbitration, Procedural Fairness, and the Rule of Law', in Schill S (Ed.), *International Investment Law and Comparative Public Law*, Oxford University Press, Oxford.

Vanclay, F (2003), 'International Principles for Social Impact Assessment', *Impact Assessment and Project Appraisal*, Vol. 21, 5.

VanDuzer, JA (1999), 'What Have We Done? NAFTA States Have Concerns Regarding Investor-State Settlement under NAFTA Chapter 11', *Canadian Council of International Law Bulletin*, Vol. 25, 13.

VanDuzer, JA (2004), 'Health, Education and Social Services in Canada: The Impact of the GATS', in Curtis J M and D Curiak (Eds), *Trade Policy Research 2004*, International Trade Canada, Ottawa, Vol. 287.

VanDuzer, JA (2007), 'Enhancing the Procedural Legitimacy of Investor-State Arbitration through Transparency and *Amicus Curiae* Participation', *McGill Law Journal*, Vol. 52, 681.

VanDuzer, JA (2008), 'Foreign Investment and Development: The Role of Domestic Policy and International Investment Agreements', in Commonwealth Secretariat, *Commonwealth Finance Ministers Reference Report 2008*, Commonwealth Secretariat, London.

VanDuzer, JA, P Simons and G Mayeda (2008), 'Modeling International Investment Agreements for Economic Development', in V Qalo (ed.), *Bilateralism and Development: Emerging Trade Patterns*, Cameron May, London, 359, at 390.

VanDuzer, JA (2010), 'Mixed Signals: What Recent Developments Tell Us about Foreign Investment Policy in Canada', *Asper Review of International Business and Trade Law*, Vol. 10, 247.

Vernon, R (1971), *Sovereignty at Bay: The Multinational Spread of US Enterprises*, Basic Books, New York.

von Moltke, K and H Mann (2005), *A Southern Agenda on International Investment?: Promoting Development with Balanced Rights and Obligations for Investors, Host States and Home States*, International Institute for Sustainable Development, Winnipeg.

World Bank (1992) *World Bank Guidelines on the Treatment of Foreign Direct Investment*, World Bank, Washington, DC.

World Commission on Environment and Development (1987), *Our Common Future*, UN Doc. GA/42/427, 43.

WTO (2002), *Communication from India*, Working Group on the Relationship between Trade and Investment (2 October), Doc. No. WT/WGTI/150.

WTO (2002), 'WTO Working Group on the Relationship between Trade and Investment', Note by the Secretariat, WT/WGTI/W/108 (21 March).

Wouters, J and N Hachez (2011), 'Institutionalization of Investment Arbitration and Sustainable Development', in Cordonier Segger M-C et al. (Eds.), *Sustainable Development in World Investment Law*, Kluwer Law International, The Hague.

Wright, G (2010), 'Risky Business: The Case for Enterprise Analysis at the Intersection of Corporate Groups and Torts', available at: http://papers.ssrn.com/sol3/papers.cfm?abstract_id=1966777 (accessed 8 January 2013).

Yackee, JW (2007), 'Do BITs Really Work? Revisiting the Empirical Link between Investment Treaties and Foreign Direct Investment', Legal Studies Research Paper No. 1054, University of Wisconsin Law School, Madison.

Yackee, JW (2010), 'Do Bilateral Investment Treaties Promote Foreign Direct Investment? Some Hints from Alternative Evidence', *Virginia Journal of International Law*, Vol. 51, 397.

Zarsky, L (Ed.) (2005) *International Investment for Sustainable Development: Balancing Rights and Rewards*, Earthscan, London and Sterling, VA.

Index